THE
GREEN HOWARDS.
ALEXANDRA,
PRINCESS OF WALES'S OWN
YORKSHIRE REGIMENT.

1914-1919

W. & D. Downey]

HER MAJESTY QUEEN ALEXANDRA

COLONEL-IN-CHIEF

THE GREEN HOWARDS

IN THE

GREAT WAR

THE GREEN HOWARDS

1914–1919

by

COLONEL H. C. WYLLY, C.B.

The Naval & Military Press Ltd

Reproduced by kind permission of the Central Library,
Royal Military Academy, Sandhurst

Published by

The Naval & Military Press Ltd

Unit 10, Ridgewood Industrial Park,

Uckfield, East Sussex,

TN22 5QE England

Tel: +44 (0) 1825 749494

Fax: +44 (0) 1825 765701

www.naval–military-press.com

www.military-genealogy.com

The Naval & Military Press ...

...offer specialist books for the serious student of conflict. The range of titles stocked covers the whole spectrum of military history with titles on uniforms, battles, official histories, specialist works containing Medal Rolls and Casualties Lists, and numismatic titles for medal collectors and researchers.

The innovative approach they have to military bookselling and their commitment to publishing have made them Britain's leading independent military bookseller.

In reprinting in facsimile from the original, any imperfections are inevitably reproduced and the quality may fall short of modern type and cartographic standards.

Printed and bound by Antony Rowe Ltd, Eastbourne

THE
GREAT WAR
1914—1918

———————

THE
THIRD AFGHAN WAR
1919

FOREWORD

Our beloved Colonel-in-Chief, H.M. Queen Alexandra, whose picture adorns this History, passed from among us on the 20th November, 1925.

Her Majesty had always taken a deep interest in Her Regiment and Her thought of Her soldiers prompted the sending of those gifts which were so deeply valued by the men at the Front. The world is the poorer in having lost this gracious, gentle, most lovable Queen.

At the outset I wish to thank our gifted historian, who has from a mass of chaff salved the grains which make our book. Colonel H. C. Wylly's reputation is too well established to need any praise from me, but I desire to thank him from the Regiment, and also Mr. K. R. Wilson, who assisted him.

I wish to thank also all those who contributed descriptions of actions and those who sent diaries, pictures and details of events, and all who helped us in any way to produce this book.

Writers of history tell us that many years must elapse before the events to be recorded can be viewed in their correct proportions. Our able and experienced historian, in compiling our Regimental History of The Great War, has collected facts and impressions from those who actually took part in, or witnessed, the events herein recorded, enabling future historians to glean the facts first hand.

This History must for ever be to us a valued record of the deeds and achievements of the gallant officers and men of our many and far-flung Battalions who fought in The Great War.

A hundred years ago the great Napoleon, no mean judge of soldiers, described our Infantry as the best in Europe; had the Great Captain lived to-day, he could truthfully have enlarged his dictum to the " best in the world." I doubt if anyone, who had not daily watched it, could conceive the dreadful and horrible conditions under which our officers and men in the front-line trenches lived and fought during the first year of the war. Experience and money did much to alter and improve matters during the later years, but it needed grit and a very high ideal of duty to withstand the privations and hardships our men endured.

The Green Howards fought on almost every front, and pulled their weight.

Our parent 1st Battalion was held back in India with some ten other Regular Battalions, needed for security. Our 2nd Battalion formed part of the Seventh Division, landing in Flanders in time for the First Ypres. Other of our Battalions fought in Flanders, France, Italy, Gallipoli, and Russia, while we had officers and men of the Regiment fighting in the Balkans, Palestine, Syria, and Mesopotamia—a fine record of service. But, alas! it took a heavy toll in young lives, as our book in the Parish Church at Richmond testifies, but there is no record of those countless others who, by their noble unselfishness, high ideals of duty, and iron endurance, proved themselves worthy sons of Yorkshire and of the Regiment to which it is our proud privilege to belong.

EDWARD S. BULFIN,
General,
Colonel, The Green Howards.

WALMER, KENT,
1st December, 1925.

CONTENTS

CHAPTER VI

THE 2ND BATTALION

1918–1919

CHAPTER VII

THE 1/4TH (TERRITORIAL) BATTALION

1914–1918

CHAPTER VIII

THE 1/5TH (TERRITORIAL) BATTALION

1914–1918

CHAPTER IX

THE 6TH (SERVICE) BATTALION

1914–1915

CHAPTER X

THE 6TH (SERVICE) BATTALION

1916–1919

EGYPT—FRANCE

CHAPTER XI

THE 7TH (SERVICE) BATTALION

1914–1916

CONTENTS

CHAPTER XVIII

THE 12TH (SERVICE) BATTALION

1915–1918

CHAPTER XIX

THE 13TH (SERVICE) BATTALION

1915–1919

CHAPTER XX

1914–1919

APPENDICES

PLATES

MAPS

xiii

THE
BATTLE HONOURS

" Malplaquet,"

" Alma,"   " Inkerman,"   " Sevastopol,"

" Tirah,"

" Relief of Kimberley," " Paardeberg," " South Africa, 1899–1902,"

" Afghanistan, 1919."

THE
BATTLE HONOURS

THE GREAT WAR

(24 Battalions)

" YPRES, 1914, '15, '17 "
" Langemarck, 1914, '17 "
" Gheluvelt "
" Neuve Chapelle "
" St. Julien "
" Frezenberg "
" Bellewaarde "
" Aubers "
" Festubert, 1915 "
" Loos "
" SOMME, 1916, '18 "
" Albert, 1916 "
" Bazentin "
" Pozières "
" Flers-Courcelette "
" Morval "
" Thiepval "
" Le Transloy "
" Ancre Heights "

" Ancre, 1916 "
" ARRAS, 1917, '18 "
" Scarpe, 1917, '18 "
" MESSINES, 1917, '18 "
" Pilckem "
" Menin Road "
" Polygon Wood "
" Broodseinde "
" Poelcappelle "
" Passchendaele "
" Cambrai, 1917, '18 "
" St. Quentin "
" Bapaume, 1918 "
" Rosières "
" Lys "
" Estaires "
" Hazebrouck "
" Kemmel "
" Scherpenberg "

" Aisne, 1918 "
" Drocourt-Quéant "
" Hindenburg Line "
" Canal du Nord "
" Beaurevoir "
" Selle "
" VALENCIENNES "
" SAMBRE "
" FRANCE AND FLANDERS
1914–1918 "
" Piave "
" VITTORIO VENETO "
" Italy, 1917–18 "
" SUVLA "
" Landing at Suvla "
" Scimitar Hill "
" Gallipoli, 1915 "
" Egypt, 1916 "
" Archangel, 1918 "

DEDICATION

To

THE GLORIOUS MEMORY

OF

7,500

GREEN HOWARDS

WHO GAVE THEIR LIVES

FOR

THEIR KING, MOTHERLAND AND EMPIRE

IN

THE GREAT WAR.

" Their Name Liveth for Evermore."

2ND BATTALION.

THE MENIN CROSS ROADS.

THE GREEN HOWARDS

IN

THE GREAT WAR

CHAPTER I

1914

THE BEGINNING OF THE GREAT WAR

IT has over and over again been said that we, as a nation, were wholly unready for the war which came upon us in August, 1914; but this is only true so far as concerns the people in general and the politicians in particular, for in 1914 the Army of this country was probably better prepared for war on the continental scale than it had ever been before. In the years that immediately preceded the outbreak we had been able to draw, as in the long past, a very rich and varied experience from our many Indian and Colonial wars—which if they had taught us nothing else had educated our soldiers in the art of improvisation, in readiness to adapt themselves to novel and difficult situations, and in the making use of scanty materials; while very much indeed had been learnt from the experiences and even from the mistakes of the war of some twelve years previously in South Africa. During the three years which that war endured, the Regular Army of Great Britain, too weak in numbers for the services then asked of it, had been strengthened by large reinforcements from the Militia, Yeomanry, and the Volunteers, and by large contingents from the military forces of the Dominions and the Colonies; and the British military authorities had learnt at great expenditure of lives and money to realize the more serious of our defects of training, organization and armament, and had taken steps to remove or at least to remedy them.

When the South African War came to an end, and political parties had ceased their inevitable bickerings as to which of them was responsible for its occurrence and for the defects of its management, much was done for the improvement of matters military ; an Army Council was set up, a General Staff was organized, extra provision was made for a reserve of officers for the Army ; and the Regular Army and the Army of the Second Line were both re-organized for war on a greater and more workman-like scale than had ever before been attempted or even contemplated. The Regular Army was organized in an expeditionary force of six infantry divisions, each of three brigades, and one cavalry division, the total war establishment of each infantry division being eighteen thousand of all ranks, with seventy-six guns, and twenty-four machine guns ; the Yeomanry became the second line of cavalry and was organized in fourteen brigades ; while the Volunteers, who had hitherto been no more than independent groups of varying corps, were converted into a local militia under the title of " the Territorial Force," and were grouped in fourteen divisions organized on the lines of the Regular Army. The old Militia was re-named " the Special Reserve " and became once again as of old a draft-producing body for the Regular Army on the outbreak of and during war.

Further, much was done to improve military training for all branches, regular and second line, and mobilization schemes were practised, with the result that " in every respect the Expeditionary Force of 1914 was incomparably the best trained, best organized and best equipped British Army that ever went forth to war. Except in the matter of co-operation between aeroplanes and artillery, and use of machine guns, its training would stand comparison in all respects with that of the Germans. Where it fell short of our enemies was first and foremost in numbers ; so that, though not ' contemptible,' it was almost negligible in comparison with continental armies even of the smaller States." *

It is not proposed here to give any detailed account of the events which preceded and led up to the outbreak of the Great War ; and it will probably be amply sufficient for the purposes of a purely regimental history if certain dates are here briefly set down as showing their relation to the military happenings which followed. On the 28th June the heir to the throne of Austria-Hungary was assassinated at Serajevo, the capital of Bosnia ; nearly a month later—on the 23rd July—the Cabinet of Vienna presented an ultimatum to the Serbian Government ; on the 25th Austria declared war on Serbia ; on the 29th Russia ordered first, partial, and two days later, complete mobilization of her armies ; on the 1st August Germany declared war on Russia, and on the 3rd against France, having already on the previous day presented something of the nature of an ultimatum to the Belgian Government, setting forth that Germany possessed certain intelligence of the intention of the French military authorities to advance on the

* *Official History of the War*, Vol. I, pp. 10 and 11.

Meuse by Givet and Namur, and demanding unresisted passage for the German Armies through Belgian territory. On the 2nd August the German troops crossed the Polish and French frontiers and on the 4th that of Belgium ; on the same day Great Britain declared war on Germany.

On the 5th and 6th August meetings of the British Cabinet were held and were attended by the leading Ministers, by Field-Marshal Lord Kitchener, who had become Secretary of State for War on the 6th, by Field-Marshal Sir John French, the Commander-in-Chief designate of the Expeditionary Force, and by the heads of the Admiralty and War Office, and it was then decided that for the present only the Cavalry Division and four Infantry Divisions should be sent to France, embarkation commencing on the 9th ; that the regular regiments forming the peace-time garrisons of India and South Africa should at once be brought home ; and that the British Expeditionary Force on arrival in France should be concentrated in the region of Le Cateau and Avesnes.

The decision was further come to that the Expeditionary Force should be organized in three Army Corps, and these were commanded, the I. Corps by Lieutenant-General Sir Douglas Haig, the II. by Lieutenant-General Sir James Grierson, and later, on his death a few days after his arrival in France, by General Sir Horace Smith-Dorrien, the III. by Lieutenant-General Sir William Pulteney, and the Cavalry Division by Major-General Allenby.

None of the battalions of The Green Howards were included in the original Expeditionary Force. When the war commenced the Regiment consisted of no more than five battalions all told—two Regular, one Special Reserve, and two Territorial, and of these the 1st Battalion was stationed in India and the 2nd in the Channel Islands, while the Headquarters of the remaining three were at Richmond, Northallerton and Scarborough respectively ; but, as was the case with every other infantry regiment of the British Army, The Green Howards underwent very great expansion as the war went on, with the result that before hostilities had been more than a very short time in progress The Green Howards had increased to no fewer than twenty-four battalions, viz. :

2 Regular—1st and 2nd Bns.
1 Special Reserve—3rd Bn.
6 Territorial—1/4th, 2/4th, 3/4th, 1/5th, 2/5th and 3/5th Bns.
8 Service—6th, 7th, 8th, 9th, 10th, 11th, 12th and 13th Bns.
2 Reserve—14th and 15th Bns.
2 Labour—16th and 17th Bns.
1 Home Service—18th Bn.
2 Garrison—1st and 2nd Garrison Bns.

of which twelve battalions served overseas and in practically every theatre of war—in France, Flanders, Italy, Gallipoli, Egypt, Russia, and India.

There is no more remarkable feature of the Great War than the extraordinary and rapid expansion of the Army of Great Britain. Prior to August, 1914, the training provided for the Territorial Force was comparatively slight ; fourteen days annually in camp, a short and simple musketry course, and certain drills during the evenings at the various battalion headquarters, was hardly a sufficient training to fit the Territorial soldier to meet fully trained men of the continental armies ; and the training afforded and demanded was probably calculated rather on what the non-professional soldier would readily accept than on what was militarily desirable. That this was realized by the authorities seems evidenced by the fact that the scheme introduced in 1907 provided for a period of six months' home training for all Territorial soldiers, prior to their employment on active service in the field. But under Section XIII of " the Territorial and Reserve Forces Act of 1907," it was distinctly laid down that " while any part of the Territorial Force shall be liable to serve in any part of the United Kingdom, no part of the Territorial Force shall be carried or ordered to go out of the United Kingdom " ; so that it is clear that the Territorial Force was a body primarily intended to be used for purposes of Home Defence only. It had, however, always been taken for granted that at any time of national emergency a very large percentage of the officers and other ranks composing the Force would readily come forward and offer themselves for service overseas ; already during the years of peace since the formation of the Territorial Force, it had been open to all ranks to accept such an Imperial obligation, but the opportunity had not been very freely accepted, with the result that out of an establishment of 300,000 no more than 17,621 men had undertaken the General Service Obligation.

On the 10th August Lord Kitchener, as Secretary of State for War, sent a note* in the following terms to the Director-General of the Territorial Force :

" Lord Kitchener desires to be informed as soon as possible which of the Territorial Battalions and other units :

1. Volunteer for service abroad.
2. Partially volunteer ; if so, how many of each category, officers by ranks.
3. Desire to form part of the Home Defence Force not leaving the country."

On the 4th August the embodiment of the Territorial Force had been

* The original document, in Lord Kitchener's handwriting and in pencil, is preserved in the Museum of the Royal United Service Institution, Whitehall.

decreed under Army Order No. 281, and on the issue being put before their subordinates by the Commanding Officers of Territorial units the response was immediate and hearty, something like eighty per cent. of the officers and men volunteering for service abroad, and intensive training was at once put in hand. It very soon, however, became apparent that if and when such an Imperial Service unit went overseas, an extra or reserve organization would be needed to take its place in the general scheme of home defence, and also to provide drafts and reinforcements for the unit abroad ; and as a result Army Order No. 399 was issued on the 21st September, authorizing the County Territorial Force Associations to raise a Home Service unit for each unit of the Force which had been accepted for Imperial Service. Even this expansion of the Territorial Force was very soon found to be inadequate to meet the huge scale upon which operations were being conducted in all parts of the world, and also in view of the wholly abnormal wastage which was to be anticipated ; and consequently on the 24th November instructions were issued from the War Office directing that when an Imperial Service unit embarked and was replaced at home by its Reserve unit, a *second* Reserve unit was at once to be raised at the depot or peace headquarters of the original unit.

So much for the expansion of the Territorial Force, and we may now consider the creation of the New Armies composed of the Service Battalions.

On assuming control as Secretary of State for War, Lord Kitchener not only realized as did few others that the war would be a very long one, but he grasped the need for immediate and immense augmentation of the Army, far beyond anything with which existing organizations were able to grapple ; but there remained no Regular Army basis upon which to build up new forces. He might of course have expanded the Special Reserve which in itself was partly regular ; he might have made use of the Territorial Force organization which already provided the framework of fourteen mounted brigades and the same number of infantry divisions ; or it was open to him to create entirely new formations. The objections to the first course were that it would disorganize the Special Reserve of the Regular Army already committed to the campaign, that the number of the Special Reserve units was too small, and that they were composed almost exclusively of infantry. The main objection to the second of the three alternatives was the inadequacy of the framework upon which to raise the hundred divisions upon which Lord Kitchener had already decided ; duplication and reduplication of those small nuclei would eventually entail practically new formations ; further duplication would render them immobile ; while Home Defence would be paralysed, and the possibility of using any units already existing and organized for reinforcements would be neutralized.

Lord Kitchener therefore decided to create entirely new divisions, while retaining the Special Reserve for its maintenance functions, and at the same time fostering the recruiting, training and eventual duplication of the Territorial Force in order to relieve the Regular Army in overseas garrisons, and to supply immediate unit reinforcements to the field army ; and further, as soon as the Territorial Divisions, not broken up for these two purposes, were sufficiently trained, to put them into the field as complete divisions. The new divisions were to be created as armies each of one hundred thousand men—popularly known as " Kitchener Armies."

No part of Lord Kitchener's administration of the Army has been more largely and more adversely criticized than this decision to create entirely new armies, instead of making use of the already existing machinery of the Territorial Force Associations for providing an expansion of the formations controlled by them.   The reasons for the course which he followed may be found in the address which the Field-Marshal made to members of the House of Commons on the 5th June, a few days before he left England on his last voyage.   He said : " When I took over the office of Secretary of State for War, I found myself confronted with a complicated emergency.   The pre-war theory worked out by the General Staff on instructions from the Government of the day had been that, in certain eventualities, we should dispatch overseas an Expeditionary Force of six divisions in all, or, in round numbers, one hundred and fifty thousand men ; that the Territorial Force should take over the defence of these islands ; and that the Special Reserve should feed the Expeditionary Force.   On this basis, the business of the War Office in event of war was to keep the Army in the field up to strength and to perfect the arrangements for Home Defence.

" My immediate decision was that, in face of the magnitude of the war, this policy would not suffice.   Whether our armies advanced, retired, or held their ground, I was convinced that not only had we got to feed the existing Expeditionary Force, and maintain an adequate garrison here and in India, but, further, we had to produce a new army sufficiently large to count in a European war.   In fact, although I did not see it in detail, I must ask gentlemen of the House of Commons to recognize that I had, rough-hewn in my mind, the idea of creating such a force as would enable us continuously to reinforce our troops in the field by fresh divisions, and thus assist our Allies at the time when they were beginning to feel the strain of the war with its attendant casualties.   By this means we planned to work on the up-grade while our Allies' forces decreased, so that at the conclusive period of the war, we should have the maximum trained fighting army this country could produce. . . .   I must point out here that the building of these armies was only a part of the task.   The Expeditionary Force had to be kept going, and the Territorial garrison of these Islands had to be kept up to strength and given the training necessary to enable them to take the field against equal numbers of trained troops, and most splendidly have they realized our expectations."

On the 8th August, 1914, Lord Kitchener asked for one hundred thousand men, and within a fortnight he had them in camp; on one single day the enlistments totalled over thirty thousand—indeed the men came in faster than equipment could be provided for them. While, therefore, the existing Territorial units were preparing themselves for war, and in some cases were relieving the overseas garrisons of Regular troops recalled from India, the Colonies and Mediterranean stations to form the 7th, 8th, 29th Divisions and those of the Indian Army Corps, and while additional battalions of Territorial units were being raised, side by side the creation of the New Armies proceeded with remarkable rapidity and enthusiasm, and, taking everything into consideration, with really extraordinary smoothness.

The following was His Majesty the King's message to his Army:

" You are leaving home to fight for the safety and honour of my Empire.

" Belgium, whose country we are pledged to defend, has been attacked and France is about to be invaded by the same powerful foe.

" I have implicit confidence in you, my soldiers. Duty is your watchword, and I know your duty will be nobly done.

" I shall follow your every movement with deepest interest and mark with eager satisfaction your daily progress; indeed, your welfare will never be absent from my thoughts.

" I pray God to bless you and guard you and bring you back victorious."

To every soldier of the British Army who left England for France Field-Marshal Lord Kitchener addressed the following letter:

" You are ordered abroad as a soldier of the King to help our French comrades against the invasion of a common enemy. You have to perform a task which will need your courage, your energy, your patience. Remember that the honour of the British Army depends on your individual conduct.

" It will be your duty not only to set an example of discipline and perfect steadiness under fire, but also to maintain the most friendly relations with those whom you are helping in this struggle. The operations in which you are engaged will, for the most part, take place in a friendly country, and you can do your own country no better service than in showing yourself in France and Belgium in the character of a true British soldier.

" Be invariably courteous, considerate and kind. Never do anything likely to injure or destroy property, and always look upon looting as a disgraceful act. You are sure to meet with a welcome and to be trusted ; your conduct must justify that welcome and that trust.

" Your duty cannot be done unless your health is sound, so keep constantly on your guard against any excesses. In this new experience you may find temptations both in wine and women. You must entirely resist both temptations, and while treating women with perfect courtesy, you should avoid any intimacy.

" Do your duty bravely.

" Fear God.

" Honour the King."

THE GREEN HOWARDS

" MALPLAQUET,"

" ALMA," " INKERMAN," " SEVASTOPOL,"

" TIRAH,"

" RELIEF OF KIMBERLEY," " PAARDEBERG," " SOUTH AFRICA, 1899–1902."

CHAPTER II

THE 1ST BATTALION

1914–1919

INDIA. THE THIRD AFGHAN WAR

WHEN the Great War opened in August, 1914, the 1st Battalion The Green Howards had been some six years and a half on foreign service. It had gone to Egypt from Aldershot in February, 1908, and had arrived in India just four years later, its first station in that country being Sialkot. When war was declared, however, the Battalion was quartered at Barian, with a detachment at Sialkot, and the Indian Army List for July of that year gives the following distribution of the officers at that date belonging to it :

Lieutenant-Colonel G. Christian, D.S.O., in command ; Majors W. L. Alexander (on leave out of India), C. V. Edwards, G. B. de M. Mairis and M. D. Carey ; Captains C. H. de P. Bunbury, B. H. Leatham (depot), H. V. Bastow, K. W. L. Simonet, B. L. Maddison (depot), R. S. Ledgard (adjutant, on leave out of India), L. F. Lanyon and C. N. Jevelund ; Lieutenants T. C. Mintoft, A. C. Hooton, G. B. Worsdell, G. N. N. Smith (station staff officer, Barian), H. F. Blackwood, E. J. Richardson (depot), R. G. Atkinson (on leave out of India), B. Cuff, M. U. Manly (on leave out of India), G. L. Compton-Smith (on leave out of India), H. S. Bagnell (on leave out of India), S. R. W. Bennedik and G. W. E. Maude ; Second-Lieutenants E. G. C. Le Sueur, J. R. F. Errington and A. Beatson-Bell ; Lieutenant W. T. Howes was Quartermaster.

At this time there were 52 battalions of British Infantry quartered in India and Burma—17 in Bengal, 14 in the Punjab, 12 in Bombay, 6 in Madras, and 3 in Burma, and the immediate concern of the military authorities in London was to bring home as speedily as possible all the British portion of the garrison of India that conceivably could be spared to form the new divisions getting ready to proceed to France, replacing these in India by units of the Territorial Force which had already been invited to volunteer for such foreign service. Before the end of September ten

9

battalions of British Infantry had already left India, some of these proceeding direct to France with the two divisions of the Indian Army Corps, others voyaging to England to join the 8th Division ; by the end of the year fifteen more battalions had sailed for one or other of the many theatres of the World War ; and by the beginning of 1915 there were something less than a dozen battalions of British Infantry left in India, while the places of those which had gone to the war were filled by fine, strong battalions of the Territorial Force, of which from first to last over fifty-five thousand officers and other ranks served in India.   It is worthy of mention that, when asking Territorial units to undertake this service, Field-Marshal Lord Kitchener gave them a definite promise that "at the end of six months he intended to bring them home from India and replace them by less well-trained troops," while he further promised them that they should "share in all the honours of the war just as if they had gone to France."

The 1st Battalion The Green Howards naturally hoped that it would early be sent home from India to join one of the new divisions, and in a letter, dated the 30th September from Barian in the Murree Hills, to *The Green Howards' Gazette*, the writer says: "We are not one of the regiments which have been called for, but have no reason to think that our turn will not come before long, and the sooner the better."

At this date the Battalion had five companies at Headquarters, one at Attock guarding the very important bridge over the Indus, and two at Sialkot.   Of the officers who had been on leave at home when the war broke out, Major Alexander had been appointed to the 2nd Battalion, and Lieutenants Atkinson, Manly, Compton-Smith and Bagnell had rejoined the 1st Battalion *per* the *Dongola* ; while Captain Lanyon was at Samasata on railway duty, Lieutenant Cuff was at the Musketry School at Changla Gali, and Second-Lieutenant Le Sueur was attached temporarily to the Mountain Battery at Bara Gali; then of the non-commissioned officers, ten had been selected to proceed to England to assist in the training of the new armies ; these were Colour-Sergeants Stalker and Drew, Sergeants Newman, Staveley, Wicks, Morley, Dane, Myhill, Ayton and Smith.

The war had naturally somewhat disturbed the reliefs of British regiments in India, and there were orders and counter-orders as to where the 1st Battalion The Green Howards was to proceed on leaving the Murree Hills at the beginning of the cold weather of this year.   Early in October it was announced that the Battalion was to relieve a battalion of the North Staffordshire Regiment in Victoria Barracks at Rawal Pindi, being itself relieved at Sialkot by a battalion of the Gloucesters, and Captain Bastow proceeded to Rawal Pindi with an advance party to take over barracks. This order was, however, almost immediately cancelled on the grounds that the Gloucesters were being sent home at once, The Green Howards remaining at Sialkot. A few days later it was announced that the original order was to hold good, and in October the Battalion marched from the Murree Hills down to Rawal Pindi, and entrained from there for Delhi, remaining here only a few weeks before returning to Rawal Pindi, where it occupied Victoria Barracks in the Aldershot of Northern India.

"On November 29th," writes the Battalion correspondent of *The Green Howards' Gazette*, " an urgent wire arrived from Delhi ordering us to mobilize at once and proceed to Kohat. The detachment on manœuvres at Hassan Abdal received the wire at 11 p.m., and spent the night in the business of packing up and entraining. But there being no room in the train for the mules of the machine-gun section, that gallant body, under their redoubtable commander, undertook, on the spur of the moment, the thirty-mile march back to Rawal Pindi, where they arrived in barracks at 11 o'clock on the following morning—several lengths in front of the remainder who had come by train. The same evening . . . the Battalion* left for Kohat. Exactly what was happening on the frontier no one knew ; whether it was merely a rising of the tribes or an invasion by the Amir of Afghanistan with three hundred thousand men, led by German officers, was not certain ; but no one had any doubt that there *was* something considerable happening, and that we should probably be in the thick of it in a day or two."

The trouble at this time emanated in Waziristan, that five thousand square miles of hilly country lying on the western border of the Indian Empire, and forming the connecting link on the Afghan frontier between the districts of Kurram and Zhob. The expeditions sent into the country of the Wazirs have been many and costly, and the political relations of the Indian Government with this people have not been any the less difficult and delicate by reason of the claims made by the Amir of Afghanistan in 1884, and not definitely repudiated by us until 1892, to establish his supremacy over the Wazirs. The position of Waziristan was then defined to the Amir as one of complete independence, qualified by our right to hold direct relations with the people ; and in 1893 certain "protected" areas were formed in Wana and Tochi, administered by political officers, a loose form of control being exercised over the people outside these areas.

In October and November, 1914, many attempts were made to stir up fanaticism along the frontier, and at the end of November certain mullahs in independent territory led a *lashkar* from Khost into the Tochi Valley ; and, on the news of this gathering being received, reinforcements were dispatched to Bannu and Thal, Tank was strengthened, and a movable column was sent against the *lashkar* into the Tochi. Of the British forces then in

* Less one Company on detachment at Agra.

or dispatched to the scene of action, only the Northern Waziristan Militia was engaged, and by the second week in January, 1915, it was found possible to withdraw most of the extra troops which had been sent to this part of the frontier.

To continue the account given in *The Green Howards' Gazette* :

" Kohat, however, seemed to be pretty clear of the enemy. With the exception of a certain amount of mild surprise on the part of the inhabitants, and some disorganization of the station waiting-room staff at the unexpected appearance of so many hungry officers, things seemed to be adhering fairly closely to their normal routine.

" From Kohat we proceeded by light railway to Thal, a small frontier post in the Kurram Valley, where the fun was expected. But at Thal they told us that, though nothing had been heard of the enemy, it had been raining steadily for the past six months, and would probably rain again in the near future. The next day, while the clouds gathered overhead, we worked at our portion of the perimeter of the entrenched camp we were to occupy. At about 9 p.m. it began to rain ; by 10 o'clock it was pouring and continued to pour the whole of that night, the whole of the next day, and part of the following night, till the whole camp was reduced to a gigantic puddle, and the horrors of war were brought home to us. By a merciful providence the days following the deluge were fine ; and when we had got thoroughly dry and had completed the drainage arrangements of the camp, the order came to fill up our trenches and return to Rawal Pindi.

" After four days' march we again found ourselves at Kohat, only to learn that we were to hold ourselves in readiness to return immediately to Thal ; and after camping at Kohat a day we returned by train, convinced that at any rate this time there would be something worth doing there. But there was nothing, only a few rumours."

The Battalion remained at Thal, leaving one company at Kohat until the 11th January, 1915, when it marched back to Kohat, where, on the 16th, it entrained once again for Rawal Pindi ; here, during these movements, " A " Company had remained as a depot under Major Mairis, so that the whole Battalion was now once more united, though a good many officers and non-commissioned officers were detached on special duties, some with the arrived and arriving Territorial battalions. Lieutenant Mintoft had proceeded to East Africa in charge of a draft for the Loyal North Lancashire Regiment, while Lieutenant-Colonel G. Christian was early in the year appointed to command the Rawal Pindi Brigade with the rank of Brigadier-General, Major C. V. Edwards assuming command of the Battalion.

In February the Battalion was inspected by Major-General Townshend, C.B., D.S.O., who published the following remarks in orders :

"Major-General Townshend, on his inspection of The Green Howards in quarters, wishes to congratulate Colonel Christian on the smart appearance of the Regiment on parade, its fine physique, and the smart handling of arms. He wishes him also to inform all ranks that he feels proud to have this distinguished Battalion under his command ; more especially as it was commanded by one of his family, Colonel Townshend, some one hundred and fifty years ago. General Townshend wishes the Battalion all good luck in 1915, and also hopes that it may be shortly our good fortune to join in the present great war."

When later Major-General Townshend proceeded to Mesopotamia, Captain H. V. Bastow accompanied him as one of his staff.

During the hot weather of this year a detachment of the Battalion was quartered at Topa in the Murree Hills, and there was another detachment at Attock, but the Headquarters and greater part of the Battalion remained at Rawal Pindi ; later on, however, the Attock detachment was relieved by the 2nd North Staffordshire, when " A " Company of The Green Howards was sent up to Topa. Then towards the end of the year the Battalion went for a fortnight to Sohan to take part in manœuvres, but at the beginning of 1916 all were back again at Rawal Pindi, which was now more full than ever before of troops, British and Indian.

On the 5th and 6th May the 1st Battalion The Green Howards moved again to the Murree Hills, this year to Upper Topa where barracks had recently been built, but later in the summer these were vacated and the Battalion went under canvas, in a very rainy year, the barracks being given up to convalescents from Mesopotamia. On the 1st and 2nd November, The Green Howards moved down to the plains and re-occupied their former quarters in the Victoria Barracks, Rawal Pindi. Here the order appears to have reached the Battalion permitting the shaving of the upper lip, an indulgence as to which the Battalion correspondent of *The Green Howards' Gazette* remarks : " Some of the junior subalterns assure us that they are glad to avail themselves of the privilege and we are content to accept their word for it ! "

The Indian Army List for January, 1917, contains the following list of officers of the Battalion, which affords proof of the many changes that had taken place in its officer-corps since the commencement of the war : Lieutenant-Colonel E. G. Sinclair-MacLagan, D.S.O., temporary brigadier-general commanding brigade ; Majors M. D. Carey and H. V. Bastow, staff ; Captains R. S. Ledgard, A. C. Hooten, R. G. Atkinson, H. S. Bagnell (adjutant), S. R. W. Bennedik (Attock), and G. W. E. Maude ; Lieutenants E. G. C. Le Sueur (temporary captain, leave out of India), J. R. F. Errington, A. Beatson-Bell (attached 31st Divisional Signal Company), H. Ebourne, V. J. Barber, W. Derham, F. McGovern (attached 31st Divisional Signal Company), H. C. Lloyd, G. H. S. Hollom, A. Parrott, W. D. Clayton, T. Hayes (Supply and Transport Corps), P. Clow (adjutant and quartermaster Convalescent Depot), and F. Crowsley ; Second-Lieutenants J. W. Banner, P. W. Finch, R. Chouler (Indian Army Reserve of Officers), A. B. Wills and H. B. Morkill ; attached, Second-Lieutenants J. Baumber (13th West York-shire Regiment), W. K. Wallis (11th Lincolnshire Regiment), J. E. Hughes (9th East Yorkshire Regiment), N. J. Brewer (9th Lincolnshire Regiment), A. E. Green (10th Suffolk Regiment), J. L. Edmunds (9th Lincolnshire Regiment), H. Wigzell (10th Suffolk Regiment), J. C. Tobin (4th West Yorkshire Regiment), and E. W. Reed (11th Lincolnshire Regiment) ; with Lieutenant and Quartermaster W. T. Howes.

As to these attached officers the Battalion correspondent sympathetic-ally remarks as follows : " At the beginning of the month we welcomed nine attached officers who arrived after somewhat of a world-tour voyage of eight weeks. These are now enjoying that time-honoured and health-giving privilege of preventing the grass on the square from a too luxurious growth, and daily exhibit thereon the alertness and precision of movement so essential to the Adjutant's equanimity of mind ! "

This year passed very much like the previous one, the Battalion con-stantly drawn upon to provide officers for courses of all kinds, and non-commissioned officers for instructors of the Territorial battalions now form-ing so large a part of the British garrison of India, while occasionally officers were called for to fill gaps in regiments or among the staff at the many " fronts." Those left behind busied themselves with the practice of moun-tain warfare at Abbottabad and other suitable places, and the usual round —the plains in the cold weather and the hills in the hot—still went on. Of those whom the 1st Battalion The Green Howards sent away in drafts to other regiments in Mesopotamia and elsewhere, " Some there be which have no memorial," but *The Green Howards' Gazette* for June, 1918, tells us something of a small party of thirty-four men of the Regiment who joined the Cheshire Regiment, and of whom we read the following notice :

" Out of this number fell some of the best—Sergeant Miller, Corporal Quinn, Privates Maloney, Hurd and Lewis ; and since then we have heard of the death of Sergeant-Major Hardisty. Wounded we find Corporal Dale, Corporal Collis, Corporal Quinn, Corporal Scott (since died), Private Pugh, Sergeant Gill, Private Curley, and Privates E. Mauger and McDonald invalided. Mauger had been employed as an observer, and his place will be hard to fill ; he rendered good service during the engagements round Kut and at the Shumran Bend ; had his company officer been spared there is no doubt he would have been mentioned in General Maude's despatch. His services on board ship during the trip from Bombay to the Gulf were very valuable. He had eighteen cases of heat-stroke, but only one died ; and, considering the arrangements for hospital cases, he saved many when others might have given them up. On one case alone he poured cold water and rendered first aid from 11 a.m. until 8.30 p.m., when his services were rewarded by the recovery of a patient whose case the doctor remarked was hopeless. As a nursing orderly everyone recognized him as one of the best.

" Private Lewis was a sniper, and he too rendered valuable service. Lewis was beloved by all with whom he came in contact. A small wooden cross marks the place where his body rests near that of Corporal Scott at Kut.

" Morris, who was badly wounded, was a Lewis gunner ; he passed his course in ten days and came out first in order of merit. . . . Corporal Scott was a keen N.C.O., and his captain always spoke in high praise of him. He was wounded twice, but refused to be brought in. He longed to complete his task, and his name is on the tongue of everyone who knew him. He died as he wished—on the battle-field—his task completed."

In October, 1917, the Battalion moved to camp at Burhan, about midway between Rawal Pindi and Peshawar, and remained here until it proceeded, in January, 1918, to Peshawar. The hot weather of this year was spent at the small, more or less local, hill station of Cherat, one company remaining in Peshawar ; and when about the middle of this year India was overtaken by a terrible outbreak of influenza, which carried off no fewer than six millions of the population in three months, the 1st Battalion The Green Howards did not escape the visitation ; and when at last the epidemic had subsided the casualties had been by no means negligible, over thirty non-commissioned officers and men succumbing. The Battalion remained on in Cherat after the end of the hot weather of this year, only returning to Peshawar just before Christmas, 1918.

For the account of the services of the 1st Battalion The Green Howards in the Third Afghan War of 1919, it is thought that one can hardly do better than make use of the story contributed to *The Green Howards' Gazette* by Lieutenant-Colonel M. D. Carey, supplemented where necessary by such details as may be gathered from the Battalion War Diary.

" The disturbances which broke out in the Punjab and other parts of India during April did not at first appear to have penetrated to the North-West Frontier Province. Undoubtedly, however, there were secret and silent influences at work in and among the turbulent inhabitants of Peshawar City, which would at a given signal have blazed forth but for the watchfulness of the politicals and police, who took the necessary measures to nip any such movement in the bud. The head and centre of these disturbing elements was the Afghan Postmaster, an official permitted by us to live in Peshawar City to facilitate communication with Kabul. Meetings had been held to protest against what is popularly known as the Rowlatt Act, and a spirit of unrest was manifest. On one or two occasions shops in the bazaar and city were closed, this being part of the passive resistance movement to the above Act, but no rioting or open hostility occurred, and beyond precautionary measures on a more elaborate scale than usual, and a lot of ' standing to ' on the part of the troops, nothing unusual happened up to the end of April.

" With the advent of May, however, it became apparent that Amanullah-Khan, the newly-installed Amir of Afghanistan, proposed taking a hand in the game."

In the despatch, dated the 1st November, 1919, from the Commander-in-Chief in India, he gives the following information as to the forces at the disposal of the Kabul Government, the strength of the British Army by which these could be opposed, and the general plan of campaign which the Afghan leaders sought to carry out.

" The distribution of the Afghan Army at the end of April is believed to have been as follows : On the northern line, including Kabul, were stationed $7\frac{1}{2}$ regiments of cavalry (2,800 sabres), 29 battalions (16,500 rifles), and 110 guns, of which about 200 rifles and 4 guns were located between Kunar and Asmar on the Chitral border. On the central line, including Ghazni, were 3 cavalry regiments (1,100 sabres), 17 battalions (9,150 rifles), and 60 guns ; and on the southern line 1 cavalry regiment (460 sabres), 10 battalions (5,250 rifles), and 24 guns. The Afghan garrisons of Herat, Farah and Mazar-i-Sharif, and in the Maimana and Badakshan Districts are not included in the above and amounted to about 2,700 sabres, 11,100 rifles, and 70 guns. The force at the Amir's disposal thus comprised about 7,000 sabres, 42,000 rifles, and 260 guns, but it should be noted that at least half of his guns were either immobile or obsolete. But the Amir's real strength lay, not in his regular army (which in itself is of small account), but in the potential fighting value of the frontier tribes on either side of the Border. Expert in all forms of guerilla warfare, and amounting in the aggregate to some one hundred and twenty thousand men armed with modern rifles, many of which are provided from Kabul, these tribes are the outstanding factor in the Indian frontier problem, and it was on their co-operation that the Afghan plan of campaign was based. As far as can be judged, this plan contemplated operations on three fronts, viz. :

" (a) From Jalalabad on the Khaibar and Mohmand Sector ;

" (b) From Gardez on the Kurram and Waziristan Border, utilizing the Khost salient;

" (c) From Kandahar on the Chaman Border.

" The general idea seems to have been to push forward in the first instance detachments of Afghan regular troops, whose function was to raise the tribes on both sides of the Border. . . . The formations at my disposal at the outbreak of war (excluding units allotted to area defence) comprised 2 divisions and 2 cavalry brigades on the Khaibar line, 1 brigade in the Kohat-Kurram area, 2 brigades in Waziristan, and 1 division and 1 cavalry brigade and 2 mixed brigades in central reserve. During the course of the operations, 7 additional brigades and 1 cavalry brigade were formed, increasing the total force employed at the signing of peace to the equivalent of about 7 divisions and 4 cavalry brigades with 1 cavalry and 5 infantry brigades in reserve."

We may now resume Colonel Carey's narrative after this necessary digression.

" What motives urged the Amir thereto cannot at present be definitely stated, but be that as it may, he started the ball rolling by massing troops on his frontier, crossed the border line and seized the springs at Bagh, where is the source of water supply for Landi Kotal, our then furthest outpost up the Khaibar and garrisoned at that time by the Khaibar Rifles, since disbanded."

On the 5th May orders were issued for the mobilization of the Field Army, which in the first instance was organized in two bodies, the North-West Frontier Force commanded by General Sir A. Barrett, and the Baluchistan Force under Lieutenant-General R. Wapshare. Before the month was out, however, the troops of the Bannu and Derajat areas were separated from the North-West Frontier Force and placed under the orders of Major-General Climo, being designated the Waziristan Force.

The plan of campaign drawn up contemplated the taking of the offensive against Jalalabad with the main striking force, the object being to divide the Mohmands and the Afridis, two of the most important of the tribes likely to be implicated, cutting them off from Afghan influence and support ; to strike at any Afghan concentration within reach, and to induce the withdrawal of Afghan forces from our tribal borders elsewhere for the purpose of covering Kabul.

On learning of the Afghan movement on Bagh, " a portion of the Flying Column was at once rushed up the Khaibar to reinforce Landi Kotal, followed almost immediately by the remainder of the 1st Brigade, the 2nd Brigade from Nowshera moving into Peshawar.

" On May 8th a sudden and unexpected move on the part of the authorities

India – N.W. Frontier

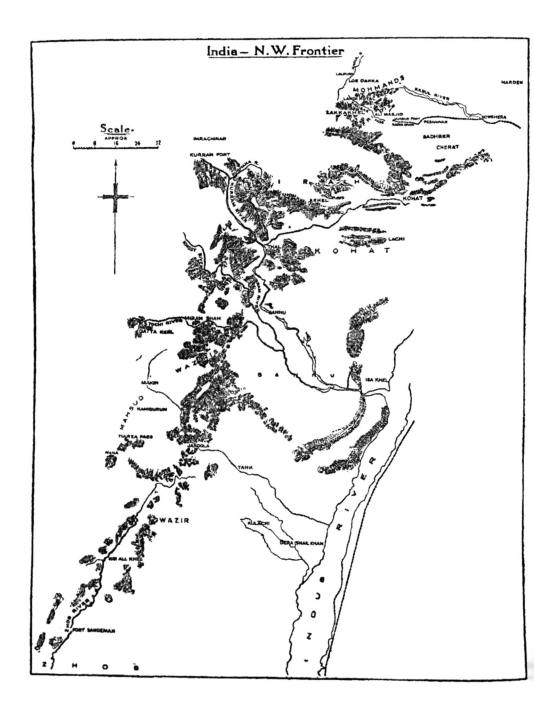

cut off Peshawar City from taking any active part in the hostilities now beginning, and severely cramped the style and activities of the Afghan Postmaster and several of his most notorious *confrères*. The city was quickly surrounded and all exits and entrances barred by troops of the 2nd Brigade and a regiment of Cavalry ; while the civil police, with the moral support of some armoured cars, raked through the city and made a large number of arrests of ' wanted ' and suspected agitators, including, of course, the Postmaster, who was ' wanted ' most of all. The arrest of the agitators effectively broke up the city conspiracy and little more trouble was given by the inhabitants during the campaign. Picquets were posted all round the city, a system of patrols instituted, all gates except one were closed, and no one was allowed to enter or leave the city—and then only during the hours of daylight—except by the Kabul Gate and under close scrutiny.

" At 6 a.m. on May 9th the Battalion took over the city picquets on the N., N.E., and E. sides of the city, and remained on duty for twenty-four hours. Nothing very stirring occurred, the extent of the inhabitants' ' offensive ' being mainly the making of faces, the hurling of violent abuse —chiefly on the part of the female portion—and, in a few cases, stone-throwing by some whom the mere threat of a shot quickly scattered. Further arrests were made and martial law was proclaimed during the day.

" Orders to completely mobilize were received on May 6th, but as one is always more or less in a state of mobilization on the North-West Frontier, little remained to be done, except the usual medical inspections, issues of stores to companies, etc. ; and I was able to report by 12 noon on the following day that the Battalion was fully mobilized in every respect and ready to move. On being relieved from our duties in the city at 6 a.m. on May 10th, we returned to barracks and spent a busy morning making final preparations to move—loading baggage, entraining mules, chargers, etc. ; and at noon the Battalion marched to the railway station and entrained for Kacha Garhi, our concentration camp, only about five or six miles from Peshawar, so that no time was gained by proceeding there by rail instead of on foot. Owing to demobilization having begun, and a large number of men being employed in various parts of India on ' non-recallable jobs,' the strength of the Battalion marching out was only 18 officers and 571 other ranks." The names of the officers were as follows : Lieutenant-Colonel M. D. Carey ; Captains G. Maude, P. Clow, and W. Howes (quartermaster); Lieutenant F. Crowsley (adjutant); E. W. Heckle, A. Lyle, E. Prestwich (Manchester Regt.), A. H. Booth (West Yorkshire Regt.), W. B. Kerr (Gordon Highlanders), E. W. Read (Lincoln Regt.), H. P. Cinnamond, M.C. (West Yorkshire Regt.), J. J. W. Fairburn (York and Lancaster Regt.);

Second-Lieutenants E. H. Hare (Royal Dublin Fusiliers), E. Brewman, and H. B. Hewitt (York and Lancaster Regt.), R. H. Marr, and G. Abbott (King's Own Yorkshire L.I.).

"With us in the 3rd Brigade were three Gurkha Battalions, viz. the 2/1st, 4/3rd and 3/11th; the last-named we found at Kacha Garhi, the other two having marched on that day to Ali Masjid, whither our Brigade Commander, Major-General A. Skeen, C.M.G., and staff had also gone. There were no orders for us at Kacha Garhi and no transport, hence the necessity of our coming five miles by train ; and our chances of getting any further in the immediate future did not look very bright, especially as the Army Commander, General Sir A. Barrett, whom I waylaid as he was returning in his car from watching an operation at Landi Kotal, whereby the Afghans were cleared off the heights overlooking that place, could hold out no hopes of providing us with necessary transport to move us for a day or two. So there was nothing for it but to settle down for the night and exercise the virtue of patience.

"Next morning of course the unexpected happened. A heated mounted orderly arrived at the same time as my shaving water with an order for us to march at 10 a.m. with a convoy of five hundred camels, using as many as we wanted for our kit and baggage, the remainder to be loaded up with supply and transport stores. Accordingly at 10 o'clock we got on the move —the sun being nicely up then and beginning to assert itself—with our long string of camels. The medical arrangements were certainly, as a distinguished officer remarked, ' top 'ole,' and consisted of a medical officer, very active and energetic, a sick assistant-surgeon, who struggled as far as Landi Kotal, after which he was seen no more, and a medical orderly strung round with a small pannier and a medical comfort haversack. As to motor ambulances and bullock tongas, there were none.

"The march was particularly hot and trying, and for the most part up-hill, and had to be done at camel pace, necessitating frequent halts which made it even more tedious. Several men were knocked out by the heat, and those who were too bad to be brought along on a camel had to be sent back to Jamrud or Peshawar as best one could, by packing them into passing lorries, or cars, or *tumtums*, whatever conveyance we happened to meet on the road. Owing to this non-provision of transport for the sick, several men who could otherwise have been brought on and would soon have recovered in camp, had perforce to be evacuated and were lost to the Battalion, thus still further depleting our small numbers. We bivouacked at Ali Masjid, and the night passed off without incident.

"At 7 a.m. the next day—the 12th May—we got on the move again, and soon after starting it was evident that the Afridis were going to provide some entertainment for us *en route*. About a mile from Ali Masjid, and at a point where the road passes through a gorge with steep and almost unclimbable hills, heavy and accurate sniping took place. To be sniped at while moving along a road in column of route, and from which it is almost impossible to take reprisals, and by marksmen one can never spot, is annoying enough, but when it came to seeing the Khaibar Rifle garrisons of some of the blockhouses designed to guard the route, either sitting outside watching the time-honoured sport, or even joining in, one was consumed by a feeling of helpless rage. It is, however, only fair to say that some of the blockhouse garrisons played up and fired back at their snipers, without, I fancy, doing them much harm. I turned a few men on as anti-snipers from the roadside, while I kept the column on the move. The party claims to have knocked one sniper off his perch on the hillside, but this was never verified. Our casualties were one killed, Lance-Corporal Richardson, a Lewis gunner, and two slightly wounded. In addition, Second-Lieutenant Marr, King's Own Yorkshire Light Infantry, attached, and one man sustained grazes, but marched on. One Lewis gun mule was also hit, but got on all right. ' A ' Company, who were finding the rear-guard, took on the snipers, result unknown.

" We were fortunate in not having more casualties, as the tribesmen had the range and had their aiming marks, consisting of white stones, etc., on the hillsides above the road. It was a lucky thing we had no camels hit, which might have held us up badly in an unfavourable position. Eventually we arrived without further mishap at Landi Kotal about midday, where we handed over our camels and went into the perimeter camp on the east side of the fort. Here General Skeen met us and we made his acquaintance, he having only taken over command of the Brigade a few days previously. The Brigade-Major, Griffith, 107th Pioneers, was, however, an old friend whom we were all glad to see again.

" Next morning we were off again " (17 officers and 504 other ranks), " moving at 4.45 a.m., as part of a force to picquet the road between Landi Khana—about four miles or so beyond Landi Kotal, at the foot of a steep hill, which had now become and remained throughout the campaign the station of the 2nd Brigade—and Lal Dakka. The object was for the cavalry force, consisting of the 1st Cavalry Brigade and one other cavalry regiment, accompanied by motor-lorries carrying three days' supplies, to pass through and occupy Dakka, which had previously been cleared by our aeroplanes doing a bit of bomb-dropping. Contrary to expectation, it turned out to be a peaceful and unopposed occupation. The Battalion was in reserve on this occasion and was not called upon to do any picqueting. It was, however, a very long and tiring day, lasting from reveillé at 3.30 a.m. until our return at 6.30 p.m., and included a seventeen-mile march, to say nothing of waiting about in the sun without any shade for five or six hours. Our rations up to this time were on the old-fashioned scale of bully-beef and Delhi biscuits, and it was not till some days later that we began to receive a more liberal allowance. We never attained the full scale, as something was invariably out of stock or unobtainable, such as oatmeal, bacon or vegetables ; but on the whole, after the first two or three weeks of the campaign, our rations were really good and sufficient, and left very little cause for complaint. Supply officers and their subordinates had to be up pretty early to prevent our good and efficient Quartermaster from getting to windward of them, and obtaining our full share, and perhaps a bit over of whatever was going. His daily visits to the ' dump ' were never unproductive.

" The Somerset Light Infantry met us on our return just short of our camp with *degchis* of tea which the men found very acceptable, and later an issue of rum was made which was even more so, and put them as right as ninepence once more.

" The next three days were spent in camp, improving the perimeter, taking our share of camp picquets, guards and the usual camp fatigues. During these days Captain Clayton, Second-Lieutenants Hartley, Ball and O'Callaghan rejoined on recall from Bombay, where they were almost in the act of stepping on board the ship that was to take them home on two months' leave prior to joining the F.S. details. Lieutenant Kerr, Gordon Highlanders, who had been attached to the Battalion for over two years, also rejoined from the School of Musketry.

" The 1st Brigade had moved to Dakka a day or two after the cavalry, and we were expecting to follow them shortly, but did not imagine we would move at such short notice as we eventually got. At 4.30 a.m. on May 17th I was awakened by the Brigade-Major coming to my tent with the news that the Battalion, in company with Brigade Headquarters, the 2/1st Gurkhas, a machine-gun company and a battery of artillery, would start at 7 a.m. for Dakka, but what had actually happened was this : On May 16th a small reconnoitring force which had gone out through the Khurd Kabul Pass, beyond the hills west of Dakka, had run their heads into it, and were followed up and harried on their return to camp. It was on this occasion that the King's Dragoon Guards carried out their charge, questions in regard to which were asked in the House of Commons. The Afghans followed up and occupied the nearer range of high hills overlooking the camp and from which they proceeded to give the camp a warmish time throughout the night, bringing up Krupp guns into position on the hills. These they failed to get away next day and they were all captured.

. . . The fact remained that the hills were occupied by the Afghans and could not be allowed to remain so. The 1st Brigade was consequently directed to attack this position at 4 a.m. on the 17th, our hurried move being to reinforce if required, and as events proved we were required badly.

" We arrived at the point where the road debouches from the hills on to the Dakka plain at 11.30 a.m., and were at once directed to move straight on to a high peak known as Somerset Hill, in the range of hills, having about one and a half to two miles of open, bare, stony plain to cross before reaching the foot of the hills. The 2/1st Gurkhas were to move on our left, while a machine-gun company and a howitzer battery supplied covering fire. The three Indian battalions of the 1st Brigade were at this time about half-way up the hill; they had suffered heavy casualties, and were unable to get on; the Somerset Light Infantry were in reserve in camp.

" I had only three companies available, and all were rather weak; ' C ' Company was on rear-guard and escort to second line transport and had proceeded straight to camp. I detailed ' B ' and ' D ' as firing line, finding their own supports, and had ' A ' Company as local reserve. The advance across the open was very steadily carried out, and at about two thousand yards from the position the fire began to grow pretty hot. As is usual in this kind of warfare, not a sign of an enemy could be seen, and it was difficult to tell where the fire was coming from; but it seemed to be from all sides except behind. It was while we were crossing the plain that poor Maude was hit, when nearing the foot of the hills. He made a speedy and apparently good recovery from his wound, which was right through the body, the bullet grazing the base of one lung and traversing the liver. He rejoined us less than four months later, to all appearance as fit as ever, but it is, I think, an undoubted fact that his subsequent sad and untimely death was due to his wound.

" On reaching the foot of the hill a certain amount of delay occurred, owing to the difficult and broken nature of the ground, and as the country was so *big*, my three weak companies seemed to be lost in the foothills. However, after some little time, the two leading companies started to climb the hill, and ' A ' got into a position whence they were able to help with covering fire. Once the companies commenced the ascent they were more or less in dead ground and, although I did not realize it at the time, the Afghans started to go as soon as we got to the hillside, having apparently come to the conclusion that as they did not stop us when crossing the open, we were for the top. Of course the howitzers and machine guns had been giving them a good basting all this time.

" It was at this point that the Brigade-Major arrived with a message that the Brigade Commander wanted me in camp, and that the Battalion was to stand fast in its present position while I went to receive fresh instructions. Having sent off the necessary orders, I accompanied Griffith to the General, who to my great disappointment told me that as the operation had been originally a 1st Brigade show, it had been decided to send the Somerset Light Infantry out from camp to pass through the Battalion and occupy the peak which was our original objective. In his accustomed cheery way, on hearing exactly the position the Battalion had gained, he remarked, ' Well, you've won the battle, but I've got another job for you if your fellows can do another four or five miles.'

" Having assured him on this point, I got my instructions, which were to collect the Battalion at the foot of the hill and move out to a small detached hill in the centre of the plain about one and a half miles south of our present position, thence to try and get into touch with a squadron of cavalry who were operating on that flank, and to send them, supported by our three companies and a section of machine guns, to round up and capture if possible an enemy mountain gun further away on our left flank, which had been very busy all day and had done some extremely accurate shooting. Fortunately for us, its shells had consistently failed to explode and merely went off like a damp squib ; it was a lucky thing for us they did as two were twice planted in the middle of our first line transport, and several landed amongst the second line as they were marching in, but in no case was any damage caused.

" It took some little time to get the three companies collected, as the two leading ones were well over half-way to the top, and, having ' smelt blood,' were naturally anxious to finish off their job. However, an order is an order, and eventually by 4 p.m. we were ready to move off on our new mission. The men were getting a bit done by this time, but there was nothing for it but to trek off to the new position and try and get into touch with the cavalry squadron. The hill was found to be already occupied by a company of the 15th Sikhs, who had been there since early morning. They were unable to give me any information about the cavalry, while two mounted orderlies whom I had been lent, and whom I sent to bring the O.C. Squadron to me, also failed to find any trace of them.

" The howitzers had been giving the enemy gun some attention and it had ceased to trouble us after we had begun to move off to our new position, and apparently it had cleared off at the same time as the general retirement of the Afghans from the main ridge took place. As there seemed to be nothing doing in this direction I made a report to that effect to Brigade Headquarters, and was jolly glad to receive a message in reply to return to camp, bringing all detachments in with me. We reached camp, a very weary and thirsty lot, at 6.30 p.m.—and what a camp ! The ground was

THE HILLS ABOUT DAKKA.

Showing the line of hills on which the permanent picquets, covering the camp at Dakka, were established.

The 1st Battalion were the first troops to occupy this ridge, which was carried out without opposition, on the day after the successful action at Loe Dakka, on 18th May, 1919.

It is a fair sample of the country that the operations took place in.

nothing but rocks and boulders, and, as I said before, it had been given a pretty warm time the night before and a large number of horses and mules had been killed. The stink—there is no other word for it—defies description, but even it, after another hour's work in building up a perimeter, added to the hardness of the ground, failed to prevent everyone sleeping soundly just where they happened to doss down.

" Our casualties were remarkably light, being, in addition to Captain Maude wounded, one man killed and three wounded. Although the fire was necessarily plunging for the most part, I can attribute our small losses to the fact that extensions, intervals and distances were very well kept and that we were on the move until we reached the foot of the hill, where we got into more or less dead ground.

" The following were awarded the Military Medal for their good work on this occasion : Company-Sergeant-Major Gill, 'B' Company, who took charge of 'B' Company's leading lines on Captain Maude being knocked out till the arrival of the next senior officer, and who steadied and encouraged the men admirably. He displayed great coolness and good leadership throughout the day. Private Kelly, 'A' Company, as a Battalion Headquarters runner was indefatigable in carrying messages under heavy fire, and when so employed lent a hand in helping with the wounded. In fact, he never stopped all day.

" Orders were issued that night for the next day's business, and next morning the Battalion moved off as an advanced guard to occupy the semicircle of hills on either side of the Khurd Kabul Pass, while the remander of the force shifted camp to a fresh site about one and a half miles along the Jalalabad Road and nearer the bank of the Kabul River. No opposition was met with except from three or four enemy snipers who were lying up in a nullah ; these were all accounted for by us and the Gurkhas. One sniper that some men of 'C' Company shot was dressed in khaki and had on black —Gurkha pattern—bandolier equipment. This, with other salvage, was called in for identification purposes. . . . The Battalion also salvaged a Krupp mountain gun and some of its ammunition. The Gurkhas, however, made the best haul of ammunition. This had been cleverly hidden, as the tribesmen, knowing how we respect their graves, had buried a lot of gun ammunition and disguised its concealment as the last resting-place of some of their dear departed, with the usual small slabs of stone at the head and foot. However, the Gurkhas nosed this out and disinterred quite a number of boxes. Except these few odd snipers, not a sign of an Afghan was seen that day, all having apparently gone off and not lingered by the way.

" Having taken up a covering position on the hills, we remained out most of the day, and eventually posted strong picquets on the selected hill-tops, which remained out until relieved the next morning, while the rest of the Battalion returned to our new camping site, which was to be our home for the next three or four weeks until a more extensive and better laid-out camp was occupied on June 11th.   One of our picquets, under Lieutenant Kerr, was attacked during the night, but the attack was not heavily pressed, and the picquet, although hastily and not very strongly sangared, owing to the short time available, was able to deal successfully with their assailants and suffered no casualties.

" We did not anticipate making a lengthy stay at Dakka, expecting a forward move to Jalalabad to take place, and preparations for such a move were, in fact, made, and there would have been little to stop us at this period.   Shortage of necessary transport and supplies, and also of men and animals, however, precluded the possibility of an early move, and our offensive against Jalalabad was confined to aeroplane bombing operations, which, from all accounts, were most effective and successful, as was also the one visit paid to Kabul by the Handley-Page machine.   The aerodrome at Dakka was just outside our perimeter, and our mess being the nearest to it we saw a good deal of the flying officers while the period of aerial activity continued on this part of the front. . . .   Every officer-airman carried a letter in Pushtu, signed by the Chief Commissioner, Sir G. Roos-Keppel, offering a reward of Rs. 10,000 to any tribesman who brought the bearer in safely in the event of his having to make a forced landing in hostile tribal territory.   Two officers of the R.A.F. were captured after a forced landing in the Bazar Valley, and were eventually returned to Landi Kotal after about a fortnight's captivity. . . .   The observer who underwent this unpleasant experience—Lieutenant Hoare—served in the Battalion for a short time before joining the Air Force. . . .

" Captain Barber joined us on 30th May, having been away for about two and a half years at Deolali, at which place he was latterly doing duty as S.S.O.   A draft of sixty-seven non-commissioned officers and men also came up to join, and some officer reinforcements.   The latter all belonged to various corps: they were Lieutenants Barclay, Dowland, Cozens and Moat.

" Our hardest and least appreciated duty during the next few weeks were the foraging expeditions to bring in corn, wood, and vegetables when we could get them.   No opposition was met with on any of these earlier expeditions, but they meant long and tiring days—a march of from eight to fourteen miles, with hard work collecting and loading up grain and wood for several hours, or else picqueting the heights and performing protective duties generally.   It was by now getting unpleasantly hot, and being out all day we invariably had one or two cases of heat-stroke on each of these expeditions. Everyone was glad therefore when the S. and T. Corps succeeded in amassing a sufficiency of fodder to keep the Force going and provide a reserve, and so obviate the necessity of our having to go out and reap corn with the bayonet or else pull it up by the roots.

" An Afghan emissary with a white flag used to come in almost daily at this period, and after several small-fry individuals had been turned down as not possessing sufficient authority to be treated with, someone of more standing eventually arrived and the so-called armistice was concluded. After this, as far as one could tell, we had no further engagements with the Afghan regulars, but it seemed to be the signal for the tribesmen, chiefly Mohmands, to become increasingly active and aggressive. Up to date we had not heard from them, barring the usual sniping, which was of almost nightly occurrence and continued so during the whole of our stay at Dakka. . . .

" By now—early June—the heat, dust and flies were all getting somewhat appalling, and although we were not having anything in the way of fighting, all ranks were getting a lot of hard work. Picquet duties in twenty-four-hour reliefs came round pretty frequently, road-making on the level and up to picquet positions, water-channel construction, pumping parties and all the usual camp fatigues, in addition to an occasional reconnaissance and foraging expedition. Until these were knocked off they all helped to fill up the days, while any spare time was devoted to improving and strengthening the perimeter defences. Nor was training neglected when men could be spared from other necessary duties. The health of the Battalion remained very good. . . .

" On 11th June the Battalion moved to its new camping ground near Sherabad Cantonment. The 3rd Brigade was now all together in a large square camp with two batteries of artillery and other details, and everyone had far more elbow room and space. It meant a longer perimeter to construct, consisting of a breastwork four feet six inches high with frequent traverses. The soil being soft loose sand, it was a difficult piece of work to complete satisfactorily ; in fact, it was not nearly completed until we were nearing the end of our stay at Dakka, but when finished it was a good piece of work. About the time we moved camp several cases of cholera occurred, but as prompt measures were taken to deal with it, it was fortunately prevented from spreading and was soon stamped out. It was, I think, imported from Ali Masjid where there was a serious outbreak, but in Dakka it was almost entirely confined to the transport *personnel*, only one European, a S. and T. sergeant, succumbing. I am happy to say we had no cases in the Battalion, every member of which had just finished being inoculated against it.

"At this period General Skeen was commanding what was known as 'Dakka Force,' consisting of the 1st Cavalry Brigade, 1st and 3rd Infantry Brigades, artillery and other details, as the G.O.C. and staff of the 1st Division were still at Landi Kotal. As he had taken the whole of the 3rd Brigade staff to form that of 'Dakka Force,' the 3rd Brigade had temporarily to find a new commander with an improvised staff. It was in turn commanded for short periods by Colonel Macmullen, 15th Sikhs, myself" (Lieut.-Colonel Carey, Green Howards), "and, finally Colonel Nicholay of the Gurkhas, until eventually a brigadier arrived to assume control in the person of Brig.-General R. O. B. Taylor, C.M.G., C.I.E. . . .

"Little occurred during this month to break the monotony of long blazing days and stuffy nights. The usual routine of fatigues, working parties, picquet duties and parades went on. We varied it once by taking part in a night operation to surround a village, but we drew a blank, although the village showed signs of very recent occupation. There was no doubt the alarm had been given by spies in camp. . . .

"News had been brought in of the gathering of a considerable *lashkar*, reported to be chiefly Mohmands, a few miles out along the Jalalabad Road, and they soon began to evince signs of activity after the celebration of the 'Id,' which marks the end of the Mohammedan's month of fasting. Attacks on the outer picquet line at night and heavier sniping became frequent, and they could be seen in the morning and evening buzzing about on the plain in front. A system of daily morning and evening cavalry reconnaissances was therefore instituted, and occasionally an operation was designed to draw the tribesmen under the fire of our artillery and machine guns; but the tribesman showed himself true to his reputation of being ever a shy bird when enticed to come and try conclusions in the open. For some time the supporting troops to the cavalry consisted of one company only, and this duty was delegated to the 3rd Brigade as long as these reconnaissances lasted.

"On 13th July the supporting company of the 2/1st Gurkhas got far more heavily engaged than usual as the tribesmen had come much closer in under cover of darkness and were on the hills this company was going to picquet. They extricated themselves after some sharp fighting at close range and claim to have inflicted considerable casualties on the enemy. In consequence of this the infantry detailed for supporting the cavalry reconnaissances was increased to three companies, with a second battalion standing by in camp and ready to move at fifteen minutes' notice if called upon. Later this was changed, a battalion and machine-gun section going out and three companies standing by in camp. The artillery had all important points registered and could be called on through a F.O.O. if required.

Nothing much beyond the ordinary exchanges happened during the next ten days, until on 23rd July, when ' B,' ' C ' and ' D ' Companies of the Battalion took their turn of this duty.   One of the Political Officer's native agents, who was met with on our way out, informed us that two of the hills we were in the habit of picqueting were already occupied by some of the enemy.   We, however, occupied all the hills except the most advanced one ; but as soon as a platoon of ' B ' Company started its advance to the latter, it was met by a fairly heavy fire, and as the approach to this hill, known as the Twin Peaks, was up a narrow spur, they were held up and prevented from gaining the summit.   A second attempt with two platoons met with no better result, and by now strong enemy reinforcements could be seen converging on this hill from all directions and the picquets on the other hills also became engaged.

" ' B ' Company was reinforced, but still Captain Barber asked for more men.   I was in telephone communication with the Brigadier and Brigade-Major and got a message to the 2/1st Gurkhas—the battalion standing by, to send out one company to reinforce me.   Very shortly afterwards I came to the conclusion that one company would not be enough, and got the remainder of the battalion sent out.   With them I was able to reinforce ' B ' and dispose of two more Gurkha companies in positions from which they were able to give good covering fire and close support to the platoons carrying out the assault on the Twin Peaks.

" In the meantime the howitzers were pounding the top of this hill with H.E., but, owing to the extraordinary good cover which existed, the tribesmen were able to shelter from this bombardment, and, directly it lifted, to come out and meet the infantry attack at close quarters.   This happened several times, and, contrary to one's preconceived ideas, the tribesmen stood up extraordinarily tenaciously to this artillery fire.   A section of No. 8 Mountain Battery subsequently came into action from a hill some way back and at a different angle from the field battery, and the effect of this fire was more searching and, under its cover, a further assault was delivered.   In the third attempt to occupy this hill, Lieutenant Hare, Royal Dublin Fusiliers, attached, Sergeant Westcott and a subadar of the 2/1st Gurkhas were killed, when practically on the summit of the hill and when leading their respective platoons.   Eventually at about 11 a.m. the fourth concerted attack gained and occupied the Peaks.   One platoon of ' B ' Company, under Second-Lieutenant O'Callaghan, and three platoons of Gurkhas composed this last attacking party.

" The British officer of the Gurkhas got the M.C. for his work in this affair, and I was disappointed that O'Callaghan, who had taken part in two of the three former unsuccessful attempts, was not awarded one also.   He brought back a trophy in the shape of a murderous-looking Afghan knife with which one of these beauties tried to behead him, but who was plugged by (I think) his platoon sergeant just in time. Hare was officially noted for a mention in despatches, as a posthumous award could not be granted him. Sergeant Wood, ' B ' Company, won the D.C.M., and Corporal-Signaller Bryant the M.M. for exceptionally fine work ; the latter was also brought to notice for his behaviour in the engagement of 17th May.

" Directly we captured this hill the enemy retired, as they had come, in all directions ; they went off quickly, but in more or less regular formation and in several extended lines. In fact their actions and methods all through were far more those of trained or semi-trained troops than the usual tactics pursued by frontier tribesmen, and there are some who maintain that they recognized Afghan regulars amongst them.

" Our casualties, in addition to Hare, came to four killed and nine wounded. We were able to collect and bring in all dead and wounded without molestation, and though the tribesmen advanced again during our withdrawal to camp, they did not press the retirement and we were able to get behind the permanent picquet line with no further casualties.

" I cannot but pay a tribute to the work of the Battalion signallers on this occasion; they worked like Trojans and kept up most excellent communication throughout, dealing with a great number of messages and reports.

" The enemy losses were reported as being one hundred and twenty, including thirty killed, and two of their leaders are said to be included in these numbers."

On the day after this action the Afghan peace delegates passed through on their way to Rawal Pindi, where a conference was opened on the 26th July, and after very protracted negotiations a preliminary peace was signed on the 8th August, being ratified a month later.

At the end of July the Commander-in-Chief visited Dakka, and in the middle of August the Viceroy also came to this part of the frontier, visiting the outer picquet line. Early in September the troops commenced to withdraw, the Cavalry Brigade and the 1st Infantry Brigade moving India-wards first, at the rate of a regiment or battalion per day. The 13th September was the day fixed for the final evacuation of Dakka, and the last night spent here was marked by the usual amount of sniping into camp.

At 4 a.m. the Brigade marched off, the 1st Battalion The Green Howards —strength only 385, including officers—forming the advance guard and baggage escort, and by midday the last of the troops had reached Landi Khana. The retirement was not followed up in any strength, but there was some tolerably persistent long-range firing by the tribesmen, which, however, caused no casualties.

The Battalion marched on each day, halting at Ali Masjid and Jamrud, and reached Peshawar, its peace station, on the 16th September.

The fighting in which the 1st Battalion was engaged does not compare with that in which other battalions of the Regiment took part on other fronts during the Great War; but certainly all ranks had anything but a " soft time." They had a very great deal of hard work in a difficult and inhospitable country, and under very severe climatic conditions during the greater part of the time; the enemy, moreover, as the history of Indian frontier expeditions shows, was by no means one to be despised, and the tactics in which they are adepts are admirably adapted for the country over which the fighting took place.

The following are the names of the officers of the Regiment, and of those of other corps who were attached to it, who served with the 1st Battalion The Green Howards in the Third Afghan War of 1919:

Officers of the Regiment: Lieutenant-Colonel M. D. Carey; Captains G. W. E. Maude, V. J. Barber, W. D. Clayton and P. Clow; Lieutenants F. Crowsley, F. Hartley, G. Ball, W. H. Mitchell and E. W. Heckle; Second-Lieutenants L. M. O'Callaghan and A. Lyle; Captain and Quartermaster W. T. Howes.

Attached Officers: Captains A. G. C. Denber * (King's Own Yorkshire L.I.), W. Moger * (Somerset L.I.), and S. J. Cozens * (Norfolk Regiment); Lieutenants E. Prestwich (Manchester Regiment), A. H. Booth (West Yorkshire Regiment), W. B. Kerr (Gordon Highlanders), C. N. Barclay * (Cameronians), A. L. D. Laskie,* D.C.M. (King's Own Yorkshire L.I.), E. W. Reed (Lincoln Regiment), H. P. Cinnamond, M.C. (West Yorkshire Regiment), J. J. W. Fairbairn (York and Lancaster Regiment), C. A. Moat * (Somerset L.I.), W. Dowland,* M.C. (King's Own Yorkshire L.I.), and A. Birkmyre * (Royal Lancaster Regiment); Second-Lieutenants E. H. Hare † (Royal Dublin Fusiliers), E. B. Newman (York and Lancaster Regiment), H. B. Hewitt (York and Lancaster Regiment), R. H. Marr (King's Own Yorkshire L.I.), G. Abbott (King's Own Yorkshire L.I.), and J. P. Williams * (East Surrey Regiment).

* Joined with reinforcements in Afghanistan.   † Killed in action.

CHAPTER III

THE 2ND BATTALION

1914

THE OPENING OF THE WAR AND THE FIRST BATTLE OF YPRES

WHEN, on the 4th August, 1914, war was declared against Germany, the 2nd Battalion The Green Howards, being quartered in the Channel Islands, was not allotted to any of the brigades or divisions constituting the original Expeditionary Force, and its immediate duties on mobilisation were to send parties to various points in the islands of Guernsey and Alderney to guard cable stations and other places of naval and military importance.

On the 6th reservists began to arrive at Battalion Headquarters from the Depôt, these coming over in charge of Captain Maddison, Second-Lieutenants Walmesley and Thorne, all of the 3rd Battalion, and the days that followed were fully occupied in musketry, in fitting out the reservists, in drawing such war stores as were available and in handing in all peace-time equipment. On the 23rd and 25th the two companies which had been stationed at Alderney rejoined Headquarters on relief by a detachment of the 3rd Battalion North Staffordshire Regiment, and finally, on the 27th, orders were received for the Battalion to embark next day. The 2nd Green Howards left Guernsey at 10 a.m. on Friday, 28th August, in two steamers, " A " and " B " Companies with Battalion Headquarters in the *Sarnia* and " C " and " D " Companies in the *Vera*, reaching Southampton Dock about 6 p.m. the same evening, and there learning that they were the first unit to arrive of the new 7th Division.

The same evening the Battalion marched out to the rest camp on the outskirts of the town, remaining there the best part of a week, during which time the other battalions detailed to form the Division began to arrive, so that when, on the 4th September, The Green Howards marched to a camp at Lyndhurst in the New Forest, the formation of the 7th Division was tolerably complete. It was commanded by Major-General T. Capper, C.B., D.S.O., and contained the 20th, 21st, and 22nd Brigades, and in the 21st Brigade, under Brigadier-General H. E. Watts, were the Second Battalions of the Bedfordshire Regiment, The Green Howards, the Royal Scots Fusiliers, and the Wiltshire Regiment.

The battalions of the new division now spent some very busy days drawing their war equipment—carts, transport animals and harness, which had to be gathered from all parts of the United Kingdom; but before long all was ready and everybody was anxiously waiting for the order to march to the port of embarkation.

" At 3.15 p.m. on Sunday, October 4th, we received our long-expected orders. At 5.30 p.m. ' A ' and ' B ' Companies marched out and were followed an hour later by ' C ' and ' D ' Companies. The two half-battalions did not meet again for three days. The right-half battalion embarked at about 10 p.m. in the Leyland S.S. *California* and set sail early next morning under sealed orders. At 4 p.m. we found ourselves off Dover, where we got more orders, and soon we were all trying to find if Zeebrügge was marked on our war maps. We arrived at Zeebrügge early on the 6th and entrained for Bruges. We were the first British troops to arrive in Bruges and our reception was a very hearty one. We were conducted to billets which had been selected for us. The officers were accommodated in private houses and the office of the Tramway Company, while the companies were put up in the tram sheds. . . . We spent the 7th October at Bruges and were joined by the left-half battalion," which had embarked in the S.S. *Victorian* and did not leave Southampton until the early morning of the 6th October, having been occupied during the whole of the 5th in embarking guns, R.A.M.C. wagons, etc.

The following are the names of the officers and of the principal warrant and non-commissioned officers who accompanied the Battalion overseas :

Lieutenant-Colonel C. A. C. King, Majors W. L. Alexander and W. B. Walker, Captains T. W. Stansfeld, D.S.O., A. L. Godman, H. W. McCall, B. S. Moss-Blundell, C. G. Jeffery, L. Peel, H. Levin and R. B. Corser, Lieutenants C. G. Forsyth, adjutant, A. E. G. Palmer, R. H. Phayre, F. C. Ledgard, machine-gun officer, and H. S. Kreyer, Second-Lieutenants L. H. Marriage, W. A. A. Chauncy, transport officer, P. C. Kidd, W. A. Worsley, H. G. Brooksbank and R. H. Middleditch ; Lieutenant and Quartermaster E. Pickard, and Captain E. S. Winter, R.A.M.C., T.F., in medical charge. Attached from the 3rd Battalion were Second-Lieutenants M. D. W. Maude, W. H. Colley, and R. Walmesley. Captain E. S. Broun remained in England to follow with the first reinforcement. R.S.M. F. C. Hatton, R.Q.M.S. M. Thwaites, Sergeant-Drummer Penniket, Pioneer-Sergeant T. Pennycuick, Sergeant-Cook F. Caulfield, Colour-Sergeant O.R.

Sergeant S. Challice, Lance-Sergeant O.R. Clerk A. Lamper and Armourer-Sergeant H. Pinner, A.O.D.

"A" Company: C.S.M. W. Mann, C.Q.M.S. W. Cooling, Sergeants E. Keane, L. Carter, J. Heaton, J. Stancliffe, W. Pinner, R. Malpress, A. E. Radford, G. Mellady and G. Mitchell.

"B" Company: C.S.M. W. Wilcox, C.Q.M.S. R. G. Lovett, Sergeants T. Fell, H. Lucas, W. Ingleson, W. Hitch, J. H. Ghiblin, G. Holroyd, W. W. Court, W. P. Phillips and G. Walton.

"C" Company: C.S.M. J. Sefton, C.Q.M.S. W. Sheay, Sergeants W. Wood, W. Neary, E. Fox, F. Taylor, H. Fraser, J. H. Bartle, J. L. Kitchen, T. E. Gray and S. Ayling.

"D" Company: C.S.M. J. Nolan, C.Q.M.S. J. Smithies, Sergeants J. McEvoy, G. Toase, T. Hey, A. Shortridge, H. Liddle, E. Longley, and W. Dimsdale.

The advance of the 7th Division having now been landed on the Flanders coast, this seems a favourable opportunity to give the reasons why this force had been put on shore in a theatre of war somewhat remote from that in which the units of the original Expeditionary Force were at the time contending.

"Throughout the operations near Paris which culminated in the Battle of the Marne, and in the pursuit which followed that battle, General Joffre had endeavoured to outflank and envelop the right, or western, wing of the German hosts. When the deadlock between the contending forces was reached in the middle of September, 1914, on the Aisne, he still sought for success by a continuation of the same manœuvre. As the Germans, on their part, also aimed at turning the open western flank of their enemies, the battle line had extended rapidly northward. . . . In their race northwards, however, the French and German divisions and corps on the threatened flank had arrived in a succession so nearly synchronous that neither side had been able to secure a strategical advantage. . . . Whilst the two armies were thus extending northward in the effort to outflank each other, it was evident that a suitable force, if it could be spared from the main action, thrown into the fray on the north, in advance of the parallel fronts, might obtain the decision that mere extension of the front seemed unlikely to bring about. . . . Early in September the British General Staff had suggested a movement from Dunkirk and Calais, and on the 16th September, General Joffre, acting on this idea, asked that all available British troops might be sent to these ports to act against the enemy's communications." *

* *Official History of the War, Military Operations, France and Belgium,* Vol. II, pp. 27, 28.

The number of British troops at this time available was, however, very small, and in the meantime the Germans had fully realised the increased importance of Antwerp and the necessity of its early capture. " Antwerp was not only the sole stronghold of the Belgian nation ; it was also the true left flank of the allied left front in the west. It guarded the whole line of the Channel ports. It threatened the flanks and rear of the German armies in France. It was the gateway from which a British Army might emerge at any moment upon their sensitive and even vital communications." *

The changes induced in the military situation by the results of the Battles of the Marne and the Aisne had made the early capture of Antwerp a matter of the first importance for the Central Powers, and as early as the 9th September the German High Command had issued orders that steps should at once be taken for the reduction of the fortress. On the 28th fire was opened from huge howitzers upon the exterior forts, and although a considerable Belgian army was engaged in the defence of the place, the situation rapidly became very grave and the allied governments were fully alive to the serious effect which the fall of Antwerp might have on the result of the campaign in the west. The Belgian Government appealed for assistance to England and France, and from the first named came the promise of the dispatch of a cavalry and an infantry division with certain naval detachments, while the French agreed to send a Territorial Division and a Brigade of Marines ; the whole made up a force of rather over fifty thousand men. The British Infantry Division began disembarkation at Zeebrügge on the 6th October, on which date the French Territorial Division and Marines were embarking at Havre or entraining for Dunkirk.

General Capper had been ordered before leaving England that he was to disembark his division at Zeebrügge and co-operate with the French contingent in supporting the Belgian Army defending Antwerp, but he was especially warned that on no account was he to run the risk of getting shut up in the fortress ; so that when on disembarkation he was urged by the local Belgian military authorities to at once entrain for Antwerp, he declined this proposal and instead proceeded with his force to Bruges, there joining General Sir Henry Rawlinson, who had recently been promoted from the command of the 4th Division to that of the British force assembling in the north.

" By 5 p.m. on the 7th," so runs the *Official History of the War*, " the Division was practically all concentrated at Bruges, and it was billeted in the town and suburbs. It now became evident that the expedition to relieve Antwerp as planned could not be carried out. Of the expected force of fifty-three thousand men, only the 7th Division had arrived, and during the

* Mr. Winston Churchill in *The World Crisis*, Vol. I, p. 332.

day the War Office forwarded news of a large enemy concentration, principally cavalry, north of Lille, which it was suggested was intended to act in the
direction of the recently landed British force.   On this day, indeed, the
German *IV. Cavalry Corps*, on the extreme flank of the main army, was
approaching Ypres, but without any knowledge of the new British forces."

In view of the information that strong enemy forces were advancing from
Lille, the 7th Division, on the 8th October, marched from Bruges to Ostend
and formed on an arc of a circle four miles outside the town to cover
the landing of the 3rd Cavalry Division.   The Green Howards, however,
marched to Klemskerk, a village near Ostend, and that day and the night
that followed were spent in a field, the Battalion moving back next day
to its former billets in or near Bruges.

While the Division was in the vicinity of Ostend, General Rawlinson had
received instructions from Lord Kitchener, under whose orders he was
directly acting, that the decision to evacuate Antwerp had now been come to,
and that his troops were to cover the withdrawal of the Belgian Army from
the line Ghent-Selzaete to the area Ostend-Thourout-Dixmude, subsequently
forming the left column of the eastward advance of the main British Army.
Accordingly the 20th and 22nd Brigades were sent on the 9th to join the
French and Belgian troops at Ghent, while the 21st Brigade and the 3rd
Cavalry Division remained at Bruges, but on the 10th moved to Beernem,
seven miles on the road to Ghent.

On the 9th October Sir Henry Rawlinson's force was placed at the
disposal of General Sir John French and became known as the IV. Corps.

On the march to Beernem, The Green Howards furnished the advanced
guard for the 21st Brigade, and on arrival " C " Company was employed on
outpost duty, being relieved next day by " D " Company.   Beernem was
left on the 12th and the Battalion marched by way of Koolscamp and
Roulers to Ypres where it arrived about noon on the 14th October, and here
some of the Green Howards were for the first time in action.   Major Pickard,
the Quartermaster, thus describes what took place :

" The Battalion marched with the Brigade up the Menin Road and after
a time I received orders to proceed to Kruisstraat and billet the Battalion
there.   This village was about half a mile from the Ypres railway station on
the road to Dickebusch.   On arrival there I rode through the village in order
to get an idea of the size of it and the type of houses it contained.   I then
came back to the Ypres side of the village and commenced to mark up the
houses for the Battalion.   Suddenly, a small boy appeared out of a by-
road, shouting ' Uhlan !   Uhlan ! '   I had my regimental quartermaster-
sergeant with me, and Sergeant Bell was actually at the door of the house.
I seized Sergeant Bell's rifle and some ammunition off him and dashed off

to the corner of the road.   There about twenty yards away were two Uhlans. My Q.M.S. and I dropped on our knees and blazed off.   The Uhlans who, in my opinion, should have charged us, turned round, crashed into each other, and dashed away, but not before we had got them both in the back.   A naval party, who had an aeroplane on the Dickebusch Road, was in Ypres when we started firing, and thought their aeroplane was in trouble, so dashed out in a light lorry.   I told them what had happened and asked them to get down the Dickebusch Road as fast as they could and try and capture those two Uhlans.   Off they went as fast as possible and returned about ten minutes later with the two.   One was an officer who was very badly wounded and died shortly after in Ypres, the second was a non-commissioned officer who was also seriously wounded in the back. . . .   My Q.M.S. and I were the first to open fire in the 7th Division."

Apparently the Battalion marching later in to Ypres also had some little excitement,for firing was heard in front, magazines were at once charged and the machine guns ordered up and all made quite sure they were in for a " scrap " of some kind.   " On arriving near Ypres we met two armoured cars who told us they had fired on and brought down a German aeroplane . . . but when the cars came up with it they found the machine intact but the pilot and observer gone.   This was the firing we heard. . . .   While we were on the road we saw a car coming down the road at a great pace.   We then discovered it contained the two German officers who had escaped from the aeroplane, they having been captured further up the road and were being brought back to Ypres.   They were sitting on the back seat with a large Gendarme between them, who was holding them firmly by the scruff of the neck and shaking them hard the whole time ; a French dragoon was standing on the step beside them, and another Belgian Gendarme was leaning over the front seat waving a large revolver under their noses.   I never saw two men look so annoyed in my life or two such awful looking blackguards ; both had lost their hats and, like all Germans, had their heads entirely shaved ; the result was not flattering.   One of them, we discovered, had got the Iron Cross for being the first man to throw a bomb on Antwerp."

" In conjunction with the 87th French Territorial Division—originally detailed for the relief of Antwerp—which was now in occupation of Ypres," so the *Official History* states,* " General Rawlinson took up an outpost line covering the town.   The marching on the *pavé* roads and the haste of the operations had been very trying to the infantry of the 7th Division, who, brought for the most part from foreign stations, were not in hard condition, and the men arrived tired and short of sleep, little guessing they were to remain unrested and unrefreshed for many days to come."

* Vol. II, p. 67.

While in Ypres the news was received that Regimental-Sergeant-Major F. C. Hatton and Regimental-Quartermaster-Sergeant M. Thwaites had been granted commissions, and Company-Sergeant-Major W. Wilcox and Sergeant W. Ingleson were then appointed to fill their places.

The 21st Brigade marched out of Ypres at 11.30 a.m. on the 15th and proceeded to a railway " Halte " about one and a half miles east, where the Brigade took up a defensive position occupying the trenches vacated by some French Territorial troops who were drawn off to the left flank. The 2nd Green Howards remained in reserve for the greater part of the day, but early in the afternoon " C " and " D " Companies under Major Alexander were moved about half a mile to the left to support another battalion of the Brigade which was covering the road leading from Passchendaele.

In Sir John French's operation orders for the 16th October, issued on the afternoon of the 15th, General Rawlinson's troops are for the first time included, and the 7th Division was now directed to move eastward between Courtrai and Roulers, with the 3rd Cavalry Division on its left, north of Roulers ; it was to keep slightly ahead of the III. Corps and co-operate with the Belgian Army ; on the 16th then, the 7th Division was moved to a covering position about five miles east of Ypres, running from the west side of Zandvoorde, through Gheluvelt to Zonnebeke, and some six miles long, and here the Division began to entrench. On this day the Battalion marched, as advanced guard to the Brigade, to Gheluvelt and on arrival here advanced about a mile east of that town to the cross-roads nine kilometres from Ypres, where a small collection of houses, with the inevitable estaminet, went by the name of Petit Kruiseecke.

Of the position here taken up and of the events of the day one who was present has given the following account :—" We were told to entrench a line which, as far as our Brigade was concerned, ran from the ninth kilo-metre stone through Poezelhoek and then back in the direction of Poezel-hoek. The 22nd Brigade carried this line on facing almost due north, and on our right the 20th Brigade continued the line facing south and south-east through Zillebeke. So, as will be seen, the Division faced roughly three ways —north, east, and south. The Battalion had to hold about a mile of ground which included the village at the cross-roads by the ninth kilometre stone, and continued from that to the left towards Poezelhoek. " A " Company had the village and the cross-roads, " B " Company was on their left, then " C," and then " D." Headquarters, to begin with, was in the village. . . .

" The men had tea and breakfast and while this was going on a small patrol which had gone out from ' A ' Company under Phayre came back very full of themselves, having captured a German patrol. They had gone down the road a bit and been fired on from a farmhouse, so they moved up against the place and saw about eight Germans run across the road from the house into a barn. They shot one as he was running. . . . The remaining Germans were summoned to surrender, and as they flatly refused to do so, Phayre set the barn on fire. Eventually they came out, but not until their boots were nearly burnt off their feet ; and when asked why they had not surrendered before, they said they had been told that the English always shot their prisoners ! They were agreeably surprised when they found that, instead of being killed, they were given some food ; and said if they had known that they would have surrendered long ago. They were reservists of the 19th Hussars, and we told them it was only fitting they should be captured by the 19th Regiment ! "

The same day Battalion Headquarters occupied the estaminet at the cross-roads and found there on the table the partly-consumed meal of some German officers who had hurriedly left on learning of the advance of the 7th Division.

The 17th October was spent in entrenching and in securing the troops against any possible enemy attack ; the line and village occupied by The Green Howards were shelled and snipers were tolerably active, but there were no casualties ; and then on the 18th the Battalion marched from its entrenchments about 11 in the morning to the village of Becelaere and became reserve battalion of the Brigade, being accommodated in very close billets ; but late that night orders were received for all transport to move back to the old position near Gheluvelt.

It was the eve of the First Battle of Ypres.

The First Battle of Ypres is officially considered to have commenced on the 19th October, 1914, and to have come to an end on the 22nd of the following month, and the part which it appears to have initially been intended that the 7th Division was to play in the battle is indicated in the orders at this date received by General Rawlinson and under which he was now acting : * " Rawlinson was to move with his right on Courtrai, keeping generally level with the III. Corps in the subsequent advance, should that prove possible ; his cavalry under Byng were to move to the north of him. I had told Rawlinson that, whilst conforming to the general move east, he must keep an eye on the enemy's detachments known to be at Bruges and Roulers, I told him I would deal with these later by means of the I. Corps, but for the moment his left required careful watching." Subsequently, so Lord French tells us, having good reason to believe that Menin was very weakly occupied on the 17th, he issued orders to General Rawlinson to move on and attack that place on the 18th.

* Lord French, *1914*, p. 219.

At the time when these instructions were issued the allied line from Albert to the sea-coast was held as follows : The Tenth French Army was disposed from Albert to Vermelles ; then came the II. British Corps between Givenchy and Laventie ; on its left was a corps of French cavalry ; next to these was the III. British Corps astride the Lys east of Armentières ; then came Allenby's Cavalry Corps ; in the Ypres Salient was the 7th Division with the 3rd Cavalry Division on its left ; while between Zonnebeke and Bixschoote the I. Corps was now coming up in line, with French cavalry and marines between it and the sea.

In the *Official History of the War* the following description is given of the town of Ypres and of the country in its immediate vicinity : " The town itself is surrounded by strong earthen ramparts faced with brick, and on the eastern and southern sides by a broad wet ditch. Standing at a corner of the coast plain, at the junction of the Comines and Yser Canals, it is over-looked on the south by the Kemmel heights and on the east by a low line of hills running south-west to north-east, marked by Wytschaete—Hill 60—Hooge—Polygon Wood—Passchendaele. The summit of this latter ridge at Wytschaete is 7,000 yards from the town ; near Hollebeke this distance is reduced to 4,000 yards ; at Polygon Wood it is again 7,000, whence it gradually trends away. Its height above the general level of the plain gradually decreases from about 150 feet at Wytschaete, to about 100 feet where the road between Hooge and Gheluvelt crosses it, and to about 70 feet at Passchendaele. . . . The ridge was, as was often said, the rim of a saucer, with Ypres in the middle of the saucer, and those inside it felt that they could do nothing without being observed. . . .

" Several well-marked spurs extend from the east side of the main ridge ; notably that of Messines, which projects nearly two miles south-eastwards from Wytschaete, and forms a barrier across the approach to Kemmel from Wervicq, Comines and Warneton ; so important is it that it was known as a ridge and not as a mere spur. . . . South of it, and separated from it by the valley of the small, but muddy-bottomed Douve, lie Ploeg-steert Wood and Hill 63. The Wulverghem spur is parallel to and west of Messines Ridge ; the Oostteverne spur lies due east of Wytschaete ; and there are others running towards Gheluvelt, Becelaere and Keiberg. Stretching out further than these spurs and connected to them by saddles, are the swells of higher ground at Zandvoorde, Kruiseecke, Terhand and Moorslede. In general, southward of Ypres the ground is a series of small ridges and depressions, while northward it gradually flattens out and be-comes featureless. The Ridge in 1914 was dotted with woods, forming an almost continuous chain from Wytschaete to Zonnebeke and giving excellent cover from view. Some of these . . . were of considerable size. . . . Between them there was often cultivated ground. Some seven miles north of Ypres lay the great Houthulst Forest. . . .

" The lower ground west of the ridge was partly grass fields and partly cultivated. It was intersected by small streams. . . . Between the fields there were often high hedges as well as ditches, and these with isolated trees in the hedgerows assisted to obstruct the view when the leaf was on, as it was in October, 1914. . . . The roads, except the few main ones radiating from Ypres, were merely mud tracks. Along them, besides the villages and occasional chateaux, were numerous isolated houses. . . ."

A few words must be said of the weather conditions during the battle : it opened in weather which was dull and misty, observation beyond a very limited distance was impossible, and for days together the morning mists enveloped everything in a thick haze well into midday. Then rain fell heavily, followed in November by snow : the fields became impassable, the soil was water-logged and the trenches were first turned into water-channels and were then frozen over.

" In the IV. Corps the morning of the 19th opened satisfactorily. Reconnaissances made the previous evening by an armoured car furnished good information as to how the German line near Menin was held. Sir Henry Rawlinson therefore ordered the 7th Division to move to the attack early," * the right flank being protected by the 2nd and the left flank by the 3rd Cavalry Division. The attack on Menin was to be carried out in three distinct phases as follows :

1st phase, an attack by the 22nd Infantry Brigade on the trenches at Klythoek from the north.

2nd phase, a combined attack by the 20th and 21st Infantry Brigades against Gheluwe.

3rd phase, a combined attack by the Division from Gheluwe and Klythoek on Menin.

The 20th and 21st Infantry Brigades were to remain in concealment ready to advance near Kruiseecke and Terhand respectively.

" General Capper placed his three brigades in line, the 20th on the right near Kruiseecke, the 21st next to it near Terhand, and the 22nd opposite Dadizeele. The Division thus faced south-east towards Menin with a front of about 8,000 yards." *

As matters turned out, in being ordered to advance to the capture of Menin, the IV. Corps and the 7th Division were given a task wholly impossible of fulfilment ; General Rawlinson was operating with inade-

* *Official History of the War, Military Operations,* Vol. II, p. 132.

quate support on a front of twenty miles, and the ultimate abandonment
of the advance was due to the sudden and unexpected appearance of two
new German Army Corps from the direction of Courtrai, the proximity
of which had been in some measure foreshadowed by the capture on the
18th by French cavalry, near Roulers, of some cyclists belonging to one
of them.

In view of the enfilade fire from Werwicq on his right flank General
Capper, commanding the 7th Division, decided to attack first with his
left, the other two brigades of the division capturing Gheluwe, and the
whole then advancing on Menin as soon as the 22nd Brigade had taken
the trenches on its front.   By noon on the 19th this brigade had advanced
nearly two miles and was now within assaulting distance of the German
trenches south of Kezelberg—two thousand yards south-west of Dadizeele
and a little more than two miles from Menin.

" The morning passed very quietly," writes a diarist of the Battalion,
" until suddenly, about 1.30 p.m. we got orders to be ready to move at
a moment's notice, and at 2 p.m. off we went, not to the attack of Gheluwe
as we thought, but back to our own entrenchments we had left the day
before.   On the way we were told that the attack on Kezelberg, though
successful, had had to be abandoned because it was suddenly discovered
that two German Army Corps were moving down on to us from the direction
of Roulers. . . .   We got back to our entrenchments about 4.30 p.m.,
that is to say, with roughly an hour and a half's daylight left."   The
Battalion was now back in its former trenches at the cross-roads at the
Ninth Kilometre on the Menin Road, and spent the night improving the
position.   On this evening the 7th Division was occupying a line from
Zandvoorde east to Kruiseecke, whence it turned north and passed behind
Becelaere to Zonnebeke, so that its left was three and a half miles in rear
of the place whence it had started in the morning, and the task of the
IV. Corps and the 7th Division now was to hold on while the I. Corps
came up on the left to the north of Ypres.

On the morning of the 20th the German artillery commenced to shell
the position very heavily, and about 10.30 a.m. General Capper sent forward
two battalions from both the 20th and 21st Brigades towards Gheluwe
and Terhand respectively.   These came under heavy fire and were shortly
ordered to fall back whence they had started, and the Germans then
followed up and an engagement spread southwards along the whole front
of the Division.   The Germans were driven back by fire ; but at 4 p.m.
they made another attack—it was also repulsed, but the enemy got within
fifty yards of the British trenches at one place, and continued his attempts
to advance until well into the night.

Of the events of this afternoon a Battalion correspondent wrote in *The Green Howards' Gazette*: " That day was our first experience of shell fire and though we had only shrapnel against us it was not very pleasant. The enemy's snipers came into action too, and wonderfully good they are in utilizing ground for cover. . . . There was a certain amount of shooting on the left during the afternoon, and when dusk fell we were able to get out of our trenches and found out what had happened generally. We were told that among the casualties in ' D ' Company, Walmesley had been killed."

" The task of the IV. Corps was to hold on while the I. Corps came up on its left. General Rawlinson's orders for the 21st October directed the 7th Division to improve its trenches, and the 3rd Cavalry Division to concentrate on the left of the line and protect the right of the advance of the I. Corps. The front of the 7th Division was a long one, and formed nearly a right angle, roughly running eastwards one and a half miles from Zandvoorde to Kruiseecke, and then four miles northwards to Zonnebeke. There was great difficulty in making good trenches, for, owing to night work and constant retirements, the loss of picks and shovels in the small number of heavy—that is full-sized—tools carried had been very great . . . barbed wire, here as elsewhere before R.E. Parks were formed, was almost unobtainable. The Germans opened the day with heavy artillery fire, mainly with ' Black Marias ' and ' Woolly Bears,' from a series of new positions, and followed this up by infantry actions. . . . The enemy made no progress, though the position of the IV. Corps was for some time very critical, owing to the 2nd British Cavalry Division on its right giving ground and to the heavy attack made against its left. . . .

" By 8 a.m. the extreme left of the Division was seriously threatened by infantry of the *52nd Reserve Division*. . . . Then followed a very determined attack by the *54th Reserve Division* and *3rd Cavalry Division* against the 21st Brigade (centre) and 20th Brigade. It was particularly pressed against the 2nd Green Howards and the 2nd Royal Scots Fusiliers of the 21st Brigade in the centre near Poezelhoek, between Gheluvelt and Becelaere. The Germans came on in wave after wave, and, despite the heaviest losses, managed for a moment to break in between the two battalions " ; but, except for a slight retirement near Zonnebeke, the line of the IV. Corps was generally retained during the 21st, though it had no reserves, and General Rawlinson had to employ his cavalry division first to safeguard his left and then his right.

So far the *Official History of the War*,* and the Battalion Diary gives no idea of the severity and the intensity of the fire this day, all it says

* Vol. II, pp. 155–157.

being : " Artillery duel continued soon after daybreak, increasing in force towards midday. Enemy made an unsuccessful attack on the left flank of our position. A few casualties caused by shrapnel " : but another diarist tells us that " early this day we saw masses of the enemy who offered very fine targets for our machine gunners who were not slow to take full advantage of them ; all companies poured in a very heavy independent rifle fire, and the enemy recoiled with many casualties. Apparently he had been massing for an attack, but the fierce fire poured into his troops made him withdraw and alter his plans."

From 7 a.m. on the 22nd October the front of the 7th Division was heavily bombarded, the enemy fire especially affecting the junction of the 21st and 22nd Brigades in front of Polygon Wood, but there was no serious infantry attack during the forenoon.

" About 3 p.m., however, when the Division had already been heavily shelled for eight hours, the German infantry was seen to be advancing over the crest of the ridge running from Becelaere to Zonnebeke, against the front of the 21st Brigade and its junction with the 22nd near Reutel. The weight of this attack fell upon the 21st Brigade and a very determined attempt was made to overwhelm it. Here the 2nd Green Howards, the 2nd Royal Scots Fusiliers and the 2nd Wiltshire were in line, and under the fierce fire these delivered as the enemy came in sight the German masses staggered, but, led by their officers, some still struggled on and even penetrated a gap between The Green Howards and the Scots Fusiliers, there being annihilated by a reserve company. The remnant of the 54th *Reserve Division* came on again, but were driven back, decimated by shrapnel, machine gun and rifle fire, and dug in where they had taken refuge, in some places only 400 or 500 yards from the British line."

In the German Official account of Ypres we are told that the XXVII. Reserve Corps " fought for the upper hand in the woods between Zonnebeke and Becelaere," and that " the well-aimed fire from the enemy's prepared positions reaped a great harvest."

One of the 2nd Battalion who was there tells us that " we could see quite clearly columns of Germans massing on our left flank ; our artillery made excellent practice, but how we prayed for more and heavier guns. On the evening of this day we heard that the enemy had broken through the line on the left. They were attacking in mass for all they were worth and fully determined to break through, but were stopped in a most gallant manner by ' A ' Company and the machine guns under Lieutenant Ledgard and by a party of our men who volunteered to attack and clear a wood under Captain Jeffery."

In this operation Lieutenant Ledgard was killed and Captain Jeffery mortally wounded, and the manner of the deaths of these very gallant officers has been thus recorded by some of those who fought beside them.

"On the day of the big German attack Lieutenant Ledgard was in command of two machine guns. Operating against us were eight machine guns and some artillery, and every few minutes he had to change the position of the guns. Backwards and forwards along the trenches, from one position to another, he was running with a heavy machine gun over his shoulder and perspiration streaming down his face. Man after man in his section was hit as they mowed down the German infantry, and eventually all were out of action except Lieutenant Ledgard and Private Norfolk. Almost at nightfall the officer was hit by a shell and he died—a great hero in the eyes of every Green Howard. Then Norfolk was the only one left and, though wounded by shrapnel, he continued unaided to work his machine gun until the attack ceased at nightfall. Private Norfolk was awarded the Distinguished Conduct Medal."

Of how Captain Jeffery this day received his mortal wound, a private soldier states as follows : " It was the beginning of the great attack to get Calais. ' D ' Company was slightly in advance and to the left of the trenches in which were Captain Jeffery—' C ' Company—and his men. The Germans attacked ' D ' Company from the front, and as the regiment on their left was forced back, it was evident that ' D ' Company would be enfiladed in their trench. They therefore retired to the right and behind Captain Jeffery's trench. On his right there was a small wood and immediately behind this was the main road to Ypres. About seven men, including Private Waller, ran through the wood and there saw, though it was getting dusk, being after 4 o'clock, a party of Germans advancing to take ' C ' Company in flank. Waller dashed back to inform Captain Jeffery, the Germans being now some fifty yards away. Captain Jeffery said,' If they are as near as this we must charge them with the bayonet : who will rush them with me ? ' Waller and about twenty men jumped out of the trench and charged, Captain Jeffery gallantly leading them, sword in one hand, revolver in the other. Before they reached the Germans Captain Jeffery was struck by a rifle bullet and called out, ' I am wounded somewhere— carry on, men, carry on ! ' "

On this day Lieutenant and Adjutant C. G. Forsyth and Lieutenant W. F. I. Bell were also wounded.

During the next four days—the 23rd to the 26th inclusive—The Green Howards, like other battalions of their brigade and division, were subjected to a tremendous shell fire, night and day, without a break. The expenditure of ammunition by the Battalion was naturally very great, especially when it is remembered that day by day the rifle strength of The Green Howards declined. Every night, under cover of the darkness, ninety-six thousand rounds of ammunition were brought up ; and on one occasion when, in the middle of the day, more ammunition was urgently required, the six ammunition carts came up, " delivered the goods," and returned without casualty among men or horses, though heavily fired on by the enemy when returning through Gheluvelt."* In the Divisional diary of the 23rd the following may be read :

> " The tenacity of this battalion (2nd Green Howards) during this and the following days of heavy fighting was worthy of all praise. Though subjected to violent shell fire and continued infantry attacks, they fought steadily on. When blown out of one trench, they moved on to the next, and never wavered."

Of the nature of the entrenchments at this period held by the 7th Division, the *Official History of the War* tells us that, " dug in sandy soil, these trenches had already lost all regular shape, and they gave little cover ; but a far more serious result than this was that the sand thrown up by shell bursts got into the barrels and mechanism of the rifles, caused bursts and jambs, and even interfered with and prevented the fixing of bayonets."

A heavy toll had been taken of the officers of the Battalion. On the 23rd Captain H. W. McCall was wounded ; on the 25th Second-Lieutenant L. Studley received wounds of which he died ; while on the day following Captain T. W. Stansfeld, D.S.O., was wounded and Lieutenant R. H. Phayre was killed.

Indeed, during the fighting since the opening of the Battle of Ypres, the losses experienced by the 7th Division amounted to 43·6 per cent of the officers and 37·2 of the men. The casualties in the 21st Brigade totalled 55 officers and 1284 other ranks, and on the early morning of the 27th it was at last relieved at the front and withdrawn into reserve at Veldhoek.

On this day General Rawlinson left for England to superintend the organization and training of the 8th Division which was to constitute with the 7th the new IV. Corps, and the 7th Division was now placed under Sir Douglas Haig in the I. Corps. In the redistribution of the front thus occasioned the 7th Division was to take up the line from the Chateau east of Zandvoorde to the Menin Road, and the result of this was that the 21st Brigade, the officers and men of which had hoped to obtain a rest of at least two days, received about 6.30 p.m. on the 27th October urgent orders to move up again to the trenches.

* The Transport Officer at this time was Second-Lieutenant W. A. A. Chauncy.

The 2nd Green Howards spent the whole of the next day under a very heavy shell fire and in the evening moved back again into reserve.

"At daybreak on the 29th October," so runs an account of the events of these days in *The Green Howards' Gazette,* "'A' and 'C' Companies went up to support the Royal Scots Fusiliers; at about 11 a.m. the Germans in great strength broke through a regiment on our left and threatened our left rear, which forced those on the right to retire about 1000 yards. Colonel King reorganized the Regiment and, collecting anyone he could find from other units, led an attack which was successful in retaking our former position and gaining another 200 yards. This advance was terrible, as the enemy simply poured shrapnel into us and our casualties were heavy. Major Walker was killed whilst in charge of his Company, 'C,' by a shrapnel bullet; his death was very much felt as we lost a very fine soldier and a good friend. Major Alexander, Levin, Marriage, Thwaites and Sykes were all wounded on the same day. . . .

"When dawn broke the Battalion took up a position which formed a salient, with 'D' Company on the left and the other companies in the order 'A,' 'C' and 'B.' We little knew what a terrible day it was going to be for us. We were fired at fairly heavily during the morning, but this caused no casualties; it was through the deadly accuracy of a few snipers who never seemed to miss, that the Battalion had a loss which those who get through this war will never forget—I refer to Colonel King; every officer and man felt his loss more than I can describe. Brown and Hatton were both killed by snipers. . . .

"All these casualties made Moss-Blundell C.O. of the Regiment—he was told about noon that he was the senior officer left. . . . At 3.30 p.m. we got a message from the Brigade telling us to retire. The message had been delayed three hours as the orderly had been cut off and had had to work his way through a wood which was full of snipers. When Moss-Blundell got this message he had to make up his mind what to do; it was one of two things—hang on till dark, or go at once and risk a larger loss of life. His mind was made up by hearing heavy firing on his left, and he took the Battalion back by companies, working from the left and starting with 'D' Company. Owing to some very bad shooting on the part of the enemy, and our men keeping their heads, we were able to get back with only eleven casualties; this did not include our losses in the trenches before we retired. We got back to our new position in the dark and were ordered to dig bomb-proof shelters behind the second line of trenches "— to a point south of the U in the word Gheluvelt on the map.

Of this retirement the Official Historian, after pointing out that the position of the Scots Fusiliers and Green Howards, north of Zandvoorde, was extremely perilous, forming as it did a pronounced salient in the line, the left of the last-named battalion being well in advance of the general line near Gheluvelt, goes on to say : " In spite of the loss of their commanding officer, and although they were only some three hundred strong, The Green Howards were not only still in possession of their ground, but had established such fire superiority over the enemy, that, like the bulk of the battalions of Smith-Dorrien's force at Le Cateau, they were able to break off the action in the middle of the afternoon, with the loss of ten men, using a covering force of only one platoon. Here, between Gheluvelt and Zandvoorde at any rate, as is known from their own account, the Germans had no zest for further losses."

Of the commanding officer of The Green Howards a general officer wrote as follows :

" Colonel King, I am sorry to say, was killed yesterday ; he was holding on to his trenches most gallantly, indeed he has done awfully well throughout ; nobody could have done better and I am most awfully sorry at losing him, and also many of the gallant fellows in his Regiment. He was splendid and I shall miss him greatly, he did such a lot of good work " ; while one of his Battalion said, " The Regiment has suffered severely, but his loss is the hardest blow of all. He was so splendid in these last days, always thinking for us, so tireless in his energy, never sparing himself in the great strain of responsibility which fell so entirely on him after Forsyth was wounded. We all loved and admired him." Another brother officer pays the following tribute : " I do wish the C.O. had lived to hear what the generals said about our Regiment and to read the splendid report they sent in. What is left of the Battalion has come through with flying colours. The Colonel could not have died a more gallant death. Right in the front trench he was, leading and cheering on the men. He was shot by a rifle bullet and death was absolutely instantaneous. He died like the true British officer he was, facing the enemy and doing his duty to the end."

Of such a man it may perhaps not inappropriately be said, as Clarendon said of Falkland : " Whoever leads such a life need not care upon how short warning it be taken from him."

Another officer of the Regiment who fell in this battle and whose loss was very deeply mourned was Captain L. Peel, then serving with the divisional cyclist company. On the night of the 23rd October, this company was ordered to attack a farm on the 20th Brigade front, between Gheluvelt and Klein Zillebeck, occupied by enemy machine gunners and snipers. Captain Peel made a preliminary personal reconnaissance and then attacked the farm, entering the building, but finding it too strongly defended to be held. The attackers had to fall back, but the last seen of Captain Peel, he was wounded, but fighting hand to hand in the midst of the enemy, his sword in one hand and revolver in the other.

" Saturday, the 31st October, 1914, was to prove one of the most critical days in the history of the British Expeditionary Force, if not of the British Empire . . . it will always be remembered for the more dramatic fighting near Gheluvelt. . . . A decisive victory " (for the Germans) " seemed assured ; for everything pointed to the British being completely exhausted. And they may well have appeared so to the enemy. The line that stood between the British Empire and ruin was composed of tired, haggard and unshaven men, unwashed, plastered with mud, many in little more than rags. But they had their guns, rifles and bayonets, and, at any rate, plenty of rifle ammunition, whilst the artillerymen always managed to have rounds available at the right place at critical moments." The line held firm, and at 7 p.m. on the 1st November, so the *Official History of the War* tells us, " the troops of General Capper and Lord Cavan were fatigued and worn out to the last degree. Though they seldom had a field of fire of more than thirty to one hundred yards, and no more obstacle in front of them than a wire fastened from tree to tree, and had been pounded by a numerous heavy artillery, they had held their ground with feeble effectives against the whole *39th Division* and brigades of the *4th Bavarian* and *30th Divisions* on either flank of it." *

On the 1st November the following message from the I. Corps was passed to The Green Howards through the Brigade and Division :

" Please congratulate the Yorkshire Regiment on their stout performance ; "

and this was forwarded by the Brigadier with the following addition :

" I am very pleased to send this on to you and I entirely concur."

In the position now taken up, the Battalion was ordered to hold on at all costs, wire was put up, and here The Green Howards remained in hourly and even momentary expectation of attacks which were now no longer so strongly pressed, and suffering many casualties from the enemy's high-explosive shells. On the 4th the Battalion again reverted to a position in reserve, occupying dug-outs about which shells fell at all hours of the day and night. Here Captain R. B. Corser and Second-Lieutenant H. G. Brooksbank were wounded ; but on the other hand a much-needed draft of eighty-eight non-commissioned officers and men arrived as a first re-inforcement under Lieutenant S. P. Gladstone.

On the afternoon of the 5th November a welcome message was received

* *Official History*, Vol. II, pp. 303, 304, 358.

to the effect that the 21st Brigade was about to be relieved by the 15th, and during the night that followed the Battalion was withdrawn out of the line and marched to Locre, reaching this village about 6 a.m. on the 6th. The men had been on the march since 10 the previous evening, and were so worn out by the march and the long days and nights in the trenches, that, on entering the field where they were to be given a hot meal before moving off to the billets which had been made ready for them by an advance party under the quartermaster, they lay down and were all fast asleep in a few minutes!

"Never," writes one who saw the remnant of the Battalion, "never did I again see during the war men in such a sorry plight. We had lost 10 officers killed, 18 wounded and 655 other ranks killed and wounded, of which about 250 were killed. What was as fine a Battalion as there was in the British Army, which had started the battle about 1000 strong, was now reduced to one captain, three second-lieutenants and less than 300 gallant men, but with the spirit of the old Green Howards still in their blood. The nucleus was there on which we soon built up the Battalion again."

In his report on the part played by the 2nd Battalion The Green Howards in the First Battle of Ypres, Major-General Capper wrote as follows:

"This Battalion during the fighting before Ypres occupied a very exposed position to the north of the cross-roads east of Gheluvelt. On one occasion, while in this position, the enemy succeeded in occupying a wood in the left rear of the Battalion. 'A' Company and the Machine Gun section had to be brought from the right flank to deal with the situation. This party gallantly and successfully drove the enemy from the wood, but lost the Machine Gun officer (Lieutenant Ledgard) and two other officers, besides many men. On the 24th, 25th, and 26th October, this Battalion was subjected to a tremendous shell fire and continual attacks, but never wavered. The enemy had the exact range of their trenches and endeavoured, systematically, to blow them in all along the line. The officers and men, however, showed a splendid spirit, and as they were blown out of one trench, moved into the next and never retired."

The Major-General then referred to the work of the 21st Brigade, in which the 2nd Green Howards were serving, and went on to say:

"When this Brigade was withdrawn from the front position near Ypres after nearly three weeks' continuous fighting, its effective strength, counting Brigade Headquarters, stood at 11 officers and 750 men."

So ended the part played by the 2nd Battalion The Green Howards in the First Battle of Ypres, though fighting actually endured for some days longer.   Of the work done by his thin, battered line General Rawlinson said :

"After the deprivations and tension of being pursued day and night by an infinitely stronger force, the Division had to pass through the worst ordeal of all.   It was left to a little force of thirty thousand to keep the German Army at bay, while the other British corps were being brought up from the Aisne.   Here they clung on like grim death, with almost every man in the trenches, holding a line which of necessity was a great deal too long—a thin, exhausted line—against which the prime of the German first-line troops were hurling themselves with fury.   The odds against them were about eight to one ; and when once the enemy found the range of a trench, the shells dropped into it from one end to the other with terrible effect.   Yet the men stood firm and defended Ypres in such a way that a German officer afterwards described their action as a brilliant feat of arms, and said that they were under the impression that there had been four British army corps against them at this point.   When the Division was afterwards withdrawn from the firing line to refit, it was found that out of 400 officers who set out from England there were only 44 left, and out of 12,000 men only 2336."

CHAPTER IV

THE 2ND BATTALION

1914–1915

NEUVE CHAPELLE. THE SECOND BATTLE OF YPRES. THE BATTLE OF LOOS

THE Battalion spent only a few hours in the vicinity of Locre, proceeding the same afternoon to Bailleul and crossing the Franco-Belgian frontier under the command of Captain Moss-Blundell, who had with him five officers only—Lieutenants Kreyer, Maude and Gladstone, Second-Lieutenant Chauncy and Lieutenant and Quartermaster Pickard. But this small officer-corps was still further reduced in the course of the 8th November, when the 2nd Green Howards moved with their Brigade up to Ploegsteert in support of the 11th Brigade, holding a position about two kilometres to the east of that village; for on this day Captain Moss-Blundell, Lieutenants Maude and Gladstone were all taken ill and were sent to hospital, leaving Kreyer, Chauncy and Pickard as the only officers with some two hundred and twenty other ranks.

While here the enemy persistently shelled the village of Ploegsteert, and the officers and men of the Battalion had to occupy dug-outs in rear, and the work upon which the Battalion was engaged during the three days spent here—digging trenches for the 11th Brigade, which at this time was composed of fragments of some fourteen different battalions—was very seriously interfered with.

On the 12th the Battalion was withdrawn to billets between Bailleul and Neuve-Eglise, and here received orders to be prepared for a move to Bac St. Maur, south-west of Armentières, but there was no change for some days yet, and on the 16th a large draft joined from Havre—five officers and five hundred and thirteen non-commissioned officers and men, bringing the strength of the 2nd Green Howards—with some other accretions—up to over one thousand all ranks.

On the 16th the 21st Brigade marched by Sailly to Fleurbaix, when two battalions went into the trenches while The Green Howards and the Royal

Scots Fusiliers remained in billets as brigade reserve, and here the routine followed was that battalions were three days in and three days out of the trenches.

In this neighbourhood several weeks were now passed.

On the 2nd December another draft arrived comprising three subaltern officers—Lieutenant C. G. Briggs (West Yorkshire Regiment), Second-Lieutenants W. Bosley (Dorsetshire Regiment) and J. D. Wyatt (Northamptonshire Regiment), and seventy-six other ranks, the whole being in charge of Captain B. H. Leatham, who on arrival assumed command of the Battalion, and on the 14th marched it to Nieppe ; and of the days spent here and of those that immediately followed a Battalion correspondent wrote at the time : " On December 14th we had a welcome change by getting orders to move to a different part of the line, where we stayed until the 18th December. This change did the Battalion a great deal of good, for it gave us a chance to do some marching as it was not in the trenches. . . . When we got back to our old quarters " (near Fleurbaix) " we were ordered out for a night attack on the German trenches." The 22nd Brigade was to open the attack at 4.30 p.m., followed by the 20th and that later by the 21st, but the attack by the 22nd Brigade failed, while that delivered by the 20th was only partially successful. " We waited six hours formed up on one of the darkest, wettest and coldest nights we have experienced, but in the end we were not used. That we must have got to our objective I am certain, as we were all in the best of trim for it. It was while waiting that Second-Lieutenant Pickup was wounded, and I regret to say we had one man, Private J. B. Jones, killed and eight other men wounded. Since this event we have had nothing particular to relate. The weather, if possible, has got worse, except for one little spell of frost, and rain in torrents, wind and even a thunderstorm have visited us. On December 23rd Major W. L. Alexander rejoined and took over command of the Battalion ; he has quite recovered from his wound and seems very fit. A draft of one hundred and twenty N.C.O.'s and men joined the same day. We spent Christmas Day in our billets. It was a beautiful frosty day and the ground was all white. We had a quiet day, plum puddings galore, and other additions from home. H.M. Queen Alexandra sent us 874 pound-tins of excellent plum pudding which was much appreciated. Then their Majesties the King and Queen sent every officer and man a Christmas card. Perhaps what caused the greatest interest was Princess Mary's present ; every one serving in the country at the time received this present and it gave the greatest pleasure.

" Christmas has caused strange happenings in the trenches. The Germans illuminated their trenches and asked for an armistice to bury some of their dead. This extended to a mutual peace which lasted over the New Year. ' If you do not shoot we will not,' was the arrangement. So we strolled about our respective entrenchments and were glad of the freedom to improve them and our dug-outs ; and really it was a blessing for us as the weather was the worst we have had. Some of us had interviews with the Germans to arrange this mutual understanding, and the men exchanged cigarettes and cigars and other souvenirs. But this private arrangement could not last and besides was rather disconcerting ; war is again being waged and the potting at each other's heads has once more begun."

The heavy and continuous rain had reduced the trenches to a deplorable condition, and in places the water was above the men's knees ; if pumping ceased for any reason, the trenches became flooded, while the parapets were continually giving way. In January and February, 1915, matters sensibly improved, the water was got under and the floors of the trenches were planked ; so that when on the 2nd March the Battalion marched to Estaires, the relieving corps, the 5th Canadian Battalion, found conditions markedly better than they had been earlier in the winter.

On the 7th March the 2nd Green Howards moved into billets in Laventie, and here on the 9th orders were received for an attack in which the Brigade was to take part on the following day, for the 7th Division was now to be employed in the early fighting of this year, the objects of the operations being the capture of Neuve Chapelle and the pushing as far forward as possible of the British line. The main offensive was in the hands of the First Army, supported by troops of the Second Army and by certain units from the general reserve. In these operations the 7th Division of the IV. Corps was to be actively engaged, especially about the village of Aubers ; and all ranks of Major-General Capper's command entered upon the battle heartened by the following order issued by the G.O.C. IV. Corps :

> " The attack which we are about to undertake is of the first import-
> ance to the Allied cause. The Army and the Nation are watching the
> result, and Sir John French is confident that every individual in the
> IV. Corps will do his duty and inflict a crushing defeat on the German
> VII. Corps which is opposed to us."

The British line opposite Neuve Chapelle was held as follows from right to left : the Indian Corps, 8th Division, 7th Division and 6th Division, and the attack was to be opened by the 8th Division and the Meerut Division of the Indian Corps ; but in his despatch of the 5th April, 1915, Sir John French imputes blame to the G.O.C. IV. Corps for not having brought his reserve brigades more speedily into action and pressed the advance when this was checked by the disorganization caused by the violent nature of the attack, and by the passage of the infantry through the enemy's trenches and the buildings of the village.

At 2.30 a.m. on the 10th March the 2nd Battalion Green Howards left their billets in Laventie and assembled in the reserve trenches, advancing at 9 o'clock to the support trenches of the 23rd Brigade in the Rue Tilleloy ; some few casualties were caused by machine gun fire when crossing the open, but there was no loss from the enemy's artillery.   It was not, however, until 2 p.m. that the Battalion moved across from the British line to the German trenches, crossing these and taking up a position with " D " Company on the left astride a second German trench running almost at right angles to the first one, their position here being a marked salient ; the remaining three companies were on the right, some of the men in an orchard and some in open ground, where they were a good deal troubled by rifle and machine gun fire.   There was here some delay before any order to advance further was received, but by dark the companies had got well forward and were then checked by two strong German redoubts.   The casualties so far had been surprisingly few, but all now began to entrench hard, knowing that a bombardment might be expected with the dawn.

The left company—" D "—was thrown back some 150 yards on the left rear, but the Battalion line was in touch with the 2nd Royal Scots Fusiliers on the right and the 2nd Wiltshire Regiment on the left.

During the course of the night many Germans who had fled before the surprise attack on Neuve Chapelle returned to their trenches, and when morning broke were occupying a position within 300–30 yards of the line of the 21st Brigade.   There was, however, no enemy counter-attack on the morning of the 11th as had been anticipated, and the British were not here in sufficient strength to attack the two redoubts.   A very brilliant attack was made on the enemy by the Battalion bombers under No. 8191 Corporal W. Anderson, who, with only nine other men, succeeded in bombing out and capturing sixty-two Germans in a trench opposite the left of The Green Howards. This day there were many casualties in the Battalion, some caused by the shells from our own guns ; and of the officers Second-Lieutenant G. Cuttle, who had lately joined from the Artists' Rifles, was killed while showing his men where the parapet needed strengthening, and Captains B. L. Maddison, C. R. White and W. K. Rollo, Lieutenant D. Paton and Second-Lieutenant R. C. Bentley were wounded.

Shortly before dawn on the 12th the Germans made a counter-attack upon the three right companies of The Green Howards, but this was completely stopped by rifle and machine-gun fire and the enemy fell back, leaving behind him from four hundred to five hundred dead.   Somewhat later some of the enemy crept up and occupied a trench on the left, whereupon

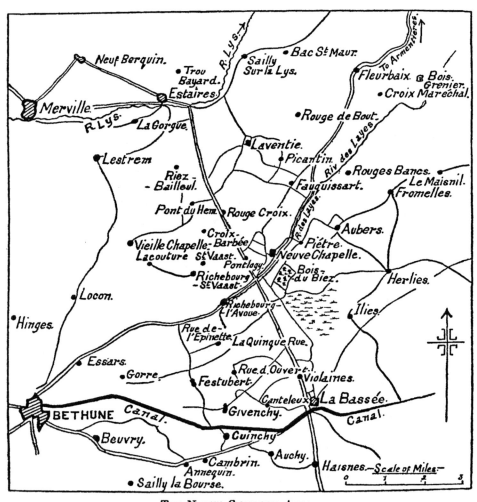

THE NEUVE CHAPELLE AREA.

Corporal Anderson again assembled his bombers and led them to the attack, directing also parties of riflemen who were sent up to assist.   This non-commissioned officer showed the greatest gallantry, fearlessly exposing himself on the top of the parapet, firing thence on the enemy with his rifle and then jumping down to hurl bombs among them ; when his own supply ran short he threw back the German bombs.

At about 11.30 a.m. the British guns began a very heavy bombardment of the German redoubt opposite the Battalion left, whereupon four hundred of the enemy came out and gave themselves up.   Part of the left rear company was then sent forward to fill the gap on the left of the advanced companies, and the Battalion now experienced some loss from the cross fire from the redoubt still remaining in German hands and from the enemy shelling of their old trenches.   This day two officers of The Green Howards were killed—Captain O. Oakes and Second-Lieutenant M. E. B. Crosse—the latter while working his machine gun ; Lieutenant A. E. Robinson, Second-Lieutenants H. L. Hollis, F. C. Pyman, A. J. Pickup and W. K. Walters were wounded, and Second-Lieutenant J. D. Wyatt was missing.

During the night of the 12th–13th the position was consolidated, and then during the early hours of the 13th the Battalion was relieved and ordered back to reserve trenches, Lieutenant H. S. Kreyer, D.S.O., being hit during the withdrawal ; on the 14th The Green Howards were called back to the front, but were not wanted, and so moved back into billets at Laventie.

The casualties during the operations of the 10th–14th March inclusive amounted to 3 officers and 90 other ranks killed, 11 officers and 182 non-commissioned officers and men wounded, and 1 officer and 24 men missing.

The following Order was published by the G.O.C. 7th Division :

" The Divisional General has now received the reports of the fighting near Neuve Chapelle between the 10th and 14th March.   He desires to express his sense of the steady conduct of the 2nd Battalion Yorkshire Regiment, whereby great damage was done to the enemy. The behaviour of the grenade throwers was particularly gallant, especially that of Corporal Anderson and his small party.

" The Divisional General much regrets the losses sustained by the Battalion."

Corporal Anderson, who was among the " missing " at the close of these operations, was awarded the Victoria Cross for his gallantry, in the *London Gazette* of the 22nd May, wherein may be read :

" No. 8191.   Corporal William Anderson.

" 2nd Bn. Alexandra Princess of Wales' Own Yorkshire Regiment.

" For most conspicuous bravery and devotion to duty at Neuve Chapelle on March 12, 1915, when he led three men with bombs against a large party of the enemy who had entered our trenches, and by his prompt and determined action saved what might otherwise have become a serious situation.   Corporal Anderson first threw his own bombs, then those in possession of his three men (who had been wounded) amongst the Germans ; after which he opened rapid rifle fire upon them with great effect, notwithstanding that he was at the time quite alone."

Of the appearance of the German trenches one of the Battalion wrote as follows at the time : " One's impression was that we have nothing to learn from them, except perhaps their excellent system of sniping loopholes.   The trenches were insanitary and dirty.   An enormous amount of rifles and equipment was lying about, and well-made packs full of comforts and clothing of all kinds.   Many boxes of good cigars were found and a lot of tobacco.   Helmets were the most sought-after trophy and there were dozens of them, both of the old black kind and the new pattern blue-grey ones.   In parts the Germans were evidently much troubled with water and had by no means got it in hand ; few pumps were to be seen."

For some little time now the 2nd Battalion The Green Howards was not seriously engaged : from the 16th to the 25th March it was in billets at Estaires, on this latter date moving into trenches about one and a half miles north of Fauquissart ; but on the 31st the Battalion went into Corps reserve at La Gorgue, where for a fortnight it enjoyed a complete rest.   From here on the 14th April a move was made to reserve billets about one mile north-west of Pincantin, going up from here four days later to the trenches and then on the 25th back again to billets at Laventie ; only three days were passed here, for on the 28th the Battalion marched to Strazeele, between Bailleul and Hazebrouck, and went into billets at Rouge Croix, the 21st Brigade being here kept as a reserve to the troops now engaged in the Second Battle of Ypres, which, having opened on the 22nd April, continued until the 24th May.   It was in this battle that the Germans made use for the first time of poison gas, which occasioned some reverses to the British, and the Commander-in-Chief now decided to concentrate all the efforts of the First Army on the southern point of attack.   " To this end," so runs the despatch of the 15th June of this year, " the 7th Division had been brought round from the IV. Corps area to support this attack, which was timed to commence on the night of the 15th (May), the 7th Division being placed on the right of the 2nd, and advancing with it and the Indian Division against the German trenches extending from Richebourg l'Avoué in a south-westerly direction."

The 2nd Battalion The Green Howards had now received substantial reinforcements both in officers and men : during March and April the following drafts arrived—272, 25, 30, 166—also the undermentioned officers : Major T. W. Stansfeld, D.S.O., Captains F. E. Fish and A. J. Richardson,

Lieutenants J. D. Hallifax and G. L. Nevile, Second-Lieutenants W. Gray, J. Lloyd-Jones, A. E. Belcher, K. R. Anderson, E. H. Fisher, A. Todd (Durham L.I.), J. H. Butlin (Dorsetshire Regiment), L. Coker (Essex Regiment), W. Sheay, A. H. Eames, J. O. Pritchard-Barrett, A. Pyman, F. C. Pyman, and A. J. Pickup.

The Battalion left Rouge Croix on the 4th May and moved gradually nearer to the point of attack, at 1 a.m. on the 9th marching to the cross-roads half a mile south-east of Rouge de Bout, and for this day the plan of attack was as follows : The 8th Division was intended to break the German line opposite Rouges Bancs and thence advance on Fromelles, while the 7th Division was to follow through the gap made, deal with certain defended points and then move on to Aubers, Le Plouich and La Cliqueterie, where it was to effect a junction with a division of the Indian Corps advancing from a point further south ; it was hoped that in this way the Aubers Ridge would be secured. The 1st Division was to move on the right of the Indians. Unfortunately the attack by the 8th Division on the 9th was only partially successful, and the 7th Division did not for some days get beyond the support trenches, the Battalion being in brigade reserve in the Rue de l'Epinette. It was not until the 12th that the services of the Battalion were required, when " C " Company and the machine-gun section went into the trenches, " D " Company following next day. On the 14th the Second Battalion experienced a great loss in the death of its commanding officer, Lieutenant-Colonel W. L. Alexander being killed by a shell fragment from one of our own guns. At the time he and Major Stansfeld were moving up through a communication trench to visit " C " and " D " Companies, and to see as much as possible of the ground over which the coming battle was to be fought. The trenches occupied by these two companies were much shelled and " C " Company had some sixteen casualties this day.

In company with the 2nd Division the 7th was to deliver its attack in the direction of Violaines, having its right some one hundred and fifty yards south of the Rue de Cailloux ; the 2nd Division was to attack late on the night of the 15th, and, if successful, again early the next morning with the 7th Division : the projected advance was one of about one thousand yards.

In the 7th Division, in this operation known as the Battle of Festubert, the 20th and 22nd Brigades were in the front line, while the 21st was held in reserve. " During the 14th and 15th," writes a Battalion correspondent, " our guns had been systematically bombarding the German trenches, and at 2.45 a.m. on the 16th those of us who were asleep (there were not many) were awakened by a terrific bombardment which lasted half an hour. At 3.15 the infantry assaulted and carried the German first-line trenches, and in some cases their second line. During this time our Brigade was in reserve.

. . . It was during this first assault at 3.15 a.m. that poor Sheay received the wound from which he afterwards died. He was at the time actually firing one of his machine guns in order to make absolutely sure it was trained on that part of the German parapet which our troops were now attacking ; a bullet ricocheted off the gun and hit him in the head. . . . In him we lost, I may almost say without any exaggeration, the best machine-gun officer in the British Army."

On the 17th " D " and " A " Companies were sent forward to support the Scots Fusiliers and " B " Company moved up into the place vacated by " D," " C " Company remaining in the British trench line. Later, " D " Company was sent up into the firing line on the right of the Royal Scots Fusiliers and helped that regiment to consolidate its position. About 4 o'clock in the afternoon Battalion Headquarters, " B " and " C " Company and the machine-gun section were all withdrawn and marched by way of Rue de l'Epinette and Festubert to the right of the British attacking line, " A " and " D " Companies remaining with the Royal Scots Fusiliers. While this move had been taking place the two remaining battalions of the 21st Brigade had been engaged in an only partially successful attack on the enemy's position about La Quinque Rue, and during the course of the night Battalion Headquarters, " B " and " C " Companies and the machine-gun section also moved up towards La Quinque Rue and the firing line and there dug themselves in.

About 9 p.m. this night " A " and " D " Companies of The Green Howards were withdrawn to billets in the Rue de l'Epinette, but the remainder of the Battalion remained in their entrenched position until the evening of the 18th, when they fell back to the first captured German trench, and about the same time the two other companies moved to the old British second-line trench on the south of the Rue de Cailloux. Finally, on the evening of the 19th the whole Battalion, on relief by the Canadians, marched to Gonnehem, north of Bethune, and was there accommodated in billets.

During these operations the Battalion losses amounted to 6 officers and 25 non-commissioned officers and men killed or died of wounds, 2 officers and 135 other ranks wounded, while 8 men were missing ; during the battle upwards of 150 Germans surrendered to The Green Howards. The names of the officers who were killed were Lieutenant-Colonel W. L. Alexander, Captain F. E. Fish, Lieutenants H. S. R. Montesole (Royal Sussex Regiment), J. D. Hallifax and E. H. Fisher, and Second-Lieutenant W. Sheay.

During the action a draft of two hundred and two rank and file arrived under Captain P. Hanbury and Lieutenant J. R. A. Rigby, but these remained for the time with the transport in rear, joining headquarters at Gonnehem on the 20th.

On the 27th the 7th Division was inspected in a field near Busnettes by General Joffre, who afterwards wrote the following letter to Sir John French :

> " The splendid bearing of the British troops who marched past me in the course of my recent visit reflects the greatest credit on officers, non-commissioned officers and all ranks.
>
> " I thank you for having afforded me the great pleasure of saluting your fine regiments ; and I request you to be so good as to convey to them my admiration of their soldierly appearance.
>
> " Please accept, Monsieur le Maréchal, my most sincere regards."

In the middle of June the 7th Division was again engaged in the neighbourhood of Givenchy, but the weight of the attack and the greater proportion of the losses seem to have fallen upon the 21st Brigade in general and The 2nd Green Howards in particular. On the afternoon of the 14th the Battalion proceeded to the trenches near Givenchy, and, preparatory to assaulting the German line next day, took over from the Scots Guards a portion of the British trench line east of Givenchy, " A " and " B " Companies manning the fire parapet, " C " Company being located in Givenchy Keep, Marais Redoubt, and in some billets near Windy Corner (800 yards west of Givenchy Church), while Battalion Headquarters and " D " Company were at Windy Corner.

Early on the 15th the Battalion was assembled ready to attack—" A " and " B " Companies and the machine-gun section in front, each company having a frontage of some two hundred yards, and " C " and " D " Companies being in support in rear. " And so," writes one who participated, " a few minutes before 6 everything was ready, the men in grand form and full of confidence, and only waiting for the signal to jump over the trenches and rush across the one hundred and fifty yards to the first German trench. As soon as our heavy bombardment commenced the Germans replied very violently, aiming especially along our parapet, and at 2 minutes to 6 their machine-gun and rifle fire commenced. This was difficult to understand as we thought no one could be living in that German trench. At 6 o'clock to the minute the signal went, a mine exploded under a portion of the German trench away to the right, and without the slightest hesitation, and in spite of a regular hail of bullets and continuous shells, the men, most gallantly led by their officers and non-commissioned officers, rushed out to the attack. . . .

" But our hopes of getting across were stopped ; the Germans were able to line their trenches and simply stand up and shoot, for no covering fire could be brought to bear on them. In spite of this, a party of twenty men of ' A ' Company, under Second-Lieutenant Belcher and Sergeant Whitlock, reached the German line, drove out and killed some German bomb throwers, and pressed a few yards beyond this trench, but could not get any further. However, they hung on until 10 p.m., when they were able to get back to our lines, bringing their wounded with them. It was a fine achievement carried out with great boldness. It must be noted that the German line could not be seen from our trenches, as it was on the reverse side of a slope and the ground was covered with long grass and standing corn—this made it impossible to follow what was going on throughout the line.

" The attack was carried out by ' A ' and ' B ' Companies, and they advanced until every man was killed or wounded or pinned to the ground by rifle and machine-gun fire and hand grenades. These two companies had roughly a total strength of 360 men ; about 70 came back. Of the 13 officers who went over the parapet 5 were killed and 5 wounded and 1 wounded and missing. The loss of our officers is very severe, and as far as can be ascertained the details are as follows : Captain Nevile was shot while advancing ; he cannot be traced, but we still cling to the hope that he may have been wounded and come in. His subalterns, Lieutenants Graham and Pritchard-Barrett, were killed leading their platoons ; Second-Lieutenant Belcher was twice wounded, once after he got to the German trench and again on his way back ; Second-Lieutenant Coker was wounded leading his platoon. Of ' B ' Company officers, Captain Raley was killed almost on the parapet, when leading his company out of our trenches ; Lieutenant Hadow was killed by a shell while coming back to Headquarters to report ; Second-Lieutenants Henderson and Eames were wounded when leading their men over the parapet ; Second-Lieutenant Lloyd-Jones was with the bombers on the left and was wounded while throwing grenades at the Germans ; and Second-Lieutenant A. Pyman was killed while going out to find a position for his machine guns. It is a long list of gallant officers and we deplore the loss of those killed, especially of Captain Nevile, whose fate is uncertain. True to his sporting nature he had armed himself and his subalterns with hunting-horns—a blast was to be blown on them on reaching the first German line. . . . It should be added that a few men, under Sergeants Foster and Malpress, also reached the German trench. Sergeant Malpress was killed on the parapet, and Sergeant Foster, who took his place, was wounded there.

" After the attack was held up we were subjected to a severe bombardment again which lasted all night. We were eventually relieved and got clear of the trenches about 2 a.m. on the 16th and remained in some reserve trenches for two nights, when we were sent back to billets to refit "—to Les Harisoirs, one mile east of Mount Bernenchon, where two officers, Second-Lieutenants C. F. Webb and T. Tweddell, and one hundred and fifty other ranks joined the Battalion.

The following losses were suffered in this action : 5 officers and 33 non-commissioned officers and men killed, 5 officers and 231 other ranks wounded, 97 men missing, and 1 officer and 12 men wounded and missing.

The Commanding Officer published the following complimentary order :

> "The Commanding Officer wishes to congratulate and thank all officers, N.C. officers and men of the Battalion, especially those of 'A' and 'B' Companies, for the most gallant way they carried out the attack on the enemy, strictly according to orders, and he assures them that it was no fault of theirs that the attack failed. No Battalion could have gone straighter or done more than they did to make it successful, and it was purely owing to the superiority of the enemy's fire, and inability to support the attack with covering fire, that it failed.
>
> "He feels confident that when the Battalion is called on again to attack the enemy, they will worthily uphold the traditions of the Regiment, and will act with the same bravery and dash that they did in the last attack. He deeply deplores the losses of our gallant comrades who set us such a noble example."

For many weeks now the 2nd Battalion The Green Howards was not engaged in any events of special importance ; it was very much moved about, spending a considerable portion of the time in billets and occasionally returning to the front to take its share of trench duty. Many drafts arrived from the Base and the supply of junior officers was well maintained, but on the other hand two thoroughly experienced and valuable officers were taken from the Battalion, when Captains Leatham and Forsyth were appointed as commander and second-in-command respectively of the 2nd Wiltshire Regiment ; but early in July Lieutenant-Colonel W. H. Young joined from the 2nd East Yorkshire Regiment and took over command of the 2nd Green Howards from Major Stansfeld.

On the 1st July the Battalion marched to Berguette, the 7th Division having now been transferred from the IV. to the I. Corps, when the following was published in IV. Corps orders :

> "The IV. Corps Commander desires to place on record his high appreciation of the very gallant services rendered by the 7th Division during the nine months he has had the honour of having them under his command. He cannot allow their transfer to the I. Corps to take place without expressing his gratitude to every officer, non-commissioned officer and man for the admirable spirit displayed at all times by the Division, sometimes under most trying circumstances, and he trusts that at some later date he may welcome them back to the IV. Corps."

During this month The Green Howards, when up in the line, were either in the trenches just north of La Quinque Rue or occupying forts and redoubts near Richebourg St. Vaast, and when at rest were billeted either near Lacouture or at Paradis near Merville. August again was a month of many moves ; the opening days were passed at Gonnehem, where a fortnight was spent ; the middle of the month the Battalion was in trenches near Le Casan, where the German guns were very active and some casualties occurred ; but during the greater part of September the Battalion alternated between Bethune, Noyelles and Vermelles, being at this last-named place when the Battle of Loos opened.

At this time the officers of the 2nd Battalion The Green Howards appear to have been distributed as follows : Lieutenant-Colonel W. H. Young, in command, Major T. W. Stansfeld, D.S.O., Captain A. A. Chauncy, adjutant, Lieutenant E. Pickard, quartermaster, Lieutenant F. C. Pyman, transport officer, Lieutenant P. A. Forster, machine-gun officer, Lieutenant D. A. Laird, R.A.M.C., in medical charge, and the Rev. C. Cryer, chaplain.

> " A " Company : Captain M. Thwaites, Lieutenant R. C. Bentley, Second-Lieutenants T. Tweddell, C. G. Oliver, H. G. Tozer, W. E. P. Waterfield and F. W. Smith.
>
> " B " Company : Captain N. T. Wright, Lieutenant A. J. Pickup, Second-Lieutenants C. F. Webb and K. R. Henderson.
>
> " C " Company : Captain P. Hanbury, Lieutenants J. R. A. Rigby and W. Gray, and Second-Lieutenant W. H. O. Hill.
>
> " D " Company : Captain E. J. Richardson, Lieutenants S. Brooksbank and G. B. Lancaster, Second-Lieutenants E. W. Loyd and J. O. McIntyre.

In his despatch of the 15th October, 1915, Sir John French wrote that " it was arranged that we should make a combined attack from certain points of the Allied line during the last week in September. The reinforcements I have received enabled me to comply with several requests which General Joffre has made that I should take over additional portions of the French line. In fulfilment of the rôle assigned to it in these operations, the Army under my command attacked the enemy on the morning of the 25th September. The main attack was delivered by the I. and IV. Corps between the La Bassée Canal on the north, and a point of the enemy's line opposite the village of Grenay on the south. . . . The general plan of the main attack on the 25th September was as follows : In co-operation with an offensive movement by the Tenth French Army on our right, the I. and IV. Corps were to attack the enemy from a point opposite the little mining village of Grenay on the south to the La Bassée Canal on the north. . . . The attacks of the I. and IV. Corps were delivered at 6.30 a.m. and were successful all along the line, except just south of the La Bassée Canal."

At 5.50 a.m. on the 25th September an intense bombardment of the enemy's trenches commenced, lasting forty minutes, at the end of which time the infantry advanced to the attack ; in the 7th Division the 20th and 22nd Brigades were on the right and left respectively, the 21st in support.

" At the moment the assault took place, we were to leave our assembly trench and follow up along a communication trench to our original front line,

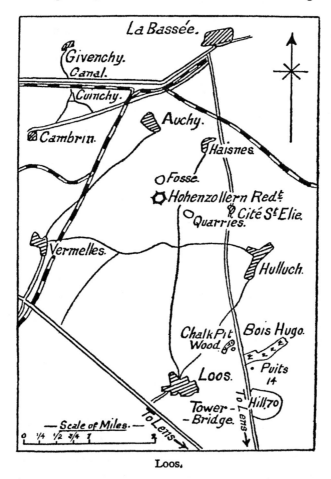

Loos.

occupy that front line and wait for orders. This communication trench, however, was about a mile long, and owing to our being suddenly held up from one cause or other, it took us fully two and a half hours to get the whole of the Battalion up into the front line. It must be remembered that we could only go up in single file ; the delay did not matter very greatly as we were fully an hour in our old front-line trenches before we got any orders to move.

F

" About 10 a.m. we received an order which told us that the 20th Brigade had taken Gun Trench and the 22nd had taken the Quarries, and that our Brigade—the Wiltshires on the right, supported by the Bedfords, and our Battalion on the left supported by the Cameron Highlanders, with Royal Scots Fusiliers in reserve—was to go through these two brigades and attack some cross-roads on the north-east corner of Hulluch.   Colonel Young then gave the order for the Battalion to get out of the trenches and advance in artillery formation in the direction of our objective.   He had already moved ' C ' and ' D ' Companies into the old German front line.   These orders were carried out.   On our arrival at the Quarries, Colonel Young ordered ' C ' and ' D ' Companies to advance towards Cité St. Elie and Hulluch, finding their own firing line and support ; they were supported by ' B ' Company and he kept ' A ' in reserve.

"' C ' and ' D ' Companies then advanced in the direction ordered, and, when they got within about three hundred yards of the above-named villages, found the Germans in great strength, holding a trench which ran along the edge of the villages, while there were machine guns in the houses.   Captain Hanbury, commanding ' C ' Company, came back himself and reported that he thought it was impossible to advance any further unless the enemy's position had undergone a very thorough bombardment.   By this time ' B ' had reinforced ' C ' and ' D ' Companies, and these three companies now started to dig themselves in with their entrenching tools, and by dusk they had a very good trench from which they could all fire and which also gave them a certain amount of cover from shell fire.

" Battalion Headquarters and ' A ' Company moved up into the Quarries, where they found those of the 22nd Brigade who had not been hit ; the Cameron Highlanders also came up into the Quarries and filled up the gap between the left of ' D ' Company and the right of the 22nd Brigade.

" It was most difficult to get communication with the Brigade in spite of the efforts of Sergeant Lucas, the signalling sergeant, who spent most of the day laying or repairing lines from the old British trench to our new Headquarters.   The Quarries themselves were about four hundred yards long by two hundred yards broad, and were rather irregular in shape. Captain Laird, the medical officer attached to the Battalion, brought his stretcher-bearers up to the Quarries almost as soon as the Battalion arrived there, and formed an aid post in one of the big dug-outs, in which he could get about fifty or sixty lying-down cases.

" At about 4 in the afternoon the Colonel was going round one part of our lines, and I was going round another, when we heard cheering from the direction of Haisnes.   We watched with our field glasses and saw parties of men coming out of this village.   It was difficult to see who these were, but we eventually discovered that it was the advanced troops of the division on our left who had been driven out by a Bosche counter-attack.   However, they only fell back a short distance and joined up with the left of the 22nd Brigade.   This division, I may say, had done exceptionally well ; they had taken the whole of the Hohenzollern Redoubt and Fosse 8, and had, as I said before, got into Haisnes itself.   When it was dark I accompanied the Colonel round the Battalion line ; the men by that time had started to improve their own trenches with the picks and shovels they carried.   We had up to then had a certain number of casualties ; Gray had been hit in the body, McIntyre had been badly hit through both legs and eventually died of wounds in Germany, while Bentley had been wounded in both legs too and a good many of the N.C.O.'s and men had been killed or wounded.

" ' A ' Company had in the evening been put in on the left of the Camerons to strengthen the line there, as we rather feared a counter-attack from the direction of Haisnes.

" On our arrival back at Battalion Headquarters an order came to say that on the following morning the Brigade was to attack Hulluch ; and in order that this attack might be carried out, the Cameron Highlanders were to withdraw from the Quarries at once, and our Battalion was to withdraw when the 22nd Brigade had relieved us.   We then made arrangements for the 22nd Brigade to relieve us at 11 p.m."

At 11 p.m. Headquarters and " A " Company commenced to withdraw, and the process of relief was just starting about 11.15 when some Germans were seen in front and fire was opened upon them, while at the same time heavy firing was heard beyond the northern end of the Quarries, and a few minutes later it was reported that a small body of the enemy was then actually in the Quarries.   Lieutenant Hill and a bombing section were sent to deal with them, but this officer was almost at once reported to be hit, and Colonel Young, still thinking that the enemy could only be a very few in number, dispatched Lieutenant Brooksbank and a platoon to turn them out. However, a message soon came back from this platoon saying there were at least fifty Germans in the Quarries and that Lieutenant Brooksbank had been wounded.   It was now midnight and " D " Company under Captain Richardson was just ready to withdraw, so he was now ordered to clear the Quarry, supported by " B " Company ; as this officer was moving to comply with the order, he was mortally wounded, while immediately afterwards Captain and Adjutant Chauncy was also hit.

The situation was now serious ; the trench was held by " C " Company of The Green Howards and eighty men of the South Staffordshire Regiment, who were facing both ways, and fighting was going on in the Quarries. About 2 a.m. on the 26th the British guns opened a heavy fire on the position, and the troops here had to be withdrawn to the cover of the nearest quarry. An orderly went off with the adjutant to try and get in touch with the Wiltshires, while Colonel Young and the C.O. of the South Staffords moved to the other quarry to see if communication thence was still open, reaching the dug-out where the telephone had been to find it in German hands and, being fired at, they were obliged to retire, for it was clear that the enemy was in occupation of the Quarries in force.

The troops here were now led out south towards the Hulluch Road, but had only moved some three hundred yards when they were fired into by an advancing line of Germans, and so fell back into a German communication trench ; from here they began to move south-east, and then struck to the south and finally came in touch with the Royal Scots Fusiliers and the Wiltshires, who were engaged about Breslau Avenue in forming a defensive flank. Here also were " B " and " D " Companies who had found themselves not strong enough to deal with the Germans in the Quarries. " B," " C " and " D " Companies now held the line here throughout the 26th with the Wiltshire Regiment and were the whole time subjected to heavy sniping. This day Lieutenants Pickup, Rigby and Cressy were killed.

During the early half of the 27th the situation remained unchanged so far as the Battalion was concerned, but at 1 p.m. The Green Howards were concentrated in the front British trenches, and during the whole of the night that followed furnished working parties of three hundred men to strengthen the position held by the Cameron Highlanders. During the course of this day Lieutenant Loyd, who had already been slightly wounded, was again hit in the jaw, and Sergeant-Major Wilcox was also wounded ; while Major-General Capper, commanding the 7th Division, was mortally wounded when visiting the trenches held by the Battalion ; he was succeeded in command of the Division by Major-General H. E. Watts, C.B., C.M.G. It was not until 10 on the evening of the 28th that The Green Howards moved, when they advanced some little distance and entrenched on a line in rear of the Royal Scots Fusiliers and extending from the Hulluch Road to Breslau Trench. The night was very dark and digging in the chalky soil was not easy work, but by the morning of the 29th good cover had been obtained against the very persistent enemy snipers.

During the 29th there was a heavy and sustained bombardment by both sides, and many heavy shells fell near the Battalion, doing, however, but little harm. At night " A " Company was sent forward into the front line on the right of the Scots Fusiliers and on the south of the Hulluch Road, Captain Thwaites being unhappily killed by a shell just after the move of the company was completed. The shelling continued throughout the 30th, followed in the evening by bomb attacks on Gun Trench ; in the evening the

Battalion was under orders to relieve the Royal Scots Fusiliers, but any movement of this kind was obviously impossible, and the most that could be done was to send " D " Company up to take up a new support position in a trench some twenty-five yards in rear of Gun Trench, so as to be at hand in case of the Scots Fusiliers needing reinforcement. Bombing sections were also sent to the Fusiliers and to the Bedford Regiment on their left—or, more accurately, on the left of the enemy, who had now occupied some one hundred yards of this trench. In view of the situation here, at 9.30 p.m. Colonel Berners, Royal Scots Fusiliers (now in command of the 21st Brigade *vice* General Watts to command of the Division), directed Lieutenant-Colonel Young to turn the Germans out with the bayonet.

" B " and " C " Companies accordingly advanced on this mission, but on reaching the support trench, where was " D " Company, it was found that a wire entanglement ran the whole length of the trench in front, thus making the operation very much more difficult. There was one gap in the wire, through which men were dribbled, extending on the further side, but the German flares showed up the movement and the enemy machine and rifle fire concentrated on this spot made the execution of the operation impossible, even with the assistance of bombing parties attacking from either end of the trench. The trench was eventually blocked and the position held as it was. There were many casualties in the Battalion during this night, including Captain Wright wounded, but these were in a measure made good by bringing up and sending to " B " Company a draft one hundred and one strong which had just arrived from the Base.

At last, late on the night of the 30th the Battalion was relieved by the Highland Light Infantry, and billets at Le Préol were reached by a very weary lot of officers and men at 4.30 on the morning of the 1st October.

The casualties sustained by the 2nd Battalion The Green Howards in the Battle of Loos between the 25th September and the 1st October inclusive were heavy ; they amounted to 6 officers and 32 other ranks killed or died of wounds, 3 officers and 187 non-commissioned officers and men wounded, 5 officers and 7 men wounded and missing, 2 officers and 96 other ranks missing, 1 officer gassed ; the names of the officers who were killed were Captain M. Thwaites, Lieutenants J. R. A. Rigby and A. J. Pickup, Second-Lieutenants G. E. L. Cressy, H. G. Tozer and W. H. O. Hill ; wounded were Captains A. A. Chauncy, adjt., and N. T. Wright, and Second-Lieutenant E. W. Loyd ; wounded and missing were Captain E. J. Richardson, Lieutenants T. Brooksbank, R. C. Bentley and W. Gray, and Second-Lieutenant J. C. McIntyre ; Captain D. A. Laird, R.A.M.C., and Second-Lieutenant C. F. Webb were missing, while Second-Lieutenant F. W. Smith was gassed.

In spite of these heavy losses the strength of the Battalion was tolerably well maintained, for drafts of officers and men came out at frequent intervals, and even on the 2nd October, the day after coming out of action, the strength stood at 14 officers and 735 other ranks.

During the remainder of the year 1915 the 2nd Battalion was not engaged in any important actions, but was a good deal moved about, particularly during the months of November and December. While still at Le Préol, the Battalion was considerably worried by the enemy rifle grenades, the British possessing at the time but very few of these missiles with which to retaliate. On one occasion, however, a message arrived from the German trenches, delivered by the agency of a grenade from which the explosive had been removed ; it was as follows :

" My dear friend,—

     " I hope you are very well. Have you had enuf ? What makes Mr. Gray ? Have you any more gas ? "

On the 15th the Battalion was at Essars, moving thence at intervals of one or two days to Gonnehem, Manqueville, Hinges, Le Quesnoy, Givenchy and L'Ecleme, where the end of the month found it in very scattered billets. Early in November The Green Howards went to the neighbourhood of Bethune, where mining and counter-mining was the order of the day, and as to these activities Major Pickard relates the following as occurring at the end of November : " Two Bosche miners came over and surrendered and gave us information that they were going to explode four mines under our front line at 7 the following morning. We accordingly withdrew our men to safe positions whence they could fire on the enemy when he should attempt to occupy the craters he would have made. Right to the minute next morning *three* of the mines went up, but not *four*, so the Company was held back for some considerable time, until it was not considered safe to keep them in rear any longer in view of the possibility of an attack. ' A ' Company then occupied the same trench as before, but had hardly got into position when up went the fourth mine with two officers and about twenty men. The two officers and all the men except eight were dug out, but these eight poor fellows could not be found. It was the first war experience of the two officers : they had just come out from England and I had only taken them up the line the night previously. They thought it was a very good start ! Both were badly shaken and had to go to hospital ; one lost some teeth."

Colonel Young gives this story as follows : " Two German deserters came in on the 29th November and reported that a mine would be exploded at 7 next morning. On this our sappers arranged to blow a counter-mine which it was hoped would destroy the German one. Our mine was blown up at 4.20 a.m., and we seized and consolidated the crater in face of a very hot fire.

We then held our front very lightly in view of the possibility of the German mine going up, which it did at 7.20 a.m., with the result described by Major Pickard. Half an hour later I was blinded by a bullet hitting an iron loophole we had got up in the new crater, and was in hospital for four or five days."

These two officers were Second-Lieutenants W. D. Clayton and B. A. Nuttall.

Early in December the 7th Division was transferred to the Third Army, and on the 6th The 2nd Green Howards marched to Lillers and there entrained for Saleux, which was reached about 9 p.m., when the Battalion marched to billets in the villages of Oissy and Dreuil, Headquarters, " A " and " D " Companies being in the former and the remainder of the Battalion in the last-named place.

By this date many of the new formations were reaching France from England, and it was realized that the units of the New Army would need the support, guidance, experience and example of those of the Regular Army who had seen more of modern continental warfare. Battalions, and even in some instances brigades, were transferred to the New Army Divisions to give them the necessary stiffening, and in the case of the 7th Division, the 21st Brigade was taken bodily out of it and was transferred to the 30th Division, its place in the 7th Division being taken by the 91st Brigade from the 30th.

On the morning of the 19th December the 2nd Battalion The Green Howards left Oissy by march route, spent the night at Canaples, and joined the 30th Division next day at Fienvillers ; the Division at this time was commanded by Major-General W. Fry, C.V.O., C.B., and was composed of the 21st, 89th and 90th Infantry Brigades, and formed part of the XIII. Army Corps under Major-General W. N. Congreve, V.C., C.B., M.V.O.

The 21st Brigade now contained the 18th King's, 2nd Green Howards, 2nd Wiltshire and 19th Manchester Regiments.

At Fienvillers, in billets, Christmas Day was spent, and the following message from His Majesty the King was published for the information of all ranks :

"Another Christmas finds all the resources of the Empire still engaged in war, and I desire to convey, on my own behalf and on behalf of the Queen, a heartfelt Christmas greeting and Our good wishes for the New Year to all who, on Sea and Land, are upholding the honour of the British name. In the officers and men of my Navy, on whom the security of the Empire depends, I repose, in common with all my subjects, a trust that is absolute. On the officers and men of My Armies, whether now in France, in the East, or in other fields, I rely with an equal faith, confident that their devotion, their valour and their self-sacrifice will, under God's guidance, lead to Victory and an honourable Peace. There are many of their comrades now, alas, in hospital, and to those brave fellows, also, I desire, with the Queen, to express Our deep gratitude and Our earnest prayers for their recovery.

"Officers and men of the Navy and Army, another year is drawing to a close, as it began, in toil, bloodshed and suffering ; but I rejoice to know that the goal to which you are striving draws nearer into sight.

"May God bless you and all your undertakings."

In the week immediately preceding Christmas, a change had been made in the command of the British Expeditionary Force, on the 19th December General Sir Douglas Haig having taken the place of Field-Marshal Sir John French, who, on leaving France for England, issued the following valedictory order :

"In relinquishing the command of the British Army in France, I wish to express to the officers, non-commissioned officers and men with whom I have been so closely associated during the last sixteen months, my heartfelt sorrow in parting with them before the campaign, in which we have been so long engaged together, has been brought to a victorious conclusion. I have, however, the firmest conviction that such a glorious ending to their splendid and heroic efforts is not far distant, and I shall watch their progress towards this final goal with intense interest, but in the most confident hope.

"The success so far attained has been due to the indomitable spirit, dogged tenacity which knows no defeat, and the heroic courage so abundantly displayed by the rank and file of the splendid Army which it will ever remain the pride and glory of my life to have commanded during over sixteen months of incessant fighting.

"Regulars and Territorials, Old Army and New, have shown these magnificent qualities in equal degree. From my heart I thank them all.

"At this sad moment of parting my heart goes out to those who have received lifelong injuries from wounds, and I think with sorrow of that great and glorious host of my beloved comrades who have made the greatest sacrifice of all by laying down their lives for their country.

"In saying good-bye to the British Army in France, I ask them once again to accept this expression of my deepest gratitude and heartfelt devotion towards them, and my earnest good wishes for the glorious future which I feel to be assured."

CHAPTER V

THE 2ND BATTALION

1916–1917

THE BATTLE OF THE SOMME. THE BATTLE OF ARRAS.
THE THIRD BATTLE OF YPRES

D URING the first six months of the year 1916, the 21st Brigade saw little or no fighting of a serious nature: the 30th Division had only very recently arrived in France from England and had much to learn ; and these months were passed in a tolerably quiet area where it was possible gradually to break in the new levies, of which the Division was mainly composed, for the work that was before them.

Early in January the 2nd Battalion The Green Howards was at Sailly Laurette, moving thence to Bray and relieving here a Battalion of the 5th Division, who joyously informed the new-comers that Bray was never disturbed, that they had been there five months and had only sustained three casualties !

" It was something new for us to be in such a quiet part of the line," writes a Battalion correspondent. " Bands played in the square by the church and crowds of men turned out to listen. Estaminets were open, and men could get what they liked to eat and drink from the various shops in the town, which did a very flourishing trade. The routine which the Division adopted here was for our Brigade four days at Bronfay Farm, four days in trenches at Carnoy, four days at Bray and four days at Bronfay Farm, so that out of sixteen days we really only spent four days where one could have proper billets."

There seems, however, to have been a considerable amount of shelling, and casualties were not few.

Here the Battalion remained until the 14th March, when it moved to Corbie, whence two companies were sent to Amiens and Ribement respectively for work with the R.E. A fortnight was spent here and another couple of weeks at St. Sauveur, The Green Howards then marching back again to Corbie. At the end of May the Battalion was in trenches near

Maricourt, where all were issued with the new steel helmets and new pattern anti-gas respirators. Here on the 2nd June the French XX. Corps took over the sector on the right, including the trenches up to this held by " A " Company of the Battalion, leaving " B " and " C " Companies in the front line, and the last named being now in charge of the extreme right sector of the whole British line in France ; " A " Company was in support and " D " in reserve.

" On one of the nights we were in this part of the line," we read in a diary—this was actually on the 3rd June—" we had a working party out constructing a listening post. On one of the men looking up out of the trench in which the party was working, he saw a foot suddenly appear over the top of the parapet. Without asking any questions he seized the foot and pulled the owner down into the trench, when what was his surprise to find he had got hold of a tiger in the shape of a regimental-sergeant-major of the pre-war German Army, who fought like the very deuce to get free and had to have a crack over the head with an entrenching tool before he could be taken to Battalion Headquarters. He was in charge of a patrol and had left his men some distance in rear, and said that he had heard our men working and was very anxious to find out what we were doing. He was over six feet in height and a fine stamp of a soldier. He burst into tears of rage in our Headquarter dug-out on arrival, and said he would much rather have been killed than taken prisoner. He had nearly seventeen years' service in the regular army. Promises of leave had been made to anyone who made an important capture of enemy troops on this front for some time past, and it was very important we should get to know whom we had opposite us. . . . The man who captured the German R.S.M. was given £5 and a month's furlough to England, and after a reward like this we had to stop men going over the top on their own account at night in the hopes of bringing in a scalp."

Towards the end of June the Division was back about Corbie again, and on the 23rd the Battalion was in Trigger Wood, which contained a great many guns of all calibres, British and French, from which opened next day a six days' bombardment, ushering in the Battle of the Somme of this year.

For some time past it was very evident that a great Allied offensive was in contemplation ; considerable reinforcements had now reached the British Army in France ; and the recent introduction of compulsory service had made easier the provision of drafts. The allied commanders had decided upon an offensive during the summer, but were only in doubt as to the exact date when the attack should take place, and it was eventually determined that it must begin as near the end of June as possible, and that it must be a combined one, since neither the French nor their allies were in a position to attack single-handed. There were now four British armies in the field ; the Second about Ypres, the First about Neuve Chapelle, the Third about Arras, and the Fourth, commanded by General Rawlinson, between Albert and the Somme and joining on to the left of the French. The attack then was to be carried out by the Fourth British Army, now disposed from Gommecourt to Maricourt ; and by the Sixth French Army, under General Fayolle, whose troops held a line from Maricourt to the village of Foy.

The position to be assaulted consisted of two strong systems of defence, the first running north for 3,000 yards from the Somme near Curlu, then west for 7,000 yards to the vicinity of Fricourt, and then due south. The second, between the Somme and the Ancre, was situated some 3,000–5,000 yards in rear of the first, and both contained several lines of deep trenches with bomb-proof shelters, all protected by broad belts of wire.

From right to left the British Corps were disposed in the following order : XIII., XV., III., X., VIII., and VII. ; and of the first phase of the Somme battle, which commenced on the 1st and closed on the 14th July, General Haig wrote in his despatch that " the enemy's second main system of defence had been captured on a front of over three miles. We had again forced him back more than a mile, and had gained possession of the southern crest of the main ridge on a front of over six thousand yards. . . . Our line was definitely established from Maltz Horn Farm, where we met the French left, north along the eastern edge of Trônes Wood to Longueval, then west past Bazentin-le-Grand to the northern corner of Bazentin-le-Petit Wood, and then west again past the southern face of Pozières to the north of Ovillers."

So much for the general results of the fighting of the first fourteen days of the battle, and we must now see what part the 2nd Battalion The Green Howards played in it.

The objective of the 30th Division, attacking on the right of the XIII. Corps, was the important village of Montauban, and the Division advanced with the 89th Brigade on the right and 21st on the left, covering the divisional front as the 55th Brigade covered that of the 18th Division on the left.

At 7.30 a.m. on the 1st July the Battalion was in Headquarters Avenue Trench, but two platoons of " D " Company, under Second-Lieutenants Parisotti and Dickinson, had been detailed as " cleaning-up " platoons with the 18th Battalion King's and 19th Battalion The Manchester Regiment respectively. The battle-strength of The 2nd Green Howards on this day was 24 officers and 688 other ranks, the residue remaining in the Bois des

Tailles with the 1st Line Transport ready to move up as reinforcements when required.

The front to be attacked by the Brigade extended from the junction of Glatz Redoubt with Dublin Trench on the right to the railway line on the left, the assaulting battalions being the 18th King's and the 19th Manchester, while The Green Howards were in support of these and were responsible for occupying and consolidating the German front and support lines on these being captured. The Battalion was ordered to advance in two lines of columns of sections, and to this end companies were arranged in the line in alternate half-companies.

The leading line, composed of " A " Company, under Second-Lieutenant Brooke, D.S.O., and " B " Company, commanded by Captain Wylde, advanced at the appointed hour, followed three minutes later by " C " Company (Captain Maude) and " D " Company under Lieutenant Rowley. Immediately after crossing No-Man's Land " A " Company came under heavy machine-gun fire from the left front and suffered severely, Second-Lieutenants Brooke, Henderson and Colk being wounded, Brooke mortally, while Lieutenant Denman was killed, only some thirty men of the company reaching the German trench under a corporal. There were many losses in other companies, in " B " Second-Lieutenant G. E. Layton-Bennett being killed and Captain Wylde and Second-Lieutenant Myers wounded, while the second line also suffered, Second-Lieutenant Niblett being wounded and the Battalion sustaining some two hundred casualties in crossing No-Man's Land ; but the survivors pushed on, reached the German trenches pointed out to them as their objectives, and at once set to work consolidating their gains. While thus engaged a German machine gun, which had escaped notice up to now, suddenly opened fire ; this was located by Lance-Corporal W. Parkin, who made for it single-handed, killed the two men composing the detachment and captured the gun ; this was then at once handed over to the Brigade Machine Gun Company, who brought it into action against the enemy.

It was now 3 p.m. and the C.O. decided to hold the front German line only and withdrew " B " Company into it, when the position was occupied by the companies of the Battalion in the following order from right to left— " C," " D," " B," and " A " ; of the Battalion's Lewis guns only five were now in working order, and these were disposed so as to cover the flanks. In the meantime the 90th Brigade had gone through the others and had occupied the village of Montauban about 9 a.m., but of the two " cleaning-up " platoons of The Green Howards, that under Second-Lieutenant Parisotti had been practically " wiped out " while crossing No-Man's Land, only one or two men under Corporal Peat reaching the enemy trenches, where they did excellent work, holding up a party of Germans, who were bombing their way up from Valley Trench, until Second-Lieutenant Dickinson's platoon arrived upon the scene. This officer, with commendable promptitude and decision, seeing the state of affairs, at once got his men on to the parapet and overwhelmed a superior body of the enemy, who promptly surrendered.

The work of consolidation was continued until dusk, but the trenches had been so battered by our bombardment that communication was difficult, and in places the line of the original trench could not be traced. There were several alarms during the night, but no attack developed. On the 2nd large parties were told off to clear the battle-field, and many arms— rifles, machine guns and minenwerfers—with a great deal of equipment were collected. There was a good deal of enemy shelling, but this gradually grew less violent, and at 7.30 p.m. the Battalion was withdrawn to Headquarters Avenue, remaining here all through the 3rd, clearing the ground and burying the dead, and then on the evening of the 4th, on relief by a battalion of the South African Brigade, marching back to the Bois des Tailles. The 5th was spent in reorganizing and cleaning up, in receiving congratulations from the Brigadier and Divisional Commander on the behaviour of the Battalion, and in hearing the thanks of the Commander-in-Chief for the " successful attainment of the task demanded of the 30th Division."

On the 6th the 21st Brigade learnt that it was next day to make an attack upon Trônes Wood, which was connected up on the German side by good lines of trenches with Maltz Horn Farm on the south, with Guillemont on the east, and with Waterlot Farm on the north—each of these points being from four hundred to seven hundred yards away, while Trônes Wood itself was commanded by a large number of heavy guns. The 2nd Green Howards paraded on the evening of the 6th to return to the trenches, but then learnt that the attack was postponed, and it was not until the early morning of the 8th that the Battalion marched off by Talus Boisée to a position just west of Bernafay Wood with orders to attack and capture the southern portion of the wood. When this was achieved, the 2nd Wiltshire were to attack Maltz Horn Alley from the cover of Trônes Wood, their right joining on to the French, who were making an attack at the same time. The 19th Manchester were disposed in trenches in rear, available for support ; while the 18th King's were detailed to provide carrying parties. Battalion Headquarters was at La Briqueterie.

At 7.15 a.m. " C " Company (Captain Maude) entered Bernafay Wood, followed in succession by the Battalion Bombing sections, by " D " Company (Captain Belcher), " B " (Second-Lieutenant Hubbard) and " A " Company (Captain Colley).

At 8 a.m., under severe shell fire, which caused a certain number of casualties before starting, and under the added difficulties of getting through the wood, " C " Company passed through and commenced to cross the open ground between Bernafay Wood and Trônes Wood. For the first eighty yards of this advance the rising ground afforded a certain amount of cover, but on " topping " this a very heavy machine and rifle fire was opened on the advancing troops from the edge of Trônes Wood, and the whole of the front line was hit almost to a man. Some few of The Green Howards got into Trônes Alley, a communication trench between the two woods, and Lieutenant Field, with the Battalion bombers, endeavoured to bomb up it and get into the wood, but snipers located among the branches of trees defeated this attempt ; and now, seeing that in the absence of a powerful and prolonged artillery preparation, any direct attack was hopeless, a withdrawal to Bernafay Wood was ordered at 8.30 a.m. Even here, however, there was small respite : the Germans bombarded the wood heavily and without intermission throughout the day with great guns ; the cover was indifferent and the Battalion could do no more than just hold on under this severe shelling ; casualties were many and the evacuation of the wounded was a matter of the gravest difficulty ; the strain was unceasing, and it was with great relief that at 7 that evening orders for a withdrawal were received, when " A " Company went back to La Briquet-erie and the remaining companies—what was left of them—to Head-quarters Avenue.

During this week the losses in the 2nd Battalion The Green Howards had been many and grievous : killed were Second-Lieutenants C. B. Brooke, D.S.O., P. D. Denman, G. E. L. Bennett, W. D. Hubbard, H. B. Laird, A. C. Strugnell and T. D. Strathern, and 71 non-commissioned officers and men ; wounded were Captain J. G. Wylde, Second-Lieutenants K. R. Henderson, P. Colk, J. F. Myers, L. Parisotti, S. A. Vincent, I. K. Thomson, A. E. Niblett, J. Trickett, B. J. Wilkinson and J. B. Freeland, and 309 other ranks, while 35 men were missing—a total of 433 casualties all ranks out of 712 officers and men who went into action !

The Battalion now made several short moves—on the 11th to Morlan-court, on the 13th to the village of Vaux-sur-Somme, next day to Vecque-mont where it entrained for Ailly-sur-Somme, marching from there to Fourd-rinoy, where it was inspected by Major-General J. S. M. Shea, C.B., D.S.O.,* now commanding the 30th Division, who thanked The 2nd Green Howards for the good work done during the past fighting ; then on the 19th the Battalion was back again at Morlancourt, only to leave there again next day for a bivouac in a valley to the west of Bois Caffet. The Battalion was by

* He had taken over from Major-General Fry on the 17th May.

this approximately up to strength again, having received, though there had hardly yet been sufficient time to assimilate, drafts amounting to 12 officers and 309 other ranks, almost wholly made up of non-commissioned officers and men of some thirteen different regiments; the officers were all of junior rank—Second-Lieutenants E. P. Davy, H. S. Hobby, A. Miller, D. K. Moir, N. F. McCarthy, J. B. Cutts, C. C. Bramwell, G. E. Richards, F. Middlehurst, L. Hanson-Abbott, W. C. Mills and J. F. B. Delap.

During the three weeks' fighting since the 1st July the British forces had gained a footing on the main enemy ridge, but only on a comparatively narrow portion of it, and it was necessary to widen this front before the advance could be followed up.   It was in the first place necessary to bring up the right British flank in line with the centre, and in order to do this Guillemont, Falfemont Farm, Leuze Wood, Ginchy and Bouleaux Wood— localities all naturally strong and elaborately fortified—must be captured. " An advance by the Fourth Army on the 23rd July on a wide front from Guillemont to near Pozières found the enemy in great strength all along the line, with machine guns and forward troops in shell-holes and newly-constructed trenches, well in front of his main defences.   Although ground was won, the strength of the resistance experienced showed that the hostile troops had recovered from their previous confusion sufficiently to necessitate long and careful preparation before further successes on any great scale could be secured." *

The 21st Brigade of the 30th Division was now to attack the village of Guillemont, and on the 22nd July The 2nd Green Howards, under Major Richards, marched to the assembly position on the early afternoon of this day, and reached Glatz Redoubt about 4.30 p.m.   At 9.30 all moved forward to the north of Trônes Wood, being heavily shelled while going up, one 5·9 c.m. shell falling in the middle of a platoon and causing several casualties.   By 2.30 on the morning of Sunday, the 23rd, all were ready and waiting for zero hour, fixed for 3.40 a.m.—" A " Company under Second-Lieutenant Scoby on the right and " B " (Captain Rowley) on the left, with " D " and " C " Companies in support and reserve under Captain Belcher and Captain Maude respectively.   The 3rd Division was attacking on the left, while on the right of the Battalion was the 19th Manchester Regiment.

By reason of the darkness, and a smoke barrage put up by the 3rd Division, the true direction could not be kept, touch was lost and never regained with the other assaulting battalions.   Some platoons of The Green Howards reached the trench south of Guillemont, but found the wire uncut and were then obliged to retire owing to enfilade rifle and machine-gun fire.   " D " Company, with what was left of " A " and " B," did manage

* Sir Douglas Haig's despatch of the 23rd December, 1916.

to struggle on to the trench north of Guillemont, beat off two counter-attacks and consolidated their gains. The position was then taken over by the 3rd Division and the companies fell back on " C " Company in the Assembly Trench ; and then at 7 that evening the Battalion was withdrawn to Happy Valley, where it saw the rest of the month out.

The casualties had again been by no means light, amounting as they did to over 250 killed, wounded, and missing : Second-Lieutenant D. K. Moir and 9 other ranks were killed, Second-Lieutenants H. H. Scoby, M. A. C. Jubert, J. B. Cutts, C. C. Bramwell and L. Hanson-Abbott, and 151 non-commissioned officers and men were wounded, while Second-Lieutenants J. Perry and W. C. Mills and 90 men were missing.

August was a quiet month for the Battalion, passed at Citernes, Robecq and Givenchy, where it arrived on the 11th and was distributed in some eight or nine " keeps " in the village line ; the rest of the month was spent at Gorre or Locon. The Division was now in the First Army, but about the middle of September it was moved again and then joined the Fifth (Reserve) Army, and The Green Howards went into a training area at Naours, where the command of the Battalion was assumed by Major H. F. Bidder, Lieutenant-Colonel Young being at the time on leave on medical certificate, while Major Richards had recently been wounded.

Naours was left again on the 4th October and the Battalion proceeded by motor-bus and march route by way of Ribemont and Pommiers Redoubt to Brigade Reserve in Switch Trench, but when on the 13th it marched up to the support area the column was very heavily shelled and several casualties were occasioned, of the officers alone five being hit, Second-Lieutenants H. Phillips and W. W. Watson being killed, and A. Miller, E. A. Bull and E. J. Rapp being wounded, the first named mortally.

On the 17th and 18th the Division was engaged in an attack near the Le Transloy Ridges in the Gueudecourt area, the first task allotted to the 2nd Green Howards being the capture of a portion of Bayonet Trench, forming a defensive flank on the right, while at the same time a bombing party was to work up Bite Trench to its junction with Bayonet Trench. For the direct attack of Bayonet Trench three companies were detailed— " D," " C " and " A " in that order from right to left—two platoons of " B " were to form the defensive flank, the remaining two assisting in the attack and supplying carrying parties if called upon. Half the Battalion bombers under Lieutenant R. A. Field were to work up Bite Trench, the remainder moving with " D " Company and making a block in Bayonet Trench. The three attacking companies were to move in two lines, each company having two platoons in the front line and two in the second, the men moving at two paces interval with ten paces between the lines.

During the evening of the 17th the companies were assembled in New Trench and in the front line to the right of it, and shortly before zero the men lay down in two lines, one along the tape which had previously been laid out, and the other ten yards in rear of it. A Vickers Maxim gun team, one of two allotted to the Battalion, got into position in rear of the right of " C " Company.

The enemy gave no sign that he was aware of what was happening, and at zero the two lines rose and moved forward, incurring but few casualties, and all three companies arrived in an irregular line from twenty to fifty yards from Bayonet Trench, where the men dropped into shell-holes and waited to get together before finally going on to the assault. The enemy had by this opened short bursts of machine-gun fire from the right and hurled a good many bombs, but he used but little rifle fire.

The right and centre companies—" D " and " C "—had closed up until they consisted of groups of six or seven men each, somewhat irregularly spaced, from twenty to thirty yards from the German trench, and " D " only waited to charge forward till its rear line was nearer. The O.C. " C " Company was struck on the head by a fragment of a bomb and stunned when within a few yards of the enemy trench, and unhappily at this moment the left company—" A "—which had by this lost both its officers, and was under the fire of a machine gun on the left and also of rifles, wavered and fell back, and this movement unfortunately spread all down the line and could not be checked. Only two unwounded officers remained now with the attacking line, and thus the whole line fell back, the flanking parties conforming.

One minute after zero, Lieutenant R. A. Field, with a subsection of Battalion bombers, attacked up Bite Trench by moving along the top ; but the enemy had recently dug a trench (known as " X " Trench) parallel to and some one hundred and fifty yards from Bite Trench, which bent round to meet Bite Trench about midway between the Bombing Block which was there and Bayonet Trench. This " X " Trench was found to be full of Germans, who opened a heavy rifle and bombing fire on Lieutenant Field's party, forcing them to jump back into Bite Trench, whence they engaged the enemy in " X " Trench from behind a wire Block which covered the opening to " X " Trench. Lieutenant Field, however, got on to the top again, moved round the wire Block and got into " X " Trench again ; here he met a German whom he shot with his revolver, and then finding the trench inconveniently full of the enemy, he went back and rejoined his party. It now seemed to Lieutenant Field that there appeared to be no reasonable chance of bombing the enemy out of " X " Trench. The supporting company had been delayed and was not yet up, and reports

G

of the failure of the attack on Bayonet Trench reaching him, he withdrew to the original Block. On the next day the Battalion was relieved by the 18th King's and withdrawn to Flers Support Trench, whence during the next few days the Brigade, having been relieved by the 53rd Australian Brigade, marched via Pommiers Redoubt to Dernancourt.

In the action of the 18th the losses in the 2nd Battalion The Green Howards totalled 214 of all ranks, made up as follows : killed, Lieutenant B. E. Gill and 15 others ; wounded, Captain H. F. Blackwood, Second-Lieutenants H. H. Fraser, G. F. Kershaw, J. B. Girling, A. O. Lister and R. M. Somerset and 153 non-commissioned officers and men ; wounded and missing, Second-Lieutenants N. F. McCarthy, J. F. B. Delap and T. E. Robinson, and missing, 36 men.

On the 23rd October Major H. F. Bidder left the Battalion on transfer to England for employment on the Home Establishment, and Major C. V. Edwards of the Regiment assumed command in his place.

At the end of this month the 2nd Battalion The Green Howards were at Bailleulmont, an area described in the Battalion diary on first arrival as " very quiet," but the Germans shelled it at times, causing some loss, while, when the Battalion moved about the 19th November to Bailleuval, owing to some necessary redistribution of the divisional front, the Germans opened upon this village a very heavy shell fire for some two hours in the evening, whereby six men of the Regiment were killed and Second-Lieutenant E. J. Rapp and thirteen other ranks were wounded ; the officer had only returned a few days after recovery from an earlier wound.

In this neighbourhood the Battalion spent the end of the year, and on the 31st December the officers of the 2nd Battalion The Green Howards were thus distributed : Captain W. H. Colley, in command, Second-Lieutenant G. P. Lund, acting-adjutant, Captain F. Dallimore, R.A.M.C., in medical charge, Second-Lieutenant W. B. Cornaby, transport officer, and Regimental-Sergeant-Major J. T. Colver, acting-quartermaster.

" A " Company, Second-Lieutenant W. Jackson ; " B " Company, Second-Lieutenant H. Smith ; " C " Company, Second-Lieutenants A. Newbury and H. Dean ; " D " Company, Second-Lieutenant F. Whaley.

On leave, Major C. V. Edwards, Captains G. N. N. Smith, M. D. W. Maude and T. W. Baron, Lieutenant A. O. Lister, Second-Lieutenants J. T. Evans, E. J. Rapp, H. Hargreaves, E. P. Davy, H. B. Whitfield and Lieutenant and Quartermaster E. Pickard.

On command, Lieutenant-Colonel W. H. Young, Captain E. C. W. Rowley, Second-Lieutenants A. E. J. Belcher, A. Dickinson, J. H. O'Halloran and H. J. Whiting.

A HEAVILY-SHELLED VILLAGE.

October, 1916.

Attending courses of instruction, Lieutenant R. A. Field, M.C., Second-Lieutenants H. N. Bright and T. Connelly.

The end of the Battle of the Somme had advanced the British line on the left bank of the Ancre close up to the villages of Pys and Grandcourt, where the German positions ran from the spur above Beaumont Hamel along the ridge north of Beaucourt and then across the Ancre, enclosing Grandcourt, Miraumont and Pys. In rear of this was a strong second line, in front of Bucquoy and Achiet-le-Petit, Grévillers and Loupart Wood to the Albert-Bapaume road, whence it continued south-east past Le Transloy to Saillisel. This system, known as the Le Transloy-Loupart line, had behind it a third line in course of construction, covering Rocquigny, Bapaume and Ablainzeville.

With the last shots of the battle, winter set in with unusual severity—wet, mist, frost, and snowstorms, and the energies of the troops were principally directed, during the ensuing six weeks or more, to the improvement of the trenches and of the communications in rear of them, while preparations were made for driving the enemy from the remainder of the Beaumont Hamel spur as soon as active operations should again become possible.

By the beginning of the year 1917 the British front had been increased to one hundred and twenty miles, held from north to south, or left to right, in the following order of armies; the Second about Ypres, the First in the Armentières district, the Third thence to the south of Arras, then came the Fifth, while the Fourth joined on to the French.

The 2nd Battalion The Green Howards spent the early part of January about Bailleulval and Le Souich, refitting, training the drafts which here joined and cutting wood in the forest of Lucheux, this work all greatly interfered with by heavy falls of snow. Then about the 26th the Battalion moved to Mondicourt, and was employed on a new railway there under construction ; but after some ten days of this work the Battalion marched via Humbercourt and Beaumetz to Achicourt, where it moved up into the line, relieving a battalion of the 14th Division ; here " A " Company was in the front line, " B " Company in Agny and the remainder of the Battalion in reserve in Achicourt. When relieved The Green Howards were in divisional reserve in Beaumetz, furnishing many working parties, particularly on the construction of a Corps cable trench in Beaumetz and Berneville. Then at the end of the month the Battalion moved to Arras, where it was for some days employed under the R.E.

By this time the Germans were everywhere falling back, and more than once the 30th Division was under orders to move forward and help to take up the pursuit. By the 19th March, however, " our advance had reached a stage at which the increasing difficulty of maintaining our communications made it imperative to slacken the pace of our pursuit. South of Peronne, the River Somme, the bridges over which had been destroyed by the retreating enemy, presented a formidable obstacle. North of Peronne, the wide belt of devastated country over which the Somme battle had been fought offered even greater difficulties to the passage of guns and transport." *

For a few days The Green Howards returned to Mondicourt, where Major W. D. Grant, of the Yorkshire Dragoons, joined for duty, moving then to the divisional training area at Bailleulval, and then on the 28th March found themselves near Ficheux, holding an outpost line west of Hénin-sur-Cojeul, a small village of some thousand inhabitants six miles south-east of Arras, with a small stream, the Cojeul, running through it. About three thousand yards to the north-east is a low ridge between Héninel and Neuville Vitasse, on which the Germans had sited that portion of the Hindenburg front line known as the Cojeul Switch. Hénin itself is on level ground, fairly well wooded, with gardens and orchards on the east of it, while the houses of the village, though badly battered, had for the most part the walls still standing. Skirting the north-west side of the village and leading right into the British position was a deep and wide German communication trench known as Nagpur Trench; this played an important part in the two attacks made upon Hénin by the Battalion.

" It evidently being considered that the enemy would attempt no very determined defence of Hénin, the Battalion was ordered to make an attempt to ' squeeze ' the Germans out of it on the night of the 30th–31st March, and two companies—' A ' under Captain G. N. Smith, and ' B ' commanded by Captain R. A. Field—were detailed for the task, their objective being to endeavour to place posts quietly round the village and then induce the enemy to leave it. The hostile garrison consisted of four hundred of the 99th Regiment of Prussian Infantry, a set of stubborn fighters as we were soon to prove, while the belief of our higher commanders that they might easily be shepherded out of the village was somewhat too optimistic. ' B ' Company made a fine attempt to succeed, reaching a point in line with the centre of the village in Nagpur Trench, where they captured a machine-gun post and a few prisoners. Here a gallant little subaltern, Smith, who had recently joined from a public schools battalion, showed his mettle by assaulting an enormous Prussian, thus proving that his heart was bigger than his body. After dawn the enemy became too aggressive for any forward positions to be held, so our advanced parties were withdrawn into our outpost position. Field as usual had behaved gallantly

* Despatch of the 31st May, 1917.

and performed several feats of daring. Much useful information about Hénin was obtained as a result of this small affair.

"Our casualties were, Second-Lieutenant Whaley and 6 other ranks killed, 18 men wounded, and the same number missing."

Among the missing was Sergeant Adair of the Battalion, who was captured and kept by his captors in the village, and " all through the following day they ignored his requests for food and water. This Sergeant Adair might have overlooked, but what he could not so easily forgive was the fact that they made him wheel a barrow. His exercises with the barrow do not appear to have been designed with any practical end in view, since for the greater part of the day it was empty ! Still the fact remains that for several hours a British sergeant wheeled a German barrow, while two German privates, with fixed bayonets, marched behind. Senior N.C.O.'s who chance to read these lines will sympathize with the indignation that surged through Sergeant Adair's breast at this indignity ! In the early hours of the following morning one of the Germans chanced to lean his rifle against a neighbouring wall. This was the opportunity for which Sergeant Adair had been waiting. He seized the rifle, put a bullet through the chest of the owner and instantly made off. The other private seems to have been so astonished at this irregular proceeding that he let the fugitive get well away before deciding to take action. Then only one of several shots he fired did any damage—a flesh wound in the leg. Sergeant Adair got into a shell-hole just as day was breaking, and here he had to remain all day, for as often as he made an attempt to move out he was sniped at from the village. At nightfall, however, he was able to get away unobserved and had just strength enough to crawl back to our lines."

" The Battalion was now ordered to make a strong attack on the village of Hénin on the early morning of 2nd April, and the force to be employed was composed of the following troops under Lieutenant-Colonel C. V. Edwards :

" 2nd Battalion The Green Howards.

" 2 Companies 19th Battalion The Manchester Regiment.

" 2 Stokes mortars of the 21st T.M. Battery.

" 2 machine guns.

" 30 other ranks of the Brigade Pioneer Company.

" The plan of attack was as follows : ' B ' Company under Captain Field and ' C ' under Lieutenant Bright, on left and right respectively, were to make a direct attack on the front of the village ; two platoons of ' A ' Company (Captain Smith), with two Stokes mortars and one machine gun were to advance up Nagpur Trench on the left of the village ; the two remaining platoons of ' A ' with one machine gun were to advance round the right of the village ; while ' D ' Company, under Captain Baron, was to follow in support of the frontal attack. The two companies of the 19th Manchester were detailed to follow as ' moppers-up,' but they were late in reaching the rendezvous and took small part in the ensuing action. Battalion Headquarters was established in a shallow ditch one hundred and fifty yards east of the Mercatel-Boiry Road, some twelve hundred yards from the front edge of Hénin.

" It was laid down in Operation Orders that as soon as the village was captured, posts were to be established on the flanks and beyond it as under : Nos. 1 and 2 on the right or south-east edge ; No. 3 at the far or east end ; Nos. 4 and 5 on the far or north-west edge of Hénin, these posts all being consolidated and prepared against counter-attack. ' B ' Company had been detailed for forming No. 3 post, but as this company did not succeed in entering the village the post was not established, and a gap was thus left through which a number of the enemy escaped, heavily fired on from No. 2 post.

" Dawn was late and the morning dark. The artillery barrage opened at 5.15 a.m., and the enemy at once sent up showers of rockets and Very lights of all colours. The various units of the attacking force followed the barrage as ordered, the right flank of the centre group moving straight through the right of the village up to the place where No. 2 post was to be found ; on the extreme left the advance was equally successful and Nos. 4 and 5 posts were established. Unfortunately ' B ' Company on the left centre was held up at the edge of the village and failed to enter, being faced by several strong points defended with much determination. Captain Field, intrepid as ever, pushed on and was found later lying dead near the Mairie, which the enemy had evidently used as a strong rallying point. On the right, though the advance had been successful, the enemy rifle fire had been very heavy, and Second-Lieutenants Evans and Bright were wounded and the machine-gun officer, Lieutenant Wordsworth, M.G.C., killed. On the left Second-Lieutenant Jones had pushed forward and established No. 4 post early, capturing fifteen Germans, but later was violently counter-attacked from the village, losing practically all his men, and was himself badly wounded and captured. The Germans placed him in a shed, where he was found in the afternoon when the village was finally in our hands. From ' B ' Company Second-Lieutenant Wright with some fifteen men had dug a shallow trench just outside the village, and every one of them was picked off by sharpshooters in the village. A pity, as undoubtedly a dash to another position would have saved most of them. It seems that in the absence of direct orders Wright was unwilling to move, and so, with his men, he died at his post.

" Wright, who had joined us only a few days previously, was a boy of barely nineteen, but he had already driven an ambulance for the French at Verdun while he was still too young to join up. He was a promising musician too, and had composed music in the trenches in his field notebook, which unfortunately was missing when his body was found later.

" Meanwhile the supporting company—'D'—under Captain Baron had, in accordance with instructions, been digging in just outside the village ; but finding that the left centre company was making no headway, it came up to the edge of the village to assist. Here it was held up by strong points till early in the afternoon, when Captain Baron's determination proved effective, and the enemy were forced to yield. During the morning Captain Smith came back from the left to report to Battalion H.Q. and there received orders to collect all the men he could and advance into the village from Nagpur Trench towards the Mairie ; this he at once proceeded to do. At the same time a platoon under Lieutenant Snelling was working its way back from No. 2 post through the village—a very useful piece of initiative on the part of this officer, for in the village he captured three German chargers, one of which eventually became the C.O.'s charger !

" Our efforts were now beginning to tell, and at 2.30 p.m. the C.O. was able to ring up the Brigadier and report that Hénin was ours. The Brigadier, General Goodman, who had only recently joined the 21st Brigade, afterwards said that the news was so unexpected that he fell off his chair with surprise ! He might have known that when The Green Howards are given a job to do they see it through.

" Nos. 3 and 4 posts were soon established by Captain Smith's party, the remnants of the Manchester Regiment being collected to form the garrison for No. 3, while later on fifty men of the 2nd Wiltshire, who had been carrying up reserve ammunition, were told off to No. 4.

" At 4 p.m. it started to snow heavily, and every one was pleased to hear that the 16th Battalion Manchester Regiment was on its way to relieve us. The relief was completed by 1 a.m. on the 3rd and Battalion H.Q. arrived back at its billet in Bellacourt about 4 a.m.—a long and cold ride through the snow. The C.O. and Adjutant had been so occupied with the two actions that they had not had a wink of sleep for seventy-two hours on end, and the adjutant (Lund), after partaking of a heavy supper—or perhaps breakfast would be more correct—was so drowsy that he fell with a crash fast asleep into the fireplace !

" This was the first serious action the Battalion had taken part in since it left the Somme, somewhat war-weary, the October before, and no doubt the fight, although severe, with its final brilliant success, was the re-making of it. The action of course is not well known, and was of only local tactical importance, but it was a Battalion affair, planned and organized by the Battalion commander and carried through by the company officers and men in face of stiff opposition. The Prussians who held the village were a hard-bitten lot of men, the prisoners all being fine upstanding fellows. The Commandant of the village, a tall, rather unbending Prussian, was captured by one of the smallest men in the Battalion, but one of its stoutest fighters, who conducted him back in triumph to Battalion Headquarters. Captain Baron was appointed commandant of Hénin in his place till relieved by the incoming regiment. On the following day the

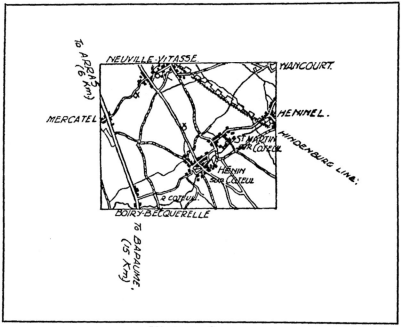

HÉNIN-SUR-COJEUL.

Divisional Commander paid a special visit to congratulate the Battalion on its success.

"The casualties sustained by the Battalion in this action were : killed, Captain R. A. Field, M.C., Second-Lieutenant H. M. Wright, and 62 other ranks ; wounded, Lieutenants A. F. Robinson and J. Pyman (A.S.C. attached), Second-Lieutenants J. T. Evans, A. T. Jones, H. N. Bright (Manchester Regiment attached), T. Connelly, and 96 non-commissioned officers and men, while 8 men were missing.

"Captain R. A. Field was a sad loss to the Battalion. This young officer—he was only twenty-two, though he looked older—was ranching in Canada when the war broke out and, leaving his property all standing, he at once hurried to England. Well known for his gallantry throughout the Division, he was bombing officer during the Somme Battle, and was appointed adjutant in November, 1916, but resigned this post to take command of ' B ' Company. His name was submitted for the Victoria Cross, but it is believed that owing to some temporary alterations in the rules for posthumous awards his name failed to get through ; there could have been no other reason.

"Our doctor—Captain F. Dallimore, M.C., R.A.M.C.—had his aid-

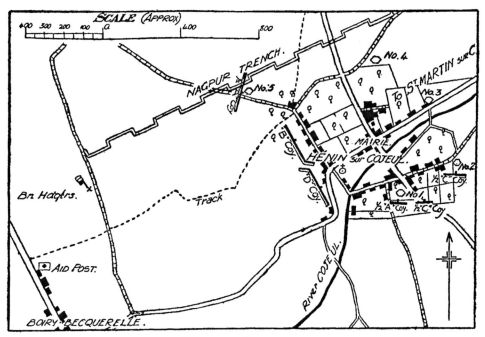

HÊNIN-SUR-COJEUL,
2nd April, 1917.
(Situation about 9 a.m.)

post in a house on the outskirts of Boiry-Becquerelle, where he dealt with the wounded with his usual care."

The enemy casualties were : killed, 90, actually counted in the village ; wounded, estimated at not less than 200 ; prisoners, 2 officers and 37 other ranks.

The 2nd Battalion The Green Howards could not for long be spared out of the line in view of the major operations which were now about to commence and which are known as the Battle of Arras ; for the prosecution of these preparations on a very large scale had for some time past been going forward. The front to be attacked by the Third and First Armies under Generals Allenby and Horne, on right and left respectively, " extended from just north of the village of Croisilles, south-east of Arras, to just south of Givenchy-en-Gohelle, at the northern foot of Vimy Ridge, a distance of nearly fifteen miles. It included between four and five miles of the northern end of the Hindenburg Line, which had been built to meet the experience of the Somme Battle." *

The 30th Division was now in the VII. Corps (General Snow) in the Third Army ; the Corps contained the 14th, 21st, 30th and 56th Divisions, and of these the three first named were in the first line in the order 21st, 30th and 14th from right to left, the 30th Division having immediately in its front the village of Wancourt.

Of the opening of the battle the British Commander-in-Chief states in his despatch that " the general attack on the 9th April was launched at 5.30 a.m. under cover of a most effective artillery barrage. Closely following the tornado of our shell fire, our gallant infantry poured like a flood across the German lines, overwhelming the enemy's garrisons. Within forty minutes of the opening of the battle practically the whole of the German front line system on the front attacked had been stormed and taken. Only on the extreme left fierce fighting was still taking place for the possession of the enemy's trenches on the slopes of Hill 145 at the northern end of the Vimy Ridge.

" At 7.30 a.m. the advance was resumed against the second objective. Somewhat greater opposition was now encountered, and at the hour at which these objectives were timed to have been captured strong parties of the enemy were still holding out on the high ground north of Tilloy-les-Moffleines, known as Observation Ridge, and in Railway Triangle."

On the 7th April the Battalion moved from Bellacourt *via* Agny to Blaireville, in readiness for the part it was to take in the operations commencing on the 9th, and in regard to which all ranks for some days previously had been under instruction.

For the opening day of the Battle of Arras The 2nd Green Howards were told off as follows :

(i) 146 non-commissioned officers and men under Captain G. N. N. Smith, M.C., were to move with the 18th King's as " moppers-up."

(ii) 126 other ranks under Captain W. H. Colley were to accompany the 2nd Wiltshire Regiment as " moppers-up."

(iii) 40 other ranks, under Second-Lieutenant E. J. Rapp, were to move with the 21st Stokes Mortar Battery as carriers.

* Despatch of the 25th December, 1917.

(iv) 21 other ranks were to be held in reserve as escort to the 21st
    Mortar Battery.

The part of the enemy line to be attacked by the 21st Infantry Brigade
was immediately to the east of Neuville Vitasse ; the preliminary bombardment was very light, and the Division had to advance in daylight over
some two thousand yards of open ground before arrival at the enemy
wire.   During this advance a hare was kicked up and actually chased by
some of the men !

The first party of The Green Howards followed the first wave of the
King's and advanced as ordered over the open ground until the King's
were held up by the German wire which our shells had failed to cut.   The
party of the Battalion then pushed right up to the leading line of the first
wave of the King's and established itself in shell-holes on the left, close
up to the wire, joining these up during the day by digging trenches, and
here the party remained under shell and rifle fire until relieved about 1 a.m.
on the 10th.

The second party of The Green Howards followed the second wave of
the Wiltshire Regiment, which halted on its first wave reaching the German
wire ; but the " moppers-up " of the Battalion moved on steadily until
fifty yards from the first wave, which had been unsuccessful in finding gaps
in the wire.   The first wave then fell back, leaving the second party of
The Green Howards in front, where they remained for some little time until
ordered by Second-Lieutenant Camm to withdraw to the St. Martin-
Neuville Vitasse road, where Second-Lieutenant Camm established himself—
his right fifty yards from Nepal Trench in touch with the 89th Brigade.
This party remained here until it was also relieved early on the morning
of the 10th.

The forty carriers remained throughout with the Stokes Mortar Battery,
its final position being on the Hénin-Neuville Vitasse road.

The 2nd Green Howards sustained the following casualties : killed,
Second-Lieutenant E. J. Rapp and 23 other ranks ; wounded, Second-
Lieutenants R. R. Taylor, W. B. Taylor, P. Snelling, J. H. O'Halloran
and B. C. Camm, and 84 non-commissioned officers and men ; and missing,
2 men.

On relief the mopping-up and carrying parties joined Headquarters
at Blaireville, but thereafter there were several moves before, on the 18th,
the Battalion moved to the Cojeul Switch in the Hindenburg Line, relieving there the 2nd Royal Scots Fusiliers in Divisional Reserve.   On
the afternoon of the 23rd The Green Howards again moved forward with
orders to support the 18th King's and 19th Manchester, crossing the Cojeul
River just west of Héninel and halting in the trenches and under cover of

banks about three hundred yards south-east of the river. Here The Green Howards came under heavy shell fire, and " D " Company incurred some five-and-twenty casualties. After consulting with the O.C. 18th King's, The Green Howards moved to the east about 8.30 p.m. in order to reinforce the 19th Manchester, who, with the 18th Battalion of the same Regiment, were attacking a line overlooking Cherisy. For this the frontage allotted was very wide. The Manchester Regiment had not been given time to fully grasp the plan of attack, and the enemy trenches were penetrated at isolated points only. When, about 10.30 p.m., The Green Howards arrived at the Headquarters of the 19th Manchester, information was received that the only troops left in the German trenches were some thirty or forty men of the Manchester Regiment ; so two companies of the Battalion were sent forward to occupy a portion of the enemy trenches. This was successfully carried out by " C " and " D " Companies under Captains Colley and Baron respectively, while the two remaining companies were sent to Wancourt Tower to gain touch with the 150th Brigade on the left.

Communication was established with this Brigade at 2 a.m. on the 24th, and at Wancourt Tower were found men of the 4th and 5th Battalions The Green Howards and of a Border battalion of the 50th Division. One company, under Lieutenant Newbury, was sent to occupy the German front line between the two companies on the right and the 150th Brigade on the left ; while at 3 o'clock Second-Lieutenant Camm pushed on with his company to seize certain quarries, and at the same time Lieutenant Newbury's company was ordered to occupy the German support line.

" Lieutenant Camm's advance to the quarries, some eight hundred yards over unknown ground, was a great achievement," writes Colonel Edwards. " These quarries—there were three, although the map only showed one—had been very strongly held by the enemy on the morning and evening of the 23rd, and had undoubtedly been the reason why our two attacks had failed. The ground in front and for several hundred yards to the flanks of the quarries was covered thickly with dead and wounded. About 11 a.m. on the 24th the Battalion started its interesting advance to the Cherisy Ridge. This was more or less an independent advance, encouraged by our brigadier, General Goodman. We had no one on our flanks and no artillery support ; in fact, after moving forward some three hundred yards, our own field artillery opened on us, but was stopped by the F.O.O., who discovered his mistake before much damage was done. The Bosche resistance was slight and the Battalion reached the top of the Ridge without difficulty, and the 2nd Wiltshire were hurried up after us. Our troubles were not over, for about 4 p.m. our 60-pounders, misled I believe by an aeroplane, started to bombard us, and for two hours we were forced to admire the accurate shooting of our own gunners! Our casualties from this fire were two killed and five wounded.

" We were now a long way in advance of the 50th Division on our left, and about 5 p.m. we watched them attempting to come up into line. The Germans were ready for them and they were only partly successful. We managed to help them a bit with rifle and Lewis gun fire. During our advance we walked over two German 8-inch howitzers, but omitted to label them, which the King's Battalion of the 89th Brigade did, and I believe these howitzers now adorn the Town Hall in Liverpool."

Early on the 25th the Battalion was relieved and moved back, first into support and later to Cojeul Switch, finally marching on the 29th into Arras and there entraining for Linzeux ; then the month of May found the 30th Division in the salient south-east of Ypres, where it occupied a position on the flank of the Battle of Messines of the 7th June, coming in for what a correspondent describes as " some of the backwash," but taking no part in the battle itself.

Then for some time the Battalion was at rest in the training area at Zouafques, but at the beginning of the last week in July it was moved up to the Dickebusche Huts in readiness for a daylight raid which had been arranged on the German front lines. " C " Company, under Captain E. G. C. Le Sueur, penetrated to Jeffery Reserve Trench, following the barrage steadily for the allotted distance, but as the barrage went on, the raiding party had to come back without any artillery protection, and the enemy was able to fire heavily upon it as it fell back from Jackdaw Beek. One German officer and ten of his men were brought back prisoners, but Captain Le Sueur and Lieutenant J. B. Freeland and 9 men were killed, 34 were wounded and 2 were missing.

On the evening of the 28th July the 2nd Battalion The Green Howards moved into the line on Observatory Ridge in readiness for the Third Battle of Ypres, which opened on the 31st, and it was now in the II. Corps under Lieutenant-General Jacob, composed of the following divisions in order from left to right : the 8th, 30th and 24th, with the 18th in support. The ground in front of the II. Corps, which was on the extreme south of the Fifth Army, was covered by a number of woods ; Sanctuary Wood and Shrewsbury Forest covered practically the whole of the Corps front, behind these was Stirling Castle Ridge, and in rear of this again were Glencorse and Polygon Woods and Inverness Copse.

In the 30th Division the 21st and 90th Brigades were in the first line and the 89th was in support, while the objective of The 2nd Green Howards was a line slightly beyond the eastern edge of Bodmin Copse, an advance of one thousand and fifty yards : zero hour on the 31st July was at 3.30 a.m.

" Forty minutes before zero the whole Battalion assembled in No-Man's Land and lay down to await the barrage. Immediately in front of us the enemy was carrying out a relief, which we duly discovered later, so we did not suffer much from shell fire, our casualties being about a dozen from one unlucky shell that dropped into ' B ' Company. Companies were commanded as follows : ' A ' by Captain Lund, ' B ' by Captain Bunting, ' C ' by Lieutenant Newbury, and ' D ' by Lieutenant Watt in the absence of Captain Baron, who was kept out on this occasion. The morning was dark and misty, which made it difficult to keep direction, and the ground was very much broken up by shell fire, the Bosche trenches being practically obliterated. What resistance there was came from concrete pill-boxes, of which there was a large number. Our barrage was very severe, and the thermite shells that were used lighted up the whole country-side. Our two leading companies, ' A ' and ' C,' reached their objective, Jeffery Reserve Trench, with little, if any, opposition ; ' B ' and ' D ' then passed through and on into Bodmin Copse, ' D ' going straight to its objective, but ' B ' Company, losing direction, somewhat to its left. As we advanced, the 24th Division appeared to be inclining too much to its left, and thus shouldering us off our own true line. On its objective, ' D ' Company captured a large concrete shelter and slew a number of Germans. Here ' D ' consolidated with the 1st Royal Fusiliers and various other regiments on its right. The actual distance advanced by this company was nine hundred and sixty yards.

" ' B ' Company, meanwhile, had halted away to the left and was joined by ' A ' as a reinforcement. This was as far as the II. Corps got that day. Two more bodies of troops were due to pass through us in further attacks, but although Bodmin Copse became packed full of troops, not another man managed to advance beyond our front line.

" During the night I brought ' A ' and ' B ' Companies up on ' D's ' right and moved parties of other units away to make room for them, leaving Lund in charge of our front line. It started to rain during the afternoon and did not stop for nearly six weeks. Our front line was not too happily situated, the Dunbarton Lake being in front with Tower Hamlets Ridge overlooking it. We held on to this position until the night of the 3rd August, when we were relieved by the 2nd Buffs. The attack by the II. Corps had not been a great success, while the Corps away on the left had gained all its objectives ; this Corps had won its first only. The reason is difficult to find ; resistance was not great, but darkness, loss of direction, inability to read a map in a new shell-stricken area, difficulties in assembling—all had something to do with it. The 2nd Battalion may have been lucky to have been the first to go over the top, but the fact remains that it got there and then knew where it was.

" Our aid post was in Tor Top Tunnel, and for four days and nights our medical officer, Clark, worked like the true Scotsman that he is. The Battalion on relief moved back to Chateau Legard, where Pickard was waiting for us with unlimited supplies of hot rabbit-pie."

The casualties suffered by the Battalion in these operations amounted to : killed or died of wounds, Second-Lieutenants H. S. A. Turner, J. W. Brown, M.C., and 19 other ranks ; wounded, Second-Lieutenants G. C. Kindersley, V. F. B. Sanders, M.C., H. Child, H. R. Watt, M.C., H. L. Hannam, H. Dean, and 173 non-commissioned officers and men ; missing, 34 men.

From this area the 30th Division proceeded to and took over the slightly less muddy, but much more tranquil, Messines-Wytschaete front, and during the remainder of the year 1917 the 2nd Battalion The Green Howards had no share in any very serious fighting. The events of the latter half of the year are thus described in brief by the commanding-officer :

" Our stay in the Wytschaete Ridge area during the autumn was a pleasant one. The weather was good, and, after the first week or so, when we got some of the backwash from the battle going on in the Salient, not too trying. Our front line was at the bottom of the eastern slope of the hill below Oostaverne and was not too comfortable down there, as there was no continuous line and the ' carries ' were long. Battalion Headquarters were more comfortably placed—Torreken Farm, Prince Ruprecht's dug-outs, Lancaster House near 15-inch Corner and Derry House—all being above the average. Our transport lines were also well situated in a small ruined farm close to French Farm and known as Tea Farm. The main building soon became a comfortable mess, much appreciated by visitors from the trenches. The windows actually contained glass, but where Pickard obtained it from I never learnt.

" It was when we were in support near Irish Farm that some three hundred sailors from the Dunkirk flotilla were billeted on us for a couple of days. They swarmed all over the Ridge, and the Bosche must have thought that there was going to be a naval invasion of his trenches.

" About this time Mr. Asquith in a tin hat paid us a visit to the Ridge, much to the joy of our ' D ' Company commander, who happened to be a staunch supporter of his politics. The Wytschaete Ridge was, of course, quite a show place for visitors, the two mine craters near Spanhoek Mollen being about the biggest in France or Belgium. I saw them four or five days after they were blown up, and they were then about eighty yards deep and one hundred and twenty across. Our reserve brigade's headquarters were on the western slope of Kemmel Hill, and I spent a very pleasant fortnight here during October. At this time the hill had not been greatly 'straffed,' but later on, in May, 1918, it became the centre of a very violent struggle and was sadly knocked about. General Hunter-Weston was our Corps commander, and it was during an inspection of the 21st Brigade, in the middle of one of his famous speeches, when he was describing how near the end of his tether the Bosche was, that the troops suddenly broke out into loud cheering. From about fifteen thousand feet above our heads a German 'plane could be seen descending in flames. After a quick glance upwards the Corps commander quietly remarked— 'The beginning of the end'!

" In November the 30th Division was relieved by Australians and moved back for a fortnight to Steenvoorde, where the Battalion was billeted in farms just north of the town. Later in November the Division went back to the Salient, the front line being a few hundred yards west of Gheluvelt and Polderhoek Chateau. Divisional Headquarters were at Westoutre and the battalions in reserve about Reninghelst, Scottish Wood and Swan Chateau. Life during December was uneventful, some shelling at first, which gradually died down. Two support battalions were again in Tor Top Tunnel, Hedge Street, and Canada Tunnel."

"SOMEWHERE IN FRANCE."

January, 1918.

CHAPTER VI

THE 2ND BATTALION

1918–1919

THE BATTLE OF THE SOMME, 1918. BATTLE OF ARRAS. BATTLE OF THE SCARPE. BATTLES OF THE SELLE AND OF THE SAMBRE. THE RETURN HOME

DURING the fighting on the Western Front in the course of the past year many substantial successes had been gained, and as stated in the Commander-in-Chief's despatch on the Cambrai operations, " the sudden breaking through by our troops of an immense system of defence has had a most inspiriting moral effect on the Armies I command, and must have a correspondingly depressing influence upon the enemy." In nearly every one of the more distant theatres of war also the Allies had gained many victories, but, after all, the effect of those distant operations was only an indirect one upon the progress of the war in Europe, and here the balance of power had swung dangerously against the British and their Allies.

" The disappearance of Russia as a belligerent country on the side of the Entente Powers had set free the great bulk of the German and Austrian divisions on the Eastern Front. Already, at the beginning of November, 1917, the transfer of German divisions from the Russian to the Western Front had begun. It became certain that the movement would be continued steadily until numerical superiority lay with the enemy. It was to be expected, moreover, that large numbers of guns and munitions, formerly in the possession of the Russian armies, would fall into the hands of our enemies, and at some future date would be turned against the Allies." *

Roumania, too, overpowered in front, and with treason on her flanks and in her rear, had been compelled to make terms with the Central Powers ; and despite the fact that powerful Austrian forces were confronting the Italians on the Piave, some of the British and French divisions which had been sent to Italy to help to hold the line there after the disaster of Caporetto,

* Despatch of the 20th July, 1918.

had been hastily recalled to France in view of the enemy massing on this front.

The great efforts made by the British armies during 1917 had left them at a low ebb both as regards training and numbers; the ranks had to be refilled, and it was eminently desirable that the new-comers should be thoroughly trained; but the fresh ground which had been wrested from the enemy needed much to be done in the way of development, while the officers and men had to pass from the offensive methods of the last few months to a study of the defensive tactics which the new situation, caused by the defection of Russia and Roumania, seemed likely to impose upon the Western Allies, until at least America might be expected in some degree to restore the balance in our favour.

" At the same time," so we read in the despatch above quoted, " a change took place in the organization of the forces. Under instructions from the Army Council, the reorganization of divisions from a 13 to a 10-battalion basis was completed during the month of February. Apart from the reduction in fighting strength involved by this reorganization, the fighting efficiency of units was to some extent affected. An unfamiliar grouping of units was introduced thereby, necessitating new methods of tactical handling of the troops and the discarding of old methods to which subordinate commanders had been accustomed."

In consequence of the above the 21st Brigade was reduced from four to three battalions, the 19th Manchester being taken out of it and the officers and men distributed among the 17th and 18th Battalions of the Regiment, and the 21st Brigade was now composed of the 2nd Battalion The Green Howards, the 2nd Battalion The Wiltshire Regiment, and the 17th Battalion The Manchester Regiment.

On the 2nd January, 1918, The 2nd Green Howards moved to Hedge Street Tunnel, Ypres, Major Birch being at this time in command, and here something of a disaster befell the Battalion, which had then just received orders to move by train to the neighbourhood of Amiens on relief by troops of the 20th Division. Under date of the 4th January, Major Pickard thus records what here took place : " Went up to Hedge Street Tunnel about 11 a.m. to arrange details for the move next day with the C.O. Very cold, ice was lying thick on the ground. I had never been down this particular tunnel previously and I was much surprised at the intense heat in the tunnel and mentioned the fact to Birch. The tunnel was very well built and had bunks all along the length off the main alley-way. It was strongly timbered and in the various messes the woodwork was covered with hessian canvas ; this I thought was very dangerous in case of fire. I stayed some hours and fixed up everything for the move and then returned to the transport lines at Reninghelst and left by lorry shortly after to arrange billets at Wallon Cappel.

" The 20th Division was due to relieve our division, but failed to arrive, and the relief of our Battalion was therefore delayed one day. Shortly after the time we should have been relieved had the 20th arrived to time, a fire broke out in the Tunnel, and from what the Medical Officer, who was with Headquarters at the time, stated, it appears that about midnight, looking up to the ceiling of the Tunnel, he saw a streak of flame. He at once gave the alarm, and everybody was roused and told to get out of the Tunnel as quickly as possible. Before many seconds had elapsed the Tunnel was one mass of flame and black smoke. Lieutenant Picken saved many lives by his brave conduct in staying at the bottom of the stairs and pushing and guiding the men which way to go, as it was impossible for them to see. The C.O. (Major Birch) was seen to be moving about, and it was thought that he would be able to get out ; but it appears that as soon as he learnt that every-one was not out of the Tunnel, he went back into the flames again to see if he could save anyone. He was not seen alive again. He and the adjutant—Lieutenant Dean—and the whole of the officers of ' B ' Company—Captain B. C. Camm, M.C., Second-Lieutenants G. P. Smith, J. Symon and W. Barber, also one R.E. officer, an officer of the Shropshire L.I., and a Church of England Brigade Chaplain, and twelve men of the Battalion were burnt to death. All these men belonged to our Battalion Headquarters staff, many of them were signallers and most of them had been with the Battalion during the whole of the war.

" The Tunnel had to be sealed up to localize the fire, and when it was re-opened some days after by the 20th Division the bodies of our men were found in the various bunks wearing their gas helmets. Except where was part of a man's body lying in the main alley there were no marks of burning on the bodies, but everything in the main alley was charred up."

On the 10th January the Battalion marched to the railway station at Steenbecque and entrained for Longeaux, the Division having now been transferred to the Fifth Army area, and on arrival at Longeaux, The Green Howards marched to billets in Moreuil, south of Amiens : a couple of days only were spent here and then the troops moved on by Hangest to Solente. " This," writes one then with the Regiment, " was quite new country to us. We crossed the trenches which had been occupied since the early days of the war near Damery, then marched through Roye, Champien, and then to Solente. This country had been in the occupation of the enemy since 1914, and it was most interesting to meet people who had had the enemy living amongst them for the past three years. As we marched through we saw German prisoners of war repairing houses which had been damaged by shell fire, and it did me good to see these men being made to make good the damage they were responsible for.   The country round the trench area was so different to what we had been used to in the north.   Here it was scarcely damaged except where the trenches had been made.   One envied the men who had held this part of the line for any length of time.   There was none of the mud and slush we saw in the north."

From Solente the Battalion moved for a week to Flavy-le-Meldeux, then to Crissoles, and then on through Chauny to Roupy Wood, taking over the sector from the French and occupying pre-war forts near Liez and La Fère. " We found this a very quiet area, we never heard a gun fire for days, and it seemed almost uncanny after our years of living in the constant noise of guns firing and shells bursting."

On the 2nd February there was a further move, to Cailloul, and on the 4th to Guiscard, moving back to Flavy for ten days, then going to Dury, and then on the 22nd February to Aubigny, where some days were profitably spent in training.

" Our divisional front," writes another Battalion correspondent, " was now immediately in front of St. Quentin, astride the Ham Road.   Battalion Headquarters in the line were either at Manchester Hill, near Francilly, or at Dallon.   Billets in rear were at Etreillers, Aubigny, Vaux, Fluquières, or Dury.   At Aubigny we received a large draft from our 10th Battalion which had recently been disbanded, and they brought their drum and fife band, under their drum-major, and a large amount of new equipment and instruments.   Unfortunately the Germans captured all this a little later.   Captain Read from the 10th now became our adjutant.   Life in the front line at this time was remarkably quiet, the Bosche being busy with preparations for his offensive, and our troops working hard on wire, trenches, dug-outs, and cable trenches to meet it.   The weather in February, March and April was delightful, a great contrast to the spring of 1917.   When not digging we were busy training—General Maxse saw to that ! "

When the German offensive opened on the 21st March, Lieutenant-Colonel Edwards was in temporary command of the 21st Brigade, while Captain Lund was commanding the 2nd Battalion The Green Howards.

A German offensive on a large scale was by no means unexpected.   " Towards the middle of February, 1918, it became evident that the enemy was preparing for a big offensive on the Western Front.   It was known from various sources that he had been steadily increasing his forces in the Western theatre since the beginning of November, 1917.   In three and a half months twenty-eight infantry divisions had been transferred from the Eastern theatre and six infantry divisions from the Italian theatre.   There were reports that further reinforcements were on their way to the west, and it was also known that the enemy had greatly increased his heavy artillery in the western theatre during the same period. These reinforcements were more than were necessary for defence, and, as they were moved at a time when the distribution of food and fuel to the civil population in Germany was rendered extremely difficult through lack of rolling stock, I concluded that the enemy intended to attack at an early date.

" Constant air reconnaissances over the enemy's lines showed that rail and road communications were being improved and ammunition and supply dumps increased along the whole front from Flanders to the Oise. By the end of February, 1918, these preparations had become very marked opposite the front held by the Third and Fifth British Armies, and I considered it probable that the enemy would make his initial effort from the Sensée River southwards. . . . By the 21st March the number of German infantry divisions in the Western theatre had risen to 192, an increase of 46 since the 1st November, 1917."[*]

The order of battle of the Fifth Army, upon which the brunt of the German attack fell, was on the 21st March from north to south as under :

The VII. Corps (Congreve), a front of 14,000 yards from Gouzeaucourt to Ronssoy.

The XIX. Corps (Watts), a front of 13,000 yards from Ronssoy to south of Pontruet.

The XVIII. Corps (Maxse), a front of 18,000 yards from Pontruet to the St. Quentin–Vendeuil Road west of Itancourt.

The III. Corps (Butler), a frontage to the south of Barisis of 30,000 yards, protected somewhat along 14,000 yards by the River Oise.

" In a wet season this protection would have been great ; but very little rain fell between January 1 and March 21. Marshes dried up, and the water channels narrowed and became shallow and fordable ; so the river had little defensive value."[†]

In the XVIII. Corps the divisions were in the following order from north to south : 61st—30th—36th, with the 20th in reserve ; the 30th Division, now commanded by Major-General W. de L. Williams, C.M.G., D.S.O., had two brigades in front line, the 90th on the left, and the 21st on the right, with the 89th in reserve.

In an account of the events of the 21st March furnished by Captain G. P. Lund to *The Green Howards Gazette*, he states that " forty-eight hours prior to the attack commencing, two German soldiers entered the Fifth Army lines and gave the time, date and place on which the attack would take place.

[*] Despatch of 20th July, 1918.
[†] Sparrow, *The Fifth Army, in March 1918*, p. xix.

This was the first definite information that the attack would be on our front." This statement is borne out by General Ludendorff,[*] who tells us that " on the 18th or 19th March two men deserted from a trench mortar company. Judging by notes found by us in the enemy's lines, or according to prisoners' statements, they are alleged to have given information of the impending attack."

On the 20th March the Battalion was billeted at Fluquières, about two miles in rear of the " forward zone," in what was known as the " battle zone," at a devastated village called Roupy. The position was a strong one, a defended locality with the main Ham–St. Quentin Road running through the centre. The Battalion had orders in the event of attack to man the battle trenches at Roupy ; the position which each company had to take up had previously been thoroughly reconnoitred, every man knew where he had to go, and companies were instructed to move off independently as soon as the message was received from Brigade Headquarters—" Man Battle Positions."

Of the eve of the great offensive Major Pickard has left the following account on record : " I was staying in a small cellar-like place about fifty yards from the cross-roads. I laid down that night ready dressed in order to be able to turn out without delay. I found it impossible to sleep : I thought the night would never pass, and I went out of my billet about 3 a.m. The night was deadly silent, and what surprised me most was to find the country enveloped in a very thick fog,[†] as the previous evening had been particularly clear with no sign of fog. I wondered if it was some devilish scheme of the Bosche, preparatory to the launching of the attack. I also felt firmly convinced in my mind then that an attack was going to take place. I went back into my ice-cold cellar, but could not rest, so walked round to see that all the carts were quite ready and the horses harnessed up. This took some time, and when I returned to my billet it would be about 4 a.m. I sat down on the trestle bed and waited for what was to come. About 4.30 a.m. I distinctly heard the boom of a heavy gun. Immediately the whole country resounded with the noise of artillery and the screaming of shells. I rushed out to order the drivers to hook their horses in and get ready to move. The shells were now falling very fast in the village, particularly near the cross-roads by which the majority of our carts would have to go. . . . It must be borne in mind that the fog was the thickest it was possible for one ever to experience—not a black fog, but perfectly white ; yet it was impossible to see further than a couple of yards at the outside."

[*] *My War Memories*, Vol. II, p. 596.
[†] There has been much discussion as to whether the fog did or did not assist the enemy attack, but General Gough says—*The Fifth Army in March, 1918*, p. 60—" the fog favoured our Fifth Army."

The forward battalions of the 30th Division on this morning were the 2nd Battalion The Wiltshire and the 16th Battalion The Manchester Regiments, and at the usual hour the Division sent out a couple of patrols, each a platoon strong. " One was a patrol from the 2nd Wiltshire. Out it went into the gathering white mist and disappeared ; it was never seen again. The other patrol had men from the 16th Manchester ; and at 4.40 a.m., when German shells began to seek for the lives of men, it was in No-man's-land and so cut off. But it took its chance nonchalantly—or shall we say cigarettefully ?—dodging from crater to crater ; and after 7 o'clock it made its way back into our forward zone, where it fought all day long ; and then with half its men lost, it withdrew into and through the battle zone. From eight battalions in the front zone of Maxse's Corps less than fifty men returned. All had fought to the very last." *

On the German bombardment commencing the Battalion was ordered to man battle stations, when the companies at once got clear of the village and were in position in the Roupy defences by 6.30, having suffered some half-dozen casualties, which, in view of the violence of the shelling, was very little. The fog was at this time so thick that nothing could be seen of the S.O.S. calls from the front line, and it was not until about 11 o'clock in the morning that a report came in that the enemy had succeeded in penetrating the British front line of resistance.

It was just after this that Colonel Edwards returned from Brigade Headquarters and reassumed command of The 2nd Green Howards.

About midday the fog suddenly lifted and some little time later Lieutenant Capp of the 2nd Wiltshire Regiment arrived at Battalion Headquarters stating that the support redoubt, the Epine de Dallon, had been surrounded and passed by the enemy, and that he, Lieutenant Capp, and the six men with him were all that had managed to get away. About the same time, " B, " the left front company of The Green Howards, reported that Germans were in a quarry some eight hundred yards distant. " We now saw the enemy advancing towards our position. They presented a very fine target for artillery fire, but, owing to most of the guns being on the move, we could get no weight of shell fire. Consequently he massed his troops in a valley between the quarry and Roupy with very few casualties. About 1.30 p.m. the enemy attacked our left front, but without success. The battalions on our flanks reported no enemy attack, so it was evident that they were anxious to get to the main road—in the direction of Savy.

" About 4.30 p.m. the second strong attack commenced, the enemy having massed troops taken from the left. Heavy artillery fire. Our own artillery short. The enemy attacked persistently for more than an hour,

* *The Fifth Army in March, 1918*, p. 65.

with large casualties, and about 5 p.m. he gained a position on our left front, and Second-Lieutenant Cownley, in command of ' C ' Company, was ordered to counter-attack. This he did under very heavy machine-gun fire and without success, the few who gained the German front line being overpowered and taken prisoners ; and by 6.30 p.m. the enemy had gained the Battalion front line trench, though the platoon keeps, immediately in rear, still held out. During the night the 17th King's were sent up with a view of making a counter-attack, but owing to the darkness and their not being familiar with the ground and the defences, they lost time and connection and were made use of to reinforce the platoon keeps and Roupy redoubt. During both these attacks the German aircraft were very active, flying low over our position and firing Véry lights to show the different strong points.

" The morning of the 22nd was again very foggy, and under the cover of the mist the enemy attacked again about 7 a.m., continuing to press on the greater part of the day. Early in the morning he penetrated our left flank and began to fire upon us with machine guns from the north-west corner of Roupy, a strong attack against the platoon keeps being delivered about midday. At 2.30 p.m. Colonel Edwards was wounded ; at 3 o'clock the battalion on the right was withdrawn ; and by 4 p.m. the right and left platoon keeps had been captured by strong enemy forces, while at this hour the Germans opened a strong attack from both flanks, using trenches already captured to mass their troops, on the left making use of the cover offered by the ruined village, and bringing machine guns to bear on us from the left rear. The situation on the extreme right—the south side of the Canal—was also very bad, the attackers having advanced to a position south of the Canal at Ham, some seven miles in rear of our position at Roupy at 5 p.m.

" The enemy continued to attack from both flanks, and our position was untenable, so we withdrew to a system of trenches between Roupy and Fluquières, but as these trenches were only three feet deep they afforded no protection ; so after a short time we withdrew to the Fluquières defences, where we found troops of the 20th Division. In this position we were very heavily shelled as the German gunners had these defences taped, so about 6.30 we withdrew through Fluquières and took up a position on the ridge between Fluquières and Aubigny, where the Battalion was reorganized. Here we were almost immediately attacked by the enemy, and about 6.45 p.m. a despatch rider arrived with orders to withdraw to Ham, where we were told to proceed to Maille-Villette, where we found billets."

" We got rations up to them quite easily this day and had them all cooked in the travelling kitchens for the Battalion," writes the quartermaster.

In his despatch on the Great German Offensive, Field-Marshal Sir Douglas Haig said of the 30th Division that, on the 21st, " About Roupy and Savy all hostile attempts, in which tanks were used, to break into the battle positions of the 30th Division, under command of Major-General W. de L. Williams, were repulsed with the heaviest losses, our troops carrying out a number of successful counter-attacks. In this sector, the advancing German infantry frequently bunched together and offered good targets to our artillery and machine guns."

" At Roupy and Savy, where German tanks led the attack," writes the author of *The Fifth Army in March, 1918,* " Williams fought finely with the 30th Division. . . . Williams had twenty-four machine guns well posted in his battle zone, and their teams had deep dug-outs, from most of which the guns could be fired. They suffered little from casualties during the bombardment ; and their turn came when the foe, after pushing patrols forward, assailed the battle zone, coming on in waves sometimes, and sometimes in small columns that bunched. Into these large moving targets our machine gunners fired, one gun using in all about twelve thousand rounds, and two others about thirty-five thousand. Attack after attack was shattered, and the many Germans who clustered into the quarry on the north-east of Roupy had terrible experiences, bullets ripping through them and strewing the ground with many dead and wounded. Yet the German attack did not give in. It went below ground into trenches, or sought shelter behind ridges and rallied itself for another grapple. . . . At midnight the 17th Manchester and 2nd Bedford held the whole of their battle positions, while the 2nd York " (The Green Howards), " after a hard struggle against big numbers often renewed, had lost no more than their front and support lines, retaining their keep."

And of the services of the 30th Division on the 22nd March the Commander-in-Chief has told us that " after repulsing heavy attacks throughout the morning, the 30th Division were again attacked during the afternoon and compelled to give ground. Our troops, fighting fiercely and continuously, were gradually forced out of the battle zone on the whole of this front, and fell back through the 20th Division and the 50th Division holding the third defensive zone between Happencourt, Villéveque and Boucly, in the hope of reorganizing behind them."

By this time, the evening of the second day of the German offensive, all available reserves at the disposal of the Fifth Army had been used up, and only some French troops were within supporting distance of the fighting line. " There remained, therefore, no course open but to fall back on the bridge-head positions east of the Somme. Accordingly, at 11 p.m. on the 22nd March, orders were issued by the Fifth Army Commander that the troops of the XVIII. Corps should fall back during the night behind the line of the Somme south of Voyennes, in touch with the III. Corps on their right ;

while the XIX. and VII. Corps endeavoured to secure the main Peronne bridge-head on the line Croix-Molignaux-Monchy Lagache-Vraignes, and thence northwards along the third zone of defence to the junction with the Third Army about Equancourt.   These withdrawals were carried out under constant pressure from the enemy, covered by rearguards of the 20th, 50th and 39th Divisions, which were constantly in action with German troops."*

At 4 a.m. on the 23rd the enemy was reported as having broken through the Aubigny defences, and preparations were made for immediate withdrawal from Maille Villette, and the Battalion marched to Golancourt, where, at 10 o'clock, it was directed to fall back in the direction of Ercheu, but on the march thither fresh orders were received, and The Green Howards then marched to Esmery Hallon, took up a position there and at once began to " dig in."   At 8 on the morning of the 24th " we observed our troops withdrawing from the Somme Canal defences, and at 9 a.m. the enemy advanced on our left.   We counter-attacked successfully through the woods northeast of Esmery Hallon ; about this time our right flank was reported to be withdrawing, and at 9.30 the troops on our immediate right fell back.   At 10 a.m. enemy machine guns suddenly opened on us from the woods on our right flank, so we withdrew through the village and got rather scattered ; we then reorganized on the north-west of the village and retired by sections, fighting a rear-guard action to the Canal east of Moyencourt and Ercheu. The Battalion was now separated into two parties, the one going with the details of the 21st Brigade to Ercheu and the other remaining on the Canal, towards which the enemy advanced in skirmishing order about 5 p.m., but was scattered by our artillery and rifle fire.

" 25th.   8 a.m.   Enemy cavalry reconnoitred opposite us, and at 10 o'clock the Germans advanced from the Esmery Hallon direction and from the north-east, but were held in check on our front ; but at 3.30 in the afternoon the French on our right retired, while the situation on our left was rather obscure.   About an hour later .the enemy machine guns enfiladed us from the right and we fell back under fire, one party going to Villersles-Roze and another to Roze.   These parties united again on the 26th, and the Battalion then proceeded to Folies, where the 21st Brigade was reorganizing and where the Battalion once more took up a defensive position." On this day Captain Lund rejoined and assumed command of the Battalion ; he had been sent back on the night of the 21st to take command of the reinforcements, and on Lieutenant-Colonel Edwards being wounded, Captain Read had exercised command.

On this day, the 26th March, it was decided to place the supreme control

---

* Despatch of the 20th July, 1918.

of the operations of the Western armies in the hands of General Foch, who then assumed command.

On the 26th the 30th Division was holding the Bouchoir-Rouvroy line, but next day the enemy managed to possess themselves of Bouchoir and began an attack upon the 2nd Green Howards. " D " Company was sent forward and attached to the 59th Brigade to fill a breach in the front line, and pressed on until the whole line retired, then taking up a position along the road running south-east from Folies. In the evening two more companies of the Battalion—" B " and " C "—were put into the front line, while " D " was relieved by the 17th Manchester Regiment. On the 28th the Germans attacked again, pressing back the right flank towards Arvillers and the left towards Beaufort ; but finally about midday the Battalion received orders to fall back on the French, who were holding a line through Le Quesnel, and about 1.30 p.m. the relief was effected, and the weary Battalion, gathering its remnants together, marched by Mezières, Villers-aux-Erables, Moreuil and Morisel to Rouvrel, where The Green Howards had their first night's rest since the opening of the battle on the 21st March.

On the 29th what was left of the three battalions of the 21st Brigade was organized into the 25th Composite Battalion under Major Rapson of the 2nd Wiltshire Regiment, with orders to remain ready to move wherever required at half an hour's notice ; about noon this day the Composite Battalion was ordered to march to Raineval to reinforce or support French cavalry, but these orders were cancelled and the troops remained stationary until the following day, when they marched to Saleux, south-west of Amiens, and there entrained for the St. Valery area, and marched then to Sallenelle. Here nearly a week was spent in reorganizing and refitting and making good deficiencies of all kinds.

The 2nd Battalion The Green Howards had gone into action on the 21st March at a strength of 23 officers and some 600 other ranks, its company commanders at the outset being—" A " Company, Second-Lieutenant R. N. Picken, " B " Company, Lieutenant J. S. A. Bunting, " C " Company, Second-Lieutenant J. J. Cownley, and " D " Company, Second-Lieutenant J. W. Walker, all of whom became casualties, the Battalion being reduced to 5 officers and some 200 other ranks.

The casualties among the non-commissioned officers and men totalled 410, while of the officers Lieutenant-Colonel C. V. Edwards, Lieutenant J. S. A. Bunting, Second-Lieutenants R. N. Picken, J. S. Smith, W. Rowell, D. W. H. Lean and J. Foreman were wounded ; wounded and missing were Second-Lieutenants J. W. Walker * and N. Morant † ; while missing were

* Became prisoner-of-war.   † Died of wounds in German hands.

Second-Lieutenants W. W. Vasey,* G. F. Lockwood, E. Howard, J. J. Cownley * and L. H. Barker.*

The first stage of the enemy's offensive had now weakened, though it did not close until the 5th April. The crisis had been great and its extreme gravity had been appreciated by His Majesty the King and his Cabinet, as may be read between the lines of the messages which reached the Field-Marshal in France when the danger was finally surmounted ; from the King came the following :

> " I can assure you that the fortitude, courage and self-sacrifice with which the troops under your command are so heroically resisting greatly superior numbers is realized by Me and My people. The Empire stands calm and confident in its soldiers. May God bless and give them strength in their time of trial."

On behalf of the British Government the Prime Minister wrote :

> " The British Cabinet wishes to express to the Army the thanks of the nation for its splendid defence. The whole Empire is thrilled with pride as it watches the heroic resistance offered by its brave troops to overwhelming odds. Knowing their steadfastness and courage whenever the honour of the Country depends on their valour, the Empire awaits with confidence the result of this struggle to defeat the enemy's last desperate efforts to trample down the free nations of the world. At home we are prepared to do all in our power to help in the true spirit of comradeship. The men necessary to replace all casualties, and the guns and machine guns required to make good those lost are either now in France or already on their way, and still further reinforcements of men and guns are ready to be thrown into the battle."

When the Germans were at last checked on the Somme, the High Command prepared to attack the British front in Flanders, north of the La Bassée Canal, and for this their preparations were well in hand. Such an attack offered substantial advantages, since in the prolonged fighting in the south the British Commander-in-Chief had not only called up and made full use of the whole of his reserves, but he had brought some ten divisions from the northern to the southern area and had replaced these by battle-worn divisions from the Somme fighting. In the north the British front would, in a normal spring, have been to some extent safeguarded by the very marshy nature of the country, but the spring of 1918 had been unusually dry and by April the northern front was almost everywhere readily passable. Further, in this area the British communications were indifferent, there being but the one line of railway running from St. Pol by Béthune and

---

* Became prisoners-of-war.

Hazebrouck to Calais and Dunkirk, some portions of it consisting of a single line of rail only, while the German communications were especially good, there being a great double line from Ostend to Douai and Cambrai with many feeders and auxiliary routes.

The German plan was to make here a limited offensive only, pushing through between La Bassée and Armentières with the object of capturing Béthune, thereafter seizing Hazebrouck and occupying the hills north of Bailleul. Then, when the British should have retreated, and as many French divisions as could be spared had been sent north to their assistance, the advance against Amiens was to be renewed. For the initial German attack nine divisions were available, and to meet these there were six British and one Portuguese divisions only, all greatly exhausted and weakened by the recent fighting.

On the morning of the 5th April the 2nd Green Howards marched from Sallenelle to Woincourt and there entrained for the Poperinghe area, left the train at Proven and marched to camp at St. Sixte, moving again in the afternoon of the 6th to dug-outs in the Canal bank on the left of Ypres and being temporarily attached to the 90th Brigade ; here the 30th relieved the 1st Division, and was now in the XV. Corps, commanded by Lieutenant-General Sir J. B. Du Cane, of the First Army under General Sir H. S. Horne.

" On the 12th April the Battalion moved forward to Cane Post in the support position ; this was well forward and amongst all the ground which had been so hardly fought over in the severe battles which had raged and had devastated the surrounding country from the 31st July, 1917, until the Passchendaele fighting of that year came to an end. Without exaggeration there was not a yard of ground anywhere in this area which had not been churned up by shell fire. It was quite a usual thing to come across a body lying in a shell-hole which was full of water and which from long standing had become quite clear. Elephant shelters had been erected near the support positions, but when the enemy opened his offensive in this part of the line, he soon made short work of the shelters."

In the Battalion diary under date of the 13th April it is stated : " Received orders in early morning to occupy battle positions on account of suggested withdrawal to the Steenbeek Line " ; and then under date of the 16th : " Withdrawal to Steenbeek Line complete by 6 a.m." The explanation of the movements indicated in these entries is to be found in the Field-Marshal's despatch of the 25th July, 1918, para. 62, wherein we read : " In order to set free additional British troops for the battle and to delay the execution of any plans which the enemy might be entertaining for extending the flank of his attack to the north, I approved of putting into execution the scheme for the gradual evacuation of the Ypres Salient. The first stage in this withdrawal had been carried out on the night of the 12th–13th April, since which date our position on the Passchendaele Ridge had been held by outposts only. On the night of the 15th–16th April the withdrawal was carried a stage further, our troops taking up positions along the line of the Steenbeek River and the Westhoek and Wytschaete Ridges."

About 3 on the afternoon of the 16th the enemy opened a very heavy gun fire, under cover of which they were seen to be advancing to occupy the ground which the British had vacated ; all the morning of the day following the shelling of the back areas and the new line taken up was heavy, but before midday The Green Howards had been relieved by the 10th Regiment of Belgian Infantry and had begun moving back to White Mill Camp, which was reached at 1 a.m. on the 18th.

Here a large draft of officers of junior rank joined : Lieutenants J. C. Storey, G. F. Mitchinson, W. H. Porter, G. A. Bowler, A. E. Malins, T. H. T. Bale and H. H. Fraser ; Second-Lieutenants F. C. Ainley, V. W. W. S. Purcell, H. R. B. Bailey, W. Jackson, R. S. Beaumont, A. Dockray, H. R. R. Bicknell, C. H. Marsden and B. Wahl.

There is not very much of importance to record during the remainder of the month of April—it was a period of alarms and excursions, raids and counter-raids, of constant shelling and resultant casualties, Second-Lieutenants W. P. Burkett and T. H. T. Bale being killed, Lieutenant A. E. Malins was gassed, and Lieutenant T. C. W. Sandilands and Second-Lieutenant J. S. Branscombe were wounded ; then on the 1st May the Battalion moved to the neighbourhood of Ouderdom, being shelled out of one camp there and finding little less peace in the second to which it moved. The 6th found The Green Howards up in the line near Voormezeele, where they relieved a South African unit, and where the enemy guns were very active, firing considerably with gas shells.

" At 3.15 a.m. on the 8th the enemy laid down an exceptionally heavy bombardment on our front line and support trenches, lasting four hours and causing many casualties, while the trenches were practically obliterated."

At 7.15 a.m. the Germans made an attack in force upon the Battalion front line, and this having been captured by the enemy he made for the present no further advance, and at 7 in the evening a counter-attack was ordered to be made by two battalions of the 19th Brigade assisted by the 30th Composite Brigade. the battalion of the 19th Brigade detailed to attack on this front appears to some extent to have lost direction, and a company of the Manchester and what remained of " C " Company of The Green Howards, with two companies of the 17th King's, joined in the counter-attack, gaining all objectives, though at a very heavy cost, but not being

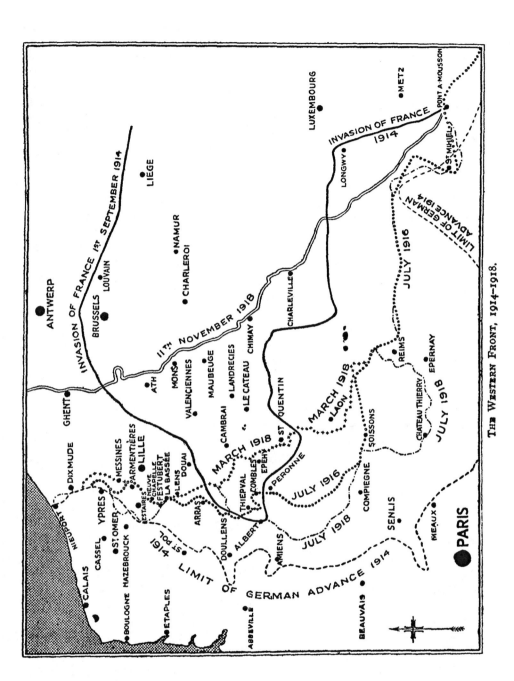

THE WESTERN FRONT, 1914–1918.

111

able to hold in sufficient strength what ground was gained. Consequently when the enemy came on again about 9 in the evening, he was able to re-establish himself in the front line. The support line was, however, held until the early morning of the 9th when the two remaining companies of the 17th King's relieved what was left of The Green Howards, and these were taken out of the line and withdrawn to St. Lawrence Camp.

" Thus ended a month of very severe fighting, during which we were in no fewer than four divisions, purely as a temporary measure and owing to the way in which divisions were smashed up. The 30th Division, being very much reduced in strength, was formed into one brigade and lent to another division ; the brigade was in turn decimated and was then formed into one battalion with our Battalion staff administering it. The enemy had now captured Kemmel Hill, and Locre, which had escaped damage so far during the war and which was the last village in Belgium which we marched through when we left Ypres in 1914, was soon in total ruin ; while Bailleul, which all British soldiers who were ever in it during the war had a great liking for, soon suffered the same fate as Locre."

During these last operations the 2nd Battalion The Green Howards had lost 9 officers and 284 non-commissioned officers and men killed, wounded and missing ; the casualties among the officers were distributed as follows : killed, Second-Lieutenants J. Fawcett, A. Shann and A. J. Dawes ; wounded and missing, Captain C. Davison, Second-Lieutenants J. Henderson, J. Halliday, J. G. Campbell and J. E. Hibbert. This last-named officer with Second-Lieutenant Shann and a number of men were buried by a shell, and Second-Lieutenant Hibbert was the only one who was dug out alive, remaining wounded and a prisoner in German hands until the end of the war.

On the 14th the Battalion proceeded in motor-omnibuses to the Watten area and by the 16th was quartered at Mazingarbe, where The 2nd Green Howards left the 30th Division, in which they had served for nearly two years and a half, and now joined the 32nd Brigade commanded by Brigadier-General Foord, D.S.O., of the 11th Division under Major-General Davies. The Green Howards were the only regular battalion in this division, the remainder being all New Army units. At Mazingarbe the Battalion absorbed the 6th Battalion Green Howards—some 21 officers and 640 other ranks.

The other two battalions in the 32nd Brigade were the 9th (Yorkshire Hussars) West Yorkshire Regiment and the 6th York and Lancaster Regiment.

" The line held by the 11th Division extended in front of Hulluch. The Quarries, well known to the Battalion in September, 1915, were just on our front, and at this time were practically in No-Man's-Land. Loos was away to our right, ' The Tower Bridge ' being still a conspicuous landmark. When we were in support at Vermelles, Battalion Headquarters were billeted under the brewery. The system of tunnels in our lines in this sector must have been the most extensive in France. It was reported of them that a man could walk underground from Loos to La Bassée Canal, a distance of nearly seven miles. They were lofty and dry, with light railways, electric light and ventilation fans, and branches extended from Battalion H.Q. right up to the front line."

For some considerable time now—as time was measured on the Western Front—the Battalion took no part in any large scale operations ; early in June, Lieutenant-Colonel Lawrence assumed command, being later relieved by Lieutenant-Colonel Edwards, who had been temporarily commanding a brigade, and then towards the end of August, when Colonel Edwards again left to take command of the 64th Brigade, Major H. Cooper took his place with The 2nd Green Howards.

The Battalion was now attached to the Canadian Corps in position near Monchy-le-Preux and was at first in brigade support ; the 11th Division actually, however, belonged, with the 51st Division, to the XXII. Army Corps.

On the 31st August the Battalion moved slightly forward under the orders of the Canadian Corps and captured the village of Hamblain-les-Prés, the opposition experienced being but slight, while the casualties were only twenty wounded, including Second-Lieutenant L. H. Barker ; and the next few days were occupied in consolidating the captured position, and in salvage work over the area. Then, on the 11th September, Lieutenant-Colonel B. T. Burbury, M.C., having taken over command, the Battalion moved first into Arras, on the 19th to Bethencourt and Tinques, and on the 24th to the Buissy Switch line at Vis-en-Artois, where it was in reserve to the Canadians, moving up on the 26th to a position to take part in the " Battle of Cambrai and the Hindenburg Line," as the Field-Marshal calls it in his despatch of the 21st December, 1918, but which is now more usually described as the Battle of the Canal du Nord.

The place of the 11th Division in the XXII. Corps had now been taken by the 4th Division, while the 11th was now in the Canadian Corps with the 1st, 3rd and 4th Canadian Divisions and Brutinel's Brigade, both these Corps forming the First Army under General Sir H. Horne.

" On the 22nd September orders were issued by G.H.Q. for :

" (a)   The First Army to attack on Z day ; to capture the heights of Bourlon Wood and secure its left flank on the Sensée River, and operate so as to protect the left of the Third Army. . . .

" On the 25th September Z day was fixed for the 27th.   During the

I

25th and 26th the Canadian Corps (which included the 11th Division) concentrated south of the Arras-Cambrai road ; the 2nd Canadian Division, which till then had been holding the Corps front, was relieved by the leading brigades of the 4th Canadian Division, 1st Canadian Division and 11th Division, and went into Corps reserve. Twenty-four Tanks (7th Battalion) moved up to their assembly positions west of the Canal. The 56th Division relieved the Canadian Corps north of the Arras-Cambrai road. We then had in the line nine divisions (4th Canadian, 1st Canadian, 11th, 56th, 4th, 51st, 8th, 20th, 24th). In support, 3rd Canadian Division. In reserve, four divisions (2nd Canadian, 49th, 66th, 47th) and 1st Cavalry Brigade. Total, fourteen divisions." *

The orders for the Canadian Corps were to attack with the 4th and 1st Canadian Divisions on the right and left respectively and force the Canal line between the northern end of Mœuvres and Lock 3, the 4th Division taking Bourlon Village and Wood and the line from Fontaine Notre Dame to the Copse five hundred yards south of the Arras-Cambrai road ; the 1st Canadian Division was to capture Sains-les-Marquion and extend the line of the 4th on the north as far as Sauchicourt Farm. The 3rd Canadian and 11th Divisions were to follow in rear of the two above named, the four divisions reorganizing on the captured line in the order 3rd Canadian, 4th Canadian and 11th Division from right to left, and advancing to capture the Marcoing line and Raillencourt, Haynecourt, Epinoy and Oisy-le-Verger.

The attack was opened at 5.30 on the morning of the 27th September with an intense bombardment by the British guns of the Canal front, the line of the Sensée River, and north of the Scarpe as far as Oppy, and against the Lens defences ; while Bourlon Wood had been systematically shelled for ten days with mustard gas, the success of this action being seen later when the wood was entered by our troops, abandoned German guns testifying to its recent occupation and the effective nature of the gas bombardment.

The two front line divisions of the Canadian Corps, having formed up some four hundred to six hundred yards from the west bank of the Canal, rushed the canal on the Mœuvres-Lock 3 front, carried the enemy posts west of the Canal, and also the rifle-pits and trenches some two hundred to five hundred yards beyond it, and, pushing on under stubborn resistance, by 7.30 a.m. the Marquion line up to Keith Wood was in the hands of the Canadians. In the meantime the leading brigades of the 11th and 3rd Canadian Divisions had moved up from their assembly positions west of the Canal in readiness to cross, in the 11th Division the 32nd and 34th Brigades being on the right and left respectively and the 33rd in support.

* Major-General Anderson, " The Crossing of the Canal du Nord," *R.U.S.I. Journal*, May, 1922.

THE ADVANCE ON THE HINDENBURG LINE.

September, 1918.

Moving up from the Buissy Switch line about 10 a.m., The Green Howards had crossed the Canal du Nord near Baralle about 1 p.m., and the 11th Division now came up on the outer flanks of the 1st Canadian Division, which simultaneously closed inwards, the whole line of the Canadian Corps then advancing, supported by field artillery batteries which had been moved across the Canal, and acting on the lines of open warfare, while a heavy artillery barrage from guns west of the Canal also assisted this part of the attack.

The 11th Division now attacked north-east and north with its two leading brigades on a converging front, the right brigade being directed on Epinoy, and passing through a thick wire-belt running east and west between the Marquion and Marcoing lines.

The diary account must now here be followed. " The Battalion commenced to attack Epinoy about 3 p.m., moving forward in columns of platoons, ' D ' Company being in reserve. By 6 p.m. the village had been reached, the advance being much slower than had been intended, for though little or no enemy artillery fire or serious opposition was encountered, the British barrage was at times uncertain ; but the south-eastern outskirts of Epinoy were found to be still defended by two or three machine guns, and ' A '—the right company—suffered rather heavily from enfilade fire on entering the village—Captain W. O. Hall being seriously wounded and Lieutenant A. L. Vick killed—before the machine guns were silenced and the detachments captured. By 7.15 that evening the village was entirely in British hands and posts were established and a line of resistance thrown out."

The Green Howards had captured some hundred prisoners, including a battalion commander, with five field and several machine guns ; besides the 2 officers above mentioned Lieutenant A. Newbury was wounded, while 7 men were killed, 46 wounded, and 5 were missing.

The night passed quietly, and on the 28th patrols were sent out and the position was consolidated and further advances made, the 3rd and 4th Canadian Divisions capturing Fontaine Notre Dame, Raillencourt and Sailly and the Marcoing line as far north as the Cambrai-Douai Road ; the 11th Division advanced into the south-western outskirts of Aubencheul-au-Bac and on the left worked down to the Sensée Canal and joined hands with the 56th Division north of the Bois de Quesnoy ; the 1st Canadian Division, which was well in advance, remained stationary. On this day the 2nd Battalion The Green Howards suffered much from heavy gas shelling and machine-gun fire and sustained many more casualties—2 officers and 18 other ranks being killed, 4 officers and 102 non-commissioned officers and men being wounded or gassed, while 7 men were missing—the total casualties in the two days' fighting amounting to 9 officers and 185 other ranks.

Of the officers Second-Lieutenants J. Stanbridge and B. S. Appleyard this day were killed, while Captain H. E. B. White, M.C., R.A.M.C., the medical officer, Second-Lieutenants C. F. Cox, W. A. Stewart and A. Grant were wounded or gassed.

Captain White's place as medical officer of the Battalion was taken by Captain Phelan of the United States Army.

On the 5th October there was a conference of commanding officers, when an attack was planned for the morning of the 8th on Aubencheul-au-Bac and on the Canal—the opening of the Cambrai battle of this year; the 19th West Yorkshire attacking with the 33rd and 168th Brigades on the right and left respectively, " A " and " B " Companies of the Battalion being detailed as a support to the West Yorkshire Regiment.

" 6th. Blustery, cold morning. Second-Lieutenant W. R. Hall, temporarily in command of ' A ' Company, wounded by shell in early hours of morning. Lieutenant F. Tenney took daylight patrol of ' D ' Company out from Quarry to Railway and established a post there—no enemy encountered. At dusk ' D ' Company was ordered to push patrols down to Canal. Enemy set fire to Church at Aubencheul. 33rd Brigade, on our right, later advanced through our patrols and occupied Canal. 1/4th London Regiment, on our left, pushed patrols through Aubencheul and down to Canal bridges and linked up with the 6th Lincolns of the 33rd Brigade. Our patrol was then withdrawn and ' D ' Company occupied the Sunken Road, while two platoons of ' A ' took over Quarry from ' D,' ' C ' Company extended its position to left and joined up with ' D ' Company,' B ' and Battalion H.Q. remaining unchanged. . . . These operations affected the results to be gained by the projected attack on the 8th.

" 7th. Quiet, cold but fine. Battalion was relieved at night by 6th Lincolns, who extended their area to include ours. Battalion came back to area just south of Souchy l'Estrée. Bivouacked in trenches.

" 8th. Quiet, fine. Companies engaged in cleaning up.

" 9th. Quiet, fine. About noon orders were received from Brigade to be in readiness to move at half an hour's notice, it being reported that enemy had evacuated position east of present position. At 3 p.m. orders were received to move via Haynecourt, Sancourt and Blécourt to Cuvillers. Arrived Cuvillers about 7 p.m., occupying trenches about two hundred yards south-south-west of Cuvillers. . . .

" 11th. Rain from 9.30 till noon. About 2 p.m. orders were received that the Battalion was to follow 6th York and Lancaster Regiment (who were in close support of the Canadians) and to be responsible for protecting the left flank of the Canadians from Hordain northwards along the line of the

Scheldt Canal, to cross the Canal by two bridges indicated on the map, and to cross and be in position by 9.30.   On arrival at Canal it was found that the first of the two bridges named did not exist, and the two leading companies then proceeded along the towpath towards Thun l'Eveque for about three hundred yards to a temporary and partially destroyed bridge left by the enemy.   Lieutenant-Colonel B. T. Burbury, M.C., leading the Battalion, was half-way across this bridge when it snapped in the middle, but Colonel Burbury was able to pull himself up on the far side, having a very narrow escape from falling into the Canal.   It was now impossible for the two leading companies to cross here, so they went on to the lock at Thun l'Eveque. Here the enemy put down a barrage, and also on the towpath on the south-eastern side of the Canal, causing 26 casualties, but the Battalion crossed here and took up a position in rear of the Château d'Eswars."

On the 12th October the Battalion was withdrawn to Cuvillers on the 11th Division being relieved by the 2nd Canadian Division, moving on the following evening to Sailly-Raillencourt and remaining here until the 20th, when it marched to Thun St. Martin and on the 26th to Haspres.   " The enemy had left Haspres only a few hours before we entered it.   The bridges over the River Selle had been blown up and had to be made good by our R.E. ; this they soon did.   We found only a solitary inhabitant here and there, who had in each case remained hidden in the cellars of the houses. The remainder of the residents had been compelled to move out of their homes and march to Valenciennes.   The buildings were more or less intact, for the enemy had not had time to complete the destruction of the village ; but they had found time to smash nearly all the furniture in the houses and also the pictures, and had fouled and otherwise ruined the bedding.   The condition of the insides of the houses was a disgrace to a civilized race as the Germans are supposed to be.   Excreta and urine were over everything. When the inhabitants were released and came back to their homes they were horrified at the wilful damage which had been done.   It was very touching to see the women and children burst into tears when they saw the condition of their homes, and they saw them, moreover, after our men had spent two days cleaning them up. . . .

" Soon after we occupied Haspres the inhabitants commenced to dribble back.   The Bosche released them from Valenciennes.   They had very little food of any description, so we organized the civilians who lived in our area of the village into parties and allotted them one party to each company. The men were eager to help those poor people in their distress and willingly offered a portion of their rations to them until proper arrangements could be made by the French authorities to feed them.   The men dubbed these parties their No. 5 Platoon ! "

The end was now drawing very near, and the Battalion had only one more general engagement in which to take part—the Battle of the Sambre—the 11th Division now again forming part of the XXII. Corps.

Leaving Haspres on the 2nd November, the Battalion marched for Artres, coming at Quermaing under shell fire and having its medical officer, Captain Phelan and seven men wounded and one killed, and dug in on the 3rd on high ground between Artres and Presseau.   On the 4th The Green Howards advanced again in support of the West Yorkshire, assisted on the 5th in the capture of the village of Roisin, and then took over the front line.   The 6th was a very wet day, but early that morning the Division again moved forward, the enemy falling back in their front, and the objective of the Battalion being the Bavay-Montignies main road—" A " and " B " Companies in front, " C " in support, and " D " in reserve.   When east of Meaurains the leading companies came under very heavy machine-gun fire and casualties mounted up, while not much progress could be made ; indeed, as the Field-Marshal says in his despatch :   " The 11th and 56th Divisions, having crossed the Aunelle River and captured the villages of Le Triez, Sebourg and Sebourquiaux, were counter-attacked on the high ground east of the Aunelle and pressed back slightly."

The advance was, however, resumed on the 7th, and by 11 o'clock the Battalion was through the village of Gussignies and making for the high ground in front of the final objective.   This was gained and the Battalion dug in along the road.   The Green Howards had now fought their last fight in the Great War, for that evening they were relieved and marched back by way of Meaurains, Eugnies, Crosse Haie, to Georgnies Chaussée, where on the 11th November the news of the signing of the Armistice reached them.

" The officers and men," writes one who was then present, " took the news very calmly, it seemed too good to be true."

During the advance from the 2nd to the 11th November the casualties incurred by the Battalion were as follows : killed, Second-Lieutenant D. Leonard and 30 non-commissioned officers and men ; wounded, Lieutenant H. G. Atkin, M.C., Second-Lieutenants W. Hall and J. Walker and 130 other ranks, while Second-Lieutenant F. Tenney and 11 men were missing.

His Majesty the King was among the first to send his congratulations to the Army on the successful termination of the long war, and the following are the words of His Majesty's gracious message to his soldiers, sent through the Secretary of State for War :

" I desire to express at once, through you, to all ranks of the Army of the British Empire, Home, Dominion, Colonial and Indian troops, my heartfelt pride and gratitude at the brilliant success which has crowned more than four years of effort and endurance.   Germany, our most formidable enemy, who planned the war to gain the supremacy of the world, full of pride in her armed strength and of contempt for the small British Army of that day, has now been forced to acknowledge defeat.   I rejoice that in this achievement the British forces, now grown from small beginnings to the finest Army in our history, has borne so gallant and distinguished a part.   Soldiers of the British Army, in France and Belgium, the prowess of your arms, as great in retreat as in victory, has won the admiration alike of friend and foe, and has now, by a happy and historic fate, enabled you to conclude the campaign by capturing Mons, where your predecessors of 1914 shed the first British blood.   Between that date and this you have traversed a long and weary road, defeat has more than once stared you in the face, your ranks have been thinned again and again by wounds, sickness, and death, but your faith has never faltered, your courage has never failed, your hearts have never known defeat. With your Allied comrades you have won the day.   Others of you have fought in more distant fields, in the mountains and plains of Italy, in the rugged Balkan ranges, under the burning sun of Palestine, Mesopotamia, and Africa, amid the snows of Russia and Siberia and by the shores of the Dardanelles.   Men of the British race who have shared these successes felt in their veins the call of the blood, and joined eagerly with the Mother Country in the fight against tyranny and wrong.   Equally those of the ancient historic peoples of India and Africa, who have learnt to trust the flag of England, hastened to discharge their debt of loyalty to the Crown.

" I desire to thank every officer, soldier and woman of our Army for services nobly rendered, for sacrifices cheerfully given, and I pray that God, Who has been pleased to grant a victorious end to this great crusade for justice and right, will prosper and bless our efforts in the immediate future to secure for generations to come the hard-won blessings of freedom and peace."

After the promulgation of the Armistice the 2nd Battalion The Green Howards went for a fortnight into rest billets at Georgnies Chaussée, and then moved to Helesmes to the east of Valenciennes, where a draft of nearly three hundred recruits was awaiting its arrival.   Some considerable time was spent here, and it was while in this garrison that on the 29th December the Colours of the Battalion arrived from home and were taken over with the usual ceremonial.

The Battalion now began daily to decrease in numbers as men went home for demobilization or to join other battalions intended to form the Army of Occupation in Germany ; of these The 2nd Green Howards supplied two drafts both of officers and men. Then early in 1919 Major Pickard, the quartermaster, left to join the 3rd Battalion of the Regiment, his place being taken by Lieutenant Pyne of the Buffs. Major Pickard came out to France with the 2nd Battalion, and was one of the few of any rank who served continuously with it from the beginning of the war to the Armistice, and his services are not likely to be forgotten by his comrades. The rest of the staff of the Battalion was changed times without number, but Major Pickard remained, a tower of strength to the many new-comers and a very present help in time of trouble to his older comrades.

When, in February, 1919, Admiral Sir David Beatty paid a visit to the Headquarters of the First Army, the Battalion furnished a Guard-of-Honour under the command of Captain J. S. A. Bunting, M.C., and the Army Commander afterwards wrote thanking Lieutenant-Colonel Burbury for " the splendid Guard-of-Honour."

From this time on, the strength of the Battalion very rapidly grew less, and the last draft of five officers and forty-eight other ranks left on the 7th April, when the Battalion was down to Cadre strength and was on the 12th moved from Helesmes to Denain, where all the Cadres of the Division were to be concentrated. Then on the 10th June the Cadre of the Battalion left Denain and on the 12th reached a dispersal camp at Boulogne, finally embarking here on the 14th for Dover.

The following composed the Cadre : Lieutenant-Colonel B. T. Burbury, M.C., Captain A. E. L. Belcher, M.C., Lieutenant F. C. Ainley, Second-Lieutenant F. G. S. Weare, Regimental-Sergeant-Major J. Colver, D.C.M., Regimental-Quartermaster-Sergeant G. Wilson, Bandmaster F. Andrews, Company-Sergeant-Majors H. Burridge, O. Garbott, M.M., L. Thewlis and G. Holroyd, Company-Quartermaster-Sergeants J. Goodall and H. Carter, Sergeants W. Raine, W. Brown, C. Broadbent, H. Hoyland and F. Hampshire, Lance-Sergeant C. Horne, Lance-Corporals G. Hill, M. Hunton, E. Cragg, S. Human, T. Coad and B. Holditch, Privates E. McCuniff, C. Hellings, W. Carter and R. Harris, Bandsmen E. Lewis, H. Sullivan, G. Doudney, R. Devaney, F. Hopkins, F. Wheatley, T. Baker, J. McGuinness, L. Balmer, T. Walton, F. Cooke, H. Gepheart, F. Batchelor, J. Cragg, A. Cox, A. Campbell, G. Ballock and C. Joyce.

Richmond was reached early on the morning of the 15th, and next day the 2nd Battalion Cadre was accorded a civic welcome, marching to the Square where all the people received the officers and men with hearty cheers, and the Mayor, Mr. G. R. Wade, J.P., made a speech, to which Lieutenant-Colonel Burbury replied in suitable terms. All then adjourned to a banquet and concert at the Town Hall, and next day all officers and men who could possibly be spared were granted a month's leave to visit their homes.

CHAPTER VII

THE 1/4TH BATTALION

1914–1918

THE SECOND BATTLE OF YPRES. THE FIRST BATTLE OF THE SOMME. THE THIRD BATTLE OF YPRES. THE BATTLE OF ARRAS. THE BATTLE OF THE LYS. THE SECOND BATTLE OF THE SOMME. THE SECOND BATTLE OF THE AISNE

WHEN, at the end of July, 1914, the European situation began to be strained, the 4th (Territorial) Battalion of The Green Howards had gone to Deganwy Camp in Wales for the annual training with the York and Durham Infantry Brigade. The last two days of the first week of the training were full of alarms and excursions of all kinds, and on the 3rd August the Battalion camp broke up and each company proceeded at once to its own Headquarters. Two days later came the order to mobilize, when the Battalion collected all but eleven of those who were on its strength; of the eleven one was dead and three were known to be at sea, so that the absence of only seven men was unaccounted for.

The reassembled Battalion remained five days concentrated at North-allerton, then moved for a week to Newcastle, and finally joined a brigade camp at Hummersknott Park, Darlington, where the Battalion soon found itself practically at war strength.

The Army List for August, 1914, shows the following officers as belonging to the 4th Battalion: Colonel A. F. Godman, C.B., V.D., Hon. Colonel; Lieutenant-Colonel M. H. L. Bell, V.D., in command; Major H. G. Scott; Captains H. C. Matthews, B. Jackson, A. Graham, R. A. Constantine, G. H. Bowes-Wilson, W. W. Constantine, J. V. Nancarrow, and B. H. Charlton; Lieutenants W. F. Mott, J. Maughan, N. W. Stead, T. H. Hutchinson, L. P. l'Anson, T. W. P. L. Chaloner, G. W. Samuelson, and A. C. P. de la P. Beresford-Peirse; Second-Lieutenants C. R. Scate, E. Williams, C. C. Jervelund, A. J. B. Richardson, and H. T. Fawcett; Captain G. D. P. Eykyn, adjutant; Lieutenant W. H. Colton, Quartermaster Major H. L. de Legh, R.A.M.C., and Surgeon-Captain C. B. Whitehead, medical officers; and the Rev. H. C. Holmes and the Rev. F. L. Perkins, chaplains.

On it being announced from the War Office that if 80 per cent. of the Battalion were to volunteer for service abroad, it would be permitted to embark as a unit, no less than 90 per cent. of the 4th Green Howards did so volunteer, while at Northallerton there were very soon nearly two hundred recruits eagerly waiting to join the Battalion as vacancies occurred.

In October the 4th Battalion moved to Newcastle, remaining here until orders were at last received to embark for France, and then, leaving Newcastle at 9 a.m. on the 17th April, 1915, the Battalion proceeded by train to Folkestone and there embarked for Boulogne, which was reached at 2o'clock on the following morning. From the wharf the companies marched to a camp on the hills behind the old town, and here a very cold night—what remained of it—was passed. By 10 p.m. on the 18th, however, all were on the move again and took train for Cassel, from which the Brigade marched some few miles and then billeted in certain villages, the 4th Green Howards being accommodated in Godwaersvelde. Here a halt of some four days was made.

The Battalion now formed, with the 5th Green Howards, the 4th East Yorkshire Regiment and the 5th Durham Light Infantry, the 150th Brigade of the 50th Division, the Brigadier being Brig.-General J. E. Bush, and the Divisional Commander Major-General Sir W. Lindsay, K.C.B., D.S.O.

On the 22nd the Germans made their infamous gas attack, whereby a portion of the line, held by a French division on the flank of the Canadians, had been of necessity abandoned and the Germans had succeeded in capturing the bridge at Steenstraate and some works south of Lizerne ; but the Canadians were still in possession of the line immediately in front of St. Julien.

During the night of the 22nd–23rd the Battalion was ordered to stand to, and on the morning of the 23rd April it marched to the Poperinghe-Vlamertinghe Road and was conveyed from this point in buses to " C " Huts at Vlamertinghe, the remaining battalions of the Brigade concentrating here also.

At 1 a.m. on the 24th the whole Brigade moved out to the Canal, the 5th Battalion passing over, but the 4th remaining for the present on the western bank ; and as far as could be learnt the situation was that the Germans had pressed their attack on Ypres, the Canadians had suffered many casualties from the poison gas, and there was a very wide gap in the British line to the north-east of Ypres.

During the morning the 4th Battalion lay under an intermittent but never very heavy shell fire, whereby Lieutenant Tugwell and four or five men were wounded ; but soon after midday orders were received for the 4th Green Howards to move forward and cross the Canal by a pontoon bridge, then proceed to Potijze and place themselves at the disposal of and under the orders of any brigade commander who appeared to be in need of help. Advancing at once, the pontoon bridge was found to be under tolerably heavy shell fire, but all four companies were lucky enough to get over without loss, though they had hardly crossed when a shell hit and wrecked the bridge, leaving the machine gun, limbers and medical officer's cart on the other side of the Canal.

At Potijze a Canadian staff captain met the Battalion, explained the position of affairs so far as it was known, and gave orders for the 4th Green Howards to occupy a line of trenches to the north-east of Potijze Château ; on arrival here, however, it was found that these trenches, at the time heavily shelled, were occupied by the remnants of a Canadian brigade, so the Battalion was then ordered to dig a support line of trenches. Very shortly, however, a message came to hand from the 27th Division Headquarters, then occupying the Château, to the effect that the situation was critical, that the Germans had occupied St. Julien and, it was believed, Fortuin also, and that their further advance must be checked. It was *hoped* that other troops might be able to assist in a counter-attack on St. Julien, but in any case the 4th Green Howards were to make good Fortuin and push back the enemy into St. Julien and further if possible. The operation was to be carried out without delay, though it was admitted that both flanks would be in the air and that no support either by guns or by other infantry could be afforded.

The Battalion now advanced, made its way through the wire in front of the trenches and then deployed into artillery formation, moving forward, under cover of a slight rise of ground on the left, in a north-easterly direction, parallel to the Wieltje–Fortuin road, under a fairly heavy shell fire, which, however, did very little damage. Having gone forward for the best part of a mile, the Battalion had to close somewhat in order to cross a deep and muddy stream, and then, deploying again, proceeded in dead ground until it came level with Fortuin, where it again met with shell fire and a certain amount of long-range machine-gun fire, chiefly from the left flank. The line now changed direction, the two leading companies taking shelter in a sunken road opposite the village of Fortuin, which, so far as could be judged, was only lightly held.

St. Julien could be seen from here and appeared to be occupied in considerable force, while the enemy advanced parties were holding the banks of a muddy stream some five hundred yards south of St. Julien ; the ground between the sunken road at Fortuin and this stream was level grassland. Some two hundred yards south of the stream, however, there was a slight fold in the ground which seemed to give promise of affording a suitable

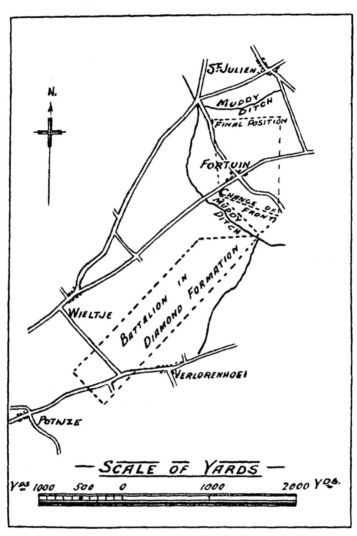

ST. JULIEN.
(24th April, 1915.)

124

position from which to attack and drive in the advanced German posts, and two companies of the Battalion, now advancing by rushes, this position was occupied, the enemy falling back on St. Julien.

The other two companies were held back in reserve on the left, as this seemed to be the more exposed and dangerous flank.

At this point the adjutant of the 4th East Yorkshire appeared and reported to the officer commanding the 4th Green Howards that his Battalion had been sent up as a support, that his C.O. and second-in-command had both been killed, and he asked for orders, whereupon the two reserve companies of the 4th Green Howards, reinforced by two of the East Yorkshire, were directed to prolong the line to the left, while the other two East Yorkshire companies remained in support. Both battalions lost heavily while crossing the open level ground, but the enemy was driven back into St. Julien and held there, while a platoon of the Royal Irish Fusiliers came up on the right and prolonged the line on this flank.

The Commanding Officer of the 4th Green Howards had previously been warned that, owing to the immediate scarcity of troops, it was inadvisable to lose many men unless some really definite advantage could be gained ; it was clear that any attempt to cross the stream between the British line and St. Julien would entail very heavy casualties in view of the volume of machine-gun and rifle fire which the enemy could bring to bear ; while the primary object of the operations—holding up the German advance at this point—had been attained. The two battalions, therefore, merely hung on to the ground gained until darkness set in, when orders were received to fall back on Potijze Château. This was carried out without hindrance or molestation.

In this the first action of the 4th Battalion The Green Howards, who had been thrown into the fight within a week of landing in France, the losses had been heavy. Major H. C. Matthews, Captain and Adjutant G. D. P. Eykyn, Captain J. V. Nancarrow, Lieutenant L. P. l'Anson and Second-Lieutenant E. Darwin with ten other ranks were killed, Second-Lieutenant H. B. Blackett and fifty-nine non-commissioned officers and men were wounded, while seventeen other ranks—some of whom turned up later— were wounded and missing.

On the 25th General Sir H. Plumer, commanding the II. Corps, sent a special messenger to thank the 4th Green Howards for the good work they had done on the previous day.

" Thus passed several days," writes a Battalion correspondent of *The Green Howards Gazette*, " during which we occupied first one trench and then another, never more than a few hours in any one ; and all the time good old Hutchinson and his transport turned up regularly with our rations.

We then went back to the rest huts from which we started, for a few days so-called rest during which we were shelled intermittently. Our worst day we had ten casualties, among whom was Lieutenant Beresford-Peirse. Of the huts we saw little, as they were practically uninhabitable. Back we went to a new set of trenches; these we were in for five days, shelled from front and flank, gassed and attacked. During this period we were lent to another division commanded by General Bulfin. We had our first touch of gas on May 1st, and also were attacked on the 2nd; our casualties during this time being thirty-four killed, among whom was Company-Sergeant-Major Preston, six officers and seventy-four other ranks wounded, the officers being Captain N. W. Stead, Lieutenants A. R. Welsh, C. Sproxton, J. K. Stead and H. N. Constantine, while among the non-commissioned officers and men wounded was Company-Sergeant-Major Wilkinson; Lieutenant E. Williams was gassed.

"Perhaps the best thing done during this time was by Major H. L. de Legh, who got fifteen wounded men out of a burning cellar under heavy shell fire."

From the 9th to the 12th May the Battalion was in reserve trenches at Brandhoek, where Captain P. C. du S. Leather, Lieutenant G. F. Lucas, Second-Lieutenants D. McLaren, L. Yorke and G. H. Hutchinson joined; on the 12th and 13th it was in dug-outs behind the Château north of Vlamertinghe, and spent the 14th in Ypres attached to the 84th Brigade. Leaving Ypres on the 15th the Battalion marched to the railway embankment, and was here until the 21st, attached to one cavalry brigade after another, and having one officer—Second-Lieutenant W. P. Orde-Powlett—killed, and Major de Legh and twenty men wounded.

Here five officers joined or rejoined—Captain A. J. Dorman, Second-Lieutenants E. F. Hutchinson, E. Beresford-Peirse, E. Jones and G. W. Dawson.

From the railway embankment the Battalion was sent to a camp south of Vlamertinghe for a couple of days, moving up on the evening of the 23rd May to the trenches astride the Menin Road at Hooge, and here on the early morning of Whit-Monday the second great German gas attack fell upon the 4th Green Howards. "From trench to trench we fought," so runs the account in the Battalion diary, "and thank Heaven stuck to our trenches, but at great cost. Lieutenant H. W. Cummins and Second-Lieutenant E. F. Hutchinson* were killed, Captain W. W. Constantine, Captain A. Graham, and Lieutenant C. C. Jervelund were gassed and taken to hospital, and when on the 25th the Battalion, or what was left of it, got back to huts the casualties among the non-commissioned officers and men stood at thirty killed,

---

* He had only joined two days previously.

seventy wounded and ninety-eight wounded and missing ; these latter were almost all accounted for in different hospitals, either wounded or gassed. Where all ranks did well perhaps special mention may be made of Captains Leather and Bowes-Wilson, Lieutenant McLaren and his machine gun, and Captain Charlton who was acting adjutant. Company-Sergeant-Major Myers again distinguished himself ; Company-Sergeant-Major Bainbridge was splendid ; Privates Perry and Ekins also deserve mention. One man got into the machine-gun emplacement of one of our Hussar regiments, where he found only the officer working the gun and stayed with him until he, the man, was killed.

"At night the remainder of the garrison of our trenches were relieved and straggled back, Captain Bowes-Wilson and his company getting in about 3.30 on the 25th ; then Captain Leather, then Captain Dorman, then Captain Constantine and Captain Charlton last. The men were nearly exhausted and all were suffering from gas more or less—they had been in the very centre of it. Captains Charlton and Bowes-Wilson, though they did not go to hospital, were in a terrible state. Major de Legh, though suffering from neuritis, worked like a slave among the men who were lying about being sick at intervals. Captain Leather's work in getting the remnants of the Battalion back was splendid. So ended the 24th and 25th May, 1915."

The Battalion remained in these hutments until the 6th June, during which time Captain R. A. F. Montanaro joined and took over the adjutancy ; and then there was a move to trenches in Sanctuary Wood, and while up in this part of the line there were nearly twenty casualties, which included Captain G. H. Bowes-Wilson killed, and Captain P. C. du S. Leather badly wounded. For the next few weeks the Battalion was in and out of the trenches, chiefly in the vicinity of Armentières, incurring slight but recurring casualties, and at the end of August the strength of the 1/4th Battalion The Green Howards was as under :

Trench Strength	.	.	18	Officers	and	411	Other	Ranks.
Transport .	.	.	2	,,	,,	60	,,	,,
Garrison Employ, etc.	.	3	,,	,,	50	,,	,,	
Attached	.	.	1	,,	,,	10	,,	,,

On the 27th October, while in rest billets in Armentières, Lieutenants Welsh, Constantine and Hutchinson, and sixty other ranks—fifteen selected from each company—proceeded to Bailleul to take part in a review by H.M. the King. They were conveyed to Bailleul and back by motor-lorries, and the following message was circulated after the review by General Plumer :

"His Majesty the King desires me to say that he was very pleased with the soldierly bearing of the troops and all he saw."

From the 12th November to the 17th December the Battalion was training near Merris, and then, marching to Bailleul, entrained there for Poperinghe, and by the evening of the 18th was accommodated in huts at Dickebusch. " It took an hour and a half to get the Battalion settled in the various huts. The state of the ground was awful, deep mud everywhere, fortunately it was fine. We were all very sorry to leave our comfortable farmhouses, where we had been for five weeks."

There was a threat of a gas attack early on the 19th and The Green Howards " stood to," but when all chance of this passed off the Battalion marched by Zillebeke to trenches in Armagh Wood, having the 4th East Yorkshire Regiment on the left and the Durham Brigade on the right, and all were now kept very busy repairing and draining the trenches under a desultory shell fire from the enemy. Christmas Day of this year was spent in rear in the Railway Dug-outs, and New Year's Eve in Divisional Reserve in the Dickebusch hutments.

On the 3rd January, 1916, it was announced in orders that Lieutenant-Colonel Bell had been found medically unfit for active service and had been ordered to return to England. " An old complaint, which necessitated a severe operation no longer than two years ago, had reasserted itself, and those who knew the Colonel well were surprised that he was able for nine months to stand the physical strain and discomforts of trench warfare. This is not the place to speak of all that the Colonel has done for the Battalion, or of his enormous popularity with all ranks. The behaviour of the Battalion during the first few weeks in Flanders is sufficient testimony to his work at Hummersknott and in Newcastle during the period of training. No commanding-officer ever lived more completely for and in his unit than did Colonel Bell, and to have served under him on active service was a liberal education "—so runs the tribute from one of his subordinates.

The command of the 1/4th was now assumed by Major H. G. Scott, who, a few days later, had to go to hospital, when his place was taken by Major L. A. Barrett, M.C., Northumberland Fusiliers.

In this month five officers joined: Second-Lieutenants R. G. Harrowing, H. N. Laing, C. A. Taylor, K. L. Harris and I. H. Scarth, and then on the 12th February the Battalion for the first time occupied trenches round Hill 60. " There are certain times by which we date things," says the Diary, becoming somewhat gloomily retrospective ; " the first period from 24th April to 2nd May, 1915, when we came back for the first time from the Ypres Salient through the troops occupying the trenches of the shortened line, then four days' rest at Steenvoorde, and then by degrees worked our way up to Railway Wood, and then the gassing on May 24th. This tour in the trenches will be remembered with those times. ' W ' Company took over trenches 37 Left and 37 Left Support and 38 Trench ; ' X ' Company took over Centre Trench, Switch 39 Trench and 39 S ; ' Y ' Company took over Trenches 40, 41 and 41 S ; ' Z ' Company took over Trenches 47, 47 S and 48 ; the 4th East Yorks were on our left and the 8th South Staffords of the 17th Division on our right.   The relief passed off quietly and the night was fairly quiet.   We had in close support one company of the 5th Green Howards in Railing Cutting and one company in dug-outs in the Sunken Road.

   " 13th.   Save for continual sniping and a good deal of ' sausaging ' on the part of the Germans and the sending of rifle grenades, things were pretty quiet all day and all night.   Work of repairing trenches and communication trenches went on uninterruptedly.

   " 14th.   The Dump was shelled at intervals during the day, but every-thing was comparatively quiet until 3 p.m., when the Germans began to bombard us. . . .   At 5 p.m. the enemy exploded a mine under H.1. bomb-ing sap, but did not attempt to occupy the Crater.   The bombardment con-tinued until 8 p.m., when it slackened slightly.   It was then possible to take account of the damage done by the Germans : thirteen men had been killed and five men badly bruised by the explosion of the mine.   Two trenches were breached in two places, and the Lewis gun in another was buried, but this was dug out during the height of the bombardment.   The edge of the Crater was held immediately after the explosion and work commenced dig-ging through to it.   The support and communication trenches were very much knocked about and all the latter blocked. . . .   As soon as the bom-bardment slackened work on repairing was at once commenced.   Two men were dug out alive from the trench near the Crater, and one man picked up alive after having been blown forty yards, but he died soon after he had been brought in. . . .   The South Staffords reporting that they were out of bombs, thirty-six boxes were sent to them.

   " 15th.   At midnight 14th–15th the bombardment commenced again and continued for an hour and a half, but the damage done was not so great as on the previous occasion.   The South Staffords reported that they were short of bombs, and ten men from the 5th Green Howards and ten snipers were employed carrying for them.   The result of the bombardment was only slight, but the communication trenches were again a good deal knocked about. . . .   At 6 a.m. all communication trenches were reported clear and the trenches practically repaired.   A patrol went round the Crater and found no trace of the enemy.   The rest of the day passed quietly till 3 p.m., when the bombardment recommenced and continued intermittently until 8 p.m., when it quieted down again.   At 10 p.m. the South Staffords reported little or no progress in their counter-attack.   Not much damage was done by the bombardment except the usual blocking of communication trenches, which, however, were cleared before morning. The work of digging into the Crater was hampered by bodies having to be removed from the trench as it was cleared. Work was commenced at 7 p.m. digging a new trench round behind the Crater.

"16th. The day was fairly quiet. The 5th Green Howards took over the Bombing Sap in 48 Trench and Glasgow Cross. . . . The new trench behind the Crater was dug to across the Zillebeke Road, and the old trench out into the Crater cleared. . . . The old Communication Trench was also made passable. . . .

"17th. During the night and all the day the situation was fairly quiet. Good progress had been made with all the work of repairing and renewing ; the 8th South Staffords wired to the C.O. : ' On relief by 7th Border Regiment we all wish to express our appreciation and thanks to you and to your Battalion for your assistance and generous supply of bombs and carrying parties during the last two days. Your help has been very much appreciated by all ranks of this Battalion.'

"18th. Situation fairly quiet and all work had progressed satisfactorily. We were relieved at night by the 8th Durham L.I. . . . We suffered during the last tour of the trenches casualties to the extent of two officers, Second-Lieutenant J. W. Daglish and Captain J. Maugham, and twenty-two non-commissioned officers and men killed, three officers and sixty-two other ranks wounded. Lieutenant A. R. Welsh died of wounds."

The fighting above described in the Battalion diary was included in what is known as "the Operations at the Bluff," the eastern point of the narrow ridge, only some thirty to forty feet above the level of the plain, on the northern bank of the Ypres-Comines Canal ; this was the objective of the enemy in the attack which he had opened on the 13th February against the front held by the 17th, 50th and 24th Divisions, in order from right to left, and as a result of which some six hundred yards of front line trenches immediately north of the Bluff, and held by the 17th Division, were captured and retained by the Germans for something over a fortnight.

An attack to regain these trenches was undertaken on the 2nd March by the 3rd and 17th Divisions, and the assistance given by the battalions of the 50th Division is thus described in the war diary of the 1/4th Green Howards :

"1st March. Snow on ground and hard frost at night. Owing to the counter-attack on the Bluff the next morning a demonstration from trenches held on the left was ordered, smoke bombs to be used if the wind was favourable, but it was not. The demonstration consisted of bursts of Lewis-gun fire and individual fire to be kept up for twenty minutes ; this caused the enemy to retaliate. Casualties, three other ranks wounded.

" 2nd. A further demonstration was ordered for the next morning at 5.32 a.m., smoke bombs again to be used if wind favourable ; it was not. The same methods were adopted as on the 1st. The Bird Cage was trench-mortared and a mine sprung. The enemy retaliated and enfiladed our trenches the whole day. Two platoons of ' Y ' Company moved to close support trench."

As a result of the attack by the 3rd and 17th Divisions the whole of the ground which had been lost was recovered, and the Battalion remained in the front line until the 8th, having sustained a loss of Lieutenant G. H. Hutchinson and three other ranks killed, Second-Lieutenant K. L. Harris and twenty-four men wounded. On withdrawal from the front the Battalion went for a few days to the Hop Factory at Poperinghe, moving on the 14th to dug-outs in close support near Goldfish Château, and here on the 17th Lieutenant R. M. Howes and a small reinforcement of twenty-nine men joined ; but on the same day Major L. A. Barrett was killed while going round the trenches, and was succeeded in command by Major F. F. Deakin.

On the 30th March the 4th Green Howards moved by Bailleul to Locre and took over from the 28th Canadian Battalion, relieving Canadian troops in the various small forts and dug-outs about Kemmel Château, and here the Battalion spent the first anniversary of its joining the British Expeditionary Force in France. Of the officers who at that date were on the strength of the Battalion the following were still remaining : Captains Charlton, Fawcett, Rowlandson, Stead and Howitt, Lieutenants Thornton and Constantine. The following had been the losses sustained during the twelve months : Officers : killed or died of wounds, 14 ; wounded, 26 ; gassed, 3 ; shell-shocked, 1 ; otherwise injured, 1. Other Ranks : killed or died of wounds, 163 ; wounded or gassed, 478 ; missing, 6 ; and captured, 4.

For something like a month now from the 23rd April the Battalion was in very scattered and uncomfortable huts at Locre or in still more uncomfortable and insanitary billets in the rest area about Flêtre, where two very small drafts arrived under Second-Lieutenants Miller and Tugwell, and where also the medical authorities, with a somewhat strained sense of humour, returned one man who had been undergoing dental treatment, carefully labelled as follows :

" To be supplied with soft diet and a mouthwash for two months until his gums have hardened."

On the 26th May the 4th Green Howards returned to Locre *en route* to the trenches near Kemmel Shelters, where casualties at once began to be incurred and where five junior officers joined : Second-Lieutenants C. Hawdon, H. M. Hollingsworth, A. Coates, M. W. Macnay and E. R. Richardson, and of these the first-named was killed in a raid upon the enemy's lines

on the 26th June. It was not until the month of September, however, that
the 50th Division was called up to take an active part in the Somme Battle
of this year, which had been raging since the 1st July. " The general plan
of the combined Allied attack which was opened on the 15th September was
to pivot on the high ground south of the Ancre and north of the Albert-
Bapaume Road, while the Fourth Army devoted its whole effort to the rear-
most of the enemy's original systems of defence between Morval and Le
Sars. Should our success in this direction warrant it, I made arrangements
to enable me to extend the left of the attack to embrace the villages of Martinpuich and Courcelette."* The 50th Division, now commanded by Major-
General P. S. Wilkinson, was in the III. Corps (Lieutenant-General Pulteney),
which covered the whole front from Martinpuich down to High Wood ; the
50th Division was in the centre, facing the various German trenches which
linked Martinpuich with High Wood, and had the 47th Division on its right
and the 15th on the left. The III. Corps was on the extreme right or north
of the Fourth Army, containing three Army Corps and commanded by
General Rawlinson.

The latter half of August and the early part of September had been
spent by the 4th Green Howards training about Millencourt, which was
left on the 10th of this month when the Battalion went up into Brigade support in Shelter Wood, then very greatly congested with troops of two divisions, and where all ranks were employed during the next three days in working at cable trenches, deepening the existing advance line, making dressing
stations and preparing dumps, all under a good deal of enemy shelling,
while the rain which fell at night made the ground very slippery and the
carrying of stores arduous, difficult and slow. Then on the evening of the
14th the Battalion moved to the place of assembly in Eye and Swansea
Trenches, these having to be reached over the open as the communication
trenches were so congested, and the Germans, opening fire, caused some
forty casualties.

" At 6.30 a.m. the infantry assault commenced," so we read in the despatch already quoted from, " and at the same moment the bombardment
became intense. Our new heavily armoured cars, known as ' Tanks,' now
brought into action for the first time, successfully co-operated with the
infantry, and coming as a surprise to the enemy rank and file, gave valuable
help in breaking down their resistance."

In the Brigade attack the Battalion was in the centre with the 5th Green
Howards and 4th East Yorkshire Regiment on either flank, while of the
4th Battalion companies, " Z " was on the right, " X " in the centre, " W "
on the left, and " Y " was carrying company. The first, second and final

* Despatch of the 23rd December, 1916.

objectives were all carried in succession, but as the right division of the Corps met with very severe resistance in the capture of High Wood, the right Battalion of the 150th Brigade was unable to get up in line with the 4th Green Howards, whose right was consequently in the air at the junction of Prue Trench and Martin Alley; but the Battalion held the line reached all that day and throughout the 16th under very heavy shell fire which caused many casualties. The 17th and 18th were spent in consolidation, and on the 19th the Brigade was relieved and withdrawn to a line south of Bazentin-le-Petit Wood, all the men wet through from the rain which had been falling for some hours, all utterly spent and weary.

The 20th and 21st were devoted to such reorganization as was possible, and on the 22nd the 4th and 5th Green Howards of the 150th Brigade returned to the front line, the 4th Battalion occupying Sixth Avenue and the intermediate line.

The weather had been so bad that it was impossible to push the advantage gained, but at 12.35 p.m. on the 25th September, after a heavy bombardment commenced early the preceding morning, a general attack by the Allies was launched on the whole front between the Somme and Martinpuich. There had been considerable redistribution of divisions, and the 50th Division was now to attack with the 1st on its right and the 23rd on its left; in front of the 50th was the important village of Eaucourt l'Abbaye. By nightfall the greater part of the objectives were in our hands, and for the 26th it was ordered that the 1st and 50th Divisions were to attack and capture the German trench line running from Flers, the 23rd Division then passing on and completing the final captures. The two battalions of The Green Howards were ordered to attack the enemy trenches at 11 p.m. in conjunction with the 1st Division, the 5th Durham Light Infantry working up Crescent Alley. By some mistake, however, the 1st Division did not attack, and when the 4th Green Howards got into the German trenches they found themselves with both flanks in the air, were driven out by a strong counter-attack, and were ordered back to Starfish Trench to reform. From here they were sent into divisional reserve and were occupied during the next two or three days in rearranging the companies and allotting to them the men of such reinforcements as were available.

The Commander of the British Expeditionary Force tells us in his despatch of the 23rd December of this year that " on the afternoon of the 1st October a successful attack was launched against Eaucourt l'Abbaye and the enemy defences to the east and west of it, comprising a total front of about three thousand yards. . . . Bomb fighting continued among the buildings during the next two days, but by the evening of the 3rd October the whole of Eaucourt l'Abbaye was in our hands."

In this action the Battalion was not especially actively engaged, though it sustained many casualties, the 150th Brigade being in support to the 151st which attacked the Flers line; when, however, the 4th Green Howards were withdrawn on the 3rd October to billets in Albert, the losses suffered since the 15th September amounted to 7 officers and 75 other ranks killed or died of wounds, 20 officers and 250 non-commissioned officers and men wounded, and 47 missing—a total of 399 all ranks killed, wounded and missing; in the Diary we read, however, that " considering the ground won and the fact that the right flank was always in the air, and in the night attack of the 26th *both* flanks, the casualties are not excessive."

The following are the names of the officer casualties: killed or died of wounds, Captain T. S. Rowlandson, Second-Lieutenants R. B. Abrahams, W. J. Hayton, H. N. Laing, E. L. Perris, R. S. Omand and E. Richardson; wounded, Captain W. W. Constantine, Lieutenants T. G. Thornton, J. Millar, G. A. Tugwell and R. F. Williams, R.A.M.C., Second-Lieutenants A. S. Brentnall, C. B. Prior-Wandesforde, A. D. Scott, M. W. Macnay, R. S. Forrest, V. A. Bell, H. E. Aust, J. Robson, C. J. Minister, H. L. Harrison, R. M. Howes, D. P. Hirsch, H. G. Scott, J. B. Hudson and W. L. Batty; but when on the night of the 24th–25th the Battalion went up to the front again Second-Lieutenants Hudson and Batty, who though wounded had remained at duty, were killed during the relief with two other ranks, while eleven more men were wounded. Two days later Second-Lieutenant A. Coates was killed in the trenches.

Against these very heavy losses in officers only five joined or rejoined during this month: Captains C. Sproxton and C. N. Carleton-Stiff, Second-Lieutenants W. L. James, R. E. Edwards and G. R. Cole.

The 4th Battalion The Green Howards remained in this area until the 30th November, when the Brigade marched to Contay for a month's training, and here Christmas Day was passed, while on the last day of the year the Battalion moved to huts near Bazentin-le-Petit.

During January, 1917, the 4th Green Howards moved from Bazentin-le-Petit to Fricourt and from there to Buire, doing a good deal of useful work out of the line, for in this month only four days in all were spent in the front trenches; the Battalion was still very weak, for its wastage does not appear to have been in any way made good, and it was working with companies of an average strength of well under a hundred and with only three officers per company. On the 10th February a move was made to Foucaucourt, whence on the following night it relieved parties of the 18th and 218th Regiments of French Infantry, and here became the right battalion of the whole British Army. March was spent about Belloy and Bayonvillers, and then on the 30th the Brigade set off for the Arras area, where the Allied offensive of this year was almost due to commence and where the 50th Division was to join the XVIII. Corps ; marching by Bonnay, Molliens-au-Bois, Naours, Longuevillette, Houvin-Houvigneul, Lignereuil and Noyellette, Arras was reached on the 12th April, and on arrival here the Battalion was accommodated in caves in the Faubourg Rouville ; the journey was by march route the whole way, the weather rainy in the earlier stages and Arctic towards the end ; the roads were mostly by-roads and the going none too easy.

The front here lay for the most part from Wancourt Tower to the River Cojeul ; when in support the Battalion occupied Niger Trench, and when in reserve was in deep German dug-outs and trenches in the recently captured Harp. The front line trenches afforded little cover against the " heavy stuff " which the enemy was continually sending over, and on the very first day of the tour in the front line nearly all the sergeants of " W " Company and Second-Lieutenant Welbourne of " Y " were knocked out.

The 50th Division was now to take part with the VII. Corps in the Second Battle of the Scarpe, where the British troops attacked on a front of about nine miles from Croisilles to Gavrelle, the high ground west of Cherisy being assailed by the 15th, 30th and 50th Divisions.

During the night of the 22nd–23rd April the Battalion moved into position for the operations of the following day, " W," " X " and " Z " Companies in the front line in that order from right to left—" W " to the south and the others to the north of the railway. The barrage opened at 4.45 a.m. on the 23rd and proved very accurate and heavy, the German reply being chiefly from field guns, except for the 105 and 150 mm. barrage along the bed of the Cojeul and westward of Wancourt. The 4th Green Howards suffered some few casualties from this barrage and also from our own, the initial advance of which seems to have been at rather a slow rate. During the advance " W " Company on the right met with considerable opposition from machine-gun and rifle fire from the enemy front line and had to take up positions in shell holes some fifty yards away ; here they remained until they had established a fire superiority over the enemy, when, reinforced from the rear, they rushed the trench and took many prisoners, finding the trench full of dead and wounded Germans.

" X " Company in the centre of the Battalion front experienced less opposition and reached their objective rather earlier, but had some thirty casualties from enemy fire, artillery and machine guns.

At Zero hour " Z " Company on the left or north was facing north-east, but it swung round, aligned itself with " X " Company, and was able to arrive at the first German line with less opposition than either of the other companies. The Battalion was now, however, considerably thinned, but was still a continuous line, and moved east to the German support trench, which did not run parallel to it, being a switch of the front line.   This was reached at 5.25 a.m. and was found to be a broad trench literally filled with dead Germans.   At this time there were no other troops observable immediately on either flank of the Battalion, but continuing to advance, it captured the three guns of a howitzer battery, and then proceeded to dig itself in along a line one hundred to two hundred yards west of the first objective.

Enemy rifle and shell fire had now practically ceased in this part of the field, but machine-gun fire was increasing in intensity and a particularly deadly stream of bullets being directed on the Battalion left, Captain Hirsch —now the only officer here remaining—established a defensive flank with half of " Y " Company, which dug in along a line above and parallel to the river.   With what remained of the 4th Green Howards—some one hundred and fifty men—he decided to hold his position and sent back for reinforce-ments and ammunition.   " A " Company of the 5th Durham Light Infantry came up with rifle ammunition and with orders to endeavour to extend the line on the right across the railway and, if possible, get touch with the East Yorkshire Regiment ; the company did succeed in establishing itself beyond the railway, but found its right again in the air.

At 7.15 a.m. Captain Hirsch, already wounded, was killed, and what was left of the Battalion was for a time commanded by Second-Lieu-tenant Luckhurst of the Regiment, but then serving with a Trench Mortar Battery.

The residue of the Battalion maintained itself near the first objective— " W " Company swung back and forming a defensive flank facing south-east, and " Z " Company slightly thrown forward—for something over an hour and a half ; but by 7.30 a.m. the enemy was seen massing for a counter-attack, one party creeping down the low ground by the Cojeul River, another coming from the direction of the trenches in front of Vis-en-Artois, while a third on the right rear, at first taken for men of the East Yorkshire, was now recognized as German.

A retirement by successive phases was now initiated, first to the German second line, then to their first line, and finally to the British front line, the whole under heavy machine-gun fire and directed by a handful of junior non-commissioned officers, who kept the line unbroken and under admirable control, fighting a rear-guard action to cover the general retirement, and by 8.10 a.m. all who remained had re-occupied the old British front line.

Since the 21st the 4th Battalion The Green Howards had had three officers killed, seven wounded and one missing, believed killed, while the losses in killed, wounded and missing among the other ranks totalled three hundred and fifty-two.   The officers killed were Captains D. P. Hirsch, V.C., and G. A. Tugwell, and Second-Lieutenant I. H. Scarth, while Second-Lieutenant W. Luckhurst was missing, later assumed to be killed.

For the remainder of the day the Battalion, under Major Stead—who came up from Brigade H.Q. in the afternoon—remained in support to an attack made by other battalions of the Division, moving back in the evening to Wancourt and next day to the citadel at Arras.

From here the Brigade went by train on the 26th April to Mondicourt, and thence by road to Famechon, which was reached very early on the morning of the 27th. Here a small draft of forty men only came to join from the 3/4th at Catterick, and on the 1st May the Division marched east again in order to be in position in support of the final attacks of the long-enduring Arras Battle, returning again on the 5th to Famechon, breaking the journey *en route* at Bayencourt. At Famechon twelve days were very pleasantly spent, and then the Division marched east once more on the 18th and passed the rest of the month at Douchy-les-Ayettes and Bayencourt.

The 16th June found the Battalion up in the front once more in the Hindenburg Support, and here some casualties were caused by enemy shell and rifle fire, and at least as many more by his poison gas, four officers and four other ranks being killed by gas, one officer and fourteen other ranks were wounded, one officer and sixteen other ranks were gassed ; the officers who died were Captain J. E. Bryden, the medical officer, Lieutenant C. B. Prior-Wandesford, Second-Lieutenants W. E. Pacey and C. J. Perkins ; Second-Lieutenant R. S. May was wounded, and Lieutenant J. S. Bainbridge was gassed. The reinforcements this month were bigger as regards officers than as regards other ranks ; of these last only five arrived to replace wastage, but six officers joined the Battalion, Captain L. Newcombe, Second-Lieutenants P. L. Leigh-Breese, G. H. Perkins, F. D. Farquharson, R. K. Smith and W. Thornton.

On the 27th the enemy opened a very heavy bombardment and then attacked the posts of the Battalion about Wood Trench ; the attack was repulsed and the enemy suffered many casualties, but it was while endeavouring to carry up more ammunition to his comrades holding Wood Trench that Company-Sergeant-Major Hopper of the 4th Green Howards was killed. These bombardments and attacks were renewed from time to time and were especially heavy on the 19th July when the Battalion was distributed in Swift and Snipe Trenches, Wren Lane, Martin and Avenue Trenches ; and on this day the Germans were on the point of penetrating the front of the battalion on the left when the Lewis guns of the left company of The Green Howards opened on the enemy flank and broke up the attack. On this day Captain Sproxton, the adjutant, was killed.

During the night of the 25th–26th a raiding party, led by Second-Lieutenant D. J. E. Lamb, left Wren Trench at 11 o'clock and advanced on the German post in Cable Trench. Here they found the wire was uncut, in spite of the previous efforts of our artillery, but the officer, Corporal Hammond and Lance-Corporal Horn climbed over the wire and entered Cable Trench, finding it and the neighbouring trenches all empty. After spending some time here searching for the enemy, the party had to fall back as dawn was breaking, being under enemy machine-gun fire most of the time, whereby Second-Lieutenant Lamb was wounded with two of his men.

During July Captain C. Sproxton and 12 other ranks had been killed, Second-Lieutenants C. Lamb, H. G. Cole and P. L. Leigh-Breese and twenty-eight men were wounded and three were gassed ; while on the 31st the effective strength of the Battalion stood at 28 officers and 654 non-commissioned officers and men. The reinforcements continued, however, to be very meagre, and, so far at least as the " other ranks " were concerned, did not go anywhere near to making up the wastage ; only 18 non-commissioned officers and men appear to have joined during July and August, with 7 officers—Second-Lieutenants J. S. Beall, J. S. Robson, G. G. W. Mackay, E. L. Fowler, J. Elgey, T. J. Dickson and T. V. O. Thomas. Late in September, however, a strong reinforcement of 180 other ranks arrived, so that when in the latter part of October the Battalion found itself in the Elverdinghe area, it contained 37 officers and 928 non-commissioned officers and men ; the 37 officers included 5 who now joined for the first time—Second-Lieutenants H. E. Webb, T. S. George, R. W. M. Close, N. Scorer and S. M. Oliver.

The latter part of November was spent at Touruchem near Watten, " in very good billets in ideal surroundings," and there the strength of the Battalion was more than maintained by the arrival of drafts totalling 172 other ranks with 8 officers—Lieutenant C. N. Carleton-Stiff, Second-Lieutenants J. R. Cook, T. L. Beynon, W. Fletcher, W. E. Cook, W. H. Jones, L. Brewin and W. H. Ibbetson ; but during November and December—the latter part of this last-named month was spent at Brandhoek—2 officers—Lieutenants H. C. Hale and T. Taft—and 13 other ranks were killed or died of wounds, Lieutenant R. M. Howes and 28 other ranks were wounded, and 2 men were missing.

The greater part of the months of January and February, 1918, were spent in the neighbourhood of Ypres, where at the end of February Captain S. R. Dobinson, Second-Lieutenants F. E. Lonsdale, J. G. Hardwicke, W. A. Cliffe and T. A. Hyslop, M.C., joined from the 10th Battalion of the Regiment ; but when the great German offensive opened on the 21st March the 4th Green Howards were engaged in training at Ignaucourt, receiving sudden orders this day to be ready to move at short notice. At 5.15 that afternoon the Battalion marched to Guillaucourt and entrained for Brie, and on arrival here at midnight entered upon a six-hours' march which brought the Battalion to a position which was taken up near Hancourt—the 4th Green Howards being the centre battalion of the Brigade, with the 4th East Yorkshire on the right and the 5th Durham Light Infantry on the left. The 50th Division was now in reserve to the XIX. Corps, and the position it was ordered to take up was between the Omignon and Cologne Rivers, on a front which had been partly wired.

In the absence of any special account of the fighting that now ensued and in which the 4th Green Howards were for some days engaged, it is proposed to give the story as it appears in the Battalion diary.

" 22nd March. The 66th Division retired through our line, which then became the front line. At 6.30 p.m. the 5th Durham L.I. on our left was pressed back and our left company started to retire. Lieut.-Colonel B. H. Charlton and the adjutant, Captain J. S. Bainbridge, went up to rally them and were both killed. A new line of defence was now established in some old trenches in rear of Battalion Headquarters at Hancourt.

" 23rd. Early in the morning orders were received to retire to a line running from Vraignes to Bouvincourt, where the 4th East Yorkshire and the 5th Green Howards were in the line and the 4th Green Howards were in support. During the morning ordered to retire to a prepared line on the River Somme, and the retirement of the other two battalions of the Brigade was covered by the 4th Green Howards, who fought a rear-guard action all the way back to Le Mesnil-Bruntel. On reaching this place Brigadier ordered one company of the Battalion to hold the high ground east of Brie until all the British troops had passed through ; and this company afterwards covered the retirement of all troops across the Somme at this point and held the enemy in check until all the bridges except one had been destroyed, and this was demolished immediately they had crossed the river by it. This company then went on to Belloy-en-Santerne, where it rested for the night, while the rest of the Battalion joined the Brigade at Villers-Carbonnel.

" 24th. In the afternoon the Battalion was ordered to report to the 24th Brigade for duty and marched to Marchelpot, where we spent the night.

" 25th. In the morning the Battalion, with the 4th East Yorkshire on its left, was directed to attack the enemy who had crossed the Somme by the bridge at St. Christ, and the attack was to have been supported by some French troops, a tank, some armoured cars and an artillery barrage, but none of these arrived upon the scene and operations were postponed from time to time until, about 10 a.m., the enemy himself attacked. The line was, however, held east of Licourt until the Germans worked round our flanks ; one company of the 4th Green Howards fought on until they were surrounded, the remaining companies falling back for half a mile in the direction of Misery, holding an old trench here for seven hours. But at about 6 p.m., as touch could not be obtained with any other unit and rifle ammunition was running short, Lieut.-Colonel Wilkinson of the 4th East Yorkshire, who had taken over command of the troops immediately at hand, ordered a retirement to the railway line northward of Misery. Half an hour after reaching this position a further withdrawal was ordered to a line east of Fresnes, where, during the evening, touch was obtained with the 150th Brigade, and orders were received to join it at Ablaincourt ; this place was reached about midnight.

" 26th. Early in the afternoon the Brigade withdrew through Lihons to Rosières-en-Santerre, which place was reached about 5 p.m., and the Brigade dug in here—facing south-east—and held the position throughout the night and all the following day. We were in support with the 4th East Yorkshire on our left ; the 5th Green Howards and the Durham L.I. were in the front line.

" 27th. Throughout the morning the enemy attacked the position taken up on the 26th, but was repulsed. Towards the evening the enemy pushed up on the north of Rosières and we sent two platoons to reinforce the line on the left. These platoons, with the exception of one officer and two other ranks, eventually became casualties.

" 28th. At 1 a.m. the Brigade withdrew to a line at Vrely, facing north-east. At 8 a.m. a further retirement was ordered to some old trenches on the high ground south-east of Caix, and this position was held until the flanks gave way between 11 a.m. and noon. We then retired through Beaucourt-en-Santerre to Villers-aux-Erables, where we were ordered back to billets at Jumel where the night was spent. . . .

" 29th. At 5 p.m. the Battalion was ordered to report at a point east of Mezières, the strength being now about three hundred. On arrival at a point about six hundred yards north of Mailly-Raineval on the Mailly-Morisel Road at 10 p.m., we were informed that the enemy was occupying Moreuil, and the Battalion therefore withdrew to the wood west of Mailly, where the night was spent.

" 30th. At 8 a.m. the Battalion left the wood to return to the transport lines at Jumel, but on arriving there we were informed that the transport had moved to Boves, whither we marched, arriving there at 6.30 p.m. to find that the transport had moved to Sains-en-Amienois. The night was spent at Boves.

" 31st. Left Boves at 10.45 a.m. and arrived at Sains-en-Amienois at 12.30 p.m., from where we marched on to Saleux, entraining there for Rue. This place was reached at 11.30 at night, and we then marched to billets at Estrées-le-Crecy."

On the 2nd April the Battalion moved to Béthune, remaining here until the retreat ended, and being very busily engaged in the reorganization so greatly needed after the very heavy losses which had been sustained in all ranks since the 23rd March.

The casualties totalled 7 officers and 24 other ranks killed, 11 officers and 147 non-commissioned officers and men wounded, 1 officer and 10 men wounded and missing, 3 officers and 168 other ranks missing—in all 22 officers and 349 non-commissioned officers and men killed, wounded, and missing.

Of the officers there were killed in action Lieut.-Colonel B. H. Charlton, M.C., Major H. Brown, D.S.O., M.C., Captain and Adjutant J. S. Bainbridge, Acting-Captains D. Spurway and C. N. Carleton-Stiff, Lieutenant S. R. Dobinson and Second-Lieutenant T. A. Hyslop, M.C.; wounded were Lieutenants M. W. Macnay, R. Edwards and H. L. Harrison, Second-Lieutenants J. G. Hardwick, T. L. Beynon, W. Fletcher, W. L. Snowball, N. Scorer, A. R. Stein, D. J. E. Lamb, M.C., and R. Campbell; wounded and missing was Second-Lieutenant W. E. Cook, while Acting-Captain A. R. Powys, Second-Lieutenants G. A. Green and W. L. Thornton were missing.

Reinforcements were hurried out to the units of the British Army which had been so greatly reduced in numbers during the recent very severe fighting, and during April no fewer than twenty-two officers and eight hundred and two other ranks joined the 4th Green Howards, the majority of these from home, but a considerable proportion of all ranks who had recovered from recent wounds; but the numbers, large as they may appear, were none too many in view of the many further casualties which the Battalion was this month to sustain.

The officers joining or rejoining were Major R. E. D. Kent, Captains T. H. Blair, A. C. P. de la P. Beresforde-Peirse, F. A. Foley and A. L. Goring, Lieutenants P. L. Leigh-Breese, C. K. Kelk, R. Gates, T. A. Robson, J. A. Hamlyn and T. Wiggins, Second-Lieutenants A. W. Appleby, F. D. Harley, A. G. V. Marsh, L. S. Gray, J. A. Naylor, W. R. Holmes, P. J. Godfrey, A. E. Bedford, A. E. Kennington, J. H. Derrett and W. A. Shooter.

Early on the morning of the 8th April orders were received to leave Béthune, for the 50th Division was now required to play its part in the Lys Battle then opening, and was directed to move via Neuf Berquin to Laventie. Proceeding by light railway to Rue Montigny, in the evening orders were issued that the 50th Division was to relieve the Portuguese troops in the line on the following night. These orders were followed early next morning by one placing the Battalion under "one hour's notice to move," and in the course of the morning it marched to Trou Bayard where its Brigade was assembling. Arrived here about midday the 4th Green Howards were directed to hold a line west of the river at Sailly-sur-Lys ; this was reached about 2 p.m. and the work of " digging in " commenced.   The front ran from Rouge Maison Farm on the right to the temporary bridge south of the Factory on the left, and three companies occupied the line, the fourth being in reserve at Battalion Headquarters ; the 4th East Yorkshire Regiment was on the right and the 21st Middlesex on the left.   To stay any enemy advance a foot-bridge in the front was destroyed and all preparations were made for the demolition of the bridge at Sailly.   When by 4 p.m. all Allied troops east of the Lys had withdrawn to the western bank, an unsuccessful attempt was made to blow up the Sailly bridge, but the bridge was held and its passage denied to the enemy, who suffered heavy casualties in attempting to force it.   He managed, however, to pass the Lys to the north, and during the evening formed a line at right angles to the Battalion front, running along the road from Bac St. Maur through Croix du Bac to Point Vanuxeem.

The despatch of the 20th July, 1918, says that " the weight and impetus of the German attack overwhelmed the Portuguese troops, and the enemy's progress was so rapid that the arrangements for manning the rear defences of this sector with British troops could scarcely be completed in time." The enemy was, however, held throughout the night on the line which had been here taken up.   About 11 on the morning of the 10th the troops occupying the line opposite Point Vanuxeem, viz. at right angles to the front of the 4th Green Howards, were driven back, so that the left flank of the Battalion was exposed and, being at the same time strongly assailed in front, The Green Howards were compelled to fall back in line with their left—a line one hundred to three hundred yards east of and parallel to the Trou Bayard-Le Point Mortier road ; here the 4th East Yorkshire were on the right and the 5th Green Howards on the left.   This line was held all night, but the Germans attacked next morning, the 11th, in great force and a further withdrawal became obligatory, during which units became considerably disorganized.   Later in the day the battalions of the 150th Brigade were directed to assemble at the cross-roads west of Doulieu, remaining there till 1 a.m. on the 12th ; but at 4.30 in the afternoon these orders were changed and Vierhouck was named as the place of assembly.   Some of the Battalion succeeded in reaching this place, but others took up a position and tried here to rally such of the troops as were falling back from Neuf Berquin at this time, eventually rejoining the Brigade in the evening at Arrewage.

The whole of the 12th was passed in taking up and falling back from one position after another, incurring many casualties, but causing great loss to the enemy, and by night La Motte-au-Bois was reached, where some huts were occupied and rest was obtained.   At daybreak on the 13th, however, these huts were heavily shelled and had to be vacated, and at 8 a.m. the

Battalion was ordered to march to the neighbourhood of Le Parc, where the 50th Division was assembling. Late in the afternoon this place was reached, and next day and the 15th working parties were supplied to dig trenches south of the Bois des Vaches, while many stragglers came in during these days and rejoined the ranks of the 4th Green Howards, which was finally, at the end of the month, able to reorganize in quiet at Courville, whither it proceeded by train on the 27th.

Again, for the second time within something like a month, had the Battalion lost many of its best ; 2 officers and 21 other ranks had been killed or had died of wounds, 3 officers and 216 non-commissioned officers and men had been wounded, 1 officer and 115 other ranks were missing, while 1 man was wounded and missing. The officer-casualties were : died of wounds, Major A. Graham and Captain F. D. Farquharson ; wounded, Second-Lieutenants H. A. Clidero, W. H. Ibbetson and H. E. Webb ; while Second-Lieutenant W. A. Cliffe was missing.

The IX. Corps, commanded by Lieutenant-General Sir A. Gordon, and composed of the 8th, 21st, 25th and 50th Divisions, had, as the story of one of its battalions testifies, suffered very heavily in the recent fighting,* and when the Lys Battle was over it was relieved by French troops, and sent down to rest and recuperate in what was described with undue optimism as " a quiet sector." This formed part of the French front in Champagne, and its outpost line extended from Loivre, a village about five miles north-north-west of Reims, to the eastern end of the Chemin des Dames about a mile west of Craonne. Here it came under the orders of General Duchêne.

" These divisions had been heavily engaged during the past month, three having been twice and one (25th) three times withdrawn from the battle line and again engaged after being reformed. They, therefore, had few experienced officers and men when they arrived in Champagne, and were again filled up by immature and half-trained lads fresh from home whose training had to be completed. In these circumstances the divisions could not be considered fit for heavy fighting for some time to come. Notwithstanding this, they were ordered into the front line almost at once by the French Commander, who countered the British objections by declaring that as the front was a quiet one, and as no attack was to be expected, it would be possible to continue the training of the troops while in the line, and that the French divisions, urgently required elsewhere, could thus be relieved."†

On the 4th May the 4th Green Howards moved from Courville to Maizy, spent a few days here in training, and then on the 8th went into reserve billets at Beaurieux.

---

* The IX. Corps had lost 1,600 Officers and 35,000 Other Ranks since the 21st March.
† *Sir Douglas Haig's Command.* Vol. 2, p. 232.

The ridge known as the Chemin des Dames was held by four divisions of the British IX. Corps—the 50th, then the 8th about Jouvincourt, the 21st about Neufchatel, with the 25th in reserve on the extreme left wing at Craonelle. " Against an attack in grand style the Chemin des Dames was not only a bad position, as too narrow, but it was in the front line. Purely tactical considerations pointed to its occupation by a line of outposts, strong only in machine guns, the first real position of resistance being organized on the heights on the left or south bank of the Aisne."*

The French seem to have made up their minds that no German attack would here take place, Marshal Foch himself being persuaded that, if the enemy attacked again anywhere, it would be between Montdidier and Arras ; but the British Corps Commander on the spot, while considering a German attack here improbable, believed that if such did take place it would be delivered in great force with the object of outflanking the Allied forces north of the Aisne, driving them towards the sea, and thus preparing the way for a subsequent advance on Paris from a broad base.

As a matter of fact the Germans made a surprise attack on the Chemin des Dames position on the 27th May, and how extreme was the surprise may be gathered from the following message received by General Gordon from the French Headquarters on the 25th : " In our opinion there are no indications that the enemy has made preparations which would enable him to attack to-morrow."

" On the morning of May 26th," so General Gordon tells us, " the troops of, and attached to, the IX. Corps were disposed as follows : 21st Division holding over seven thousand five hundred yards of the front line from near the village of Loivre (held by the 45th French Division) to Berry-au-Bac on the Aisne, with headquarters at Chalons-le-Vergeur ; 8th Division holding the next ten thousand yards round Cæsar's Camp and up to a point about half-way between Jouvincourt and Corbeny, with headquarters at Roucy ; 50th Division another eight thousand yards to the source of the river Ailette where they joined hands with the 22nd French Division in the wooded valley lying north of the narrow steep-sided Craonelle plateau forming the eastern end of the famous Chemin des Dames. The 50th Division had their headquarters at Beaurieux. Each of the Divisions held the front line with all three of its brigades, and they were covered by their own divisional artilleries, which, in the case of the 8th and 50th, were supplemented by three batteries each of French field guns. By permission of the Army Commander the 21st Division was also helped by the field batteries of the 25th Division which was in Army Reserve round Montigny."

Early on 26th May definite information was received from two prisoners

* R.U.S.I. Journal, August, 1922.

that an attack on the IX. Corps front would be made next morning, preceded by a bombardment commencing at 1 a.m.; this began at the appointed hour and lasted until 4.30, when the German infantry left their trenches and advanced to the assault. "The enemy," so General Gordon states, "at first made most progress on his right, being reported in Ailles and on the crest of the plateau by 5.15 a.m., while at the same time he was moving through Chevreux. This threatened the left of the 50th Division, and the 5th Yorks made a determined counter-attack on the eastern end of the Chemin des Dames. It was, however, unsuccessful and they were overpowered. The Germans crossed the ridge and advanced so far that they began to enter the village of Beaurieux from the west, and the 50th Division H.Q. had to make a hurried retirement."

On the 26th the 4th Green Howards, which had been in reserve at Beaurieux, moved forward and took up a support position round Craonelle and La Hutte. When on the next morning the enemy bombardment commenced, his heavy gas shelling was felt as far back as Maizy. "The enemy broke through on our left and pushed on towards Beaurieux, arriving there about 10 a.m. He also came through on our right, using tanks over the flat country to the east of Craonne, and then also came on from there towards Beaurieux and there surrounded the brigade in the line, advancing thence on Maizy. All the troops in Maizy, and the few who were able to effect a retreat from Beaurieux, then made a stand on the hills to the south of the village; but by midday the Germans had made a big advance on the left of the British Corps front and against the whole of the XI. French Corps, and had succeeded in crossing the Aisne at many points. The troops of the 50th Division now fell back, first to a position at Glennes, and later in the day to one on the hills north of Fismes, which was held during the night."

Early on the 28th May the enemy heavily attacked this position and a further retirement was made, the 21st Division to the spur between Trigny and Prouilly, and the 8th and 50th, now greatly reduced in numbers, continuing the line on the south bank of the Vesle to a point about two miles west of Jonchery. What was left of the 4th Green Howards had fallen back with the French, and, having expended all its ammunition, managed to join the 50th Division near Arcis-le-Ponsart, where the night was passed.

On the 29th the 4th Green Howards assisted to occupy a position at Romigny, and on this day the 8th and 50th Divisions, still further reduced and exhausted, were placed under Major-General Henneker, the commander of the former.

The 19th British Division now came up as a reinforcement from the VIII. Corps, near Chalons, and on the night of the 30th the line taken up ran from Rosnay through Tramery to Lhéry, but by this time four of the British Divisions engaged barely exceeded the ordinary strength of one. On the 31st a position was taken up from Bligny to Champlat, and though during the next few days the enemy made many determined attacks, he was unable to achieve any substantial success—the line was held.

Of the resistance offered by these battle-worn divisions the French commander, General Maistre, wrote as follows to General Sir A. Gordon :

> " Avec une ténacité, permettez-moi de dire, toute anglaise, avec les débris de vos divisions décimées, submergées par le flot ennemi, vous avez reformé, sans vous lasser, des unités nouvelles que vous avez engagées dans la lutte, et qui nous ont enfin permis de former la digue où ce flot est venu se briser. Cela, aucun des témoins français ne l'oubliera."

Again had the 4th Battalion The Green Howards suffered grievous loss, the toll of the missing being especially heavy : Lieutenant-Colonel R. E. D. Kent, Captain H. N. Constantine and three men were killed, Captain T. H. Hutchinson and Lieutenant G. S. Mitchinson with fifty-two other ranks were wounded, while no fewer than twenty-three officers and five hundred and sixty-six non-commissioned officers and men were missing ; the Battalion may be said to have practically ceased to exist. The missing officers were : Major L. Newcombe, Captains R. A. Constantine, A. L. Goring and H. M. Howes ; Lieutenants V. W. W. S. Purcell, C. K. Kelk, J. F. Johns, R. Gates, R. W. M. Close, J. C. Story, T. Wiggins, T. A. Robson, H. R. Burn-Bailey and G. G. W. Mackay* ; Second-Lieutenants H. E. Webb,* C. W. Stirk, W. H. Jones, A. W. Appleby, V. H. Derrett, H. A. Clidero, W. H. Shooter, H. R. Holmes and A. G. V. Marsh.

The 4th was now formed into No. 2 Company of the 150th Composite Battalion, of two platoons each of the 4th and 5th Green Howards, Major A. C. Barnes, D.S.O., assuming command of the 150th Battalion, and Captain T. R. K. Ginger, M.C., being in command of No. 2 Company ; and as such all played their part in the defence of the Montagne de Bligny so long as the German attacks continued. During June some small reinforcements arrived, bringing the Battalion strength up to sixteen officers and three hundred and sixty other ranks.

But on the 16th July, when at Limeux, the 4th Battalion The Green Howards was reduced to a Training Cadre and sent to Rouxmesnil, and in September to Le Touquet, where on the 31st October the active share in the prosecution of the war by the Battalion, then consisting of nine officers and eighty-five other ranks, seems to have come to an end.

---

* Also wounded.

CHAPTER VIII

THE 1/5TH BATTALION

1914–1918

THE BATTLE OF YPRES, 1915. THE BATTLE OF THE SOMME, 1916. THE BATTLE OF YPRES, 1917. THE BATTLE OF ARRAS. THE BATTLE OF THE SCARPE. THE BATTLE OF THE SOMME, 1918. THE BATTLE OF THE AISNE, 1918.

ON the 26th July, 1914, the 5th Battalion The Green Howards had arrived at Deganwy Camp, in Wales, for the annual training, but at this date the European situation was already serious, and on the very next night a Special Reserve Section received orders to proceed at once to Scarborough. On Sunday, the 2nd August, the Battalion was called upon to furnish a second Special Service Section, and at 8 a.m. next morning orders were given for camp to be struck and for the troops to be ready to move at a moment's notice. At this time, however, the railway lines were greatly congested, and the Battalion could not be entrained until 2.30 in the afternoon: and since the orders were that the men should be sent to their homes, the train followed a somewhat circuitous route in order to pass through the headquarters station of each company, and consequently Scarborough, the Battalion Headquarters, was not reached until 2 a.m. on the 4th August.

At 6 p.m. on the same day mobilization orders were received and notices to rejoin were at once sent out to all ranks of the Battalion.

The Officer Corps of the 5th Battalion was composed as follows on the 1st August: Colonel the Earl of Faversham, V.D., Hon. Colonel; Lieutenant-Colonel Sir M. Sykes, Bt., in command; Majors J. Mortimer and W. A. Wetwan, V.D.; Captains C. H. Pearce, J. B. Purvis, G. J. Scott, G. C. Barber and F. W. Robson; Lieutenants D. H. Walker, T. E. Dufty, C. C. Pickles, J. S. Wadsworth, G. A. Maxwell, F. Woodcock, E. R. Spofforth and H. Brown; Second-Lieutenants R. Green, R. C. Bentley, A. F. Clarke, W. Vause, G. B. Purvis and H. S. Cranswick; Lieutenant S. Grant-Dalton, Adjutant; Lieutenant R. Rennison, Quartermaster; Captain E. O.

Libbey, R.A.M.C., Medical Officer; the Rev. B. N. Keymer and the Rev. C. H. Coates, Chaplains.

During the forenoon of the 5th August the companies from out-stations reassembled at Scarborough and the Battalion then entrained again at 2 p.m. the same day, reached Hull a couple of hours later and was distributed in various billets in the city, spending the ensuing days in digging trenches in connection with coastal defence works. " H " Company, under Captain Thomson, was placed in charge of some German vessels and prisoners which had been captured.

On the 8th, the 5th Green Howards marched fifteen miles to Aldborough and remained there until the 12th, when they marched to Whitedale and entrained for Darlington, being billeted for some days in the local Drill Hall until the camp, which was now preparing in Hummersknott Park, was ready for the accommodation of the troops on the 19th August. When the dry summer weather changed, this camp became very damp, so on the 16th October the Battalion moved to billets in Newcastle-on-Tyne, and remained here until the 15th April, 1915, when the advance party left *en route* to the front.

The advance party, consisting of the Battalion transport and details, eighty strong, under Captain J. A. R. Thomson, with Lieutenants G. A. Maxwell and J. S. Wadsworth, transport officer, and Second-Lieutenant G. B. Purvis, machine-gun officer, left on the above date for Southampton, where they arrived at 6 on the morning of the 16th, sailing at 7.30 p.m. and reaching Havre about midday on the 17th. These were followed at 11 a.m. on the 17th by the remainder of the Battalion, which went direct by train to Folkestone, crossing over from there in the transport *Onward* to Boulogne.

The following officers left England with the 5th Battalion The Green Howards: Major J. Mortimer, Captains C. H. Pearce, J. B. Purvis, G. C. Barber, F. W. Robson and E. G. C. Bagshawe; Lieutenants T. E. Dufty, F. Woodcock, E. R. Spofforth, H. Brown and R. Green; Second-Lieutenants A. F. Clarke, W. Vause, H. S. Cranswick, G. Thompson, E. M. Thompson, F. H. H. Barber, H. E. Gorst, F. J. Dymond and D. P. Tanks; Captain and Adjutant S. Grant-Dalton, Lieutenant and Quartermaster R. Rennison, Captain A. Perl, R.A.M.C., and the Rev. B. Wolferstan, Chaplain.

A very cold and uncomfortable evening was spent at Boulogne in St. Martin's Camp, and at midnight the Battalion marched to the railway station and proceeded thence by rail to Cassel and on by a very hot and trying march to Steenvoorde. Here three days were passed, the Division being in Corps Reserve, and in view of the very heavy cannonade which could be heard going on in the front nobody was surprised to receive orders that the Battalion was to move up nearer to the front on the 23rd. At 1.30 p.m. on this day the 5th Green Howards were loaded on to motor-buses and were carried by way of Abeele, Poperinghe and Vlamertinghe to a camp at Brielen, north-west of Ypres, meeting *en route* hundreds of Belgians flying from Ypres and carrying with them their poor household gods in every description of conveyance; while there were also some few stragglers from the Allied armies, who had been driven back by the gas, here lately used for the first time, and against which there were then no respirators or gas helmets.

" At 1 a.m. on the 24th the whole Brigade was ordered to occupy the Yser Canal bank, west of Ypres. The position allotted to the 5th Battalion was the extreme left of the British line, the troops on our immediate left being Algerian Zouaves of the French Army. Owing to the French division having received the brunt of the gas on the 22nd, they had been driven back and at Steenstraate the Germans had been able to cross the Yser Canal. From the position we occupied the enemy line was about three hundred yards north-east of the Canal, and although we were in support of the British Army, from our position on the extreme left, linked with the French, there were none of our troops between us and the Germans.

" During the early hours of the morning of the 24th we were not disturbed by fire of any kind, but about 10 a.m. the enemy opened a heavy shell fire against our position, but luckily for us he was out in his estimation of the range and most of his shells passed over our heads, though ' B ' Company had two men wounded. About midday the Battalion was directed to proceed to Potijze and place itself at the disposal of any brigadier requiring assistance. After crossing the Canal by the pontoon bridge we moved on to Potijze in diamond formation, leaving Ypres on our right and St. Jean on the left, the Germans being now engaged in attacking the latter place, and the noise of the fire was terrific, the Canadians being on the point of evacuating St. Jean as we were passing. It appeared that at St. Julien matters were worse, for here the enemy had broken through, but a powerful counter-attack was being organized by Brig.-General Hull, and on arriving at Potijze we were told off to the Canadian Division and occupied the left of the British line before St. Julien.

" The counter-attack did not succeed in driving the enemy out of St. Julien, so from this time until 4 a.m. on the 25th the Canadians and we held on to the position, and at that hour we were ordered to retire to make room for the Seaforth Highlanders and Royal Irish Fusiliers, who were coming up to relieve us and the Canadians, the latter for a much-

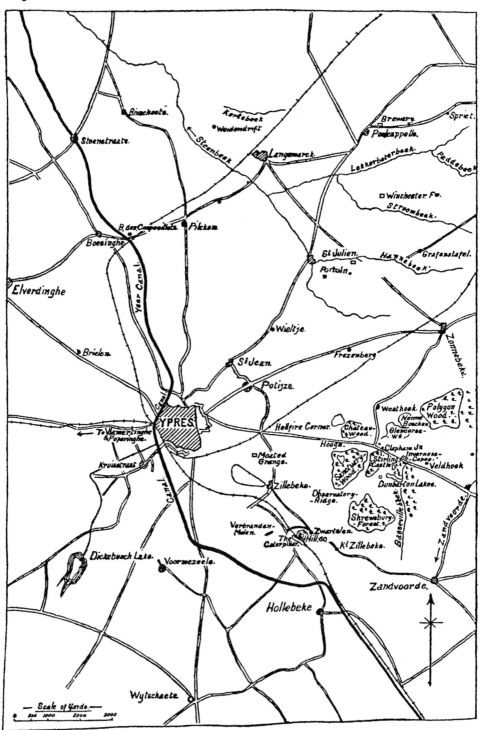

THE YPRES AREA.

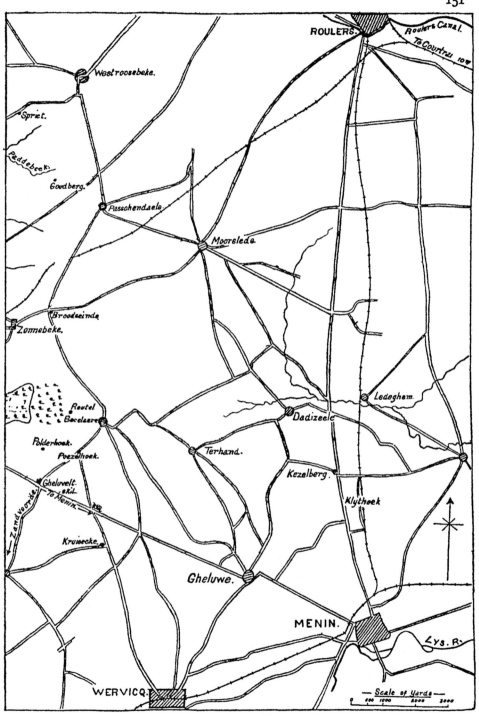

ROULERS—MENIN.

needed rest, and us in order that we might support any unit requiring assistance. We now halted in a field just south of the Zaaerebeke stream, near the road to Wieltje, where we rested until 8 a.m., when we learnt that the Canadians and the two battalions relieving them had been attacked by gas and forced back. The 5th Green Howards at once hurried forward, and, having crossed the Zaaerebeke stream, we were advancing towards St. Julien when we were met by a very heavy shrapnel fire and in less than five minutes suffered sixty casualties, among these being the adjutant, Captain Grant-Dalton. The companies at once deployed, and took up a line facing St. Julien and Fortuin, opening fire on the advancing Germans. About 10 a.m. these halted and appeared to be consolidating the trenches they had captured, while we also dug for ourselves such cover as we could with our entrenching tools.

" The Brigade-Major now noticed a farm-house in our front and in order to prevent the enemy creeping up and occupying it, he sent forward Captain Barber and part of ' D ' Company to hold it ; but on arrival they were met by very heavy shell and machine-gun fire, Captain Barber and Lance-Corporal Dell being killed and the remainder falling back again under very heavy fire. Our orders were that the position *must* be held at any cost as there was no support or second line upon which we might fall back." Here Sergeant H. Joy was also killed.

" On the 26th April the Lahore Division and the 149th Brigade of our Division advanced upon St. Julien and succeeded in entering and, for a time, occupying the southern portion of the village, but were eventually driven back to a line on our left—south of St. Julien ; we held our position until the night of the 27th and by that time a new line had been formed which ran slightly north of our line, occupied in our immediate neighbourhood by the Royal Fusiliers.

" On the night of the 27th we relieved a battalion of the London Regiment about three-quarters of a mile to the north-east of the position previously occupied ; here we were out of sight of St. Julien, but not out of shell fire, and suffered rather severely from this, for the trenches here were very wide and shallow. We held on here for two days, during which the enemy made no attempt to advance, but persistently shelled us, while his aircraft were constantly overhead. During these days we lived on our emergency rations and on such water as we could collect in the small holes in the bottom of the trenches, for our transport could not get up.

" On the night of the 29th we were relieved by the 4th Battalion of our Regiment and marched back to camp at Brielen, only to find no rest here as we were heavily shelled by the enemy's long-range guns, and had to quit the huts in the camp and dig shelter trenches for ourselves close by. After a day or two we were roused out by reports of another gas attack, hundreds of gassed men passing through us, and we marched down to the Poperinghe-Ypres Road and lay there waiting for whatever might turn up."

During these days the Battalion had one officer—Captain G. C. Barber—and twenty-three men killed, Captain and Adjutant S. Grant-Dalton and one hundred and six non-commissioned officers and men wounded, of whom six died of their wounds.

From this camp the Battalion moved by Brandhoek and Abeele to Steenvoorde, where on the 4th May The 5th Green Howards were inspected by the Commander of the British Expeditionary Force, Field-Marshal Sir John French, who made the following most flattering remarks :

"I have come this morning to express to every single officer and man how much I admire the splendid behaviour of the Battalion in the fighting which has gone on during the last ten days. The 5th Yorkshire Regiment has suffered heavily. You have had one officer killed, one officer wounded, twenty-eight men killed and one hundred and five wounded. When you came out here you were called upon very hurriedly and you had very little preparation. Things do come that way—very suddenly—in war. The call came through the disgraceful conduct of the people who are fighting us, who call themselves soldiers, but who behave in a very unsoldierlike way. In the circumstances we could not wait and had to do the best we could. I do not want to go into the details of that fight, because there were other British soldiers engaged. I want particularly to talk of the splendid conduct of the men of the Northumbrian Division, and especially of your Battalion. I wish to compliment every one of you, and I am very grateful to you for all you have done. I think your conduct magnificent. Whenever I am speaking of Territorial soldiers I find it very difficult adequately to express how strongly I feel on the subject. I had a good deal to do with Territorial soldiers before the war when I was Inspector-General of the Forces, and I have always said that when the Territorial Force was called upon and put to the test it would not be found wanting. A good many of our countrymen did not agree with me. But you have shown right well that not only were you not found wanting, but that you were capable of taking your place and fighting splendidly in accordance with the best traditions of the British Army. Your conduct has been superb. Nothing is more difficult than to come out in the ordinary way of routine as you did, and then suddenly to be called upon to fill a breach that had so suddenly been occasioned. You showed a spirit of splendid patriotism months ago when, leaving your work and homes, you volunteered for foreign service, though originally you had only taken the responsibilities of home defence. This you did for the defence of the British Empire, and whilst others remained behind, you have come here to do your duty and have done it and have set a magnificent example. I am sure that when your fellow-countrymen fully realize your magnificent behaviour, they will thank you as I thank you now. I feel confident that you will keep up the splendid record that you have established whenever you are called upon."

May was a month of many moves—to the neighbourhood of Vlamertinghe, then to Brielen, then to trenches in Sanctuary Wood, where Second-Lieutenants W. A. Turnbull, O. Barton and H. P. Bagge joined; then called out for the great German gas attack of Whit-Monday, 24th May, and hurried up to Zouave Wood, near Hooge; and though not actually employed in the front line the Battalion experienced a number of casualties these days, and lost Captain T. E. Dufty killed and Lieutenant Clarke wounded. Remaining in these parts during June and through half of July the usual wastage was incurred, two more officers—Lieutenant H. E. Gorst and Second-Lieutenant W. A. Turnbull—and several other ranks being among the casualties; and then on the 17th July the 5th Green Howards marched away to billets at Pont-de-Nieppe, three-quarters of a mile west of Armentières, where Captain D. H. Walker, Second-Lieutenants L. T. Tracy, I. A. Sleightholm, C. H. Rose, P. D. J. Waters and E. G. S. Corry joined from England. A few days later Second-Lieutenants E. M. Robson and J. S. Robson also arrived, while on the last day of the month Lieutenant F. Woodcock was wounded in the trenches east of Houplines.

It was not, however, until the 12th November that the 5th Battalion The Green Howards was accorded a real rest, when it marched from Armentières to rest billets near Outtersteene, some two and a half miles west of Bailleul, where a full month was very happily and peacefully spent, it being the 19th December when the Battalion was sent back by train to Poperinghe, marched thence to Dickebusch and so up to the trenches. Here on the very first day in the trenches some half-dozen casualties occurred, Captain J. A. R. Thomson and Second-Lieutenant C. H. Dell— the latter only commissioned some six weeks previously—being wounded, while on the day following Captain G. J. Scott was killed. " Our loss," writes a Battalion correspondent of *The Green Howards Gazette,* " is great. Several of us have lost a very personal and sterling friend and the Battalion one of its most popular and experienced officers. All he has done for the Volunteer Force in general and the Battalion in particular will never be known, for he invariably *did* things and said little."

The month of January, 1916, was spent in the region of Hill 60 and Sanctuary Wood, where on the 11th Lieutenant H. S. Lambert was killed when out with a wiring party, while on the 26th Captain D. H. Walker was also killed when superintending work outside the parapet.

During February, the Battalion occupied more or less the same trenches as during January, and on the 16th of the month there was a determined attack on the British lines, of which The Bluff, held by the 17th Division, a very important observation point south of the Ypres Salient, was the centre. The German bombardment was severe and deadly and The Bluff was captured, the bombers of the Battalion being employed during the action in carrying up bombs to the front, but it was not otherwise engaged.

On the 27th Lieutenant E. M. Thompson was killed while superintending repairs to the parapet of his company's trench.

The 5th Battalion The Green Howards remained in the vicinity of Sanctuary Wood till the 9th March, when it proceeded to billets in Poperinghe, having a few days previously taken part in a demonstration made by the 50th Division, during which The Bluff was recaptured by the 76th Infantry Brigade. In this fighting the Battalion had Lieutenant E. R. Spofforth and five men killed, Captain J. A. R. Thomson, Second-Lieutenant E. H. Weighill and twenty-seven other ranks wounded. Then on the 14th the Battalion moved to Dickebusch, and at the end of the month to Locre, while in the trenches here two Poles of the 212th Reserve Regiment giving themselves up to one of the companies of the 5th Green Howards. Preparations were on hand all this time for a great offensive against the Messines Ridge ; this, however, did not materialize owing to the destruction of a great ammunition dump near St. Omer.

During May the 5th were chiefly at Eecke, a few miles north-west of Bailleul, where, on the 27th, the Battalion was inspected by General Sir H. Plumer, commanding the Second Army. Next day the Battalion moved to Locre, being here for some days in divisional reserve, then from the 4th June onwards taking its share of the ordinary trench work and working parties, the casualties for the month being five killed, and Lieutenant R. Green and thirty other ranks wounded. On the 10th July a raid on a considerable scale was carried out on an enemy mine crater, the party discarding their steel helmets and blackening their faces so as to avoid detection during the advance. The raiding party was under the command of Captain H. Brown, D.S.O., and consisted of three officers— the other two being Second-Lieutenants H. P. Bagge and E. R. Saltonstall—and thirty-three non-commissioned officers and men, the objects being to obtain identifications, to kill Germans, and to discover whether a certain crater had any mine shaft. Of the enemy one man was captured and fifteen men were killed, while of the raiding party Captain Brown and Second-Lieutenant Bagge and eleven other ranks were wounded.

The enemy's artillery was particularly active between the 16th and 21st of this month, during which period Captain E. G. C. Bagshawe, Second-Lieutenants W. A. Turnbull, E. W. Brodrick, J. Jacobs and P. L. N. McInnes and eight other ranks were killed, Second-Lieutenants H. A. Fagan and G. W. Smith with thirty-eight non-commissioned officers and men were wounded.

On the 7th August the Battalion returned to billets at Eecke, and four days later entrained at Bailleul for Doullens, marching from here to Bernaville, where three days were spent, and then moving on by Flesselles and Molliens-au-Bois to Millencourt in the III. Corps area, where the remainder of the month was passed in preparing the 50th Division and its units for the coming Battle of the Somme.

On the 9th September the Battalion moved from Millencourt to Lozenge Wood in reserve to the 44th Brigade of the 15th Division, and then next day up to Pioneer Alley and Swansea Trench; and when at 6.30 a.m. on the 15th, the 5th Battalion The Green Howards advanced to the attack from between High Wood and Martinpuich, the 50th Division had the 47th and 15th on the right and left, while the 5th was on the left of the Division with the 4th Battalion of the Regiment on its right; the Battalion had Second-Lieutenant W. Featherstone killed while moving up into the line.

Just before the attack opened Lieutenant-Colonel Mortimer, in command of the Battalion, was killed by a shell while on his way to the assembly trenches, his men hearing the news just prior to the assault, and the subsequent success of the Battalion was, as a writer has said, " his due, for it was his work, his encouragement, and his personality that were alone responsible for it "; while of him his General said : " He was the soul of his Battalion, the pride of the Brigade, and an example to us all."

The 5th Battalion The Green Howards, with the 4th, reached its objective and clung to it under very heavy shelling, but when relieved early on the morning of the 19th by a brigade of the 23rd Division and withdrawn into divisional reserve, the 5th had had four officers and forty-eight other ranks killed, eleven officers and one hundred and sixty-two non-commissioned officers and men wounded and twenty-seven men missing —a total of two hundred and fifty-two casualties.

The names of the officer casualties are : killed, Lieut.-Colonel J. Mortimer, C.M.G., Captain F. Woodcock, Second-Lieutenants G. S. Phillips and W. R. Lowson ; while the wounded were Captain H. Brown, D.S.O., M.C., Lieutenants E. M. Robson and G. Harker, Second-Lieutenants P. H. Sykes, A. G. Winterbottom, C. Martin, C. R. Hurworth, C. H. Dell, W. H. Game, W. Rennison and J. S. Purvis.

Major C. H. Pearce now took over command in place of Colonel Mortimer.

There was renewed fighting during the last week of the month, when the Battalion was called out again, and before on the 29th it was sent back to Mametz Wood to reorganize and refit, four more officers—Second-Lieutenants T. J. Dickson, A. J. L. Ramm, E. A. Lister and I. A. Sleightholme—and seventy other ranks had been wounded while seven men had been killed. For some few days now in the early part of October the Battalion was training at Baizieux, moving then back to Mametz Wood on the 11th and being employed on road-making until the end of the month—a job of work which was not so safe as it sounds, since over sixty casualties were incurred while engaged upon it. The last month of the year the Battalion alternated between Baizieux, Bécourt and Mametz Wood, where it was when the year 1917 opened.

The whole of January was spent in this area, but on the 30th there was a move to Buire-sur-Ancre for training, while in February there were several minor moves—from Buire-sur-Ancre to Morcourt, thence to Bois St. Martin, then to Berny-en-Santerre, thence to Fresnes Wood, and then to Bois St. Martin and Triangle Wood. The latter part of March was passed by the Battalion in comparative quiet—so far, that is, as intensive training permitted—at Bayonvillers, while the month of April up to the 11th spent in Corps Reserve near Arras, after which the 5th Green Howards were sent to the caves east of the town, remaining there some days in support.

On the 29th April the Battalion was sent up to occupy Nepal Trench, and on the 23rd and 24th was engaged with the 50th Division in the operations known as the Second Battle of the Scarpe, being brought forward at 4.45 in the morning of the first day in support of the 4th East Yorkshire Regiment which was attacking, and the 5th Green Howards were used to meet a German counter-attack which had succeeded in forcing our troops back to their original front line. The Battalion held on here until 6 in the evening, when two battalions of the 151st Brigade came up and all three went forward together. This attack was entirely successful and the line gained was held all night. In these operations the losses suffered by the Battalion were again heavy, 3 officers and 16 men being killed or dying of wounds, 3 officers and 118 other ranks were wounded, while 2 officers (later reported killed) and 55 non-commissioned officers and men were missing. The names of the officers were: killed, Captain W. Vause, M.C., Lieutenants J. E. G. Herbert and F. B. Whitehead, Second-Lieutenants W. H. Game and R. E. M. Hofmeyr; wounded, Major H. Brown, D.S.O., M.C., Lieutenants W. Rennison and G. F. Rodgers.

On the 24th the Battalion was relieved by the 2nd Battalion of the Regiment and marched through Arras to Halloy, where it remained in billets until the 1st May, reorganizing and refitting, moved then to Coigneux on transfer to the II. Corps, and was on the 2nd at Ficheux in Corps Reserve for the attack next day by the Third Army, at the Third Battle of the Scarpe. On the 4th the 50th Division was transferred back to the XVIII. Corps and the Battalion came again to Halloy, only to be hurried off to Coigneux on the 17th, the Division now rejoining there the VII. Corps and being held in Corps Reserve for the attack by the 33rd Division on the Hindenburg Line on the 20th May. At the end of this month the Battalion was once more in Chestnut Camp, Coigneux, where a reinforcement of ten officers and seventy-seven other ranks joined.

At the beginning of the first week in June The 5th Green Howards were occupying the front line trenches once more west of Fontaine-les-Croisilles in the right sub-sector, and here on the 26th the Battalion, with the 5th Durham Light Infantry on its left, attacked the German position northwest of Fontaine, the objectives being Rotten Row and certain cross-roads indicated on the map by numbers. The attack was carried out by " A " Company, under Second-Lieutenant E. G. S. Corry, with " D " Company in support, and " C " in reserve in Shaft Trench. The objective was gained at once and several dug-outs in Rotten Row were successfully bombed. " A " Company then dug itself in, making use of an old German trench along the west side of Rotten Row, but the attack had inclined rather too much to the left and the cross-roads were not included in the captures of ground made. When daylight came on the 27th the company found itself completely isolated from any support, these having moved up to the assembly trenches, and at 5 a.m. the enemy attempted to counter-attack from the direction of River Road. This attack was, however, driven off by machine-gun fire and bombs, and " A " Company maintained its position all through the 27th, being relieved at night by a company of the 4th East Yorkshire Regiment.

The company captured four prisoners and one machine gun, but lost Second-Lieutenant E. G. Stewart-Corry and four men killed, eleven wounded and one missing.

On the 10th July the Battalion was up in the sub-sector west of Cherisy, at the Quarry, when Lieutenant-Colonel C. H. Pearce was wounded and Major J. A. R. Thomson took over command ; and on the 19th the enemy, who for some days previously had been showing an unusual activity, suddenly early in the morning put down a heavy barrage on the front and support lines along the whole of the Brigade sector, then attacking at three points, the most westerly of which was at Dead Bosche Sap on the extreme right of the Battalion front. A party of three or four Germans succeeded in penetrating the front line at this point, but they were driven out by the garrison of one of the trench posts and fled, leaving one non-commissioned officer dead in the trench, besides several sacks of bombs which they had abandoned in their flight. The enemy bombardment cost the Battalion fifteen killed and eighteen wounded.

A few days later Second-Lieutenant J. H. E. Winstone was wounded.

From the 1st to the 3rd August the Battalion was in Brigade reserve, from the 4th to the 10th it was about Neuville Vitasse, busy supplying working parties for the line ; then came a spell in the trenches ; finally from the 19th to the end of this month being about the Hindenburg Line providing working parties for tunnelling companies. Here on the 5th September the front was subjected to an enemy gas bombardment, one officer—Second-Lieutenant T. A. Williams—and nineteen other ranks, one of whom died, being affected. Every day here produced a few casualties, and on the 1st October Lieutenant G. S. Bailey and several men were wounded ; but on the 5th there was a move, by Boisleux-au-Mont to Achiet-le-Petit, and then to Miraumont, whence the Battalion proceeded by train to Cassel, spending a few days here and going on by way of Broxelle, Door-naert, Wormhoudt, Provins and Elverdinghe, and then going up on the 26th to the front line near Marsuin Farm with Battalion Headquarters at Egypt House, where almost immediately after arrival Captain G. F. G. Rees and seven men were hit. On the 28th and 29th the casualties were more serious, amounting to seventeen non-commissioned officers and men killed, three officers—Lieutenants J. D. Bryden and H. G. Amis and Second-Lieutenant A. Philips—and fifty-nine other ranks wounded.

On the 10th November the Battalion was at last accorded a period of rest of a rather longer duration than usual, being sent by rail and march route to La Commune, near St. Omer, where it remained until the 2nd December, then went for a few days' training to Zudrove, and then was sent to the neighbourhood of Brandhoek, which was reached on the 10th, being greeted on arrival by a bomb from a German aeroplane, whereby one man was killed and five injured, in addition to twenty transport animals. In fact, the month of December was to prove rather a costly one for The 5th Green Howards, since in the course of it three officers were killed or died of wounds, the result of a direct hit upon " C " Company's Headquarters, nine other ranks were killed, while one officer and thirty-one non-commissioned officers and men were wounded ; the officers who were killed were Lieutenants F. G. Danby and F. Green and Second-Lieutenant W. H. Coles, while Lieutenant T. H. Gaunt was the officer who was wounded.

Christmas Day, 1917, was passed up in the front line, happily without any casualties, while the Battalion saw the old year out in Toronto Camp in the Brandhoek area.

On the 2nd January, 1918, the Battalion was sent for two days to Whitley Camp in the Potijze area, moving on then to the neighbourhood of Steen-voorde, and on the 16th entrained at Godwaersvelde for Serques, near St. Omer, where it was accommodated in billets and where battalion training went on steadily for some ten days, before going to the Potijze area in relief of a Battalion of the 33rd Division. Nothing of any importance occurred in the month of February, during the latter portion of which the 5th Green Howards were again at Serques; but when on the 21st March the great German offensive of this year opened the Battalion had been for the past ten days training at Demuin, where on this day a warning order was received to be prepared to move at four hours' notice.

The actual order was issued at 5.30 p.m. when the Battalion entrained at Guillancourt, arriving at Brie at 5 a.m. on the 22nd and then marching at once to Hancourt. No further movement was made until 1 o'clock in the afternoon, when the 5th Green Howards were sent forward to dig in on a line which had been selected, the 66th Division now withdrawing through the 50th. This position was, however, only maintained until 11 that night, when a line in rear near the cemetery at Vraignes was taken up, with the 4th East Yorkshire on the right, the 8th Durham Light Infantry on the left, and the 4th Green Howards in support in rear. Here the Brigade remained all through the night, receiving orders at 8 on the morning of the 23rd to withdraw along the main Mons *–Brie Road, the 4th Green Howards to cover the retreat to Mons. The Battalion was at this time engaged with the enemy who was enveloping the right flank and withdrawal was not easy, but this was effected, and from Mons to Brie the 5th Green Howards fought a rear-guard action on the north side of the Mons–Brie Road with the 4th East Yorkshire on the right and the 8th Durham Light Infantry on the left. The Somme was crossed at Brie about 3 p.m., the Brigade here passing through the 23rd Brigade of the 8th Division, and, marching on, the Battalion rested for the early part of the night in a quarry near Villers-Carbonnel.

Soon after midnight—at 1 a.m. on the 24th, to be exact—came orders to fall back at once to Belloy-en-Santerre and spend what remained of the night there: this was done and a certain amount of rest was obtained, but at 2 o'clock on the afternoon of this day, the Brigade was directed to move to Marchelpot to reinforce the 8th Division, reporting to the 25th Infantry Brigade. On arrival here, however, the 5th Green Howards

* A small village between Brie and Vraignes in the angle formed by the junction of the Cologne and Somme Rivers: not to be confused with the town of the same name in Flanders.

were impressed by the G.O.C. 24th Brigade and told off to a certain position, filling a gap in the line on the high ground north-east of Licourt and east of the Licourt–Cizancourt Road, with the Northamptonshire Regiment on the right and the 1st Battalion Sherwood Foresters on the left; by about 9.30 p.m. the Battalion was in the position designated, two companies being in the front line and two in support immediately north of the village of Licourt; but very early in the morning of the 25th one of the supporting companies was sent closer up to the front line.

About 9 a.m. one of the battalions from the right was obliged to fall back, whereupon the enemy occupied part of Licourt. The two front-line companies of the 5th Green Howards and those of the Sherwood Foresters, however, maintained their ground, " B " Company of the former, under Lieutenant Hepton, holding on until the end, the officer and many of his men being captured, and only a very few succeeding in effecting their retreat. Then, at about 10 a.m., Battalion Headquarters was established on the Licourt–Villers Carbonnel Road to conform to the situation on the right and a defensive flank was formed, but this unfortunately, but unavoidably, was in the air. Half an hour later the enemy wholly occupied Licourt and enfilade fire caused the Battalion, and the 4th East Yorkshire Regiment beside it, to withdraw and take up a fresh position in rear and to the north-west, the left now being on the St. Christ–Marchelpot Road and the right on the copse on Hill 102. The right was still in the air, but the left was in touch with the Devonshire Regiment, which was some little distance away.

Here the 5th Green Howards and 4th East Yorkshire held their ground from 9 a.m. to 5 p.m., eighty men of the Worcester Regiment, commanded by Captain Thompson, M.C., 5th Green Howards, being sent forward to form a defensive flank facing south on Hill 102.

At 5 in the afternoon both the commanding officers present agreed upon a withdrawal, as the flank was in the air, no orders had been received and repeated demands for ammunition had met with no response; and the 5th Green Howards and 4th East Yorkshire accordingly fell back on Misery, where a staff officer of the 24th Infantry Brigade met the two battalions and ordered them to take up a position along the railway from the Villers Carbonnel–Marchelpot Road crossing northwards. No further orders came to hand, and as it appeared that the enemy was now working round the exposed right flank, the two commanding officers decided upon withdrawing towards Fresnes, taking up a line from Mozaucourt northward on the west side of the road, with the 8th Durham Light Infantry on the right. At 8 in the evening an unsigned order was received from the 24th Brigade to fall back to Ablaincourt, and here the 4th East Yorkshire and the 4th

M

and 5th Battalions of The Green Howards occupied front-line trenches immediately east of the village—in the order as given from north to south. The remains of the 150th Brigade were now formed into one battalion under Colonel Wilkinson of the 4th East Yorkshire.

During the night the G.O.C. 24th Brigade sent for Lieutenant-Colonel Thomson of the Battalion, thanked him for all he and his officers and men had done, and told him he might be required to fight a rear-guard action in the case of further withdrawal being decided upon.

At 8 a.m. on the 26th the enemy again attacked, and the O.C. 2nd Worcestershire Regiment being now in command of the 24th Infantry Brigade, he issued instructions from his H.Q. at Vermandovillers for a general retirement to the Rosières line in echelon of battalions from left to right. This order does not appear to have been thoroughly understood, for, as the left battalion withdrew, one from the extreme right did so also, with the result that there was no little confusion, the withdrawal of the Composite Battalion (150th Brigade) was made very difficult, and the whole of the rear-guard platoon of the 5th Green Howards was either killed or captured.

The retirement continued through Vermandovillers, where the battalions reorganized, and the 150th Brigade Composite Battalion moved across country in artillery formation, taking up a position in support of a line running from the road junction south of Rosières. The retirement was now unmolested except by enemy aircraft, but as night began to come on the enemy advance was reported as approaching by the 8th Durham Light Infantry who were holding the front line.

The night passed quietly, however, except for enemy guns which were in action almost continuously, and there were some casualties from our own guns, one or two of which—one 18-pr. in particular—were firing short. Lieutenant-Colonel Wilkinson, commanding the Composite Battalion, was here wounded, and Lieutenant-Colonel Thomson of the 5th Green Howards assumed command. By 8 on the morning of the 27th the Germans were in possession of Meharicourt and opened on the position with machine guns, finally launching an attack about 7 p.m., but were driven back with heavy casualties. At midnight Colonel Thomson was given verbal orders by the G.O.C. 24th Brigade to retire to trenches immediately in rear of his present position and in front of the Rosières–Vrély Road, from north of Vrély Village to the light railway, the Composite Battalion being distributed in depth. Finally, at 4.30 on the morning of the 28th, there was a conference of commanding officers at the 24th Brigade H.Q. in Rosières, at which the decision when and how to withdraw was left to battalion commanders but the Composite Battalion finally retired, acting as flank guard to the

6th Durham Light Infantry which was falling back to take up a position in the valley south of the Caix–Rosières Road; and eventually, about 11 a.m., the Composite Battalion was in position on the high ground south of Caix, with the 8th Durham Light Infantry on the right, and the 6th Durham Light Infantry still further to the right, the left being in the air. No further orders were received until 4.30 p.m., when a cyclist orderly brought a written message from the 24th Brigade saying, " You will proceed to Moreuil." The Composite Battalion accordingly marched thither *via* Beaucourt and Mezières, and in Moreuil the men at last got some food, and the Battalion then went on to Louvrechy, where in somewhat congested billets—the village being full of French troops—the night was passed.

At 7.30 on the morning of the 29th an order was received from the 50th Division stating that this Division was now in reserve to the 20th, and directing Lieutenant-Colonel Thomson to take his command at once to the wood one mile south of Demuin and there concentrate. Here the Battalion arrived about 11.30 in the morning, took up a position in the wood and there dug in; at 5.30 in the afternoon, however, the French troops who were on the right fell back, and the enemy penetrated into the copse immediately north of Villers-aux-Erables, and also into portions of the village itself, and one company from each of the 4th East Yorkshire and 5th Green Howards, the latter under Lieutenant Crapper, was ordered to take up ground on the east side of the wood. Half an hour later the right flank gave way and Colonel Thomson was directed to launch an immediate counter-attack; one company from each of these battalions was told off, and they were about to move, when the troops on their right were withdrawn and the counter-attack was accordingly cancelled, and *all* the troops here were now ordered to fall back to a point on the Amiens–Roye Road and there dig themselves in.

At about 7 a.m. on the 30th March orders were received from the 60th Infantry Brigade that as the enemy was holding the wood north of Moreuil, Colonel Thomson must establish a standing patrol of an officer and twenty men to guard the right flank, and that in the event of any further withdrawal the Composite Battalion was to take up a position and fight a rear-guard action to cover the safe retreat of the troops across the Luce River; but at this point Lieutenant-Colonel Thomson was hit and handed over command to Captain Pollock, 4th East Yorkshire. Orders to fall back were issued about 8.30 in the morning and the line was drawn back to the Hourges side of the wood immediately south-east of Hourges; but as it was now discovered that a party of the 4th East Yorkshire was still holding out on the north side of the road in the old position, a portion of the Composite Battalion moved south and re-took the copse north-north-west of Villers.

This was about 10 a.m., but during the afternoon, owing to a flanking movement on the right, the Battalion was forced to fall back some six hundred yards, when the enemy again occupied the copse. Then at 7 p.m. the Composite Battalion once more advanced and, in conjunction with the French, counter-attacked and regained possession of the copse, capturing some seventy prisoners and re-establishing the line as it had stood in the morning.

The night of the 30th–31st March passed quietly, and the line was reinforced early on the 31st by something under fifty stragglers who had been collected. About midday the enemy put down a heavy barrage on Domart and Hourges, attacking two hours later on a frontage extending beyond both flanks of the 150th Composite Battalion. On the right the French fell back, thus permitting the enemy to outflank the Battalion and reach the rear of it, but Captain Pollock and all those with him fought desperately until the very last and inflicted severe losses on the enemy. The situation then naturally became somewhat obscure; detachments held on to the high ground north-west of the wood due south of Hourges, but the Germans worked up the valley south of the wood, and then, bringing enfilade fire to bear, caused all parties to withdraw on the 60th Brigade, which was taking up a new line north of the River Luce between Domart and Hangard. At this time two regiments of British cavalry crossed the river and began working forward south of the Amiens–Roye Road; and at about 5 in the afternoon the Composite Battalion, under orders from the H.Q. 60th Brigade, dug in on a line running north-east and south-west through Domart. Later—towards midnight—the Battalion held a line across the spur running out south-east towards the village of Domart on the right of the main Amiens–Roye Road, about three hundred yards short of Domart.

Here on the left, between the 150th Brigade—if so it may be still called —and the main road were troops of the 149th Brigade, but the right flank was still in the air.

The great German offensive of this year did not finally come to an end for some days yet, but the 50th Division had no longer any share in holding it up, for on the 1st April it passed to the reserve and on the evening of this day the 150th Brigade marched to Longeau, then next day to Saleux, and then taking the train for Rue, moved by road and motor-bus *via* Machiel to Locon, where four days were passed in billets.

The losses in the 5th Battalion The Green Howards during the ten days' practically continuous fighting from the 22nd to the 31st had been terribly heavy, amounting to 388 killed, wounded and missing: killed were 3 officers and 22 other ranks, 9 officers and 219 non-commissioned officers and men were wounded, 2 officers and 7 men were wounded and missing, while missing were 2 officers and 124 other ranks. The names of the officers who were killed were Captain C. R. Harworth, Lieutenant H. E. Evans and J. Battye ; wounded were Lieutenant-Colonel J. A. R. Thomson, Captains W. E. E. Garrod and G. Thompson, M.C., Lieutenants E. R. Winser, J. V. Townsend, Second-Lieutenants L. S. Wallgate, C. W. Stoddart, W. G. Morris and C. Crapper ; wounded and missing were Lieutenant A. Hepton and Second-Lieutenant W. N. Pearson, while missing were Lieutenant H. G. Gregory and Second-Lieutenant A. H. Strong.

Training and reorganizing went on at Locon for four days, during which the officers and men of the Composite Battalion rejoined their units so far as this was possible, and stragglers came in ; but early on the morning of the 9th the Battalion was placed under " one hour's notice to move," by reason of the line of the Portuguese Army having been pierced about Le Touret, the operations which then ensued being known as the Battle of the Lys. At 9 o'clock the Brigade moved off to Trou Bayard, where its battalions were to assemble, but the road through Estaires was heavily shelled and was to all intents and purposes impassable ; further, it was learnt that the enemy was already in Laventie, and the Battalion dug in short of this place. At 2 p.m. a short advance was attempted, the 5th Green Howards moving forward in support to the 4th East Yorkshire and taking up a line between the two farms of Bretagne and Quennelle, being entrenched here by 3.25. Towards nightfall, as a gap of some two hundred and fifty yards was found to exist on the left, Captain Parker went up with " A " Company to fill it, linking up with the 4th East Yorkshire on the left and the 5th Durham Light Infantry on the right.

Very early on the morning of the 10th the Battalion moved back, the company under Captain Parker remaining close up in support of the East Yorkshire, but rejoining some half-hour later.

Then at 4.5 a.m. the whole Battalion was moved forward in support of the East Yorkshire, and about 11 o'clock information came to hand that the enemy was over the Lys at Bac St. Maur and was occupying La Boud-relle. Three companies were then at once moved up to form a defensive flank facing east—astride the road—the fourth company being held in support ; but the three advanced companies came under direct and heavy fire from machine guns and light field artillery and suffered some loss ; and the Germans, continuing to advance along the west bank of the Lys, caused the left of the East Yorkshire to give way about the bridge, and the general line then fell back to that held by the three supporting companies of the 5th Green Howards.

This line required modification, as portions of it were driven in by the weight of the attack, but eventually that taken up was held all through the night.

In the early morning of the 11th the enemy attacked the left flank heavily, and, though the battalion on the left of them retired, the companies of the Battalion, holding a sharp salient in the line, maintained their ground till practically surrounded and many were captured, while the wounded had to be left behind, it being impossible to bring them away; those who could do so fell back to a line dug in rear by the 29th Division, with which some of the scattered men of the Battalion remained, while others were collected and placed on a support line which the 50th Division was taking up about Le Crerseobeau. Later again, in consequence of orders received, all men of the 150th Brigade were collected and formed into a very weak battalion under Lieut.-Colonel Thomson and instructed to move to Brigade H.Q. at Vierhouck.

When, however, this Battalion was marching thither, it was stopped by a staff officer and informed that the enemy was in Neuf Berquin, being now directed to form a line parallel to and on the south-east side of the road by which it was moving. This was done, but many casualties were caused by the fire of an enemy field gun. About 7 p.m. fresh orders were received—to hold on till darkness at all costs, and, if unable to maintain the position any longer, to withdraw and retire on Vierhouck, where the 50th Division was forming a line running towards Merville. The position becoming untenable about 8.30 p.m., since both flanks were in the air, Colonel Thomson withdrew as ordered, joining up about 10.30 p.m., the Battalion being rested in some houses for the night.

The 12th was spent in taking up one line after another, the troops now being greatly mixed up, and at night the Battalion was about Château La Motte, where the 50th Division was concentrating; and on the 14th, the 150th Brigade was once more able to organize, each battalion composing it contributing a company to form a 150th Brigade Battalion, first under Lieutenant-Colonel Thomson, 5th Green Howards, and then under Colonel Pike, of the 4th East Yorkshire.

On the 16th this Battalion moved to La Lacque, the 50th Division being now in Corps Reserve.

In the Battle of the Lys, the 5th Green Howards had 25 men killed or died of wounds, Captain F. B. Parker, Second-Lieutenants H. Speight and G. W. Brown and 123 other ranks wounded, while Captain E. M. Robson, M.C., Second-Lieutenants G. H. Lawson, T. A. Williams, W. H. Allis and 155 other ranks were missing, a total of 310 casualties, or a grand total of 698 between the 22nd March and the 12th April!

On the 25th April the 50th Division, under the circumstances described

in the last chapter, was transferred to what was claimed to be a " quiet
sector of the line," moving by train and motor-bus, and, having finally
detrained at Fismes, found itself in the IX. Corps under the Sixth French
Army behind the ridge known as the Chemin des Dames.

When the wholly unexpected German attack was launched against
this position on the 27th May, the 150th Brigade was occupying the
Plateau de Californie (or Craonne Plateau), with the right at the village of
Chevreux and the left at the Piste d'Orléans—a total front of some two
thousand six hundred yards.   The 5th Green Howards and 4th East Yorkshire Regiment were in the front line on right and left respectively, the
4th Green Howards being in divisional reserve at Beaurieux.   The 5th
Green Howards had three companies in front and one in reserve ; but on
warning of an impending attack being received, a reserve company of the
4th East Yorkshire was moved up and placed at the disposal of the O.C.
5th Green Howards.

About 1 a.m. on the 27th the enemy bombardment opened with every
kind and calibre of shell, including gas, heavy casualties were caused in
the forward posts on the plateau, and nearly all rearward communications
were cut within a very short time.   No infantry attack, however, developed
against the 150th Brigade front from the north, but as a result of the
successful advance made by the enemy on the right of the divisional front
and through the 22nd French division on the left, the plateau was enveloped
on both flanks by about 6.30 a.m.   The hostile barrage was maintained
to the last, and many men were in all probability captured before they
could leave their deep dug-outs.

There was no morning mist, but the smoke and dust caused by the
bombardment made observation impossible, and all Colonel Thomson was
able to report was that his H.Q. company was fighting round his command
post and appeared to be surrounded ; the Brigadier decided that no
counter-attack was likely to be successful, and he therefore gave out that
he proposed holding the intermediate line with the 4th Green Howards,
moving his Brigade H.Q. back to a point six hundred yards south of
Craonelle ; this withdrew accordingly about 7 a.m., but on arrival at the
proposed position it was learnt that the 4th Green Howards had been overwhelmed on the Mt. Hermel line and that the enemy was already approaching Craonelle from the west.   All attempts to organize any defence at
this point had then to be abandoned.   The retreat was consequently continued by Fismes, Arcis-le-Ponsart, Romigny and Champlat-Bligny to
Vert-la-Gravelle on the 31st May, where the Brigade—or what was left
of it—was re-formed.

The losses, especially in missing, had been again terribly heavy : nine other ranks only were actually reported killed, while Captain P. D. J. Waters and eleven men were reported wounded; but the "missing" amounted to twenty-five officers and six hundred and thirty-eight non-commissioned officers and men—in all six hundred and eighty-four all ranks! So that within but little more than two short months the 5th Battalion The Green Howards had suffered a total loss of one thousand three hundred and eighty-two officers, non-commissioned officers and men in killed, wounded, and missing!

On the 6th June Major D. J. Ward, M.C., of the 5th Gloucestershire Regiment, arrived to take over command, while towards the end of the month Captain A. Simkins, M.C., Royal Fusiliers, joined as second-in-command: this month raised the roll of casualties by three killed, Lieutenant and Quartermaster P. J. Foord, and nine men wounded; while on the 21st the remnants of the 5th Green Howards were formed into No. 3 Company of the 150th Brigade Composite Battalion, commanded by Colonel Wilkinson, D.S.O., the company containing Lieutenants W. H. Porter, F. W. M. Steggall, H. J. Graves, Second-Lieutenants C. S. Hill, A. W. B. Bentley, J. S. Hanson, and one hundred and fifty-one other ranks.

The latter part of June was spent in training at Broyes, and during the first fortnight of July the Battalion was at Hangest-sur-Somme, Metigny and Caumont, where four officers and thirty-six other ranks were formed into a training cadre and moved to Rouxmesnil Camp, near Dieppe; the officers of the cadre were Lieutenant-Colonel D. J. Ward, M.C., Captains E. R. Saltonstall, M.C., W. H. Porter and Second-Lieutenant C. S. Hill, while six officers and one hundred and seventy-three other ranks were sent down to the Base.

August, September and October were spent at Stella Plage Camp, near Le Touquet, where the heavy losses incurred by the Battalion and the grave difficulties of replacement led, on the 6th November,—only a few days before the end of the war—to the greatly-to-be-regretted demobilization of the 5th Battalion The Green Howards.

6TH BATTALION.
May, 1915, before Embarkation.

Back Row.—Lt. M. B. Lambert ; Lt. N. M. Bruce ; 2nd-Lt. T. W. Rutherford ; 2nd-Lt. M. Y. Simpson ; 2nd-Lt. A. E. Hall ; 2nd-Lt. A. M. Eadon.

Middle Row.—2nd-Lt. E. Frank ; Lt. I. McL. Wilson ; 2nd-Lt. J. F. White ; Lt. W. Appleyard ; Lt. C. H. Dawnay ; Lt. B. Williams, Q.M. ; Lt. E. W. Alcock, R.A.M.C. ; Lt. W. H. Haynes (did not sail) ; 2nd-Lt. S. Morris ; Lt. H. de C. Casley ; Lt. E. M. Worsley ; 2nd-Lt. L. K. Gifford-Wood.

Front Row.—Capt. W. H. Chapman ; Capt. G. A. Heron ; Capt. J. C. Morgan ; Major A. Roberts ; Lt.-Col. E. H. Chapman ; Capt. W. R. Peel ; Major W. B. Shannon ; Capt. H. Chapman ; Capt. R. Randerson.

Sitting—Capt. A. C. T. White ; 2nd-Lt. C. E. Whitworth ; Capt. G. G. Currey.

CHAPTER IX

THE 6TH BATTALION

1914–1915

GALLIPOLI

THE raising of the first of the Service Battalions of The Green Howards is first mentioned in *The Green Howards' Gazette* for September, 1914, in the following terms : " Consequent on the increase of the Army a new battalion is to be added to each regiment of the Line. This battalion of ours will be called the 6th Service Battalion, and it is being raised at Grantham. Major E. H. Chapman, who has been selected for the command of it, is thirty-nine years of age, and has been nearly twenty years in the Regiment. He took part in the Tirah Expedition of 1897–98, for which he wears the medal and two clasps. The only other officer whose appointment to the new Battalion we know of is Lieutenant and Quartermaster B. Williams, who has been specially promoted from Sergeant-Major of the 3rd Battalion. He served as Colour Sergeant of ' B ' Company in the 1st Battalion during the Boer War, and for his services was mentioned in despatches and awarded the Medal for Distinguished Conduct in the Field, as well as the Queen's Medal with six clasps and the King's Medal."

In the Army List for October, 1914 (none was published for the month of September of this year), the following officers are shown with the 6th Battalion : Temporary-Lieutenant-Colonel E. H. Chapman ; Captain J. A. S. Daniell (14th Sikhs) ; Lieutenants G. L. Compton-Smith and F. C. Shelmerdine ; Second-Lieutenants E. M. Worsley, J. Clough, R. Randerson, I. McL. Wilson, W. Appleyard, A. M. Eadon, A. E. Hall, B. Hickson, N. M. Bruce, H. de C. Casley, I. K. Gifford-Wood, W. H. Haynes, G. H. Matthews, K. L. Higgins and G. S. Currey ; Lieutenant and Adjutant H. E. Franklyn and Lieutenant and Quartermaster B. Williams.

The first official mention of the existence of the new unit seems to be contained in Army Order No. 324, published on the 21st August, 1914, wherein His Majesty approved of the addition to the Army of six divisions and Army troops, viz. the 8th, 9th, 10th, 11th, 12th and 13th Divisions; and in an appendix to this Order we find that the 6th (Service) Battalion Alexandra, Princess of Wales's Own (Yorkshire Regiment) (The Green Howards) is included in the 32nd Infantry Brigade of the 11th Northern Division. The Brigade contained also the 9th West Yorkshire, the 6th East Yorkshire and the 6th York and Lancaster Regiments, and was commanded by Brigadier-General H. Haggard, the divisional commander being Major-General F. Hammersley, C.B.

In a later Army Order—No. 382—the 8th Division was re-numbered the 14th, and finally in Army Order No. 389, published on the 14th September, Divisions 9 to 14 inclusive were included in the First New Army commanded by General Sir A. Hunter, G.C.B., G.C.V.O., D.S.O.

Raised in the first instance at Richmond, the Headquarters of the 6th Battalion moved on 5th September to camp at Belton Park, Grantham, whither an advance party had proceeded on the 27th August. "The men," writes a Battalion correspondent, "are a fine, well set-up, hardy lot, mostly miners, and very keen. In many cases they look upon this as the finest holiday they have ever had, in spite of the seven and a half hours —at one time eight hours—of work that they now put in daily; exclusive of lectures and night operations twice a week." By the 10th October the following officers appear to have joined, additional to those mentioned in the October Army List: Major A. Roberts; Captains O. Oakes, W. B. Shannon, J. C. Morgan and C. J. H. Gardner; Lieutenant M. C. K. Rhodes; Second-Lieutenants G. A. Heron, A. C. T. White, W. R. Peel, C. Dawnay and M. B. Lambert.

The Battalion remained in camp at Belton Park until well into the year 1915, the weather being for the most part very wet and the camping ground and neighbourhood very muddy, but by the end of February all ranks were tolerably completely fitted out with the 1914 equipment— made for the most part in the United States. The training of the 6th Green Howards was now so far advanced that it was permitted to take part in brigade, and even divisional training, a privilege which was no doubt duly appreciated. Then on the 25th March definite orders were received to the effect that the Battalion was to leave Grantham on the 5th April, march to Rugby and there entrain for Witley Camp, near Godalming. On this date then the Brigade left Belton Park and, marching by Sralford, Thrussington and Whetstone, reached Rugby on the 8th. "Our march on the Wednesday," we learn, "took us through Leicester, where the Division was accorded a really wonderful reception; all work was suspended and the streets were lined by an enthusiastic and cheering multitude who showered all kinds of gifts on the troops."

On the 9th the Battalion proceeded by train to Witley, where " we find the change of climate and scenery a welcome one, and the open heathland of this district is more satisfactory for manœuvre purposes than the highly cultivated and enclosed country of Lincolnshire. The weather has been delightful during the time we have been here. . . . We are going to the front from here," continues the optimist. " It is not yet absolutely certain where, but all destinations undoubtedly lead to Berlin. . . . The Battalion looks better than ever, if possible. There is a rumour that the last stage of our training will accustom us to live on one biscuit a week, but I do not believe it. It is obvious that this war will be finished by amateur soldiers. My only fear is that we shall win a great victory immediately we enter the fray, and then be disqualified as professionals. Anyhow, after we get there, the war will surely end."

The time had, however, not yet come to proceed overseas, and on the 1st May the 11th Division was inspected by His Majesty the King, who was accompanied by Lord Kitchener, and the following divisional order was subsequently issued :

> " His Majesty the King has desired the G.O.C. to convey to the troops his appreciation of the splendid appearance and steadiness of the men on parade yesterday. His Majesty also remarked on the good condition of the horses. Finally His Majesty said to the G.O.C., ' It has been a very great pleasure to me to see such a splendid body of men, and I desire you to so inform the troops.' "

Towards the end of June the American-made equipment was withdrawn and British-made substituted, and then at long last, at 5 o'clock in the afternoon of the 30th June, " the longed-for and welcome news arrived that we were to go on active service the following evening. Previous to this the men had all been issued with khaki drill and helmets, and all men on leave had been recalled. June 30th and July 1st were a very busy time for company commanders, and one was unable to get through all that has to be done on mobilization, so had to be content with getting through the most important. We left Witley Camp in two parties of half-battalions on the evening of the 1st July and arrived at Liverpool early on Friday morning. A mile march to the docks and we embarked in H.M.T.S. *Aquitania*, the largest ship afloat. She carried our brigade and two battalions of the 34th Brigade—six battalions in all, and in addition the divisional and brigade staffs. We sailed about midday on Saturday, the 3rd July, and were escorted by two destroyers to a point between the Scilly Islands and Cape Ushant at about 5 a.m. on the Sunday morning. Ten minutes after their departure a German submarine fired a torpedo at us, she missed us a few feet astern—her torpedo being diverted by our immense wash. With the exception of those on watch everyone was in his berth, and on the alarm sounding there was some confusion, but not a vestige of panic. Shortly after passing Gibraltar another German submarine was sighted, but luckily for us she was engaged in taking in oil fuel at the time. The Island of Lemnos was reached early on the morning of Saturday, the 10th July, and we disembarked the following day, this place being our advanced base.

"We have learnt since that the Germans intended getting us at one of three places, two being where we sighted the submarines and the third off Alexandria, at which port we were expected."

The following are the names of the officers who landed in Mudros Bay on the 10th July with the 6th Battalion The Green Howards : Lieutenant-Colonel E. H. Chapman ; Majors A. Roberts and W. B. Shannon ; Captains J. C. Morgan, G. A. Heron, H. Chapman, W. R. Peel, (Adjutant) R. Randerson, A. C. T. White, G. G. Currey and W. H. Chapman ; Lieutenants B. Williams, (Quartermaster) E. M. Worsley, W. Appleyard, N. M. Bruce, H. de C. Casley, I. McL. Wilson, A. E. Hall, C. H. Dawnay and M. B. Lambert ; Second-Lieutenants A. M. Eadon, L. K. Gifford-Wood, E. Frank, J. F. White, M. Y. Simpson, C. E. Whitworth, S. Morris and T. W. Rutherford ; Captain the Rev. F. King, chaplain ; and Lieutenant E. W. Adcock, R.A.M.C., medical officer.

Since the units of the Expeditionary Force sent to the Dardanelles under the command of General Sir Ian Hamilton had effected their wonderful landing at Helles on the 25th April, they had remained in possession of the comparatively small coastal strip which their heroism had won for them, and had held on there suffering many casualties from the fire of the Turks, and even more from the climate ; but had found themselves unable, with or without the assistance of the fleet, to push through and seize Constantinople, the possession of which had been the whole aim and object of the expedition.

The troops now on the Gallipoli Peninsula had recently been reinforced, and with the additional troops which had reached him and those which were now on their way, Sir Ian Hamilton should have had available for any fresh operations against the enemy a force of thirteen divisions and five brigades, all, however, a good deal under establishment, and the whole probably consisting of no more than one hundred and ten thousand men. With the help of the new-comers, General Hamilton had now made up his mind to reinforce the Australian and New Zealand Army Corps at Anzac, and to effect a landing in Suvla Bay, proceeding from here to the capture of the hill known as Khoja Chemen Tepe, the main peak of Sari Bair, and so grip the narrows of the Peninsula. In his despatch of the 11th December, 1915, the commander's intentions are thus stated : " (1) To break out with a rush from Anzac and cut off the bulk of the Turkish Army from any land communication with Constantinople; (2) to gain such a command for my artillery as to cut off the bulk of the Turkish Army from sea traffic, whether with Constantinople or with Asia; (3) incidentally, to secure Suvla Bay as a winter base for Anzac and all the troops operating in the northern theatre."

The operations in connection with this plan of campaign were to commence on the 6th August, on which day the Army was distributed as follows :

At Anzac : the Australian and New Zealand Corps, the 13th Division, an Indian Brigade, and a brigade of the 10th Division.

At Helles : the 29th, 42nd, 52nd and Royal Naval Divisions and two French Divisions.

At Mitylene : the 31st and part of the 30th Brigade of the 10th Division.

At Lemnos : the remainder of the 30th Brigade.

At Imbros : the 11th Division.

The 53rd and 54th Divisions, with the last of the expected reinforcements, were then approaching Imbros, and it had been originally intended that these should be there landed and retained as a general reserve, but when these divisions arrived off Mudros Harbour they were hurried on to Suvla Bay without disembarking.

Some account must now be given of the general features of the Peninsula and of the disposition of the British force. The Australians held the edge of the plateau at the top of the long ravines which ran down to the sea. Eastwards the land rises in the uplands of Sari Bair until about a mile and a half north-east of the position the culminating point of Khoja Chemen Tepe is reached. On all sides the ground slopes away from the crest, distant some four miles in a direct line from the waters of the Straits. North and west a jumble of ridges falls towards the Gulf of Saros, ridges broken and confused, sometimes bare and sometimes covered with scrub jungle, and separated by dry nullahs. From a point on the shore of the Gulf of Saros, south of the Fisherman's Hut, a fairly well-marked ridge runs up to the summit of Khoja Chemen Tepe. North of this spur is a watercourse called the Sazli Beit Dere, and a little further north the Chailak Dere. Separating the two is a long spur which leaves the main range just west of Chanuk Bair; north of Chailak Dere is another ridge, and still further north a wide watercourse, the Aghyl Dere. From the Fisherman's Hut the flat ground between the hills and the sea widens north as the coast sweeps round towards Nibrunessi Cape, and beyond it is the half-moon of Suvla or Anafarta Bay, two miles wide, enclosed between Nibrunessi

Cape and that of Suvla Burnu, the north-western extremity of the Gallipoli Peninsula.

The hinterland of Suvla Bay consists of a rectangle of hills lying north of the Azmak Dere watercourse, and connected towards the east with the outflankers of the Khoja Chemen Tepe system.

The north side, lining the Azmak Dere and breaking down into flats two miles from the sea, is a blunt ridge, rising as much as eight hundred feet, of which the western part is Yilghin Burnu, called by our troops Chocolate Hill. The eastern side of the rectangle is a rocky crest, rising in one part to nearly nine hundred feet, and falling shorewards in two well-marked terraces. Between the three sides of the hills, from the eastern terraces to the sea, the ground is nearly flat. Along the edge of Suvla Bay runs a narrow causeway of sand, and immediately behind it is a salt lake, partly dry in summer, but easily converted by rain into a swamp. East of this the hills and flats are patched with farms and low jungle, mostly dwarf oak, and on the edge of the terraces the scrub grows into something of the nature of woodland ; everywhere the plain is seamed by dry watercourses.

Two villages are important points of the Suvla Bay hinterland—Little Anafarta, on the slopes of the south-eastern angle of the enclosing hills, and Big Anafarta, two miles south across the watercourse of the Azmak Dere and just under the northern spurs of Khoja Chemen Tepe. The road connecting the two Anafartas runs south to Boghali Kalessi on the Straits.

The 6th Battalion The Green Howards passed some ten days on the Island of Lemnos, and was then ordered to Imbros, where it arrived on the 20th July, and here rather over a fortnight was spent : " Bivouacked on a sandy plain, very plain and exceedingly sandy, no shelter of any kind, about two miles from Kephalos Harbour. There were a great many troops here, rest camps for the Indians and Australians, also Territorials from Gallipoli. We rested there several weeks, being very hard-worked in the interim, getting on parade at 5.45 a.m. We started doing constant practices of night attacks, including night landings from lighters, which might start at 7 or 8 p.m. and end at any time up to 3 a.m. During this period inoculation for cholera took place, two injections at a week's interval. We were also inspected by General Sir Ian Hamilton, who was very complimentary in his remarks, and said he expected great things from the Division. We were supplied with maps of the district round Smyrna and the coast of Asia Minor."

Of the comparative merits of the new divisions now joining his force General Hamilton says : *

* *Gallipoli Diary*, Vol. I, p. 328.

"Three days ago," this was written on the 24th June, "we asked the War Office to let us know the merits of the three new divisions. The War Office replied placing them in the order 11th, 13th, 10th, and reminding me that the personality of the Commander would be the chief factor for deciding which were to be employed in any particular operation. K. now supplements this by a cable in which he sizes up the Commanders. Hammersley gets a good *chit*, but the phrase, ' he will have to be watched to see that the strain of trench warfare is not too much for him ' is ominous. . . . On these two War Office cables Hammersley and the 11th Division should be for it."

Then after seeing the new divisions at Imbros, General Hamilton wrote in his diary under date of the 4th August : " Have been out seeing the New Army at work. Some of the 11th Division were practising boat work in the evening, and afterwards a brigade started upon a night march into the mountains. The men are fit, although just beginning to be infected with the Eastern Mediterranean stomach trouble : i.e. the so-called cholera, which saved Constantinople from the Bulgarians in the last war." *

The time was now at hand when the new British offensive was to be launched, and for this the plan of attack necessitated four separate actions as here indicated :

(1) A feint was to be made at the head of the Gulf of Saros, as if to take the Bulair Lines in flank and rear ; (2) a strong offensive was to be made in the Helles area against Achi Baba with the hope of attracting the Turkish reserves to Krithia ; (3) the Anzac Corps was to endeavour to gain the heights of Khoja Chemen Tepe and the seaward ridges ; (4) a simultaneous and new landing was to be effected in Suvla Bay. If the Anafarta Hills could be seized and the right of the Suvla Bay force linked up with the left of the Australians, the British would hold the central crest of the uplands running through the western end of the Peninsula, cutting the Turkish communications and leading to the capture of the Achi Baba and the Pasha Dagh tableland.

On the eve of the operations General Sir Ian Hamilton issued the following order :

"Soldiers of the Old Army and the New !
"Some of you have already won imperishable renown at our first landing, or have since built up our footholds upon the Peninsula, yard by yard, with deeds of heroism and endurance. Others have arrived just in time to take part in our next great fight against Germany and Turkey, the would-be oppressors of the human race.

* *Ibid.,* Vol. II, p. 49.

" You, Veterans, are about to add fresh lustre to your arms. Happen what may, so much is certain.

" As to you, Soldiers of the New Formations, you are privileged indeed to have the chance vouchsafed you of playing a decisive part in events which may herald the birth of a new and happier world. You stand for the great cause of Freedom. In the hour of trial remember this, and the faith that is in you will bring you victoriously through."

On the 6th August the forces at Helles and at Anzac opened the attack ; the former were so far successful that they distracted the attention of the enemy from the main operations in the north, while the Australians, after severe fighting and many losses, secured touch with the right wing of the Suvla Bay troops at Susuk Kuyu on the Azmak Dere on the 12th August.

The force intended to land at and operate landwards from Suvla Bay was in the first instance composed of the 10th, 11th, 53rd and 54th Divisions, composing the IX. Corps, commanded by Lieutenant-General Sir F. W. Stopford, and for these three landing-places had been selected : " A," north of the Salt Lake, and " B " and " C " to the south-west of it ; and we may now follow the account of the events of these days as given by an officer who took part in them with the 6th Battalion The Green Howards.

" Suddenly, about 10.30 on the morning of the 6th, company commanders were told that the move was coming that day. There was an officers' conference at 2.30 ; maps were supplied to us of the Suvla Bay district, and the Colonel issued orders for the Battalion's action. ' A,' ' B ' and ' C ' Companies, under Major Roberts, second-in-command, were to land at the beach south of the Salt Lake, proceed up the beach about one hundred yards and form line ; then to wheel half-left, which would bring us north, and attack the hill Lala Baba. The orders were—no loading, bayonet only. ' D ' Company were to be in a separate lighter with Headquarters, and were to picquet the south end of the Salt Lake. The orders for the Brigade were to move north of Lala Baba along the spit of land by the sea, move east round Salt Lake to a certain point, then turn south to Ali Bey Chessun. It was not known if the Salt Lake contained water at this time of the year. The men carried two days' iron rations, which they were told would have to last four, two empty sandbags, and, of course, full water-bottles, these being filled half an hour before we moved out. Instructions were given that, as it was not known when they could be refilled, no water was to be used during the night. The men also carried two hundred and twenty rounds of ammunition. We travelled exceedingly light, leaving our packs and wearing a haversack on the shoulders. Everyone had a white patch sewn on the corner of his haversack and wore two white armbands, also a little triangular piece of tin cut from a biscuit box, tied on to the corner of the haversack. This had been found very effective in a line of infantry attacking hills, as it shows up clearly like a heliograph, and enables the gunners to support an attack very close to the enemy.

"We marched out at a quarter to four and were loaded on to two lighters which were towed by destroyers, these also being packed with troops. We were towed from the bow of the destroyer, steering ourselves. The lighter too had a little engine of its own which can do about six miles an hour. It was an exceedingly dark night, almost pitch black. As we neared the Peninsula we travelled slower and slower, eventually creeping along. There were searchlights moving from the direction of Achi Baba; two of these seemed to pick us up."

The three brigades of the 11th Division were to land and move forward as follows : the 32nd Brigade was to land at Suvla Point and then, moving north of the Salt Lake, take Yilghin Burnu and the high ground north and east of it. The 33rd Brigade was to land at a point marked " C," and while two battalions dug in on a line from the Salt Lake to the sea, the other two were to follow the 32nd Brigade. The 34th Brigade, landing at a point marked " P.P.," was to advance on the left of the 32nd Brigade.

"We had been told by the Colonel that our Brigade was covering the landing and the 6th Yorkshire was covering the Brigade ; so that the Yorkshire Brigade in that respect had been honoured by selection. As we neared the shore under our own engines we were greeted with a burst of rifle fire. 'C' Company had received certain separate instructions; they were on the left flank of the line, the companies* being disposed—'A' centre, 'B' right flank, and 'C' left. 'C' Company was responsible for taking the small hill, marked 20 on the map, near the cape opposite the Salt Lake, also for the duty of clearing that little cape of the enemy, it being expected that a signal post would be situated there.

"Owing to the landing being effected under fire we did not act altogether according to the programme. We could only get the men off the lighters in file, mostly in single file. The officers landed first and marshalled the men as they came off. As they moved forward from the seashore they were immediately engulfed in the darkness of the night, it being impossible to see a body of troops at a few yards' distance. When about twenty-five men of 'C' Company had disembarked, Lieutenant Lambert came back and said they were ready to move off. Lambert then returned to his company and I did not see him again. The two companies must have moved off without waiting for us, and it seemed to me that they may have

* " A " Company, Captain Morgan ; " B," Captain Heron ; " C," Major Shannon ; " D," Captain Chapman.

been drawn by the fire which was slightly to our right when we moved north. When our company had disembarked and had been put in line facing north with flank platoons in fours, we moved north, the left flank having instructions to keep touch with the sea.

" We came to Hill 20, a low ridge but very rocky and very steep, and the part which I climbed necessitated the aid of hands as well as of feet. On this we found a good Turkish trench which we occupied without trouble. I then moved up and down the company—firing going on all the time on our right flank—and spoke to the officers and also to Company-Sergeant-Major Simpson. No. 10 Platoon was on the right flank as I had given them orders to clear the little Cape. I saw Lieutenant Appleyard marshal this platoon and proceed to his allotted work. There were two little rises marked on the map down to the Cape. I ordered him to rush them both, bayonet everybody he found there (as I did not want any prisoners at that time of night) and smash up the signalling apparatus, if any, cut the wires, etc., and rejoin me on Hill 20. We then waited a short time, during which I received a message from Lieutenant Appleyard that he was at the bottom of the first hill and asking for No. 11 Platoon. As I had not expected there would be more than a score of men at the signalling post, I sent orders to carry on with No. 10 Platoon only. Just then I heard a heavy burst of rifle firing to our front and saw a red flare burning on the crest of Lala Baba. The crest showed up clearly against the sky-line, it being the only thing one could distinguish. I heard a faint cheer also, but did not hear any indication of complete success. I therefore ordered the company, less one platoon, to advance. We halted before we got quite to the base of the hill, and I gave instructions to Lieutenant Worsley to take our right flank and endeavour to keep the line complete. Lieutenant Wilson was on the left flank and I moved about the centre.

" Captain A. C. T. White had been left at Imbros sick, Lieutenant A. M. Eadon also sick, and Lieutenant C. Dawnay, reserve machine-gun officer, were left as first reinforcement with 160 men." Disembarking strength of the Battalion was 25 officers and 750 other ranks.

" On arriving at the base of Lala Baba I ordered a charge and we ran up the hill. About three-quarters of the way up we came upon a Turkish trench, very narrow and flush with the ground. We ran over this and the enemy fired into our rear, firing going on at this time from several directions. I shouted out that the Yorkshire Regiment was coming, in order to avoid running into our own people. We ran on and about twelve paces further on, as far as I can judge, came to another trench ; this we also crossed and again were fired into from the rear. I ordered the company to jump back into the second trench, and we got into this, which was so narrow that it

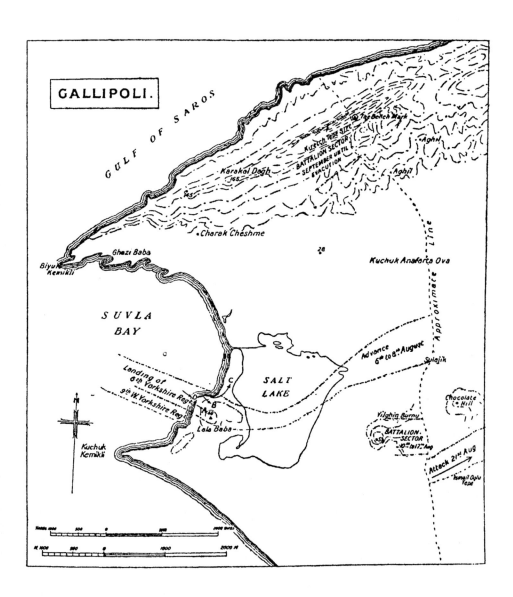

GALLIPOLI.

GULF OF SAROS

The Bench Mark

Kiretch Tepe SITE
BATTALION SECTOR.
SEPTEMBER UNTIL
EVACUTION

Aghn

Karakol Dagh
165

Aghil

165

Charak Cheshme

28

Kuchuk Anaforta Ova

Ghazi Baba

Biyuk
Kemikli

SUVLA
BAY

Advance
6th to 8th August

Sulajik

Approximate Line

Landing of
6th Yorkshire Reg.

9th W. Yorkshire Reg.

C

SALT
LAKE

Chocolate
Hill

B

Yilghin Burnu

Lala Baba

BATTALION.
SECTOR
10th to 17th Aug

Kuchuk
Kemikli

Attack 21st Aug

Ismail Oglu
Tepe

179

was quite impossible for one man to pass another, or even to walk up it unless he moved sideways ; another difficulty was that if there were any wounded or dead men in the bottom of the trench it was impossible to avoid treading on them in passing. There was a little communication trench running from right to left behind me, and whenever I shouted an order a Turk, who appeared to be in this trench, fired at me from a distance of apparently five or ten yards. One of our men on my left was sitting on a prisoner, and there were four wounded or dead men just in the bottom of the trench. I chucked out several Turkish rifles, in case they were shamming, and took a clip from one of them which I brought home as my sole trophy. I had some difficulty in getting anybody to fire down the communication trench in order to quiet the enterprising Turk, who was endeavouring to pot me with great regularity, but eventually got him shot. We had at this time not picked up any of the remainder of the Battalion, so far as I could ascertain. I therefore ordered another charge over the crest of the hill which was just in front of us, and we ran on shouting that the Yorkshires were coming.

" A little way down the reverse slope we came to some groups of men, several of whom were lying about apparently awaiting orders, and one group on the left was ' scrapping ' with some Turks in a trench a few yards distant from them. In response to shouting I got an answer from two directions and picked up Lieutenant Whitworth and Second-Lieutenant Simpson. These were all the officers then present. I formed such of the Battalion as could be collected into a line facing north, and we charged down to the base of the hill facing the further beach—afterwards known as ' A ' Beach—where another brigade was to land—the 34th. I expected to find a Turkish trench commanding this beach and gave orders to occupy it when we came across it, which we duly did ; and I instructed Lieutenant Whitworth with his platoon to ' mop up ' round the crest of the hill generally, and clear out any Turks who might still be lurking there. It was so dark that it was impossible to see if the ground was clear or not, and the enemy, having the advantage of knowing the ground, would of course slip about out of our way. I heard Lieutenant Whitworth encouraging his men round the crest of the hill. Second-Lieutenant Simpson was very lame, having fallen down a ten-foot trench and hurt his back, and could only hobble along. I then heard that Major Roberts was wounded and that the Colonel was killed.

" I sent back a message at 12 o'clock " (midnight) " to the Brigadier to say that the Yorkshire Regiment had taken Lala Baba and occupied the trenches on the base of the north side commanding the further beach, and that we had lost practically all our officers. A little later we heard a battalion coming up the crest of the hill. We waited for them to join us at the base of the hill, but they did not do so. I went half-way up the hill and found that it was the West Yorkshire and shouted to them to come down as the Yorkshire Regiment was at the base of the hill; I directed them to our right flank, where they fell in between ourselves and the Salt Lake. At about 2.15 or 2.30 a.m." (on the 8th August) " the Brigadier arrived with the remaining battalions of the Brigade and they lay down close to our rear. I reported to the Brigadier and asked him if he had received the written message I had sent back by an orderly, to which he replied, ' No.' I heard afterwards the man had had his helmet shot off as he was going back, delivered his message to the Division, and was detained there as an orderly. I acquainted the Brigadier with the fact that we were only 2½ officers and that we were unable to continue in advance of the Brigade. At this time I had no idea what losses we had suffered in the ranks, but so far as my own company was concerned I had no officers, no quartermaster-sergeant and no company-sergeant-major. Later I learnt that Lieutenant Wilson was bayoneted and Lieutenant Worsley shot through the lungs. We received orders to follow in support of the Brigade, which advanced, about 2.30 or 2.45 a.m., north along the sandy spit."

At 2.12 a.m. this day General Stopford, commanding the IX. Corps, had sent off the following message to General Sir Ian Hamilton, then at Imbros: " As far as can be ascertained 33rd Brigade hold line the sea about 91.I.9. to Suvla east corner of Salt Lake to Lala Baba inclusive. North of Salt Lake 31st and 32nd Brigades extended east of Azmak 117 U. preparatory. Brigade advancing, having followed retreating enemy towards line diagonally across 117 X. and 117 D. One battalion, latter Brigade, occupy high ground about square 135 X."

" As the Brigade moved north," to continue the Battalion account of this day's happenings, " we were mixed up with portions of the 34th Brigade, whose lighters had grounded before they reached the shore; those getting ashore had therefore to wade, the lighters being unable to return and bring the rest off the destroyers. The 32nd Brigade therefore received orders to halt, lie down, and let the 34th Brigade get clear. This never occurred, as portions of them kept landing in boats belonging to the ships. While we were waiting, as the Battalion seemed somewhat small, we went back to see if we had got them all up from the Lala Baba trenches. It was naturally very difficult to handle the men with only Whitworth and myself able to run about. We got some men up. . . . We found one telephone wire in our final trench on Lala Baba and cut it, and we also sent back a few prisoners, but not very many. I heard later that quite a few, who had been lying *perdu* meanwhile, surrendered as it became light. When we had got what was left of the Battalion together I found that the Brigade had gone on; and we seemed to be with the Northumberland Fusiliers and Lancashire Fusiliers.* I heard that the Brigade had crossed the Salt Lake, so started off in that direction.

"We moved in lines of platoons in fours. The enemy were using shrapnel. The Salt Lake was more or less dry; you could walk across it, and we came to the bank on the east side, which would be its boundary when full. There was a disposition on the part of the troops to occupy this, so, as we were very short of officers and I thought it would be difficult to get a move on if we once halted, I ran up the bank and called to the Battalion to advance; it was still fairly dark at this time. Just over the crest of the bank troops were grouped in an irregular line forming clumps of men, the units seeming to be much mixed. The country was plain, with scrub patches and occasional trees. The hills east seemed to be about a couple of miles distant, and those to the north about half or three-quarters of a mile. I tried to get the men in my vicinity to keep the advance going, as, although there was a fairly heavy rifle fire, like most night firing much of it was high and the shrapnel was also badly timed and was bursting high. The high explosive was generally carrying on to the beaches. I saw Lieutenant Dutton of the West Yorks here, and we got quite a move on at this time, occasionally getting a steady double, but there was not sufficient order.

"A fairly heavy enfilade fire was coming from the hills north. I moved along to the left flank, thinking that if we could get up the nearer hills first, we could sweep along these and stop the enfilade fire, bring the left flank forward and charge in a sort of half-moon. I found on the left flank a thin line of men with some non-commissioned officers, but the line was ragged. I pushed them up level and, walking down to the extreme left flank, I found Captain Lupton of the West Yorks and ordered him to advance in section rushes from the left, he leading the first section, and I would push the rest up to him. . . . In this manner we got quite close to the foot of the hills—about hundred and fifty to two hundred yards I should judge— but had then become separated from the main body."

At this time the narrator was seriously wounded by shrapnel and had to fall to the rear, and his account of this day's happenings consequently comes to an end.

The losses in the 6th Battalion The Green Howards, particularly in officers, had been very heavy, 16 officers and about 250 other ranks being killed and wounded; killed were Lieutenant-Colonel E. H. Chapman, Captains J. C. Morgan, W. Chapman and R. Randerson, Lieutenants H. de C. Casley, N. M. Bruce and I. McL. Wilson, Second-Lieutenants

* Of the 34th Brigade.

E. Frank and J. F. White, while Major A. Roberts died of his wounds;
wounded were Captains G. A. Heron and W. R. Peel, Lieutenants C. H.
Dawnay and E. M. Worsley, and Second-Lieutenant M. Y. Simpson. Then
three company-sergeant-majors were killed, viz. Wright of " A," Simpson
of " C " and Holcom of " D " Company, while as the Regimental-Sergeant-
Major, W. Mann, was wounded, the whole of the Battalion Headquarters
had been " knocked out " within an hour of the landing.

At 10.50 a.m. this day General Hamilton at Imbros received the following message from General Stopford at Suvla : " Approximate position of
troops under General Hammersley this morning. Two battalions 33rd
Brigade from sea to south-east corner of Salt Lake ; will be moved forward
shortly to connect if possible with Anzac troops. Two battalions 33rd
holding Yilghin Burnu. Position of hill 500 yards east Yilghin Burnu not
yet certain. From Yilghin Burnu 31st Brigade holds line through Baka
Baba cross-roads, thence north to about 118.0.2. 32nd and 34th Brigades
ordered forward from Hill 10 where they spent night to line 118 M.R.W.
to fill gap with 10th Division. Detailed information of 10th Division not
yet definite ; will report later. Consider Major-General Hammersley and
troops under him deserve great credit for result attained against strenuous
opposition and great difficulty."

During the 7th, as is common knowledge, the whole Corps remained
quiescent, beyond that about midday the 6th Green Howards took up an
outpost position on Hill 10 ; but no doubt owing in some degree to the
Brigade Commander, Brigadier-General Haggard, having been severely
wounded, reorganization in the units of the Brigade seems to have been
slow. At 10 on the morning of the 8th, however, the Battalion was sent
forward to a position between Hill 53 and Sulajik, and on this day and the
next was in action some two miles inland and a mile to the north of Scimitar
Hill ; this hill was, however, never taken, though one battalion of the
11th Division, the 6th East Yorkshire, advanced past Anafarta Sagir to
Tekke Tepe.

On the night of the 9th the reinforcements were landed which had been
left at Imbros under Captain White, and he now assumed command, but
the Battalion remained in the trenches all the 10th, having Second-
Lieutenant S. Morris killed and incurring five other casualties ; finally
withdrawing on the night of the 11th–12th under heavy fire and by small
parties and assembling on the cliff due west of Lala Baba, where reorganization was begun. Nothing in the way of training could, however, be
attempted since the companies were, owing to shell fire, confined to a strip
of beach twenty yards in width immediately below the cliff, but ammunition
was replenished and platoons were reorganized ; and on the evening of the

12th the Battalion again moved forward to the fire trenches on the east slopes of Hill 50, where the front line lay in the valley while the Turks held the crest of Hill 70, some six hundred yards distant only.

The 11th Division now remained comparatively inactive for some days while Sir Ian Hamilton was maturing his plans for a fresh attack upon the Turkish positions in this part of the Peninsula ; " with a little sniping and patrolling by night," writes an officer of the 6th Green Howards, " we lived a life quite like the trench existence we later experienced in France. The drawbacks were the heat, the want of water, the flies—daily increasing —and the dry rations. The want of water had a great influence on the ultimate failure ; it reduced strength and caused men to give up attempts that they would have carried out in a cooler climate ; the wells were known and sniping guns were trained on them. The most famous character in the Battalion—Sergeant Bayge—went out against orders to fetch water from an open well ; we watched him draw his water, but a shrapnel burst over him and wounded him badly. In the first few days snipers hidden in trees played the same game on us."

On the 19th Major M. Wood, of the 9th West Yorkshire Regiment, assumed command of the Battalion, and on the 20th, being again in the line to the south of Hill 50, orders for the forthcoming attack were that evening issued : the 53rd and 54th Divisions were to hold the enemy from Sulajik to Keretch Tepe Sirt, while the 11th and 29th Divisions were to storm Ismail Oglu Tepe, two brigades of the 10th Division and the Mounted Division being held in reserve. " My special object," so Sir Ian has told us, " was the hill which forms the south-west corner of the Anafarta Sagir Spur. Ismail Oglu Tepe, as it is called, forms a strong natural barrier against an invader from the Ægean who might wish to march direct against the Anafartas." Further, in accounting for the comparative failure of the enterprise the General states that the 32nd and 34th, the leading brigades of the 11th Division, lost direction and moved north-east instead of east, while the 33rd Brigade, following in support, not only fell into the same error, but became divided, with the result that the attack by the 29th Division on the left of the 11th, directed upon Scimitar Hill, failed equally, the whole force being obliged to fall back to the original position under cover of night.

The orders were that the 32nd Brigade was to attack Hill W. on the east of Ismail Oglu Tepe, where if successful it was to dig in while the 33rd Brigade passed through and captured Hill 101.

General Hamilton has thus described the hill which was to be stormed by the 11th and 29th Divisions : " The hill rises three hundred and fifty feet from the plain, with steep spurs jutting out to the west and south-west, the whole of it covered with dense holly-oak scrub, so nearly impenetrable that it breaks up an advance and forces troops to move in single file along goat-tracks between the bushes."

The following account is from the pen of one of the few officers of the Battalion who came out of action alive : " On our front the first Turkish line was parallel to ours and about four hundred yards away ; the second, eight hundred yards distant, was at the base of Ismail Oglu Tepe, a hill some three hundred feet high.   Between lay fields thick with hedges, bushes and cultivation, but with no vestige of cover except an occasional shallow drainage ditch some 18 inches deep.

" At 3 p.m. the bombardment opened, it looked very grand and we were cheered by the imposing sight, but we found out afterwards that the flat trajectory of the naval guns had done no damage to the Turkish trenches, which were deep and well concealed.   At 3.30 we went over, advancing on a compass bearing of somewhere about 70° magnetic, and, officers being scarce, we had only one—Gifford-Wood—with a small party by which we were to take direction.   They must have been shot down early.   The official despatch attributes some of the failure to the loss of direction in our part of the line ; I suppose that is true, but I cannot imagine now how direction could have been kept.   The shrapnel fire was heavy, the enemy machine guns had a clear target, the ground was intersected with low hedges at all angles and the men conformed to these, while the officer-casualties were heavy," all the officers who landed with the Battalion having been killed or wounded within the first fourteen days.

" Company-Sergeant-Major Green and about one hundred men got into the first Turkish line on the right ; I got in on the left in the valley that runs north-east towards Hill 70, but I could only find wounded men. I went on a little up a communication trench, could find no one in the space between the two lines, came out into the open and was immediately hit twice in the leg by a burst of machine-gun fire.   I got back by the way I had come and was eventually hit in the knee-cap by shrapnel, and for the rest of the day had a good view of the proceedings from behind a fragment of stone-wall.   On the left the Yeomanry Division were doing their very fine charge, dismounted, to Hill 70—then the thick scrub caught fire and their chance was over.   On our front and to the right was the weak link ; there could be no movement over the flat plain that was not enfiladed from north and south.   The parties who were in the front line—I believe it had been thinly occupied of set purpose—could not get on or organize owing to the machine-gun fire ; and the final attack was over by 4 p.m.

" Sergeant-Major Green and his party stayed out until the next day, but being without orders or reinforcements came back to our lines on the morning of the 22nd.

" I think some mention should be made of Captain B. Williams, the quartermaster ; commissioned at the outbreak of the war, he was in command of the Battalion for a short time at the end of August, 1915, and went to Egypt, France and North Russia with it.   I am certain that never, except for a few days on the Somme when the front line was unapproachable, did he fail to see the rations into the hands of companies throughout the whole war.   His adventures at Suvla when, not knowing a word of Hindustani, he brought up a convoy of native drivers with pack mules to the front line, are a story in themselves.   Once he took them into the Turkish lines and had to sort out the Indian from the Turk."

When on the 22nd August the Battalion moved back to the beach in reserve it was only 285 strong and had sustained the following casualties among the officers :   killed, Captain G. G. Currey, Second-Lieutenants T. W. Rutherford and W. Appleyard ; wounded, Major M. Wood, Captain A. C. T. White, Lieutenant A. E. Hall,* Second-Lieutenants A. M. Eadon,* L. K. Gifford-Wood,* and C. E. Whitworth.

The 6th Green Howards were now formed into a composite battalion with the 8th Battalion West Riding Regiment under Captain Fletcher, and while taking their full share of trench duty, occupied the time spent in rear in reorganizing and in assimilating the large reinforcements in officers and other ranks which joined for duty during the month of September, the majority of these from the 3rd and 11th Battalions of the Regiment.   These reinforcements amounted in other ranks to 788 with 11 officers—Captain Tyrrell, Lieutenant K. Hutchence, Second-Lieutenants A. H. B. Shipley, H. Bowman, R. A. Law, E. A. Martin, J. Huggins, W. A. Bond, H. T. Holdstock, W. A. Boot and B. S. Jennings.

The diaries for September and October contain little more than the repeated statement, " Nothing to report," but at any rate several more officers joined the Battalion, now for the greater part of the time in the vicinity of the Karakol Dagh :   Lieutenant J. A. Groves, Second-Lieutenants O. S. Melhado, H. S. Oppe, J. W. Walker, W. A. Kirkwood and F. E. Briscoe ; but casualties went on steadily mounting up, and young Jennings, who only joined on the 29th September, died of wounds on the 7th November, and Oppe, joining on the 10th October, was killed by a sniper on the 5th of the following month.

By this time the military authorities in the United Kingdom, realizing the costly nature of the operations in Gallipoli, and the difficulty of pro-viding adequate reinforcements, having due regard to the claims of other war-theatres, had decided upon the evacuation of the Peninsula.   On the 16th October Lord Kitchener cabled to Sir Ian Hamilton to return home

* Since presumed killed.

in order that the War Cabinet might have the benefit of his views on the situation, and informing him that General Sir Charles Monro had been appointed to take command in his place. On the 17th General Hamilton issued the following farewell order to his troops:

> " On handing over the command of the Mediterranean Expeditionary Force to General Sir C. C. Monro, the Commander-in-Chief wishes to say a few farewell words to the Allied troops with many of whom he has now for so long been associated.
>
> " First, he would like them to know his deep sense of the honour it has been to command so fine an Army in one of the most arduous and difficult campaigns which has ever been undertaken; secondly, he must express to them his admiration of the noble response which they have invariably given to the calls he has made upon them. No risk has been too desperate, no sacrifice too great.
>
> " Sir Ian Hamilton thanks all ranks, from generals to private soldiers, for the wonderful way they have seconded his efforts to lead them towards that decisive victory, which, under their new Chief, he has the most implicit confidence they will achieve."

General Monro arrived on the Peninsula on the 30th October, reported strongly against continuing the struggle and urged early and complete evacuation; and his views being accepted by Lord Kitchener, who arrived a few days later, the necessary orders for withdrawal were issued in the early part of November. These could not, of course, be at once given effect to, for there was very much to be done and many arrangements to be made; and at Suvla and Anzac, which were to be first evacuated, there were over eighty thousand men with guns, horses and mules and an abundance of stores of all kinds, all to be brought away from open beaches in the face of a very brave and resourceful enemy, whose trenches in some places were no more than twenty yards distant from those of the British.

Late in November Second-Lieutenant Kirkwood was killed and Lieutenant Melhado was wounded, while eight officers reported themselves for duty, the majority of these from the 11th Battalion : Lieutenant J. L. James; Second-Lieutenants T. R. Brown, B. Stott, H. C. Hurst, C. L. Bayliss, C. E. Hurst, J. F. Faithfull and I. C. MacFarlane; also fifty other ranks. Then on the 17th there was very heavy rain, flooding the trenches and breaking down the parapets, followed a week later by a blizzard of great severity, many men dying of exposure at their posts and some ten thousand sick having to be evacuated from the Peninsula. On one day twenty-two men of the Battalion were sent to hospital suffering from frostbite.

On the 30th November a message was circulated by the Corps Commander, now Lieutenant-General Byng, " congratulating all ranks on their good work and determination under very trying weather conditions in the trenches."

At the time when the decision to evacuate the Gallipoli Peninsula was arrived at, there were five divisions at Suvla—the 11th, 13th, 29th and 53rd, and the Mounted Division, but the 29th and 53rd were almost at once brought round to Helles, so that on the date—the 10th December—when the evacuation at Suvla actually commenced there were only three divisions remaining to be embarked.

" In the rear of the front line trenches at Suvla the General Officer Commanding IX. Corps broke up his area into two sections, divided roughly by the Salt Lake. In the Southern Section a defensive line had been prepared from the Salt Lake to the Sea and Lala Baba had been prepared for defence, on the left the second line ran from Karakol Dagh through Hill 10 to the Salt Lake. These lines were only to be held in case of emergency —the principle governing withdrawal being that the troops should proceed direct from the trenches to the distributing centres near the Beach, and that no intermediate positions should be occupied except in case of necessity." *

From the 10th to the 18th December the withdrawal proceeded gradually until by the latter date the garrisons had been reduced to the numbers determined upon.

On the 14th Second-Lieutenant W. A. Boot, 1 sergeant and 1 private left as an advance party to take over a camp at Imbros, and these were followed on the 18th by 5 officers—Lieutenants B. Williams, quartermaster, J. W. Walker, J. L. James and J. J. Taylor and Second-Lieutenant T. R. Brown, and 491 other ranks ; on the next day the actual evacuation of the positions began, Lieutenant J. A. Groves, Second-Lieutenants I. C. Mac-Farlane and R. B. Bingham and 121 men moving off *via* Oxford Circus to the Beach ; at 10 p.m. Captains J. R. Earle and W. R. Peel and Lieutenant R. J. Aherne, R.A.M.C., with 102 other ranks from Headquarters and Green Lane followed to the Beach, being joined *en route* by Major H. Chapman and 1 private ; and at midnight Second-Lieutenant L. A. Gordon and 14 machine gunners also proceeded to the place of embarkation.

The last party of The 6th Green Howards—Captain N. P. Shepherd-Turneham, Lieutenant F. E. Briscoe, Second-Lieutenants R. A. Law, H. Bowman, H. C. Hurst and H. A. R. Biziou, and 107 non-commissioned officers and men—fell in at 1.30 a.m. on the 20th and also made for the shore, and by 5.30 a.m. on the 20th the last man had left the trenches at Suvla. Later in this day the whole Battalion had disembarked at Imbros.

* General Monro's despatch of the 9th March, 1916.

General Sir Charles Monro issued the following appreciative order on the manner and successful conduct of the evacuation of the Peninsula :

" The arrangements made for withdrawal and for keeping the enemy in ignorance of the operation which was taking place, could not have been improved. The General Officer Commanding the Dardanelles Army, and the General Officer Commanding the Australian and New Zealand and IX. Army Corps, may pride themselves on an achievement without parallel in the annals of war.

" The Army Corps staffs, divisional and subordinate commanders and their staffs, and the naval and military beach staffs, proved themselves more than equal to the most difficult task which could have been thrown upon them. Regimental officers and men carried out, without a hitch, the most trying operation which soldiers can be called upon to undertake —a withdrawal in the face of the enemy—in a manner reflecting the highest credit on the discipline and soldierly qualities of the troops.

" It is no exaggeration to call this achievement one without parallel. To disengage and to withdraw from a bold and active enemy is the most difficult of all military operations ; and in this case the withdrawal was effected by surprise, with the opposing forces at close grips—in many cases within a few yards of each other. Such an operation when succeeded by a re-embarkation from an open beach, is one for which military history contains no precedent.

" During the past months the troops of Great Britain and Ireland, Australia and New Zealand, Newfoundland and India, fighting side by side, have invariably proved their superiority over the enemy, have contained the best fighting troops in the Ottoman Army in their front, and have prevented the Germans from employing their Turkish Allies against us elsewhere.

" No soldier relishes undertaking a withdrawal from before the enemy. It is hard to leave behind the graves of good comrades, and to relinquish positions so hardly won and so gallantly maintained as those we have left. But all ranks in the Dardanelles Army will realize that in this matter they were but carrying out the orders of His Majesty's Government, so that they might in due course be more usefully employed in fighting elsewhere for their King, their Country and the Empire.

" There is only one consideration—what is best for the furtherance of the common cause. In that spirit the withdrawal was carried out, and in that spirit the Australian and New Zealand and the IX. Army Corps have proved, and will continue to prove, themselves second to none as soldiers of the Empire."

CHAPTER X

THE 6ᵀᴴ BATTALION

1916–1919

EGYPT—FRANCE. THE FIRST BATTLE OF THE SOMME. THE BATTLE
OF MESSINES. THE THIRD BATTLE OF YPRES.
NORTH RUSSIA

THE 6th Battalion The Green Howards remained at Imbros throughout the month of January, 1916, and here Captain W. R. Peel assumed command in place of Major H. Chapman, who was admitted to hospital. On the 12th a draft joined from Mudros —Major C. R. White, Second-Lieutenants A. H. B. Shipley and R. S. Butterfield, and 49 other ranks—Major White then relieving Captain Peel. On the 21st and 26th Lieutenant James, Second-Lieutenant Boot, and seven non-commissioned officers and men left as an advance party—the words " proceeded overseas " are no doubt intended to cast the veil of mystery over their possible destination—and then on the 2nd and 3rd February the Battalion embarked in two parties for Mudros Harbour, 3 officers and 239 other ranks in the one party and 17 officers and 869 other ranks in the second. On arrival in Mudros Harbour the whole went on board the *Empress of Britain*, sailed on the 5th and disembarked by companies at Alexandria on the afternoon of the 7th. From here the Battalion proceeded to a camp at Sidi Bishr.

On the next day seven more officers joined or rejoined, when the officer corps of the Battalion appears to have been composed as follows : Majors C. G. Forsyth, D.S.O., in command, and C. R. White ; Captains J. K. Earle, W. H. Peel, F. E. Briscoe, K. Hutchence and N. P. Shepherd-Turneham ; Lieutenants G. G. Gummerson, J. W. Walker, J. A. Groves, J. J. Taylor, W. J. Charsley, J. L. James and H. Bowman ; Second-Lieutenants A. H. B. Shipley, R. A. Law, J. F. Faithfull, W. A. Boot, J. H. Derrick, R. B. Bingham, L. Barnett, I. C. MacFarlane, T. R. Brown, H. G. Taylor, R. S. Butterfield, C. E. Hurst, H. C. Hurst, L. C. Gordon and H. A. R. Biziou ; Lieutenants A. C. Dandria and J. Huggins arrived later in the month.

During the next few days several officers and non-commissioned officers were detached on courses of instruction and others were taken for extra regimental employ, while parties joined from or were transferred to the 11th Base Depot; but on the 12th March the Battalion made a move, proceeding in two parties, of 15 officers and 442 other ranks and 15 officers and 494 other ranks respectively, by train to El Ferdan, where all went into a camp half a mile to the north-east of the railway station on the east bank of the Suez Canal. Here on the 16th eight officers—Lieutenant F. P. Croshaw, Second-Lieutenants C. S. M. Weldon, T. T. Shipman, G. F. Stout, G. B. Andrews, A. G. Pryor, S. K. E. Hildersley and J. E. Dobson—and 400 other ranks were attached from the 11th Base Depot.

The railway had at this time only penetrated some six miles into the desert east of the Canal, and the task of the Battalion here was to dig a line of defence—a very difficult job in view of the shifting character of the ground hereabouts. Apart from the fact that water was scarce, the conditions for training were ideal, the men were healthy, sickness contracted on the Peninsula disappeared, and the Battalion was soon in a high state of efficiency.

The 6th Green Howards remained about El Ferdan until the middle of May, when they moved to railhead and took over part of the outpost line, but all must have felt that something was in the air when on the 18th June orders were received that attached men and officers and other ranks surplus to establishment were to be held in readiness to move. Further orders quickly followed, and on the 22nd the Battalion, having been relieved by one from the 42nd Division, marched back to El Ferdan, left here again on the night of the 24th and arrived next morning at Alexandria Docks, where it embarked in the *Arcadian*, strength 35 officers and 979 non-commissioned officers and men, and sailed next day on a north-north-westerly course.

Of the divisions evacuated from the Gallipoli Peninsula which had found a temporary abiding place in Egypt, six had, by the 31st May, been re-embarked for service in France or Mesopotamia, leaving only the 11th and two Australian divisions, and before June had come to an end these had also left for France.

The *Arcadian* arrived at Marseilles on the afternoon of the 1st July and disembarking early next morning, the 6th Green Howards at once entrained and proceeded by Orange, Macon, Nuits St. Favier, Montereau and Ecoivres to billets at Arras, whence on the 17th the Battalion marched to and took over trenches south of Agny.

During the last few months considerable reinforcements had reached the British Army on the Western Front, while the difficulties of recruiting had been lightened by the introduction of compulsory service in Great Britain.

There were now four great British Armies in the field, the Second about Ypres, the First opposite Neuve Chapelle, the Third covering the ground down to Arras, and the Fourth holding the line from Albert to the Somme, where it joined the French.   In rear was another Army known as the Reserve, later as the Fifth Army.

The Battalion remained about Agny until early in September, taking no part in the Somme Battle now in progress, but was then brought up to Senlis, and on the 8th, at 9.10 in the morning, moved off by companies at seven minutes' interval *via* Bouzincourt to Brigade Reserve dug-outs at Crucifix Corner, near Authuille, next day taking over front-line trenches.

The 11th Division was now, with the 18th, in the II. Corps (Lieutenant-General Jacob) of the Reserve or Fifth Army commanded by General Sir H. Gough.

In the fighting which for some time past had been in progress many successes had been achieved and much ground had been won, but " on my left flank the front of General Gough's Army bent back from the main ridge near Mouquet Farm down a spur descending southwards, and then crossed a broad valley to the Wonderwork, a strong point situated in the enemy's front-line system near the southern end of the spur on the higher slopes of which Thiepval stands.   Opposite this part of our line we had still to carry the enemy's original defences on the main ridge above Thiepval and in the village itself, defences which may fairly be described as being as nearly impregnable as nature, art, and the unstinted labour of nearly two years could make them. . . .   An important part of the remaining positions required for my assault on them was now won by a highly successful enterprise carried out by the 11th Division on the evening of the 14th September, by which the Wonderwork was stormed." *

On the night of the 14th September the 32nd Brigade of the 11th Division was detailed to carry out an attack on the enemy position, his trenches in Turk Street being the primary and the Wonderwork itself the final objective, and the assault was to be undertaken by the 8th Duke of Wellington's Regiment and 9th West Yorkshire on the right and left respectively, while on the left of the West Yorkshire Regiment the 6th Green Howards were to make a bombing attack.

At 6.30 p.m. a very heavy artillery barrage from every gun that could be brought to bear was opened upon Turk Street, and three minutes later the front attacking wave of " D " Company of the 6th Green Howards left its assembly trench and assailed the enemy Trenches 91–69.   These had somehow remained untouched by our artillery and the attacking force was met by heavy rifle and grenade fire, but nevertheless some of them at least

* Despatch of the 23rd December, 1916.

reached the objective and, assisted by a platoon of the West Yorkshire which arrived as a reinforcement, Trenches 91–69 were gained by a bombing attack about midnight; a bombing block was then established at about seventy yards from 91 Post. The enemy counter-attacked violently with bombs at least three times during the night, but on each occasion was successfully repulsed; the losses in the Battalion, in this its first fight on the Western Front, had been serious, Lieut.-Colonel C. G. Forsyth, D.S.O., and Second-Lieutenant C. E. Hurst being killed, Captain J. K. Earle and Second-Lieutenant T. T. Shipman wounded, and Second-Lieutenant I. C. MacFarlane wounded and missing, while the casualties among the other ranks numbered one hundred and thirty.

Of the death of Lieutenant-Colonel Forsyth something more must be said: A report had been received that " D " Company was in difficulties; it proved to be unfounded, but Colonel Forsyth at once went up to the extreme front, where he was shot through the head. He was one of six brothers who served in the war and five of them were killed in action. He was marked out for advancement and the 6th Battalion owes him a very great debt.

The whole of the 15th was spent in consolidating Princess Street and Trenches 91–69, and early in the day the enemy remained tolerably quiet; but towards evening he opened a strong bombardment of the line held by the Battalion, followed at 10.15 by a determined attack on Trenches 91–69, Posts 68, 78 and 46, gaining possession for a time of a portion of Trenches 91–69. A counter-attack was then made, the enemy was driven out and the lost ground regained and held, all attacks elsewhere being repulsed.

Early on the 16th the Battalion was relieved and marched to rest billets at Hedauville, where both the divisional and corps commanders congratulated the 32nd Brigade on the success of the operations.

On the 19th, at Bouzincourt, Major W. B. Shannon, D.S.O., Captain C. H. Dawnay, Lieutenant J. T. Colbert and Second-Lieutenant H. C. Hill joined for duty with some twenty other ranks, and the Battalion then moved by Mailly Maillet and Englesbelmer to Martinsart, whence it was sent up to trenches north of Ovillers, and here, under unusually heavy enemy shelling, it remained some three days. The 6th Green Howards had, however, barely reached their billets at Bouzincourt, when they were ordered to move to Crucifix Corner and, marching off at 1.20 p.m. on the 26th, " A " and " D " Companies occupied Ribble Street, while Headquarters and " B " and " C " and the Lewis gunners were in dug-outs to the south of Crucifix Corner.

At 11.30 a.m. on the 27th the Battalion received orders to move in support of the 34th Brigade into Ration and Sulphur Trenches, and " C "

Company marched off first, the other companies following at five-minute intervals; having arrived here, further orders came to hand for the 6th Green Howards to attack at 3 p.m. a portion of the German line—Hessian Trench and Stuff Redoubt—the 9th West Yorkshire attacking on their right. " C " and " B " Companies of the Battalion went forward to Zollern Trench, the remainder following in support, but at 3 p.m. a message was received that the attack was postponed. This information does not, however, appear to have reached the West Yorkshire companies, which went on, having commenced their advance some few minutes before; and their direction being in some degree lost owing to the opposition met with and the difficulties of the ground, they entered and captured Stuff Redoubt instead of Hessian Trench, the objective assigned to them.

At about 4 in the afternoon, " B " and " C " Companies of the 6th Green Howards advanced, captured Hessian Trench West and took there some eighty prisoners and two machine guns, while others of the Battalion moved on to Stuff Redoubt, where they found the West Yorkshire in possession, and the two battalions here, being much mixed up and greatly reduced in numbers, Major White, Green Howards, formed a composite battalion and took command. About 8.45 p.m. he reported as follows to the Brigade: " Yorkshire Regiment holding Hessian Trench West from R.20.d.9.1. to R.21.C.4.5.; mixed force West Yorkshire and Yorkshire holding R.21.C.1.8. to R.21.C.8.7., latter point inclusive, where much fighting is going on."

During the night which followed two companies of the 8th Duke of Wellington's Regiment were sent up as reinforcements to the West Yorkshire and Green Howards and occupied Zollern Trench; and early on the morning of the 28th orders were received that an attack would be made in the evening, and that the task allotted to the troops in Stuff Redoubt was to bomb round the enemy flanks. Again was the attack postponed and again did the order for postponement fail to reach the troops; the attack was consequently launched and ground gained, but this could not be held owing to lack of rifle ammunition and bombs, and the combined battalions fell back to their original positions.

On the 29th at midday the attack was renewed, only to fail again for the same reason, and the Germans towards evening counter-attacked, but were bloodily repulsed. The greater part of the next day was tolerably quiet except for a certain amount of shelling, but late in the afternoon three bombing attacks were made, the enemy was driven back, the gap between Hessian Trench and Stuff Redoubt was closed and the captured ground was consolidated; and then on the night of the 30th the battle-worn remnants of these two battalions were relieved by troops of the 25th Division, and the 6th Green Howards—all that was left of them—marched *via* Bouzincourt to hutments at Varennes.

Again had the casualties in the Battalion been cruelly heavy, totalling fifteen officers and three hundred and eighty-one other ranks killed, wounded and missing. The officers who were killed were Captain N. P. Shepherd-Turneham, Second-Lieutenants A. H. B. Shipley, H. C. Hurst and G. F. Stout; wounded were Major W. B. Shannon, Captain K. Hutchence, Lieutenant J. T. Colbert, Second-Lieutenants H. O. Vick, C. E. Sowry, G. B. Andrews, N. K. Maclean and L. A. Gross.

Of the result of these operations the British Commander-in-Chief stated in his despatch that " with the exception of his positions in the neighbourhood of Sailly Saillisel, and his scanty foothold on the northern crest of the high ground above Thiepval, the enemy had now been driven from the whole of the ridge lying between the Tortille and the Ancre."

During the month of October—spent by the Battalion at Beaumetz—reinforcements arrived in parties varying in strength from 8 to 159 non-commissioned officers and men, so that by the end of the month 19 officers and 427 other ranks had joined, and the wastage was replaced so far as mere numbers were concerned; the officers joining were: Lieutenant E. G. Butcher; Second-Lieutenants J. F. Myers, G. F. Fillingham, A. Eade, V. B. Elliott, W. Dresser, R. J. Darvall, J. L. Derrick, A. L. Duddell, F. Hollingsworth, W. B. Vautier, F. R. Laver, H. G. Atkin, J. D. Brydon, G. H. Gilbert, A. L. B. Childe, H. Laxton, R. Campbell and H. Lawrence.

In these parts the Battalion remained for some considerable time—casualties being few, but there was much sickness—and it was not until nearly the end of February, 1917, that a move was made, when the 6th Green Howards found themselves attached to the II. Corps in the 7th Division area, for employment on working parties about Bertrancourt, finding daily some six officers and three hundred other ranks for work in digging a pipe line near the Acheux–Bertrancourt Road, or in unloading ammunition, but being relieved after some three weeks of this work and going into billets at Vauchelles-les-Authies.

Here a very strenuous time was spent in training of all kinds, in the attack, bombing, bayonet fighting, artillery formations, musketry and gas-helmet drill.

On the 18th May the Division was transferred from the Fifth to the Second Army area, and the Battalion proceeded by train *via* Abbeville, Calais and St. Omer to Bailleul, marching from there to a camp north of Meteren, and now finding itself in the X. Corps reserve of the Second Army. The Division received the thanks of the Fifth Army Commander for the work done during the past nine months.

The Division had been brought here to take part in the Battle of Messines of this year, for which preparations on a large scale had been for some time past in progress, and the attack now to take place was to be carried out by the troops of the Second Army, commanded by General Sir Herbert Plumer, the actual front to be assailed extending from a point opposite St. Yves to Mount Sorrel inclusive, a distance following the curve of the salient of between nine and ten miles. The final objective was the Oosttaverne Line, which lay between these two points.

The Second Army was composed, from right to left, of the II. Anzac Corps, the IX. Corps and the X. Corps, the IX. in the centre containing the 11th, 16th, 19th and 36th Division, the 11th Division being in support to the north of Kemmel.

At 3.10 a.m., nineteen great mines having been exploded under the German defences, our guns opened and the infantry attack was launched, the enemy's first trench system being captured without any very serious resistance being encountered.

On the night of the 6th June the 6th Green Howards had moved into the Corps Reserve position to the south-west of Kemmel, seven officers and one hundred and thirteen other ranks having been left behind as reinforcement and reorganization *personnel*; and on the 19th the Corps front was held by the 11th Division on the right and the 19th on the left. For the events of the ten days that followed there is very little information to be gathered; for the 9th to the 20th the Battalion diary merely says, " see attached," but no very detailed narrative is to be found, the Brigade diary does not say much and the 11th Division G.S. diary is not especially communicative. It seems, however, that on the 12th the 32nd Brigade relieved in the front line a brigade of the 25th Division and thereby extended the right of the 11th Division and of the IX. Corps to the Blauwepoorte Beek. On the 14th a number of raids were carried out along the front in conjunction with the II. Anzac Corps on the right and the X. Corps on the left, all objectives being gained, an advance of some six hundred yards was made, and upwards of two hundred prisoners were taken. Finally, on the 19th the relief of the 32nd Brigade commenced and was completed by 2 a.m. on the 20th, when the Division moved back to Merris, south-west of Bailleul; there were shortly, however, further moves, and by the 23rd the Division had joined the VIII. Corps of the Fifth Army and the 6th Green Howards were then in a camp to the west of Houtkerque.

During this period in the line—between the 9th and 20th June—Major Peel and Second-Lieutenant Batt were wounded,

During July the Battalion remained for the most part in a training area, but on the 1st August the 11th Division relieved the 51st—which had suffered heavy casualties in the Third Battle of Ypres attack of the previous day—in the XVIII. Corps, the 6th Green Howards moving up to the Yser Canal dug-outs, whence on the 11th they relieved the front line, sending out patrols at night to discover the enemy's positions.

"Towards the middle of August," we read in Sir Douglas Haig's despatch, "a slight improvement took place in the weather, and advantage was taken of this to launch our second attacks east and north of Ypres, on a front extending from the north-west corner of Inverness Copse to our junction with the French, south of St. Janshoek." Four Army Corps took part in this attack, and they were aligned in the following order from left to right : XIV., XVIII., XIX., and II., the XVIII. containing the 11th and 48th Divisions on left and right respectively. The 11th Division was thus in the centre of the attack, where the defence was very obstinate and where, the ground being too waterlogged to admit of the enemy making deep dug-outs, he had constructed a number of strong points, known as "pill-boxes," built of reinforced concrete often many feet thick ; these were, moreover, heavily armed and strongly manned.

At 3 a.m. on the 14th the Battalion outposts were withdrawn to the left bank of the Steenbeek and the companies formed up there preparatory to an advance, "A" Company attacking on the right with two and a half platoons and one and a half in support to occupy the old line of posts ; two platoons of "B" Company immediately in rear to occupy a prepared position on the west bank of the Steenbeek ; and "C" Company on the left with two and a half platoons in front and one in support to occupy the old line of posts. The barrage came down at 4 o'clock and the advance commenced ; "C" Company gained its objective on the left, but "A" was held up on the right by hostile machine-gun fire from certain dug-outs which had been uninjured by our guns, and was several times attacked during the day, but these attacks were easily beaten back by rifle fire.

The shelling was intense all through the day, and when at night the Battalion was withdrawn to dug-outs in the east bank of the Canal, it had had twenty men killed, Second-Lieutenants C. S. M. Weldon and W. F. Jelley and sixty-three other ranks wounded, while twenty-six men were missing.

During the rest of the month the weather was deplorable, but nevertheless the line was advanced on the front of the XVIII. Corps by small local operations, resulting in the capture of some hundreds of prisoners and of a gain of ground of some eight hundred yards for two miles on this front. On the 26th "A" and "B" Companies were attached to and in close support of the Duke of Wellington's Regiment and took over a line of trenches on the north bank of the Lekkerboter Beek. Next day, the 27th, at 1.55 p.m., Second-Lieutenant F. E. A. Postill and No. 1 Platoon of "A"

Company attacked the White House, the 115th Brigade being on the left and the Duke of Wellington's Regiment on the right. The platoon came almost at once under very heavy machine-gun fire: the officer was hit, and only Sergeant Cleary and six men managed to reach the objective. Two sections of the same company were sent up to reinforce, but all, except two men, failed to arrive, and what was then left of the original party, finding itself in danger of being cut off, withdrew to Pheasant Trench at 8 p.m.

At 3 in the afternoon " B " Company of the Battalion had been called upon to send up one platoon to reinforce the line, when Second-Lieutenant G. W. Howarth went forward with No. 6 Platoon, but coming under heavy machine-gun fire this party suffered several casualties, including the officer. Captain J. L. Derrick then went up to try and lead the party by a safer way, when he was killed. In all, this day cost the Battalion 1 officer and 8 men killed, 2 officers and 44 other ranks wounded, and 2 men missing.

The 6th Green Howards spent the first three weeks of the month of September in the vicinity of Poperinghe, and then on the 24th moved by rail to Reigersberg, and marched from there to dug-outs in the Yser Canal bank, remaining here during the night and then taking over the front-line trenches, or rather shell-holes, where during the three days of the tour the Battalion came in for very heavy shelling and lost 1 officer—Second-Lieutenant A. L. Duddell (died of wounds)—and 29 other ranks killed, and had 63 men wounded. On relief, the Battalion went by march route and motor-'bus to Houtkerque.

The 11th Division was now to be employed in the attack against the main line of the ridge east of Zonnebeke, the front of the principal attack extending from the Menin Road to the Ypres Staden railway, a distance of about seven miles. The Division—still in the XVIII. Corps and the Fifth Army—was to attack the Poelcapelle line, and was again on the left of the Corps front, having on its left the 4th Division of the XIV. Corps.

The 6th Green Howards left Houtkerque by 'bus at 10 a.m. on the 7th October and arrived at Siege Camp at 2 in the afternoon, the move being conducted in very cold and rainy weather; and here orders were received to move up to the line and relieve the left battalion of the 33rd Brigade that night. This was done, " A " and " B " Companies occupying the outpost line, while " C " and " D " were in support at Pheasant Farm Cemetery, the relief, by reason of the bad state of the ground, not being completed until 3.40 on the morning of the 8th. This day orders were received for the carrying out on the 9th of an attack the details of which had previously been made known, but the weather was so stormy, and the night so exceptionally dark, that some of the runners sent out lost their way and the companies in the front line did not get their orders until the early hours of the 9th.

Then when, on the evening of the 8th, an attempt was made to put out the tapes, these were drowned by the rain, and they were not in position until 2 a.m. on the 9th, so that company officers were unable to make any previous reconnaissance of their forming-up places and the assembly was thus much hindered. However, the Battalion was finally formed up at 4.30 a.m. on the 9th.

The enemy's shelling was very heavy during the forming-up, but there was no actual hostile barrage, while that by our guns was not very well defined, and some of the heavy batteries seemed to be firing very short.

There was little opposition in the village until the fork in the roads opposite the Brewery was reached, and some one hundred to two hundred prisoners were sent back to the Battalion; but at the Brewery itself heavy machine-gun fire was met with from Meunier House and from the direction of String Houses, and though several of the concrete " pill-boxes " north-west of the Brewery were captured, the general line reached could not be held and a line was finally dug some short distance in rear. During this consolidation many casualties were caused by machine-gun and rifle fire at close range and from both flanks. The light trench mortars attached to the Battalion were early destroyed by shell fire and consequently failed to come into action, while the state of the ground prevented the co-operation of the tanks, the absence of which was much felt. At the time of " digging in " the Battalion was not in touch with other troops on right or left, so that both flanks were in the air.

At 11.15 a.m. a company of the 8th Duke of Wellington's Regiment was moved up in close support, while rifle ammunition and a supply of bombs were sent up rather later with a party from the 34th Brigade, which came up with great coolness and gallantry to Captain Dawnay's headquarters in broad daylight.

There were various rumours and reports of the enemy massing for attack, but nothing of the kind materialized, and the remainder of the 9th was quiet except for some sniping and machine-gun fire, though about 5 p.m. some forty of the enemy reoccupied the dug-outs north-west of the Brewery, causing an advance post of seven men to fall back; it had, however, already been decided to withdraw this post.

The night of the 9th–10th was taken up with reorganization, with gaining touch with the battalions on the flanks and in evacuating the many wounded; but early in the morning the enemy guns again became active, putting down a very heavy barrage, though no attack followed, and the rest of the day may be described as quiet. During the night that followed the 6th Green Howards were relieved by a battalion of the 18th Division and marched back to Irish Farm, where they entrained for the Serques area.

Of the work of the troops the despatch states that " the 11th and 4th Divisions, advancing on both sides of the Poelcapelle road, stormed the western half of that village, including the church, and captured the whole of their objectives for the day " ; while the same despatch gives the general result of the attack in the following words : " The success of this operation marked a definite step in the development of our advance. Our line had now been established along the main ridge for nine thousand yards from our starting-point near Mount Sorrel. From the furthest point reached the well-marked Gravenstafel Spur offered a defensible feature along which our line could be bent back from the ridge."

The losses in the Battalion had been heavy, amounting to 7 officers and 228 non-commissioned officers and men killed, wounded and missing, made up as follows : killed, Captain J. F. Myers, Second-Lieutenants F. Welford and R. Galtry and 38 other ranks ; wounded, Lieutenants H. Firth and A. Eade and 169 non-commissioned officers and men ; missing, Second-Lieutenants C. H. Burriss and J. G. Huntrods and 15 men.

While at Serques Second-Lieutenants C. F. S. Osmond, G. M. Puckrin, M. McCoach and A. Prime and seventy other ranks joined as reinforcements ; and then, following upon two or three minor moves, the Battalion was sent to Mazingarbe, and from here went up into the Brigade support line between Loos and Lens, and was there employed in working parties, building fire-steps in the reserve line and deepening and improving the communication trenches. The 6th Green Howards remained in these parts until well into December, experiencing at the end of November losses from the enemy guns whereby Second-Lieutenant C. F. S. Osmond and twelve men were killed, Captain C. L. Baylis, Second-Lieutenants C. H. Cross and B. S. Appleyard and seventeen other ranks were wounded. Christmas Day found them at Leclème, and the end of the year and the opening of 1918 in a training area south-east of Chocques.

During January and February of this year the Battalion was stationed mostly in the great chalk tunnels at the Cambrin front, where on the 12th February six officers—Captain S. Cranswick, Second-Lieutenants W. Bullock, L. H. Barker, E. G. Sharpington, C. W. Goodlass and A. W. Tovell —and one hundred and sixty-one other ranks joined from the 7th Battalion of the Regiment, and where on the 27th Captain F. R. Milholland died of wounds received in the trenches the previous day.

When the great German offensive opened on the 21st March the 6th Green Howards were in Brigade reserve in Mazingarbe, and moved at once into the left sector of the Brigade front upon which an attack was momentarily expected, but this not materializing several raids were carried out to see what the enemy was doing and to identify the corps in the front ; and in one of these, undertaken during the night of the 30th–31st March, Second-Lieutenant L. M. Evers and one man were missing, believed killed, and four other ranks were wounded, while a few days later Second-Lieutenant W. Bullock was wounded when on a covering party.

The time was now at hand when the active services of the Battalion in France were to draw to a close, and on the 16th May, when at Mazingarbe, the 6th Battalion The Green Howards was absorbed by the 2nd Battalion of the Regiment, ten officers and fifty non-commissioned officers and men forming a cadre training staff attached to the 30th Division for training the American Army, and this party then proceeded to huts at Coupigny, where also the surplus *personnel*—three officers and two hundred and ten other ranks—was temporarily accommodated prior to moving on to the Base.

Lieutenant-Colonel C. R. White, who had commanded the Battalion since September 1917, was now sent home sick, and died some six years later. For long he had struggled against illness, in fact it may be doubted whether he had ever really been fit enough to be passed for field service.

The Cadre was then sent to Mille Bosc and later to Martainville and Maigneville, where it was employed in training the 130th and 139th Regiments of United States Infantry. This work continued until the 27th June, when the Cadre, then at Pierregot, marched to St. Leger and there received orders to proceed to England. Taken by 'bus next day to St. Riquier, the Cadre entrained there for Abbeville and Boulogne, embarking at the last-named place in the *Henrietta* on the 30th June and arriving at Folkestone the same afternoon. From here the Cadre was taken by train to Aldershot and reached Mychett Camp late at night.

The next few days were taken up in receiving and posting to companies the various drafts which began to arrive, and the following list shows the remarkably heterogeneous—not to say, polyglot—character of the *personnel* composing the re-made 6th Battalion of The Green Howards in July :

17th.	31	Other Ranks from the			3rd Battalion Green Howards.
18th.	5	,,	,,	,,	4th Battalion Green Howards.
	3	,,	,,	,,	East Yorkshire Regiment.
20th.	30	,,	,,	,,	3rd Battalion Seaforth Highlanders.
	9	,,	,,	,,	3rd Battalion Scottish Rifles.
	10	,,	,,	,,	Garrison Battalion, Highland L.I.
	8	,,	,,	,,	Depot, Black Watch.
22nd.	4	,,	,,	,,	5th Battalion Lancashire Fusiliers.
	32	,,	,,	,,	Tyneside Garrison Battalion.
	36	,,	,,	,,	Cannock Chase Reserve.
	4	,,	,,	,,	4th Battalion Sherwood Foresters.

22nd.	4 Other Ranks from the Argyll and Sutherland Highlanders.
17 ,, ,, ,,	York Defences.
26 ,, ,, ,,	3rd Battalion Welch Regiment.
23rd. 19 ,, ,, ,,	3rd Battalion Royal Scots Fusiliers.
4 ,, ,, ,,	Cameron Highlanders.
11 ,, ,, ,,	4th Battalion Seaforth Highlanders.
3 ,, ,, ,,	3rd Battalion Scottish Rifles.
24th. 28 ,, ,, ,,	4th Battalion Gordon Highlanders.
16 ,, ,, ,,	3rd Battalion Gordon Highlanders.
25th. 5 ,, ,, ,,	Scottish Borderers.
34 ,, ,, ,,	5th Argyll and Sutherland Highlanders.
3 ,, ,, ,,	Scottish Rifles.
1 ,, ,, ,,	Gordon Highlanders.
26th. 12 ,, ,, ,,	2/6th Norfolk Cyclists.
20 ,, ,, ,,	5th Battalion South Staffordshire Regt.
20 ,, ,, ,,	3rd Battalion Green Howards.
7 ,, ,, ,,	3rd Battalion Highland L.I.
27th. 1 ,, ,, ,,	7th Battalion Sherwood Foresters.
28th. 11 ,, ,, ,,	Royal Scots.
2 ,, ,, ,,	King's Own Scottish Borderers.
30th. 2 ,, ,, ,,	488th (H.S.) Employment Company.
31st. 6 ,, ,, ,,	4th Battalion Northumberland Fusiliers.

The same varied kind of recruitment went on all through August, and by the end of this month the strength of the resuscitated Battalion appears to have stood at 23 officers and 1,321 non-commissioned officers and men, less a party of 385 other ranks who were passed " unfit " by a medical board.

After a few weeks spent at Margate the Battalion returned to Mychett Camp at Aldershot, and finally on the 13th October the 6th Green Howards entrained in two parties for Dundee, being on arrival here accommodated partly in the Western Barracks and partly in the Bell Street Drill Hall, finally embarking on the 16th in the *Tras-os-Montes* and sailing at 1 p.m. next day, escorted by two torpedo boat destroyers. *The Green Howards' Gazette* for April and May, 1919, gives the following nominal roll of the officers who were serving with the Battalion on its arrival in the North Russia Expeditionary Force : Lieut.-Colonel G. P. Lund, M.C. ; Major E. Munday (Lancashire Fusiliers) ; Captain C. H. Dawnay, M.C., B. Williams, M.C., D.C.M., quartermaster, T. E. G. Bailey, K. R. Henderson, F. B. Parker, J. T. Whetton, V. B. Elliott and G. B. Andrews ; Lieutenants H. C. Hill, A. C. Mills, M.C., H. V. Hart, M.C. (London Regiment), C. N. Corlett (Highland Light Infantry), and A. O. Etches (R.A.S.C.) ; Second-Lieutenants C. W. Goodlass, C. V. Proctor, H. Hendry (Lancashire Fusiliers), R. S. Robinson (Suffolk Regiment), H. E. Mason, W. S. J. Wood, N. Wilson, J. R. Wood, R. Plumpton, O. E. Bunting, C. N. Marshall, M.C., B. C. Postle, W. Higgins (Lancashire Fusiliers), O. F. Barkes, F. March, M.M., W. R. Martine (Highland Light Infantry), T. Seggar, G. Richardson, M.C., and Lieutenant P. W. Putnam, R.A.M.C.

Something must now be said as to the objects of this new expedition of which the 6th Green Howards were to form a part.

During the earlier part of the Great War, the Baltic and Black Sea ports being practically closed by the enemy, Murmansk on the Kola Gulf, ice-free all the year round by reason of the presence of a branch of the Gulf Stream, was first used for the conveyance to the Russian Army of military stores sent by ship from England ; but following upon the revolution in Russia this port became something of a menace in that it formed a favourable base of operations for German submarines which might be brought thither overland by railway through the interior of Russia, and thence to the harbour of Murmansk, which had been joined to the internal railway system by a military line completed in 1917. Consequently, in June, 1918, a small detachment composed of infantry and marines had been dispatched to protect the port and the large amount of stores of all kinds which had there been accumulated. Major-General F. C. Poole, C.B., C.M.G., D.S.O., had been sent to Murmansk at the same time with orders to assume command of the Allied Forces in North Russia, and with instructions to organize the Czecho-Slovaks, of whom there were said to be some twenty thousand *en route* to Archangel and Murmansk ; and these with any local troops he might be able to raise were to form the bulk of his force.

The following account of the voyage of the Battalion was contributed to *The Green Howards' Gazette* for January and February, 1919 : " I do not think anybody was impressed with their first view of our new transport, a 10,000-ton ex-Norddeutscher-Lloyd liner. She looked dirty and had a heavy list to port, and when we embarked we found that she *was* dirty and generally in an insanitary condition. We left Dundee on the 17th, escorted by two destroyers, the *Vortigern* and *Versatile*. The sea was choppy, and towards evening the crowd of sightseers on deck had dwindled considerably. Next morning the sea was calmer and nearly everybody reappeared to see the Shetlands, the last, as we supposed, that we should see of the British Isles for some considerable time.

" At 10.30 that night a boiler burst and filled the engine-room with steam. The Lascars were, with some difficulty, prevented from panicking and the ship quieted down. Our position then was roughly forty miles north of the

Shetlands, and near to one of the big mine-fields, towards which we were drifting. Messages were sent for tugs, but as these were slow in arriving one of the destroyers took us in tow, and towed us into Swarbacks Minns in the Shetlands, and we lay here for three weeks, occupying our time with fishing over the side and going ashore for route marches. Experts were working on the boilers, and finally made the ship capable of proceeding to Invergordon for further repairs. Consequently, on 6th November, the ship crept out of Swarbacks Minns and, with the usual escort, sailed towards Scotland. The steering gear broke early next morning, and owing to a strong head wind we were unable to make more than one knot per hour. However, we reached the Orkneys and took refuge in Inganess Firth, anchoring with the auxiliary anchors, as the main anchors had failed the last time they were weighed.

" The gale grew stronger, and at 5.30 a.m. on the second day we were there the ' Boat Stations ' signal was blown and we were duly assembled by our respective boats. As it grew lighter we saw that we had drifted nearly on to the cliffs ; distress signals had been put up and destroyers and tugs came to our assistance. Some of the men were taken off and landed, but as it grew lighter the gale died down and it was found possible to tow the transport off. This was done, and next day we were towed into Kirkwall harbour. Some of us went ashore that day and met the men who had been taken off in the boats. They had had a wonderful reception from the people of Kirkwall, and did not wish to leave—the arrival of the transport in harbour had apparently in some cases come as an anti-climax to their account of the shipwreck !

" We lay in Kirkwall harbour for about a fortnight, and then transhipped to a sister ship of our first transport " (the *Huntsend*), " but as different as possible in every way. We sailed the day after, on the 21st, and arrived in Murmansk on November 26th."

" The small British force, barely more than a company, which had landed the previous June (1918), ably assisted by a company of Royal Marines who were already there, by locally raised levies and certain Finn troops, had held a German force of several thousand men in Finland in a state of uncertainty during those critical months preceding the Armistice, when every available German was needed on the Western Front. There were numerous forces, hostile to one another, operating in the area, and known by different colours ; those immediately affecting us were the ' Reds ' and the ' Whites.' The ' Reds,' who had established a Soviet Government in that part of Russia occupied by them, and had acknowledged Lenin and Trotsky as their leaders, were composed of various nationalities, but were mainly Russian, assisted by a certain element of Finns who had revolted earlier in the year against German aggression in their own country and had been forcibly thrown out. The ' Whites ' were, generally speaking, the Allied troops, but included also those Finnish troops which were actually then in Finland. The latter, who had thrown out of their country the ' Red ' Finns previously mentioned, were pro-German, but anti-Bolshevik ; towards us they were neutral, maintaining a strict outpost along their frontier and not hesitating to shoot any troops, Allied or Bolshevik, who approached it. Therefore amongst our enemies, the ' Reds,' were anti-Germans, pro-Bolsheviks ; whilst our ' White ' neighbours—who later endeavoured to co-operate with us—were pro-German, anti-Bolshevik !

" On our side at that time there were, in addition to departmental services, the company of Royal Marines previously mentioned, a company of the Royal Fusiliers,* some machine gunners, and a handful of Canadians, all of whom had been in the country for some time ; three British Battalions —the 6th and 9th† Green Howards and the 11th Royal Sussex—a machine-gun company and a trench mortar battery ; and several thousand Russian troops, mostly undergoing training, a company of French Skieurs, some French gunners, a battalion of Serbians—veterans who had fought their way from the south—a battalion of Italians, a battalion of about 1,400 ' Red ' Finns, a large regiment of locally raised Karelians, with a proportion of British gunners and sappers.

" The Karelian Regiment, led by British officers and N.C.O.'s, consisted of several thousand volunteers enlisted from the region known as Karelia, extending from the Finnish frontier to the White Sea, between the neighbourhood of Kandalaksha in the north and Soroka in the south.

" The whole force, which was distributed amongst two Brigade areas, was under the command of Major-General Sir C. C. M. Maynard, K.C.B., C.M.G., D.S.O., whose G.H.Q. was at Murmansk. In the north, under Brig.-General M. N. Turner, C.B., C.M.G., C.B.E., was the 236th Infantry Brigade, which covered the area from Polyarni Krug—on the line of the Arctic circle—to the Murman coast. In the south, under Brig.-General G. D. Price, C.M.G., was the 237th Infantry Brigade, which covered the area from Polyarni Krug to the south." ‡

The 6th Battalion The Green Howards was in the 237th Brigade.

The *Huntsend* was moored off the jetty at Murmansk at 2.30 p.m. on the 27th, but the bulk of the troops remained for the present on board, the men being employed on working parties and, in such spare time as remained to them, going for route marches.

---

* Picked men from the 29th and 30th Battalions.   † Evidently an error for 13th.
  ‡ The above is taken from an article, " With the Murmansk Expeditionary Force," in the *R.U.S.I. Journal* for November, 1921.

At the time when these reinforcements landed at Murmansk the general situation and the dispositions to deal with it were roughly as follows : the idea was to hold the Bolsheviks in the south while remaining ready to deal with any raids from Finland against our lines of communication.   There was a strong Allied garrison at Petchenga, a small outpost at Reshtikent, and small posts along the railway between Murmansk and Kandalaksha. The Kandalaksha area and the safety of the line of communications was entrusted to the " Red " Finn battalion, which, besides holding various points on the railway, had posts at Vabinski, Tolvanto, Tumsa, Ruva and Kananen, watching the " White " Finns.   Further south, in the large area west of the Kem district, the Karelian regiment guarded the railway line. The southern front, which at this time was about the line of Olimpi, was held by miscellaneous detachments of British, Canadian, Serbian, French, and Russian troops.

On the 30th November " D " Company moved off to Drovonha ; on the 2nd December " A " Company left the ship and moved into billets in Murmansk ; on the 3rd and 4th Battalion Headquarters and " C " Company entrained at Murmansk for Kola, immediately south of Murmansk on the railway and only half an hour's journey ; and on the 4th half of " B " Company also took up billets at Murmansk, the rest of the Company remaining in the *Huntsend* until accommodation could be found for them on shore. Accommodation here was wholly inadequate, and many departments, etc., had to be housed in trains, causing, of course, a very serious drain on the meagre rolling stock available.   There was a great deal of thieving of Government stores going on, and one of the first duties allotted to " A " Company on landing was the searching of the houses in the town for stolen food-stuffs ; various articles were discovered, and in the inevitable scrimmage one of the inhabitants was killed and another wounded.

It was not until the 6th December that the remainder of " B " Company was able to find billets in Murmansk.

The duties and fatigues were very heavy : the thieving propensities of the people made the use of large guards necessary over all Government stores ; there were many escorts required for trains, and there were heavy fatigues for hewing wood and drawing water ; and all these duties were carried out in a temperature varying from freezing-point to 30° Fahrenheit, while snow was thick on the ground, and during the month of December there was little more than three hours' daylight each day.

" The clothing of the force was special for the climate, and was issued in three scales, Mobile, Semi-Mobile and Sedentary, according to the nature of the work to be performed by each individual.   The Mobile scale consisted of wind-proof blouses, trousers, hoods and mitts, worn over a sweater, and

Petchenga

MURMAN Gulf

Alexandrova

Restikent

MURMANSK

KOLA

Loparskaya

Pylozero

P LAND

Olenya

Imandra

Octa Kanda

LAP LAND

Khibinski

KANDALAKSHA

Tolvanto

Tumsa

Kandi

Knyajya Guba

Ruvan

Kananen

ARCTIC CIRCLE

Polyarni Krug

MURMAN COAST

KARELIA

WHITE SEA

Regozerska

Sayavaga

Rukhnava

ARCHANGEL

Kurgievska

KEM

Maslozerska

Avodinska

SOROKA

Keltegarska

Olimpi

Varotska

Sagela

Sumpshi Posad

Onega

Uroza

Volmasalmi

Podanski

Jolokina

Maselja

Ostretcha

MEDVYEJYA GORA

POVYEBETS

Svyalnavoloi

SCHUNG

Konchozero

PETROZAVODSK

LAKE ONEGA

THE

MURMAN PENINSULA

Scale

0 10 20 30 40 Miles

0   50 versts

FINLAND

207

the warmest possible underclothing, while on the feet were large leather-soled canvas boots.   The Semi-Mobile scale was similar to the Mobile, excepting a reduction in the quantity of underclothing and the substitution of woollen mitts and a fur cap for the windproof mitts and headgear of the latter.   The Sedentary scale included the boots and fur cap of the Semi-Mobile scale, but in other respects consisted of Service dress clothing, with specially warm underclothing, and a large great-coat made of skin and lined with sheep's wool."

On Christmas Day a tragedy befell the 6th Green Howards, Second-Lieutenant R. Plumpton being found murdered in a ravine near Murmansk. It was not for some days that any evidence could be found implicating anybody, but on the 14th January, 1919, a party from " B " Company made a raid upon certain Russian quarters, and here the dead officer's watch and certain stolen Government stores were discovered.   The owner was tried and shot on the 5th February.

On the 9th of this month the Battalion found a detachment at Loparskaya, a short distance south of Kola ; but on the 20th orders were received for the Battalion to prepare to move to join the Archangel Force, and all mobile kit was handed out, while heavy baggage was given in for dispatch by sea.   Headquarters and " A " Company started first, entraining on the evening of the 24th and moving off early the following morning, " B " and " C " Companies remaining for the present in Murmansk under Major Munday.   " D " Company joined the train at Loparskaya, and the combined wing then continued the journey until Soroka was reached, where the two companies detrained on the afternoon of the 28th—" D " Company taking up billets in Soroka, while Headquarters and " A " Company marched to Shijem.

The reason for the transfer of troops from the Murmansk to the Archangel Front was that during the past weeks the Bolsheviks had made stronger and stronger efforts to drive the Allied forces out of Archangel, and these were often hard put to it to maintain their extended positions against superior forces.   " The passing of over two thousand men of General Maynard's Murmansk force as reinforcements from Soroka to the Archangel Front by land route, a distance of four hundred miles, using local sleighs, was a military achievement of which all could well be proud." *

During the 1st to the 3rd March the Headquarters Wing, 6th Green Howards, was engaged in making preparations for a sleigh journey to join what was known as " the Elope Force," and on the 4th a start was made by " D " Company, " A " moving twenty-four hours in rear.   The route followed was Sumski-Posad, Schisne, Kolesma, Nukta (where a change of

* General Ironside's despatch of the 1st November, 1919.

sleighs was made), Uishma, Koskora, Onega, Perog, Korelski, Usolia, Bolshiozerki and Obersaskaya, where it took train for Barkaritza and moved on the 15th into billets, spending the next day in cleaning up for an inspection by General Ironside on the 17th and in getting ready to move off again on skis. The advance was continued by this Company on the 18th, and it arrived at Bistokuria on the 21st and made preparations to join in an attack on the enemy in support of the Slavo-British Legion at the village of Zempzova.

In the meantime the remaining three companies of the Battalion had been following up in rear—" B " and " C " Companies having left Murmansk on the 4th March—but when these last named had reached Onega and " A " Company had arrived at Barkaritza, they were hurriedly moved forward on the 22nd to Chinova ready to attack the town of Bolshiozerki, of which the garrison of French troops had been overwhelmed in a surprise attack by Bolsheviks.

" D " Company, in support of the Slavo-British Legion, attacked Zempzova on the 25th, and in the action which ensued had two men killed and three wounded, while on falling back the following day it had two officers and several men admitted to hospital suffering from frost-bite. The attack was to have been renewed on the 27th, but the idea was abandoned owing to a thaw setting in, and on the 29th the Company withdrew to Chuga.

On the 23rd " A," " B " and " C " Companies attacked Bolshiozerki, but the assault failed and the companies were called off at 8.40 p.m., " A " and " C " Companies going to Usolia and " B " to Chinova ; they had sustained the following casualties : Captain F. B. Parker, Lieutenant H. V. Hart and one man killed ; Second-Lieutenant O. F. Barkes and fourteen other ranks wounded ; and two men missing and wounded. On the 24th the companies reorganized and " B " patrolled the Bolshiozerki road, and on the 1st April the three companies were at Chinova preparing for a second attack upon this town in conjunction with one from the Obersaskaya side. " A " and " C " attacked with " B " in reserve, but again was the attack unsuccessful, while Captain T. E. G. Bailey and two men were killed, Lieutenant C. W. Goodlass, Second-Lieutenant F. March and ten other ranks were wounded, and two men were missing. On retirement " A " and " C " Companies were sent to Usolia and " B " to Chinova, while " D " Company moved to Bistokuria.

For some reason which is not stated " C " Company was now broken up, its *personnel* being distributed between " A " and " B " Companies, and these were kept busy reorganizing, patrolling and strengthening the defences of their posts ; and on the 10th April " B " Company was relieved by Russian troops at Chinova and joined Headquarters at Usolia, with one platoon at

P

Chequevo. On the 17th, on news being received that the Bolsheviks had evacuated Bolshiozerki, this was occupied by troops from the Obersaskaya side, with which " A " and " B " Companies of the Battalion co-operated, being subsequently employed in cleaning up the place, which was found to be in a most insanitary state, many dead lying about and the village full of typhus. By the 22nd the Companies were in billets in Archangel Prestyn, where the rest of the month of April seems to have been passed.

During the same time " D " Company had been more actively employed. On the 6th April it had left Bistokuria and proceeded by Kaptchepski, Rakoula and Emetskoe to Bereznik, where it arrived on the 9th, reported here to the Dwina Force Headquarters and was sent on to join the Vaga Column, marching next day to Ust-Vaga and there occupying blockhouses for two days. Relieved here on the 12th by some of the King's Liverpool Regiment, the Company marched to Mal-Bereznik, and was here engaged in trench-digging and in cleaning up the village, but returned to Ust-Vaga on the 21st and took over the defence of the place. On the 25th this Company was on the move again, crossing the Vaga—a tributary of the Dwina—in small boats, spending the night at Navalock, and arriving on the 26th at Shushuga, where an attack was daily expected and in expectation of which the garrison " stood to " two nights in succession. The Diary tells us that " a party of Bolos attempted to surrender, but was driven off by machine-gun fire " ; but, undeterred by this somewhat unfriendly reception, one " Bolo " does appear to have managed to effect a surrender to " D " Company, and announced that his friends had decided against further attack " as it was impossible to take the village." For a time the enemy appeared to have wholly withdrawn from the neighbourhood, but the Company continued actively to patrol, wire and strengthen the defences, and as on the 3rd it was found that the enemy had returned and seemed to be engaged in the preparation of gun-positions, it was decided to attack him. On the 6th May, then, under cover of the fire from a monitor and the Canadian and Russian artillery, the Company attacked the enemy and drove him from his positions, capturing two machine guns, four prisoners, and a great quantity of stores.

Driven from here, the Bolshevik troops occupied another position at Touglas, which was again attacked and occupied on the 18th by Russian troops supported by " D " Company of the 6th Green Howards.

There seems now to have been something of a lull in the operations so far as the Battalion was concerned, and soon after the middle of June it appears to have been more or less concentrated about Bakaritza.

By this time the British Government seems to have realized that, as stated by General Lord Rawlinson in his despatch of the 11th November, 1919, " the forces at the disposal of Generals Ironside and Maynard were few in number and composed of low-category men selected originally as unsuitable for service in France, and further severely tried by the rigours of an Arctic winter.   The dispatch of reinforcements was necessary before the operations imposed on us by the decision to withdraw from North Russia in the autumn could be undertaken.   Two infantry brigades, under the command of Generals Grogan and Sadleir-Jackson, were sent accordingly in June to the Archangel Front to effect the relief of the tired troops and generally strengthen our position."

With the arrival of these fresh troops, the gradual withdrawal of those which had been in these parts since the previous autumn seems to have commenced, and as early as the 16th June one officer and thirty other ranks of the 6th Green Howards embarked in the *Pretorian* for England and demobilization ; this party was followed on the 23rd by another officer and sixty-eight non-commissioned officers and men, and on the 16th July by a third party of six officers and one hundred and twenty-five other ranks, who embarked at Archangel in the *Czar*.   Other small parties followed at intervals, until on the 31st August there remained but three officers and two hundred and eighty-four other ranks for evacuation from North Russia ; on this date General Ironside inspected available officers and men at Michigan Camp, Bakaritza, when in a farewell speech he thanked all ranks for the help they had afforded him during the past winter.

CHAPTER XI

THE 7TH BATTALION

1914–1916

THE FIRST BATTLE OF THE SOMME

THE 7th (Service) Battalion of The Green Howards was raised at Richmond in the very early days of the war, the command of it being given to Major R. D'A. Fife of the Reserve of Officers of the Regiment, and in Army Order No. 382 of the 11th September, 1914, the new Battalion was posted to the 50th Infantry Brigade of the 17th Division of the Second New Army. The 50th Brigade was composed of the 10th Battalion of The West Yorkshire Regiment and the 7th Battalions of The East Yorkshire Regiment, The Green Howards and of The York and Lancaster Regiment.* The Brigadier was Brigadier-General C. T. Reay, C.B., the Divisional Commander was Major-General W. R. Kenyon-Slaney, C.B., while the Second Army was under the command of Lieutenant-General the Hon. Sir F. W. Stopford, K.C.M.G., K.C.V.O., C.B.

The Brigades were told off to Wool, Lulworth and Wareham, and within a very few days of being raised the Battalion moved to this last-named station from Richmond—on the 7th September, 1914.

Of the class of men who joined the Battalion a correspondent, writing in *The Green Howards' Gazette* for December, writes as follows : " We are all very proud of our 7th Battalion. Most of the men must have enlisted during the time that the standard of height was temporarily increased, for we have a splendid lot of fellows, and they are the type of recruit from which good soldiers are made. They are very keen on their work, their only grievance being that they cannot be sent to the front at once." The same correspondent gives the following list of the officer corps of the Battalion at the end of November : Lieut.-Colonel R. D'A. Fife ; Majors A. G. Cartwright, R. B. Turton (commanding " B " Company), R. L. Dudding (commanding " C " Company) and I. E. Rivis (commanding " D " Company) ;

---

* In December the 7th York and Lancaster Regiment became divisional troops (Pioneers), and was replaced in the Brigade by the 6th Battalion Dorsetshire Regiment.

212

Captain W. B. Hunton (commanding " A " Company) ; Second-Lieutenants A. J. W. Barmby, adjutant, R. W. S. Croft, M. R. Steel, L. V. C. Hawkes, R. F. Howard, F. H. Hyland, F. W. Crabtree, R. Blyth, S. B. Kay, C. W. Lamb, C. G. Weston, L. W. Goldsmith, N. S. C. Johns, A. D. David and D. J. Wilson, with Lieutenant and Quartermaster E. Arnsby.

At Wareham the Battalion was at first accommodated in tents, but before the winter really came on it was moved into huts, though for some little time no luxuries were provided in the way of beds, tables, or forms, while there was nothing in which to cook the rations except camp-kettles, and even the Christmas dinner had to be eaten with the floor for a table and a folded blanket for a tablecloth ! With the beginning of the New Year musketry and practice in digging trenches set in with great vigour, though it is remarked that the extreme narrowness of the trenches of real Flanders pattern caused serious alarm and despondency among those N.C.O.'s of the pre-war army who possessed what tailors describe as " difficult " figures !

In the spring * there was an unusually large crop of rumours of moves ; it was said that the Battalion was to go to Codford ; later, that Sutton Veney was to be the station of the Battalion ; but finally the 7th Green Howards received definite orders to proceed to Romsey by march route at a very few hours' notice. Wareham was left on the 27th May, 1915, and Romsey was reached in four days of ideal marching weather ; the Battalion had been there little more than a week, however, when it was ordered to prepare to move again, this time to Wilkworthy Camp, Lydford, and an advance party was actually sent thither ; but these orders were cancelled and The Green Howards remained on at Romsey, being sent in parties by train to Lark Hill Camp, Salisbury Plain, to complete their musketry. When the final orders for a move came they arrived rather unexpectedly, and as the final date of departure for France was uncertain, officers and men were unable to avail themselves of the usual forty-eight hours' embarkation leave ; but since most of those belonging to the Battalion came from the north, they were able to console themselves with the reflection that such short leave would not have been of much use had the offer of it been made to them.

" The last days in Romsey were busy ones. We had to complete our mobilization, and it seemed wonderful how everything turned up and was issued almost at the last moment. Our move to the port of embarkation was quite uneventful. At Guildford the band of the West Surreys gave us a send-off, and it seemed quite like old times to hear the Regimental March Past again on a band, followed by ' Auld Lang Syne.' "

* In January the command of the 17th Division had been assumed by Major-General T. D. Pilcher, C.B.

At 10.30 p.m. on the 13th July the 7th Battalion sailed from Folkestone for France at a strength of 30 officers and 937 other ranks, arriving at Boulogne at 3.30 on the morning of the 14th and marching to the Rest Camp at Ostrove, where the Chevalier Milliard of the 6th French Hussars joined the Battalion as interpreter. The following are the names of the officers accompanying the Battalion to France : Lieutenant-Colonel R. D'A. Fife ; Majors A. G. Cartwright and W. B. Hunton ; Captains E. V. Slater, R. A. Young, R. E. Cotton, L. E. P. Jones and L. W. Goldsmith ; Lieutenants A. J. W. Barmby, adjutant, L. V. C. Hawkes, R. G. de Quetteville and D. J. Wilson ; Second-Lieutenants M. R. Steel, L. A. D. David, T. Huffington, G. A. Tomlin, transport officer, H. B. Coates, W. D. Wilkinson, J. H. F. Clarke, and H. K. C. Hare ; Lieutenant and Quartermaster J. Dickson.

During the days that immediately followed the Battalion had a varied experience of several camps. On the 15th it entrained at Pont-de-Briques on a train also containing the Battalion transport and machine-gun section which had crossed to France by way of Southampton and Havre, and arrived in the evening at Remilly-Wirquin, moving thence by way of Arques to Steenvoorde, where The Green Howards were inspected by General Sir H. Plumer, now commanding the II. Corps. Here the company commanders were sent up into the 3rd Division trenches to glean what experience so fleeting a visit might afford them, while the remainder of the Battalion carried out various tests with the gas helmets which had been issued.

On the 23rd July The Green Howards marched to La Clytte, when they occupied huts, and Lieutenant D. J. Wilson was wounded while conducting a party to the trenches to be attached for instruction to another battalion ; and on the same day Second-Lieutenant J. H. F. Clarke and eight non-commissioned officers and men were wounded and two men were killed. Then on the 24th " A " Company under Major Hunton went for a four-days' tour of duty to the trenches, and the remaining companies sent three platoons to the trenches every twenty-four hours. Finally the Battalion, now being no doubt considered to have been sufficiently " blooded," on the night of the 2nd–3rd August relieved the 1st Wiltshire Regiment in the trenches at Voormezeele, having one man wounded during the relief. " We had it fairly quiet the first night," writes a Battalion correspondent, " but the following day the Germans left cards on us in the shape of a few shells. ' C ' Company, who were in the support trenches, got them rather badly, and a shell burst in one of their trenches killing Captain L. E. P. Jones, Privates Moore and Wills, and wounding seventeen others. This has been our worst bit of luck so far. The loss of Captain Jones came as a shock to all of us.   He was a keen soldier, ready to tackle any job that came his way, and was very popular with the men of his company."

The 17th Division had now taken over the St. Eloi sector and remained on this front until early in October ; here the 50th Brigade worked with the 51st, doing tours of eight days in the line and eight days at Reninghelst. " The trenches were quiet except for mortars, and fairly comfortable ; the march to and fro was some seven miles ; Reninghelst itself was not amiss, though the huts were indifferent."*   Quiet is no doubt a relative term, but possibly officers and men recently out from England did not find trench life exactly dull, and so far as the 7th Battalion The Green Howards was concerned it was probably lively enough, and casualties were by no means few, as may be seen from the pages of the Battalion diary.

On the 5th August a draft of seventy non-commissioned officers and men came out from England, bringing the strength of the Battalion up to 26 officers and 961 other ranks ; and on the 9th the 7th Green Howards were for the first time in the war concerned in a major operation, being required, with the battalions immediately on the right and left, to open fire on the enemy early that morning with a view of diverting his attention from the British attack then taking place at Hooge.   In retaliation the Germans shelled heavily the communication trenches and the roads in rear, but the Battalion suffered no casualties.   The Green Howards remained in the front line until the 14th, on which day Lieutenant F. W. Crabtree was killed by a German sniper.   Latterly, while in these trenches about Voormezeele the men had been chiefly employed in strengthening the parapets and traverses and in digging new trenches, the difficulty of this last-mentioned work being materially increased by the number of dead who appear to have been buried hereabouts.   Not much was seen of the enemy, but his snipers were very efficient, their work being assisted by the fact that the German trenches were on high ground overlooking those of the British.

When back at rest at Reninghelst an accident occurred on the 19th during bombing practice, a bomb exploding prematurely in the bomber's hand, whereby one man of the Battalion was killed and Second-Lieutenants T. Large and G. D. Preston and two men were wounded.   When up in the Voormezeele trenches again in the middle of September, it was noticed that the Germans had planted a red, white and black flag between the opposing lines, and on Lieutenant R. W. S. Croft going out, accompanied by Lance-Corporals Griever and Stewart of " C " Company, it was found that the staff of the flag was attached by wires to several bombs.   Cutting the wires the party brought the flag into the British lines, when it was discovered that another bomb was still attached to the flag, but as this bomb had a

* *The History of the 50th Infantry Brigade,* p. 15.

bullet hole through it, it was looked upon as harmless : it exploded, how-ever, while in the hands of Lance-Corporal Griever, killing him on the spot.

Towards the end of September the 7th Green Howards and some other battalions went into Corps Reserve, and were not permitted to leave camp, since this was the time when the British were attacking at Hooge and La Bassée and our Allies in Champagne ; while here three officers—Second-Lieutenants H. R. Ballinger, J. Driscoll and W. Evers-Swindell—joined for duty from the Cadet School.

On the 5th October the Brigade marched by way of Poperinghe and Abeele back to Steenvoorde, the Battalion going into approximately the same billets as it had occupied in the previous July, in farms between Steen-voorde and Godwaerswelde ; " and after eighteen days spent in rest and training, especially in the use of bombs and Lewis gun, the Brigade marched eastwards again towards Vlamertinghe to take over the Hooge sector from the 9th Brigade. Rest billets were at Busseboom, in a detestable camp of intolerable filth, where a fetid and evil-coloured liquid oozed up from ground which Belgian labour had surfeited with manure. Nor were any steps taken until the very end (unless indeed the offer of a staff officer to provide a steam-roller to squash out the mud was intended seriously) to improve this disgusting spot. Back to an obscure slough, which was each day discovered to be more and more repulsive, troops had to come, after exacting hardships in the trenches. The distance through Ypres was nine miles along miserable roads ; and after early frosts there was heavy and continuous rain, which converted many trenches into quagmires. . . . Warfare was not violent, though at times the shelling was severe. But the enemy was in a dominating position ; and if it was an honour to guard the Menin Road, the call on physical endurance and determination was very severe."

Here on arrival the Battalion took over a line from the 1st Lincolnshire of the 3rd Division, from Hooge Stables on the Ypres–Menin Road on the left, to Sanctuary Wood on the right—" D " Company being on the left, " B " on the right, " A " Company in support and " C " in reserve at Kruisstraat.

On the 26th Colonel Fife went to Poperinghe to command a composite battalion, when representatives of the 17th Division were inspected by His Majesty the King.

The month of November passed tolerably quietly, but on the 1st, Lieutenant C. G. Weston was killed while in charge of a working party in rear of the trenches at Hooge.

In the middle of December Major Warburton, 14th Durham Light

Infantry, was attached to the Battalion as second-in-command, and shortly after his arrival—on the 19th—the Germans discharged gas against the fronts of the 6th and 49th Divisions, and violently bombarded the British lines east and north-east of Ypres. The 50th Brigade was at this time in divisional reserve, but the battalions composing it were ordered to stand to during the 19th and 20th, though The Green Howards were not called upon to move, as no enemy infantry had penetrated the British front. The trenches, the roads about Ypres, and the towns of Ypres, Vlamertinghe and Poperinghe were all violently bombarded, 42 cm. shells falling in Vlamertinghe ; while the effects of the gas were felt in the rest camp, situated some twelve thousand yards from where the gas was liberated, though no one in the Battalion was really seriously affected.

Two battalions of the 50th Brigade were sent forward through Ypres to construct an emergency breastwork, and part of this served as a front line in the great German offensive of 1918.

Christmas Day, 1915, was spent by The Green Howards in Ypres, in billets in the ramparts and in the cellars of ruined houses, while the last day of the year they were up again in the trenches, where, so the Diary informs us, there was " considerable artillery activity on both sides, few casualties " ; the sick wastage of the Brigade seems also at this time to have been remarkably low.

Early in January, 1916, the 50th Brigade was relieved by the 72nd, and on the 5th the 7th Green Howards entrained at the Quentin siding at Poperinghe and detrained again at Audruicq, half-way between St. Omer and Calais, occupying rest billets in the village of Polincove, and the Division now being in the Nordausques area, where all lived for a month in comfort and decency and proceeded to repair the many ravages of the last three months, training reserves of machine gunners, route marching and refitting. This quiet period ended on the 6th February, when the battalions composing the Brigade moved forward again by train *via* Godwaersvelde to the Reninghelst area, the 7th Green Howards going to billets at Dickebusch. Here " on February 12th the Germans attacked the British line on a broad front north of Pilckem, and on 14th February attacked and captured the trenches held by the 51st Brigade on the Bluff, north of St. Eloi, and those five hundred yards north of it. The attack was preceded by an intense bombardment and the explosion of several mines, which destroyed much of the trenches, the Bluff being a mound of considerable importance on the north side of the Ypres–Comines Canal. At the time of the German attack the 50th Brigade was in divisional reserve at Reninghelst. Local counter-attacks on the night of the 14th failed to regain the Bluff, and at about 2 a.m. on the 15th the Dorsets, West Yorkshires and East Yorkshires were moved forward—the Dorsets to Dickebusch, West Yorkshires to Scottish Wood, and East Yorkshires to 51st Brigade Headquarters.

" Previously, on the 14th, the Yorkshire Regiment " (Green Howards), " who were moving up to relieve the 12th Manchester Regiment of the 52nd Brigade, were stopped and ordered to take up positions in G.H.Q. line, north of Voormezeele. Two companies of the Yorkshire and two of the West Yorkshire Regiment were ordered during the night 14th–15th to be attached to the 10th Lancashire Fusiliers of the 52nd Brigade, who were holding the trenches immediately south of the Canal. None of these companies were engaged in the actual fighting at the Bluff, but all had plenty to do carrying bombs, and suffered a number of casualties. The remaining two companies of the Yorkshire, after being employed on bomb carrying, remained during the night of the 15th–16th in the G.H.Q. line, and the other two companies of the West Yorkshire stayed in Scottish Wood. It was a bitterly cold night and the move was carried out in a storm of sleet."

Other attacks failed, and " the task of the recapture of the Bluff was taken up by the higher command, and the Division held the trenches during the preliminary bombardment, which lasted from February 21st to March 2nd. . . . Very severe retaliation fell on the trenches held by the 50th Brigade south of the Canal and upon Spoil Bank, causing some one hundred and fifty casualties." *

During the operations of the 14th to 17th, inclusive, the Battalion had Captain S. B. Kay and Second-Lieutenant L. A. D. David wounded and some fifty other casualties.

By the middle of March the Brigade was again on the move, marching by Bailleul to Armentières, where on the 28th it took over the Lys sector, and the command of the 50th Brigade was now assumed by Brigadier-General W. T. B. Glasgow, C.M.G. The trenches told off to the Battalion were immediately north of L'Épinette and in front of Pont Ballot ; they were in excellent condition, compared with those in the Ypres Salient, being well revetted, duckboarded and drained, while the front line here was not held throughout its whole length, but only in certain strong " localities," the portions of trench in between being wired.

" This period ended on May 12th, when the 1st New Zealand Brigade came in with the Australians, and the Brigade marched back through Estaires, the Forest of Nieppe, and Arques to the Nordausques area in order to train for the great summer battle of the Somme. The month that followed was one of the happiest of all the time spent in France. The weather was perfect, the country full of growing crops and fruits. Quarters were comfortable, if not luxurious, and training, though intensive, was enjoyable. Units

* *History of the 50th Infantry Brigade*, pp. 19 and 20.

were exercised mainly in assaults on trench systems and in semi-open warfare. Conditions produced a feeling of fitness in mind and body such as had not been known since England was left, and *morale* was heightened by the expectation of taking part in great events."

Then on the 11th June the Division commenced to move down to the Longeau area, joining the Fourth Army, commanded by General Sir H. Rawlinson ; the Battalion moved by train to Amiens and marched thence *via* Bussy and Morlancourt to trenches immediately south of Fricourt, where on the 13th The Green Howards relieved a battalion of the 7th Division in the Maple Redoubt Sector ; on the following day a dug-out was knocked in by a shell and seven men of " D " Company, occupying Maple Redoubt, were killed.

" On June 23rd," writes Colonel Fife in his diary, " I received the Brigade orders for the attack on Fricourt. The 7th Battalion was detailed to make the assault with the 7th Battalion East Yorkshire Regiment in support. The 10th Battalion West Yorkshire Regiment on our left was under the orders of the 21st Division, and the 6th Battalion Dorsetshire Regiment was to be in Brigade reserve. The Brigade orders stated that our attack was not to take place at the time of the general attack, and that I should receive orders later telling me when our attack was to be made. It was made clear that the capture of Mametz Village, to the east of Fricourt, by the 20th Brigade, and of positions to the north-west of Fricourt by troops of the 21st Division, were preliminary operations which were intended to threaten the flanks and rear of this very strong position and to render our attack easier. The 22nd Brigade was to attack simultaneously with The Green Howards, and was to push in between Mametz Village and the eastern outskirts of Fricourt. . . .

" It appeared to me that the key to the village of Fricourt was a salient, known as Wing Corner, opposite to the extreme right of our line. I knew that this salient held machine guns which could enfilade almost the whole of the front which had been allotted to our assault, and in front of our left centre was another salient, known as Wicket Corner, which could also bring enfilade machine-gun fire to bear on our left as it advanced. Wing Corner was the nearest point to our line, and I formed the opinion that it was of the utmost importance to capture it first in order to silence the enemy machine guns. The method of the assault as ordered by the Higher Command was that, on leaving the trenches, the successive waves were to throw themselves flat on the ground and crawl forward behind the artillery creeping barrage until it lifted beyond the enemy's front trench, when the remainder of the intervening ground was to be crossed as fast as possible. . . . We had of course practised crawling, and as far as I recollect had found that fifteen yards a minute for men in battle kit was fairly good going."

At 10 p.m. on the 26th June the 7th Green Howards marched to Ville and went into billets in houses and barns, thus escaping some of the heavy rain which fell that night ; and at about the same hour the following night the Battalion moved up to the trenches in front of Fricourt. Only twenty-five officers accompanied the Battalion, the remaining nine being left at Ville under Captain Carruthers, 7th West Yorkshire Regiment. The three companies detailed for the assault were placed as follows : " A " Company in the front-line trenches on the right, " B " in the support trenches in Kingston Avenue, and " C " Company in the front-line trenches on the left, while " D " Company, forming the Battalion reserve, garrisoned Bonte Redoubt.

By this time very heavy rain had made the trenches practically impass-able, so the attack on Fricourt was postponed for forty-eight hours, the Battalion remaining in its position, and during the 30th the enemy heavily shelled the Cemetery held by " A " Company and the front line generally ; several casualties were sustained, and Second-Lieutenant Griffith being wounded he was replaced by Lieutenant Wilkinson, who was called up from Ville. The Companies were now commanded as follows : " A " Company, Major R. E. D. Kent ; " B," Captain L. G. Hare ; " C," Captain R. W. S. Croft ; and " D " Company, Captain H. L. Bartrum.

A heavy bombardment of the whole German position was maintained by the British guns throughout the night of the 30th June–1st July, the enemy retaliating half-heartedly and directing his fire mainly on the front-line trenches, but doing little damage, except to those about the Cemetery.

" At 3 a.m. on the 1st July the bombardment was intensified and con-tinued up to 7.30, when the great moment came, and for many miles to our right and left the British and French Armies opened the assault. It was a bright summer morning and visibility would normally have been good, but the smoke clouds were so dense that nothing could be seen from our position. Only the fact that our artillery fire had lifted and the increased rattle of machine guns showed that any new phase had begun.

" We knew that on our left the 10th West Yorkshire of our Brigade, though temporarily under orders of the 21st Division, were attacking, but could see nothing of their progress, though a report from Captain Bartrum, ' D ' Company, on the higher ground behind us, stated that their first wave had crossed No-Man's Land with hardly any casualties. This, I believe, was the case, but a tragic fate later overtook this fine Battalion. . . . Owing to the dense clouds of smoke and to the terrific noise, we were for some time entirely dependent for news on telephone messages from Brigade H.Q. and the reserve company, ' D ' ; but at 9 a.m. I received a message from

' B,' my centre company, which was of the gravest importance. The message was to the effect that ' A ' Company on the right had left its trenches and had assaulted the enemy's position at 8.20. This seemed so incredible that I could hardly believe that it was true, but immediately sent the adjutant to ascertain. To my horror, Lieutenant Barmby returned almost immediately to say that there was no doubt whatever that the statement was correct. A few minutes later a message from ' A ' Company came back with a report from Lieutenant Wilkinson, who stated that he and those of the company who were left were lying out in front of our wire ; that Major Kent and Lieutenants David and Tenney were wounded, and that they were being heavily fired on by machine guns and snipers."

Colonel Fife now ordered " D " Company to take the place of " A " in the Cemetery Trenches, and had a company from the 7th East Yorkshire placed at his disposal by the Brigadier to use as Battalion reserve. Owing to the action of " A " Company the fire by the British guns were considerably reduced, as the gunners were hampered by the knowledge that the remnant of the Company was lying out in No-Man's Land and in closest proximity to the German wire ; as a result the enemy wire was practically intact in front of the Cemetery when the attack came to be launched in the afternoon.

At 2.30 p.m. " D," " B " and " C " Companies went " over the top " in succession from the right, but the advance was a very desperate effort. " Although only a few yards behind our own front-line trench and on much higher ground," wrote Colonel Fife, " we could see nothing immediately in front, owing to the slope ; but the deafening cracking of the enemy's machine guns and rifles, which began the moment that the first wave of men crossed the parapet, showed clearly what was happening. Three hundred yards away I saw the enemy's trenches bristling with bayonets and lined with steel helmets, while more and more of them poured into their trench opposite our left, coming from what was known as the Tambour, which it was supposed that our artillery had made untenable. Opposite to our centre and right, where the enemy's trenches were much nearer, I could see nothing owing to the dust and smoke ; but it was evident that the assault was under enfilade fire from both flanks and that it would be a miracle if it succeeded against such a storm of bullets."

Officers and men of the three attacking companies were literally mown down and were finally brought to a standstill half-way across to the enemy trenches, where a ditch afforded some slight protection to those who were so fortunate as to reach it unscathed—but these were no more than a handful, thirteen officers and over three hundred other ranks having become casualties in about three minutes' time. Major Cotton went forward to see if it were possible to collect enough men for another effort, but the commanding officer decided, and the brigadier agreed, that any attempt to put in the reserve company and to make a further advance would only lead to the useless sacrifice of more lives. The enemy's fire now slackened, but broke out again with renewed fury when any movement was made or any of the wounded attempted to crawl back.

Many gallant deeds were performed by both officers and men ; the runners and stretcher bearers especially distinguished themselves ; while among the wounded Captain Harper, the medical officer, and the Reverend Father Potter worked untiringly.

About 6.15 p.m. the 6th Dorsetshire Regiment relieved the 7th Green Howards, the Battalion fell back and the wounded were brought in, but the dead still lay thick upon the ground. " Here and there some gallant man had gone forward apparently alone ; one or two had almost reached the enemy's wire, through which there were only four narrow openings, and one had got to within a few yards of the enemy's trench, where he lay with a bomb in his hand."

The casualties in the Battalion were very heavy ; " A " Company had only 32 unwounded survivors out of 140, " B " lost 70 out of 160, " C " had 97 casualties out of 177 non-commissioned officers and men engaged, while " D " Company, of which only three of its four platoons took part, lost 61 out of 130. The total casualties are given as officers, killed 5 and wounded 10, while 336 non-commissioned officers and men were killed, wounded and missing. The names of the officers who were killed were Lieutenant H. A. M. Hillman, Second-Lieutenants L. A. D. David, H. B. Coates, J. H. F. Clarke and H. G. Hornsby, while wounded were Major R. E. D. Kent, Captains L. G. Hare and H. W. S. Croft, Lieutenants R. G. de Quetteville and C. W. Lamb, Second-Lieutenants W. T. Fry, F. Tenney, F. C. Griffiths, B. C. Camm and R. A. Mann.

On the morning of the 2nd July the 51st Brigade was able to occupy the village of Fricourt without opposition, the enemy having evacuated his trenches during the night ; in the meantime the 7th Green Howards had gone back to Heilly, where they were joined by a draft of forty-six other ranks, and where congratulatory messages were received from the Brigadier and from the G.O.C. 17th Division, who wrote that " owing to the self-sacrifice of the 7th Battalion The Green Howards the village of Fricourt was occupied the following day without a shot being fired."

The 3rd and 4th July were spent at Ville, the 5th at Méaulte, where the Battalion received orders on the 6th to move into Brigade reserve during the attack about to be made on Contalmaison and Mametz Wood ; the fighting strength now was only some three hundred and sixty non-commissioned officers and men.

" On the 7th," writes Major Cotton in his diary, " marched in the early morning to Fricourt Village. For the most part the dead still remained unburied and a great number were still lying where they had fallen. The remainder had been collected together and were subsequently buried close to the road leading from the cemetery to the village. Several hours spent waiting in Fricourt. The village was now full of field guns and field howitzers of all calibres, which had been brought up very quickly. We moved up during the afternoon to Fricourt Wood—a nasty wet afternoon it was too. The Battalion H.Q. was at the eastern point of the wood, while most of the troops were in a trench called Railway Alley in front of us, with ' C ' Company in the wood in rear. . . . During the night the Battalion again moved forward and relieved the 6th Battalion Dorsetshire Regiment in the trenches south-west of Mametz Wood—' A ' and ' B ' Companies in the front line, ' C ' and ' D ' in support. . . . The 7th Battalion East Yorkshire Regiment was on our left and the 38th Division on our right.

" 8th. At 1.22 a.m. a bombing attack was ordered on Quadrangle Support Trench to take place at 6 a.m. It was postponed until 7 a.m. The 51st Brigade was to co-operate on the left and the artillery was to barrage the enemy communication trenches. At 7 a.m. ' B ' Company began moving up the trench towards the objective, but the men soon became exhausted owing to the indescribable state of the trenches ; the mud was over the men's knees and they could hardly move. However, they got about one hundred yards down the trench leading to their objective when they came under heavy cross machine-gun fire and were held up. The whole success of the venture depended on rapidity of movement, an impossibility with the trenches in the state they were. The 51st Brigade on the left was like-wise held up, both attacks failed and the Company withdrew to its former position in Quadrangle Trench.

" At 5.30 p.m. a second attack was ordered—7th East Yorkshire Regi-ment " (Green Howards) " attacking at 5.50 p.m., with 6th Dorsetshire Regiment attacking on the right and at a different hour. The orders were to rush up Quadrangle Alley Trench to its junction with Quadrangle Support and establish the necessary stops. Thirty minutes later, after a further bombardment, the troops were to work north-west and join hands with the 51st Brigade coming south-east from Pearl Alley. Lieutenant Hare was in command of ' B ' Company, which was detailed for the attack. This attack also failed for the same reasons as the former one. The absolute impossibility of *rushing* any trench knee-deep in mud does not appear to have been realized by the Division. Hostile machine guns enfiladed the trench almost the whole length of the distance to be traversed and the blown-in sides of it gave absolutely no cover whatever to the attacking troops.

" 9th. A third bombing attack on exactly similar lines was ordered at 12.15 p.m., the preliminary bombardment lasting an hour and a quarter, but this attack also failed, and it was suggested to the Brigade that a night attack over the open might succeed. At 11.20 p.m. Captain Barmby with ' C ' Company attacked the above-mentioned trench junction once more, this time over the open, a company of the R.E. being detailed to construct a strong point at the trench junction when captured, while the bombing squads were to move north-west and join hands with the 51st Brigade coming to meet them. This attack likewise failed, mainly, it was thought, through the 51st Brigade starting too early and alarming the enemy in our front.

" 10th. The 38th Division on our right attacked Mametz Wood at 4.15 a.m., the 50th Brigade ordered to co-operate and push up Quadrangle Alley and the railway and, if possible, get a footing in Wood Support. Later the objective of the 38th Division was altered in some degree. The Battalion did not move during the day, but materially assisted the attack of the 38th Division by directing Lewis and machine-gun fire on the strong points and trenches held by the enemy. . . . The enemy could be plainly seen retiring into the wood and leaving a number of dead on the way. . . .

" 11th. At 1 a.m. the Brigade was relieved by the 21st Division . . . and the Battalion marched from the trenches, waited several hours at Grovetown Siding, and eventually entrained at midday for Saleux. Detraining here the Battalion was conveyed part of the way by lorries to Molliens-Vidames. We arrived at 10.30 p.m., and went into billets feeling more dead than alive."

The losses of the Battalion since the 2nd July amounted to 1 officer killed and 2 wounded, and of the other ranks 104 killed, wounded and missing, the *total* losses incurred in the Somme fighting of this year having been, killed, 6 officers and 73 other ranks; wounded, 12 officers and 322 non-commissioned officers and men; while missing, believed killed, were 44. The one officer killed during the later operations was Lieutenant C. D. McIntyre, while the two wounded were Captain A. J. W. Barmby and Second-Lieutenant F. R. Milholland.

The entraining strength at Grovetown, exclusive of transport proceeding by road, was 349 all ranks.

On the 15th July the Battalion marched seventeen miles to Bellancourt, east of Abbeville, where reinforcements arrived of five officers and ninety-one other ranks—the officers being Second-Lieutenants H. P. Gregory, R. T. Rudge, C. I. Eyre, B. House and G. D. Stansfield; and here Major-General P. R. Robertson, C.B., relieved Major-General Pilcher in command of the Division. The Battalion was on the move again on the 22nd, and marched by Condé, Hangest and Ribemont to Dernancourt, where the Division was inspected by the Corps Commander, General Horne; but by the beginning of August the Division was in the line again near Longueval, the Battalion being in some old German trenches, known as Pommiers Redoubt, about a mile east of the village of Mametz.   Here there were many conflicting orders for an attack which never materialized, and on the 13th the Battalion marched back to the old camp near Dernancourt, entrained on the 15th at Mericourt, and on arrival at Candas marched thence by way of Heuzecourt, Bonnières, Doullens and Bayencourt to Hébuterne, which was reached on the 19th August, where The Green Howards took over trenches overlooking Gommecourt Wood, which was very strongly fortified, Battalion H.Q. being in the ruins of Hébuterne.

"The enemy's front line," writes Colonel Fife, "lay in a shallow dip, but behind it his trenches were in tiers up the opposite slope, and were so sited as to afford excellent covering fire to his front line."

The 17th Division remained in these parts until the 22nd September, when it was sent into the Third Army training area, marching by Occoches and Maizicourt to Drucat, three miles north of Abbeville, where the Battalion and 50th Brigade Headquarters were billeted and where, in very pleasant weather, training of all kinds set in.   The ration strength of the 7th Green Howards was now 36 officers and 305 non-commissioned officers and men.

"It was a stirring time, for good news was continually arriving.   The capture of Flers, Courcellette and Martinpuich had been followed by that of Lesbœufs, Morval, Combles and Thiepval, and we were hard at work preparing for our next share in the advance."

"On the 5th October the Brigade was once more on foot and after daily marches found itself again in the trenches by the 9th.   Vigorous preparations were pushed forward, but on the 18th the 144th Brigade suddenly came in and the 17th Division set its face to the dismal south.   As if railways had ceased to be, it spent five consecutive days on the road, and on the 22nd reached Méaulte, for which familiarity had bred loathing.   The weather had turned bitterly cold and wet, and formed a fitting prelude to the vile winter that followed and its unimaginable miseries.

"On October 29th the Brigade relieved the 23rd Brigade in the Lesbœufs sector.   The leading battalions marched from Mansel Copse straight to the front line." (The Green Howards to a bivouac between Bernafay and Trones Woods.) "The going was very bad; traffic congestion and control regulations separated the Lewis gun limbers from their companies, and from Ginchy onwards the way lay across a filthy wilderness of shell-holes and sloppy mud which grew worse nearer the front.   Outgoing battalions were in a state of utter exhaustion, and there was the utmost

Q

difficulty in effecting a relief with incoming troops, themselves in great distress. . . . If the mud of the Salient had been bad, this was even worse ; trenches deemed impossible there, were here the normal place of habitation. The mire in the front lines was hip-deep and could only be dealt with by hand ; neither spades nor scoops were of any use. Men became imprisoned and could not be released in some cases for over twenty-four hours. . . . With powers of physical resistance lowered by exposure, the fight against trench feet became more difficult, and many of the new drafts were not hardened. The trenches themselves were a maze and the line intricate ; men of different units and even strange divisions, hopelessly lost, were adopted for a night until they could be sent off by daylight. The back areas and headquarters were continually shelled, and of all the sunken roads in France which have earned execration, that one north of Lesbœufs was surely the most tormented." *

The ration strength of the 7th Green Howards on the last day of October was 30 officers and 726 other ranks.

On the 3rd November the Brigade front line was held by two battalions, the 7th Green Howards on the left and the 7th East Yorkshire Regiment on the right. The day opened with the ordinary enemy shelling, which became intense by 2 p.m., and at about 4 o'clock four lines of enemy troops advanced against the 7th Lincolnshire Regiment of the 51st Brigade, who were on the left of The Green Howards. The Lincolns reported to Colonel Fife that the enemy had penetrated and were holding a portion of trench in their line, and that, having run out of bombs, they were unable to bomb them out.

" I sent Second-Lieutenant Watt, our bombing officer," writes Colonel Fife, " with Sergeant Hornby and a detachment carrying a supply of bombs. On receiving these, the Lincolnshire bombers made a sudden and most successful attack on this piece of trench, killing forty-eight of the enemy and taking thirty-five prisoners with four machine guns. In this enterprise the Lincolns were assisted by Second-Lieutenant Watt, Sergeant Hornby and their men, who were reported to me by the O.C. Lincolnshire as having behaved with the greatest gallantry. Second-Lieutenant Watt was wounded in the face, and our doctor ordered him to leave the trenches, though he wished to remain at duty. All day the enemy's shelling was heavy and we had a good many casualties, including Second-Lieutenant Eyre, who was wounded. . . . Early in the morning of November 4th we took over some more line from the Lincolns, and ' D ' Company under Captain Bartrum, which had been left in camp, arrived to take the place of ' B ' Company, which had relieved the Lincolns. The enemy's shelling was fairly heavy all day. In the afternoon I received orders to carry out a small attack on the following

* *History of the 50th Infantry Brigade*, pp. 30, 31.

morning against a short length of trench opposite to the right of our front line, which rested on a road leading to Le Transloy. I was told not to employ more than forty men. The East Yorkshire were to attack simultaneously with one company on our right, and attacks on a larger scale were to take place to the north and south. The attack was to be made at 11.10 a.m. I detailed ' A ' Company for this purpose, assisted by covering fire from ' B ' Company's Lewis guns and a Vickers-Maxim. The Brigade also promised assistance from Stokes mortars.

" At 10 o'clock on the 5th our artillery opened a heavy fire, which intensified to a barrage on the enemy's front line at 11.10. Soon after 12 o'clock the O.C. East Yorkshire received a report that the objective had been gained and that the enemy could be seen ' running like hell ' . . . and the Yorkshire report also stated that it was believed that one company had gained its objective. This was to some extent corroborated by a report from Lieutenant Robertson of ' A ' Company, though he added that he believed our losses to be heavy and that Captain Goldsmith was wounded. I sent an order to Captain Kay to report on the situation, and at the same time warned Captain Bartrum, commanding ' D ' Company, to be ready to support with his platoons if necessary. The orderly sent to Captain Kay returned saying that he could not find him, and I heard later that Captain Kay had been wounded.

" The situation continued to be obscure, for there was no telephone communication, and, owing to the mud, it took at least four hours for an orderly to reach the front line and to return ; this, although the distance was not more than five hundred yards.

" As I had been ordered to repeat the attack at 10 p.m. if it had not succeeded in the morning, I sent Captain Bartrum forward with his company at dusk, telling him, if he found that ' A ' Company had been successful, to occupy the trench from which that company had advanced ; otherwise, to renew the attack. Lieutenant Huffington, the Battalion signalling officer, went as guide to ' D ' Company. . . . He returned at 8 p.m. I remember that though he was an exceptionally tall man, well over six feet, he had been above his waist in mud. He told me that ' A ' Company had failed in their attack, that Captain Goldsmith had been killed and that Captain Kay and Second-Lieutenant House had been wounded. I heard afterwards that Captain Goldsmith had been shot for the second time while being carried away on a stretcher, and that three stretcher-bearers had been deliberately shot by the enemy. Captain Bartrum sent me word that he intended to renew the attack at 10 p.m., and I sent Second-Lieutenant Walton forward with his platoon to reinforce Captain Bartrum."

Unfortunately, just ten minutes before this attack was due to commence, but too late to issue any counter-orders, instructions came from the Brigade that the attack was not to take place unless the East Yorkshire attack in the morning had been successful. This assault had failed, although the sixty men making it had been seen to gain their objective, and it was supposed that all were killed or taken prisoners, as none of them returned.

Captain Bartrum's attack was made, but failed before the enemy's heavy machine-gun fire, and these operations had proved very costly, the two battalions taking part having had nearly three hundred of all ranks killed, wounded and missing. In the 7th Green Howards Captain L. W. Goldsmith, Second-Lieutenants A. C. Goodall and R. T. Rudge and twenty-seven other ranks were killed, Captain S. B. Kay, Second-Lieutenants H. R. Watt, H. P. Gregory, C. I. Eyre and S. J. House and seventy other ranks were wounded, while ten men were missing.

The Battalion was relieved on the night of the 6th and went back to a camp near Montauban. "Our march from the trenches," writes the C.O., "was very miserable, for the mud was in places waist-deep and the men were much exhausted, several falling in the ranks. The boots of two men were, to my knowledge, sucked off by the mud, from which their comrades pulled them by means of a rope, and one man's trousers were lost in the same way. One of these men found two left-foot boots to continue his march in, and another obtained a pair from a dead German, which he declared were the most comfortable that he had ever worn. We were fortunate in having no casualties on the march back, though there was a good deal of shelling."

On the 14th November the Guards Division relieved the 17th which proceeded by march and rail to Molliens-Vidames, in the Amiens rest area, where in very wintry weather training was carried on and the men quickly recovered from the mental and physical strain of the past weeks. Here some "Bantam" drafts arrived, and by the end of the month the ration strength of the Battalion was 16 officers and 622 other ranks, the effective strength being 26 officers and 754 non-commissioned officers and men. Here too a change occurred in the command of the 50th Brigade, Brigadier-General C. Yatman, C.M.G., D.S.O., taking the place of Brigadier-General Glasgow.

The Battalion moved to Mericourt l'Abbé on the 14th December, the Division being here in Corps reserve, and Christmas and the remainder of this year were spent in the trenches at Lesbœufs or in Carnoy Camp, Guillemont; the trenches are described as "a horrible scene of desolation. The whole landscape was one sea of mud and slime. Dead men and fragments of men lay everywhere. . . . A lowering winter sky and driving rain completed the picture. From the support line to the front trenches the ground rose slightly to a low ridge, and being on the reverse slope was not

under direct fire from the enemy's trenches. . . . The state of the communication trenches which led to the front line was such that everybody
preferred to take their chances across the open. . . . In the trenches the
mud was thigh-deep. . . .

" As the enemy was inactive, our casualties were not numerous, though
there were a few cases of trench feet, all among men for whom no rubber
boots had been available. That there were not more cases of this malady
was due to the untiring efforts of Captain Harper, our medical officer, who
instituted a system of having the men's feet rubbed at intervals by stretcher-
bearers. At this time the water in which the men stood in the trenches was
often freezing, and even rubber boots were no protection against the deadly
cold of this icy slush. Captain Harper also used to go round the trenches
during the night carrying thermos flasks full of hot soup, for which many a
shivering wretch must have blessed him."

CHAPTER XII

THE 7TH BATTALION

1917–1918

THE ACTION OF SAILLY-SAILLISEL. THE BATTLE OF ARRAS. THE THIRD BATTLE OF YPRES

W HEN the year 1917 opened, the 7th Battalion The Green Howards was in Brigade Reserve at Guillemont, but on the 2nd January the Battalion relieved the 12th Manchester Regiment in the trenches to the east of Morval. The disposition of the divisional front had now somewhat changed ; the Australian Corps having taken over the left battalion front of the left brigade group the previous evening. The Green Howards now occupied Lincoln and Bennett Trenches, and became the right battalion of the left brigade group, with the 7th Lincolnshire Regiment on the right, and the 7th East Yorkshire Regiment on the left. One company of the Battalion—" A "—was in the front line, two half-companies of " B " and " D " were in support, while " C " Company was in reserve ; the remaining platoons of " B " and " D " Companies occupied a large dug-out.

There were no communication trenches to the front line, which was found to consist of what had become a narrow canal with islands at intervals, each island being occupied by a picquet with Lewis guns. No communication between these points was possible during daylight, or from them to either the support line or to Battalion Headquarters.

A bombardment of the enemy trenches on the Battalion front had been ordered for the morning of the 3rd January, and Colonel Fife had been directed to detail an officer as observer, and had told off Second-Lieutenant A. James for this duty, warning him not to expose himself unnecessarily ; but unfortunately this young officer was killed by a sniper while looking out from his observation post.

" I cannot pass over the story of this very trying time," writes Colonel Fife, " without alluding to the admirable work of Captain and Quartermaster Asbrey, to whom, with Captain Harper, the Battalion owed its comparative immunity from sickness. When leaving the trenches, at a half-way halt near Guillemont, we used to be met by the ' cookers ' full of hot tea, and a large sandwich was provided for every man. Further, on arrival at the huts where we were to rest, there was more hot tea and more sandwiches, with a dry change of trousers, shirts, and socks. It is impossible to exaggerate the value of these comforts to men who had been standing in icy water and mud for two or three days and nights."

The 50th Brigade was relieved by the 87th on the 13th January, when the Battalion marched by way of Méaulte to Corbie, which was reached on the 14th, where training, interfered with a good deal by snow, was commenced ; and on the 22nd the 7th Green Howards paraded for the presentation by the Brigadier of the Diploma of the Royal Humane Society to Battalion-Sergeant-Major Adolfo, for gallantry for attempting to save Lance-Corporal Hamilton, who was drowned in the Somme near Condé on the 23rd July, 1916.

Major Mairis, D.S.O., had now rejoined the Battalion and had assumed the duties of second-in-command.

On the 25th the Battalion moved to Bronfay in lorries, marching thence to Fregicourt, from where on the following day it moved up to the trenches under Major Cotton, and took over the left sector of the right brigade group near Sailly-Saillisel, " B " and " C " Companies on the right and left respectively of the front line, " D " in support, and " A " Company holding strong points in rear. " B " Company occupied nine forward posts, and had one platoon in Bean Trench, with the 10th King's Royal Rifles on the right ; " C " held three forward posts with the remainder of the company in Crow Support Trench ; " D " Company had three platoons in Crow Support Trench, and one platoon in South Copse Strong Point ; while " A " Company had two platoons in Château Strong Point, and two in Cushy Strong Point. Battalion Headquarters was at the Château.

Here the Battalion remained until the 28th, when it went into Brigade reserve in dug-outs and cellars in Combles, moving up to the front line forty-eight hours later, coming out again on the 1st February, and going back by train from Guillemont to Bronfay Farm Camp, having had eight casualties in this last tour of trench duty, including Corporal Fox, the Battalion sniping corporal, who was killed.

On the afternoon of the 2nd, the C.O. saw all the company commanders and explained the plan of a forthcoming attack, which was rehearsed on marked-out ground, " A " and " B " Companies furnishing the assaulting waves, " C " following with the materials and wire with which to consolidate the position after capture, while " D " Company was to be in Battalion reserve. As it would be necessary to *reverse* the trench when captured, and the ground was frozen too hard to dig, something had to be provided to allow of the men firing over the parados of the trench, and for this purpose some ammunition boxes and planks were obtained to be used as improvised fire-steps. Practice with rodded Mills pattern grenades was carried out by the bombers, and the Battalion had reason afterwards to be thankful for the degree of proficiency arrived at.

The following are extracts from the operation orders drawn up by Colonel Fife:

" On February 28th the enemy's front line trench between U.14.b.85.25 and U.15.c.05.70 will be assaulted and consolidated as part of our front line system. The assault will be assisted by an intense bombardment which will begin at zero hour, the advance of the assaulting troops being covered by a creeping barrage.

" During the night of the 7th–8th February the Battalion will be disposed as follows: 'A' Company in posts 17 to 6 inclusive; 'B' Company in posts 5 to 1 inclusive; 'C' Company in Bean Support and New Support; 'D' Company, less the garrisons of Posts 'A' and 'B,' in Cane Alley. Two squads of Battalion bombers will be attached to 'A' Company, and two squads to 'B' Company. All consolidating material will be placed immediately in front of the parapet of 'C' Company's trenches during the night, and each man will stand to at the usual time opposite to the material which he is to carry.

" The assault will be carried out in two lines by 'A' and 'B' Companies, each on a front of two platoons, with two platoons in the second line. The formation of each line will be that laid down in orders recently circulated. The second line will follow the first at a distance of forty yards. A third line, consisting of the whole of 'C' Company, less Lewis gunners, will follow the second line at a distance of fifty to sixty yards. This line will act as carriers of consolidating material, bombs and ammunition, the men wearing battle kit with slung rifles.

" 'D' Company, less the garrisons of Posts A and B, will be in reserve.

" The signal for the assault will be the commencement of an intense bombardment by seventeen batteries of 18-pounders, forming a barrage on No-Man's Land and the enemy's trenches. The moment the bombardment begins, the three lines will leave their trenches. The two assaulting lines will deploy at three paces interval with the right on No. 17 Post, and the left on No. 1 Post, the first line advancing five paces before deploying to enable the second line to deploy clear of the Posts. The third line will advance as soon as possible after the men have picked up their loads, the right flank stepping short to enable the left to close up into the alignment."

7TH BATTALION.

SAILLY-SAILLISEL.

8th February, 1917.

It is proposed now to follow the account of the action as told by Colonel Fife in *The Green Howards' Gazette*.

" The trench to be attacked was on the highest point of ground over-looking what had been the village of Sailly-Saillisel, and the front to be captured was about one hundred and eighty yards. Our main front trench was four hundred to five hundred yards from the enemy's, but between the two was a chain of twelve detached posts, those on the flanks being only about fifty yards from the enemy, the line of posts curving backwards towards the centre until it formed a re-entrant in shape like the hind leg of a horse with the hock towards us. In the attack the posts on each flank were to be held by Lewis guns and bombing detachments, similar assistance being given by the East Yorkshire on our right, also holding detached posts, and by the Northumberland Fusiliers of the 52nd Brigade on our left. During the night preceding the attack the attacking companies were to assemble in groups in the detached posts, nine posts being allotted to them. Zero hour was fixed for 7.30 a.m. on February 8th, at which time the companies were to leave their posts and deploy between the outer flanks before advancing. This manœuvre under heavy fire, and the fire was likely to be heavy, would be a severe test of drill and discipline, and the fact that it was successfully carried out speaks well for the Battalion.

" The 12th Manchester Regiment was holding support trenches at Sailly-Saillisel, and two companies of this Battalion were placed at my disposal.

" On February 6th I went up to the trenches, where, from an observation post, I tried to learn more than the photographs could show me, but I could only see a rough expanse of snow and ice, which our guns were shelling. After returning to Combles to see the Brigadier, I returned to the trenches at about 10 p.m., and went over the ground over which the advance was to be made. It was a bright moonlight night, but the ground was so broken up and covered with stumps of trees that movement was most difficult. The water in the shell-holes had all been frozen into solid masses of ice, which in their turn had been upheaved by the bursting of more shells until the whole surface resembled a frozen Arctic Sea, with large floes of ice heaped at every conceivable angle. In order to give the men's feet some grip on the ice, it was decided that they were to put each foot into an empty sandbag, the string of which was to be tied round the leg below the knee.

" The morning of February 8th was bright and sunny, though intensely cold. The barrage for our assault opened rather raggedly, some of the guns beginning to fire at 6.28, and, from my position on the left flank, I was horrified to see that some guns were shooting short, their shells actually bursting behind the third wave of men.   There was no chance of stopping these guns, as it was impossible to know which battery or batteries were at fault, and the whole affair would be over long before a telephone message could get through.   A few minutes later, one of our aeroplanes, which had been flying very low above the enemy's trenches, turned and flew swiftly homewards.   I felt sure that this meant that the attack had been successful, and shortly afterwards a message arrived from Captain Wilkinson, commanding 'A' Company, which confirmed this belief.   'A' and 'B' Companies were in possession of the whole objective, but had lost heavily, and 'C' Company, who were for the most part carrying the materials for consolidating, had suffered even more from our own artillery, with the result that quantities of bombs and wire had not reached their destination.   The reserve company, 'D,' had also contributed carriers and was now very weak.   A counter-attack was, of course, imminent, and it was necessary at once to organize and dispatch more bomb-carrying parties from the men available.

"Batches of prisoners to the number of eighty, including two officers —all, I think, of the 94th Regiment—were sent back under escort.   They and their escorts were having an unpleasant time as the enemy were now shelling us heavily.   Captain Huffington, commanding 'B' Company, was reported wounded, also Second-Lieutenants Griffiths, Purcell, Collett, Jolly, and Black.

"The enemy was now making vigorous counter-attacks.   A frontal effort was destroyed by Lewis gun and rifle fire before the enemy had deployed, but bombing attacks on both flanks were more threatening, and at one time both our flanks were slightly pressed in owing to our supply of bombs running short.   The company of the 12th Manchester Regiment under my orders was fully employed in carrying more bombs, and I now obtained another company of this Battalion from Combles.   Major Mairis undertook the organization of bomb-carrying parties from the dump, where he had a horrible time under shell fire ; at a critical moment the discovery of a large store of German hand-grenades in the captured trench did much to save an unpleasant situation.   By 3.15 p.m. the enemy had made five counter-attacks which had all been beaten off, and the whole of the original objective remained in our hands.

"I then put Lieutenant Hare in command of 'B' Company in place of Captain Huffington ; the latter, a most able and gallant officer, had remained in command of his company after being wounded, but had been hit again and was now dead.   The combined strength of 'A' and 'B' Companies in the captured trench was only seventy, and 'C' Company had lost heavily, as also had ' D,' the casualties among the carrying parties having been numerous.

" It seemed probable that the enemy would make another counter-attack between sunset and the rise of the moon, and I moved the newly-arrived Manchester company into our old front line in support of Captain Bartrum, who was holding the line of posts with what remained of ' D ' Company. The enemy, however, appeared to have had enough of counter-attacks and contented himself with shelling us very heavily. Some wiring parties sent by the Brigade reached us at about 6.30 p.m., and I provided them with white coats in order that they should be less conspicuous against the snow. At 7 o'clock a company from a battalion in the 51st Brigade, on its way to relieve part of a battalion on our left, arrived at Battalion Headquarters, and the officer in command explained to me that they had been diverted from their line of advance by the shelling and were waiting for a lull. There was at the moment a lull, but I told this officer that he had come to the worst possible place, and that he would do well to get on to his destination as quickly as possible. Unfortunately he did not take this advice, but put his company into a trench just outside Battalion Head-quarters, where he and two other officers and many of the men were killed by shells a few minutes later.

" A number of our stretcher cases had been placed in a cellar at Head-quarters to await removal, and about this time a shell blew the place in, killing most of the men and wounding all the others for the second time. Among these was Second-Lieutenant Collett, a splendid young officer, who died from his wounds a few days later. The stretcher cases were now moved into Battalion Headquarters, but this was only a cellar with a thin roof, from which bricks fell in showers whenever a shell burst near it.

" The Brigadier of the 52nd Brigade was so generous in the matter of reinforcements that by 9 p.m. I had all four companies of the 12th Man-chester Regiment at my disposal, and made arrangements, if the enemy should get into our captured trench, to turn him out again at once by a bayonet charge. But except for some desultory bombing on the flanks, the enemy did nothing more, and during the night the new front was well covered with wire. It was fortunate that throughout the day and night the enemy's guns never shortened their range sufficiently to hit the trench which his infantry had lost, so that the highly tried men who had taken the trench had not to endure shell fire in addition to their other troubles.

" The Battalion had behaved splendidly, and it was difficult to single out names for reward ; but the honours of the day certainly remained with Captain Wilkinson, whose fine leading of ' A ' Company during the assault had been crowned by the dogged manner in which he remained completely master of the situation and beat off counter-attacks."

As to this the *History of the 50th Infantry Brigade* says that " after the position was captured the enemy made several counter-attacks, but they were all repulsed, largely owing to the gallantry of Captain W. D. Wilkinson, who was commanding the right company. . . . With the assistance of the Engineers the position was consolidated during the night, and was re-named ' Green Howards' Trench.' "

" Stretcher bearers, carrying parties and messengers all behaved magnificently, working all day under heavy shell fire in the open. Captain Harper, R.A.M.C., showed the greatest coolness in getting the wounded under shelter, and Private Cumings, an officer's servant at Headquarters, displayed great gallantry in helping the wounded when the cellar in which they had been placed was blown in. Despite the heavy losses, which deprived us of so many gallant comrades, it was in high spirits that the Battalion, on being relieved by the 10th West Yorkshire next day, returned to camp. We received messages of congratulation from Sir Douglas Haig, General Rawlinson, commanding Fourth Army, and Lord Cavan, our Corps Commander. The last named visited our camp on February 11th, and said a few words to each company. Major-General Robertson, commanding 17th Division, also visited us."

On relief the 7th Green Howards marched back to Bronfay.

The strength of the Battalion in the trenches before the attack opened was about 330 all ranks, and the casualties were : killed or died of wounds, Captain T. Huffington, Second-Lieutenants F. C. Griffiths, B. O. Jolly, T. T. Collett, and 68 non-commissioned officers and men ; wounded were Second-Lieutenants V. W. W. S. Purcell, K. E. Black, and 118 other ranks, while 4 men were missing—a total of 196, or close upon 60 per cent. of the trench strength of the Battalion !

The 7th Green Howards were only three clear days out of the trenches, when, very weak in numbers, they returned to those at Sailly-Saillisel on the 13th.

Of the thirteen commanding officers who had accompanied the 17th Division to France, Colonel Fife of the Battalion was the only one remaining, with the sole exception of the C.O. of the Lancashire Fusiliers, who, having been wounded, had spent several months in England, and the end of Colonel Fife's period of command was now very near. " At about 10.30 p.m. on the 13th," he writes, " I started to go round the trenches, and as Captain Harper, our medical officer, was also making his tour, we went together. The shelling was fairly heavy on the way up until we reached the recently captured trench, where all was quiet. At about 3 a.m. Captain Harper,

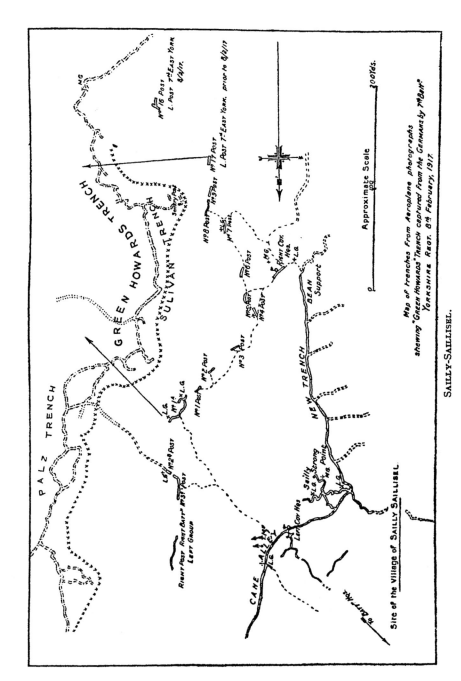

Map of trenches From Aeroplane photographs
shewing "GREEN HOWARDS" TRENCH captured From the GERMANS by MᶜBᴀɪɴ"
YORKSHIRE Rᴇɢᴛ. 8ᵗʰ February, 1917.

SAILLY-SAILLISEL.

and I started to return to Headquarters, and as soon as we left the front line came in for a lot of shelling and had one or two narrow escapes. We had accomplished about two-thirds of our journey when a 5·9 shell burst about five yards from us, instantly killing poor Harper and knocking me over, but although my clothes were riddled by pieces of shell, the only serious damage was to my left arm. With this, broken in three places, I hobbled along until I met an orderly of a machine-gun company, who kindly helped me to Headquarters. As my arm did not heal completely until the war had been over for more than two years, I never rejoined, and am glad to have been spared the bitterness of seeing the Battalion broken up. In conclusion, I must add that I do not believe any commanding officer was more fortunate in those who served under him than I was, or that there existed a more gallant, uncomplaining lot of officers, non-commissioned officers and men than those I had the honour to command.

" The death of Captain Harper distressed me very much. A more gallant, kindly and conscientious medical officer did not exist, and he was universally beloved in the Battalion."

Major Mairis, D.S.O., who had temporarily been commanding the 9th Northumberland Fusiliers, now reverted to his own Battalion and assumed command.

On the 19th, the 7th Green Howards marched to Méaulte, remaining here until the end of the month, moving thence on the 1st March to Warloy, and on the 14th *via* Beauval and Bonnières to Vieil Hesdins, where " we seem to have struck ideal quarters at last, and for once there was no grumbling to be heard, except from the confirmed pessimists who prophesied that they were too good to last long," as we are told by Lieutenant-Colonel Cotton, who had taken up the pen of Battalion correspondent when Colonel Fife had dropped it.

Since the last action the Battalion had received some much-needed reinforcements in both officers and men—Second-Lieutenants F. A. Foley, H. C. Radley, L. A. Mullaney, G. S. Townsend, C. S. Hill, R. R. Humphrey, J. H. Palin, and J. F. Mowett, and Lieutenant T. R. Groom, and 243 other ranks joining by the end of March, when the effective strength of the Battalion rose to 29 officers and 843 non-commissioned officers and men.

In this area, throughout the month of March and until the end of the first week in April, the Division rested and trained for the forthcoming offensive at Arras. In the original scheme drawn up by the British Commander-in-Chief his efforts were to have been directed against the German forces holding the salient between the Scarpe and the Ancre, into which they had been pressed as a result of the Somme Battle ; and the Fifth Army was to have operated on the Ancre front while the Third Army attacked from the north-west about Arras. For various reasons, which need not be considered in a purely regimental history, these plans had to be modified, and the First and Third Armies were now to capture Vimy Ridge and Monchy-le-Preux, while the Fifth Army exerted pressure from the south against the front of the Hindenburg Line.

The Battalion was still in the XVIII. Corps (Lieutenant-General Sir I. Maxse) of the Third Army, commanded by General Sir E. Allenby, and this Army contained four Army Corps—VI., VII., XVII., and XVIII., and also the Cavalry Corps under Lieutenant-General Sir C. Kavanagh. In the Third Army the Corps stood from north to south, or right to left— XVII., VI., VII., while the XVII. Corps was in rear, containing, in the same order, the 33rd, 50th, 17th and 29th Divisions; this Army covered the front on either side of the Scarpe from Thélus in the north to Croisilles in the south. It was decided, however, that the 17th Division should be attached to the Cavalry Corps, its rôle being to follow the cavalry on their moving forward after the initial attack. The 50th Brigade was to move behind the 3rd Cavalry Division along the main Arras–Cambrai Road, while the 52nd Brigade marched in rear of the 2nd Cavalry Division along a parallel road to the south of the main road.

The general attack was timed to commence at 5.30 a.m. on the 9th April on a twelve-mile front south-east and north-east of Arras, and on this day the Brigade was concentrated about Agnes-les-Duisans, the Battalion being rather close-billeted in Montenescourt under orders to be ready to move at fifty minutes' notice.

The cavalry began moving forward in the morning and the Brigade followed about 3.15 p.m., the 7th East Yorkshire leading, followed by the 10th West Yorkshire and the 6th Dorsetshire Regiment, the 7th Green Howards bringing up the rear with one platoon as rear-guard; but progress was so slow, owing to the desperately congested state of the road, that the Battalion did not make a start until 4.45 in the afternoon, while by 6.30 the head of the column had only reached the outskirts of Arras and was here halted, the rear battalion closing up about 8 o'clock in the evening.

"During the afternoon cavalry had been brought up to positions east of Arras, in readiness to be sent forward should our infantry succeed in widening this breach sufficiently for the operations of mounted troops. South of Feuchy, however, the unbroken wire of the German third line constituted a complete barrier to a cavalry attack, while the commanding positions held by the enemy on Monchy-le-Preux Hill blocked the way of advance along the Scarpe. The main body of our mounted troops was accordingly withdrawn in the evening to positions just west of the town."*

* Despatch of the 25th December, 1917.

The 50th Brigade was now ordered to bivouac where it had halted, and as it was snowing heavily a miserable night was spent in the open. "Next day the cookers were sent forward and the Brigade moved into billets and cellars in Arras. Everyone was cold, hungry and wet, but reports from the front were encouraging in spite of the weather. Several thousands of Germans were taken prisoners, and it was a cheerful sight to see some two thousand, with fifteen to twenty officers, including a haughty-looking regimental commander, being conducted to the rear under a cavalry escort. The first day of the battle went well. Vimy Ridge was stormed by the Canadians, and our troops got well forward east and south-east of Arras. . . . Owing to the atrocious weather, the cavalry were hopelessly handicapped from the start and lost a large number of horses. The 17th Division ceased to be in support of the cavalry at 4 p.m., and on the 11th came under the orders of the VI. Corps with orders to relieve the 15th Division in the line," and on this night the 50th Brigade took the place of the 44th north and north-west of Monchy-le-Preux ; but the relief was so complicated a business, and the congestion outside Arras was so great, that the relief was not finally completed until 5 a.m. on the 12th, the Battalion having by then had one man killed and Second-Lieutenant A. B. Bacon and six men wounded by shell fire.

The 7th Green Howards were now in Brigade reserve in the old German support line. The 29th Division was on the right and the 4th on the left of the 17th Division ; and the line held by the 50th Brigade extended from just short of the north-west corner of Monchy-le-Preux to just south of the River Scarpe, along a sunken road running north-west from Monchy-le-Preux towards Fampoux.

During the next ten days the Battalion moved up to and back from the front line, and when the second phase of the Battle of Arras opened on the 23rd April, the 7th Green Howards were " resting " in some old German dug-outs in the Railway Triangle east of Blangy. In his diary of this date Lieutenant-Colonel Cotton tells us that " the main attack on a frontage of many miles * was delivered at 5 a.m. after a perfectly terrific bombardment —I have never heard anything like it. The whole line advanced, but not to a very great extent. On the front held by the 17th Division not much progress was made owing to the heavy machine-gun fire from across the river. At 2 a.m. the Battalion moved to the old German support line east of Arras, with the 7th East Yorkshire Regiment on the right. The 50th Brigade was in support, the 52nd in Divisional Reserve, while the 51st Brigade assaulted. Several attacks were made by this Brigade, but they all failed, and the casualties were heavy. Attack renewed by 6th

* The despatch says, "nine miles from Croisiles to Gavrelle."

Dorsetshire Regiment and 10th West Yorkshire Regiment with a similar result. During darkness our Battalion passed through these two battalions and dug in on a new line in front of them. This was occupied by ' A,' ' B ' and ' C ' Companies before daylight, with ' D ' Company in support near Lone Copse. ' D ' also garrisoned two posts. The 7th East Yorkshire Regiment was on our right. I went up to the old German trenches north of the Scarpe, but could see little of what was going on.

"24th. The enemy shelled the new front line all day. Few casualties. . . .

"25th. At 3.30 a.m. ' A ' Company made a demonstration against the northern part of Bayonet Trench. This operation was to assist the bombing attack by the East Yorkshire Regiment on our right. Several killed and wounded. At 9 a.m. patrols went out from all four companies and reported Bayonet Trench still occupied by the enemy. Shelling continued all day. During the night the Battalion was relieved and returned to Railway Triangle," moving next day in lorries to huts at Fosseux and there resting in beautiful weather.

Between the 9th and the 25th April the Battalion had had 14 men killed, 4 officers—Second-Lieutenants A. B. Bacon, R. R. Humphrey, J. Palin, G. S. Townsend, together with some 13 other ranks wounded, while 14 men were missing; but when at Fosseux 3 officers—Lieutenant E. D. Clarke and Second-Lieutenants W. A. Thacker and F. D. Harling—joined or rejoined, as did a draft of 59 non-commissioned officers and men, and the effective strength of the Battalion at the end of the month was 30 officers and 861 other ranks.

Having spent some days in reorganizing and refitting, the Brigade moved back to Arras on the 1st and 2nd May in motor-omnibuses, the Battalion on arrival being billeted in St. Nicholas suburb, where on the 4th a fire broke out and a large dump of shells and small-arm ammunition caught fire; there were many narrow escapes from the exploding shells, two men of The Green Howards were injured, and the Battalion lost most of its equipment, Lewis guns and mess carts, etc. Between the 9th and 11th the 17th Division took over the front held by the 9th Division in trenches north of the Scarpe.

On the night of the 11th May " B " and " C " Companies of the Battalion were in Clover Trench, and " A " was in Cushion Trench, and in the early hours of the following morning " B " and " C " moved forward and occupied some new assembly trenches which had been dug by another battalion during the night, " A " and " D " taking the place of " B " and " C " in Clover Trench. Then at 6.30 the 4th and 17th Divisions joined in an attack which now opened along the whole Corps front, the objective of the 17th

Division being Cupid Trench, one hundred yards north of the Railway, to Curly and Cash Trenches, and thence to a point about four hundred yards north-west of it in Charlie Trench to the 50th Brigade operating on the right, and Charlie and Cuthbert Trenches to the 52nd Brigade operating on the left. In addition both Brigades were to establish posts in Cuthbert and Cod Trenches.

The 50th Brigade attacked on a two-battalion front, the 7th Green Howards being on the right and 7th East Yorkshire on the left.

The following is Colonel Cotton's account of the action of the 12th :

" The attacking companies went forward under a very effective shrapnel barrage in two waves of two companies each, " B ' Company on the right of the first wave and ' A ' on the right of the second, each wave being composed of two lines. ' A ' and ' D ' Companies detailed a mopping-up party, consisting of one officer and thirty men from each, to clear Crook Trench, which ran roughly at right angles to their objective. Dust and smoke from the barrage made observation impossible once the attack was launched. At 7.30 a.m. a message was received from Lieutenant H. A. Wilkinson, reporting that Captain R. W. S. Croft, ' C ' Company, had been killed and that all objectives had been gained with the exception of the junction of Curly, Cupid and Crook Trenches, and that the troops were consolidating the position. Touch was maintained with the 1st Battalion Rifle Brigade on the right, but the left flank was exposed, as the 7th East Yorkshire on the left had been unable to gain their objective. Further attempts were made to secure this trench-junction, but by dusk it was unoccupied by either side.

" At 12.30 p.m. Second-Lieutenant Collins made a most gallant reconnaissance on the left flank, and confirmed the fact that the junction of the three trenches was unoccupied, and also the eastern end of Crook Trench. At 10.30 p.m. Second-Lieutenant Fox led a bombing attack and established a block in Curly Trench, north of the coveted junction, and eventually succeeded in occupying the junction itself after encountering very strong opposition. The Battalion had fought splendidly, but it had lost some brave officers and men.

" 13th. Incessant fighting continued all next day in the neighbourhood of the ' stop ' in Curly Trench. The Battalion held its own, however, and was ably assisted by the Stokes mortar battery firing from Crook Trench. At 10 p.m. an attempt was made to push forward northwards in Curly Trench in conjunction with an above-ground attack by the 7th East Yorkshire Regiment. This attack failed, but Lieutenant H. A. Wilkinson, seconded by Second-Lieutenant E. V. Fox, by dint of hard fighting made their way yard by yard to one hundred yards beyond the ' stop.' This success was only temporary, and the enemy forced us to yield ground, eventually leaving us with a net gain of only a quarter of that distance. Wilkinson and Fox were both severely wounded, and only three officers were left with the companies after this operation. Wilkinson, though severely wounded, gave detailed orders to Second-Lieutenant Hill, the sole remaining officer in the front line, before he allowed the stretcher-bearers to remove him, and insisted on being carried to Battalion Head-quarters to make his report.

"The men in the front line were becoming very exhausted, and there was a shortage of drinking water. Two companies of the 6th Dorsetshire Regiment were sent up about midnight to reinforce the front line, and the remnants of 'A' Company withdrew about 4 a.m. on the 14th to the Fam-poux–Gavrelle line on relief by the Dorsets, while the three remaining com-panies stayed in support to the Dorsets, to which they were temporarily attached, being heavily shelled all day by 4·2, and 5·9-inch shells. At 2.30 a.m. on the 15th, 'B,' 'C' and 'D' Companies were relieved by a company of the 7th Lincolnshire of the 51st Brigade, and joined Battalion Head-quarters and 'A' Company at a camp near St. Nicholas, near the Candle Factory where 'A' Company had arrived during the night.

"The Battalion had gone into the trenches on the 9th May with 18 officers and 436 other ranks, coming out on the 15th with only 5 officers and 228 other ranks. Second-Lieutenant Hill was the only surviving officer out of the 14 who went into action with their companies, the remaining 4 being with Battalion H.Q."

The casualties were : killed, Captain R. W. S. Croft, Second-Lieutenants G. S. R. Roper, M.C., F. W. Banner, W. A. Thacker, and 23 other ranks ; wounded, 9 officers and 130 non-commissioned officers and men ; missing, 42 men—total casualties, 208. The nine wounded officers were Captain H. K. C. Hare, Lieutenants H. A. Wilkinson, E. D. Clarke and T. R. Groom, Second-Lieutenants E. V. Fox, D.C.M., T. F. Mowatt, F. D. Harley, C. I. Eyre, and B. Rouse.

It was during this action that the first Victoria Cross was gained in the 17th Division, the recipient being No. 242697 Private T. Dresser, "B" Company, 7th Battalion The Green Howards, and the announcement of the award is made as follows in the *London Gazette* of the 27th June, 1917 :

"For most conspicuous bravery and devotion to duty.

"Private Dresser, in spite of being twice wounded on the way, and suffering great pain, succeeded in conveying an important message from Battalion Headquarters to the front line of trenches, which he eventually reached in an exhausted condition.

"His fearlessness and determination to deliver this message at any cost, proved of the greatest value to his Battalion at a critical period."

From the 16th to the 21st the Battalion remained near St. Nicholas resting and reorganizing, and, some small reinforcements arriving from the Brigade Depot, " A " and " D " and " B " and " C " Companies were temporarily amalgamated and numbered Nos. 1 and 2 Companies respectively. The 7th Green Howards then returned to the front line, where they endured considerable shelling and where Second-Lieutenants Nicholson and Sherwood joined ; and then on the 28th the 50th Brigade moved back by rail to the Halloy area, and remained there at rest until the 19th June, when it returned once more to Arras and neighbourhood, taking over the line occupied by the 102nd Brigade, while the 7th Green Howards went back to their former quarters near St. Nicholas. From now until the end of September the 17th Division held the line north of the Scarpe, the brigades interchanging and doing a fortnight in the line and a week at rest in the St. Nicholas Camp ; the front held by the Division was some two thousand nine hundred yards in length and extended from due east of the Chemical Works to within six hundred yards of Gavrelle.

This was on the whole a quiet sector, which was perhaps as well since the 7th Battalion The Green Howards was still rather weak in numbers, but casualties mounted up and two officers—Second-Lieutenants T. H. Eyre and T. Sykes—were killed. There was a certain amount of raiding and counter-raiding and patrols from both sides were very active ; Lieutenant Bielby conducted a very daring raid on Wart Trench in July, while, when, in the middle of August, the Germans attempted a raid on the Battalion trenches, they were chased back to their own lines by Lance-Corporal Rayner and several of them were killed and wounded ; and in appreciation of these and similar efforts by other units the Commander of the Third Army, General Sir J. Byng, received the following message from the Commander-in-Chief :

> " The Commander-in-Chief congratulates you and your troops on the repeated successes gained in your local operations, which show spirit and skill. These successes help appreciably in the general plan."

On the 25th and 26th September the 50th Brigade marched for rest to the Ambrines area, the Battalion being accommodated in rather poor billets at Izel-les-Hameau ; and, having now been joined by two drafts of 178 and 149 other ranks, the numbers of the Battalion were very greatly augmented, the effective strength being, at the end of September, 31 officers and 953 non-commissioned officers and men. Here the Division was in the VI. Corps.

As early as the 19th September there had been rumours of a probable move from the Arras front, while a few days later came news of the great German offensive in Italy ; and on the 4th October the 17th Division began moving by train to the Ypres front, where it joined the XIV. Corps, commanded by General Lord Cavan, in the Fifth Army under General Sir H. Gough. By the 11th the 17th Division had relieved the 29th in the centre section of the Corps front east of Langemarck, the 51st Brigade being in the front line, the 50th in support in trench shelters about Langemarck and Pilkem, and the 52nd Brigade in reserve. The Division was now to take part in the Battle of Ypres of this year which had been raging since the 31st July.

"On the evening of the 10th October, the Battalion made a further advance to Whitemill Camp, near Elverdinghe, and the next day to the Yser Canal. It poured with rain. The place selected for the camp was nothing but a bare spot, ankle-deep in mud and water. There was no shelter whatever until the evening, when a very few bivouacs were procured, and proved quite inadequate for even half the Battalion. The trench strength was 18 officers and 490 non-commissioned officers and men. The night of the 13th–14th found us moving forward to the relief of the 51st Brigade in the front line. The relief was carried out with the greatest difficulty in pitch darkness and pouring rain. The so-called guides lost their way more than once. The only tracks leading to the front line were duck-boarded for miles and shelled at intervals all night long. Troops could only move in single file, and in this inky darkness it was an easy matter to miss the track, which turned and twisted to avoid the enormous shell craters which covered the entire country. The front line consisted of a series of occupied shell-holes, with no cover or protection from shell fire or the weather. The bottom of these shell-holes was filled with water, and the sides were slipping in all the time. It was no consolation to know that the enemy was in the same plight as ourselves. . . . Battalion Headquarters was in an old fortified house, known as Olga House. The Battalion held the right half of the divisional front with the 10th West Yorkshire on the left. Front and support lines were similar waterlogged shell-holes devoid of cover. The country was flat, every movement could be seen by the Germans, and their snipers were particularly active. Hostile aircraft flew low over the forward area and fired machine guns at the men in the shell-holes and at anyone going up the broken duck-board tracks. The whole front was heavily shelled all day."

On the night of the 16th–17th the 50th Brigade was relieved, and went back to the camps in the Proven area, west of Elverdinghe, and then on the 21st the whole 17th Division returned by train to the rest area at

Recques, west of St. Omer, and here remained training until the end of the first week of November. While at Proven the Battalion was in Persia Camp, to the south-west of the town.

The casualties had been tolerably heavy while in the line, Lieutenant J. W. Brown and seven men had been killed, Second-Lieutenant Goodlass and fifty-eight other ranks had been wounded or gassed, while fifteen men were missing.

While in this camp the drum and fife band was restarted, and very soon reached a high state of efficiency and helped the men through many a weary march.

In the Recques area the 7th Green Howards were in billets at Landrethem-les-Ardres, seven miles from Audruicq. Here Second-Lieutenant E. E. Briggs joined, and the Rev. Father McPolin took the place of the Rev. Father Potter, who had been invalided home. At the end of October the effective strength of the Battalion was 38 officers and 973 other ranks, with a ration strength of 30 officers and 848 non-commissioned officers and men ; but on the 1st November there were 40 officers on the roll, distributed as follows : Lieutenant-Colonel G. B. de M. Mairis, D.S.O., in command ; Major R. E. Cotton, second-in-command ; Captain L. W. C. Hawkes, adjutant ; Captain F. R. Milholland, assistant adjutant ; Lieutenant L. G. Collins, signalling officer ; Second-Lieutenant A. N. Strong, intelligence officer ; Lieutenant G. A. Tomlin, transport officer ; Captain R. C. Briscoe, medical officer ; the Rev. Father O. McPolin, R.C. chaplain ; Lieutenant E. Asbrey, quartermaster ; Second-Lieutenant M. Wilkinson, assistant quartermaster.

> "A" Company : Captain W. D. Wilkinson, D.S.O., M.C., Second-Lieutenants S. Bott, Lewis gun officer, H. G. Stephenson, C. L. King, J. W. Bywell, S. A. Mullaney, attached Brigade H.Q., and E. E. W. Armstrong.
>
> "B" Company : Captains R. G. de Quetteville, M.C., and F. A. Foley, Second-Lieutenants C. S. Hill, J. D. Moylan, F. W. Hudson, J. Goodway, C. W. Tunnicliffe, and O. J. Stanton.
>
> "C" Company : Captain F. Cranswick, M.C., Second-Lieutenants F. M. McCarthy, T. N. Barker, G. S. Townsend, F. H. Whitwell, E. E. Wood, and E. E. Briggs.
>
> "D" Company : Captain H. L. Bartrum, Lieutenant C. Bielby, M.C., Second-Lieutenants R. C. Sharpington, W. J. Lucas, O. Dockray, C. W. Goodlass and A. W. Tovell.

On the 7th December the 17th Division finally left this area and moved by rail and road, and by Elverdinghe, Audruicq, Nortkerque, Bayenghem-les-Eperlecques, St. Omer and Bapaume to Beaulencourt, just north of Le

Transloy, German aeroplanes dropping several bombs during the detraining of the Division. The 17th Division was now in the V. Corps in the Third Reserve Army, and at two hours' notice to move. The *History of the 50th Infantry Brigade* states that the period spent at Ypres, "short as it was, and although there was little or no fighting for the Brigade, was nevertheless one of the most horrible times spent in France, owing to the incessant rain, appalling mud, and general beastliness of the surroundings ; no attempt will be made to describe further the conditions, which will be only too well remembered by those who were there. Altogether the Brigade was in the front line for sixteen days, and the following list of casualties incurred during that period testifies to the severity of the enemy's shell fire. 7th Yorkshire Regiment (Green Howards) : wounded, 1 officer ; other ranks, killed, 15 ; wounded, 92 ; missing, 23."

The total losses in the four battalions of the 50th Brigade amounted in this period to : killed, 6 officers and 103 other ranks ; wounded, 16 officers and 486 other ranks ; while 28 men were missing.

"Our camp here," writes Lieutenant-Colonel Cotton, "was close to Sailly-Saillisel, and it was interesting to go over the ground where the Battalion had fought in February, when we captured 'Green Howards Trench' from the Germans. The trenches were nearly obliterated with high grass and weeds, but some of the old duck-board tracks remained, and there was still equipment, rifles, bombs, and ammunition of all sorts lying about. Many wooden crosses marked the graves of those who had fallen, and it was not easy to recognize the old positions even after a short nine months. Battalion Headquarters under the remains of the château was a mere hole : a heavy shell had hit the cellar fair and square and broken through, leaving fragments of our wire beds, half buried in earth and brick-work, sticking out to mark the spot. Frost and snow continued, but in spite of the weather some training was done.

"21st. Our men had their Christmas dinner, as we were due once more for the trenches, and there was every likelihood of our being there on the 25th.

"22nd. We marched to Bertincourt in the afternoon. The enemy had not left us much in the way of billets, and here again trees had been wantonly cut down. At 8 p.m. the well-known sound of the enemy's aeroplanes was heard overhead and bombs began to fall in the streets and on the houses. One man was killed and five wounded close to Battalion Headquarters. The heaviest loss that night was in the transport lines, some two miles away, and Captain Tomlin, the transport officer, for one, will never forget it. Seven of the N.C.O.'s and men were killed and fifteen wounded. Two bombs fell right in the lines and forty-three horses and mules were killed, or had to be shot, besides eight more slightly wounded. Only four animals in the lines were uninjured. The four company cobs were killed, and also that of Major Cotton. A large proportion of the animals had come out to France with the Battalion.*

" 23rd. The Battalion marched to the trenches in the Cambrai salient north of Havrincourt Wood, and occupied the old front line from which the Cambrai Battle started on 20th November. The 51st and 52nd Brigades were in the front line and the 50th in Divisional reserve. The weather was very cold with an icy wind blowing, and the trench was muddy and deep in half-melted snow and slush. . . . Christmas Day was a dreary affair; it froze hard, which improved the going over the open, but the trenches remained muddy and slippery. Some of the companies were in tents in the open, and the German aeroplanes at this time came regularly every night and bombed camps and billets.

" 27th. In the afternoon we moved forward to the front line and took over the trenches in front of Flesquières. The enemy line was a considerable distance away. ' A ' and ' C ' Companies held the foremost trench with ' B ' and ' D ' in support. The latter were far too close up and so was the Battalion Headquarters under the church in the village. The front trench was continuous, though narrow, and commanded an unusually good field of fire. Graincourt could be plainly seen, and part of Bourlon Wood in the distance. On the way up to the trenches, past Havrincourt, the enemy began shelling the road on which the Battalion was marching, and No. 4 Platoon of ' B ' Company lost its commander, Second-Lieutenant Goodway, and Sergeant Kirk killed, besides two men wounded. There was absolutely no protection from the bitter wind and snow for the front troops, but they stood it remarkably well, and little sickness was reported among them. The enemy shelling was not very heavy; one man was wounded on the 28th; and on the 30th, the 63rd Division on our right, near La Vacquerie, was attacked by the enemy, the hostile shelling extending to our front. Flesquières and all the trenches, both front and support, came in for a heavy bombardment with 5·9-inch howitzer shells mixed with gas. Second-Lieutenant Bullock and five men were slightly gassed.

" 31st. We were relieved and moved back to the old Hindenburg support line. The Battalion was now in Brigade reserve with a trench strength of 23 officers and 486 other ranks."

The Battalion remained here for three days and then, on the 3rd January, 1918, moved up to the front line again, " B " and " D " in the

* *The History of the 50th Brigade* says, p. 47 : " Eight men and forty-nine animals were killed and twenty-four men and nine animals wounded. The terribly destructive effect of bombs is exemplified by this incident, for only two bombs were dropped in the camp."

advanced trenches, and " A " and " C " in support ; and at the end of four days the 7th Green Howards went back to Phipps' Camp, near Bertincourt, the Division now for some weeks holding the line with two brigades in front and one in reserve. The enemy here showed an unusual amount of enterprise, and on the 18th January a party of Germans attacked three of the left posts of " A " Company, capturing one man and three Lewis guns, while one man was killed and six were wounded. Private Harris was also captured, but managed to break away and got back safely to our lines.

The strength of the Battalion had for some little time past been low, and at the end of January the trench strength was only 18 officers and 504 other ranks, no drafts appearing to have been received during the previous three months. For some little time past rumours of the possible disbandment of the Battalion had been in circulation, causing great depression among those " in the know " ; but it was not until the 4th February that the decision was publicly announced, the date fixed for final disbandment being the 15th February. The only consolation in the matter was that officers and men were to be distributed among other battalions of The Green Howards.

The Company officers and other ranks were finally posted as under :

To the 6th Battalion The Green Howards : 10 officers and 249 other ranks from " C " and " D " Companies.

To the 12th Battalion The Green Howards : 10 officers and 241 other ranks from " A " and " D " Companies.

To the 13th Battalion The Green Howards : 8 officers and 216 other ranks from " B " and " D " Companies.

The 6th Battalion was at this time in the 11th Division of the First Army, and the 12th and 13th Battalions were in the 40th Division of the Third Army.

To the 6th Battalion went Captains E. Cranswick, M.C., F. A. Foley, and F. R. Milholland ; Second-Lieutenants A. H. Strong, E. E. Briggs, O. J. Stanton, L. H. Barker, W. Bullock, C. W. Goodlass, and A. W. Tovell.

To the 12th Battalion went Captain W. D. Wilkinson, D.S.O., M.C. ; Second-Lieutenants G. H. Royce, S. Bott, C. L. King, J. Bywell, J. H. Morton, J. Binns, E. L. Downs, M. Wilkinson, and A. V. Deans.

To the 13th Battalion went Captain R. G. de Quetteville, M.C. ; Lieutenant L. G. Collins ; Second-Lieutenants C. S. Hill, F. W. Hudson, H. Storch, T. W. Tunnicliffe, E. E. Wood, and W. J. Lucas.

Of the remaining officers, Lieutenant-Colonel G. B. de M. Mairis, D.S.O., was shortly appointed to command the 6th Battalion Dorsetshire Regiment ;

Major R. E. Cotton became second-in-command of the 10th West Yorkshire Regiment; Captain L. V. C. Hawkes and Lieutenant and Quartermaster E. Asbrey went to the 7th Entrenching Battalion; Lieutenant G. A. Tomlin and Second-Lieutenant R. A. Mullaney, M.C., were attached to the 50th Brigade Headquarters; and Captain R. C. Briscoe, R.A.M.C., the medical officer, joined the East Yorkshire Regiment.

By the 13th February disbandment was practically completed, and after an existence of just on three and a half years, of which two years and seven months had been on active service in the field, the 7th Battalion The Green Howards ceased to be.

There can be no question but that it had throughout worthily upheld the fine traditions of the Regiment.

The Memorial to the Battalion, erected at Fricourt, is so far the only one set up by the Regiment in any theatre of the Great War.

The names and ranks of those who fell are inscribed, together with the following :—

To

THE GLORY OF GOD

AND IN UNDYING MEMORY OF

THE OFFICERS, NON-COMMISSIONED

OFFICERS AND MEN OF THE

7TH BATTALION, ALEXANDRA

PRINCESS OF WALES' OWN YORKSHIRE REGT.

GREEN HOWARDS,

WHO FELL NEAR THIS PLACE

JULY 1ST, 1916.

" Their Name Liveth for Evermore."

THE MEMORIAL AT FRICOURT.

CHAPTER XIII

THE 8TH BATTALION

1914–1917

THE FIRST BATTLE OF THE SOMME. THE BATTLE OF LOOS. THE THIRD BATTLE OF YPRES

IN Army Order No. 388 of the year 1914 we read the following:
"XVIII. Augmentation of the Army. 1. With reference to Army Order I. of 21st August, 1914 (Army Order 324 of 1914), and Army Order XII. of 11th September, 1914, His Majesty the King has been graciously pleased to approve of a further addition to the Army of six divisions and Army troops.

"2. These divisions will be numbered from 21 to 26. . . ."

And then in an appendix we find that the 23rd Division is to consist of the 68th, 69th and 70th Infantry Brigades, and that the 69th is to contain the 10th (Service) Battalion The West Riding Regiment, the 8th and 9th (Service) Battalions of The Yorkshire Regiment (Green Howards), and the 11th (Service) Battalion of The West Yorkshire Regiment. The commander of the 23rd Division was Major-General J. M. Babington, C.B., C.M.G., and the 69th Brigade was commanded by Brigadier-General F. S. Derham, C.B., while these six new divisions were to be included in the Third New Army under Lieutenant-General Sir A. E. Codrington, K.C.V.O., C.B.

The 8th Battalion was formed at Richmond, where the original enlistments took place, but the place of assembly for the Division was Frensham, and on the 28th September Major E. G. Caffin arrived there with no other officers, a sergeant-major, a quartermaster-sergeant, and 1,070 other ranks, the majority of the men being drawn from the industrial and mining districts round Middlesbrough and in the east of the county of Durham. In the first instance, Colonel C. J. Spottiswoode, formerly of the 2nd Battalion of the Regiment, was offered the command, but he was almost at once compelled to resign by reason of ill-health, and the command was then assumed by Major Stephen from the 11th Battalion West Yorkshire Regiment; and the following is the list of the officers who during the next few weeks joined and were serving with the Battalion : Lieut.-Colonel A. J. Stephen ; Major E. G. Caffin ; Captains J. Riky ("B" Company) and S. Robinson ("D" Company) ; Lieutenants T. L. Webb ("A" Company) and F. Dodgson ("C" Company) ; Second-Lieutenants J. D. Delius, J. Tilly, G. M. C. T. Whitehead, A. R. Thomson, C. S. Simpson, H. F. Nicholls, E. N. Player, A. J. Peters, B. Jessop and R. Evers ; Captain A. C. W. Cranke was adjutant and Lieutenant C. Ridsdale was quartermaster.

The Battalion had many moves—from Frensham to Aldershot, thence to Folkestone, and from there to Maidstone ; but it was stationed at Bramshott Camp when towards the end of August, 1915, when the war had been more than a year in progress and all were beginning to wonder if it was to be brought to an end without their assistance, orders were received for embarkation for France. At 4.15 p.m. on the 26th the 8th Battalion The Green Howards, less the machine-gun section and the transport which had left during the very early hours of the morning, marched to Liphook Station and entrained in two parties for Folkestone. Headquarters and "C" and "D" Companies formed the first party, and these reached Folkestone at 9.45 p.m. and embarked at once, arriving at Boulogne Harbour at 11.20 that night. The two remaining companies had followed almost immediately, for they reached Boulogne little more than an hour later, when the whole Battalion marched to the rest camp, some two and a half miles distant.

Very little time was spent here, for early in the afternoon of the 27th the Battalion left the rest camp for the railway station and started off by rail for Watten, arriving here about 10 o'clock at night and marching to billets at Monnecove, where something over a week was passed in training all ranks generally for trench warfare, while parties of officers and other ranks were sent to machine-gun and bombing classes in the vicinity. On the 5th September the Brigade left this neighbourhood and, marching in great heat by St. Omer, Arques, Wallon Cappell, Hazebrouck, Vieux Berquin, Steenwerck and Croix du Bac, found itself about the 13th in the vicinity of Erquinghem, whence battalions went for instructional purposes up to the trenches. Here the 8th Green Howards experienced their first casualties in the war, Second-Lieutenant W. V. Fenton and one man being wounded, while during the next few days other losses occurred.

The Battalion was now in the Bois Grenier sector south of Armentières, the Division being in the IV. Corps under Lieutenant-General Pulteney.

On the 20th October the 24th Brigade joined the 23rd Division from the 8th, the 70th Brigade being transferred from the 23rd to the 8th Division in its place.

At this period the Battle of Loos was just over, and the Allies were preparing for the next offensive, but it had been found that the new armies, admirable as had been their home training and magnificent as was the material of which they were composed, needed further experience and training in working in large bodies ; and here, in the comparatively quiet sector of Armentières, the 23rd Division was excellently well placed for assimilating all that the older divisions had at heavy cost learnt during the thirteen months that the war had already endured ; while the enemy on this front seemed concerned rather with improving his position and getting ready for the winter than with courting attacks from the British.

Towards the end of February, 1916, the 23rd Division was relieved and moved south to the Bruay area, the relief being completed by the 28th of the month and the 8th Green Howards being billeted at Steenbecque ; but the same evening orders were received from the IV. Corps Headquarters that the 23rd Division was to relieve the 17th French Division from the Souchez River as far as Boyeau de l'Ersatz, the relief commencing on the 7th March and the 69th Brigade taking over the front line.

The Battalion entrained at Steenbecque at 8.30 on the 29th for Camblain Chatèlaine and marched thence some six miles to Ruitz, finally on the 7th relieving French troops in a heavy snowstorm in the centre sector of the Brigade frontage about Gouay Servins ; this relief was a long and tedious business and was not completed until 3 a.m. on the 8th. The line here was in a very bad state of repair, while, the enemy's trenches being sited on the high ground of Vimy Ridge, he commanded practically the whole of the Allied lines ; so that no one can have felt any really serious regret when on the 12th the 23rd Division was relieved in this sector by the 47th Division and the Battalion marched to Bruay, where company and platoon training was carried out for a few days, moving thence on the 19th to Hersin, when the Division took the place of the 2nd in the left or Angres sector of the IV. Corps front. The Green Howards relieved the 24th Battalion Royal Fusiliers in the left sub-section of this sector.

Here the enemy guns were found to be very active ; the British artillery retaliated, while trench mortars and rifle grenades were constantly in use.

On the 10th March Brigadier-General T. S. Lambert had assumed command from Brigadier-General Derham.

In this sector, or in a manœuvre area behind it, the 8th Green Howards remained until the end of June, when on the 24th the Division entrained for Longeau, near Amiens, whence the Battalion marched to billets at Bertangles, remaining here a few days preparing to take its share in the Battle of the Somme of this year, of the objects and general scheme of the operations connected with which something has been said in an earlier chapter. The 23rd was not intended to be one of the Divisions to be initially employed; on the eve of the battle the British Divisions in the front line, counting from right to left, from Maricourt to Hébuterne, were the following: 30th, 18th, 7th, 21st, 34th, 8th, 32nd, 36th, 25th and 4th, while immediately available for support in whole or part were the 17th, 49th and 23rd Divisions, with a fourth, the 3rd Division, under orders to come south from Belgium.

During the night of the 1st July The Green Howards moved up to Bazieux Wood, on the following day to Albert, and on the 3rd to bivouacs on Tara Hill, where that morning, under instructions from III. Corps Headquarters, the 69th Brigade was placed at the disposal of the 34th Division, which was holding a line opposite to and south-east of La Boisselle; and in consequence of these orders the Brigade took up the line Usna Hill—Tara Hill—Bècourt Wood, two battalions holding the front, while the two others, of which the 8th Green Howards was one, remained in reserve. On the 4th the front-line trenches opposite Sausage Redoubt were reconnoitred, and during the same night "A," "B" and "C" Companies dug a communication trench from the old British front line to Sausage Redoubt.

The 69th Brigade had been detailed to capture Horseshoe Trench on the 5th July, zero hour being fixed at 4 a.m., and the attack being made by the 10th West Riding and 11th West Yorkshire Regiments, but the attack was unsuccessful under the very heavy bombing counter-attacks delivered by the enemy. The 8th and 9th Battalions of The Green Howards were now ordered to relieve the two battalions in front at 6 in the evening and make a fresh assault, but before this hour the West Riding and West Yorkshire Regiments had again attacked, stormed and captured the trench, while the Battalion, supporting with four machine guns and two Stokes guns, assisted to complete the defeat of the enemy, many prisoners and several enemy machine guns being taken this day by the Brigade. The whole of Horseshoe Trench was now occupied, and that night the 8th Green Howards held a portion of the newly-captured line. Next day, the 6th, the Battalion was relieved by troops from the 68th Brigade and marched back to bivouacs in rear, having during these operations had four men killed or died of wounds and three officers and eighty-six other ranks wounded, while one man was missing.

On the 8th the greater part of the 69th Brigade marched to Albert, but the 8th Green Howards moved close up to the trenches immediately in front of Bècourt Wood, and on this day and the next, before falling back to their former bivouacs, The Green Howards were heavily shelled and the Battalion Headquarters dug-out was blown in.

The Brigade was now warned that on the morning of the 10th it was to move off to the attack on Contalmaison, and on this day the disposition of the Division and of the 69th Brigade was as follows : the other two brigades of the Division were opposite the southern and western approaches to the village of Contalmaison, and the 69th Brigade was to pass through these to the attack ; the Brigade was deployed in two lines behind Bailiff Wood, lying due west of Contalmaison, attacks upon which had already unsuccessfully been made two or three days previously. In the first line of the Brigade were the 11th West Yorkshire, in the second the 9th Green Howards, while the 8th Battalion was some five hundred yards in rear, the rest of the West Yorkshire Battalion being in reserve at Scots Redoubt. The attack consisted of two operations ; the capture of Bailiff Wood and the trenches north of it, and that of Contalmaison and the trenches to the west. (See map, p. 295.)

The following is the account of the part taken by the 8th Green Howards as given in the Battalion Diary : " The Battalion advanced to the attack at 4.50 p.m. from the Horseshoe Trench and came under shrapnel fire from Contalmaison Wood. As the Battalion advanced further, and when within about five hundred yards from the village, heavy machine-gun and rifle fire was opened on them by the enemy from the front and left flank. On reaching Trench 23–41 the wire was found to be practically intact and proved a serious obstacle, while a second obstacle in the shape of a hedge and wire netting held up the line outside the village and fifty per cent. of the casualties occurred between the trench and hedge. This obstacle was, however, surmounted and the line advanced to the village, firing on the enemy who were now retreating. At this point unexpected machine-gun and rifle fire took the men in rear and caused some further casualties, not more than four officers and one hundred and fifty men reaching the village. Eight German officers and one hundred and sixty men were captured, exclusive of one hundred wounded Germans found in dug-outs. Six machine guns and thousands of rounds of ammunition were also taken.

" Immediate steps were taken to consolidate, and a line was selected which extended from the Château through the Vieux Manoir to Point 84. It was not the best line of defence, but was chosen in view of the small number of men available, and by daylight on the 11th the line was dug.

" At 7.30 p.m." (on the 10th is meant) " a small party of Germans appeared at the Cutting, but were dispersed by machine-gun fire. Our right was exposed, and at 9 p.m. a party of about forty of the enemy were seen to be lining the hedge north from Point 93 ; these opened fire and the situation was critical ; but Major Western made a barricade across the road and was reinforced by more men from this and from the 9th Battalion, and the enemy were kept in check and finally dislodged by the further aid of a bombing party from the 9th Battalion and the fire of a Lewis gun from a house. At 11 p.m. the Battalion was reinforced by two companies of the 11th West Yorkshire and the 10th West Riding Regiment. These got into touch with the unit on the right and the situation became satisfactory. The village was shelled all night and during next day, but no counter-attack was launched. Our patrols were out all night and enemy patrols in the Cutting were fired on."

On the night of the 11th the Battalion was relieved and marched back to billets at Belle Vue Farm, and next day the whole Brigade was sent back to billets at Franvillers and Molliens-au-Bois for a rest.

In a Special Order of the day, dated the 11th July, General Babington wrote :

> " The G.O.C. the Division cannot allow the action of the 69th Brigade on July 10th to pass without special recognition. Nothing could have exceeded the steadiness and gallantry with which they carried out the attack and bore themselves in the hard fighting that followed. The example of gallantry and devotion to duty which they set calls for the highest admiration, and the Division is proud to possess such gallant comrades in their ranks." *

On the 15th the Battalion paraded with the Brigade before the IV. Corps Commander, Lieutenant-General Sir W. P. Pulteney, when he thanked all ranks for their services.

The losses in the Battalion on the 10th July had been heavy in this its first general action : 6 officers and 19 other ranks had been killed, 6 officers and 241 non-commissioned officers and men were wounded, while 1 officer and 27 men were missing. The names of the officers are : killed, Captains C. S. Simpson and F. Dodgson, Lieutenant M. G. Hume-Wright, Second-Lieutenants R. L. Bains, A. H. Darling and N. Rowley.

The 23rd Division now spent the next few days in Corps reserve, and during this period much-needed reinforcements reached the 8th Battalion The Green Howards, amounting to two hundred and thirty-four non-commissioned officers and men ; but the diary contains no reference to the arrival of any officers to replace the recent heavy wastage. The Division was back in the line again on the 25th and 26th, relieving the 1st Division in the III. Corps area ; and thereafter for the next ten days the Battalion was in Albert, which was under constant shell fire, particularly

---

* A Memorial Stone will be found on the east side of the valley due west of Contalmaison, marking the point of junction of the 8th and 9th Battalions ; it is inscribed, " In Memoriam, Francis Dodgson, Captain 8th Yorkshire Regiment, who fell here, 10.7.16."

by gas shells, the effect of which was much felt. Working parties were sent up almost daily to the front to improve a trench in front and to the left of Lancashire Trench, and another from Contalmaison Villa to Yorkshire Trench, but the enemy did not permit very much work to be done.

Since the 29th July attacks had been going on for the capture of what was known as Munster Alley, but the 8th Green Howards were not called upon to take a hand until the 5th August, when they relieved a battalion of the 68th Brigade in front of the Switch. " No sooner had we got in," so we read in the diary, " than the C.O. and Lieutenant J. Tilly were wounded and Major B. C. M. Western blown down a dug-out. The enemy kept up a very heavy barrage all night, and at 3.30 a.m. and 4 a.m. on the 6th made two determined attacks on Munster Alley Post. These were both beaten off by the occupants of the Post, who displayed great coolness.

" The Battalion received orders to attack and capture about one hundred yards more of Munster Alley at 4 p.m. and to clear Torr Trench. The heavies had been bombarding Torr Trench and Munster Alley up to the Switch, and the howitzers were bombarding the Switch itself for two hours in the morning and since 3 p.m. in the afternoon. The scheme was for a platoon to attack overland from O.G.2, a little to the right of Point 41, and simultaneously the Munster Post occupants were to start bombing up Munster. At 4 p.m. the attack was made and proved quite successful, in fact slightly more was gained than was asked for. A double block was made well above the junction of Torr Trench, but we had to fight hard to keep it. Torr Trench was rendered innocuous by a block covered by a Lewis gun. The Battalion was reinforced by two and a half companies of the 11th West Yorks."

This somewhat meagre account hardly seems to do justice to the very fine work this day of the Battalion, but is happily supplemented and expanded by the following, taken from the story of this afternoon's happenings as told by the historian of the West Yorkshire Regiment,* who says : " At 4.15 p.m. picked bombers from the 8th Yorkshire Regiment after previous artillery bombardment, having orders to carry and hold the junction of Torr Trench and Munster, and to establish double blocks in each trench at least fifty yards beyond the junction, rushed forward to the attack. The enemy was encountered near the junction, but was at once driven back and followed one hundred and fifty yards beyond the junction. Two prisoners were taken and a number of Germans killed. Heavy opposition was then encountered and the leading party, when endeavouring to make a block, was driven back twenty yards. Here another block was made, and eventually two others further back. During all this time heavy

---

* *The West Yorkshire Regiment in the War*, Vol. I, pp. 249, 250.

shell fire continued and counter-attacks were made by the enemy, but the gallant Yorkshiremen held their position. Two Lewis guns were then brought up to cover Munster Alley and Torr Trench, but the latter had been completely blown out of existence by the Divisional artillery. At 9 p.m. the Yorkshire Regiment, who for five hours had been bombing and attacking continuously, was relieved by part of the 11th West Yorkshires. . . . By this time Torr Trench, Munster Alley and the surrounding ground were hardly recognizable. Shell fire had tumbled and blown the defences to bits and all around lay German dead."

To this Lieutenant Bush adds : " One Company of the Battalion, under the personal supervision of Major Western, undertook the attack. The party of picked bombers, all volunteers, were led by Second-Lieutenant G. M. Lister, one platoon by Second-Lieutenant Lawson, and a third by Second-Lieutenant Cole. No. 12067 Private W. Short, one of the bombers, was wounded in the foot, but refused to fall to the rear, and later, when his other leg was shattered, he continued, as he lay in the trench, to adjust detonators and straighten the pins for his comrades." Private Short died of his wounds. He was awarded a posthumous Victoria Cross in the *London Gazette* of the 9th September, 1916, wherein it is announced as under :

> " For most conspicuous bravery. He was foremost in the attack, bombing the enemy with great gallantry, when he was severely wounded in the foot. He was urged to go back, but refused and continued to throw bombs.
>
> " Later his leg was shattered by a shell, and he was unable to stand, so he lay in the trench adjusting detonators and straightening the pins of bombs for his comrades. He died before he could be carried out of the trench. For the last eleven months he had always volunteered for dangerous enterprises, and had always set a magnificent example of bravery and devotion to duty."

Major B. C. M. Western now assumed the command of the Battalion, which he held till severely wounded on the 27th August, 1917.

On the 7th the Battalion was relieved and proceeded to Scots Redoubt, and next day, the 15th Division having relieved the 23rd, The Green Howards went by train to Pont Rémy, stayed in that neighbourhood twenty-four hours only and then moved on again by Bailleul and Steenwercke to Papot, which was reached on the 22nd ; trenches were taken over on the 25th, and Second-Lieutenant R. Oakley was killed during the course of the relief. Early in September the 23rd Division went to the training area about St. Omer, remaining here but a few days only, and then on the evening of the 10th, entraining at St. Omer for the Somme area, it arrived at Longeau on the 11th, from where the 69th Brigade marched through Amiens, Coisy and Poulainville to a camp in Henencourt Wood, where the 12th, 13th and 14th were spent. On the 15th sudden orders were received and the Brigade marched to Millencourt, and on the 18th took over the trenches from a brigade of the 15th Division, the 8th Battalion The Green Howards going to reserve trenches near Bazentin-le-Petit Wood. From here the Battalion was employed in carrying and working parties and in sending up companies and platoons to support the sister battalion of the Regiment in the front line. There was useful patrol work to be done also, and Second-Lieutenants Ross and Heron were complimented by the G.O.C. on their services in this connection. The work entailed a certain amount of risk and attendant loss, and by the end of the month Second-Lieutenant W. Swain and two men had been killed, and Second-Lieutenants Bush and Killacky and one man wounded.

By this time the 24th Brigade had reverted to the 8th Division and the 70th Infantry Brigade had rejoined the 23rd.

Nearly the whole of the high ground from Morval to the Ancre had been captured, with the sole exception of that near Thiepval, but, since the enemy still commanded the country about Combles from the ridges of Sailly-Saillisel and Le Transloy, the seizure of these was also necessary, the more that their possession would assist any Allied advance to and capture of the German last system of defence in front of Le Transloy and Beaulencourt, south of Bapaume and west of Lafont Wood. On the 1st October the Fourth Army attacked Flers Trench, and by the evening of the 3rd the whole of Eaucourt l'Abbaye was in British hands; in this operation the 70th Brigade only of the 23rd Division took any part.

On the 2nd, the 8th Green Howards had moved up to that part of the line to the right of the Le Sars Road and took over the line with " A " and " D " Companies in front, " B " in the trench behind Destriment Trench and " C " Company in Zigzag Trench. As the front and communication trenches here were in a very bad state of repair, it was fortunate that the enemy was not very active, though casualties did occur from an enfilading fire he was able to bring to bear.

The diary account of the events of the next few days runs as follows:

" 4th. The enemy shelled Headquarters dug-out heavily with 5·9's and it had to be vacated. That evening a platoon of ' C ' Company and the Battalion bombers attacked the trench and sap in O.G.2 to the immediate right of the Bapaume Road, the 10th West Ridings attacking O.G.2 on the left of the road. Our attack succeeded, but the latter failed. The position was consolidated and blocked. Three counter-attacks were driven off by us.

" 5th. Early this morning a fourth counter-attack was driven off by us. There was considerable enemy shelling between 6 p.m. and 8 p.m. This night our heavy artillery shelled that portion of the trench captured by us on the 4th, killing two sergeants and several men, and we had to retire to our old position, which we handed over on relief to the 9th Yorks," (Green Howards) " and the Battalion moved into support in Prue, Starfish and Martin Alley and Push Trenches. During this period in the trenches the weather was abominable and communication, telephonic and other, was very difficult, while the enemy's artillery was very active. Our casualties for the period were: killed, 19 other ranks; wounded, Lieutenant N. E. O. Story, Second-Lieutenants R. F. Wilson, A. W. Ross, A. P. Jackson and F. Ayton and 86 other ranks; shell-shocked, 5 men, and missing, 1 man. . . .

" 7th. The 68th and 69th Infantry Brigades assaulted and captured Le Sars at 1.45 p.m. ' C ' Company was sent up to reinforce the 9th Yorks in Le Sars, remaining there until the 9th was relieved. A heavy barrage was put on Martinpuich Ridge during the attack, one of our orderlies being killed.

" 8th. Le Sars was held and we provided working parties for carrying purposes as before. The 15th Division relieved the 23rd this day. The Battalion was relieved by the 7th Cameron Highlanders and marched to Scots Redoubt, arriving there about 10.30 p.m."

Next day the 8th Green Howards marched to billets in Albert, and on the 11th the Corps Commander inspected and congratulated the 69th Brigade on the work it had done during its second tour of duty in the Somme area.

In these final operations the Battalion incurred further losses, amounting to ten men killed, thirty-five wounded, three missing and one shell-shocked.

On the 12th October and following days the 23rd Division entrained at Albert for the X. Corps area, the Battalion detraining at Hopoutre on the 15th and marching to billets at Poperinghe, where the usual trench warfare was entered upon; but from now until the end of the year the Battalion was not concerned in any event of importance, while even when the year 1917 opened there was no unusual activity on this front, and much time was given to patrol work, and a raid carried out by the Battalion in February seems worthy of special mention.

At 3 a.m. on the 20th then a raiding party of twenty-eight non-commissioned officers and men under Lieutenant F. C. Miller entered the enemy's trenches in the front of the Battalion. A Bangalore torpedo was used to cut a passage through the wire, and during the time that the raiding party was in the enemy trenches the British guns maintained a box barrage. All the arrangements worked well, and the party entered the German lines without opposition, but as these had earlier been evacuated no prisoners were taken. The party remained for half an hour in the German trenches and returned without having suffered any casualties. Congratulations reached the Battalion on the success of the arrangements from the Commander of the Second Army and from the Brigadier.

For some six weeks from the end of February, 1917, the Brigade was in a training area about Houlle, but by the 14th April it was back again in the neighbourhood of Ypres, where The Green Howards furnished many working parties for the Royal Engineers, mainly for carrying stores up to the front line at night, and when out of the front line being accommodated in Toronto Camp or in scattered farms about the village of Steenvoorde; but there is very little worthy of record until the 3rd June, when the 69th Brigade was concentrated in the Ouderdom area in readiness to take part in the fighting for the Messines-Wytschaete Ridge. The 23rd Division was still in the X. Corps of the Second Army.

" The group of hills known as the Messines–Wytschaete Ridge lies about midway between the towns of Armentières and Ypres. Situated at the eastern end of the range of abrupt isolated hills which divides the valleys of the River Lys and the River Yser, it links up that range with the line of rising ground which from Wytschaete stretches north-eastwards to the Ypres–Menin Road, and then northwards past Passchendaele to Staden. The village of Messines, situated on the southern spur of the ridge, commands a wide view of the valley of the Lys, and enfiladed the British lines to the south. North-west of Messines the village of Wytschaete, situated at the point of the salient and on the highest part of the ridge, from its height of about two hundred and sixty feet commands even more completely the town of Ypres and the whole of the old British positions in the Ypres Salient."*

The British position in the Ypres salient had long been very unsatisfactory : it was completely overlooked, it was difficult to defend at any time, and in the event of a serious attack would be very costly to maintain, and it would be greatly improved by the capture of the Messines–Wytschaete Ridge and of the high ground extending thence north-eastwards. It had been decided that the reinforcements received, coupled with the quality they had shown, justified an attempt to capture the ridge being made so soon as the spring offensive in the south had come to an end.

On the night of the 5th June, the 8th Battalion The Green Howards left for the trenches, passing the 2nd Battalion of the Regiment *en route*, and meeting on the way with heavy enemy shelling with occasional bursts of lachrymatory and gas shells, and some eleven casualties were incurred. Headquarters and " B " and " D " Companies with two platoons of " C "

* Despatch of 25th December, 1917.

went to Larch Wood Tunnels, while " A " Company and the rest of " C " went to Strong Point No. 9.   The 6th June passed uneventfully and all rested as much as possible in preparation for the great events that were awaited.*

At 2 a.m. on the 7th, "A" Company and two platoons of " C " moved up to Panama Canal and Jackson Avenue, and half an hour later the whole Battalion was ready in the assembly trenches, all in high spirits and eager to move forward.   On both sides now the shelling died away, but the enemy kept on sending up Very lights from Hill 60.

At 3 in the morning of the 7th the men got out of their assembly trenches and lay down in front of them, and ten minutes later nineteen great mines exploded simultaneously beneath the enemy's defences, the British guns opened a heavy bombardment, and the infantry went forward.   The advance was difficult as the darkness was intense, but it was steadily maintained, Captains Lambert and Pearson handling their companies with much skill, moving round the great craters with which the front was studded, broadening their front, closing and changing direction as became necessary.   The Red Line was captured with great dash, while " C " Company under Captain Atkinson advanced upon and captured the two mine craters ; consolidation was in progress by 3.20.

Battalion Headquarters had started in front of the leading wave, but on reaching Deep Support, it was so far in front of the Battalion that a halt had to be called.   At 3.20, however, a further advance was made, and by 3.30 Headquarters was established on the eastern slope of Hill 60 at the Mound, in accordance with the instructions received from the Brigade. In the meantime " A " and " B " Companies, having hardly checked on the Red Line, had pushed on to the Blue Line close under the British barrage. These companies slightly overran the Blue Line owing to the fact that as the companies drew near the enemy bolted from the shell-holes they were occupying and the men could with difficulty be held back from pursuit ; further, the enemy trenches had been so knocked about by shell fire that it was not easy to recognize the line they had occupied.   Both companies now sent patrols forward.

At 3.40 " D " Company passed through in artillery formation and occupied the Black Line, meeting little or no opposition and having hardly any casualties ; but now, as the troops on right and left were not yet up in line, a slight withdrawal took place in order to establish touch.   The rest of the morning was then spent in reorganizing, consolidating, bringing up material and stores and in putting strong points in a state of defence.   Finally, on

* In the Messines Battle, companies were thus commanded: " A," Captain Pearson; "B, " Captain Lambert ;   " C," Captain Atkinson ;   and " D," Captain Reed.

the night of the 10th–11th June, " B," " C " and " D " Companies were relieved and went back into reserve in the copses near Zillebeke, " A " Company remaining in the front line until the following night, when the whole Battalion moved by lorry to Montreal Camp.

The losses had been heavy : killed or died of wounds were Captain E. N. Lambert, Second-Lieutenant W. Buckle and 35 other ranks ; wounded were Captain B. L. Pearson, Lieutenant A. G. McCullock, Second-Lieutenants C. W. Jones, J. L. Armstrong, J. T. Shaw, W. H. Mitchell, H. J. Smith and A. T. Dudley, and 195 non-commissioned officers and men, while 15 men were missing.

On the afternoon of the 13th the 8th Green Howards marched to the Berthen area, where they were billeted in barns, and where on the 17th General Babington, commanding the 23rd Division, inspected the Battalion and congratulated all ranks on the success attained on the 7th June.

At the end of the month this area was left, the Battalion moving *via* Godwaersvelde to Alberta Camp, one mile south of Reninghelst ; here eight young officers joined on first appointment—Second-Lieutenants R. R. Crute, J. H. McNicholas, L. C. Dickens, W. Lister, F. C. Vernon, C. A. Bottomley, E. Clegg, J. H. Morrison and J. Mills ; and from here on the 30th the Battalion moved up to the front once more, taking over a line of trenches slightly in advance of those which The Green Howards had assaulted on the 7th of the month. The line now consisted of a series of posts ; the day was very rainy, and the position of the enemy was not easily made out.

Early in July the Brigade went back by road and rail to the neighbourhood of Steenvoorde, where a big draft of two hundred and nineteen non-commissioned officers and men, fifty per cent. of whom had not been out before, joined the Battalion ; a few days later a further draft of sixty-four other ranks arrived. By the 13th the Battalion had gone back to the front again, when the new draft was at once " blooded," the enemy shelling causing some thirty casualties in " D " Company, two officers—Second-Lieutenants Mills and Morrison—both newly joined, being wounded. Here, or hereabouts, the 8th Green Howards remained until the 26th, when they marched to Caestre and there entrained for St. Omer, and on arrival here marched by way of St. Martins, Tatinghem and Quelmes to very comfortable billets in Acquin. Here in very pleasant and warm weather training of all kinds and courses of every description were entered upon. There was a change of quarters on the 9th, when the 8th Green Howards marched to Houlle, when the Division found itself in the XVIII. Corps, commanded by General Sir I. Maxse, of the Fifth Army. A very profitable month was passed in this area, and then on the 24th the Battalion moved by train to

Abeele in the Wippenhoek area, the Division being transferred to the II. Corps, but remaining in the Fifth Army.

On the 27th, while reconnoitring the trenches which the Battalion was about to take over, Lieutenant-Colonel B. C. M. Western, D.S.O., was severely wounded by a shell, when Major R. C. Grellet assumed command of the Battalion in his place.

The preparations for the third attack in the Third Battle of Ypres had now been completed, and the 20th September had been chosen for the date of the assault, the front to be attacked extending from the Ypres–Comines Canal, north of Hollebeke, to the Ypres–Staden Railway, north of Lange-marck, a distance of just over eight miles along the line held by the British ; the average depth of the objectives was one thousand yards, increasing to a depth of a mile in the neighbourhood of the Menin Road.

On the eve of the attack the 8th Green Howards were in camp near Dickebusch, but left camp in two parties in the afternoon and evening, and in heavy rain, for the line, the 69th Brigade attacking Inverness Copse at 5.45 a.m. on the 20th ; but in the action the Battalion did not act as a unit, its companies being all separately engaged. The companies were now commanded as follows : " A," Captain Boys ; " B," Captain Miller ; " C," Lieutenant Heron ; and " D," Captain Tilly.

" A " Company moved into New Cut fifteen minutes after zero, and at 2.30 p.m. was directed to report to the O.C. 10th West Riding Regiment, who ordered the Company to proceed to the Strong Point " N," and support the right of the Green Line ; two platoons accordingly dug in in front of this Strong Point, and at dusk Second-Lieutenant Summerville, with two Lewis gun sections, was attached to " A " Company of the 10th West Riding Regiment. These dispositions remained unchanged until " A " Company of the 8th Green Howards was finally relieved.

" D " Company was also attached to the 10th West Riding Regiment for the attack on the final objective and moved up to the Clapham Junction–Stirling Castle area on the night of the 19th–20th, lying down in the open behind the ridge until zero hour on the 20th, when the Company moved into Jasper Lane and remained here for three hours. It then advanced on the right of the Australian Division and on the left of the 10th West Riding Regiment, assisting in the capture of the final objective at about 11 o'clock in the morning. Here the Company consolidated and, the enemy making no counter-attack, it was finally relieved on the night of the 23rd–24th.

" C " Company moved up to the Blue Line at 11.30 a.m. on the 20th to act as reserve to the Green Line. At 6.30 on the morning of the 21st it took over from two companies—" B " and " C "—of the 10th West Riding

Regiment in the front line, being in its turn relieved on the morning of the 22nd and moving to Sanctuary Wood, leaving here early on the 24th.

"B" Company had proceeded to Wellington Crescent Trench on Yeomanry Ridge at 11 p.m. on the 19th and remained there during the night, but on the following morning the Company was ordered to move to the assembly position in New Cut at fifteen minutes after zero hour, carrying with it all consolidation stores, and on reaching the assembly position still more stores were drawn. Three hours after zero "B" Company of the 8th Green Howards followed the West Riding Regiment "over the top," moving in half-platoons in artillery formation. The barrage which the enemy had laid on Inverness Copse was passed through with some casualties, and the Company reached its objective—the four dug-outs near a tower known as Strong Point "I." These dug-outs were, however, found to be destroyed, so the Company dug in round them. Reconnoitring parties were sent forward to the Green Line at Northampton Farm and Strong Point "O" to clear up the situation and to find out the positions of the other companies. An hour after arrival at the objective the O.C. West Riding Regiment ordered two platoons of "B" Company, 8th Green Howards, to reinforce the Green Line, and Nos. 5 and 6 accordingly proceeded thither and dug in. The two remaining platoons were ordered to form Strong Point "N" and act as supports to the Green Line. These two platoons also carried forward the consolidation stores brought up by the Company.

During the night of the 20th–21st the platoons in the front line carried on consolidation, and by the morning a continuous line had been dug.

At 7 p.m. on the 21st the enemy opened a heavy barrage on the forward area, and large numbers of Germans were seen massing as though for a counter-attack, but they were dispersed by artillery and Lewis-gun fire. More good work was done during the night of the 21st–22nd, and then on the following night the Company was relieved and proceeded to Sanctuary Wood Craters, being finally sent back on the morning of the 24th to Alberta Camp, near Reninghelst.

During these operations Major R. C. Grellet, the commanding officer, and Lieutenant W. E. Bush, the adjutant, were both wounded; temporary command of the Battalion was assumed by Captain E. Boys, but on the 27th, just before the 8th Green Howards returned to the line about Sanctuary Wood, Captain Boys was again relieved in command by Major A. C. Barnes, D.S.O., of the 9th Battalion, who was himself relieved on the 1st October by Major M. R. C. Backhouse, D.S.O., Northumberland Yeomanry.

The month of October was spent in and out of the line, while in the line the Battalion occupying trenches about Reninghelst, and when out of it going to Micmac and other camps. On the 14th the troops were gratified by the receipt of the following message :

> " The Army Commander has desired that his appreciation of the conduct of all ranks of the 23rd Division during the operations from the 27th September to the 2nd October, 1917, should be conveyed to all units concerned. The manner in which the line was held and the several counter-attacks repulsed reflects great credit on all the troops engaged."

The drafts that came out during this month were, in regard at any rate to "other ranks," very small, and at the end of the month the strength of the Battalion was 43 officers and 803 other ranks ; during that time 9 officers and 107 non-commissioned officers and men had joined, the officers being Second-Lieutenants C. J. Roddam, H. L. Oakley, D. Fullerton, N. Millar, L. Hart, K. C. Bruce, H. Oldfield, F. Summerscale and F. G. Parker ; while during the same period Lieutenant C. H. Sparshott, Second-Lieutenant T. E. Hardcastle and 45 men had been wounded, 32 were killed, and 1 was missing. On the 31st October, the Battalion paraded in drill order and marched to Leulinghem, where the Brigade was inspected by Field-Marshal Sir Douglas Haig, the strength of the 8th Green Howards on parade being 26 officers and 540 other ranks.

For some little time past there had been rumours that the 23rd Division might very shortly be transferred to another and a distant theatre of war, and on the 7th November the Battalion marched from Acquin, where it had been quartered for rather more than a fortnight, and moving by Longuenesse, entrained at Wizernes for Italy in two parties—Headquarters, " C " and " D " Companies at 5 p.m. on the 8th, and the remainder of the Battalion at 2 o'clock on the morning of the 9th.

An explanation must now be given of the sudden transfer of several Allied divisions from France and Flanders to Northern Italy.

During the month of October Austria, assisted by German forces, had made repeated and desperate attacks upon the Italian troops on the Isonzo and Carnia fronts, but the earlier of these were repulsed, and there seemed at the time no reason to fear that our Allies would not be able to hold their own. On the 24th October, however, the Austro-German troops, under cover of a thick fog, made a very powerful attack along a twenty-mile front, and succeeded in breaking through the line of the Italian Second Army at Tolmino, Caporetto and Plezzo. The Italian Second and Third Armies then fell back behind the line of the Tagliamento River, losing 18,000 prisoners and 1,500 guns.

In response to the appeals for assistance now made by the Italian Government, the War Councils of Great Britain and France agreed to send help, and seven French and five British Divisions were hurriedly dispatched to Italy ; but before these had reached the scene of action the enemy had gained further successes and our Allies had fallen back to the line of the Piave, where the enemy advance was at last checked. The five British divisions detailed to proceed to Italy left as under :

The 23rd Division on the 9th November.
The 41st　　　,,　　　　,,　　12th November.
The 7th　　　,,　　　　,,　　19th November.
The 48th　　　,,　　　　,,　　23rd November.
The 5th　　　,,　　　　,,　　 1st December.

These were all placed under the command of General Sir Herbert Plumer, then in command of the Second Army on the Western Front, and the whole formed part of an Anglo-French force under the French General Fayolle.

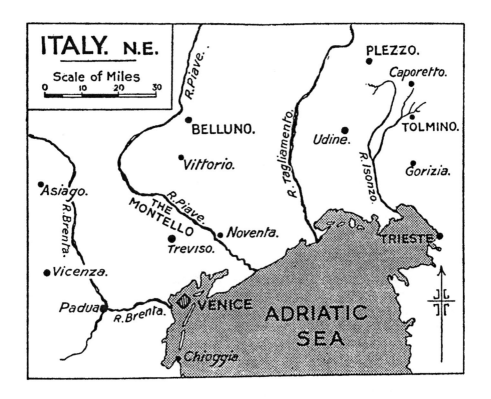

CHAPTER XIV

THE 8TH BATTALION

1917–1918

THE OPERATIONS IN ITALY. THE BATTLE OF VITTORIO VENETO

GENERAL SIR H. PLUMER, who arrived in the Italian theatre of war in advance of the units of his new Army, has given the following account * of the military situation there as he found it: "It was certainly disquieting. The Italian Army had just received a very severe blow, from which it was bound to require time to recover and reorganize. . . . The Italian retreat had been arrested on the River Piave, but it was uncertain whether they could hold this line, and in the first instance it was arranged that, in conjunction with the French, two of our divisions should move forward on arrival to the hills north and south of Vicenza, where a stand could certainly have been made. The forward march was well carried out. The marches were necessarily long, as time was, or might have been, important. . . . By the time we reached the above position the general situation had improved, and it was suggested that we should take over the Montello sector with the French on our left, to which we agreed. The Montello sector is a feature by itself and an important one. It acts as a hinge to the whole Italian line, joining as it does that portion facing north from Monte Tomba to Lake Garda, with the defensive line of the River Piave covering Venice, which was held by the Third Italian Army. We took over the line on the 4th December and at once got to work to organize the defences in depth. . . . December was an anxious month."

On the 23rd Division leaving France the following farewell order was issued by Lieutenant-General Sir T. Morland, commanding X. Army Corps:

"G.O.C. and All Ranks 23rd Division.

"It is with much regret that I have again to part with you from the X. Corps. The Division has served with the Corps for a year with

* Despatch of the 9th March, 1918.

a few short intervals, and during this period it has taken part in the Messines operations and those from 20th September onward. The Division has done all that was asked of it, and has invariably retained the captured ground. Throughout it has shown a fine fighting spirit and dash in attack, and resolution and dogged determination in defence.

" In wishing you good-bye I am confident that you will maintain your fine reputation wherever you may be called upon to serve."

The trains conveying the Battalion passed through Paris, Lyons, Marseilles, Toulon, Cannes, San Remo, Savona, Sampierdarena and Busalla ; and on the morning of the 13th November the first party of the 8th Green Howards detrained at San Antonio and then marched by Mantua and Castelluchio to billets at Rivalta, where the companies arrived at 6.30 in the evening, being joined only an hour and a half later by the left half-battalion. Only a very few days were spent here, for on the 19th the Battalion started with the 69th Brigade on its long march of one hundred and twenty miles to the Montello sector of the front, moving by Gazzo, Concarmarise, Minerbe—where General Plumer saw the Division on the road—Noventa, Coleredo, Sossano, Belvidere, Barbarano, Mossano, Nanto, Castegnero, Lurnignano, Costozza, Longare, Grumolo, Camisano, Grossa, Bonzonella—crossing the river Brenta *en route*—Castelfranco and Valla to Edifizio, where on the 29th November the march came to an end.

The 23rd Division now joined the XIV. Corps, commanded by General Lord Cavan, who forwarded the following letter to General Babington, commanding the Division :

" The Corps Commander having seen all arms of your Division at different points of its historical march, congratulates you and all ranks on :
(i.) The good march discipline maintained throughout.
(ii.) The smartness of the transport.
(iii.) The fine spirit of the men in spite of their fatigue."

To this the General Officer Commanding the 23rd Division added the following :

" The G.O.C. feels proud to command a Division which has gained such praises, and confidently relies on all ranks to maintain its reputation in any circumstances."

The strength of the 8th Battalion The Green Howards on the 30th of November was 35 officers and 827 other ranks.

It was not until the 2nd December that the Division moved up to the line, two brigades being in the front and the 69th Brigade being on the right ; the Battalion, at a trench strength of 27 officers and 546 other ranks, relieved the 135th Regiment of Italian Infantry, and " A," " C " and " D " Companies were in front, with " B " in support in rear. There was a certain amount of shelling during the few days that the Battalion held the front, but very light compared with what the officers and men had been accustomed to in France, and all ranks were able to give much-needed attention to sanitation and the construction of proper dug-outs. During the hours of darkness patrols under Captain Miller and Second-Lieutenant Sommerville attempted to find crossing-places over the Piave, but some of the many channels into which the stream was divided were too deep and the current running too swiftly to be forded.

The Montello itself was a hill some one thousand yards in length, lozenge-shaped and nearly one thousand feet high ; the view from the summit was very fine, to the north the mountains, and to the east the enemy lines, being visible ; looking south was the Piave running through the Venetian plain, and in the far distance the sea.

On the 10th December the Battalion incurred its first casualties in the Italian theatre of war, two men being wounded in " A " and two in " D " Company. This month again a patrol examined the river, Second-Lieutenant Sommerville, Lance-Corporal Sewell and Private Prudhoe, all of " A " Company, reconnoitring the island in the Piave opposite the front of the Company, but they were unable to cross the deep channel on the further side of the island to reach the north bank. No sign of any enemy was seen.

During December some one hundred and thirty non-commissioned officers and men arrived in drafts and the following officers—Second-Lieutenants D. Fullerton, S. Layfield and J. W. Wilkinson ; while the medical officer, Lieutenant N. Sherrard, R.A.M.C., left to join the 69th Field Ambulance and was succeeded by Captain Picken, R.A.M.C.

On the 30th December a memorandum was circulated in the XIV. Corps which must have been a matter of immense pride and gratification to all ranks of the 69th Brigade ; it ran as follows :

> " 1. The Corps Commander is thoroughly aware of the amount and excellence of the work on defensive lines which has been carried out by all units in the Corps, and has no complaints to make on this head.
>
> " 2. At the same time every one can learn, and he is of opinion that the work done in the sector held by the 69th Infantry Brigade of the 23rd Division is in advance of anything that is being carried out at the moment, both as regards organization of labour and as regards the tactical dispositions.
>
> " 3. He wishes all units of the Corps to study, and, where possible,

to imitate the system which is to be seen in this sector. He wishes therefore G.S.O.'s 1. and C.R.E. of divisions and all brigadiers to visit this sector at as early a date as possible, and in any case before January 3rd ; the arrangement to be made direct with G.O.C. 23rd Division.

"4. There are many points of interest to be seen. Special attention is called to :

(*a*) The combined action of machine and Lewis guns with trench mortars in defence.

(*b*) The amount of tunnelling work which is carried out by men who are not trained as tunnellers. Units have complained that they have no tunnellers available, but the G.O.C. 69th Infantry Brigade has clearly proved that tunnellers can be produced from any unit.

(*c*) The excellent interior economy and cleanliness. Every dug-out has its rifle-rack in which rifles are standing as clean as if in a barrack-room.

"5. If it were possible, and can be arranged with the G.O.C. 23rd Division, the Corps Commander would like Battalion Commanders to visit these lines in addition to the officers enumerated above."

Then on the last day of the year General Plumer, commanding the British Forces in Italy, visited the Brigade front and afterwards issued the following Special Order of the Day :

"After visiting various parts of the Brigade front to-day, the Commander-in-Chief expressed to the Brigade Commander his high appreciation of the work done and of the system of defence, and desired him to give all ranks his good wishes for a very happy New Year."

Reinforcements had continued to join the Battalion in drafts of varying strength, and Captain A. V. Richardson, M.C., Second-Lieutenants K. C. Bruce and F. Summerscale had joined, or rejoined, and on the 31st December the Battalion strength stood as high as 40 officers and 963 non-commissioned officers and men.

From General Plumer's despatch covering this period it is easily to be seen that December was, as stated, an anxious month ; several German divisions had been located among the Austrian troops east of the Piave, and it was expected that an attack would be made. The British had begun to organize the defences directly they took over the line and with every day that the defences grew stronger the sense of security deepened, and by the beginning of the year 1918 the situation on this front was well in hand. January passed tolerably quietly, but the patrol work was very good, and on two occasions during this month did patrols sent out by the 8th Green Howards succeed in crossing to the further bank of the Piave, on the second occasion encountering a strong enemy post which opened fire but inflicted no casualties; in this work Second-Lieutenants Bruce and Wilkinson were conspicuous.

During January four officers and some sixteen men joined the Battalion.

Meanwhile, the British Army in Italy, short as was the time during which it had served in the country, had already won golden opinions from all, from H.M. the King downwards, who had come in contact with the officers, non-commissioned officers and men composing its units, as may be seen from the following letter written by the British Ambassador in Rome to Mr. Arthur Balfour, dated Rome, 8th January, 1918:

" Sir,—

" The following quite unsolicited testimonial as to the impression which British troops are making in Italy will undoubtedly be of interest.

" The President of the Council observed yesterday that he could not allow the opportunity to pass of expressing his unqualified admiration of the British troops which had been sent to Italy. He had just come down from the front, and in saying what he did he felt he was echoing the opinion of General Diaz and also of the King of Italy. His Majesty said he could not find words to express adequately his appreciation of these troops. There had not been a single case of indiscipline or any subject of complaint. I have also been shown a private letter from an Italian officer, unknown to me personally, to a friend of his, in which he writes—' I am at the district headquarters where you may send me a few lines. I have almost all my time done service in the immediate neighbourhood of the British troops. They are marvellous. I am not speaking of their discipline, which is perfect, but of the singular delicacy of feeling which distinguishes officers and soldiers. When they leave a billet which they have occupied, not a chair is out of its proper place. Their cleanliness is so great that you would not find a straw on the ground. So also with their camps, where hundreds of wagons and quadrupeds have stopped—they do not leave any trace of their passage. No one even takes a glass of water without asking leave.'

" Such exemplary conduct cannot fail to have the most beneficial effect on our relations, and I feel most grateful to the Supreme Command in Italy for having inspired the forces sent to this country with such a high ideal of their obligations."

On the 13th February there was a distressing accident when an officer and some other ranks of the Battalion were examining an enemy shell; this suddenly and unaccountably exploded, killing Captain F. Hiley and seriously wounding three sergeants and one private soldier.

In the middle of this month the 23rd Division, on relief by the 41st, moved *via* Pederiva, Posmon, Busta, Casell and Altivole to Brioni and Loria, remaining here until the 25th, when it returned to the Montello sector; but about four weeks later there was a change of front, as the Division was now to take over part of the line on the Asiago Plateau, and marching by Lisiera, Monticello, Villaverla and Thiene, the Battalion proceeded to the Granezza area and on the 29th relieved the 2nd Battalion the 27th Regiment of Italian Infantry in the Reserve Brigade area at Monte Langebisa.

" Some description of the Asiago Plateau position is necessary for the reader to understand the sector taken over by the British forces. The Venetian plain extends northwards to a line running roughly east to west through Marostica, Breganze, Thiene and Schio. Just north of this line the ground rises abruptly to an average height of four thousand to four thousand five hundred feet. The Asiago Plateau is a sort of natural basin in the Alps and is some seven miles in extent from east to west, and three miles from north to south. The central point of the plateau is the town of Asiago (3,000 feet), a well-known pre-war winter sports resort. The plateau is bounded on the south by pine-covered mountains of a depth of about four thousand yards to the point where the mountains slope steeply down to the plain. To the north lies a higher and deeper range of mountains guarding the Southern Trentino, and merging back gradually into the high Alps. At the western end the plateau narrows down to the gloomy ravine of the Val D'Asse, where the opposing front trenches are close to one another on each side of an impassable gorge some two thousand feet deep. To the east the plateau again ends in the rugged heights on each side of the Brenta. The plateau itself consists of undulating cultivated land freely sprinkled with villages, and perfectly adaptable for ordinary military operations.

" The importance of the position may be judged when the point is grasped that this was the only part of the whole Italian mountain front where the operations of ordinary attack were possible. From the enemy point of view the temptation to start an offensive in this sector must have been irresistible. The Austrians were well served by a first-class road running from north to south from their railheads at Levico and Caldonazzo; their positions dominated ours, and they had only to overrun our front line to a depth of four thousand yards to stand on the edge of the mountains overlooking the plain, with no further obstacle nearer than the Adige to a subsequent advance." *

There was at this time every inducement for the Austrians to attempt such an offensive, since the success of the great German attacks recently

* Barnett, *With the 48th Division in Italy,* pp. 36 and 37.

T

made against the Western Front had rendered necessary the sudden recall of certain of the Anglo-French divisions sent to Italy in consequence of the Caporetto disaster.   General Sir Herbert Plumer had been recalled to France and left Italy in the middle of March, while by the 3rd April four French divisions and the 5th and 41st British Divisions had been withdrawn from the neighbourhood of the Piave and sent back to France. The command of the British forces remaining in Italy was, on the departure of Sir Herbert Plumer, assumed by Lieutenant-General the Earl of Cavan.

"During April," wrote Lord Cavan, "signs continued to accumulate that the enemy contemplated an offensive astride the Brenta, but it was not until the middle of May that it appeared probable that this operation would be combined with an attack across the Piave.   By the end of May the general plan of the enemy for their forthcoming attack could be already foreseen.   Subsequent events proved that the Italian high command had made a forecast correct in nearly every detail." *

At the end of May Brigadier-General Lambert, C.M.G., was promoted from the command of the 69th Brigade to that of the 32nd Division, his place being filled by Brigadier-General Beauman.

The months of April and May passed comparatively quietly, but the work of our patrols was incessant, and much useful intelligence was obtained as to the dispositions of the enemy and the condition of his defences ; the British artillery was very active, but the enemy guns made but little reply ; rumours continued to grow as to the probability of an early enemy offensive, though it was not until June opened that any reliable information was obtained as to the intentions of the Austrians.

Early on the morning of the 8th June a successful raid was carried out by "D" Company divided into three parties ; the first party, under Captain Tilly, M.C., and Second-Lieutenant Wilkinson, consisted of two platoons, while the other two parties, each one platoon strong, were commanded by Second-Lieutenants Lister and Oldfield respectively.   At zero hour the British guns bombarded Morar and the raiding parties moved forward, but at once found that the enemy were on the alert—it was supposed they were "standing to" at the moment—and at once machine-gun and rifle fire opened from Morar and from the enemy front line, while trench mortars also attempted to put down a barrage round Morar from a point which could not be located.

No. 1 Party of the 8th Green Howards seems to have rather lost direction, for instead of attacking Morar from due east, the bulk of the party reached the south-east corner of the village, where Captain Tilly

* Despatch of the 14th September, 1918.

was unfortunately very severely wounded ; Second-Lieutenant Wilkinson succeeded, however, in getting through the wire with a few men and exterminated an enemy post of three men.   No. 2 Party made gallant and repeated attempts to force an entrance to the village from the south, but the enemy resisted stoutly with bombs and machine-gun fire, while the wire proved much stronger than had been expected.   Still this second party did most valuable work in keeping the garrison fully occupied, and so gave No. 3 Party a fine opportunity, of which they were not slow to take advantage.   This party, admirably led and handled by Second-Lieutenant Oldfield, forced a passage through the wire on the west of Morar, meeting there a sentry-post of which one man was killed and another captured. The house at the south-western angle was then rushed and ten more prisoners taken.

The raid had now been in progress half an hour and as its objects had been gained, Second-Lieutenant Lister, now in command, judged it advisable to retire without searching the houses further, and the retirement was successfully carried out despite a light barrage put down by the enemy's guns.

The loss of Captain Tilly, who died of his wounds, was greatly felt ; he met his death going forward alone to reconnoitre a better line of approach when he found his party held up by strong wire, and the success of the raid was very largely due to his careful organization and fighting spirit.

Three men of the Company were slightly wounded in this affair.

On the 15th June the Austrians attacked on two fronts, the one of twenty-five miles from St. Dona di Piave to the Montello, the other of eighteen miles from Monte Grappa to Canove, the whole of the British sector being involved and the 23rd and 48th Divisions being engaged.

" The British front was attacked by four Austrian divisions.   It was held by the 23rd Division on the right and the 48th Division on the left. On the front of the 23rd Division the attack was completely repulsed. On the front of the 48th Division the enemy succeeded in occupying our front trench for a length of some three thousand yards, and subsequently penetrated to a depth of about one thousand yards.   Here he was contained by a series of switches, which had been constructed to meet this eventuality.   On the morning of June 16th the 48th Division launched a counter-attack to clear the enemy from the pocket he had gained ; this attack was completely successful, and the entire line was re-established by 9 a.m." *

On the night of the 14th June the 23rd Division was disposed as under : " The 70th Infantry Brigade occupied the right section of the Divisional

* Lord Cavan's despatch of the 14th September, 1918.

front covered by the 102nd Brigade R.F.A.; the 68th Infantry Brigade, in occupation of the left section, were covered by the 103rd Brigade R.F.A. The 22nd Brigade R.F.A. of the 7th Division, sent for the proposed attack of June 18, also supported the front. The 70th Infantry Brigade held two battalions in the front line, one battalion in support in the second line, and one battalion in reserve, of which two companies were immediately in rear of the second line—one at Pria dell' Acqua and one at Granezza.

" The 68th Infantry Brigade held their battalions in the front line, the second line being garrisoned by one company from each of the flank battalions and one company from the battalion in brigade reserve. The remaining companies of the reserve battalion were placed at and in rear of Mt. Torle." *

At 4 a.m. on the 15th the 8th Green Howards were ordered to move immediately and in fighting order to Granezza, and on arrival here at 7.30 instructions were received to occupy the so-called " Marginal Line " immediately south of Granezza. This was done, the companies being disposed in the following order from right to left—" D," " C," " B " and " A "; Lewis-gun positions and rifle posts were selected, and a hot meal was prepared. It was now learnt that, after a heavy bombardment, the enemy had attacked in force at dawn, but had only succeeded in gaining a footing on a very small portion of the front line near San Sisto ; but the right of the 48th Division at its junction with the 23rd had been pressed back.

At about 2 p.m. " A " and " C " Companies were directed to report at once at Brigade Headquarters at Granezza, and on arrival here they went forward to reinforce the 70th Brigade on the right.

Rather more than an hour later, Battalion Headquarters with the two remaining companies was ordered to report to the G.O.C. 68th Brigade at Monte Kaberlaba, and on arriving here about 5.30 p.m. they were told off to reinforce the left flank of the Division at dusk. The two companies —" B " and " D "—finally arrived in position in the second-line trenches on Monte Kaberlaba South at 11 o'clock at night and came under the orders of the O.C. 10th Battalion Northumberland Fusiliers. Major Boys now took command of the second line, the defenders of which were the two companies of the 8th Green Howards and one company of the 10th Northumberland Fusiliers. The two companies—" A " and " C "—sent to the 20th Brigade had in the meanwhile been disposed of as follows : " A " in support of the 8th York and Lancaster Regiment, and " C " as a reinforcement to the 9th York and Lancaster, two platoons going up into the front line, where one of them collected three machine guns and a number of prisoners. The night passed quietly and the 16th was uneventful, the

* *History of the 23rd Division*, p. 253.

Austrians making no attempt to renew the attack, having lost over one thousand prisoners, seven mountain guns, seventy-two machine guns and twenty flammenwerfer.

"Torrential rains brought the Piave down in flood and added to the embarrassment of the enemy. Many of his bridges were washed away, and those which remained were constantly bombed by British and Italian aviators. By means of a succession of vigorous counter-attacks the enemy was gradually pressed back again both on the Piave and the mountain fronts. As a result, not only was the original front line entirely re-established, but that portion of the right bank of the Piave, between the Piave and the Sile rivers, which had been in Austrian hands since November, 1917, was cleared of the enemy. Captured orders and documents proved beyond doubt that the enemy's plans were extremely ambitious, and aimed in fact at the final defeat of the Allied forces in Italy. The result was a complete and disastrous defeat for Austria." *

On this day the following orders were published, the first from Lord Cavan to the 23rd and 48th Divisions, the second from the Sixth Italian Army Command to the Allied forces generally :

"Owing to the staunchness of the 23rd Division and the determination of the 48th Division to lose no ground to the Austrians, our positions have been maintained. My sincere thanks to all ranks."

Sixth Italian Army Order of the Day.

"Yesterday the Army of the Plateau sustained and repulsed the fierce attack which the enemy, very superior in numbers, launched against our front. From Cesuna to Kaberlaba, from Pennar to the mountains of Val Bella and Pizzo Razea ; on the Cornone and in Val Brenta ; British, French and Italian troops, emulating one another in gallantry and valour, held and defended the lines which were entrusted to their bayonets. The enemy attack, intended to overthrow our defences and reach the edge of the plains, was contained and broken. The ancient foe of right and civilization was once more shown the faith and spirit with which our troops are animated.

"With the greatest pride and feeling I salute the British, French and Italian troops and their Commanders, both Infantry and Artillery, who struck consternation into the hearts of the enemy. I would add a grateful tribute to our heroic dead, and finally I am sure that the Army will join me in repeating from the bottom of our hearts the inspiring motto which is ringing to-day from the North Sea to the Adriatic—' Non Si Passa.'

(Sd.) " L. MONTUORI, Lieut.-General.
" Commanding Sixth Italian Army."

* Despatch of the 14th September, 1918.

On the 17th the 8th Battalion The Green Howards moved into Brigade reserve, Headquarters and " C " Company at Pria dell' Acqua, and the other three companies between that place and Malgafassa Fort. During the progress of this Austrian attack the Battalion had one man killed and five men wounded.

On the 22nd June Major J. C. Bull, M.C., 10th Battalion West Riding Regiment, assumed command of the Battalion, which at this time was busily employed in putting up wire on the San Sisto Ridge—a ridge one thousand yards long, three hundred broad, where was the junction of the British and French lines, steep on the near side and sloping and wooded towards the enemy; late in July, however, Major Grellet rejoined on recovery from his wound and relieved Major Bull, who then took over the duties of second in command.

July, August and part of September went by without any incidents of outstanding importance, but early in this last month, as it seemed unlikely that offensive operations were to be undertaken in Italy in the near future, it was decided to send some of the British troops in that country back to France. In accordance with this idea the 7th, 23rd and 48th Divisions were reduced each from thirteen to ten battalions, one battalion being taken out of each of the three brigades of which each of these divisions was composed; while the 7th and 23rd Divisions were ordered to stand by ready to return to the Western Front so soon as two battle-worn divisions should arrive from France to take their places in Italy.

Under this arrangement the 9th Battalion The Green Howards was taken out of the 69th Brigade and, proceeding to France, joined the 74th Brigade in the 25th Division.

At the time when action was expected to be taken on the decisions come to, the 8th Green Howards were in camp at Carriola; and in order that the 23rd Division might be ready to move back to France without delay, it was, about the middle of September, relieved by troops of the XII. Italian Corps, the 8th Green Howards being relieved on the 25th by the 49th Italian Infantry Regiment of the Parma Brigade, when it proceeded by lorry and by march route from Carriola to billets at Pagana near Vicenza, arriving there on the afternoon of the 26th. Here Lieutenant-Colonel Backhouse met the Battalion and assumed command.

As a result of the tactical situation in France, and consequent demands on rolling stock, the proposed exchange of divisions was postponed from day to day, while the situation in Italy also changed, and finally the 7th, 23rd and 48th Divisions all remained in the country.

About this time the air was full of rumours: that peace would shortly be proclaimed; that an early Allied offensive was under consideration;

but all that was known was that Bulgaria had surrendered and that Austria-Hungary had begged President Wilson to use his good offices in the arrangement of an armistice. General Diaz, the Italian Commander-in-Chief, had with great secrecy been perfecting his arrangements for undertaking offensive operations at a very early date, and on the 13th October there was a conference of Allied Commanders at Comando Supremo, where plans for the forthcoming offensive were explained and discussed.

"The general plan for the main attack was to advance across the Piave with the Tenth, Eighth and Twelfth Italian Armies—to drive a wedge between the Fifth and Sixth Austrian Armies—forcing the Fifth Army eastwards, and threatening the communications of the Sixth Army running through the Valmarino Valley.

"The Fourth Army was simultaneously to take the offensive in the Grappa sector.

"The task allotted to the Tenth Army was to reach the Livenza between Portobuffole and Sacile, and thus protect the flank of the Eighth and Twelfth Armies in their move northwards.

"The co-ordination of the attacks of the Tenth, Eighth and Twelfth Armies was entrusted to General Caviglia, the commander of the Eighth Italian Army.

"On 11th October the Headquarters of the Tenth Army, the Army which had been placed under my command, were established near Treviso.

"The Tenth Army in the first instance was to consist of the XI. Italian and XIV. British Corps." *

The XIV. British Corps, now commanded by Lieutenant-General Babington, contained the 7th and 23rd Divisions, and the latter of these was under the command of Major-General H. F. Thuillier, C.B., C.M.G. ; the 48th Division remained in position on the Asiago Plateau, temporarily under the XII. Italian Corps.

On the 7th October the Battalion had moved to billets in the Ronca area, where it received a very cordial welcome from the inhabitants, who had never had British troops billeted among them before ; and after remaining here rather less than a week, The Green Howards moved on by rail and road *via* Creazzo, Villaverla and Mogliano to Maerne in the Treviso area, where the XIV. Corps was concentrated by the 16th. Here General Babington caused the following farewell order to be published on leaving the 23rd Division to take up the command of the XIV. Corps :

"It is with no ordinary feelings of regret that Major-General J. M. Babington, K.C.M.G., C.B., relinquishes the command of the 23rd Division, with whom he has served since it was embodied more than

* Despatch of the 15th November, 1918.

four years ago. No commander has ever received more wholehearted support from all ranks than he has during that entire period. By the exemplary conduct in billets and most marked gallantry in the field, the Division has made a name for themselves of which they may well be proud; in more than three years of hard fighting they have never once failed to gain their objective in the attack, or lost any ground in the defence. Major-General Babington thanks all ranks from his heart for their devoted services, and, in bidding them farewell, assures them that his pride in them is only equalled by his affection for them."

On the 21st October the Battalion had moved up nearer to the front and that night was billeted in a group of farmhouses at Carita, about two miles from the front line; the following afternoon the companies marched to support positions on the left of the British front, being thus disposed : " B " and " D " Companies at Casa Barchese, " C " at Casa Castelli, and " A " Company at Casa Giare.

During the night of the 23rd–24th two battalions of the 7th Division crossed the main channel of the Piave to the island known as Grave di Papadopoli and, surprising the Austrian garrison, captured the northern half of the island, the remainder of the island falling into our hands on the following night, in anticipation of which the 8th Green Howards had at dusk moved up to the river bank and the transfer across the main Piave channel to the island shortly after commenced. For this operation small flat-bottomed boats, each holding six men and manned by Italian boatmen, were provided.

" We were all amazed at the swiftness of the current and the skill with which the Italians managed their boats, manœuvring them, by means of a paddle and helped by the current, to a spot some way downstream on the further bank.

" ' A ' Company, under Captain J. T. Shaw, commenced the passage, and we were rather perturbed to see the first boat-load turn turtle in midstream, the men, weighed down by their arms and equipment, having great difficulty in keeping afloat, but luckily the current swept them several hundred yards downstream and all were able to get safely ashore, and the rest of the Company was ferried over without any casualty in spite of the enemy searchlights and machine-gun fire.

" ' B ' Company, under Captain F. C. Miller, was just beginning to cross when orders were received to stop for the night as the river was rising, so that ' A ' was left marooned on the island, digging themselves in there while the remaining companies returned to billets. Next night— October 26th—the rest of the Battalion was ferried safely across; the

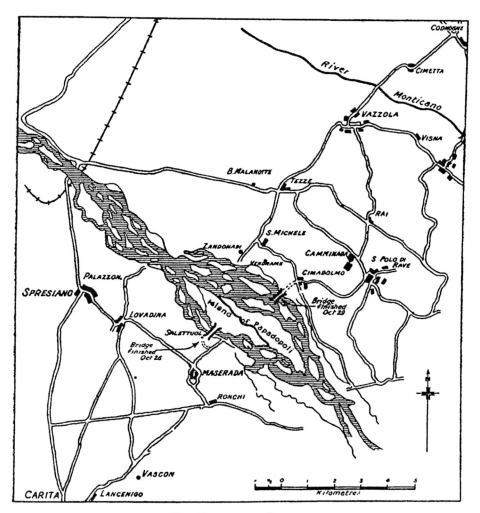

CODROGNE

River

Monticano

CIMETTA

VAZZOLA

VISNA

B. MALANOTTE

TEZZE

RAI

S. MICHELE

ZANDONADI

CAMMINADA

S POLO DI RAVE

VENDRAME

CIMADOLMO

Bridge
finished
Oct 29

PALAZZON

SPRESIANO

Island of Papadopoli

LOVADINA

SALETTUOL

Bridge
finished
Oct 26

MASERADA

RONCHI

VASCON

CARITA

LANCENIGO

0   1   2   3   4   5
Kilometres

THE CAMPAIGN IN ITALY.

281

enemy by this time, however, was well aware of the business in hand and shelled us continuously, but the companies dug themselves in and escaped serious loss.

"At 3 a.m. on October 27th the march began across the mile and a half of river bed. It was quite dark and raining, so that the Battalion moved in column of fours, led by ' A ' Company under Captain Shaw, who had taken a compass bearing previously on an identified building in the enemy position in the village of Zandonadi. It was a curious sight to see the Battalion moving forward, wading through small streams and climbing over sandbanks in complete silence, except for the crunching of the men's boots on the shingle and the bursting of an occasional enemy shell —luckily not accurate. By 6 a.m. the Battalion was deployed in its assembly position in touch with the 10th West Riding Regiment on the left and the 7th Division on the right. It was close on 6.45 a.m. before we got within four hundred yards of the enemy front line, which occupied the top of a high grassy bank. In the half-light we could see between us and the enemy another stream about sixty feet in width and very swift, and it was not without certain misgivings that we contemplated this obstacle. At 6.45 a.m. our artillery, which had hitherto remained silent, opened a terrific bombardment of the enemy's front line, while the Austrians at the same time opened a heavy machine-gun barrage on us, for we were now in full view of them. Arms were slung and the men linking hands plunged into the stream, led by ' B ' Company on the right and ' A ' on the left. The stream proved to be about four feet deep in the centre and the current was so very strong that men could not wade across unaided. Several men were killed and wounded while crossing and some of the wounded were swept away and drowned. It was very cold and raining heavily during the crossing.

"Once on the further bank the Battalion advanced with great determination on the enemy trenches : many of the Austrians left their lines and came forward with hands up to surrender, and by 7 o'clock ' A ' and ' B ' Companies had captured the first line from Zandonadi to a point some four hundred yards west of it. We lost quite a number of men in crossing the open ground between the river bank and the enemy's first line of trenches, but luckily the wire in front was not very thick.

"The 7th Division, having experienced considerable difficulty in crossing, was not in touch, so that our right was in the air, but touch was established with the 10th West Riding Regiment prior to crossing the last channel of the river, and so Colonel Backhouse decided to advance to the final objective of this day's operations.

" ' B ' Company was on the right and moved on the left of the Zan-

THE RIVER PIAVE.

27th October, 1918.

donadi–Tezze Road, with ' A ' on its left, and ' C ' and ' D ' in support, but the enemy seems to have been so surprised at the attack, accompanied as it was by so heavy a shell fire, that he quickly gave way, isolated posts were soon mopped up and many prisoners were taken, while by midday the Battalion had reached its final objective, the Tezze–Borgo Malanotte Road. The captures this day made included six guns and some four hundred prisoners. The night passed fairly quietly, though the Austrians attacked a company of the 11th West Yorkshire Regiment in a village on the left of the line.

" The advance was resumed at 12.30 p.m. on the 28th, ' D ' and ' C ' Companies now leading, under Captains R. Atkinson and C. A. Sparshott respectively, and the forward movement now received but small artillery support, except from the ' heavies,' which fired mainly on road junctions ; very little opposition was met with except from isolated snipers, and by 3 p.m. the advance had brought us to within a mile of Vazzola, and another mile further on was the River Monticano, where it was thought that the enemy would make his next stand. Orders having been received from the Brigade to send forward a company during the night to endeavour to seize the bridge over the Monticano, Colonel Backhouse directed Captain Shaw to undertake this operation with ' A ' Company, ordering him not to become involved with a larger force than his own, since he could not expect support until the advance was resumed next day. ' A ' Company accordingly moved forward with one platoon under Second-Lieutenant Summerville in front, No. 2 in close support, and the other two in rear. Vazzola was reached without incident and was found unoccupied, the inhabitants, who were overjoyed to see British troops and gave us a hearty welcome, reporting that the enemy had been clearing out during the day and that the last of them had only been gone an hour or two.

" The advance continuing up the Vazzola–Cesiola Road towards the Monticano, Second-Lieutenant Summerville quickly reported that he had seized the bridge, but on Captain Shaw going forward he found that it was a bridge over the canal about five hundred yards short of that over the river ; and on advancing further it was discovered that the enemy was holding in strength the Monticano Bridge and the bank of the river. It was now nearly dawn on the 29th, so Captain Shaw consolidated a position on the canal bank.

" At 8.30 the Battalion continued the advance with ' B ' Company leading and a squadron of Northamptonshire Yeomanry in front, and on arrival at the canal passed through ' A ' Company, which was now drawn into reserve. Captain Miller was then ordered to attack the Monticano Bridge, supported by ' C ' and ' D ' under Captains Atkinson and Sparshott. The enemy was here well supplied with machine guns, but the attack was very determined, and after very severe fighting ' B ' Company secured a footing on the further bank by 10 a.m. ' D ' Company, on fire being opened on the left, was ordered to prolong ' B ' Company's left, ' C ' to support the general advance, while ' A ' was in reserve, but this reserve was almost at once reduced to two platoons as the right flank was exposed, while ' C ' Company was soon absorbed into the front line. At the actual forcing of the bridge the dispositions of the Companies were—one platoon ' B ' Company and two of ' A ' on the right; three platoons ' B,' three platoons ' D ' Company on left in touch with 11th West Yorkshire Regiment. The shell fire of the enemy was now very heavy, but ' C ' and ' D ' pushed across the bridge and, working to the left, manœuvred the enemy out of his position on the left bank of the river. Many prisoners were taken in this phase of the battle. The advance was continued to the outskirts of Cimetta, our final objective for the day, in the face of heavy opposition, the enemy contesting every yard, his artillery fire being very heavy, his machine guns, cleverly sited in the vineyards, causing many casualties.

" At this juncture Colonel Backhouse felt constrained to use his reserve, and ' A ' Company was put into the fight on the right of ' B,' so that the whole Battalion was now extended along the whole front, fighting in one line in very enclosed country. The western outskirts of Cimetta were reached at noon, but here, as the troops of the 7th Division had met with very stubborn resistance, ' A ' and ' B ' Companies again became very heavily engaged, several serious counter-attacks being delivered by the enemy against the 7th Division and these two companies; some little ground was lost, but the 8th Green Howards continued to hold the line of the brook three hundred yards south of Cesiola against many determined attacks.

" It was in repelling one of these that Second-Lieutenant Summerville was killed. This gallant officer, who, throughout the operations, had shown absolute disregard for his own safety, took a Lewis gun and crawling out in front of our line, single-handed took on an enemy machine gun. He was unfortunately killed by machine-gun fire while performing this very gallant deed, which undoubtedly did much to maintain our line intact.

" At about 3 p.m. in the afternoon the 91st Brigade of the 7th Division succeeded in getting forward on our right flank and consequently relieved the situation on the right of ' A ' Company; and the 9th York and Lancaster Regiment was now passed through the 8th Green Howards to the final objective, thus bringing to an end the share of this Battalion in the Battle of Vittorio Veneto and in the Great War."

On the 30th the 23rd Division went into Corps reserve, the remaining troops continuing the advance to the Tagliamento, and the 8th Battalion The Green Howards marched from Cesiola to billets in Borgo and Bibano near Orsago.

In the three days' fighting the Battalion had Second-Lieutenant J. Summerville, M.C., M.M., and seventeen other ranks killed, Captain C. H. Sparshott, Second-Lieutenants H. Oldfield, M.C., J. H. Morrison, B. Ainsworth, L. C. Dickens, K. C. Bruce, and ninety-seven non-commissioned officers and men wounded, while three men were missing.

In the battle No. 13820 Sergeant W. McNally, M.M., of the Battalion, won the Victoria Cross, for service described as follows in the *London Gazette* of the 14th December, 1918:

> "For most conspicuous bravery and skilful leading during the operations on the 27th October, 1918, across the Piave, when his company was most seriously hindered by heavy machine-gun fire from the vicinity of some buildings on a flank. Utterly regardless of personal safety he rushed the machine-gun post single-handed, killing the team and capturing the guns.
>
> "Later, at Vazzola, on 29th October, 1918, when his company, having crossed the Monticano River, came under heavy rifle and machine-gun fire, Sergeant McNally immediately directed the fire of his platoon against the danger-point, whilst he himself crept to the rear of the enemy position. Realizing that a frontal attack would mean heavy losses, he, unaided, rushed the position, killing or putting to flight the garrison and capturing a machine gun.
>
> "On the same day, when holding a newly-captured trench, he was strongly counter-attacked from both flanks. By his coolness and skill in controlling the fire of his party, he frustrated the attack, inflicting heavy casualties on the enemy.
>
> "Throughout the whole operation his innumerable acts of gallantry set a high example to his men and his leading was beyond all praise."

General the Earl of Cavan in his despatch on the Battle of Vittorio Veneto made special mention of the Battalion in the following words:

> "The enemy had rapidly occupied the line of the River Monticano, and on this line he offered his last serious resistance. During the evening of the 29th October and the morning of the 30th October the passages were forced and the enemy skilfully manœuvred out of the remainder of his defences, chiefly by the very gallant work on the part of the 8th Battalion The Yorkshire Regiment. From this moment the retreat became a rout."

During the course of and subsequent to the termination of the operations the following congratulatory messages were received ; from the Division :

> " Divisional Commander congratulates General Beauman on the successful result of the operations and desires him to convey to all units engaged his—the Divisional Commander's—cordial appreciation of the fine dash and spirit with which they overcame the difficult obstacles and opposition encountered."

From the Corps Commander :

> " My very best thanks and congratulations to all ranks on the excellent work they have done and the great success they have obtained. I am more than proud to command such troops."

From the Army Commander :

> " Once more I beg you to convey to all ranks my high appreciation and congratulations on the advance to-day in spite of opposition, fatigue and difficulty of supply. It is a military feat of which they may well be proud."

From the Commander-in-Chief :

> " I am well aware of the exhaustion of the two British Divisions and the cold nights and difficulties of sleep. I am sure they will realize the necessity of completing the task that they began so heroic-ally, and I ask all ranks confidently to press forward. The XIV. Corps must keep the lead after being easily first over the water."

Events now followed one another with great and startling rapidity ; the Battalion was on the 1st November at Bibano, when news was received of the conclusion of an armistice between the Allies and Turkey ; at Palse on the 4th it was announced that an armistice had also been signed with Austria-Hungary and that it was to come into effect from 3 p.m. that day ; and at once congratulatory messages again began to come in :

Major-General Thuillier wrote :

> " The Divisional Commander wishes to express to all ranks of all units engaged his admiration of the gallantry, devotion and good dis-cipline displayed throughout the operations."

General Sir J. M. Babington, the Corps Commander, telegraphed :

> " On the conclusion of hostilities with Austria-Hungary I heartily congratulate and thank all units of the XIV. Corps for the part they have played in bringing the war one step nearer the end. By their gallantry and devotion to duty they have contributed in no small

degree to this happy conclusion, and I am proud to have shared with them their triumph in the glorious success which has been gained."

Then General Lord Cavan sent his troops the following welcome message :

> "1. The following message has been received from His Majesty the King by the Army Commander : 'With all my heart I congratulate you and the XIV. Corps upon the splendid victory achieved fighting side by side with the Italian troops of the Tenth Army, resulting in the Armistice which takes effect from to-day. For your great services I thank you.—GEORGE R.I.'
> "2. An Armistice has been signed to-day with Austria-Hungary and the cessation of hostilities ordered. The Army Commander warmly congratulates all units of the Tenth Army on their glorious share in this historic event. Germany only remains, and until she is equally defeated there can be no peace."

On the 8th the Battalion began moving back by rail and march route across the Piave to the Vicenza area, where on the 11th news was received that Germany had followed the example of her one-time Allies and had sued for peace ; and at once training began and educational classes were started and men's minds were filled with thoughts of demobilization ; but whatever hopes may have been raised by the news of the armistice concluded with the chief enemy Power, they must have received something of a shock by the arrival on the 1st December of a draft of one hundred and seven other ranks, mostly boys of nineteen years of age, who came direct from England ; this was followed on the 18th by another draft twenty-seven strong.

On the 23rd demobilization actually commenced—the Battalion being then in the Zimella area—when the first party of twenty-eight miners proceeded to England, followed on the 4th January, 1919, by eighty-six more ; and thenceforth the strength of the 8th Battalion The Green Howards steadily declined until on the 31st January it stood at only twelve officers and four hundred and twelve other ranks, Major J. C. Bull being on that date in command.

Int his month General the Earl of Cavan returned to England, having on the 19th published the following Special Order of the Day :

> "Soldiers of the Italian Expeditionary Force !
> "To-morrow I hand over the command to Lieut.-General Sir J. Babington after more than a year in Italy. I want to thank every officer, non-commissioned officer and man of you for your pride in your units, which is the essence of discipline, and for all the unforgettable

work that you have done in the mountains and on the plains.   No Commander ever had his task made so easy for him, owing to the loyalty, steadfastness and enthusiasm of you all.

" I wish you all the happiest possible furlough on return to England —good football, good beer, good friends—and after a holiday a real good job.   With all my heart I thank you, and I hope you will not forget the kindness and hospitality of our Italian friends."

There is but little more to record; the process of disintegration was hastened by the departure on the 18th February of Second-Lieutenants E. E. Hirons and F. B. Harper and one hundred and forty-five other ranks who had volunteered for service with the Army of Occupation, these leaving to join the 8th York and Lancaster Regiment at Fiume.   This left The Green Howards so weak in numbers that the Battalion was now organized into Headquarters and one company, this last under command of Captain F. C. Miller, M.C.

Late in the month what remained of the Battalion—eighteen officers and two hundred and ten other ranks—moved to Montecchia di Crosara, where it was speedily reduced to Cadre strength of four officers and forty-six non-commissioned officers and men.

The following figures show the rate of demobilization since the Armistice :

In December, 1918, 68 non-commissioned officers and men.

,, January, 1919, 238   ,,   ,,   ,,

,, February, ,,   221   ,,   ,,   ,,

The re-enlistments were, for two years, 9 other ranks ; for three years, 3 other ranks ; and for one year, 17 other ranks.

Twelve officers and 164 other ranks remained on temporarily to serve in the Army of Occupation.

CHAPTER XV

THE 9TH BATTALION

1915–1917

THE BATTLE OF LOOS. THE BATTLE OF THE SOMME, 1916.
THE BATTLE OF YPRES, 1917

THE story of the 9th Battalion The Green Howards in the war is, up to the commencement of the Italian campaign at least, very largely that of the 8th Battalion of the Regiment, but it having been decided that each battalion's record should receive separate treatment, that of the 9th Battalion is here given in full at the risk of some unavoidable repetition.

The 9th Battalion then first received official recognition when it was announced in Army Order No. 388 of 1914, published on the 13th September, that His Majesty the King had approved of a further addition to the Army of six divisions and Army troops, that these divisions would be numbered from 21 to 26, and that the 69th Brigade of the 23rd Division would contain the following infantry battalions:

The 10th (Service) Battalion The Duke of Wellington's (West Riding Regiment).

The 8th (Service) Battalion Alexandra, Princess of Wales's Own (Yorkshire Regiment).

The 9th (Service) Battalion Alexandra, Princess of Wales's Own (Yorkshire Regiment).

The 11th (Service) Battalion the Prince of Wales's Own (West Yorkshire Regiment).

In the same Order the following appointments were made: to command the 23rd Division, Temporary Major-General J. M. Babington, C.B., C.M.G., and to command the 69th Infantry Brigade, Colonel F. Murray, D.S.O. The 23rd Division was, in Army Order 389 of 1914, posted to the Third New Army under Lieutenant-General Sir A. E. Codrington, K.C.V.O., C.B., the place of assembly of the Division being Frensham.

The Battalion was formed at Richmond, Yorkshire, and for a short time was commanded by Colonel H. C. F. Vincent, C.M.G., late Indian Army, but on the 28th September it was moved to Frensham, where on the 10th of the following month Major H. G. Holmes, of the Reserve of Officers of The Green Howards, was appointed to the command with the rank of Temporary Lieutenant-Colonel, and he took over on the 14th, by which date the following officers were doing duty with the new Battalion : Lieutenant-Colonel H. G. Holmes, Major C. E. Ross, Captain H. A. S. Prior, Lieutenants L. Crawley-Boevey and W. L. S. Beckett, Second-Lieutenants A. C. L. Parry, E. Collier, W. T. Wilkinson, W. F. Greenwood, F. Hermiston, R. G. Pettle, G. K. Thompson, R. H. Tolson, C. Barraclough, A. B. H. Roberts, P. M. Courage and A. C. Barnes, Lieutenant and Quartermaster E. R. Wall.

The Battalion remained at Frensham until early in December, when it moved to Aldershot, where Christmas and the New Year were spent ; and then about the 20th February, 1915, the 23rd Division marched to Folkestone, between Maidstone and Ashford being inspected by Field-Marshal Lord Kitchener, the Secretary of State for War. Folkestone was reached on the 29th February, after a very creditable march in which the average distance covered each day was sixteen miles, though on one day as much as twenty-five miles was marched. The Brigadier-General published the following in orders :

> " The G.O.C. Brigade wishes to express his appreciation of the fine spirit shown by the Brigade and its excellent conduct on the march from Aldershot to Folkestone. The march was a higher trial than any which the Brigade has so far had to undergo ; and the manner in which it acquitted itself gives great promise of the future."

In the summer of this year the Battalion was stationed at Bramshott, where on the 23rd August orders were received to prepare for embarkation for France, and at 4.22 a.m. on the 25th the first party—3 officers, 106 other ranks, 72 horses, 23 vehicles and 9 bicycles—left Liphook Station for Folkestone. This party was followed on the 26th by the rest of the 9th Green Howards in two detachments ; one train left Liphook Station for Folkestone at 6.55 p.m., carrying 15 officers and 455 other ranks, while the second, which started some 40 minutes later, contained 12 officers and 434 non-commissioned officers and men, the total embarking strength thus being 30 officers and 995 other ranks.

Embarking at Folkestone the Battalion arrived at Boulogne in the very early hours of the 27th, marching to and spending the greater part of the day in camp at Ostrahove ; but at 9.30 the same night it entrained at Pont-de-Briques railway station and was carried to Watten, marching from there by way of Mentque to Nortbecourt, which was reached about 9.40 a.m. on the 28th. Just a week was spent here in billets and then the Battalion moved to Vieux Berquin where instruction in trench warfare at once commenced under the guidance of the 1st Royal Scots and 2nd Cameron Highlanders. By the end of September the 9th Green Howards had taken over trenches " on their own " in the La Vesée section, and here on the 28th September they suffered their first war casualty, one man being wounded by shrapnel.

The Battalion had now reached the front at a time when the period of comparative stagnation which had endured during the summer months had come to an end and the Allies were already engaged in the offensives at Loos and in Champagne.

The Battalion remained for some considerable time in the Bois Grenier sector, south of Armentières, the small drafts which arrived from time to time being sufficient to replace the trifling wastage experienced in a comparatively quiet part of the line.

" The Battalion," writes the correspondent of *The Green Howards' Gazette*, " let in the New Year in fine style by making a very successful raid on the German trenches, for which we had the honour of receiving three Military Crosses and six Distinguished Conduct Medals." The raid was organized by Major H. A. S. Prior and led by Captain G. K. Thompson, who had a party one hundred strong under his command. The losses were one man killed, one officer—Second-Lieutenant B. I. Wilkins—died of wounds—" an officer who was loved and respected by all who came in contact with him "—and fourteen other ranks were wounded.

On the 1st March the 23rd Division was ordered by the G.O.C. IV. Corps to relieve the 17th French Division on the Souchez River sector, the relief to be completed by the 8th and the 69th Brigade being detailed to take over the front line ; and at 3 a.m. on the 6th the 9th Green Howards were in occupation of the left sub-sector of the Souchez sector, when out of the line being in billets at Fosse 10 in the Angres sector.

In a letter dated the 22nd March the Battalion correspondent writes : " We have had a fair share of casualties during this time. We have lost Second-Lieutenant B. I. Wilkins, who died from wounds on the 6th January ; we have also had four officers wounded, but hope that they will all recover and be able to rejoin the Battalion. Our losses among the other ranks have been one Company Sergeant-Major and twenty-three N.C. officers and men killed in action, seven N.C. officers and men died from wounds and eighty-seven officers and men wounded. We were all very sorry to lose our old friend Major E. G. Caffin, second-in-command of the Battalion, but heartily congratulate him on his promotion to Lieut.-Colonel to command the 11th Battalion Northumberland Fusiliers, and wish him the best of luck and success with his new unit. Captain A. C. Barnes has left us and gone on the Brigade Staff, where we expect to hear more of him. Second-Lieutenant Bampfield has been appointed A.D.C.to the G.O.C., Second-Lieutenant Laycock has gone to a special company R.E., and Second-Lieutenant Rapp to the Trench Mortar Battery."

The Battalion remained during the greater part of April, May and June either in the front-line trenches in the Angres sector or in billets and in training near Hersin, and it was only towards the end of June that the 23rd Division was ordered to move south to the scene of the Somme battles. On the 24th June the 9th Green Howards entrained at Berguette for Longueau, and on arrival there about 11 o'clock in the morning they marched to billets at St. Sauveur. Here it was learnt that the Division was to move on the night of the 1st–2nd July to the Baisieux area ; then early on the morning of the 3rd the Division received orders from the III. Corps Headquarters to place one brigade at the disposal of the 34th Division, at that time holding the line opposite to and south-east of La Boisselle. The 69th Infantry Brigade was so detailed and, moving forward during the day, occupied the line Usna Hill–Tara Hill–Bécourt Wood.

The account of the fighting at Horseshoe Trench and Contalmaison, and of the movements which led up to it, will now be taken from that drawn up by one who himself took part in these operations, though not actually with the Battalion.

" On June 24th the Battalion detrained at Longueau, just east of Amiens, and marched through the town of Amiens to St. Sauveur, a small village nestling in the valley of the Somme. Those who had previously been in any doubt as to the reasons for this move southward, could scarcely have now failed to realize that business was intended after viewing the scenes of activity which prevailed at Longueau sidings, which were being used for the detrainment of our troops and of the French. It was while waiting at St. Sauveur, however, that these suspicions of a great offensive became definitely confirmed, and the general idea of the part to be played by the Battalion assumed a more concrete form. The 23rd Division was not intended to take part in the initial assault on the German front line, but was a reserve division of the III. Corps, commanded by Lieut.-General Sir W. P. Pulteney, K.C.B., D.S.O., under whom the Division had previously served at Armentières.

" Every day at St. Sauveur the Battalion waited anxiously expecting the news to arrive that the great offensive had at last been launched. The weather could hardly, however, have been more unsuitable for military operations : the rain was incessant and the ground was sodden ; and it was not until the 30th June that the Battalion was called upon to move forward to Croisy. From here a night march was made on July 1st to Baisieux, where the Battalion bivouacked in some woods to the west of the village. Here many rumours began to be received of the doings of the 8th Division, the wounded from which were being evacuated along this route. The 8th was a Division in which many of us took a special interest owing to the fact that the 23rd Division had given it the 70th Infantry Brigade in exchange for the 24th during the autumn of 1915. The terrible casualties which our old comrades had suffered in the initial struggle filled the Battalion more than ever with a desire to get forward and participate themselves in the great battle which could now plainly be heard taking place a few miles away. It was therefore with a great feeling of satis-faction that the 9th Green Howards moved forward on the evening of July 2nd to bivouacs just outside Albert on the fringe of the battle area.

" When dawn broke on July 3rd it was realized that at last the supreme test was at hand. There was a thrill of expectation and excite-ment in the air. All were outwardly calm and impassive, but yet each man felt within him that the days were at last approaching for which all had been preparing for over two years, and each asked himself whether he would be able to apply all the lessons which he had learnt and fulfil all his highest hopes and ambitions.

" The sun poured down upon the little town of Albert. On all sides were signs of great activity ; the sky was dotted with observation balloons and aeroplanes were busily engaged upon their morning tasks. Fresh troops were passing up to the line, while small parties of wounded kept filtering back. Guns revealed themselves at every turn—such a concen-tration of artillery as the world had never before witnessed, nor indeed had deemed possible. During the course of the day the Battalion moved from its bivouacs through the town of Albert, passing under the great cathedral, and seeing for the first time the golden figure of the leaning Virgin Mary, who seemed as though she might at any moment fall with the Holy Infant in her arms and be dashed to pieces on the stones and rubble beneath : an impressive figure which the Battalion was to pass many times during the succeeding months, and which was to remain for many an imposing symbol, giving her message to all who entered the vast and terrible battle-fields beyond. From the cathedral we moved up the main Bapaume Road, keeping close to the houses and walls to avoid notice by the enemy until the Usna–Tara Ridge was reached. Here a pause was made while parties went forward to reconnoitre the maze of trenches which lay on the slopes of the ridge beyond and to try and form some appreciation of the general situation.

" The artillery which the enemy possessed in this sector was almost wholly concentrated upon the front system, and interfered but little with our preparations behind the line.   One could stand unmolested on the forward slope of the Ridge and look across the valley at what remained of the village of La Boisselle, where one could make out the tide of battle ebbing and flowing as our men bombed their way forward, or the Germans, emerging from hidden trenches and dug-outs, launched their local counter-attacks.   It was the portion of the line just to the south-east of this village that the 9th Green Howards were to take over that evening, headquarters being established at Chapes Spur.   The Germans still clung obstinately to the trenches on the crest of the Ridge, and it was realized that a preliminary action would be necessary to clear this area before any attempt could be made to capture the village of Contalmaison beyond.

" On the 4th July bombing attacks were made by the Battalion and by the 11th West Yorkshire, but progress was slow.   The enemy fought with skill and determination, constantly counter-attacking; the trenches were much damaged and full of débris, the dead still lying everywhere in them ; shell, rifle and machine-gun fire was continuous ; and great difficulty was experienced in conveying messages, water, food, ammunition and other supplies to the places where these were most urgently needed, very few men being available as guides in the maze of broken ground. Large portions of the area were a mass of shell craters through which passages had to be cut or trodden by successive carrying parties.

" On July 5th at 4 a.m. an attack was made by the 11th West Yorkshire and 10th Duke of Wellington's Regiment, but the success was nullified by a heavy counter-attack by the enemy, which drove our advanced posts back to their original line.   Up to midday but little advance had been made, while during the morning Captain A. F. Atkey, commanding ' A ' Company, was killed by a sniper while observing, and Lieutenant J. Gibson met his death in a bombing attack.

" The objective of the 69th Infantry Brigade was a trench known as the Horseshoe Trench, running from Lincoln Redoubt to Scots' Redoubt on a curved line of about fifteen hundred yards and strongly held by the enemy.   During the afternoon parties of the 10th Duke of Wellington's and the 11th West Yorkshire again gradually pushed the enemy back on the right, and the 8th Green Howards, who had previously done much good work carrying up stores, were now ordered forward to relieve the 11th West Yorkshire, but the latter remained continuously in action during the day.   After a long day's fighting our artillery fire and the exertions

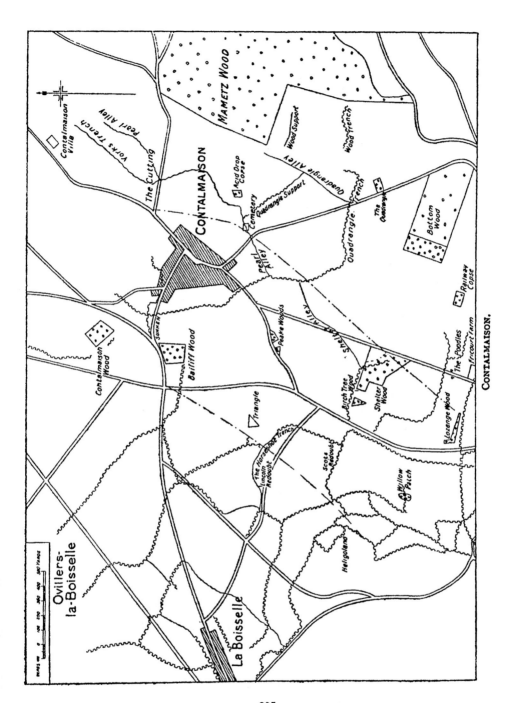

CONTALMAISON.

295

of the infantry began to have their effect on the right, and by 5.45 p.m. over eighty Germans had been captured on that flank. Orders had been issued for an attack over the open to be delivered by the 9th and 8th Green Howards and the 10th Duke of Wellington's, but owing to the progress made on the right these orders were cancelled at the last moment as regards the two last-named battalions, and the attack was made at 6 p.m. by the 9th Battalion The Green Howards only.

"Immediately after leaving the trenches the attacking companies came under a heavy fire and suffered severely, Captain W. T. Wilkinson, commanding 'C' Company, being killed and several other officers being hit; but in spite of these losses the attack was completely successful and the Horseshoe Trench was occupied, one hundred and forty-six Germans and two machine guns being captured by the Battalion.

"During this advance our line was enfiladed by a German machine gun, which caused many casualties. Seeing this, Second-Lieutenant D. S. Bell, entirely on his own initiative, followed by Corporal Colwill and Private Batey, crept towards it and then charged it suddenly across the open. Second-Lieutenant Bell shot the German gunner with his revolver and destroyed the gun and the remainder of the gun-team with bombs. By this gallant action a critical situation was undoubtedly met, and for his act Second-Lieutenant Bell was awarded the Victoria Cross. Unfortunately this very gallant officer did not live to hear of the honour which had been bestowed upon him, for he fell a few days later at Contalmaison when endeavouring to perform a somewhat similar act.

"The thanks of the Corps and Divisional Commanders were received by the 69th Brigade as a result of the operations of the 5th July; and on the morning of the 7th the Divisional Commander addressed the Battalion on parade and, in thanking all ranks for their work at Horseshoe Trench, said :

"'The Division is proud of you. It is unnecessary for me to say I am proud of you—I always have been. You have made a great name for yourselves, your Division and your Brigade. I don't wish to say any more, but again I thank you.'

"The total casualties sustained were one hundred and eighty-nine, including nine officers, those killed being Captains A. F. Atkey and W. T. Wilkinson, Lieutenants J. Gibson and F. Hermiston, Second-Lieutenant C. G. Wyld, and Captain J. C. Rix, R.A.M.C.

"During the 4th and 5th July rain fell heavily, turning the country into a quagmire and making all movement very difficult.

" On July 6th the 69th Brigade was relieved in the front line during the night, but few found much rest on the sodden ground in front of the line of our guns which remained continuously in action by day and by night.

" Attacks on Contalmaison went on during the 7th and 8th July and parts of the village were more than once entered, but it was still held in strength by the enemy, whose concealed machine guns were difficult to locate and deal with. The capture of the village was, however, a necessity prior to the further operations of the Army, and on the 10th July the 69th Brigade was ordered to assault and hold Contalmaison. From 4 p.m. artillery fire was concentrated on the village and all approaches to it, while the attack was arranged to be delivered under a barrage moving gradually back by definite periods, allowing the infantry to follow close behind in its progress through the village and search out and destroy machine-gun nests or German survivors who did not surrender. The assault was to be preceded by the complete capture and consolidation of a line facing north of Bailiff Wood, lying to the west of Contalmaison ; this duty was allotted to two companies of the 11th West Yorkshire Regiment. The village itself was to be attacked from the west by waves of infantry, and, as no other forming-up place was available, this advance had to be carried out in the open from positions nearly fifteen hundred yards from the objective.

" Some parts of Bailiff Wood and its neighbourhood had already been seized by other brigades of the Division.

" The work of the 11th West Yorkshires was well done ; several counter-attacks were driven off and in spite of all opposition the left flank of the main advance was made secure with the help of trench mortar batteries and machine guns.

" The main assault was delivered by the 8th and 9th Battalions Yorkshire Regiment " (Green Howards) " from a distance of between twelve hundred and fifteen hundred yards, zero hour being 4.50 p.m. The enemy's artillery soon observed the movement, Very lights being fired in profusion by the German infantry calling for artillery support. No finer sight has been seen than the advance of these brave Yorkshiremen in quick time across the open amid bursting shells and all the machine-gun and rifle fire that the enemy could bring to bear against them. The trenches named for the starting-point were found, some of them, to be wholly destroyed ; nearly all were at an angle which necessitated correction of alignment after starting, but there was no hesitation ; officers and men fell into their places and the long advance went on without a check. The 9th Green Howards on the left first reached the enemy's main trench and, bursting through the wire, entered the village. The sight of the gleaming bayonets was too much for the enemy who ran in all directions, only to be shot down by artillery and machine-gun fire from guns which had earlier been placed in position to flank the village. In accordance with orders received, the Battalion wheeled to its left in Contalmaison and took up a position in some old German trenches facing north ; this line was at once consolidated, while search parties continued to destroy and demoralize all opposition.

" Over one hundred prisoners and two machine guns were captured.

" On the right our 8th Battalion had perhaps greater difficulties to contend with. Here most of the enemy machine guns were located, his barbed wire was in places found almost intact ; a valley raked by fire had to be crossed, while a further unexpected obstacle was found in an unknown line of wire netting behind the German trench and bordering the village itself. It was here that most of the casualties occurred in this Battalion ; but in spite of their losses officers and men pushed rapidly forward and hunted the retreating enemy to the end of the village ; eight German officers and one hundred and sixty men were captured, as well as enemy machine guns. How many of the enemy were killed it is difficult to estimate, but that large numbers suffered from our machine guns and artillery when trying to escape from the village was clearly seen by our artillery observing officers and others. During the night the position in the captured village was consolidated, the 8th Green Howards digging themselves in on the east side and joining up on their left with the 9th Battalion, who, as already stated, had taken up a position facing north in some existing German trenches. The occupation of the village was not concluded without counter-attack, for about 7.30 p.m. a party of Germans emerged from the cutting north-east of the village, but these were dispersed by the fire of their own machine guns which were turned on to them by the 8th Battalion.

" The south-east of the village was also much exposed owing to the scarcity of men, both Battalions having suffered severely, and about 8 in the evening the enemy opened rapid fire from the cover of a hedge near Contalmaison and for some few minutes the situation was critical. Major Western, 8th Battalion, then made a barricade across the road under fire, and men of the 8th Green Howards, together with a party of bombers under Second-Lieutenant D. S. Bell, who had been sent by the O.C. 9th to reinforce the 8th, attacked the enemy with extreme gallantry and drove him back, suffering, however, some casualties, amongst them being Second-Lieutenant Bell himself : this officer, who had, as previously stated, already been recommended for the Victoria Cross, now met his death, again leading his men in a critical situation, which his gallantry and self-sacrifice turned into a success.

" Reinforcements and supplies of ammunition were sent up during the night, the first of the former to arrive being two companies of the 11th West Yorkshire Regiment, quickly followed by the 10th Duke of Wellington's, who, after their long weary days in the trenches, did a night's work in strengthening the new defences of Contalmaison ; but, like the rest of the Brigade, the Spirit of Victory was with them and fatigue was for the time forgotten.

" On the evening of July 11th the Battalion was relieved in the front line and came back to the vicinity of Bellevue Farm.

" Such briefly is a summary of the first visit of the Battalion to the Somme battle-field, the history of one week's strenuous fighting : a week so filled with incident that to those who look back on it every line might be elaborated into a complete chapter. Twice within five days had the Battalion been called upon to carry out attacks on an extensive scale over the open country against some of the most strongly fortified positions that have been known in modern warfare. In each case the attack had been gloriously successful and the Battalion had covered itself with honour. On the 15th July the Corps Commander, Lieut.-General Sir W. Pulteney, addressed the Brigade in the following terms :

" 'General Lambert, Officers and Men of the 69th Brigade.

" 'I have come down here this morning to express my satisfaction and gratitude for the excellent work this Brigade has done in the recent operations. I think you can look back upon the work you did in connection with the taking of the Horseshoe Trench and later in the capture of Contalmaison with every satisfaction. The two events you will keep on record to your credit for ever.

" 'The operations which were carried out yesterday morning were only made possible by the taking of Contalmaison. The taking of Horseshoe Trench was essential because it was a danger to the Corps on our right, and the capture of Contalmaison forms a pivot for further operations.

" 'In addition to the Infantry I must also thank those who supported them—the Artillery, the Trench Mortar Battery, Machine-Gun Company, Signallers and Stretcher Bearers.

" 'What I think you have learnt is, that it is not only essential to take positions, but also to hold them, and when face to face with the Bosche you find yourselves much the better men. I can only say that I wish every success in the future to the 69th Brigade.'

" The price which had been paid for such decisive results was, however, a heavy one. When the roll was called in the village of Contalmaison on the night of the 10th July, there were present besides the Commanding Officer, Lieut.-Colonel H. G. Holmes, and the Second-in-Command, Major H. A. S. Prior, only five subaltern officers and 128 other ranks, while of the seven remaining officers, two, Major Prior and Second-Lieutenant Bingham, had been wounded ; in all three officers and 13 other ranks had been killed, 11 officers and 192 non-commissioned officers and men were wounded, while 24 men were reported missing, and in the week's fighting the 9th Battalion The Green Howards had sustained losses in killed, wounded and missing to the number of 23 officers and 415 other ranks.   The names of the officers who were killed or died of wounds received on the 10th were Major V. L. S. Beckett, Lieutenant D. S. Bell and Second-Lieutenant T. T. Wood.

" Many of the bravest and best who had served with the Battalion since its formation had been lost for ever.   When the Battalion fell in at Bellevue Farm on the morning of the 12th July to march back for a well-earned rest, the gaps in the ranks were brought home to the few survivors. It required the utmost determination and self-control on the part of all to prevent personal feeling and sentiment ruling the day, and to be able to set out with renewed fearlessness and energy on the great task of re-forming a battalion which should be worthy of those who had fallen, and make it fit to carry on the great traditions they had given and the magnificent example they had set."

Well has Mr. John Masefield said that " Contalmaison was won by the manhood of our men."

The award of the Victoria Cross to Second-Lieutenant Donald Simpson Bell is thus announced in the *London Gazette* of the 8th September, 1916:

> " For most conspicuous bravery.   During an attack a very heavy enfilade fire was opened on the attacking company by a hostile machine gun.   Second-Lieutenant Bell immediately, and on his own initiative, crept up a communication trench, and then, followed by Corporal Colwill and Private Batey, rushed across the open under very heavy fire and attacked the machine gun, shooting the firer with his revolver and destroying gun and personnel with bombs.
>
> " This very brave act saved many lives and ensured the success of the attack.
>
> " Five days later this gallant officer lost his life performing a very similar act of bravery."

The 9th Green Howards remained on in the Somme area, either in the front line or in reserve trenches, until the 11th August, when the 23rd Division began to leave to join the Second Army in Flanders, the Battalion entraining on that date at Mericourt and moving by Pont Rémy and Bailleul, and by Steenwerck and Papot, to Creslow Farm in the Ploegsteert area, which was reached at the end of the month; but the stay here was only a very brief one, for by the 4th September the Division was once more on the move, this time to the Second Army training ground in the neighbourhood of St. Omer. Then on the 11th the 23rd Division once more entrained for the Somme, the Battalion arriving the same day at Longueau and marching to Coisy for the night; the 12th, 13th and 14th were spent in huts and tents at Hennencourt, and on the 15th the 69th Brigade marched to Millencourt and three days later moved up into the front line and took over the trenches from a brigade of the 15th Division. "C" and "D" Companies occupied a trench called Prue Trench on the morning of 19th September; the enemy attacked "C" Company's right flank and after heavy bombing forced their way along Prue Trench and Starfish Trench for a short distance, when they were held up. Bombing continued until dusk, and the ground lost was regained later.

The 1st October found the Battalion in reserve trenches near Martinpuich. Colonel Holmes had gone home in July and Major Prior was now in command.

By this date the "wearing-out Battle" had produced considerable results; the British had captured nearly all the high ground for which so long they had been fighting, and had begun to move down towards the long valley which lay between Le Transloy and Irles. The intention now was to capture the enemy defences in front of Le Transloy and Beaulencourt, followed, if possible, by the seizure of the Sailly-Saillisel and Le Transloy Ridges themselves. On the 1st October some battalions of the 23rd Division took part in the attack by the Fourth Army on Eaucourt l'Abbaye, which was captured on the 3rd; on the 4th two battalions of the 69th Brigade attacked the Second Flers Line, west and south of the Bapaume Road; and on the 7th the 23rd and 50th Divisions were told off to capture the line from Flers to Le Sars on a front of rather more than a mile. The 23rd Division was detailed for the attack on the village of Le Sars, the 68th and 69th Brigades being on the right and left respectively. In the 69th Brigade the 9th Green Howards on the right of the Brigade front were to attack the southern portion of Le Sars.

The enemy front had been continuously bombarded from about 3.30 on the afternoon of the 6th until 1.45 p.m. on the 7th, which was zero hour for the attack by the Fourth Army; at this hour the 69th Brigade advanced and the 9th Green Howards had an officer and several men killed by shells just as they reached the cross-roads near Le Sars. Pushing rapidly on, however, the enemy machine guns were bombed and the Germans were bayoneted as they emerged from their dug-outs. There was here fierce hand-to-hand fighting, quarter was neither asked nor given, and the garrison of a strong point at the cross-roads, refusing to surrender, were all killed. The machine guns too which from the village had enfiladed and held up the 68th Brigade on the edge of a sunken road were bombed and captured by the 9th Green Howards, and the greater part of the village of Le Sars was now in British hands, when the Battalion pressed on to the east and cleared the trenches north-east of the Bapaume Road. By the evening the whole of Le Sars had been captured, all gains were consolidated, strong posts were established and touch gained with the troops on the right and left.

Early on the 8th fighting was renewed and the remainder of the Flers line was assaulted and captured, and on the 9th the Battalion, on relief by the Seaforth Highlanders of the 45th Brigade of the 15th Division, moved back to camp near Round Wood and next day to billets in Albert.

In the two days' fighting the 9th Green Howards had two officers and fifteen other ranks killed, three officers and eighty-six non-commissioned officers and men wounded, while ten men were missing.

On the 12th October the 23rd Division began moving back to the Ypres area, proceeding by rail, motor-lorry and march route, and by Longpré, Conteville, Hopoutre and Poperinghe to Ypres, where on the 26th it was accommodated in the Infantry Barracks, and settled down to many dreary weeks of trench warfare in the clay-country of Flanders, where when rain came it remained, flooding dug-outs and trenches alike, and where the second Christmas of the war came and went. Then in February, 1917, there was a change to a training area where a few all-too-brief weeks were spent.

At the end of April and the beginning of May the Battalion was in billets in the Steenvoorde area in Corps reserve, coming back again for a short time to the front line before moving to billets in the Boeschepe area, where, in divisional reserve, the Battalion was trained over model trenches for the forthcoming offensive of the Second Army; before, however, this opened the 9th Green Howards were employed on the night of the 20th–21st May in an important raid on the enemy trenches about Canada Street, the objects of the raid being to obtain information and identifications and to discourage the German policy of attempting to enter the British trenches.

Second-Lieutenant M. G. Robson was to be in command of the raid generally and in special charge of No. 1 Party of sixteen men who were to work to the right for some fifty yards, while No. 2 Party, under Second-Lieutenant N. Groom, containing ten other ranks, was to work for a similar distance to the left; Second-Lieutenant R. L. Christie was held responsible for the supply of all necessaries required for the raiders.

The parties were formed up in the front line by 12.15 a.m. on the 21st May, when a box barrage was put down by our guns—trench mortars, Stokes guns, machine guns, and Lewis guns—and at 1 a.m. the parties rushed forward.

The officer and bayonet men of No. 1 Party found no difficulty in entering the German trench and at once moved to the right, expecting to be followed by the remainder of the party; there was no enemy met with, but after going some thirty yards a communication trench was seen; as, however, the rest of the party was not at hand Second-Lieutenant Robson decided to go no further and returned to the point of entry, where three men joined him, and his reinforced party then moved back up the enemy trench as far as the communication trench previously seen, though by this time the enemy had opened a very hot fire with rifle grenades, and some of our own shells were falling short into the German wire. Second-Lieutenant Robson now jumped up on the parapet and threw a bomb, which drew a hail of rifle grenades and bombs in reply from the enemy, and one bomb-carrier of the party was wounded and sent to the rear. The officer and one man then moved on along the top of the parapet, but as our shells began falling short they could proceed no further; and it being now close upon the time when they had been ordered to withdraw from the enemy trench, Second-Lieutenant Robson retired his men and informed No. 2 Party of his action.

Second-Lieutenant Groom and three men of No. 2 Party entered the trench at the same moment as did No. 1, moving to the left, and two men were at once hit; the officer and third man went on, however, for some thirty yards when they came upon one of the enemy about to fire a Very light; he was fired at and bolted, pursued by the man with Second-Lieutenant Groom, who now, however, decided to return covering the withdrawal of No. 1 Party; all returned safely, five men of the two parties engaged having been wounded.

The Battalion was now to take part in the Messines Battle, of the general object of which something has been said in a previous chapter; and in the instructions issued by the 69th Brigade Headquarters it was directed that, preceded by a five days' bombardment, the 69th Brigade, *plus* two battalions of the 68th Brigade, would make an attack on Hill 60 sub-sector, while the 70th Brigade on the left attacked Mount Sorrel. At zero hour a number of mines were to be exploded and the artillery barrage would at once fall, the infantry leaving their trenches at zero *plus* two minutes and advancing, at the rate of twenty-five yards per minute, on the Red Line, the assault on which was to be carried through without halt as close up to the barrage as possible. The assault up to the Blue

Line, the second objective, was to be made by the 10th Duke of Wellington's Regiment on the right, the 8th Green Howards in the centre and the 11th West Yorkshire Regiment on the left, while the 9th Green Howards and the 12th Durham Light Infantry on the right and left respectively were to carry the third objective, the Black Line. The Battalion moved up to the trenches on the evening of the 6th June in readiness for the attack on the following morning.

The following is Lieutenant-Colonel Prior's account of the events of that day :

" The attack was made through the Blue Line at 6.50 a.m. in two lines in small columns in artillery formation—' A ' Company on the right, ' C ' on the left, supported by ' B ' and ' D ' respectively. For about the first two hundred yards the advance did not meet with very great resistance and the troops kept close up to our own barrage. After this the undergrowth became increasingly thick and snipers and machine-gun fire caused many casualties. It was with great difficulty that touch was maintained with the troops on our flanks, and for some considerable time we were well in front of them and our advance was checked by a flanking fire. The Battalion was eventually forced to dig in on the southern edge of Battle Wood owing to heavy machine-gun fire from emplacements just beyond our objective, which made further advance practically impossible. I am of opinion that the objective allotted to this Battalion was situated on low ground in the very centre of a strong, hostile position, and one which had been carefully organized for defensive purposes, with concealed machine-gun emplacements on the rising ground in front and on our flanks. For reasons which are not clear to me these emplacements did not appear to have been dealt with by our artillery. The arrangements previous to the attack were quite efficient so far as I am in a position to judge, but the signalling communication during the attack was very unsatisfactory, and I found it impossible to get in touch with the Brigade by this means until seven hours after the attack was launched, although every effort to do so was made on our part."

In this attack the 9th Battalion The Green Howards again experienced great loss, 4 officers being killed or dying of wounds and 7 being wounded, while of the other ranks 67 were killed, 178 were wounded and 9 were missing. The names of the officers are : killed or died of wounds, Captain W. R. Gamble, Second-Lieutenants F. W. Knott, G. C. Knowles and T. W. Dean ; while those wounded were Captains W. F. Greenwood and R. H. Tolson, Lieutenant S. Blore, Second-Lieutenants D. B. Almgill, M. G. Robson, R. T. Eaton and C. Read.

The rest of June was spent for the most part in the Dickebusch area, in Brigade or Divisional reserve, but well within range of the enemy guns, for on the 24th the Battalion was shelled out of one camp and had to move to another, so that by the end of the month the casualty roll had been swelled by four more killed and fourteen more men wounded. In July again the 9th Green Howards were not engaged in any serious operations, but in that month lost six men killed, twenty-one—including Second-Lieutenant W. J. Catton—wounded, and had two men missing.

During the first half of August the 69th Brigade was about Moulle in the Tilques area, doing special training in musketry and in open warfare, and was later transferred from the Second to the Fifth Army and joined the XVIII. Corps, commanded by Lieutenant-General Sir Ivor Maxse, G.C.V.O., K.C.B., D.S.O., the Battalion marching on the 24th August to Watten station to entrain and spending the whole of September in the Dickebusch, Steenvoorde, MicMac and Westoutre areas, preparing to take part in the third attack of the Ypres Battle of this year.

In the action which commenced on the 19th September the 23rd Division fought with the Australian Corps on its left; this was to take Polygon Wood, while the 23rd Division was told off to capture a line running south from the Reutelbeek stream across and just below the Menin Road.

The Battalion companies were now commanded as follows: " A," Captain Thompson; " B," Captain Maude; " C," Lieutenant Duncalfe; and " D," Captain Roberts.

The following is the report of the Battalion's share in the week's fighting which now ensued, as drawn up by Lieutenant-Colonel R. S. Hart, Sherwood Foresters, who was then in command of the 9th Green Howards:

" The Battalion left MicMac Camp at 1.10 p.m. on the 18th September and proceeded to Railway Dug-outs, where Headquarters, ' A ' and ' B ' Companies remained for the night, while ' C ' and ' D ' Companies, after having been issued with battle stores, proceeded at 5.30 p.m. to Sanctuary Wood, where they dug themselves in. During the night these latter companies were heavily shelled with H.E. and gas shells and had twelve casualties.

" At 1 p.m. on the 19th H.Q. moved up to Clapham Junction under the Menin Road, and ' A ' and ' B ' Companies moved up to the vicinity of Stirling Castle and Sanctuary Wood. At 9.30 p.m. the companies commenced to move into their assembly positions ready for attack, and all these positions were completed by 2 a.m. on the 20th. At zero—5.30 a.m. on the 20th—' A ' and ' D ' left their assembly positions and advanced towards Inverness Copse, closely followed by ' B ' and ' C ' Companies. The morning was dark and there was a considerable mist, and this, combined with the dense clouds of smoke caused by our artillery

x

barrage, rendered the question of keeping direction extremely difficult. But in spite of this, and in spite of the fact that the ground over which they were advancing was pitted with shell-holes and strewn with broken tree-trunks and barbed wire, very little loss of direction occurred until the Battalion had advanced about one hundred and fifty to two hundred yards into Inverness Copse. Here according to arrangement a halt was called for about three-quarters of an hour, the troops taking advantage of shell-holes and natural cover. Even in this early stage of the action isolated instances occurred of fighting, individual Germans who had not been mopped up bombing our men from the rear, where the enemy also fired a green S.O.S. Very light.

" During this pause troops were reorganized and the direction checked with the aid of compasses, and the men were all in the best of spirits in spite of the heavy shell and machine-gun fire, and sat in shell-holes smoking German cigars calmly waiting for the advance.

" At zero hour *plus* 80 minutes the companies commenced to move forward, and it was while advancing from this position to the Red Line that some of the heaviest fighting occurred ; for numerous small parties of Germans had remained in the wood in dug-outs and shell-holes, and many of these put up a strong resistance, attacking our men with bombs and causing many casualties by machine-gun and rifle fire. All these parties were, however, successfully mopped up, at least sixty Germans being killed in the Copse. By this time the Battalion had suffered considerably from Germans in the wood, from machine-gun fire from a strong point beyond, and from a hostile artillery barrage ; and before reaching the Red Line eight out of sixteen Company officers had been hit, including two of the Company commanders. All the same the men formed up well under the barrage ready to go forward at zero *plus* 88 minutes according to programme.

" As was anticipated the main centres of German resistance were around the line of dug-outs extending from the Tower on the north, southwards to the pond by the Menin Road. These dug-outs had hardly suffered at all from our artillery barrage, and about them the fighting varied considerably in intensity. Several hostile parties, on recognizing that they were outflanked, abandoned their machine guns and other weapons, and came forward waving small pieces of cloth which had obviously been prepared beforehand. Round several of the dug-outs, however, the fiercest hand-to-hand fighting occurred, the Germans holding out to the last and refusing to surrender. Our men here got well home with the bayonet and many of the enemy were killed both about the Tower and in the actual passages of the dug-outs themselves. Here no fewer than ten machine guns were captured, some in concrete emplacements, others in open shell-holes, while fifteen flammenwerfer, five trench howitzers and four trench mortars were also taken in this vicinity.

"While 'A' and 'D' were thus engaged in mopping-up, 'B' and 'C' passed through them and advanced towards the Blue Line. Each of these companies had at this time only one officer left, and one of these had been shot through the helmet and wounded in the hand. But in spite of this, and the heavy losses they had suffered earlier in the day both in non-commissioned officers and men, so thoroughly did each man know the task allotted to him, that formations and direction still continued to be well maintained, and each section made independently for its own special objective on the Blue Line, captured it and began to consolidate. Although this work was much hampered by the fire of enemy machine guns and snipers, the ground was soft and the men all worked so hard that, by the time the barrage moved forward to the Green Line, every man had provided himself with good cover. While this consolidation was in progress an excellent target presented itself on our left front, where a large number of the enemy was observed retiring over the Ridge. Lewis gun and rifle fire was immediately brought to bear on these, and it is thought that a considerable loss was inflicted on the enemy.

"In the meantime Battalion H.Q. had moved up to an advanced position in the German Aid Post just south of the Menin Road, arriving there at 9.15 a.m. Throughout the rest of the day the positions occupied were improved and consolidated and stores brought up, so that when a heavy barrage was opened by the enemy during the afternoon and evening in conjunction with the counter-attacks on the Tower Hamlets Ridge, very few casualties occurred.

"On the morning of the 21st it was found advisable to thin out the posts in the vicinity of the Reutelbeek where the ground was very marshy, and to transfer those men to better positions on the right of the Blue Line. Our positions were shelled by the enemy throughout the day, but with special intensity during the afternoon and evening. On the afternoon of the 22nd, as a result of the heavy casualties incurred by other battalions of the Brigade, the 9th Green Howards were called upon to take over a portion of the Green Line, when 'B' and 'C' Companies took over the positions previously occupied by 'A' and 'D'; 'A' took over the portion of the front line north of the Reutelbeek Road from the Australians; 'D' Company took over part of the front line south of the Reutelbeek from the 8th Green Howards; while Battalion H.Q. moved to a dug-out just south of the Tower.

"On the night of the 23rd–24th 'A' Company was relieved by the

8th York and Lancaster Regiment and moved to Jackdaw Craters; and on the following night Battalion H.Q. and 'C' Company were relieved by the 2/5th Worcesters, and 'D' and 'B' by two companies of the 4th King's. The 9th Green Howards, on completion of relief at 8.20 p.m. on the 24th inst., moved to Camp Area No. 1 near Dickebusch."

The losses in the Battalion had again been serious—four officers and thirty-nine other ranks were killed, six officers and one hundred and ninety-seven non-commissioned officers and men were wounded, and twenty-eight men were missing. The officers killed were Lieutenant N. Groom, Second-Lieutenants H. J. Bunker, L. Nicholson and R. M. Matthews, while the wounded were Captains G. N. Hunnybun and M. D. W. Maude, Lieutenant H. Duncalfe, Second-Lieutenants J. G. Evans, R. Wood, and B. Wahl.

The following were the officers of the Battalion who took part in the above-mentioned operations: Lieut.-Colonel R. S. Hart, Major A. C. Barnes, D.S.O., Captain and Adjutant G. N. Hunnybun, and Second-Lieutenant W. L. Blow, Intelligence Officer.

"A" Company: Captain G. Thompson, Lieutenant N. Groom, Second-Lieutenants L. Nicholson and R. M. Matthews.

"B" Company: Captain M. D. W. Maude, Lieutenant A. C. Jardine, Second-Lieutenants H. J. Bunker, J. G. Evans, and W. G. Graham:

"C" Company: Lieutenant H. Duncalfe, Second-Lieutenants H. O. R. Lewis, R. Wood, and B. Wahl.

"D" Company: Captain A. B. H. Roberts, M.C., Second-Lieutenants J. F. Guttridge, H. E. Thornton, and G. W. Sutliffe.

On the night of the 30th September the Battalion, with one company attached from the 10th Battalion Duke of Wellington's Regiment, took over the front line south of Polygon Wood from the 8th Green Howards, the front of one thousand yards being held by four companies, one company being in reserve about Verbeek Farm.

Towards 5 on the morning of the 1st October the enemy opened a very intense artillery barrage on the Battalion front and over the whole area for one thousand yards in rear; this was replied to by the British guns which were taking part in an army practice barrage. It was tolerably evident from the intensity of the fire and the activity of the enemy aircraft that an attack was imminent, and by this time all means of communication between the front line and Battalion Headquarters, visual or other, had been severed, so that every endeavour was made to re-establish touch by runners, while officers went up to the front to try and clear up the situation. By now, however, the enemy, in addition to his other barrages, was placing very heavy vertical barrages along the northern bank of the Reutelbeek and in the area south of Black Watch Corner, so that it was found to be almost impossible to get forward. It was not until 1 p.m. that the first pair of runners came back with the news that the three right companies had successfully held their ground. The situation on the left, however, about Cameron Covert, still remained obscure, and from subsequent reports it seems that the following represents what took place on that front.

About 5 a.m. the enemy opened an exceedingly intense barrage on the line running through Cameron Covert; the company holding this front " stood to " and prepared to receive an attack, and half an hour later the enemy was seen advancing against the front in successive waves, when rifle and Lewis-gun fire was at once brought to bear. Two of the Lewis guns were, however, almost at once put out of action, one by a shell and the other by a rifle bullet, and the officer in charge of the left platoon, Second-Lieutenant Wilton, was killed. About five minutes later it was noticed that the battalion on the left had been driven from its front line and that the Germans were following it up closely. For about ten minutes longer the left posts kept up a continuous rifle fire on the enemy, while another Lewis gun was brought into action in place of the two which had been damaged; but by this time the enemy had advanced past the left flank and was well in rear of the position, and in consequence of this the forward posts were withdrawn in a south-westerly direction about fifty yards in the vicinity of company headquarters; here the men were re-organized under Lieutenant Bennison, the company commander, and Lieutenant Gibson, of the 69th Trench Mortar Battery, thereafter going forward to counter-attack. During this advance both these officers became casualties, and a fresh enemy attack compelled a retirement to a position about one hundred and fifty yards in rear of the old front line in order to secure the left flank against envelopment by the Germans. Here, assisted by some of the Leicestershire Regiment, a determined stand was made.

While the above was happening on the northern edge of Cameron Covert, the rest of the company, who were on the southern side of a small marsh with the one company of the 10th Duke of Wellington's Regiment, managed to hold their ground. Two strong attacks were here made by the enemy, but each time they were driven back by rifle fire, Second-Lieutenant Lewis, here in charge of the sector, behaving in a most gallant manner, encouraging his men and organizing an effective resistance; on the enemy establishing a footing in the trench on his left, this officer led a bombing attack, drove out the intruders and rescued his platoon Lewis gun. Unfortunately Second-Lieutenant Lewis was shortly after killed by a sniper. A third German attack was made upon this position, but was again held up short of it, and the enemy then began to dig in in front of the trench just east of an old line of German barbed wire which was there. Under cover of darkness the post then withdrew to the line of the remainder of the company, and a defensive flank was then formed by the company of the 10th Battalion Duke of Wellington's Regiment which established three posts on the left.

By midnight on the 1st October the situation had become rather more settled, and on relief a line running about one hundred and fifty yards in rear of the former positions was handed over in this sector to the 5th Division.

The German attacks were delivered with the greatest determination, and were made in conjunction with artillery fire of unprecedented intensity, great damage being done to the Battalion trenches by guns which enfiladed them from the south-east and brought concentrated fire to bear on the positions of the 9th Green Howards about Cameron Covert.

During these operations the enemy made great use of aeroplanes; four of these flew very low over the Battalion lines before dawn and continued to work in conjunction with the German infantry throughout the day. Many casualties were caused by the machine guns of these aeroplanes firing from close range on the forward positions and even on the wounded who were being brought back to the rear. The German aircraft were fired at by both Lewis guns and rifles, and one was seen to fall in rear of the enemy's lines. The losses in the 9th Battalion The Green Howards on the 1st October amounted to four officers and thirteen other ranks killed, fifty-two non-commissioned officers and men wounded and 16 men missing. The officers killed were Lieutenants M. Bennison and J. Gibson, Second-Lieutenants R. B. Wilton and H. O. R. Lewis, M.C.

On the 13th October the Battalion was again called upon to take over the front line—only six out of the twenty-one officers who had gone over with the Battalion on the 20th September now remained—the portion here allotted being a frontage of five hundred yards—two hundred yards east of the area of the Polygon Wood action. Great difficulty was experienced in reaching the top of Passchendaele Ridge from the Hooge Craters on the Ypres-Menin Road, as there was only a single track of duckboards which had been carefully registered and was heavily shelled. It was quite impossible to make one's way across the sea of mud and shell-holes which stretched on either side. Corpses of men who had attempted to take short cuts, or who had been blown off the track, could everywhere be seen drowned in the mud.

There is little to be said about the next few days; the fighting had assumed more and more the character of a battle of material, the whole of Passchendaele Ridge was heavily bombarded from south and east by day and night; during daylight enemy planes flew up and down the line observing and directing the fire, and no retaliation by the British infantry seemed to have the slightest effect upon them.   All that the infantry could do was to sit in their trenches up to their waists in mud and water, firing at any German aircraft that flew unpleasantly low.

This small portion of the line was held for four days at a cost of Captain A. C. M. Millar, M.C. (died of wounds) and 71 casualties among the other ranks out of an original total of three hundred and ten.

The following officers were with the Battalion during the fighting about Cameron Covert : Lieut.-Colonel R. S. Hart, D.S.O., Majors J. W. Chambers and A. C. Barnes, D.S.O., Captains A. C. M. Millar, M.C. (killed) and C. H. Botting, M.C.

" A " Company : Captain G. Thompson, M.C., Lieutenants K. W. R. Horner and W. T. Ellis.

" B " Company : Lieutenant A. C. Jardine, M.C., Second-Lieutenants G. W. Sutliffe and W. G. Graham (killed).

" C " Company : Lieutenant M. Bennison (killed), Second-Lieutenants W. Brown, H. O. R. Lewis (killed), and R. B. Wilton (killed).

" D " Company : Captain A. B. H. Roberts, M.C., Second-Lieutenant H. E. Thornton, M.C., and J. F. Guttridge.

The fighting of September and October had thus resulted in a loss to the Battalion of four hundred and thirty-one all ranks, killed, wounded and missing.

On the night of the 17th October, the 9th Green Howards were relieved and went back into reserve at Clapham Junction.

On the 7th October the following was published by the Second Army to the Corps, as showing what had been the intention of the enemy and how far these had been frustrated by the operations recently undertaken :

" The evidence gained from captured documents all tends to show that the enemy intended to launch a heavy attack on the Second Army front on October 3rd, and that in order to gain a better footing a preliminary attack was to be made on October 1st.   This was so heavily dealt with by the 23rd Division that it dislocated the further attack that General von Finckenstein, commanding 4th Guard Division, who was in charge of the operations, evidently decided to postpone his attack from the 3rd to the 4th October.   The result of his postponement is well known.   The Army Commander wishes the 23rd Division to be informed of the far-reaching results of their determined resistance, and to congratulate and thank all ranks concerned on behalf of himself and the Second Army."

To this the following note was added by Major-General Babington :

" With reference to the above, while some troops were more immediately engaged than others, I feel confident that whatever troops had been concerned the result would have been the same, and that the enemy will, as he has always done, meet with a heavy defeat at the hands of the 23rd Division."

The weather had now definitely broken and became cold, wet and cheerless, and another winter amid the muddy trenches of Flanders seemed in prospect, though already before the end of October rumour was busy that the Division might move to another theatre of war. The end of the month and the beginning of November were spent at Boisdinghem, and by this time definite orders had arrived for the transfer of the 23rd Division to Italy under circumstances which have already been set forth in an earlier chapter.

On the 8th November then the 9th Battalion The Green Howards moved in the morning to St. Martin-au-Laert and, entraining by half-battalions at Arques, set out on its long journey to the Italian Front.

CHAPTER XVI

THE 9TH BATTALION

1917–1919

ITALY AND FRANCE

THE BATTLE OF THE HUNDRED DAYS

MANTUA was reached on the 14th November by the leading half-battalion, which at once marched out to Sarginesco, arriving here at midnight and being joined early next morning by the remaining companies, and on the 19th the battalions of the 69th Brigade set out on their long march to the banks of the Piave. The following are the names of the places where the 9th Green Howards halted: Cade, Sanguinetto, Boschi-St.-Anna, Sossano, Piombino, Isolla, San Giorgio-di-Brendi and by S. Floriano to Venegazzo, where training in drill and musketry was carried on and where a good deal of " cleaning up " of the billets allotted seems to have been necessary. It was not, however, until the 16th December that the Battalion went into the trenches, taking over the left sub-sector of the Brigade front on the right bank of the Piave.

The weather, which had been generally fine since the arrival of the Division in Italy, had now changed and there was a good deal of rain and at times even snow. All ranks at once began to do all they could to add to the security of their positions, working on dug-outs and camouflage, improving positions for anti-aircraft guns, and wiring the shallow portions of the stream ; while many attempts were made by patrols to find crossing places over the Piave, but the depth and excessive coldness of the water defeated these early efforts. A boat was, however, secured and a wire fixed for hauling it across, when an island in the centre of the stream was searched, but no trace of any enemy was met with.

When out of the line the Battalion was in rear at Montebelluna and Sergiotto.

In the middle of February the Battalion spent some days in the Divisional rest area at Riese, and at the end of March was conveyed by lorries to the mountain area, where at Monte Magnaboschi it took over hutments from a battalion of the 12th Italian Division; then by the end of May it had again moved, this time to the Asiago Plateau, taking over the left sub-sector of the Divisional front; here the enemy was found to be very quiet, which was fortunate since on arrival in these parts the Division was assailed by what seems to have been known as "mountain fever," but was really a particularly virulent form of influenza which for a time played havoc with the officers and men, the hospital admissions in the 9th Green Howards being as many as twenty a day. About the 18th June this sickness began to abate.

Early in June the Battalion was temporarily out of the line at Cavalleto when reports of an intended Austrian attack were received, and the 9th Green Howards were moved up to a position at Spiazzi-di-Croce on the 15th, but took no active part in the Austrian repulse. A few days later, it having been decided to take the initiative and attack the enemy trenches between Ave and Sec, the Battalion was sent up to the right sub-sector of the right Brigade front; but this attack did not materialize, while the enemy remained equally inactive, even his guns doing little more than sending a few occasional shells along the front or firing spasmodically upon the roads in the rear of the British line.

On the night of the 19th–20th July a raid was carried out by a party of the Battalion against the enemy's trenches. The raiding party moved off under a barrage, but by the light of a very bright moon, at 12.4 a.m. on the 20th, but the right party unfortunately became somewhat disorganized while moving up Notts Trench owing to several shells bursting among the men, and owing also to rifle fire from a strong point in a loopholed ruined house, and lost direction. Eventually, two officers—Captain Greenwood and Second-Lieutenant Edwardes-Crate—with Lance-Corporal Watts and Private Lowther succeeded in making their way into the Railway Cutting, where, however, a party of the enemy had now lined its southern edge and were firing heavily to their front. Captain Greenwood and his small party succeeded in attacking these from the rear with rifle and revolver and inflicted severe casualties upon them; he also cleared some ten large shelters and dug-outs, killing many of the occupants and driving the remainder into the cutting where they readily surrendered. Unfortunately during this fighting Lance-Corporal Watts was shot dead at point-blank range by one of the enemy, and Captain Greenwood, finding that his party was now too weak either to complete the operation or to evacuate all the prisoners, was obliged to fall back, taking only twelve of his captives with him.

The left party encountered very strong opposition, but though met by very heavy machine-gun fire a few men under Lieutenant Sharpe succeeded in entering the cutting and advanced fifty yards up it to the east, being then held up by a strong enemy bombing party and being unable to make further progress. A third party led by Lieutenant Bingham could not get on towards Post Spur by reason of heavy machine-gun fire and had several casualties, Lieutenant Bingham himself being severely wounded.

All the parties fell back about 12.30 a.m. under machine-gun fire.

It was apparent that the cutting was, normally, occupied by a considerable number of men, for the eastern end of it was found to have a continuous line of bunked dug-outs and shelters under the southern wall. Ration dumps were seen, while a ruined house in the enemy lines was strongly held and loopholed. Of the enemy thirteen were taken prisoners and thirty were killed, while of the raiding party two were killed, fifteen—including Lieutenant E. G. Bingham—were wounded, while three men were missing.

During the first week in September the Battalion was in camp at Brusabo engaged in musketry and other training, but then moved to the reserve trenches, and was on the 11th under orders to take over the left sub-sector of the left Brigade front; but these orders were suddenly cancelled and the Battalion moved to Centrale, there to await further instructions.

As has already elsewhere been stated the British divisions serving in Italy had been reduced by nine battalions which were ordered to return to France; three of these were contributed by the 23rd Division, they being the 9th Green Howards, the 11th Sherwood Foresters and the 13th Durham Light Infantry; and on the afternoon of the 13th September the 9th Battalion The Green Howards marched to Morano and entrained for France in two parties at 3.30 a.m. and 7.30 a.m. respectively on the 14th. Detrainment took place early on the afternoon of the 17th when the Battalion marched to billets at Neuville and Oneux in the St. Riquier area, where the newly-composed 25th Division was being assembled and organized.

The 25th Division was originally raised during the later months of 1914, proceeded to France in September, and fought on the Western Front until June, 1917, experiencing especially heavy losses in the Somme Battle of that year. In the middle of June it was withdrawn from the line, when, owing to the difficulty of providing reinforcements, the Regular Battalions were transferred to other units, and the Territorial and Service Battalions composing the Division were used to feed their sister battalions in other organizations; while the Divisional and Brigade Headquarters, with cadres of their respective battalions, proceeded to Aldershot with a view to the infantry units being more speedily provided with reinforcements direct from the training centres in England. Having attained a certain growth, the Divisional and Brigade Headquarters (7th and 74th Brigades) returned to France on the 15th September, 1918, and in the neighbourhood of St. Riquier, in the area to the east of Abbeville, the 25th Division was now reformed under the command of Major-General J. R. E. Charles, C.B., D.S.O. On the 17th–19th September the nine battalions sent from Italy arrived at the Headquarters of the 25th Division, and each of the three battalions furnished from a British division on the Italian front was used to compose a brigade in the reformed 25th Division.   Thus, the three battalions from the 7th Division made up the 7th Brigade, the 9th Green Howards, the 11th Sherwood Foresters and the 13th Durham Light Infantry—all from the 23rd Division—made up the 74th Brigade, while the 75th Brigade consisted of the three battalions contributed by the 48th Division in Italy.

The 74th Infantry Brigade was commanded by Brigadier-General H. M. Craigie-Halkett, D.S.O.

The author of the history of " The 25th Division in France and Flanders," writes * in very high terms of the battalions which now joined the Division from Italy :

" With men of the best fighting age and led by experienced officers, these battalions were able to take part with conspicuous success in the heavy fighting during October, and fully justified the high reputation which they held amongst their old friends in the divisions with whom they had been associated so long and whom they were naturally loath to leave."

Since the early part of this year when the German offensive had gained such great initial successes, the situation on the Western Front had greatly changed.   American troops were arriving in daily increasing numbers, the German advance had been stayed, the Allies in their turn had taken the offensive, the German attempt to seize the Channel Ports had failed, the northern sector from Ypres to the sea had been cleared and the enemy was again back on the Hindenburg Line.

" In the meantime the 25th Division, which had completed its reorganization and been joined by the divisional troops in the St. Riquier area near Abbeville, now moved by rail on the 24th September to the XIII. Corps of the Fourth Army, and was billeted in the area midway between Albert and Amiens on the right bank of the Ancre, with Divisional Headquarters at Hennencourt.   In this area the villages had suffered considerably during the recent fighting, but a few remained habitable and offered some sort of accommodation and cover for the troops.   Nearer Albert and in the town itself no roof remained, and everywhere was to be seen the same scenes of utter desolation as throughout the old Somme battle-fields."

On the 27th and 28th September the 9th Green Howards were in billets

* Page 311.

at Albert, moving on the 29th and remaining on the 30th in hutments and dug-outs in Favière Wood in the Maricourt area.

" During the next few days the Division moved up by route march to Templeux-le-Guèrard, just behind the front line, and along with the 66th, 50th and 18th Divisions of General Morland's XIII. Corps, relieved divisions of the III. Corps on the left of the Fourth Army. Operations by the Fourth Army on the 27th September with the IX. Corps, II. American Corps, the III. Corps and the Australians had carried the British advance on this front still further ; from the north of St. Quentin the line ran west of the village of Beaurevoir, joining up with the V. Corps of the Third Army west of Le Catelet ; on the right it was in touch with troops of the First French Army near St. Quentin.

" The main Hindenburg Line, running north and south through Bellicourt, had been the scene of heavy fighting in which British, American and Australian troops had all rendered fine service. The 2nd Australian Division had successfully forced the Maisnières–Beaurevoir line four to five miles behind the main Hindenburg Line, but had not secured the village of Beaurevoir on the high ground beyond the Guisancourt Farm, about two miles to the north-west. The capture of these positions was necessary to enable artillery to be brought up and preparations made for another advance along the British front. This was the first task allotted to the 25th Division.

" On the 3rd October the 7th, 74th and 75th Infantry Brigades were concentrated at Ronssoy, Moislains and Nurlu respectively, with Divisional Headquarters at Combles. The same afternoon . . . Brig.-General Craigie-Halkett's 74th Brigade marched up Mont St. Martin in support " (The 9th Green Howards' diary for the 3rd says, " Left Moislains about 13.00 hours and marched to line south of Le Catelet "), " with the 75th Brigade at St. Emilie a few miles behind in reserve. . . . Late in the afternoon, orders were received to continue on October 4th the attack started by the Australians on the 3rd and to complete the capture of Beaurevoir and the high ground beyond it " ; and in preparation for this the 25th Division had, by daybreak on the 4th, taken up a line from the Canal des Torrens to south-west of Guisancourt Farm, altogether about three thousand yards.

The attack was opened by the 7th Brigade of the 25th Division against the German position, which was very strong and well-sited and defended by numerous machine guns concealed in buildings and along the railway, and by troops belonging to four different German divisions. The attack was only partially successful and the casualties were heavy ; but orders were given to continue operations on the 5th, as the early capture of

Beaurevoir was essential as a preliminary for an attack on a very large scale contemplated for the 7th October.

Accordingly, the 74th Brigade moved up during the evening and took over half the front now held by the battalions of the 7th Brigade with the intention of resuming the attack the next morning. The 75th Brigade also moved up to Quennemont Farm. At 6 a.m. on the 5th October the two brigades went forward, the 75th Brigade on the right with one battalion only in the front line, the 74th Brigade on the left with all three battalions in the front line; the 9th Green Howards attacked with its companies commanded as follows: " A," Captain Blow; " B," Lieutenant Wolstenholme; " C," Captain Greenwood; and " D," Lieutenant Read.

" The attack commenced well, especially on the flanks where good progress was made north of the village of Beaurevoir. The Germans at once launched a strong counter-attack, supported by large numbers of machine guns, and succeeded in forcing back our troops once more to their original line, except in the centre at Bellevue Farm, which was successfully held by men of ' A ' Company, 9th Green Howards. . . . Throughout the morning the difficulties of communication, and the uncertainty of the situation as regards the progress and exact position of the attacking troops, rendered the task of the artillery extremely difficult and made it impossible for the guns to give the infantry adequate support owing to the danger of shelling our own men. Captain Blow, 9th Green Howards, led ' A ' Company with great skill and gallantry, capturing Bellevue Farm and thirty prisoners; Second-Lieutenants Sutliffe and Taylor and Company-Sergeant-Major Goodison, when their company commanders were killed, themselves took command and showed fine qualities of leadership in the handling of their respective companies. Corporal Connell with a party of men attacked and captured a strong point, while Private Cannings himself captured a machine gun which was holding up the advance, he being wounded during the fight."

By the end of the day the village and the cemetery of Beaurevoir had been captured, and some troops of the 74th Brigade made another attempt to reach the high ground of Guisancourt Farm, but were unsuccessful; it was, however, taken on the morning of the 6th and the Farm made secure against any counter-attack, the 9th Green Howards moving forward and digging in in front of it; while the line was straightened out and parties pushed forward in the valley between Beaurevoir and Guisancourt Farm.

" During the 6th and 7th October, the line was perceptibly advanced to the north of Beaurevoir, but no further major operations took place, though preparations were made for a further advance along the whole British front on the 8th October. In the meantime, the 2nd Australian

Division on the right and the 50th Division on the left had pushed well forward, encountering but little opposition in their advance.   The artillery moved up to positions in the valley east of Guisancourt Farm and Beaurevoir, and the troops were rested as much as possible after their strenuous fighting of the past few days, though those actually in the line were heavily shelled during those two days, and consequently had very little opportunity for rest before continuing operations. . . .

" The advance made by the Division, though only some three thousand yards in depth, had been made in face of great difficulties, considerably increased by the lack of time for previous reconnaissance of the ground by the regimental officers, which proved a serious handicap in organizing the attack.   The German position was extremely strong and well chosen and had also been strongly wired.   It was stubbornly defended by troops provided with quantities of machine guns, and whose *morale*, though somewhat weakened by their defeat on the Hindenburg Line the previous week, was still good.   Casualties sustained by the Division were heavy, but were inevitable under the circumstances ; five hundred and eight Germans, including five officers, were taken prisoners.

" The evening of the 7th October, the Division held the line with all three brigades in the front line, in touch on the right with the 30th American Division of the II. American Corps, which had just finished the relief of the Australian Corps. . . .   The 74th Brigade was on the left with all three battalions in the front line, joining up with the 50th Division just north of Guisancourt Farm."

At daybreak on the 8th, however, the 66th Division came up and passed through the 74th and 75th Brigades, taking up the attack with the 7th Brigade, the two other Brigades moving back to their assembly positions about two and a half miles in rear, the 74th Brigade going then into Corps reserve and taking no part in this day's operations, which were eminently successful, all objectives being gained without much difficulty and with but small loss.   Soon after midnight on the 8th the 74th Brigade came up to the front and orders were issued for the operations of the 9th.

At 6 a.m. on the 9th the 75th Brigade advanced between Serain and Premont on a front of some three thousand yards, meeting with very little resistance, and gained the first objective on a line one thousand yards north-west of Maretz by 7.30, when the 74th Brigade came up, and in the further advance became responsible for the attack on the right half of the second objective, going forward with the 11th Sherwood Foresters in front, the 9th Green Howards and 13th Durham L.I. in support.   " Everything went well and the Brigades met with no resistance for about two and a half miles.   The country was undulating down-land, free from wire or other obstacles and progress for the troops was comparatively easy. Artillery was moving up rapidly in rear of the infantry and the 1st Cavalry Division was advancing towards the front line in expectation of a favourable opportunity being offered them to break through the retreating German lines. About 9 a.m. resistance was encountered along the railway line running north and south-west of Honnechy Village. Vigorous attacks were organized by the 74th Brigade and the 1/8th Worcesters of the 75th Brigade, dealing directly with their artillery; and after a short rest, the advance was resumed at 2 p.m. against the German rear-guards, which were here provided with numerous machine guns and some batteries of field artillery. The enemy offered considerable opposition at first, but as our troops pressed on his resistance suddenly broke, and the line retired rapidly before becoming engaged at close quarters. The village of Honnechy was soon passed, and the line established a few hundred yards east and south-east "—the 9th Green Howards " digging in " on the east side of the railway near Honnechy—" linking up with the Americans on the right and the 66th Division on the left. . . .

" Troops of the 1st Cavalry Division now passed through the infantry line north and south-east of Honnechy about 2.30 p.m., and one party captured Reumont Village, about three miles to the north, before dark, patrols reaching the Selle River about four miles beyond. . . . Intelligence reports indicated that the enemy would probably make a stand on the Selle River to the south and south-east of Le Cateau, and that a line of defence with strong belts of wire was in progress of construction on the east bank of the river.

" At 5.30 a.m. on the 10th October the Division moved forward on a three thousand yards front in the same order as on the preceding day, the 74th Brigade on the right, 75th on the left, and the 7th in Divisional reserve about two thousand yards in rear; the 74th Brigade had the 13th Durham Light Infantry in front, the 9th Green Howards about three hundred yards behind in support, and 11th Sherwood Foresters about five hundred yards behind in reserve. For the first two miles there was no opposition of any sort, but at about 8 a.m. the leading platoons came under heavy machine-gun fire from the railway embankment south of Le Cateau and from St. Benin, a suburb of Le Cateau, situated about one and a half miles to the south of the town and on the rising ground west of the River Selle. This opposition, especially from the high ground on the right flank, gradually intensified as the attack was pressed forward. At 2.30 p.m. the 74th Brigade launched their attack on St. Benin. This was successfully carried through and the enemy gradually withdrew from the village without offering much opposition." The 9th Green Howards then dug in just outside the village.

" Of the 9th Green Howards, Lieut.-Colonel R. S. Hart, D.S.O., won a Bar to his D.S.O. for his fine leadership throughout the attack. Sergeant Smith, Sergeant Dawson and Corporal Shields did very useful work with their men, the latter going through the village with patrols to gain information as to the enemy's position on the river bank. Sergeant Collinson organized and led a party against a German strong point which was holding up the advance from the flank, and won a second Bar to his M.M."

There was no further advance on the 11th, and that night the 50th Division relieved the 25th and the latter went back some six miles to the villages of Serain, Prémont, and Ellincourt, The Green Howards finding accommodation in Prémont. The inhabitants of these villages had been for four years under German rule and the welcome they accorded those whom they regarded as their deliverers was something to be remembered.

The very rapid advance of the British armies had left railhead very far in rear, and great difficulty was experienced in bringing up supplies, while as the advance went on it was found that these difficulties were intensified by reason of the systematic destruction by the retreating enemy of railway bridges and culverts, and the repair of these could not keep pace with the rate of advance.

From the 12th to the 16th October the 25th Division remained in the Serain–Prémont–Ellincourt area in Corps reserve ; on this latter date the Division again moved forward, but for some few days yet only the 75th Brigade was engaged, fighting under the orders of the 50th Division at the crossing of the Selle River, and it was not until the 23rd that the other brigades were again employed in the front.

" On the 23rd October the Fourth Army attacked with the IX. and XIII. Corps in order to form a defensive flank facing south-east for the protection of the Third Army during its operations further north, and at the same time the XIII. Corps, with the 25th and 18th Divisions, was required to advance its line sufficiently to the east to allow of the 6-inch guns being able to shell the important railway junction at Leval. The task allotted to the 25th Division was somewhat ambitious ; an advance of about eight thousand yards on a two thousand yards front, including the capture of the village of Pommereuil and the clearing of the Bois l'Eveque to a line east of the villages of Fontaine and Malgarni on the edge of the Forest of Mormal, across a tract of country much intersected by thick hedges and covered by orchards. This advance was a totally different proposition from that successfully carried out between Beaurevoir and Le Cateau. In the wood itself, felled trees and thick undergrowth made the going extremely difficult, increased by the swampy nature of the ground from the recent rain. This gave the Germans excellent cover for their nests

Y

and pockets of machine guns. Observation over the wood and line of advance was also in favour of the Germans from the high ground east of Malgarni, and for the present the line was well supported by field guns and howitzers of various calibre."

The fighting strength of the infantry of the Division was this day only 3,290 rifles, and the 7th Brigade, which was detailed for the capture of Pommereuil and a line some few hundred yards east of the village, had another battalion given it from the 75th Brigade, which with the 74th was to move in touch on the flank, the 74th advancing along the north-west edge of the Bois l'Evèque and then forming up under its cover for a further advance to the line east of the villages of Fontaine and Malgarni. As matters turned out, however, the 74th Brigade experienced considerable opposition and was not able to get up in time to join in the attack that day. On the evening of the 23rd the 9th Green Howards dug in on the edge of the Bois l'Evèque, and during this day " Sergeant Collins and Corporal Hewgill of the Battalion led their men with great determination, the latter with his section capturing a machine-gun post. Private Dyson, when his platoon officer was wounded, gallantly went forward to reconnoitre a way for his unit. Lance-Corporal Stead did valuable work as a runner under heavy fire, and Private Brown under similar conditions showed great bravery in attending to his company commander who was severely wounded.

" At 4 a.m. on the 24th October the line again moved forward, the 74th Brigade, reinforced by the 1/8th Worcesters, with the 6th Division on the right and the 18th on the left. The 6th Division, which had had heavy fighting the previous day, made rapid progress on the right, and the troops of the 7th and 75th Brigades, who had formed the defensive flank the previous evening, were withdrawn to Pommereuil. On the right of the 74th Brigade, the 9th Green Howards had ' A,' ' B,' and ' C ' Companies in the front line, commanded respectively by Captain W. R. Knott, Second-Lieutenants J. S. Wood and W. Littlefair. As the attacking waves came in to the open ground east of the wood they were met by heavy machine-gun and rifle fire from a prepared position west of Malgarni, known as the Hermann Stellung II. Line. Nothing had been previously known of this line of trenches, which was found to be protected by two strong belts of wire. Opposition was, however, soon overcome, and except for some hand-to-hand fighting in the village of Malgarni, there was little further resistance, the line of the objective, south-east of Fontaine, being in our hands by 10 a.m. . . . At 2 p.m. the Brigade moved forward to its final objective, about two thousand yards further east. This line was successfully reached by six o'clock. . . .

" Captain Knott, 9th Green Howards, and Second-Lieutenant Wood led their men during the attack with great skill and determination. Private Gilmore did most effective work with his Lewis gun team, and Private Muller with his section attacked and captured a machine-gun post which was holding up the advance.   Lance-Corporal Copley, Privates Adams, Guest and Stendall successfully delivered several messages under heavy fire, and Private Glennell gallantly went forward alone to cut some wire which was holding up the advance of his unit.   Sergeant Smith, M.M., did fine service at the head of his platoon against a machine-gun post."

During the next two days the 74th and 7th Brigades held the front with two battalions in the front line and one in support, with Headquarters at Pommereuil, and the 9th Green Howards seem to have been lucky enough to accupy billets in Pommereuil from the 31st October to the morning of the 4th November.

" During the concluding days of October and the first few days of November, preparations were pushed on for what proved to be the final advance of the Fourth, Third and First Armies, which carried the British line to the east of Maubeuge and Mons, roughly an advance of about twenty-five miles along a front of thirty miles.   Railways were repaired, bridges rebuilt, and the railheads gradually advanced close up to the fighting troops.   Thousands of prisoners and men from the Labour Corps were employed on this work, which became the main factor governing the advance of the troops. . . .   On the XIII. Corps and Third Army front, the Forest of Mormal was the chief obstacle with the River Sambre to the east. . . .

" The task before the 25th Division was to assault the German position along a front of about two thousand yards, and to advance through a very intricate and enclosed country to the banks of the Sambre Canal, about one and a half miles from the starting-point.   The crossing of the Canal, about fifty-five feet wide and six to seven feet deep, the capture of Landrecies, and the establishment of a line east of the town, completed the first ׅobjective.   An advance of a further two miles was given as a second objective so as to bring the divisional front about a mile beyond the Petite Helpe River.   This last move was, however, contingent on the successful advance on the right by the 32nd Division, which had relieved the 6th Division on the IX. Corps front.   The 50th Division was in touch on the left."

On the morning of the 4th December the 75th Brigade was to cross the Canal and capture Landrecies ; the 74th was to follow in rear, ready to assist in forcing the passage of the Canal should the leading brigade need help, finally passing through the 75th and carrying on the advance, while the 7th Brigade was in Divisional reserve; the Division this day numbered 4,190 fighting men.

By noon the canal had been crossed, Landrecies captured, and the first objective east of the town had been gained; while by 2 p.m. the 9th Green Howards, who had left Pommereuil that morning with their Brigade, had crossed the Canal north-east of Landrecies by means of bridges made of petrol tins, and had taken up an outpost line with Headquarters at a farm which had been the German artillery H.Q. One battery of 4·2 howitzers, one 8-inch howitzer and eight prisoners were captured, while by the evening the Brigade had reached a line running through Le Preseau, about three thousand yards beyond the first objective. The Battalion companies were this day commanded as follows: " A," Captain Blow; " B," Lieutenant Darvall; " C," Captain Knott; and " D," Captain Roberts.

The 75th Brigade now formed a defensive flank to the south-east in touch with the 32nd Division on the right, while the 7th Brigade was brought up to the canal.

Early on the morning of the 5th November the 74th Brigade continued the advance, the 11th Sherwood Foresters leading, followed by the 9th Green Howards and 13th Durham Light Infantry, and the 75th Brigade moving in rear in support. Very little opposition was encountered, and by 9.40 a.m. the advance guard had crossed the Petite Helpe River west of Maroilles and was pushing on through the village. There was desultory fighting all through the afternoon to the east of Maroilles, but by dark an outpost line had been taken up by the 11th Foresters and the 9th Green Howards astride the Marbaix Road, with the Durham Light Infantry in support.

The advance was continued at 6.30 on the morning of the 6th November, the 74th and 7th Brigades on the right and left of the divisional front respectively, and the 9th Green Howards leading their Brigade, " A " Company under Captain Blow forming the vanguard. The advance-guard was checked by machine-gun fire on the right and left of the road just before reaching Marbaix, but this village was occupied by " A " and " C " Companies about 2 p.m. " Had a running fight with enemy," so runs the Battalion diary, " but could not come in close contact with him. Enemy shelled village slightly about 6.30."

The outpost line outside Marbaix was held for the night by the 9th Green Howards on the right and 11th Foresters on the left, with the Durhams in support.

On the 7th the 75th and 7th Brigades went on, the 74th remaining about Marbaix, and the advance was continued towards the Avesnes–Maubeuge main road; but during the night that followed the 66th Division relieved the 25th, all three brigades of which then marched back to the Landrecies–Preux–Bousies area, the 9th Green Howards occupying billets at Bousies, where on the 11th the news reached them of the conclusion of an Armistice with Germany.

"Since leaving Le Cateau, the Division, during the two days' fighting on the 23rd and 24th October, had advanced about four and a half miles through very difficult country, including the Bois l'Eveque, a small wood half-way between Le Cateau and the Forest of Mormal. Between the 4th and 8th November it had covered another twelve miles, including the passage of the Sambre Canal in the face of a strong defence by numerous machine guns and heavy artillery. Its success was undoubtedly due to the splendid co-operation of all ranks of the various services of the Division, the finely developed *esprit de corps* of all units, and their determination to carry through an operation which required the greatest initiative on the part of the Company and local commanders on the spot."*

During the advance the losses of the 25th Division had been heavy, 50 officers and 921 other ranks having been killed, 263 officers and 4,854 non-commissioned officers and men were wounded, while 6 officers and 648 other ranks were missing—the majority of these being killed or wounded, a total loss of 6,742 all ranks.

In the same period the casualties in the 9th Battalion The Green Howards came to 8 officers and 66 other ranks killed or died of wounds, 15 officers, including the chaplain, and 388 non-commissioned officers and men wounded, and 62 men missing.† The names of the officers are, killed or died of wounds: Major G. N. Hunnybun, M.C., Lieutenants G. M.Wolsten-holme, M.C., C. Read, H. Dixon and W. H. Grimsley, Second-Lieutenants P. Helms, I. R. Edwardes-Crate and J. A. Pomfrey; wounded were Captains C. H. B. Botting, M.C., and W. F. Greenwood, D.S.O., M.C., Lieutenants R. Ward, G. H. U. Saunders and A. R. Porter, Second-Lieu-tenants R. H. Akers, H. H. Ransome, J. F. Guttridge, W. A. Sharpe, H. D. Foster, T. F. Day, C. L. Porter, T. Narrow and J. G. Anderson; with the Reverend W. E. Jones, C.F.

The 25th Division now at once began to move back from the front, and on the 13th November the 9th Green Howards were in billets at Le Cateau, where a belated reinforcement of fifty-three other ranks joined, and here they remained quietly until the 29th, when the Division moved to an area east of Cambrai, the Battalion going to billets at St. Vaast.

---

* In this account of the share of the 9th Green Howards in the Battle of the Hundred Days, heavy drafts have been made on the Divisional History.
† These figures do not altogether agree with those in the Divisional History.

Here the whole of December was spent, the battalions of the Division being employed in salvage work of all kinds in the surrounding country. Demobilization set in in a mild form on the 14th January, 1919, when one man of the Battalion was demobilized, but thereafter it continued steadily though only a few men left for home at one time; but by the end of the month, when the Battalion had moved to billets at Haussey, two officers and one hundred and forty-two non-commissioned officers and men had left.

At Haussey, on the 30th January, the King's Colour, which had arrived from England, was consecrated by the Rev. Mr. Jenkin, C.F., and presented to the Battalion by Major-General J. R. E. Charles, C.B., D.S.O., commanding the 25th Division, Brigadier-General H. M. Craigie-Halkett, C.M.G., D.S.O., being also present at the ceremony. The Colour was received by Lieutenant J. S. Wood, M.C., and Lieutenant-Colonel R. S. Hart, D.S.O., was in command of the guards on the occasion.

During February demobilization proceeded rather more quickly, no fewer than five officers and two hundred and sixteen other ranks being sent to England this month; while the gradual and progressive diminution in the strength of the Battalion was assisted by compliance with other calls which were made upon the units of the British army remaining in the theatre of war; for of the fourteen thousand men of all arms which composed the 25th Division at Christmas, 1918, about three thousand men, who had joined since the 1st January, 1916, were transferred to other divisions forming the British Army of Occupation on the Rhine, while some three hundred releasable men re-engaged for service in the post-bellum army. Of those who remained all, with the exception of those required for the cadres, had been dispatched to England by the end of March.

A few weeks later the cadres of all units of the Division returned home.

10TH BATTALION.

Witley Camp, August, 1915.

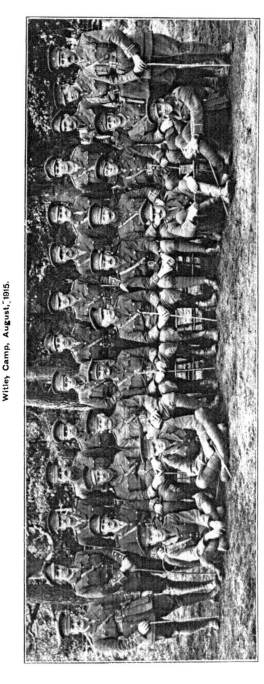

Back Row.—Lt. P. Mathison; Lt. W. H. Goater; Lt. R. M. Milne; 2nd-Lt. N. E. S. Gardner; 2nd-Lt. W. R. Knott; Lt. D. H. Wippell; 2nd-Lt. A. F. Jacob; 2nd-Lt. C. B. Bass; Lt. J. N. Barraclough; 2nd-Lt. V. D. K. Craddock; 2nd-Lt. J. S. Pratt; Capt. J. E. Lynch; Lt. E. D. O'Brien; Capt. S. W. Loudoun-Shand.

Middle Row.—Capt. C. A. McLellan; Capt. V. Fowler; Lt. and Q.M. R. Cumming; Major W. H. Dent; Col. A. de S. Hadow; Capt. A. Hollingworth (Adjutant); Capt. T. Charteris; Capt. J. C. E. Douglas; Capt. G. A. Turner.

Sitting—2nd-Lt. F. B. Parker; 2nd-Lt. W. B. Cornaby; 2nd-Lt. P. J. Sylvester; 2nd-Lt. G. B. Hornby.

CHAPTER XVII

THE 10TH BATTALION

1914-1918

THE BATTLE OF LOOS. THE FIRST BATTLE OF THE SOMME. THE THIRD BATTLE OF YPRES. THE BATTLE OF ARRAS

THE first official mention of the 10th Battalion The Green Howards is contained in the same Army Order—that numbered 388 of October, 1914—which chronicles the posting to brigades and divisions of the 8th and 9th Battalions of the Regiment; and in this Order the 10th Battalion is told off, with the 12th and 13th Battalions of the Northumberland Fusiliers and the 8th Battalion of the East Yorkshire Regiment, to the 62nd Infantry Brigade, commanded by Colonel T. G. L. H. Armstrong, of the 21st Division, under Lieutenant-General Sir E. T. H. Hutton, K.C.B., K.C.M.G. The 21st Division formed part of the Third New Army, commanded by Lieutenant-General Sir A. E. Codrington, K.C.V.O., C.B., and it was to be stationed in Halton Park between Tring and Wendover, the men being billeted in Tring and neighbourhood.

The new Battalion makes its first appearance in the Army List for October, when its officer corps contained only one captain—Temporary Captain V. Fowler, the date of whose appointment was the 3rd September, presumably that of the formation of the Battalion—11 subaltern officers, all second-lieutenants, and one quartermaster: the names of these were Second-Lieutenants D. H. Whippell, H. B. Milling, J. S. Pratt, J. N. Barraclough, B. M. Cust, O. Greenwood, J. D. Hawkins, C. G. Holman, W. R. Knott, P. J. M. Sylvester, W. Wilberforce, and Lieutenant and Quartermaster W. T. Dickenson. But in the November Army List several other, and more senior, officers appear as having joined, these being Bt.-Colonel A. de S. Hadow, in command, Majors R. E. Noyes and W. I. Wyvill, Lieutenant E. H. Sedgewick, and also Second-Lieutenant R. H. Hadow.

The 10th Battalion was in the first instance assembled at Berkhampsted, moving on the 1st October to Halton Park and going there into a so-called camp, where for the new arrivals there were certainly a few tents, but no washing places, cook-houses, or amenities of that kind. The weather was at first beautifully fine, and it was not until November that it changed for the worse, but by this time the men of the Battalion had been given blue clothing, so that they had at least a dry change of garments. On 15th November the 10th Green Howards were moved into billets in Aylesbury, ostensibly for a month only while huts were being erected in Halton Park, but all this time—having been soldiers for two months and hoping, if not expecting, to proceed early to France—the rank and file had possessed only wooden rifles, and " how," inquires plaintively the Battalion correspondent of *The Green Howards' Gazette*, " can one feel like a soldier with a wooden toy to carry about with you, knowing that before parade it had already poked the fire, cleared the kitchen sink, beaten the dog, or proved of domestic utility in other ways ? "

On 22nd May, 1915, the Battalion returned to Halton Park, where huts were now ready, and training of all kinds pursued its strenuous course ; and " at last on August 9th we began our last move for final concentration round Aldershot and marched from Halton to Witley, taking five days on the way, and marching past His Majesty the King on the borders of Windsor Forest on August 11th, and Lord Kitchener near Bagshot on the next day, arriving at Witley Camp and taking over B 2 Lines on August 13th."

The long-looked-for orders to proceed abroad finally arrived, and at 6 p.m. on the 9th September, 1915, the Battalion left Witley Camp and marched to Milford, entraining there for Folkestone ; this port was arrived at about 11.40 p.m., and, embarking at once, Boulogne was reached at 3.15 a.m. on the 10th.

The following is a complete list of the officers arriving in France with the 10th Battalion The Green Howards : Colonel A. de S. Hadow, in command ; Major W. H. Dent ; Lieutenant A. Hollingsworth, adjutant ; Second-Lieutenant V. D. K. Craddock, signalling officer ; Lieutenant E. R. Lyth, medical officer ; the Rev. O. B. Parsons, chaplain ; and Lieutenant R. Cumming, quartermaster.

"A" Company : Captains T. Charteris and J. C. E. Douglas ; Lieutenants W. H. Goater and J. N. Barraclough ; Second-Lieutenants C. B. Bass and A. F. Jacobs.

"B" Company : Captains V. Fowler and S. W. Loudoun-Shand; Lieutenant J. D. Hawkins ; Second-Lieutenants W. W. Ball, N. E. S. Gardner, bombing officer, and P. J. M. Sylvester, transport officer.

"C" Company : Captains C. A. McLellan and G. A. Turner ; Lieutenants D. H. Wippell, W. R. Knott, machine-gun officer, and G. B. Hornby.

"D" Company : Major R. E. Noyes ; Captain J. E. Lynch ; Lieutenants R. M. Milne and G. C. Ransome; Second-Lieutenants J. S. Pratt and W. B. Cornaby.

But very little time was spent in the rest camp at Boulogne, for in the early hours of the 11th the Battalion marched to the railway station and took the train for Watten, where it arrived about 7.40 a.m., and then marched to Nœux-les-Mines, halting and bivouacking or billeting *en route* at Houlle, Wittes, Ames and Burbure. Nœux-les-Mines was reached at 1 a.m. on the 25th, and all lay down in a very wet bivouac for such of the night as remained, marching on the same day to Vermelles and crossing the Bethune–Lens Road, where, for the first time, the 10th Green Howards came under shell-fire and adopted an open formation.

The Battle of Loos began this day, the 25th, the main attack being delivered by the I. and IV. Corps of the First Army between the La Bassée Canal and the village of Grenay, while the V. Corps made a secondary attack upon Bellewaarde Farm, and smaller attacks were made upon other parts of the enemy's line. On this day the Commander-in-Chief held in reserve the XI. Corps containing the Guards Division and the two New Army Divisions, the 21st and 24th, and these two last had, as stated by Sir John French in his despatch, been brought up to the line Nœux-les-Mines–Beuvry " to ensure the speedy and effective support of the I. and IV. Corps in the case of their success."

At 9.30 a.m. on the 25th, when Loos had fallen, the British Commander-in-Chief placed the 21st and 24th Divisions at the disposal of General Haig, commanding the First Army, and these had marched forward at once on receipt of orders by roads—those leading through Vermelles to Hulluch and Loos—which were terribly congested, while the country on either side was cut up by trenches and enclosed by wire ; rain also was falling intermittently.

On the afternoon of Saturday the 25th, the 62nd Brigade leading, the Division passed through the village of Loos, and the 10th Green Howards " arrived at the front trenches, as then held by the 18th London Regiment, about dusk. We inquired of the Londoners what they were doing, and they said that they had decided to dig in for the night, so we did likewise, except two platoons of ' D ' Company who pushed on a little further ; and it was then that Captain Lynch, previously shot through the wrist, but carrying on, was killed. These then fell back into line with the rest."

The two divisions were now occupying the front German trenches, the 21st on the right and the 24th on the left, with the 1st Division again on the left of the 24th ; and the orders issued this night to these three divisions were that at 11 o'clock on the 26th they were to assault the main German position.

" Having dug ourselves in fairly satisfactorily," writes O. B. P. in *The*

Green Howards' Gazette, " we were promptly moved, and had to start over again and wait in pelting rain to carry on the attack by daylight. Early on Sunday morning Major Dent called the officers together into a shed to explain what was wanted, and about 7.30 off we went up the hill, ' C ' Company leading. The attack went on all day with varying success, and it was on the Sunday, 26th, that we sustained most of our casualties. Colonel Hadow, Major Dent, Major Noyes and Captain Charteris were all killed, and we began to find ourselves the defenders in the face of a big German counter-attack. Sunday night such of the Battalion as could be found were withdrawn and told to hold a line of trenches in support under command of Captain McLellan ; these were withdrawn on the Monday morning. Meanwhile Captains Fowler and Douglas, Lieutenants Goater and Ball and about seventy men had become separated and were much further to the right in the front of the 141st Brigade ; these did not get their orders to retire till Monday morning and rejoined the rest of the Battalion in a bivouac about six miles from the firing line towards 4 p.m., Captain Fowler then assuming command."

Another historian gives the following account : " The 62nd Brigade had been hurried away separately and taken to the south and east of Loos to reinforce the 15th Division, which had sustained such losses on the 25th that they could not hold both the front and the flank. The 62nd Brigade pushed on, reached the point of danger as early as the night of the 25th, and occupied a line of slag-heaps to the south-east of Loos "—" A," " C " and " D " Companies and part of " B " Company of the 10th Green Howards on the right of the slag-heap near Loos Pylon and the rest of " B " across the road at the Chalk Pit—" where there was a gap through which the enemy might penetrate from the flank. The Brigade was only just in time in getting hold of the position, for it was strongly attacked at 5 in the morning of the 26th, the attack falling mainly upon the 8th East Yorkshire and the 10th Green Howards, who were driven back from the further side of the great dump which was the centre of the fight, but held on to the Loos side of it. The line was held all day of the 26th. More than once the fighting was hand-to-hand."

The Green Howards' Gazette correspondent goes on to say : " Little can be said of what actually happened, beyond the fact that everyone was wet, hungry (no food from Saturday morning till Sunday night) and desperately tired ; impressions left consist chiefly of the racket of machine guns and rifles, the continuous whistling of shells followed by the bang and the bubbly noise of the fuses, and the rattle of shrapnel among the Loos Pylons. Officers found themselves in command of men from three different divisions ; telephonic communication was smashed, and orders were practically an impossibility from any higher command than that of a platoon commander.

"Altogether, besides those already mentioned as killed, we lost during Saturday and Sunday, Second-Lieutenant Bass, wounded and missing, Captain Turner, Lieutenants Hawkins, Wippell and Ransome, Second-Lieutenants Jacobs, Cornaby and Hornby wounded. Two Company-Sergeant-Majors and about three hundred other ranks were killed, wounded and missing."

On being taken out of the line on the night of the 27th, the Battalion had withdrawn to a bivouac near Philosophe, where Major W. B. Eddowes, from the 13th Northumberland Fusiliers, and formerly of the Manchester Regiment, was appointed to command ; and then on the 28th the Battalion marched to Nœux-les-Mines, and there entrained for Strazeele, where about a fortnight was spent in training and reorganizing, and where drafts of eleven officers and two hundred non-commissioned officers and men joined on the 9th and 11th October ; the officers were : Lieutenant E. Collier, Second-Lieutenants A. C. Jardine, T. R. Evans, H. Such, H. Bass, B. M. Cust, G. M. Lawless, W. M. Slater, F. B. Parker, O. H. Ball, and A. R. Slater.

Strazeele was left on the 13th and, marching by Merris, Le Verrier, Steenwerck, La Menegatte, Nieppe and Pont de Nieppe, the Battalion reached Armentières next day, and here " comparatively palatial billets in this home of refuge for much-tried units put us on good terms with ourselves for the winter. Instruction in the gentle art of trench-work now proceeded apace. First the officers and N.C.O.'s went up for a daylight instruction ; then for a twenty-four hours' turn ; then a platoon from each company took over a section of trench for twenty-four hours. October 16th saw our first casualties in trench life, and 17th October our first officer casualty—Second-Lieutenant W. M. Slater, while out wiring in front and forgetting the order that all bayonets in the front line, except the sentries', shall be fixed, leaped lightly over the parapet, and was wounded !

" On October 19th another draft, of one hundred non-commissioned officers and men this time, was received, and during the 19th and 20th the whole Battalion did a twenty-four hours' tour in the trenches by companies ; finally on the 25th we, as a Battalion, took over our allotted sector and really started trench life. On the 27th a detachment—one officer and thirty other ranks—went over to Bailleul for the purpose of an inspection there by His Majesty the King during one of his visits to the front ; and on October 29th what one might call the rainy season began. The presence of at least six inches of water and several falls of the parapet occasioned great commotion in the minds of the Powers that be ; later, it was found that it was impossible to rouse their interest for anything less than six feet of water and no parapet at all !

"On November 7th Second-Lieutenant T. R. Evans was wounded while out on patrol during a mist which suddenly lifted ; on November 9th Second-Lieutenant B. M. Cust was killed, also while out in front ; Second-Lieutenant H. V. Dove joined on the 11th; and on the 24th Second-Lieutenant W. W. Ball was sniped and killed while sighting a rifle on to a German working party in the early morning.   On the 2nd December Second-Lieutenant T. E. G. Bailey joined and on the 5th Lieutenant W. H. Haynes ; six days later a shrapnel bullet caught Second-Lieutenant H. V. Dove in the open and wounded him rather severely in the head ; while, worse still, on the 18th Captain J. C. Douglas was shot through the neck, while inspecting our wire before daylight, and died in the Casualty Clearing Station : his loss was deeply regretted by all, his courage, common sense and keenness all being greatly missed, especially by 'A,' his own Company.

"Sunday, December 19th, will not be forgotten by any who had the misfortune to be in the line that day, for it was the first really heavy bombardment of trenches we had suffered * ; every kind of large and small monstrosity was hurled into them.   Some you could see coming, some you could hear, and some came without any preliminary announcement.   For their conduct on that day three men of 'D' Company—Lance-Corporal R. Hall and Privates J. Stephenson and W. Clark, and one of 'B' Company —Private T. Welsh—were all awarded the D.C.M. ; the first three for gallantly digging out the buried occupants of a dug-out in view of the enemy ; the last-named for cheery disregard of Hun hatred and the good example he set the rest of his Company.

"Second-Lieutenants D. M. Evans and H. Hume reported for duty on December 20th.   We had the good fortune to be out of the trenches on Christmas Day and celebrated the occasion fittingly "—in billets at Armentières, and from here certain fortunate individuals obtained leave to visit the United Kingdom.

Here or hereabouts the 10th Green Howards remained throughout January and February, 1916, doing their best to keep their parapets intact and their trenches drained, and losing small numbers of men almost daily from the enemy guns and snipers.   During these weeks small drafts joined, also several officers—Captain Crone, Second-Lieutenants Llewellyn, Butcher, Matthews, Kinnach, and Loney ; while Regimental-Sergeant-Major Craton

* The Battalion was now holding the Epinette Salient, and this bombardment was intended as a diversion from the German attack on the Bluff further to the north.

was invalided home, his place being filled by Company-Sergeant-Major Henderson of " D " Company.

During this time four officers were wounded—Major Shand, Lieutenant Ransome, Second-Lieutenants Cradock and Parker, Ransome and Cradock during a raid carried out by " D " Company of the Battalion against Black Redoubt, the object being to obtain prisoners and identifications, to ascertain if the enemy had installed any gas apparatus in this sector, to kill Germans and do as much damage as possible.   Five officers and forty-five other ranks took part, the officers being Captain Milne, Lieutenants Ransome and Collier, Second-Lieutenants Cradock and Dickinson.   Unfortunately the weather was misty and the enemy wire was not properly cut, while snow on the ground showed up the party, which was at once detected, and the enemy's bombs caused many casualties, so that the raiding party was forced to retire without having effected its object.   Two officers and nine other ranks were wounded and three men were missing in this affair.

During March the Battalion was twice out of the line for brief periods, once at Houplines and the second time at Steenwercke ; and then on the 31st March the Division left the Second Army and, entraining at Bailleul, moved to the Somme area, the Battalion arriving in billets at Ville-sous-Corbie on the 17th April, and being greeted on the evening of its arrival by fourteen 5·9 shells which were fired from Fricourt and fell in the neighbourhood of the billets.

The Division was now commanded by Major-General D. G. M. Campbell and was in the XV. Corps, under Lieutenant-General H. S. Horne, of General Sir Henry Rawlinson's Fourth Army.

Of the period between the arrival of the 10th Green Howards in this part of the front and the opening of the Somme Battle of this year, the Battalion correspondent wrote as follows to *The Green Howards' Gazette* : " Another week's quiet and then by easy stages up to the line ; first to the back area, then up again into the region of working parties, and finally into the trenches once more.   We started badly by getting Second-Lieutenant Kinnach slightly wounded on the first night, during retaliation for a raid by the Battalion on our right, and Second-Lieutenant Hague and his Company-Sergeant-Major Howarth on the following day by a whizz-bang in the door of their dug-out.   On the next day, April 24th, Second-Lieutenant Alexandre arrived.   The ' stand-to ' of the morning and evening of April 30th proved rather trying.   The Germans attempted a raid on our right, accompanying the effort with much trench-mortaring and other missiles, some of which we caught, Second-Lieutenant Jardine being wounded—and gas, which left us alone.   Second-Lieutenants Perkins and Harland then arrived, and our next tour in the trenches brought us

into the abominable Tambour, a most unpleasant spot, famed chiefly for
rifle grenades, canisters and casualties, and we had our share of them all,
including among the last named Second-Lieutenant Shaw. Nobody was
heartbroken when this spell of duty was over.

"Some of the sharper wits among us had already begun to think that
something was in the wind. New railways, new communication trenches,
new roads, new gun positions, were coming into being all round, and the
more inquisitive began to inquire—' What for ? '   Then in the third week in
June ten fresh officers arrived—Lieutenants G. H. V. Saunders, L. I. Collins
and R. A. Hare, Second-Lieutenants F. P. Cliff, H. A. Cornaby, A. E.
Griffin, J. L. Smith, G. S. Sarson, M. Kemp-Welch and G. H. Mather.
It was now merely a question of how soon. Then we set to work upon our
assembly trenches for use during the bombardment—deeper and narrower
ones have not often been seen. People began to talk of ' U ' days and ' Z '
days, objectives and carrying parties ; then ' U ' day arrived, the bombardment began, one more day out of the line we had in peace—when the attack
was postponed for forty-eight hours, and then on the night of June 30th
we moved up to our positions for the effort that would put to the proof the
effect, on a body of peaceful citizens, of nearly two years' soldiering." *

In his despatch of the 23rd December, 1916, the Field-Marshal states that
he had entrusted the attack on the front from Maricourt to Serre to the
Fourth Army, which contained five Army Corps ; on the extreme right or
south of this Army was the XIII. Corps and next to it came the XV. Corps
with the 7th and 21st Divisions on the right and left respectively, the 21st
Division being immediately north of Fricourt.

On the 29th June the 10th Battalion The Green Howards was in billets
at Buire, but on the following night it moved up to Queen's Redoubt in
readiness for the attack which was to take place on the following morning,
the 62nd Brigade being in divisional reserve.

"' B ' Company was detailed to follow up the Middlesex Regiment of
the right brigade and mop up the first objective just north of Fricourt,
and this company accordingly moved up to the front line just prior to zero
hour on the 1st July, which was 7.30 a.m. It was on this occasion that Major
Loudoun-Shand won his Victoria Cross for superb courage in leading his men
in the teeth of a murderous machine-gun fire, from a gun that had been
brought into action after the first wave had passed it. Unfortunately he
was not destined to live to enjoy his distinction, as, after being hit three
times, he was mortally wounded. Even then he continued to cheer on his
men, and he died just as they silenced the gun and the Huns who were

* The extracts so far made from *The Green Howards' Gazette* are from an account contributed by the Rev. O. B. Parsons ; such as follow are from the narrative of Major Goater.

causing the trouble. He was a gallant officer and was mourned by everyone in the Battalion. His Company went into action with five officers and one hundred and seventeen other ranks, and came out with one officer and twenty-seven men.

"As early as 9 a.m. orders were received to move up in support of the left brigade, and consequently the Battalion, less 'B' Company, advanced *via* Aberdeen Avenue to reinforce the Durham Light Infantry in Crucifix Trench. They pushed across No-Man's-Land into the old German front-line trench with few casualties, and then, *via* Patch Alley, to the sunken road running north and south through the village of Fricourt ; parallel with this road and about five hundred yards distant was Crucifix Trench, held by the remains of the Durhams. Just after the Battalion had reached the sunken road, the enemy put down a heavy barrage midway between it and Crucifix Trench ; but as it was known that reinforcements were badly wanted, the three Companies pushed on without a halt through the barrage and into Crucifix Trench. After a certain amount of reorganization, the order of Companies from left to right was 'C,' 'D,' 'A,' with Battalion Headquarters and the remnants of 'B' Company in support in Lozenge Alley.

"The night of July 1st–2nd was spent in the work of consolidation. At about 5 a.m. on the 2nd a hostile bombing attack on 'A' Company was beaten off, and it became apparent that the enemy was still holding a strong point known as The Poodles, immediately in front of that Company. The Battalion was ordered to attack and capture this strong point, from which part of the line, as well as all the ground in front of it, was enfiladed. The Battalion bombers under Lieutenant N. E. S. Gardner, M.C., and the company bombers of 'A' were detailed for the work. The attack resulted in some sharp bombing encounters, during which the bombers of 'D' and part of 'C' were engaged ; but after two hours' fighting, the strong point was captured and the garrison all killed or wounded. Our casualties were numerous, including three subalterns wounded, thus bringing the officer casualties up to one killed and six wounded.

"At 4 p.m. on the 2nd orders were received for an attack by the Lincoln and Yorkshire Battalions upon Shelter Wood, which lay three hundred yards in front of our position. This attack took place at 6.30 a.m. on the 3rd and was completely successful, our Battalion alone securing one hundred and fifty prisoners. By the evening 'C' and 'D' Companies had established a line from the right of the Lincolns at the corner of Shelter Wood to a point two hundred and fifty yards south where it joined the 7th Division, this being at the time the most advanced portion of the Division Front. 'A' and 'B' Companies were in support.

"The night of July 3rd–4th was given up to consolidation. On the morning of the 4th the Battalion was relieved by a battalion of the Lancashire Fusiliers and moved back to Buire. During the three days' fighting the 21st Division had taken all its objectives and had penetrated the strong enemy defensive system to a depth of over a mile."

The posthumous award of the Victoria Cross was made to Major S. W. Loudoun-Shand in the *London Gazette* of the 8th September, 1916, as under:

"For most conspicuous bravery. When his company attempted to climb over the parapet to attack the enemy's trenches they were met by very fierce machine-gun fire which temporarily stopped their progress. Major Loudoun-Shand immediately leapt on the parapet, helped the men over it and encouraged them in every way until he fell mortally wounded.

"Even then he insisted on being propped up in the trench, and went on encouraging the non-commissioned officers and men until he died."

"On being relieved by the 10th Lancashire Fusiliers in Shelter Wood the Battalion moved back to billets at Dernancourt, where it entrained in heavy rain at 6 p.m. and arrived at Ailly-sur-Somme at 11 o'clock at night; here billets were told off and everybody enjoyed a well-earned and much-needed rest. On the 7th the Battalion marched to Molliens Vidame *via* Cavillon and Oissy, billeting there, an inspection taking place next day by the Divisional Commander, who spoke highly of the work of the Battalion in the battle. Here Lieut.-Colonel Eddowes had to go to hospital, Major Fowler assuming command; the company commanders at this time were: 'A,' Captain Barraclough; 'B,' Captain Milne; 'C,' Captain Goater; and 'D,' Captain Crone.

"At 5.20 a.m. on the 11th the 10th Green Howards marched back to Ailly-sur-Somme, and entrained for Corbie, arriving at that place at 11 o'clock at night and marching on to Meaulte and there bivouacking, all thoroughly tired out, at 4 on the morning of the 12th. But early this day orders were received to move up to the front and relieve the 10th Battalion South Wales Borderers of the 38th Division in Mametz Wood and complete the capture of the same, which by this time had been partially cleared. This proved to be a long and tiring business, as the whole of the southern portion of the wood was being heavily shelled by the enemy; after many difficulties and losing a number of men, the relief was completed at 4 a.m. on the 13th, the march up having started at 7 on the previous evening. An advance was made from the positions taken over by 'B' and 'D' Companies, the wood being finally cleared by 8 a.m. The attack was made

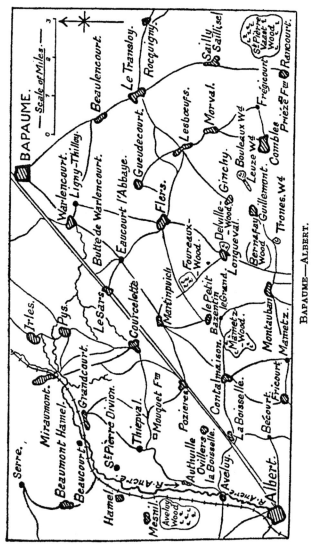

BAPAUME—ALBERT.

337

without any barrage, and there were several sharp encounters among the thick undergrowth and fallen trees, resulting in the capture of two heavy guns which were found to be two Belgian pieces from Liège. The line was consolidated on the edge of the wood, ' A ' and ' C ' Companies still remaining in their own positions, half-way through the wood, which were heavily shelled all day.

" Towards evening the shelling became intense and many casualties were suffered, including Lieutenant G. Hornby killed and Captain Milne wounded. The bearing of the men was excellent, and the Battalion and company runners and linesmen deserve special praise for the way in which they carried out their special duties ; practically all became casualties before dark. It was said at the time that the direct route from company to Battalion Headquarters could be traced by the numbers of runners and linesmen lying where they had fallen in their efforts to pass through the shelling. One signaller, Private H. George, ' C ' Company, went out in the face of this shelling no fewer than six times to repair his line to Battalion H.Q., succeeding each time, acts which gained for him the Military Medal.

" On the evening of the 13th the 110th Brigade moved up into position for an attack on Bazentin-le-Petit Wood, and Lieutenant Gardner, the Battalion bombing officer, was ordered to go out and lay tapes in No-Man's-Land for the assembly of the assaulting battalions of this Brigade ; the shelling and machine-gun fire was very heavy at the time and he was wounded as soon as he started, but in spite of this he completed his work and was awarded the Military Cross. The village and wood of Bazentin-le-Petit were captured early on the 14th, but the enemy put down a heavy barrage on Mametz Wood, again drenching it with gas and maintaining this fire throughout the 14th and 15th, many casualties being sustained.

" On the evening of the 15th the 10th Green Howards were ordered to attack and capture a trench running west of Bazentin-le-Petit Village in the north-west corner of the wood, which was still held by the enemy ; at the time the 110th Brigade and some of the Division on the right were holding a line which ran along the edge of the wood. ' C ' and ' D ' Companies under Captains Goater and Crone respectively were detailed to effect this capture, with ' A ' and ' B ' Companies in support ; and ' C ' Company formed up some two hundred yards from the objective, with ' D ' Company and the bombers on the right of ' C ' and with the right platoon just clear of the Montauban–Martinpuich Road. One machine-gun section and one Stokes gun were told off to accompany ' C ' ; zero hour was fixed for 2 a.m. The companies moved up from Mametz Wood at midnight, ' C ' Company being heavily shelled on the way up, one 5·9 shell knocking out the guides and another putting the Stokes gun and fifteen men out of action ; while

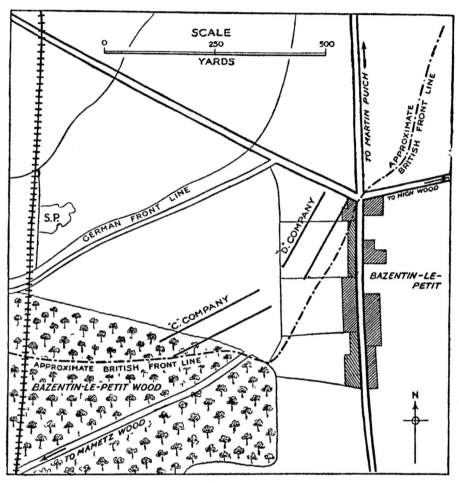

SCALE

0   250   500

YARDS

TO MARTIN PUICH

APPROXIMATE BRITISH FRONT LINE

TO HIGH WOOD

GERMAN FRONT LINE

S.P.

"D" COMPANY

"C" COMPANY

BAZENTIN-LE-PETIT

APPROXIMATE BRITISH FRONT LINE

BAZENTIN-LE-PETIT WOOD

TO MAMETZ WOOD

N

BAZENTIN-LE-PETIT.
16th July, 1915.

before the edge of Bazentin-le-Petit Wood was reached more casualties had been caused by machine-gun fire ; but the company was lined up ready to attack at 1.45 a.m. on the 16th. ' D ' Company reached its allotted position without much difficulty.

" At 2 a.m. the attack opened ; the right company had little difficulty in gaining its objective, but the enemy resistance on the left was more pronounced, and ' C ' Company bombers had a sharp encounter before they could gain access to the communication trench running at right angles to the objective. They established themselves here, however, and formed a block, and the two companies then commenced the work of consolidation. At 2.30 a.m. the enemy counter-attacked down the communication trench, pushing back our bombers, who were all killed or wounded, but two other sections quickly took their place and restored a situation which might have had serious consequences for the rest of the line, as the enemy could easily enfilade the trench from his position at the junction with the communication trench. The Battalion lost two officers and about thirty men in this operation ; the officers were Second-Lieutenants J. S. Kinnach and H. A. Cornaby, both of ' C ' Company, who were killed by machine-gun fire while crossing No-Man's-Land.

" Later in the day the Battalion was relieved and went back to Mametz Wood, which was again badly gas-shelled in the evening ; but the artillery fire was less intense on the 17th and it was possible to repair the trenches and wire the front."

This night the 10th Green Howards on relief went back to billets in Buire, which was reached early on the 18th ; leaving here again at 2.45 a.m. on the 20th the Battalion marched to Dernancourt, entrained there for Saleux and marched thence to billets at Molliens Vidame, " one of the most comfortable villages in which the Battalion had been billeted during its service overseas."

The Battalion did not remain here very long, however, for on the 22nd it was once again on the move and proceeded by march route, by motor-'bus and by train, via Amiens, Longueau, Petit Heuvin, Ternas and Manin, to underground billets in Arras, where it arrived about 1 o'clock on the morning of the 28th, and on the same day relieved a battalion of the 14th Division in Trenches 88 to one Bay north of July Avenue and in Britannia Works. Here the following officers almost at once reported themselves for duty : Second-Lieutenants E. Pepper, G. M. Lawless, A. R. Slater, and H. S. Harrison. A period of quiet but monotonous trench work now ensued ; matters here were tolerably quiet on both sides, and when out of the line the 10th Green Howards usually billeted in the neighbourhood of Agnez-les-Duisans.

On the 18th August the Battalion side-stepped slightly to the right and relieved a battalion of the 11th Division south of the Scarpe, one company going to St. Sauveur, another to the Cemetery, while the remainder of the Battalion was in billets at Arras; but on the 2nd September a move was made to Sombrin, where something of the nature of a rest was enjoyed until the 12th, by which date reinforcements had brought the Battalion up to war strength again for the first time since the Battle of Loos. While here the Brigadier inspected the 10th Green Howards and informed them that the time was at hand when they were once more to take part in the Battle of the Somme.

Moving again by march route and by train the Battalion found itself on the 15th in Becordel Camp, near Arras, and leaving this early the following morning it arrived in Potter's Redoubt, half-way between Mametz and Montauban, two or three hours later, and, moving thence up to the line, the 62nd Brigade relieved a brigade of the 14th Division in front of Gueudecourt. " The state of the ground was very bad indeed owing to heavy shell fire, and, to make matters worse, rain started to pour down and so hampered operations, which obviously would have consisted of an attack on Gird Trench and Gueudecourt by the Brigade. The weather conditions went from bad to worse, the hostile shelling and sniping increased in intensity, and everyone was impatient to get forward and drive the Hun out of Gueudecourt, from which place he was doing much damage. All the wounded were of necessity kept in the line, as the shelling was so bad that it was impossible to get them away for three days.

" On the night of the 19th–20th a portion of ' D ' Company, under Lieutenant F. B. Parker, pushed forward and established a post about two hundred and fifty yards in front of the line, which relieved the situation to a great extent. Word had been received that as the Brigade was so exhausted, the task of capturing Gueudecourt had been allotted to the 110th and 64th Brigades, and that the present line must be held at all costs. It was not until the night of the 22nd that relief arrived, and the Battalion, worn out by nearly a week of heavy shelling and hard work and abominable climatic conditions, moved back to Fricourt Camp. This rest was, however, short-lived, as orders were received on the 25th to be ready to move at an hour's notice, and at 1 p.m. the Battalion marched to a camp near Bernafay Wood, where the night was spent. On the next night—26th–27th—the 62nd Brigade relieved the 64th, and the Battalion the 10th K.O.Y.L.I., in the line south-east of Gueudecourt. Trenches here were almost non-existent, and once more a defensive line had to be made, in spite of heavy shelling and bad weather.

" On September 28th two splendid officers were lost to the Battalion,

Second-Lieutenant O. H. Ball, of ' B ' Company, being killed, and Captain W. R. Knott, his company commander, being badly wounded.

" On the following day, the 7th D.C.L.I. of the 61st Brigade of the 20th Division relieved, and the Battalion was pulled out for the last time from the never-to-be-forgotten Battle of the Somme and enjoyed a well-earned and much-needed rest at the Bernafay Wood Camp."

This camp was left again on the 1st October and, marching to Dernancourt, the train was there taken for Marle-les-Mines, and arriving here on the 10th the Division marched to Fouquereuil and took over trenches in the Hairpin Crater sector in front of Vermelles and north of Loos from the 23rd Division, the 10th Green Howards being in reserve in Curly Crescent. The trenches in this sector were bad and this probably accounts in some measure for the heavy loss experienced on the 22nd by " B " Company when occupying the Northern Crater of the Quarry Sector and Hohenzollern Redoubt, when three men were killed and eleven wounded by minenwerfers. A few days later several more casualties were occasioned by the enemy's so-called " rum-jars."

On the 18th November Major T. G. Mathias, Welch Regiment, arrived and took over command from Lieutenant-Colonel Fowler.

Christmas Day, 1916, was spent by the Battalion in the support trenches, and two days later the long-looked-for relief took place, when the 62nd Brigade had been practically continuously in the trenches since the 11th October. On the completion of the relief the Battalion marched *via* Houchin to billets at Marle-les-Mines, where the last days of the year were passed.

The Battalion remained now for several weeks in this sector, and during this time reinforcements in officers and men arrived, numbering seven officers and some hundred of other ranks ; the officers were Lieutenant N. E. S. Gardner, M.C., Second-Lieutenants J. C. Storey, W. H. Coles, M. T. J. Fairman, C. Barton, K. L. Harris, and S. H. Dobinson. By the end of January, 1917, it seems to have been considered that it was time the Division made a move, and it proceeded by train and march route to a camp at Pezelhoek, where rather over a fortnight was spent, after which the 10th Green Howards were sent on by Poperinghe, Bethune, Nœux-les-Mines and Mazingarbe to trenches north of Loos, where they took over trenches from the Leicester Regiment in the Quarries Sector ; here Second-Lieutenant M. T. J. Fairman was at once wounded during the course of the relief.

When early in April the spring offensive of 1917 opened with the Battle of Arras of this year, undertaken by the Third and First Armies, the 21st Division was on the extreme south or right of the attack, being in the VII. Corps under Lieutenant-General Sir T. D'O. Snow, of the Third Army, commanded by General Sir E. Allenby. The VII. Corps contained the 21st,

30th, 56th, and 14th Divisions in that order from right to left, the 21st Division being between Croisilles and Henin-sur-Cojeul. The uncut wire and all the elaborate defences of the Hindenburg Line lay in front of the 21st Division, so that these troops were not called on to make anything more than a holding attack, which should enable the other divisions on the left to get forward with less resistance than they might otherwise have experienced.

In the last days of March the 10th Green Howards had moved up in support to Boisleux-au-Mont, sending " A " and " B " Companies to Boyelles and Boisleux-St.-Marc respectively; but on the 1st April at dusk the Battalion advanced to the railway embankment, remaining here until the night of the 2nd, when " A " and " B " Companies were sent up to reinforce the 13th Northumberland Fusiliers just north-west of the village of Croisilles. In the early morning of the 3rd patrols were pushed through Croisilles and the Battalion, having assisted in the capture of that place, spent the remainder of the day in consolidating the ground gained. Late on the 4th the 6th Leicester Regiment came up in relief and the 10th Green Howards withdrew to billets, first at Hamlincourt and next day at Adinfer, where they remained during the 6th and 7th in very inclement weather and under practically no cover. " C " and " D " Companies had been left behind at the railway embankment under the orders of the G.O.C. 110th Brigade, and did not rejoin until the evening of the 9th, when the Battalion had moved up to Boiry Becquerelle, relieving from here the 9th K.O.Y.L.I. in the front line south-east of Henin-sur-Cojeul in front of the Hindenburg Line. Here the Battalion was ordered next day, the 11th, to assault the Hindenburg Line in conjunction with the 1st Lincoln Regiment.

The attack was duly made at 6 a.m., but the troops came upon enemy wire of unusual thickness and which had been in no way damaged by our artillery fire; the attacking battalions were consequently unable to get through and suffered heavy losses, the 10th Green Howards having two officers—Lieutenants Pratt and Kemp-Welch—killed, and Captains Bailey and Short and Second-Lieutenant Colls wounded, while some one hundred and twenty non-commissioned officers and men were also killed or wounded.

On the 13th and following day there was a general forward movement of the VII. Corps, and the 21st Division managed to carry the line forward to the high ground about one thousand yards east of the Henin stream and astride of this portion of the Hindenburg Line; but the divisions on the right and left were unable to make equal progress. On neither of these days, however, does the Battalion appear to have been actively employed, though during the 13th it was moved forward to the Henin–Croisilles Road in reserve, then going back by wings on that and the following night to Boiry Becquerelle and thence to Beaumetz, where some ten days were spent, and where Second-Lieutenants T. Pearson, W. E. A. Oxley, and W. L. Topliss reported themselves for duty.

The 21st Division was now relieved at the front by the 33rd.

The whole of the latter part of the month of May was passed in training at Heudecourt, but on the 31st the 10th Green Howards were up in the support trenches again and at once came under very heavy enemy shelling, during three days Major V. Fowler and four other ranks being killed and some twelve other ranks wounded, Captain W. H. G. Goater taking temporary command of the Battalion ; but he was himself wounded on the 6th, and Colonel Mathias, returning from leave on the 8th, then resumed command.

Nothing of an unusually stirring nature occurred until the last day of July when, the Battalion being then up again in the line, a very successful raid was carried out by a party from " C " Company under Lieutenant J. L. Smith, M.C., and Second-Lieutenant H. E. Read ; the party showed great dash and determination and a very important identification was made, while of the raiders only one man was wounded and one was missing.

On the 9th August the 10th Green Howards marched back to Moyenneville, and on the following day proceeded to and billeted at Ervillers, the Division being now transferred to the VI. Corps, on which the following 21st Division Special Order was published :

> " The General Officer Commanding has much pleasure in publishing the following order, and feels sure that all ranks will do their utmost to live up to the high opinion which the Corps Commander has formed of them during the time the Division has had the pleasure of serving in the VII. Corps.
>
> " ' On relief of the Corps Headquarters from the line, the Corps Commander wishes to convey to you, to your staff and all ranks of the 21st Division, his high appreciation of the work done by the Division during its long stay with the Corps. The complete confidence which he has always placed in the Division has been more than justified by the performance of all ranks, both in the Arras Battle and in the subsequent building up of the line. The solidarity of the line now being handed over to the VI. Corps is proof of the high quality of the troops who now hold it and who bore so distinguished a part in winning it.
>
> " ' The Corps Commander wishes the Division the best of luck and hopes some day to have the privilege of once more including it in his command.' "

For the best part of a month now the Battalion remained in the neighbourhood of Ervillers practising new methods of attack in view of the reported changes in the German system of defence, and training in the work of co-operation with contact aeroplanes.

On the 1st October the total strength of the 10th Battalion The Green Howards was thirty-seven officers and nine hundred and sixty-six non-commissioned officers and men, with a fighting strength of thirty officers and eight hundred and ninety-seven other ranks ; and on the afternoon of this day the Battalion, now in the X. Corps of the Second Army, was in No. 2 Area, H Camp, near Dickebusch Lake.

After a comfortable night the Battalion marched to and bivouacked at Zillebeke Lake, where two men were killed by shells falling among " A " Company ; and orders were now received that the 21st Division was to take part on the 4th October in an attack by the Second Army on the high ground—Reutel–Noordhemhoek–Molenaarelsthoek–Niewe–Moden.　On the right of the X.—General Morland's Corps—was the 37th Division of the IX. Corps, the divisions of the X. Corps from right to left being the 5th, then the 21st, and then the 7th on the left next to the I. Australian Corps ; the three divisions faced Polderhoek, Reutel, and Noordhemhoek respectively.

At the commencement of the action which ensued—part of the concluding operations of the Third Battle of Ypres—the Battalion was commanded by Lieutenant-Colonel T. G. Mathias, D.S.O. ; Major W. H. G. Goater, M.C., was second-in-command, and Captain H. Bass was adjutant, while the Companies were commanded—" A " by Captain J. C. Storey, " B " by Captain G. A. Turner, " C " by Captain C. H. Adwick, and " D " by Captain A. W. I. Thomson.

After all necessary battle stores had been issued the 10th Green Howards left their bivouac at Zillebeke Lake at 9 a.m. on the 3rd in order of platoons, " D " Company leading, followed by " B," " C," and " A," and the leading platoon reached Clapham Junction at midnight, meeting here the commanding officer who had gone on in front to reconnoitre the ground.　Lieutenant-Colonel Mathias now decided to himself take up " B " and " D," the front line companies, to the " jumping off " point, following and keeping in touch with the two front-line companies of the 12/13th Northumberland Fusiliers, while Headquarters with " A " and " C " Companies were to follow the corresponding support companies of the same unit which were timed to pass Clapham Junction at 1.40 a.m. on the 4th.

On arriving at Glencorse Wood, " B " and " D " Companies came under a very heavy enemy barrage and as a result lost touch with the 12/13th Northumberland Fusiliers.　The remainder of the Battalion left Clapham Junction at 1.30 a.m. in rear of the supporting companies of the Fusiliers, and also came under the same heavy fire at the same spot, but they managed to maintain touch, and, advancing, reached Black Watch Corner at 2.30, where another equally heavy barrage was met with, and an order was given for all to get what shelter they could in shell-holes. The effect of this was that touch was again lost with the 12/13th Northumberland Fusiliers, and the whole of the 10th Green Howards were now near Black Watch Corner under a heavy shell fire with no guides, and the task of regaining touch proved a formidable one. The Battalion, however, moved on and reached the "jumping off" place at 5.15 a.m., to find the 1st Battalion Lincolnshire Regiment occupying the position to which the 10th Green Howards had been told off. The fact was that the O.C. 1st Lincoln, appreciating the situation and realizing the dangerous position of the Battalion at Black Watch Corner, which he surmised must prevent it from getting into position at zero hour—6 a.m.—had moved his own Battalion up on to the left of the 12/13th Northumberland Fusiliers, and consequently the 10th Green Howards now became the reserve battalion on a line just in front of Polygon Wood, where the enemy at zero put down an intensive barrage.

The Battalion had been under heavy shell fire almost uninterruptedly from 9 p.m. on the 3rd until 6 a.m. on the 4th and had suffered serious losses, but in spite of this the *morale* of all ranks remained high. Under cover of darkness a move forward was made in the evening to a new position near the old front line in Juniper Trench, and here consolidation was put in hand. The whole of the 5th, 6th, and 7th the Battalion held on here under a particularly intense artillery fire, and both the 62nd and 64th Brigades had many casualties. The conditions in the trenches were very bad, the men standing in upwards of a foot of mud and water, and the task of the stretcher bearers was rendered extremely difficult owing to the ground being badly cut up and in many places quite impassable by reason of the heavy rain which had fallen.

Just before midnight on the 7th the Battalion was relieved and moved back to and bivouacked at Zillebeke Lake—thus bringing to an end its share in the battle of Broodseinde Ridge, wherein the behaviour of all ranks had been of the steadiest.

The losses, however, had been very heavy—one officer, Lieutenant F. P. Cliff, and seventy-four other ranks were killed, while ten officers and two hundred and forty-nine non-commissioned officers and men were wounded and missing ; the names of these officers are : Captains G. A. Turner, D. B. Parsons, and A. W. I. Thomson ; Lieutenants J. C. Storey, H. Hume, and H. W. Bird ; Second-Lieutenants T. A. Hyslop, G. A. Fowler, C. Davison, and G. S. Sarson.

During many weeks now the Battalion remained on in this Dickebusch–Zillebeke area, incurring many casualties from the enemy shelling and experiencing great difficulties in maintaining their trenches in satisfactory condition, for the rain was heavy and the slightest concussion seemed to shake down the parapets. The support line also suffered much from the German guns, since it was under observation from Polderhoek Château, which was at this time still in enemy hands. Further, the German low-flying aeroplanes were very active, so that it is not altogether surprising to find that by the end of the month the fighting strength of the Battalion was no higher than twenty-one officers and five hundred and twenty other ranks.

Much of the enemy activity at this time was no doubt something of the nature of retaliation for the attacks then taking place at Passchendaele and just south about Polderhoek Château.

On the 18th November the first of several moves was made. The Battalion marched in brigade first to the neighbourhood of Bethune, then to Bersin, then to Ottawa Camp at Mont St. Eloi, and finally to Ecurie in the Arras area, where Lieutenant Sandilands, Second-Lieutenants Crapper, Cooper, and Margerrison joined.

On the 25th November, while at Ecurie, a warning letter was received in the Division as to an impending move of the 21st Division to Italy, and on the 29th at 7.30 p.m. orders were issued for the move by rail to commence on the 3rd December. These orders were subsequently cancelled by reason of the opening of the Cambrai operations.

On the last day of the month the 10th Green Howards entrained at Maroeuil for Peronne and marched thence to Brusle Camp. The month of November, despite the absence of inclusion in any active operations, had been somewhat of a costly time for the Battalion, since in the week from the 4th to the 11th November nine men had been killed and thirty-one wounded, these last including four officers—Second-Lieutenants Martin, Jameson, Speight, and Bowler.

On the afternoon of the 3rd December the 10th Green Howards moved to Longavesnes, and the next two days were employed in reconnoitring the line which was to be taken up in divisional reserve in the event of any hostile attack between Epehy and Heudicourt, moving up some days later to the front line east of Pozières.

Here the Battalion at once began to show its mettle; on the night of the 12th Corporal Buckley, " B " Company, recaptured near the front line a German soldier who had been taken prisoner by the French and who was on the point of escaping. Then about 8 o'clock on the following morning Sergeant T. W. Thompson and Corporal G. Buckley, both of " B " Company, reconnoitred a German post nine hundred yards from the British line east of Villers–Guislains, returning with the information that no sentry was posted and that all the men of the post appeared to be asleep. On hearing this

Second-Lieutenant J. D. Smith at once called for volunteers for a raiding party, when the two non-commissioned officers above mentioned and Privates J. Rice, H. Turner, and H. Walker immediately came forward. The party—six all ranks—then went out in broad daylight, and advanced nine hundred yards to the post, which, after Second-Lieutenant Smith had personally examined it, they then attacked, killing thirteen of the enemy and bringing back with them one unwounded prisoner.

When Christmas Day came round the Battalion was occupying billets in Lieramont, the weather now bitterly cold, but the enemy, happily, comparatively inactive; on the 28th December, Second-Lieutenant H. Wray was killed; and in this area the greater part of the month of January, 1918, was passed.

The Battalion remained during January in the neighbourhood of Heudecourt, moving on the 30th by train to Moislains, and here the very stirring life of the 10th Battalion The Green Howards came to an end, for in the first week in February it was disbanded, three companies being distributed between the 2nd, 4th, and 5th Battalions of the Regiment, while the fourth was sent to the VII. Corps Reinforcement Camp.

12TH BATTALION.
Pirbright, May, 1916.

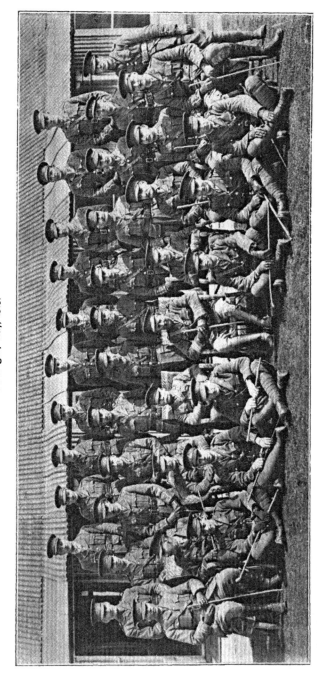

Back Row.—Lt. H. Bloom; 2nd-Lt. Miller; Lt. H. Thomas; Lt. C. W. Hogg; Lt. R. Cooper; 2nd-Lt. W. C. Macfarlane; 2nd-Lt. G. A. Dixon; Lt. S. M. Cairns; 2nd-Lt. J. Anderson; Lt. W. A. Wain.

Second Row.—2nd-Lt. V. Forster; Lt. Q.-M. J. W. Best; 2nd-Lt. A. M. Shaw; Lt. Wyatt (R.A.M.C.); Lt. Naylor; Lt. W. N. Crosby; Lt. H. Featherstone; Lt. J. A. Harris; Lt. A. W. Alcock; Lt. G. C. Cuthbertson; 2nd-Lt. J. Heron; 2nd-Lt. C. Macdonald.

Sitting.—Capt. C. C. Forster; Capt. C. M. Southey; Major J. J. O'Sullivan; Major R. B. Turton; Lt.-Col. H. W. Becher; Lt.-Adjt. T. K. G. Ridley; Capt. Alexander; Capt. A. C. Mildred; Capt. G. Stephenson; 2nd-Lt. N. Cox-Walker; 2nd-Lt. R. C. Taylor; 2nd-Lt. B. C. Peach; 2nd-Lt. H. Thomas; 2nd-Lt. C. MacKay; 2nd-Lt. H. Armstrong.

CHAPTER XVIII

THE 12TH BATTALION

1915–1918

THE BATTLE OF THE SOMME, 1916. THE BATTLE OF THE ANCRE.
THE BATTLE OF CAMBRAI. THE BATTLES OF THE SOMME, 1918,
AND OF THE LYS

THE 12th (Service) Battalion The Green Howards was raised at Middlesbrough in January, 1915, unofficially as a "Pals" Battalion, and it first appears in the Army List for February of this year as the 12th Service Battalion (Tees-side), and at this date possessed two officers only, Major (Temporary Lieutenant-Colonel) H. W. Becher, the commanding officer, and Hon. Lieutenant J. W. Best, the quartermaster. Lieutenant-Colonel Becher had served many years in the West Riding Regiment, but had retired from the Service and at the time of his appointment to command the 12th Battalion belonged to the Reserve of Officers.

About the end of this month orders were issued that the new Battalion should be organized and trained as a Pioneer Battalion, and consequently the personnel composing it was drawn mainly from the skilled artisan class, such as fitters, carpenters, blacksmiths, masons, etc. The training quarters were especially comfortably established at Marton Hall Camp, Middlesbrough, and the Battalion was in a measure fortunate in having come into existence somewhat later than the majority of the battalions of which the New Armies were composed, for by this time practically everything was forthcoming that was needed for the huge numbers of soldiers that had been recruited.

The following were some of the officers who first joined : Lieutenant-Colonel H. W. Becher, in command ; Captain and Adjutant J. J. O'Sullivan ; Lieutenant and Quartermaster J. W. Best ; Second-Lieutenants C. C. Foster, A. C. Mildred, G. C. Cuthbertson, J. C. B. Longbotham, T. K. G. Ridley, S. G. Ridley, J. H. Featherstone, and S. M. Cairns ; but in a very short time the Battalion had gathered fourteen officers and six hundred and fifty other ranks. Sergeant-Major Lawrence, from the 4th Battalion, was appointed Sergeant-Major.

After a few weeks at Middlesbrough a move was made to Gosforth, where the Battalion was accommodated in billets, and it soon grew in numbers, reaching one thousand one hundred and forty all ranks ; and, since recruits were still coming in, the formation of a depôt company was ordered. Then late in the summer of this year—on the 13th August— the Battalion was sent to Cannock Chase, being here camped on Penkridge Bank and employed in making four new rifle ranges, providing accommodation in butts and firing points so that two hundred and seventy men could fire at one time. From here it went to Badajos Barracks, Aldershot, joining there the 40th Division as the Divisional Pioneer Battalion, and moving in December to Pirbright for musketry.

It was not, however, until the summer of 1916 was beginning that the Tees-side Pioneers at last proceeded to France, being mobilized on the 27th May and embarking on the evening of the 1st June at Southampton in the S.S. *France*, the transport following in the *Invicta*. Havre was reached early the following morning and, disembarking at once, the companies marched to No. 1 Rest Camp.

The following are the names of the officers who landed in France with the 12th Battalion : Lieutenant-Colonel H. W. Becher, Major R. B. Turton, Lieutenants T. K. G. Ridley (adjutant), A. W. Alcock (transport officer), H. Bloom (machine-gun officer), N. Cox-Walker (signalling officer), J. W. Best (quartermaster), and H. D. Wyatt, R.A.M.C. (medical officer).

> " W " Company : Captain C. M. Southey ; Lieutenant G. C. Cuthbertson ; Second-Lieutenants W. A. Wain, R. C. Taylor, W. C. Macfarlane, and H. N. Thomas.
>
> " X " Company : Captain A. C. Mildred ; Lieutenants J. H. Featherstone, S. M. Cairns, and J. A. Harris ; Second-Lieutenants B. C. Peach and H. Armstrong.
>
> " Y " Company : Captain G. G. Pomeroy ; Lieutenant A. Thomas ; Second-Lieutenants C. MacNay, J. Anderson, A. M. Shaw, and G. A. Dixon.
>
> " Z " Company ; Major C. N. Wilkinson ; Captain G. Stephenson ; Lieutenant W. Naylor ; Second-Lieutenants C. W. Hogg, W. N. Crosby, and R. Cooper.

The 12th was now the Pioneer Battalion of the 40th Division, but their history is not easy to trace since they belonged to no particular Brigade in the Division, and were from time to time attached, or temporarily transferred, to other divisions or areas, where work of the kind for which the

Battalion had received special training happened to be most urgently required.

Leaving Le Havre by train on the afternoon of the day after arrival, the Battalion was taken to Rély and marched from there to Fouquières, where " W " and " Y " Companies were attached to the 15th Division and " Z " to the 1st, the fourth company going on to Mazingarbe and joining temporarily the 16th Division, all engaging in work under the Royal Engineers on the front-line trenches, making shelters, clearing the field of fire, making fire steps, etc.   At the end of June the whole Battalion was concentrated at Houchin Camp, where some three days only were spent, and then the 12th Green Howards went to South Maroc and were employed in working on the Calonne defences until the end of August, when the Battalion was sent to Loos and was there accommodated in different " Keeps," Colonel Becher being appointed Commandant of Loos and Major Turton Town-Major of Maroc.   Here some excellent work was done, by the end of September all main communication trenches being repaired, and sump holes dug up to the support line, while the billets also had been greatly improved, every man having a bunk.

The Battalion seems to have suffered its first officer-casualty on the 4th October, when Lieutenant R. N. Craig, the medical officer, was wounded.

The demand for skilled labour necessitated many moves from now onwards : on the 29th October the Battalion was back in Mazingarbe, moving on next day to Bruay, on the 31st to Marquay ; on the 2nd November it was at Moncheaux, on the 4th at Bonnières, on the 5th at Outrebois, on the 9th at Montigny, and so on by Montrelet, Beauval and Doullens to Bayencourt, where the Battalion arrived on the 14th and was there attached to the 31st Division, but worked under the orders of the G.O.C. 120th Brigade, then holding the Hébuterne sector.   On the 20th November, the Tees-side Pioneers marched on again by Halloy, Autheuille, and Berneil to Ailly-le-Haut Clocher, where at last the Battalion found itself at the end of the month in a rest area.

This quiet period only lasted until the 8th December, when the Battalion moved by rail and road and by Longpré, Pont Rémy, Mericourt and Bray to Maurepas, where it came under the orders of the C.R.E. XV. Corps for work, and was chiefly employed in repairing the Combles–Frégicourt and the Combles–Rancourt Roads, incurring here some few casualties, and on the 25th rejoining the 40th Division and going back to trench-repair work, the trenches here being in places waist deep in mud and water.

This work was continued well into the year 1917, for it was the 27th January before the 12th Green Howards went back to a camp about three miles from Bray, having during this tour in the Bouchavesnes North and

Rancourt sectors had five other ranks killed, nineteen men wounded, Company-Sergeant-Major Wattenstone and Sergeant Cook being among the killed.

At Bray the Battalion was attached to the 8th Division for rations and was under the C.R.E. XV. Corps for work.

Work of a similar character to that already described went on until well into March, when the German retirement commenced and all work on trenches was stopped, the 12th Pioneer Battalion of The Green Howards being then employed in the repair of roads, especially the Clery–Bouchavesnes Road, those through Clery, the Hem Wood–Clery Road and the Monacu–Clery Road.

On the 14th February Lieutenant H. Bloom was killed by a 5·9 shell in Abode Lane, a forward communication trench, when in charge of a working party.

During March the following officers joined from the Base—Second-Lieutenants Jennings, Champney, Temple, and Johns, and on the last day of April the strength of the Battalion stood at thirty-one officers and eight hundred and fourteen other ranks.

On this date the following was published in Fourth Army Orders :

" The General Officer Commanding the Fourth Army wishes to express his appreciation of the courage and devotion to duty displayed by No. 21365 Private H. Race, 12th Yorkshire Regiment, in salving ammunition on the occasion of the explosion of an ammunition dump on February 6th, 1917."

While the following was also published in the 40th Division this month :

" The following message received from the Commander-in-Chief is repeated for the information of all ranks :
" ' I heartily congratulate the Royal Engineers of the Fourth Army on the result of their recent efforts in restoring communication under difficult circumstances.'
" The Corps Commander has expressed to the Major-General his appreciation of the valuable assistance rendered by the Pioneers and Infantry of this Division."

The work on roads and front lines went on as before throughout June and July, and, the casualties being low in comparison with those of battalions more actively engaged, the drafts were small, only eighteen other ranks joining in June and three officers and twenty-one non-commissioned officers and men in July ; the three officers were Second-Lieutenants A. E. Lord, G. M. Clark, and C. Bird. In August Second-Lieutenants H. Fowler, F. H. B. Fraser, R. W. Turner, and E. J. Pollard arrived for duty with the service companies, together with twenty-five other ranks—nearly all men who had been out previously with the Battalion ; but on the 20th September the strength of the 12th Green Howards was temporarily reduced by one hundred and eighty-four non-commissioned officers and men being sent to the 4th Battalion of the Regiment under Second-Lieutenant MacNay, while Lieutenant Cooper took a reinforcement of similar strength to the 5th Battalion ; on the other hand three hundred and sixty-nine other ranks were received from the 1st Reserve Battalion R.E.

During September Second-Lieutenant E. Temple and three men were killed, Second-Lieutenant W. A. Wain and fourteen men were wounded.

Having now spent some considerable time in the Fins area, the Battalion moved by slow degrees to the neighbourhood of Moislains, which was reached on the afternoon of the 30th October ; the drafts were still small, only five officers—Second-Lieutenants H. G. Abbott, J. McGilley, H. Bughoff, S. F. Hutton, and T. G. Wilson—and thirteen other ranks joining or rejoining ; but the Battalion still stood at the very reasonable strength of thirty-eight officers and seven hundred and eighty-one other ranks. November was spent at Manancourt, Beaulencourt and Havrincourt—one officer—Second-Lieutenant H. H. Johnson—and fourteen men being wounded during this month, of whom one died of his wounds, while seven officers and fourteen men joined ; the seven officers were Second-Lieutenants S. F. Jowett, A. S. Larter, J. Haseman, A. W. B. Bentley, C. V. Proctor, E. Davison, and B. Bocking.

During this month the 40th Division had been engaged in the fighting at Bourlon Wood, as described in the chapter dealing with the services of the 13th Battalion, and the following special divisional order, issued on the 28th November, shows that if the 12th Battalion The Green Howards was not perhaps so actively engaged in the actual fighting as were some of the other units of the 40th Division, being employed in wiring in front of the captured positions and in repairing roads, its services contributory to the successes achieved were fully appreciated by the High Command :

> " The Commander-in-Chief personally informed the Divisional Commander that he wished all ranks of the 40th Division to be congratulated on his behalf on their recent success.
> " Great credit is due, not only to Infantry Brigades, who gave proof of fine fighting qualities and endurance, but also to the loyal co-operation and untiring energy shown by the Royal Artillery (including the Divisional Ammunition Column), the Royal Engineers, and the 12th (Service) Battalion Yorkshire Regiment (Pioneers)."

In the course of these operations Captain J. A. Harris was killed when reconnoitring the forward area.

Early in December the Battalion moved to St. Leger and was engaged mainly on repairs to the St. Leger–Croisilles–Fontaine Road, during the month one man being killed, Captain Cooper and three other ranks wounded. The Battalion appears to have won golden opinions from those for whom it worked, and one writer says in a letter to Colonel Becher, dated the 16th December : " Just a line to thank you for the very excellent work your fellows did for me last night, and to congratulate you on having such fine workmen under your command."

Work in the beginning of the New Year—1918—was considerably interfered with by the weather, severe frost being succeeded by a thaw, and that again followed by very wet weather, during which all the parapets were continually falling in. The strength and personnel of the Battalion constantly varied during January and February, for the greater part of which time it was at Mory—in January ninety-seven men arriving from England to replace one hundred transferred to the 13th Green Howards ; while in the middle of February, when the Battalion was attached for work to the 59th Division, then holding the front line, a draft of ten officers and two hundred and thirty other ranks was posted to the 12th from the 7th Battalion of the Regiment. These ten officers were Captain G. B. Wilkinson, D.S.O., M.C. ; Second-Lieutenants S. Bott, J. Bywell, G. H. Royce, J. H. Morton, A. V. Deans, F. L. Downs, C. L. King, J. Binns, and M. Wilkinson.

The following is a copy of a letter, dated 23rd February, from the G.O.C. 62nd Division to the G.O.C. 40th Division :

> " I shall be glad if I may express my appreciation of the excellent work done by the 12th Yorkshire Regiment (Pioneers) while attached to this Division.
>
> " After a long period in the trenches the cheerfulness and zeal with which the Battalion has carried out any work allotted to it, reflects the highest credit upon officers and men.
>
> " The Major-General Commanding directs me to say that the receipt of this letter has given him great pleasure. The Battalion under your command has always done all and more than was expected of it, under all circumstances, and he congratulates you on its efficiency."

When the great German offensive of this year opened, the 12th Bn. The Green Howards was occupying No. 4 Camp at Heudecourt, and having already during March received reinforcements amounting to one hundred and fifteen other ranks, it was tolerably well up to strength. Early on the 21st the German attack caused the Battalion to " stand to," and at 8.30 a.m. it moved by march route to Clonmel Camp, Hamlincourt, and manned next morning the Army line in front of Hamlincourt, with the 224th Field Company Royal Engineers on the left and the 229th on the right. Next day, the 23rd, this line was handed over to a battalion of the 31st Division, and, moving to Gomiecourt, the Battalion manned the old trenches from Ervillers to Behagnies. The hostile guns were very busy at this time and the line was heavily shelled. It was, however, held by the Battalion until the evening of the 25th, when it fell back to a position in front of Courcelles-le-Compte, one company forming a defensive flank to the north of Achiet-le-Grand and there collecting all stragglers; these were many, and the strength of the company eventually rose to nine hundred. The command of the 12th Green Howards had already twice changed hands, Major F. H. Shepperd relieving Colonel Becher on his being wounded, and he now on being hit handing over command to Major C. M. Southey.

Relieved early on the 26th, the Battalion collected its components and marched to Bienvillers-au-Bois, arriving there at midday; and then at 2 p.m., it being reported that the enemy had broken through our line at Hébuterne, the Battalion was ordered to hold a line from the windmill on the Fonquevillers–Bienvillers Road to the Bienvillers–Henescamp Road, with a brigade of the 40th Division on either flank. At 10.30 p.m., however, the 12th Green Howards were withdrawn into billets at Bienvillers-au-Bois.

Marching on by Beaudricourt, Tinques, Monchy-Breton, Dieval and Vieux Berquin, Rue-au-Bois was reached on the evening of the 31st and here, so far as the Battalion was concerned, the retreat ended.

The losses of the Battalion had been comparatively light, three men had been killed, three officers—Lieutenant-Colonel H. W. Becher, D.S.O., Major H. F. Shepperd, M.C., and Lieutenant C. Macdonald—and twenty other ranks were wounded, while four men were missing.

Congratulations to the Division now came in thick and fast: from the Corps Commander to the Divisional General:

> "As regards your fighting troops, Infantry, Artillery and Royal Engineers, I cannot speak too highly. They have made a magnificent defence, and tired as they must be with so prolonged a struggle, they have stood like a stone wall between my right and the Germans. All I can say is that I am deeply grateful and feel that they have nobly upheld the great fighting traditions of the British Army."

From Major-General J. Ponsonby, commanding the 40th Division:

> "I wish to thank the Division, one and all, for their splendid courage and behaviour. You know what the Commander-in-Chief and your Corps Commander think of you, and I can only say you have done your duty like British soldiers always do.
> "We shall no doubt be called upon again to fight for all we are

worth. We, in the 40th Division, I know, will be ready again, and I feel very proud to be the Divisional Commander of such a splendid body of men as you have proved to be. I thank you all from the bottom of my heart, and whatever may happen I feel complete confidence in the ultimate result with soldiers of your spirit and bravery under my command."

On the 30th His Majesty the King inspected the battle-worn Division, when the following order was promulgated :

" His Majesty the King visited the Division to-day and was pleased to express to the Divisional Commander his great appreciation of the gallant behaviour and bearing of the 40th Division during the recent operations. He was fully conversant with the work accomplished by the Division, and while offering his sincere congratulations thereon, he deplored the losses which have been incurred.

" The Major-General directs that the above be communicated to all ranks."

On the 2nd April the Battalion moved from Lillers to the neighbourhood of Bac St. Maur, and, after a couple of days' rest, commenced work on the tramways in the divisional area and on the making of concrete machine-gun emplacements ; and then on the 6th it became involved in the Battle of the Lys, the circumstances leading up to which will be found given in some detail in the 13th Battalion record.

At midnight on the 8th April the Battalion was billeted as follows : Headquarters and one company were at Bac St. Maur, one company was in the Rue de Quesnoy, while a third was at Sailly-sur-la-Lys, and at 4 o'clock next morning the enemy opened a heavy bombardment on each of the billets in occupation of the 12th Green Howards.

The companies all " stood to " at 6 on the morning of the 9th, but it was not until 11.15 that orders came from Divisional Headquarters for two companies to occupy a line of trenches in front of Bac St. Maur from Sailly to the Rue de Biache ; a few minutes later the third company was directed to proceed to Fleurbaix and reinforce the garrison of that place. " By noon," writes one who was this day present with the Battalion, " we had hardly a gun left in action and the line had been forced back about two thousand five hundred yards, the Portuguese Division had collapsed, and the Germans were now well round on our right flank. The line was holding well in front of Armentières, although this town suffered from a heavy bombardment. Realizing that we should have to retire at any rate to the other side of the Lys, orders were given to pack up tools and medical stores in such wagons as we had in the advanced positions, and word was sent back to the transport lines at Croix-du-Bac to send up the necessary draught animals. Good work was put in by our Company-Quartermaster-Sergeants in the way of saving the equipment of their companies. Owing to the terrible barrage on the Armentières–Estaires Road, it was very difficult to move such transport as we had on this line; the enemy naturally kept the bridges over the Lys under fire, and we were only able to get one pair of horses over from the rear."

Soon after midday the three companies of the 12th Green Howards were thus disposed: one had taken up a position on the left bank of the Lys near Point de la Boudrette with the 145th A.T. Company R.E. on the left, while the two others occupied a line from Sailly South to the Rue de la Biache, but had only been a very short time in position when the enemy attacked in great strength with many light machine guns, and there being then no troops on either flank they had to retire to avoid being surrounded. Then, after close fighting in which they captured a prisoner, these two companies eventually took up a position on the further bank of the Lys on the left of the third company near the Point de la Boudrette, holding on here until about 4 p.m., when the left of the Battalion was obliged to retire for some one thousand yards, as the enemy was working round this flank.

The first retirement of these two companies was covered by Second-Lieutenant Champney and fifteen other ranks with a Lewis gun, and it was largely due to the very skilful way in which this officer handled his party that the withdrawal was safely effected; Second-Lieutenant Champney kept the gun in action himself until the enemy was within twenty yards, when he was killed.

About 6 o'clock in the evening a brigade of the 25th Division came up with the view of attempting the capture of Croix de Bac, Bac St. Maur and Sailly; the 12th Green Howards took part in this attack, advancing on the right of the brigade, while on their right again was the 4th Battalion of the Regiment serving in the 50th Division; this attack, however, failed.

" The whole Division had now suffered very heavily, particularly the machine gunners, and by the evening the enemy had advanced about three miles and had reached the Lys. The Battalion obtained some rest that night on the line La Menegat–Point Mortier, and on the morning of the 10th manned a line at Les Haies Basses." At 2 a.m. on this day the previous evening's attack was repeated, " W " and " Y " Companies of the Battalion being in reserve, while " X " protected the right; the attack this time was at first attended with success and the river was reached, but the enemy, counter-attacking in force, drove their assailants back to their original line and eventually into Steenwerck Switch, where the 12th Green Howards—less one company—came under the orders of Lieutenant-Colonel Brown, M.C., commanding a composite battalion of the 119th Brigade. One company was withdrawn about 8 a.m. into reserve at Petit Mortier, but about two in the afternoon, on news being received from the 14th Highland Light Infantry that the enemy was attacking, this company moved up to reinforce that battalion.

" During the course of this day our companies, particularly ' X,' under Captain C. Mildred, ' W,' under Lieutenant R. Taylor, and ' Y,' commanded by Captain A. Shaw, who fell later in the day, had some good duelling with the enemy, and there was a great improvement in the shooting on both sides; one of our Lewis gunners, who had mounted his gun on a low brick incinerator, received a bullet right inside the radiator casing, but this fortunately did not put either man or gun out of action. On this day every sergeant of ' W ' Company was either killed or wounded. On the morning of the 11th April we received orders to retire to a reserve line behind Strazeele, the 31st Division having relieved ours in the line." The Battalion had suffered the great loss of three officers and twenty-eight other ranks killed, four officers and one hundred and fifty-four non-commissioned officers and men wounded, one officer and eighteen men wounded and missing, and two officers and one hundred and seventeen other ranks unaccounted for—a total of two hundred and ninety-nine casualties !

The officers who were killed were Second-Lieutenants B. C. Peach, H. D'A. Champney * and S. F. Hutton ; wounded were Second-Lieutenants A. E. Lord, G. F. W. Jennings, and S. Bott ; Second-Lieutenant A. V. Deans was wounded and missing; while unaccounted for were Captain A. M. Shaw and Second-Lieutenant J. Binns.

" We remained in reserve at Strazeele with the 119th Brigade, sending out patrols on the Strazeele–Caestre and Strazeele–Flêtre Roads, the rest of the Battalion being employed in digging a series of strong points on Strazeele Ridge ; and during the night of the 12th–13th April hundreds of motor-buses arrived with the division of Australians from the neighbourhood of Amiens, who told us of the enormous advance the enemy had made on the Somme. As we had now spent four days and four nights in fighting a rear-guard action and retiring we were pretty well done up, and were glad when we received word that our Division, which had suffered heavily in the March offensive, was to be withdrawn to rest in the St. Omer area. Considering the severity of the opening bombardment by the enemy and the fact that after four and a half hours the fighting became

---

* So reported at the time, but actually died of wounds as a prisoner in German hands.

open and machine-gun and rifle fire came into its own, the Battalion might easily have suffered very much more heavily."

On the 13th the 12th Battalion The Green Howards moved to the neighbourhood of Salperwick and Westbecourt, where Majors T. H. Carlisle, D.S.O., M.C., of the Royal Engineers, and F. Sweet, 19th Battalion Royal Welch Fusiliers, joined as commanding officer and second-in-command respectively; training was now entered upon, and a draft of three officers—Second-Lieutenants C. L. King, A. W. B. Bentley and S. F. Jowett—and one hundred and fifty other ranks was sent to the 15th Battalion of the Regiment.

While in this area the following orders were promulgated:

On the 13th from General Horne, commanding the First Army:

> "I wish to express my appreciation of the great bravery and endurance with which all ranks have fought and held out during the last five * days against overwhelming numbers. It has been necessary to call for great exertions, and more must still be asked for, but I am confident that at this critical period, when the existence of the British Empire is at stake, all ranks of the First Army will do their very best."

From the G.O.C. XV. Corps, dated the 16th April:

> "On your leaving the Corps the Corps Commander directs me to convey to you his appreciation of the services rendered by your Division during the operations of April 9th–13th."

From Major-General J. Ponsonby, commanding the 40th Division, dated the 19th:

> "The Division has again been engaged in heavy fighting, and all Battalions have fought the enemy with great courage and determination in spite of having to face overwhelming odds. The same fighting spirit continues and I know will continue in the Division. I wish General Officers Commanding Brigades to convey to the troops under their command my sincere congratulations and thanks for their gallant behaviour under trying circumstances."

At the end of April the Battalion moved, still with the 119th Infantry Brigade, to the Momelin area and was quartered at Kinderbelck; and then on the 5th May the 12th Battalion The Green Howards was broken up and formed into a Battalion Training Staff composed of ten officers and fifty-one other ranks, ten officers and three hundred and fifty non-commissioned officers and men being sent by train on the same day from Watten to the Base Depot at Calais.

* Four days only—9th–12th April—in the case of the troops transferred on the 12th from the First to the Second Army.

On the 10th the Battalion Training Staff moved to Esquelbecq and a few days later to Les Cinq Rues near Bollezeele, remaining here until the 23rd June, when it was sent by motor-omnibus to tents and bivouacs near La Belle Hôtesse.

Here on the 28th June what remained of the Battalion Training Staff was absorbed into the 17th (Garrison) Battalion the Worcestershire Regiment, of which Lieutenant-Colonel H. W. Becher assumed command, eleven officers and forty-five non-commissioned officers and men being thus posted, when the 12th Battalion The Green Howards ceased to exist.

The following were the officers thus transferred : Lieutenant-Colonel H. W. Becher, D.S.O., Majors T. H. Carlisle, D.S.O., M.C., and C. M. Southey, Captains A. C. Mildred, T. K. G. Ridley, W. N. Crosby, M.C., and H. N. Thomas, Lieutenants C. W. Hogg, R. C. Taylor, G. A. Dixon and E. Mulhall.

CHAPTER XIX

THE 13TH BATTALION

1915–1919

THE FIRST BATTLE OF THE SOMME.   THE BATTLE OF CAMBRAI.
THE BATTLES OF THE SOMME, 1918, AND OF THE LYS.
NORTH RUSSIA

THE original 40th Division was raised in December, 1914, and was re-numbered the 33rd in the following April, at the end of which month the formation of a new 40th Division was authorized.   It does not, however, appear to have been organized as a complete unit until well into the summer of this year, when the 13th Service Battalion of The Green Howards, raised in July, and to the command of which Major (temporary Lieutenant-Colonel) F. T. Tristram had been appointed, was detailed to join the 121st Brigade of the 40th Division.

Of the early history of this Battalion there is very little on record, but presumably it followed the usual course of intensive home training pursued by the majority of newly raised battalions in those hectic days until, on the 27th May, 1916, the Battalion, being then stationed at Woking under the command of Lieutenant-Colonel H. E. Falls, received orders to mobilize for active service.   Mobilization was completed the same day, and on the 4th June the 13th Green Howards, strength thirty-four officers and nine hundred and ninety-five other ranks, entrained at Woking for Southampton, which was reached the same afternoon.   The wind was then very high and the sea rough, so that the crossing was deferred until the following evening, and Le Havre was reached in the early hours of the 6th.

The following are the names of the officers who embarked with the Battalion and set out with it on the Great Adventure : Lieutenant-Colonel H. E. Falls ; Majors F. T. Tristram and W. Fox ; Captains T. Ryan, H. G. Bigg-Wither, H. Smith, J. R. Stewart, J. A. Kirby, J. A. Mansfield and T. H. C. Hopkins ; Lieutenants N. M. Vickers, C. C. Elborne, N. V. Harle, A. A. H. Jones, L. H. Jones, P. M. Phillips, T. K. Pickard and G. F. P. Worthington ;

Second-Lieutenants C. H. Wallis, J. F. Johns, P. B. Hope, H. B. Seager, H. H. Simpkin, A. W. Simpkin, D. C. R. Miller, H. J. Graves, M. W. J. Kelly, J. H. G. Bayles, H. W. Walton, F. H. Dowton and W. Scott ; Captain and Adjutant J. Virgo, Lieutenant and Quartermaster C. Johnson, and Lieutenant W. Brownlie, R.A.M.C.

Disembarkation took place at 7 a.m. when the Battalion marched to a Rest Camp some four miles north of the town ; here all rested during the day and entrained again at 10 at night, leaving at midnight and arriving at Lillers after a railway journey of eighteen hours. A march of two and a half miles then brought the Battalion to Ham-en-Artois, where all were billeted tolerably comfortably in farm-houses. The 40th Division was now in the I. Army Corps commanded by General Monro, who inspected the 121st Brigade on the 12th June.

The Brigade remained here in training for some ten days, marching on the 19th to Maisnil-les-Ruitz, where training was continued, especially in bombing, wiring, sniping, patrolling and trench work. The Brigade here was in reserve, the Battalion being held in readiness to move at six hours' notice.

While at Maisnil-les-Ruitz the first death casualty occurred, No. 23172 Private W. Green dying of bronchitis in No. 18 Casualty Clearing Station.

On the 28th June the 13th Green Howards were ordered up to Calonne for instruction and practice in trench duties—" A " and " B " Companies being attached to the 1st Battalion Cameron Highlanders and " C " and " D " to the 10th Battalion Gloucestershire Regiment, two platoons of each company being in the first-line trenches and the remainder in support ; here on the 29th, four men were killed—Sergeant W. Hemsley, Privates T. P. Taylor, C. Pasley and G. W. Gadd, and during this training period in the trenches the total casualties were eight killed and two wounded.

The Battalion returned to billets in Maisnil on the 2nd July and on the following day the 121st Brigade took over the Maroc sector from the 2nd Brigade of the 1st Division ; the relief was completed by the evening, the Battalion being placed in reserve and occupying billets in North Maroc, cellars each holding four or five men being the accommodation provided, while rations came up from Les Brebis at night. This was the commencement of a series of tours in the front, support and reserve lines alternately ; but as the trenches were in a bad state of repair, owing to the constant enemy shelling, a great deal of work on them was necessary. The chief feature of the landscape in this sector was the big Slag Heap, known as the Double Crassier, where the British and German lines ran parallel along the top, affording excellent observation to both sides and being, incidentally, the happy hunting ground of the Battalion bombers. When out of the front line here the Battalion went back to the Bois-du-Froissart and there underwent training in wood fighting.

On the 25th July Lieutenant-Colonel Falls was admitted to hospital and the command was temporarily assumed by Major Tristram, but on the 28th Major B. G. Baker was appointed to command from second-in-command of the 20th Battalion The Middlesex Regiment ; on the previous day Second-Lieutenants H. G. Abbot, R. Langley and L. A. Venables were posted from the 14th Reserve Battalion of the Regiment.

On the 3rd August Lieutenant N. M. Vickers was in command of a patrol which had been told off to reconnoitre a shell-crater held by the enemy. The party had arrived near the enemy wire when bombs were thrown by the Germans, one of which killed the officer ; he was, however, not missed at the time by the patrol, which continued to advance and reached the wire. Here the loss of the officer was realized and reported, when Lieutenant T. K. Pickard, who was on duty in the front-line trench, at once went out at great personal risk and under heavy fire, found the dead officer's body close under the German wire and brought it in. Two men of the patrol, Privates A. Gray and T. Radcliffe, were wounded on this occasion.

For this act of bravery Lieutenant Pickard subsequently received the Military Cross—the first to be awarded in the 40th Division.

When on the 4th August the Battalion was relieved and went back to Les Brebis to rest, it had been eighteen days in the front line and had incurred casualties amounting to one officer and six other ranks killed, twenty-nine men wounded and two shell-shocked.

The time was now close at hand when the Brigade was to leave the Maroc sector, but on the 25th August Lieutenant-Colonel Baker arranged the details of a raid to be carried out on the enemy's trenches from the Battalion front line, two parties being detailed under Captains H. G. Bigg-Wither and H. Smith, while Captain T. Ryan was in charge of the Advance Report Centre. The raid took place in the area of the Apex of the Triangle, Bangalore torpedoes being used for cutting the German wire, the raiding parties waiting in No-Man's-Land ready to rush the gap if found to be sufficiently cut. The torpedoes were electrically exploded from the front-line trenches, but on scouts going forward to examine the gap it was found that this was not large enough to allow of the raiding party getting through, and the men were consequently withdrawn, happily without any casualty.

During the month of August Second-Lieutenants W. H. Porter, C. F. Jennings and G. H. Perkins joined the Battalion, which on the 5th September went back for a few days' rest to the Bois-du-Froissart, the Brigade then on the 11th taking over the Loos sector from the 119th Brigade ; here the 13th Green Howards were thus disposed—" A " and " C " Companies occupying billets in the Enclosure, " B " having two platoons in the Village Line and two in Lens Road Redoubt, while " D " Company was in Duke Street ; and while occupying this sector several raids were carried out.   In an attempt to raid the enemy's trenches on the night of the 26th, the German wire was successfully blown up and the trench rushed.   Second-Lieutenant R. Langley, who was O.C. raiding party, and Sergeant Micklethwaite succeeded in entering the trenches, but Second-Lieutenant Langley was badly wounded, and Sergeant Micklethwaite made several unsuccessful attempts to raise and carry off the wounded officer, but failed, and the hostile bombing being very heavy, he and the rest of the party only got back with great difficulty.   Several other attempts to recover the officer were later made, but equally fruitlessly, and he consequently fell into the hands of the enemy.   During this month Lieutenant P. M. Phillips and five men were killed, Second-Lieutenant H. J. Graves and eight men were wounded.

On the nights of the 7th and 8th October two more raids were undertaken by the Battalion while in this sector of the line ; on the night of the 7th-8th " B " Company blew four gaps in the enemy's wire round the Long Sap, and two raiding parties under Second-Lieutenants A. W. Simpkin and L. A. Venables then entered the enemy's trenches, captured two Germans and killed five others, while the bombers also claimed to have inflicted some loss. On the following night a party of " C " Company under Second-Lieutenants Hodgson and Perkins was equally successful, entering the German trenches and occupying them for fifty-eight minutes ; they captured no prisoners, but killed some twenty of the enemy, and brought away rifles, bayonets, gas masks, identity discs, shoulder straps and other articles taken from the slain.   This raiding party had one officer—Second-Lieutenant Hodgson— and seven men wounded, one of whom died ; the officer was wounded in the knee on entering the trench, but " carried on " and was the last to come away from the German front line.

There were many congratulations for the Battalion on the success of these two raids from the Corps, Division and Brigade Commanders, and Sergeant W. Cartlidge, Corporal W. I. Brown, Lance-Corporal D. Moore and Private Gourlay were specially mentioned for excellent work.

There were several other casualties during this month, among the wounded officers being Second-Lieutenant M. W. J. Kelly, who lost his left arm.

On the 26th October the Battalion was relieved in this sector and during the weeks that immediately followed had several moves—to Les Brebis, to 14 Bis Sector, to Bruay *via* Noeux-les-Mines, to Villers-Brulin, to Rosière, to Neuvillette, to Doullens and Villers-sous-Dilly, where some few days were spent and a draft of thirty-eight other ranks joined. Then early in December the Battalion learnt that the Division was to move to the XV. Corps area, and the 13th Green Howards accordingly entrained on the 11th at Longpré and proceeded to Sailly Laurette, where the men and officers were put up in huts, and for the first time since arrival in France it was possible to form an officers' mess. Here Christmas Day was spent, but that festival was scarcely over when the Battalion moved once more as the 40th Division was to relieve the 33rd, and the 121st Brigade went into Divisional Reserve at Camp 17 Suzanne, where for the first time for over two months, the Battalion again found itself under enemy gunfire.

On the 30th December the 40th Division moved to the Bouchavesnes sector, the 121st Brigade being in reserve.

The opening days of the year 1917 found the Battalion occupying the support position in the Bouchavesnes sector, but on the night of the 5th January it took over the front line. The state of the ground here was appalling, the mud being anything from knee to waist-deep, and it was necessary to keep to the overland duckboard track to make progress to and from the line at all possible, while the ground was everywhere pitted with shell-holes, made in the previous heavy fighting in this region. On the 12th January the Brigade went up to the Rancourt sector, on the left of Bouchavesnes, where the state of the ground was as bad as that in the sector whence it had just come ; but by the end of the month the Division moved back into Corps Reserve, the Battalion being now for some days billeted in Bray for work on the rail-heads in that vicinity.

Bray was left on the 11th February for the neighbourhood of Suzanne, where some nine days were spent in camp, the Battalion then moving up to relieve a battalion of the 119th Brigade in the Rancourt sector. During one of the four-day tours of duty in the front line, the enemy put down a heavy barrage on our trench system, paying special attention to a sap held by a non-commissioned officer and a few men. Under cover of the barrage twenty-five of the enemy raided the sap and several of them succeeded in entering ; in the hand-to-hand fighting which ensued the non-commissioned officer in charge —Lance-Corporal Smith—and two of his men were killed, when Private W. Cooke rushed back for help and returning through the enemy barrage, picking up bombs as he ran, bombed the enemy out again. The leader of the raiding party was hit and brought in by Privates Cooke and Evans ; he belonged to the 114th Infantry Regiment and died after capture. Four others of the enemy party were killed and several wounded.

Private Cooke was awarded the D.C.M. for this act of valour ; he was killed at Villersplouich in May, 1917.

During the rest of the day the German shelling was heavy and two men were killed, while Second-Lieutenant E. J. Readings and two men were wounded.

To the capture by the 8th Division early in March of the ridge immediately south of St. Pierre Vaast Wood, the 40th Division guns gave what help they could, but the enemy put down a heavy counter-barrage all along the front and the 13th Green Howards were under a constant fire, but happily their casualties were low ; on the 6th March the 121st Brigade was relieved in the Rancourt sector and marched first to a camp near Maurepas and then on the 15th to the Cléry sector on the Somme. On this front the enemy was now falling back and the Battalion patrols were the first to verify this fact. On the 16th March an enemy machine gun had been noticed in a crater on " C " Company's front ; Lieutenant-Colonel Baker had decided that this crater should be seized and consolidated, and about 3 p.m. on the 17th it was rushed by a party of ten men under Second-Lieutenant Mason, when it was found to be empty, the enemy having vacated his line here. Unfortunately, on entering the crater one of the party caught his foot in a trip-wire attached to some bombs, evidently laid as a " booby trap " ; these exploded and four men of the party were slightly wounded. The three advanced companies were sent at once to occupy and consolidate the German position, which was now held by a series of strong points. Certain lines of enemy communication were reconnoitred, but it was now getting dark, and all that could be seen were some fires in the distance, from which it appeared that the Germans were burning all they could as they fell back—" according to plan " !

At daybreak on the 18th patrols pushed forward as far as Mount St. Quentin and Hill 75 north-west of Peronne, which was found to be burning. On the 21st the Battalion advanced to La Quinconce, occupying shelters in old German trenches, and was here employed in making the roads as passable as possible, the cavalry going forward and keeping touch with the retreating enemy. On the 24th March the 40th Division was withdrawn into Corps Reserve, the Battalion being in tents near Feuillicourt, remaining here until the 5th April, employed as before on road-making and mending from Haute Allaine to the crossing over the Canal near Moislains.

On the 6th the Battalion marched to Manancourt, and from here took over the front-line trenches opposite Gouzeaucourt, where on the 8th, Lieutenant C. F. Jennings was killed and three men wounded by a sniper.

On the 9th April an operation of a minor character was carried out on the left of the Battalion by the 21st Middlesex, the Battalion assisting by sending out two fighting patrols under Second-Lieutenants Miller and Relph. The operation commenced at 3 p.m., and on " going over the top " The

Green Howards' parties came at once under enemy fire. The right patrol got through without any casualty, but the left party came up against one of the German strong points, and Second-Lieutenant Relph and two men were wounded. The work was, however, well and thoroughly done and greatly assisted the 21st Middlesex in gaining their first objective. Ten days later —on the 20th—the other brigades of the 40th Division made an attack upon the village of Villersplouich, the 13th Green Howards being placed at the disposal of the G.O.C. 119th Brigade. The Battalion accordingly moved from Divisional Reserve in Etricourt to Fins at 5 in the morning and during the afternoon advanced to positions about Gouzeaucourt Wood. All went well, and on the 25th the 121st Brigade relieved the 120th in the captured village, which was then heavily bombarded by the German guns, and before being relieved on the 2nd April to return to Desart Wood, the Battalion had eleven men killed, Lieutenant-Colonel B. G. Baker, Captain J. A. Kirby and twenty other ranks wounded.

The Brigade remained about this sector until the 13th May, when a move was made to the Villers-Guislains area, going back on the 23rd to Desart Wood and so up to Villersplouich again ; from the 3rd to the 11th June the Brigade was at rest in Sorel-le-Grand, when the Battalion moved into Brigade Reserve in the Gonnelieu sector, sending out strong working parties every night to construct and wire a new front line ; and the 13th Green Howards being thereafter up to the middle of July either at Fins in reserve or in the front in the Villers Guislains sector. While here Second-Lieutenant G. H. Perkins joined, as did later Second-Lieutenant W. Birch, but on the 11th, Second-Lieutenant A. W. Wilkins was struck by a shell, dying a few minutes later.

On the early morning of the 26th July the enemy raided the right front company under cover of a most intensive barrage, but fortunately warning of the coming raid had been received the day previous from a deserter, and the British guns were prepared and put down an extremely heavy counter-barrage which inflicted severe losses on the enemy when falling back. The Battalion, however, had nearly forty casualties—five killed, six wounded and twenty-six missing.

At the end of this month Second-Lieutenants E. P. Holgate, F. T. McBain and W. Hadwick reported themselves for duty.

The usual routine went on until well into August, but on the night of the 18th-19th a minor enterprise was carried out by the Battalion against the enemy trenches with the object of annoying the Germans by blowing gaps in their wire with Bangalore torpedoes and of obtaining identifications. The operations were carried out by " B " Company, which detailed three parties :

1. Left, Bangalore Torpedo and covering party, composed of two scouts, two sappers and fourteen other ranks under Second-Lieutenant F. T. McBain.

2. Right, Bangalore Torpedo and covering party of the same strength and composition under Second-Lieutenant W. Birch.

3. A supporting party of one platoon and Lewis gun under Second-Lieutenant F. C. Walker.

On approaching the enemy wire the scouts, preceding the advance, reported an enemy working party engaged in strengthening the inner belt of the German wire. The Bangalore torpedoes were then withdrawn to a safe distance, while the parties moved forward and opened rapid rifle and machine-gun fire at the German working party. The men composing this were wholly taken by surprise, many were seen to fall, and the remainder hastily withdrew completely demoralized. Every effort was then made to bring up and explode the torpedoes, but the enemy fire now becoming very heavy, while daylight was approaching, the parties were forced to withdraw.

There was another affair on the 31st August, when at 4.30 a.m. the Germans put down a very heavy trench-mortar barrage, immediately followed by an equally intense artillery barrage, when the garrisons of the advanced front line were withdrawn and the British artillery and machine guns opened in reply. Meanwhile bombing parties were organized and, on the barrage lifting, these advanced working towards the right. No enemy was met with, but traces of exploded German stick-bombs were found in an unoccupied portion of our front-line trench, the enemy having evidently entered here and retired on finding it unoccupied.

When up in the line in the early part of September more than one attempt was made to raid the enemy trenches, notably on the night of the 4th-5th September, when parties went over commanded by Lieutenant H. H. Simpkin, Second-Lieutenants E. J. Readings, A. G. Shorthouse, and P. R. Thompson, Sergeant Rowley and Corporal Hobson ; but the Germans were here very much on the alert and nothing could be done. The 13th Green Howards were, however, ever ready to take or make opportunities for distinguishing themselves, as the following examples testify ; on the afternoon of the 19th September, Private J. G. Handley displayed great courage and initiative in rendering assistance to the pilot and observer of a British aeroplane which came down on fire about five hundred yards in rear of our front-line trenches, also salving valuable material from the burning machine. On the night of the same day Privates H. Harrison and J. H. Preece were on patrol, when within twenty yards of the enemy wire coming under heavy fire, and Lance-Corporal Griffin, one of the patrol, was mortally wounded. Passing through a barrage of rifle-grenade fire, Privates Harrison and Preece rescued Lance-Corporal Griffin and carried him into our lines.

Privates Handley, Harrison and Preece were all awarded the Military Medal, as also was Private J. Wilson, who on another occasion, when one of the scouts was killed within a few yards of the enemy wire, rushed forward and carried his comrade in, a distance of some two hundred yards, under heavy fire.

On the night of the 9th-10th the 121st Brigade was relieved, when the 13th Green Howards were conveyed by Decauxville railway to camps in the neighbourhood of Hendecourt and then on in the afternoon to Peronne. The night of the 10th-11th was spent in Peronne, and next day the Battalion was taken by train to Beaumetz-les-Logis, whence a march of six miles brought it to Barly, the allotted billeting area. Here a very pleasant time was spent amongst almost ideal surroundings until the 17th November, except for a brief interval passed in the Warluzel and Warlincourt areas. But on the 17th the Brigade marched to Achiet-le-Petit and on the following day to Rocquigny *via* Achiet-le-Grand, Bihucourt, Biefvillers, Bapaume and Le Transloy, receiving a warning order early on the 20th to be ready to move at one hour's notice.

The reasons which induced the British commander to undertake what were known as the Cambrai operations are set out in considerable detail in his despatch of the 20th February, 1918; he tells us therein that the repeated attacks made by the Allies had brought about large enemy concentrations on certain portions of the front, with a consequent reduction in the German garrisons of other sectors. It was hoped by surprise attack on one of these weakened sectors to gain a considerable local success, and of these the Cambrai front had been selected, partly because the ground was suitable for the employment of tanks, and also because if Bourlon to the north could be secured and a good flank position to the east, in the Cambrai direction, be established, " we should be well placed to exploit the situation locally between Bourlon and the Sensée River and to the north-west."

The British attack, conducted by General Sir J. Byng, commenced on the morning of the 20th November, when infantry and tanks attacked on a front of some six miles from east of Gonnelieu to the Canal du Nord opposite Hermies; and by " the end of the first day of the attack, three German systems of defence had been broken through to a depth of some four and a half miles on a wide front, and over five thousand prisoners had already been brought in. But for the wrecking of the bridge at Masnières and the check at Flesquières, still greater results might have been attained."*

* Despatch of the 20th February, 1918.

B B

The attack was resumed on the 21st November, and by the evening of this second day our troops held a line which ran approximately as follows :

" From our old front east of Gonnelieu the right flank of our new positions lay along the eastern slopes of the Bonavis Ridge, passing east of Lateau Wood and striking the Masnières-Beaurevoir line north of the Canal de l'Escaut at a point about half-way between Crèvecour and Masnières. From this point our line ran roughly north-west, past and including Masnières, Noyelles and Cantaing, to Fontaine, also inclusive. Thence it bent back to the south for a short distance, making a sharp salient round the latter village, and ran in a general westerly direction along the southern edge of Bourlon Wood and across the southern face of the spur to the west of the wood, to the Canal du Nord, south-east of the village of Moeuvres. From Moeuvres the line linked up once more with our old front at a point about midway between Boursies and Pronville." *

It was then decided that on the 22nd the operations should be continued with a view of gaining the Bourlon position and effecting the recapture of Fontaine-Notre Dame.

The account of the events of this period is contributed by an officer who was then in command of the 13th Green Howards.

" The 21st November was passed in a familiar locality—in huts near Havrincourt Wood ; the next march, on the night of the 21st-22nd, brought the 121st Brigade into camp about Vélu and Beaumetz-lez-Cambrai. The attack on the Hindenburg Line had begun, a wide breach had been made, and the German defenders, pivoting on Moeuvres to northward, had swung back their left flank, leaving free the passage of the Canal du Nord between Boursies and Gaincourt along the Route Nationale No. 29. There were very few traces of this Chaussée, indeed there was no recognizable feature left at all in the landscape after our barrage had done its business, and the sight of that descent towards the Canal was one of utter desolation. It was still light enough to get some idea of the lie of the land as I crossed the Canal some way ahead of my command, and though I had seen many a fair landscape changed into a desert on many occasions before this, it seemed to me that the scenery in this particular spot was just of the kind that Dante would have chosen as the final abode for his worst enemies had he been able to imagine such horrors as science has made possible in our day.

" However, I was not thinking about Dante at the time, but was pushing on to the Sugar Refinery, where, I was told, was the headquarters of the battalion to be relieved by the 13th Green Howards. Darkness had set in by the time headquarters had been discovered, and even then there was little information of any kind to be had. The line appeared as a jumbled

* Despatch of the 20th February, 1918.

mass of ruins of a trench system on which much care and energy had been bestowed, and the battalion which held it, having taken over from the one which captured it, had not been able to do much in the general confusion. Luckily the enemy had been badly knocked the day before and, as frequently happened, had been slow to launch any counter-offensive. In the meantime the 13th Green Howards had come up and had begun to settle down for the night. What German trenches remained were of little use for defence, since the Hindenburg Support Line, beyond which the first wave of our attack had passed on the previous day, ran almost north and south, whereas our front faced towards Bourlon, viz. to north-east.

" Brigade H.Q. was beneath the church of Graincourt in deep vaults which the retiring Germans were preparing for our reception—indeed, the pioneers entrusted with these preparations were hurrying up the steep steps of the vaults as the Brigade staff was descending it. There were also Germans still lingering in the trench system which the 13th took over on the night of the 22nd November. A German machine-gun section and crew were still ensconced in the middle of ' A ' Company's line ; however, that stout Yorkshireman, Captain J. H. G. Bayles, commanding the company, and a few of his merry men, soon ' winkled ' those Germans out of their little hole.

" The orders for the attack arrived just after midnight on the 22nd ; the hour of zero was 10 a.m. next day and the objective Bourlon Village and Wood. The 20th Middlesex were on the right of the Battalion, the 21st Middlesex in support, and the 12th Suffolk in reserve.

" The morning of the 23rd November came in with a blustering north-east wind sending cloud-shadows chasing over the undulating ground. An occasional scud of sleet made way for spells of sunshine in which Bourlon Wood to the east glowed in ragged autumn finery, while Moeuvres church tower stood out above the ruins of the village. The 13th Green Howards were drawn up with ' A ' and ' C ' Companies in front, ' B ' in support and ' D ' in reserve. By 9.30 a.m. the forms of tanks, making their way up from the south, loomed up more plainly, and the nonchalant manner in which they leant against a brick wall and then moved on leaving a ruin behind them, was much appreciated. These tanks which had been out and active for several days were as ever thoroughly up to their business, and certainly added much to the high confidence animating the 13th Green Howards.

" The advance had just begun when young Walton, the Battalion Signalling officer, was shot through the heart, probably by a German machine gun.

" The Battalion went forward behind the tanks, meeting with some resistance at first, and under a galling flank fire from machine guns. By midday the outskirts of Bourlon had been effectually cleared and organized, and all resistance swept away. The village itself was then cleared with a good deal of hand-to-hand fighting, touch being maintained in the village with the 20th Middlesex on the right. What orders had been given to the troops on the left of the Battalion I do not know ; they appear to have been ordered to wait until the leading battalions of the 40th Division should have gained their respective objectives, but even then no move was made. In the meantime the lines of communication had become unduly extended and exposed—in fact the left was in the air, and support and reserve companies had to be put in to fill the gap, into which some of the 21st Middlesex in support were also later drawn.

" By 3 p.m. the Germans considered the Bourlon position as lost and began to bombard the place, then commencing a series of counter-attacks from the front, from the north-east, and on the left flank from the northwest, which made an obtuse angle in the front line, exposing both sides of the angle to flanking fire. The Quarry in E 5 was organized, the château was held by ' A ' Company though frequently surrounded by the enemy, and the Battalion was in a position to hang on whatever befell, though unhappily there were no reserves immediately available to enable the 13th Green Howards to gain yet more ground and consolidate along the railway line. It was not till some time between 8 and 9 that evening that reinforcements arrived—a composite battalion of cavalry under Colonel Franks of the 19th Hussars, whose badge, the cypher of Queen Alexandra, made the Battalion feel happy and comfortable. The line was then taken over by the cavalry, the relief being completed soon after midnight on the 23rd, and the Battalion then returned for three days to the neighbourhood of the Sugar Refinery. On the evening of the 26th November the 13th Green Howards fell back, passing a night in the former Hindenburg Line before going back into reserve. On the march, near Havrincourt Wood, the Commander-in-Chief, Field-Marshal Sir Douglas Haig, met the Battalion and expressed his high approval of the conduct of all ranks in the attack on Bourlon."

Of the Battalion—twenty-five officers and four hundred and fifty other ranks—who went into Bourlon on the morning of the 23rd, less than one hundred came back of the non-commissioned officers and men, and no more than eight of the officers, including Battalion Headquarters. Second-Lieutenant Barrington Baker was hit early in the advance while helping a wounded Lewis gunner out of danger ; the man fell back and Second-Lieutenant Baker, also wounded by then, pulled him in again.

The following Special Order of the Day was issued by the Field-Marshal on the 24th November, 1917 :

BOURLON WOOD.

November, 1917.

" The capture of the important Bourlon position yesterday crowns a most successful operation and opens the way to a further exploitation of the advantages already gained.

" In the operations of the Third Army during the past four days the troops engaged were called on to advance under conditions different to anything ever attempted before.   The manner in which they adapted themselves to the new conditions was in all respects admirable, and the results already gained by their efforts are of far-reaching importance. Although practically all the divisions employed have already been engaged in severe and prolonged fighting this year, all arms and services have met these fresh calls on them in a manner worthy of the highest traditions of the British Army.   Infantry, artillery and aircraft have co-operated with the efficiency and complete devotion to duty in which they never fail.

" The operations on the Third Army front would in all probability have miscarried if the enemy had gained timely warning of our intentions, and a most satisfactory feature to note in connection with these operations is the complete secrecy which was maintained.   For this my thanks are due to all ranks concerned."

The Officer Commanding the 13th Battalion The Green Howards received the following letter from Major-General J. Ponsonby, commanding the 40th Division, dated 4th December :

" I had wished very much to have been able myself to see your Battalion and to tell them how gratified I was with their splendid efforts on November 23rd, but owing to so many moves I have so far been unable to do so, but will take the earliest opportunity.   Your Battalion greatly distinguished themselves throughout all those three days' hard fighting, and I hope you will convey to the men my very grateful thanks for their fine efforts and my appreciation of their soldierly qualities."

On the 27th the Battalion moved by train to Bellacourt and billets, where reorganization was taken in hand and deficiencies in equipment were so far as possible replaced.   On the 1st December, however, the 121st Infantry Brigade moved to Ervillers, where it was in reserve to the 16th Division, the Battalion finding accommodation in Belfast Camp, but moving up to the front next day and taking over a portion of the left section.

The enemy here was tolerably active, making attacks upon the divisions to the right and left, while his working parties could be heard in the front of the 40th Division ; but the Battalion was not actively engaged and suffered but few casualties.

Christmas Day was spent in Divisional Reserve at Belfast Camp, but two days later the Battalion returned to the trenches, the Division now taking over an extended front, to include that previously held by the 3rd Division. Owing to an attack recently made here by the enemy every possible precaution was ordered to be taken, all troops " stood to " daily from 6 to 6.30 a.m., and the usual working parties supplied by the support battalion were sent out nightly.

The early part of the year 1918 was spent in the same area as that in which the Division had found itself when the past year closed ; during January the weather was very inclement, alternate snow and sudden thaws rendering the communication trenches almost everywhere impassable, and reliefs had to be carried out over the top ; in February matters improved and part of this month was spent in Corps Reserve near Ervillers and in G.H.Q. Reserve at Bailleulval, where the attack in conjunction with tanks was assiduously practised. Then about the middle of March the 121st Brigade was sent to Heudecourt and was there warned to be ready to move at three hours' notice by day and at one and a half hours' notice by night.

The 40th Division was here in reserve to the VI. Corps, commanded by Lieutenant-General Sir J. Byng, and the VI. Corps also contained, in order from left to right, the 3rd, 34th and 59th Divisions.

During the night of the 20th and the early hours of the 21st March enemy gunfire could be heard, clearly indicating a heavy bombardment of our trench systems in this area. At 6 a.m. the Battalion was ordered to " stand to," and at 1.15 p.m. the 13th Green Howards were directed to march on Hamelincourt, receiving while *en route* orders to proceed across the open from Hamelincourt and occupy the front trenches of the third system of defence immediately to the east of St. Leger, in company with the 12th Suffolk Regiment. Little or nothing was known about the general situation, all that was reported was that the enemy was through our line, though it was not known to what depth the Germans had actually penetrated.

The Battalion now moved across country in diamond formation— " C " Company in touch with the 12th Suffolk on the right, " A " on the left of " C," with a platoon of " D " in support, both companies preceded by scouts ; " B " was in reserve. At midnight " A " Company reported that it had occupied the front-line trenches after some opposition, whereupon Battalion Headquarters moved up to a sunken road and the support company to a neighbouring copse, while the reserve company joined Battalion Headquarters. It was then found that " A " and " C " Companies had attempted to reach their trenches by moving up a certain communication trench, " A " Company leading, but on a patrol reporting the enemy in occupation, the companies halted in the communication trench, while Second-Lieutenant E. F. Beal with a Lewis gun team worked his way along the trench, and by bombing and Lewis gunning succeeded in dispersing or killing four enemy machine-gun detachments, capturing their guns.

" A " Company now occupied the front-line trench from the south-east corner of St. Leger Wood for a distance of two hundred and fifty yards south-south-east ; but " C " Company was met with machine-gun fire and was unable to prolong the right of " A " along the trench it was holding.

At 7 a.m. on the 22nd, Captain H. H. Simpkin with two platoons of " D " Company made a bombing attack on the portion of trench occupied by the Germans, cleared it, killed about twenty of the defenders and captured seven machine guns ; but within a very few minutes some three hundred of the enemy counter-attacked and drove out the party of " D " Company of the 13th Green Howards, Captain Simpkin being here killed and Second-Lieutenant E. E. Wood severely wounded. It being essential, however, that the portion of the trench in question, running from " A " Company's right to the left of the Suffolk Regiment at Banks Wood, should be taken, it was decided to make a frontal attack with " B," the reserve company, under Captain R. G. de Quetteville ; this thereupon attacked in a north-easterly direction along both sides of the re-entrant, artillery co-operating by putting a ten-minutes 18-pounder barrage on the trench, then lifting a hundred yards and continuing for fifteen minutes. During the first barrage the Company advanced to within fifty yards of the trench —an advance of some seven hundred yards. Then on the barrage lifting the trench was rushed, the enemy bolting and sustaining heavy casualties. Touch was now gained with the 12th Suffolk on the right and the line was complete by midday, a battalion of the 34th Division being in touch on the left.

During the rest of the day the enemy made several counter-attacks, but these were all repulsed with loss.

At 6.45 p.m. orders were received from the 121st Brigade that in the event of the 34th Division falling back, the Battalion was to retire gradually to the Army Line ; consequently when the 34th Division withdrew through St. Leger and along the crest to the north of it, the 13th Green Howards conformed about 9.30 p.m., " B " Company covering the retirement. By this time that Company was almost completely surrounded, some of the men of it were captured, and only very skilful leadership extricated this Company from a particularly precarious situation.

On arrival at the Army Line it was found that the 119th Brigade was not astride the St. Leger-Ervillers Road as had been expected, and the Battalion therefore took up a position in the Army Line with its left on the St. Leger-Ervillers Road and its right about six hundred yards to the south-east ; this position was established by 11 p.m., the right being in the air but the left in touch with the 4th Battalion Grenadier Guards.

The trench-line here was anything but ideal, being eighteen inches deep only and eight feet wide, while it was badly sited, the field of view and fire being very restricted. The night was quiet.

This position was maintained throughout the 23rd, during which the flanks of the Battalion were made more secure ; but at 2 a.m. on the 24th the 13th Green Howards were informed that they would be relieved and were then to take up a position immediately north of Behagnies. No relief took place until 10 p.m. when, the companies having, in falling back, reached the road leading from St. Leger to Ervillers, suddenly heard that the 21st Middlesex and the battalion on its right had been attacked in force, and at once reoccupied the line in conjunction with the Irish Guards. Second-Lieutenant L. Ward, who commanded the two platoons in support, saw that the attack did not immediately concern the Battalion front, so he doubled his men forward and formed a defensive flank on the right. Then, finding that the enemy were coming on in small numbers along the trench from the right, this officer sent a small mixed party of Guards and Green Howards to meet them under a sergeant of the Guards, who himself bayoneted five of the enemy and brought in a sixth as a prisoner. The two platoons under Second-Lieutenant Ward then dug in on a line at right angles to the Army Line and parallel to the St. Leger-Ervillers Road.

On the 25th the new line was consolidated and had a good field of fire and view, the St. Leger-Ervillers Road being used as a support line and held by some of the 120th Brigade. The enemy were seen in the distance during the morning on the Mory-Ervillers Road and our guns opened on them, but our artillery also caused some casualties in the Battalion, Captain W. Brownlie, R.A.M.C., the medical officer, being killed in this way some three hundred yards in rear of the line by heavy gunfire from the Hamelincourt direction.

The Guards and Green Howards were ordered to retire to the line near Moyenneville at 8 p.m. and this was accordingly done, the Battalion marching across country to Courcelles and thence to Douchy-les-Ayettes, which was reached about 5 on the morning of the 26th, where a hot meal was provided. Marching on again after a three-hours' halt, Bienvillers was arrived at about midday, the road being greatly congested, while the inhabitants of Bienvillers were now in flight, having heard a rumour that the enemy had broken through at Hébuterne with cavalry and armoured cars. The Battalion now took up a position on the ridge near the village.

During the three days that followed the retreat was continued—on the 27th to Bailleulval, on the 28th to Habarco, on the 29th to Sus-St. Leger and on the 30th to Marquay ; here the 40th Division found itself transferred to the XV. Corps with orders next day to relieve the 57th Division in the

Bois Grenier sector. The move was carried out by motor-lorries in brigade groups, the 121st Brigade " embussing " on the Save-St. Pol Road at midday on the 31st March and moving to Neuf Berquin, from where on the 2nd April the Battalion marched to and took over the left section of the Bois Grenier sector, arriving here in time for the operations known as the Battle of the Lys, wherein the Germans, brought to a stand on the Somme, were now attacking the depleted British front in the north. This front was held by the Second Army on the left and the First Army on the right, and on the left of the First Army was the XV. Corps,* under Lieutenant-General Du Cane, containing the 34th and 40th Divisions.

On the night of the 7th the enemy had opened an unusually heavy and prolonged bombardment with gas shell along practically the whole line from Lens to Armentières, and this became especially intense on the early morning of the 9th, being followed by an attack upon the northern portion of the line held by the First Army, taking advantage of a thick fog which made observation difficult. On this day the 40th Division had its 121st Brigade on the left, joining up with the 34th Division, and the 119th on the right ; the 13th Green Howards were on the extreme left of their Brigade —two companies in the line, one in support and one in reserve. At 10.30 a.m. information was received from the Brigade to the effect that the enemy was through the right brigade support and that the 20th Middlesex were holding Tin Barn Avenue ; the right support company of the Battalion— " C "—was then ordered to man Shaftesbury Avenue extending its right to Red House Post ; " D " was directed to man Tram Line Avenue and La Vesèe Post : while the front-line companies were informed as to the situation and told to hold on at all costs, another battalion forming a defensive flank along Park Row Avenue.

During the next hour or so various conflicting reports came in, attacks were made by the enemy, and his patrols attempted to get through ; and finally about noon the O.C. 20th Middlesex arrived at Battalion Head-quarters and stated that the Germans were near Red House Farm and that his battalion had been practically annihilated ; such of this battalion as remained were now placed under the command of the O.C. 13th Green Howards, and by the afternoon that Battalion, with such men as were left of the 20th Middlesex, was holding a line that exceeded three thousand yards in length. Here it was decided to stand and orders were issued to hold the line at all costs, and held it was until 4 the following afternoon when Shaftesbury Avenue fell.

Enemy attacks continued during daylight, but the night was tolerably quiet.

* On the second day of the Lys Battle the XV. Corps was transferred to the Second Army.

On the morning of the 10th the Battalion came under the orders of the G.O.C. 103rd Brigade, and all through the day attack and counter-attack went on, until at 3.25 p.m. orders to withdraw were received. The four commanding officers then present—of the 20th Middlesex, 13th Green Howards, 9th Northumberland Fusiliers and 10th Lincoln Regiment—now conferred together, when the following was resolved upon : one company of the Lincoln Regiment was to move from Halfway House to La Rolandine Farm, where the 11th Suffolk were in difficulties, and hold the line from there across the railway to the main Armentières Road ; the 13th Green Howards were to withdraw, leaving strong flank and rear guards in Shaftesbury Avenue and the front line, half of " B " and " D " Companies under Captain de Quetteville moving out and reinforcing the Lincoln Company above mentioned ; while the rest of the four battalions was to move *via* Rue Fleurie Post and Track " D " to Rue Marle and thence across the Lys by the railway bridge, the only one there remaining, concentrating at Touquet Parmentier.

Happily a mist now came on which greatly assisted to cover the retirement ; and by 5.30 all were safely past Rue Fleurie Post, though the enemy machine-gun fire was very heavy; the Germans followed up closely and Captain de Quetteville had to deploy his men and move against the pursuers. The Lys was crossed by the railway bridge and by the Pont de Nieppe, and about 7.30–8 the remnants of the Battalion reached Touquet Parmentier and there took up as good a position as the darkness permitted.

Early next day the Battalion moved into a position of support at Pont d'Achelles, and supported an attack made by the 12th Suffolk against Romain, an advance of two thousand yards being made ; the attack was, however, not greatly pressed as a further withdrawal was to be made at night. When the retirement was resumed the Battalion provided a rearguard for the Suffolks to pass through, and then, marching to a point on the Bailleul Road north of La Crèche, took up a position in support along the Bailleul main road.

The retirement was now no longer harassed ; early on the 12th the Battalion marched by way of Strazeele to Pradelles, and next day through Croix Rouge and Bavinghove to St. Martin-au-Laert and occupied billets in the village. Here reorganization was commenced and training of all kinds carried out, interrupted on the 19th by the receipt of an order to send off five hundred non-commissioned officers and men and a suitable proportion of officers to the 4th and 5th Battalions of the Regiment ; accordingly on the 20th ten officers and five hundred other ranks were dispatched, and the 121st Brigade was then re-formed under the title of No. 1 Composite Brigade, 40th Division, the Battalion being temporarily made up by one company each from the 13th East Surrey and the 21st Middlesex Regiments.

The losses in the 40th Division during this last fighting had amounted to one hundred and eighty-five officers and four thousand three hundred and seven other ranks, while those incurred on the Somme, only three weeks previously, had been at least equally heavy.

The end of April found the Battalion at Proven, engaged in digging defence lines in the vicinity of Poperinghe and Watou ; but on the 3rd May the Battalion moved to the St. Momelin area, where next day orders were received to the effect that the disbandment of the Battalion had been decided upon and was at once to be proceeded with, the following personnel being retained as a Battalion Training Staff under Lieutenant-Colonel F. Miskin, M.C. : seven officers, three warrant officers, thirteen sergeants and twenty rank and file, all personnel surplus to the above being sent *via* St. Omer to Calais.

At the end of June the Battalion Training Cadre was sent home to England and on arrival was stationed at Mychett Camp, Farnborough, and here remained for some weeks preparatory to moving to the Eastern Command, where the re-formation of the Battalion was to take place. This move was made on the 19th July when the Training Cadre proceeded to Aldeburgh, where it was found that certain of the personnel of the new Battalion—eighteen officers and fifty-eight other ranks—had already arrived and organization was steadily continued and made good progress.

In Chapter X, dealing with the services of the 6th Service Battalion of The Green Howards, some account was given of the circumstances under which British troops were sent to North Russia in the autumn of 1918. The newly constituted 13th Battalion was also detailed to join this force, and it sailed at the same time and in the same vessel as the 6th Battalion, experiencing the same maritime adventures and finally arriving at Murmansk on the 28th November, landing next day. From here the Battalion was almost at once sent off on a two-days' train journey to Popoff Island near Kem on the White Sea, the strength being now thirty-two officers and eight hundred and fifty-nine other ranks, though actually present were no more than twenty-three officers and seven hundred and twenty-three non-commissioned officers and men.

The Battalion Diary for this period only commences on the 1st February, 1919, and on the 4th of this month Lieutenant-Colonel H. E. Lavie of the Durham Light Infantry assumed command of the 13th Green Howards.

On the 1st February orders had been issued for the Battalion to leave Popoff, moving in four separate parties, and join General Ironside's force at Archangel, and, the White Sea being frozen, they were, for the most part, to march across North Russia at a time when the thermometer stood at 20–30 degrees below zero.   The four parties were made up and proceeded as follows :

No. 1. Nine officers and two hundred and eighty-eight other ranks, mostly from " A " and " C " Companies with one officer and forty-two men of " D," were to leave on the 2nd February by special train for Murmansk and move thence by ice-breaker to Archangel ; this party was under the command of Captain McCall.

No. 2. Three officers and one hundred and eighty-nine other ranks, mainly from " D " Company, were to entrain on the night of the 4th for Soroka, and proceed thence by sledge to Onega.

No. 3. Eleven officers and two hundred and twenty-six other ranks from " B " Company and some details of " C " Company, at the time stationed at Kem,—some seven miles up a shallow river—to entrain for Soroka on the night of the 5th, proceeding thence by sledge to Onega.

No. 4. All details then remaining were to leave by train on the evening of the 6th for Soroka, and go on from there to Onega by sledge.

In accordance with the above, the first party moved direct by sea upon Archangel, the remainder proceeding by train to Soroka, and then on by sledge by way of Yirma, Sumski Posad, Koleshma, Roiga, Nuksha Unejma, Malashuika to Onega, where eight men were left in hospital ; and so on by Korelskoe, Eusolia and Malozerki to Seletskoe, where on the 24th the whole Battalion, less " C " Company which remained for reinforcement purposes at Economie in the Archangel district, was finally concentrated.

By the 25th the Battalion was distributed as under :

Headquarters at Seletskoe.

Right Wing at Mejnorski.

Left Wing at Shred Mekhrenga.

Of the sledge journey Lieutenant-Colonel Lavie records :

" We were two men to each sledge, all the sledges were drawn by horses, and we moved in this way for a fortnight until we met the railway at Obozer-skaya, where we became part of the Obozerskaya Brigade and were sent on seventy-five miles to join the Seletskoe detachment.   The way this march was conducted was as follows : At about every forty miles were depots with R.A.S.C. rations for the Battalion ; we started every day about 9 a.m. and marched from one town to another, the towns being about two hours' march apart.   On arrival all the men were put into billets so as to thaw their clothes and themselves, the cold being so intense that clothing, such as greatcoats, stood up by themselves, while all food and drinks were solid blocks of ice which had to be thawed before they could be consumed. Only one event of importance occurred on the way and that was when we ran into a blizzard, the temperature dropping to 57—70 degrees below zero ; this lasted about ten hours and of course held up the march while it lasted, but no man suffered from frost-bite during the whole march."

The transfer of the 13th Green Howards from what was known as the "Syren" to the "Elope" Force had been carried out under tolerably favourable conditions and the health of the men remained good. The strength of the Battalion in these parts was now twenty-three officers and six hundred and eighty-four non-commissioned officers and men, while ten officers and one hundred and seventy-five other ranks had been retained with the "Syren" Force on the Murmansk front attached to various units.

Almost immediately after arrival on this front the services of a portion of the Battalion were called for ; on the 14th March three officers and eighty other ranks of "B" Company with four Lewis guns were sent to Rialka and Lutchino on the Dwina River front to give support to a small force there operating under Colonel Carrol ; between the 15th and 18th— on which latter date the Company returned to Shred Mekhrenga—the enemy made three attacks upon Lutchino, but these were all easily repulsed.

Then at midnight on the 19th Second-Lieutenant W. G. Butteriss, M.M., and fifty non-commissioned officers and men were sent to Obozerskaya to take part in certain operations in the neighbourhood of Bolshiozerky, coming while there under the orders of the Vologda Force.

During March there was no special activity on the Seletskoe front, but the detachment patrolled the country frequently and on two occasions encountered strong bodies of the enemy which were driven off without any loss being incurred by The Green Howards.

On the 1st April the Battalion was thus distributed : "A" and "B" Companies were at Shred Mekhrenga ; two platoons of "D" were at Seletskoe, another was at Ripolavo, the fourth was with the Vologda Force ; while "C" Company was at Bakaritza. The garrison of Shred Mekhrenga consisted at this time of the two companies of the 13th Green Howards, two batteries of field artillery, one machine-gun company, and two battalions of White Russians, as the Imperialists were called. The enemy at this time was known to be only three miles distant, and on the 5th April he attacked in force the positions at Shred Mekhrenga held by the two com- panies of the Battalion, which were in action for thirteen hours. The platoons of "D" Company were called up from Seletskoe and Ripolavo, and the enemy attack was completely repulsed, the Battalion suffering no casualties whatever, while of the enemy a hundred prisoners were taken and upwards of a hundred dead were left in front of the blockhouses.

On the 7th April the platoon of "D" Company rejoined from service with the Vologda Force ; this platoon had had some heavy fighting about

Bolshiozerky, then in possession of the enemy, and had had three men wounded ; the conditions also had been severe, the men having been obliged to camp in the woods during ten days.

During the ensuing six weeks there was no occurrence of outstanding importance, the Battalion continuing in occupation of the same posts as before, some anxiety being occasioned by the rising among the White Russians and the need for careful watching of the Russian battalions ; but about the middle of June, Battalion Headquarters and the companies, less seven officers and one hundred and twenty-one other ranks remaining behind at Seletskoe, moved in barges to Archangel Prestyn, where they were all accommodated in Michigan Camp.

Demobilization then commenced under the circumstances set forth in the latter part of Chapter X, on the 24th June one officer and ninety-nine other ranks being sent home to be demobilized, followed on the 16th July by a further party of six officers and one hundred and seventy-seven non-commissioned officers and men, who sailed for England in the *Tsar*. The Battalion Headquarters now moved to Bakaritza and by the end of August, the strength having fallen to sixteen officers and three hundred and ninety-nine other ranks, these also shortly proceeded home, when the 13th Battalion The Green Howards was finally disbanded.

THE

BATTLE-HONOURS

In recognition of the gallant services of the several Battalions, throughout The Great War, The Green Howards were awarded, in all, fifty-six Battle-Honours, as enumerated on pages xv and 401–403.

The ten, printed in CAPITALS, which are those selected by the Regimental Committee to be borne on the Colours and appointments, being as follows :—

" YPRES, 1914, '15, '17 "	" VALENCIENNES "
" LOOS "	" SAMBRE "
" SOMME, 1916, '18 "	" FRANCE AND FLANDERS, 1914–18"
" ARRAS, 1917, '18 "	" VITTORIO VENETO "
" MESSINES, 1917, '18 "	" SUVLA "

CHAPTER XX

1914–1919

The Depot

WHEN early in August, 1914, orders for mobilization were received, the 3rd Battalion The Green Howards was going through the annual training at Barnard Castle, but returned at once to Richmond by march route, and on arrival was billeted in the town. The permanent staff now returned to the Depot to assist in the mobilization of the Army Reservists, of whom over nine hundred and fifty rejoined during the first three days, and on the 6th August the first reinforcement of three hundred Army Reserve men was sent to Guernsey to join the 2nd Battalion of the Regiment : this was followed next day by a second draft of two hundred and fifty, thus completing the 2nd Battalion to war strength.

The rest of the Special Reservists—about one hundred and twenty in number—belonging to the 3rd Battalion, who for various reasons had been excused the annual training, were also mobilized and joined their companies in Richmond.

The War Depot was formed on the 7th August and comprised four officers and twenty-seven other ranks of the Army Reserve, the officers being : Lieutenant-Colonel E. M. Esson, in command ; Major H. G. Holmes, adjutant ; Major C. Organ, quartermaster ; and Major A. St. J. Seton, recruiting officer.

As more recruits were called for and the formation of the Service Battalions commenced, the Depot soon overflowed and empty houses had to be taken and billets requisitioned for recruits, as well as the old married quarters in the Castle ; while the local gentry, farmers, and townspeople were very good in furnishing blankets, rugs, and straw, recreation rooms, free suppers and all kinds of comforts for the men, of whom as many as five thousand were at one time in barracks and billets in Richmond.

On the 21st August Major and Hon. Lieutenant-Colonel C. T. Hennah joined the Depot for duty.

During September the Depot became so congested that the C.O. was directed to send five hundred men on furlough, and in order to facilitate their payment, etc., men living in Middlesbrough and Sunderland were chosen, an officer being sent every week from Richmond to these towns, where the men received their pay at the Town Halls under arrangements previously made known to all concerned.

About the end of September the Artillery Depots had become so over-crowded with recruits that three hundred and seventy-five artillerymen and recruits were sent to Richmond to be accommodated, and were there drilled by N.C.O.'s of their own arm of the Service.

Some little time prior to this Lieutenant-Colonel Hennah had taken over the duties of adjutant of the Depot.

All sick and wounded arriving in England from the Front came auto-matically on to the strength of the Depot, so remaining until posted to the Reserve Battalion on expiration of sick furlough. From first to last, from 1914 to 1919, over twenty thousand such men were dealt with by the Depot, and at one time, prior to the formation of the Command Depots, it was usual to have as many as five hundred convalescents at one time at the Depot, arranged in squads according to their degree of disability, and who, after a period of training and if sufficiently recovered, were sent to Reserve Battalions.

By July, 1915, recruiting had considerably fallen off, and orders were received to carry out a vigorous recruiting campaign in the neighbourhood of Richmond, and parties were accordingly sent out, accompanied by the 3rd Battalion Band, to surrounding towns and villages, with satisfactory results.

In January, 1916, medical boards were introduced for the examination of recruits who had been attested under the Group System, and thenceforth the officer in charge of Registration called up daily some two hundred recruits, and of those then found fit for service a certain proportion were posted to cavalry, artillery and departmental corps, the remainder then being sent off to various reserve units according to their medical categories. A medical board also sat at Middlesbrough, whence recruits were passed to the Depot for clothing and disposal.

In April of this year the first of the men were called up under the Military Service Act.

During June, 1916, the posting of recruits was commenced to the 16th (Labour) Battalion of the Regiment, then being formed at Brocklesby Camp; and in November a Substitution Company was formed, made up of low-category men posted to the Depot from various units at home.   During February, 1917, No. 2 Agricultural Company, The Green Howards, came into existence, this being designed for the replacement of fit men, also to lend out men to farmers who had insufficient labour on their land; later, this company was handed over to the Labour Corps and became the 407th and 505th Agricultural Companies of the Labour Corps, but they did not leave the Depot.

On the 16th August, 1917, Lieutenant-Colonel Esson relinquished the commmand of the Depot, Major E. G. Caffin taking his place; while some little time previously Captain B. C. Williams had been appointed adjutant *vice* Lieutenant-Colonel Hennah.

In March a considerable change was inaugurated, women of Queen Mary's Auxiliary Corps taking the place of men, where possible, in work at the Depot; while during the month following, the release of men formerly employed in and about coal mines was authorized, and large numbers of such men joined the Depot before being finally discharged from Army service.

In January, 1919, an office was opened at the Depot to deal with the demobilization of officers and other ranks, while about the same time repatriated prisoners-of-war commenced to come back, and the Depot then became a sort of clearing centre for a large number of Regular officers who had been employed with various units, such as the cadres of Service Battalions, etc.

In May, 1919, Lieutenant-Colonel E. G. Caffin retired and Lieutenant-Colonel N. E. Swan was posted to command the Depot.

This brief account of the war work of the Depot cannot be considered complete without some reference to another branch of local activities. Very early in the war it became increasingly evident that something must be done to supplement the very scanty rations which were being issued in Germany and Asia Minor to British prisoners-of-war, and to provide them with some of the comforts of which they were very greatly in need.   With this object a committee was formed at the Depot to deal with war prisoners from all the battalions of the Regiment, and a special appeal for help in money or in kind was made to the county and was at once very generously responded to. The first honorary secretary was Mrs. Esson, the wife of the O.C. Depot, and she continued to act in this capacity until she left Richmond, when the work was taken over and further developed by Mrs. Williams, who continued in office until her labours ended with the return of the prisoners at the end of the war.

Only those who were in a position to see the devoted work of these and other ladies of Richmond and neighbourhood, can judge how great is the debt owed them by the prisoners-of-war of The Green Howards.

THE 3RD (SPECIAL RESERVE) BATTALION

At the beginning of August, 1914, the Battalion was encamped at Barnard Castle for annual training under the command of Lieutenant-Colonel R. L. Aspinall, D.S.O., Lieutenant-Colonel Sir R. E. N. Gunter, Bart., being on sick leave, when, during the afternoon of Monday, the 3rd August, orders were received for the Battalion to return to Richmond forthwith. The move was carried out by a march route that evening and on arrival the men were quartered in the town, the barracks being required for the reception of the Regular Army Reservists.

As the Battalion and Depot were practically one unit, the officers and permanent staff had the dual duty of mobilizing the Reservists and of preparing the 3rd Battalion for its war station.

The order to mobilize was received on the evening of Tuesday, the 4th August, and the prepared scheme of mobilization was at once brought into operation.

Early on Wednesday morning the Reservists, eager to rejoin the Colours, were at the barrack gates, and large numbers continued to arrive during the day, so much so that the arrangements made for food and accommodation were inadequate to deal with such a large and unexpected influx on the first day of mobilization. However, emergency arrangements were made as far as possible, but many men had to sleep in sheds, etc.

Mobilization proceeded as per scheme, and the requisite drafts were sent to join the 2nd Battalion in Guernsey as soon as they were armed, clothed and equipped.

On Saturday, the 8th August, the Battalion, made up to war strength by the addition of surplus reservists, spare Depot personnel and recruits, proceeded to its war station at West Hartlepool, arriving late that night, and here it relieved the 5th Battalion Durham Light Infantry.

The 3rd Battalion Green Howards now consisted of Headquarters and four companies, stationed as follows :—

Headquarters, West Hartlepool.
1 Company, West Hartlepool.
1 Company, Hartlepool.
1 Company, Seaton Carew.
1 Company, South Gare, near Redcar.
After a little time large numbers of recruits joined day after day, some-

times in hundreds dressed in civilian clothes, and the officers and staff had
their work cut out in finding accommodation, clothing, etc., for the men.
As the Ordnance Department was, for a time, unable to cope with the unprecedented demands for uniform, the recruits had to continue to wear
their civilian clothes for a short period, but later they were temporarily
supplied with a blue uniform.

The Battalion now settled down to its duties of training drafts and
guarding the coast.

The strength was considerably depleted by the dispatch of a draft of
about eight hundred and fifty men to the 2nd Battalion, and about two
Companies were transferred to the 11th Battalion which was formed at
Darlington. Sometimes the strength was two thousand, then five hundred or six hundred, companies being formed or disbanded as the strength
fluctuated.

On the 16th December, 1914, the Hartlepools were bombarded by the
Germans, who fired about one thousand shells into the town in a very short
time. The men stood to arms at their allotted stations, and although there
were a large number of casualties amongst the civilian population and a
few soldiers of other units, there were luckily none in the Battalion. Shells
fell near two of the hired buildings in occupation of the troops, but there
was no damage of consequence. The ordinary routine of training drafts
and coast defence went on through various stages until everything was
more or less standardized and worked efficiently.

As time went on the men were made more comfortable, other and better
quarters were acquired, an officers' mess, officers' quarters and institutes
were provided, and training ground became available, all of which tended
to improve the efficiency of the Battalion; but owing to the companies
being scattered over a wide area, administrative routine and training were
much more difficult than they would have been under more normal circumstances.

For a considerable period there were constant alarms of air raids, but
although enemy airships frequently crossed the coast line at the Hartlepools and dropped bombs, no damage was done to any of the hired quarters
and there were no casualties amongst the troops. One airship was brought
down at West Hartlepool.

About March, 1919, sudden orders were received for the Battalion to
proceed to Salisbury Plain, and on arrival it was stationed at Rolleston
Camp; after a few weeks there it was transferred to Dublin.

In a short time the cadre of the 2nd Battalion arrived from France, and
on the 8th August, 1919, took over the men of the Battalion, the cadre of
which proceeded to the Depot at Richmond for disbandment.

The Commanding Officers during the period under review were :—
Lieutenant-Colonel R. L. Aspinall, D.S.O. (temporarily).
Lieutenant-Colonel Sir R. E. N. Gunter, Bart.
Lieutenant-Colonel E. K. Purnell (Lancashire Fusiliers).
Lieutenant-Colonel C. R. White, D.S.O., who commanded until disbandment.

Although it did not see any actual war service, the 3rd Battalion efficiently fulfilled its dual rôle of draft finding and coast defence, and thousands of men passed through its ranks to join the various battalions of the Regiment, and thus the old 3rd Battalion justified its existence.

The 2/4th (Territorial) Battalion

Very shortly after the war had opened it became apparent that reserve units of the Territorial Force would be needed to take the place of the already existing battalions of the Force, if and when these should be ordered abroad, and also as a feeder to replace wastage in such units. Army Order No. 399 was then issued in September, 1914, authorizing the Territorial Force Associations to form a Home Service unit for each one which had been accepted for service overseas. Even this initial expansion of the Force was soon found to be inadequate, and on the 24th November instructions were issued from the War Office conveying the decision that when an Imperial Service unit proceeded overseas and was replaced at home by its Reserve unit, a *second* Reserve unit was at once to be raised at the depot or peace headquarters of the original unit.

The question of raising a second battalion for the 4th Battalion The Green Howards was considered about the middle of August, 1914, and on the 1st September the following officers arrived at Northallerton, there to receive such preliminary military training as the majority of them required, prior to the arrival of the non-commissioned officers and men : Lieutenant-Colonel W. A. Wharton, Majors the Hon. A. Orde-Powlett and A. Fife, and Captain and Adjutant Whitaker ; Captains I. H. Hutton Squire, A. Dorman, P. C. Leather, F. Milbank, E. S. Jones, M. J. Wilson, H. Theakstone and H. Dixon ; Lieutenants J. L. Reid, J. C. Kewley, A. Wynne-Finch, A. R. Welsh, G. F. Lucas, G. D. Gardner, E. H. Pease, T. G. Thornton, C. Bolckow, H. G. Scott, T. S. Rowlandson, D. Maclaren, C. Cummins, G. Tugwell, C. E. Pease and J. K. Stead.

About the 10th September the " other ranks " began to come in, and by the end of the month the Battalion was a thousand strong, but for some time there were no uniforms, blankets or boots available for issue.

In May, 1915, when the first draft was sent out to France, the Battalion was accorded the title of "the North Riding Northern Coast Battalion," changed in the month following to "the 24th Provisional Battalion." By this time the Battalion had moved to Benton, but in July was sent to camp and later on to billets at Cramlington, with two companies at Blyth, where the winter of 1915–1916 was spent. In April, 1916, a move was made to Clacton-on-Sea, and the Battalion was there employed in digging trenches for occupation in the event of any possible landing by the enemy. In the autumn of this year Lieutenant-Colonel Wharton was invalided and the command was temporarily assumed by Major Terry pending the arrival of Colonel F. C. Bousefield.

On the 1st January, 1917, the name of the Battalion was changed for a third time, it now becoming the 18th Battalion of the Regiment ; and in April it moved from Clacton to billets in Margate and became a unit of the 222nd Mixed Brigade, Independent Force, the headquarters of the Force being in Canterbury, and the area allotted to the Battalion to guard being from Margate pier to the boundary between the North Foreland and Broadstairs. Here several air raids were experienced and one coast bombardment by a German submarine, one man of the Battalion being killed.

Many drafts were sent out to France at this time and just before the Armistice one was dispatched to Malta.

After the Armistice officers and men were gradually demobilized or sent abroad to Labour Corps in France or to Ireland, such as remained being employed in dismantling the coast defences.

3/4TH (TERRITORIAL) BATTALION

The 3/4th Battalion of The Green Howards commenced training at Northallerton at the end of April, 1915, with a nucleus of two hundred men transferred from the 2nd Line Battalion and some dozen officers who had been gazetted to the new unit. The Battalion was under the command of Lieutenant-Colonel Lord Southampton, who retained the command until he resigned in November, 1918. Lieutenant-Colonel F. F. Deakin, who had formerly commanded the 1st Line Battalion in France, took over the command on Lord Southampton's resignation.

The Battalion was fortunate in obtaining excellent headquarters in the Northallerton Grammar School, the grounds of which were of sufficient size to accommodate the large number of tents required for the unit as soon as the recruiting campaign—which, on the whole, was highly successful—commenced. The unit remained under canvas till November, by which time the camp was a field of mud and the weather was very cold. Vigorous protests having failed to produce any result, the commanding officer took matters into his own hands and commandeered all the suitable buildings in the town as billets. These included the North Riding Jail, which was admirably adapted for the purpose. This, possibly, is the first occasion on which troops were—voluntarily—billeted in a prison. Among other buildings taken over was the Workhouse. As this still left a large number of men unprovided for, the Workhouse and various other suitable buildings at Thirsk were also taken. This gap of nine miles between the two sections of the Battalion rather complicated training, but in spite of this the unit maintained the high standard it had adopted from the beginning, and the reports it received showed that its efficiency was far above the average of other similar units.

In the spring of 1916 the Battalion moved to Redcar, where it occupied billets in several large buildings. Here it not only carried on its duties as a training unit, but was responsible for a sector of coast defence. The frontage allotted to the Battalion was from the pier to Tod Point, and certain posts had to be maintained day and night. What with this, the manning of the trenches by the whole unit whenever a sea or air raid was rumoured, and emptying the trenches of the sand which filled them every time the wind blew, training was considerably hampered during this period.

In September, 1916, a scheme of amalgamation of all 3rd Line units led to the incorporation of the 3/4th and the 3/5th Battalions, which were henceforth known as the " 4th (Reserve) Battalion Yorkshire Regiment." The function of this new unit was to feed the 1st Line Territorial Battalions. A month or two later the unit was moved to Catterick, where it remained till July, 1917, after which it was transferred to Sutton, near Hull, and later to Hornsea, where it was again responsible for a sector of coast defence. During the summer months the troops were under canvas, and in the winter in the Hydro and other houses in Hornsea. The unit was finally disbanded in 1919.

THE 2/5TH (TERRITORIAL) BATTALION

This Battalion was originally raised for Home Service and began its existence on the 28th September, 1914, with the arrival of a few officers at the Grand Hotel, Scarborough, the Battalion Headquarters, Lieutenant-Colonel Chichester-Constable being in command, while Major H. de M. Leathes was adjutant. In November a move was made to Darlington, the men being accommodated in the local schools, while the officers, of whom rather over twenty had by this time been gazetted, were housed at the King's Head Hotel.

In April of the year following the Battalion moved into camp at Benton, near Newcastle, where Lieutenant-Colonel Orde-Powlett assumed command in place of Colonel Chichester-Constable, Major Leathes then becoming second in command, while Captain Moseley took over the duties of adjutant. In the following month the organization of the Battalion underwent a change, it now being divided into two separate parts, the one becoming a provisional battalion, while the other, composed of A.1. men, was formed into a unit intended for active service ; this latter then went into camp at Cramlington under Major Leathes and joined the 189th Brigade of the 63rd Division, while the remainder remained on at Benton under Lieutenant-Colonel Orde-Powlett. Later, however, the A.1. portion of the Battalion came back again to Benton, and the rest of the officers and men were sent to Scarborough to form the 3/5th Green Howards.

In August of this year Major Leathes went to the 13th Battalion of the Regiment, and Lieutenant-Colonel M. J. Wilson then took his place, with Major Milbank as second-in-command and Captain J. F. Bryant as adjutant ; during the remainder of this year the 2/5th occupied billets first in Newcastle and later in Gainsborough, where Captain C. L. Porter was appointed adjutant.

In April, 1916, the constitution of the Battalion was again altered, all the A.1. men being taken for drafts, and only officers and non-commissioned officers remaining, and these then forming another Battalion, intended for service in India, out of B.1. recruits.

In November of this year, while stationed at Catterick, orders were received that the Battalion was to proceed to India, and all were fitted out with Indian kit and given embarkation leave ; but within a very short time these orders were cancelled and the Battalion moved to Blackpool, being transferred to the 219th Brigade of the 73rd Division.

During the months from January, 1917, to February, 1918, the 2/5th was quartered in camp or billets in or near Chelmsford, and in March of the latter year it was finally disbanded.

THE 3/5TH (TERRITORIAL) BATTALION

This Battalion was raised at Scarborough in May, 1915, by Lieutenant-Colonel the Hon. T. L. F. Willoughby, late The Yorkshire Hussars, for duty on coast defence, and also with the intention of providing drafts in officers and men for the first line units of the Territorial battalions, and for the purpose of accommodating convalescents and recovered wounded until these were fit to return to the front. The Battalion was formed from a nucleus of eighty men transferred from the 2/5th, with Captain G. F. Vahey, late Sergeant-Major of the 2nd Green Howards, as adjutant. Recruiting was carried out in the Scarborough, Whitby and Malton districts, and the men were billeted in Scarborough ; the provision of instructors presented at the outset considerable difficulties, but in time these were overcome.

The permanent officers of the 3/5th were Lieutenant-Colonel the Hon. T. L. F. Willoughby, Major W. H. Williamson, late 18th Hussars, Captains G. F. Vahey, adjutant, H. Barker and W. L. Lilburn, with Lieutenant J. Orde Hume as quartermaster. The rest of the officers came and went, something like eighty going through their training with the Battalion, to which they were posted after serving for a time in Officers' Training Corps and similar organizations. Of other ranks about seven hundred and fifty were trained and sent overseas in drafts, and all—officers and men—were first rate in every way and a credit to the Regiment.

The first draft was sent to France on the 1st September, 1915.

In April of the following year the 3/5th was moved to Redcar Camp, and now became the " Reserve Battalion Yorkshire Regiment Territorial Force," and formed part of a brigade of six battalions commanded by Colonel Armstrong. In the Brigade sports the Battalion won nearly all the events, including a cup presented by the Brigadier.

In September, 1916, the 3/5th Green Howards was merged into the 4th Battalion of the Regiment, commanded by Lieutenant-Colonel the Earl of Southampton, late 10th Hussars, Lieutenant-Colonel the Hon. T. L. F. Willoughby retiring and taking over command of the 4th Volunteer Battalion, The Green Howards, at Scarborough, and retaining command of this unit until the end of the war.

THE 11TH (SERVICE) BATTALION

The 11th Battalion The Green Howards was raised at West Hartlepool in October, 1914, and as soon as formed was moved to Darlington. The staff at this time was composed as follows : Lieutenant-Colonel R. L. Aspinall, D.S.O., in command, Lieutenant-Colonel H. H. Duncombe, second-in-command, Captain A. G. Hills, adjutant, and Lieutenant C. Beastall, quartermaster ; but very soon after arrival at Darlington Captain Hills was promoted to a majority in the corps and Captain E. G. Drench was appointed adjutant.

Thanks to the labours of the quartermaster the Battalion was equipped in a wonderfully short time ; the men were billeted in the Drill Hall and in two schools in Darlington, headquarters being at the former place, and parades were held in Hummersknott Park. The Brigade contained also the 10th Battalion Northumberland Fusiliers and the 16th and 17th Battalions Durham Light Infantry, the whole forming the 89th Brigade under the command of Brigadier-General Leach, in the Third New Army. But in April, 1915, it was decided that the Third Army should become a reserve force, and the duties of the 11th Green Howards were then confined to finding drafts and reinforcements for the foreign service battalions of the Regiment.

Lieutenant-Colonel Duncombe was, about this time, transferred to another corps, his place as second in command being taken by Major R. Sandwith, C.M.G.; while on the 3rd August Lieutenant-Colonel Aspinall, D.S.O., was appointed to command the 10th Battalion The Cheshire Regiment, exchanging with Lieutenant-Colonel W. H. Benett-Dampier of that corps; further, Captain E. G. Drench was also transferred to the 10th Cheshire Regiment, and Captain E. Boys took his place with the 11th Green Howards.

In October of this year the Battalion was moved to hutments at Rugeley, and from now on the strength constantly fluctuated owing to arrivals from hospital or from other Service battalions.

A great change in organization took place in September, 1916, when all the battalions of the Brigade were turned into training battalions, the 11th Green Howards being amalgamated with the 16th Durham Light Infantry as a Training Battalion and so losing its identity; this new Battalion was placed under the command of Colonel Grimshaw.

Over 70 per cent. of the original officers of the 11th Battalion were killed in action, and one—Second-Lieutenant H. S. Bell—won the Victoria Cross in July, 1916, at Horseshoe Trench, Contalmaison, during the Battle of the Somme of that year, while serving with the 9th Green Howards.

THE 14TH (RESERVE) BATTALION

This Battalion was formed from the depot company of the 12th Green Howards and was stationed at Hummersknott, Darlington, under the command of Captain Longbotham, and became a Battalion early in September, 1915, and was then moved to Marton Hall for recruiting, which was undertaken by the then Mayor of the Borough, Alderman J. W. Bruce, who likewise raised the 12th Battalion. It was intended to find recruits for the 12th Battalion Teeside Pioneers against the time when they went overseas; but within six months of its formation the 14th Battalion was sending drafts to any Battalion of The Green Howards then overseas. For the first six months of its existence the Battalion was commanded by Major C. Bolckow and later by Lieutenant-Colonel Cartwright; and during the time it was in being the 14th Green Howards was quartered at Marton Hall, Marton, Leeds Road, Harrogate, and the Old Infirmary, Newcastle-on-Tyne, and in camp at Gosforth Park. The provision of drafts naturally caused the strength of the unit to vary almost from day to day, and whilst quartered at Marton Hall it was as high as seven hundred and fifty all ranks, but owing to the great difficulty experienced in securing both officers and non-commissioned officers with experience, during the first three months of the life of the Battalion it had to carry on with less than half a dozen officers and not more than double that number of non-commissioned officers. Approximately sixty young officers were chosen from the different O.T.C.'s then in existence, but these on joining were not immediately available for duty with the Battalion and were sent to various courses, and on their return were frequently called on to accompany drafts proceeding overseas.

On 1st September, 1916, the 14th Battalion of Green Howards ceased to function as such and was merged into the 81st Training Reserve Battalion.

THE 15TH (RESERVE) BATTALION

There is unfortunately very little to be learned of this Battalion of The Green Howards, but such as there is to be traced is here set down for record.

In or about the middle of December, 1915, Lieutenant-Colonel H. de M. Leathes took over certain details at Skipton Barracks and was ordered to form a battalion out of them, with the result that by the 15th January of the year following he had collected something under a dozen officers and about seven hundred and fifty non-commissioned officers and men, the majority of the private soldiers being lads of from sixteen to eighteen years of age.

The Battalion was now moved to Rugeley in Staffordshire, and shortly afterwards Lieutenant-Colonel Leathes was ordered to India, when the command of the new battalion was assumed by Lieutenant-Colonel L. St. C. Nicholson, with Captain C. W. C. Hutton as adjutant and Lieutenant J. B. Clark as quartermaster.

The 15th Battalion disappears from the Army List in December, 1916.

THE 16TH (LABOUR) BATTALION

The 16th Battalion The Green Howards, intended for employment as a Labour Battalion in the war area, was formed at Brocklesby Camp, North Lincolnshire, in June, 1916, the first officer to join it for duty being Lieutenant H. C. W. Woolley, who was in command for several days. In the following month the new unit proceeded overseas at practically full strength, embarking at Southampton in the *Mona Queen* and landing at Le Havre on the 12th July. The following officers sailed for France with the Battalion : Lieutenant-Colonel H. A. Hill in command, Lieutenant H. Cross, transport officer, and Lieutenant D. Rees, R.A.M.C., in medical charge.

No. 1 Company : Captain S. M. Carrington, Lieutenants H. C. W. Woolley and R. B. Cox ; Lieutenant and Quartermaster B. Anderton.

No .2   ,,   Captain H. Gaskell and Lieutenant F. Holdsworth.

No. 3   ,,   Captain S. Robinson and Lieutenant A. C. Tozer.

No. 4   ,,   Captain J. P. Hunt and Lieutenant H. Cross.

The Battalion remained at Le Havre until April, 1917, being camped in " Cinder City " and working at the docks in unloading and handling all kinds of war material and stores ; but on the 8th May all the Labour Battalions were reorganized and formed into Labour Corps, the 16th Battalion The Green Howards being made now into the 22nd and 23rd Labour Companies, under Captains Gaskell and Robinson respectively. Of these the 22nd was sent to Poperinghe and the 23rd to Bailleul, but they met once again in some heavy fighting on the Menin Road, where the 22nd Company suffered severe losses.

The life of the Labour Companies during 1917 and 1918 was very strenuous and unceasing : they made roads, railways, dumps and horse-lines ; and during that time came in for their full share of bombing and shell fire, never remaining long in one locality, but being moved about all over the whole front.

Of the men of these Companies the ordinary medical category was B.2, but some few C.1. (Home Service) men were also included. The establishment of a company was five hundred non-commissioned officers and men, the officers being a major or captain in command and four subaltern officers. The 23rd Labour Company served in each of the five British Armies, and at the time of the Armistice was stationed at Maubeuge, being finally broken up near Namur.

THE 17TH (LABOUR) BATTALION

A battalion also existed under the above title, but so far no record of its services has been received.

THE 18TH (HOME SERVICE) BATTALION

This Battalion was in the first instance known as the 24th Provisional Battalion, and was so formed, in June, 1915, from non-commissioned officers and men who had been sent to it from the 2/4th and 2/5th Battalions of the Regiment. It was then stationed at Long Benton Camp, Newcastle-on-Tyne, the first commanding officer being Colonel W. H. A. Wharton, A.D.C. to the King, who retained command until September, 1916.

During the early summer of 1915 the Battalion was sent to Cramlington, Northumberland, where it was accommodated partly under canvas and partly in billets, headquarters and " B " and " C " Companies being at Cramlington in the local school and the Workmen's Club and Institute, while the other two companies were stationed at Blyth ; later, " D " Company was sent to Horton Hutments near Cramlington, while " A " Company was transferred to Dudley and Burradon. In these parts the Battalion remained until April, 1916, when it moved to Clacton-on-Sea—while here Major C. E. Terry exercising command for some three months, until in November Lieutenant-Colonel F. C. Bousefield took over charge. Here too the title of the Battalion was altered, for in January, 1917, it became the 18th Battalion The Yorkshire Regiment (Green Howards).

The *personnel* of the Battalion was composed of men below Medical Category " A," any men found to be of this category being sent in drafts of varying sizes to reserve units in England as a rule, but in some cases drafts were sent direct to units which were preparing for service overseas, and in one or two instances drafts were forwarded direct to France, and one was fitted out for Mediterranean service. The strength naturally varied very much, at one time—when stationed at Clacton in April, 1916—the Battalion contained as many as one thousand four hundred non-commissioned officers and men, this increase being occasioned by the arrival of four hundred and eighty-five other ranks who had been posted from a provisional battalion just disbanded.

On the 29th April, 1917, the Battalion moved to Margate, where headquarters and " A," " B " and " C " Companies were stationed, " D " Company finding a detachment at Kingsgate, and here the 18th Green Howards remained quartered until after the Armistice.

Demobilization then commenced, but proceeded very slowly, not being finally completed until August, 1919, by which date the remaining details had been sent to the depot at Richmond ; during the concluding months of the existence of the Battalion Major C. E. Terry was in command again, with the rank of Lieutenant-Colonel.

In the early days the Battalion was armed with Japanese rifles, and was throughout mainly engaged in the duties of coast defence. The first two German " Gothas " brought down in England during a daylight raid fell near Margate in August, 1917, the one in the sea in the coast sector occupied by the Battalion, and the other a mile inland in flames. The three

Germans forming the crew of this last were killed, and the 18th Battalion was called upon to furnish a firing party at their funeral.

THE 1ST GARRISON BATTALION

This was raised at Pontefract in October, 1915, by Lieutenant-Colonel A. C. Tucker, and was composed of men who had been medically rejected for service in fighting units, or of those who had served overseas but were found unfit for such service but fit for garrison duty on foreign service. Drafts came from the Durham Light Infantry, from the West Yorkshire and East Yorkshire Regiments, and from the " Leeds Bantams."

On Christmas Eve, 1915, the Battalion sailed for India, arrived in Bombay on the 19th of the following month and proceeded to Ahmednagar. The Indian Army List for April, 1916, shows the following officers as serving with the Battalion : Lieutenant-Colonel A. C. Tucker, Majors E. A. Marples and W. S. Dawson (Bombay), Captains A. P. Turner (Poona), C. E. Parr, G. A. Shortt, G. Whitehead (adjutant), S. Brichta and T. C. Stafford, Lieutenants S. Cohen (Bombay), J. M. Mackay, E. C. Mackenzie, R. H. Dutchman, W. N. Harrison (Bombay), J. T. Marshall (Poona), H. H. Roskin, C. P. Groome (on leave out of India), and J. H. Holmes, Second-Lieutenants E. C. Walters, L. R. H. Tansley, D. N. Harland (Bombay), A. R. Mathar (Bombay), S. R. Macdonald, A. E. Illingworth, and S. Wallace ; Hon. Lieutenant T. Tannyane (quartermaster).

At the date of the Armistice the Battalion was stationed at Sialkot, in the Punjab, and demobilization had actually commenced when trouble broke out in the Punjab and demobilization was suspended, the Battalion being engaged in safeguarding all important centres and patrolling the country, while some two hundred non-commissioned officers and men were employed with a mobile column.

When the internal situation became easier the embargo on demobilization was removed, and drafts began to go home again in September, 1919, and by the winter of this year all officers and other ranks belonging to the 1st Garrison Battalion, The Green Howards, had left India for England.

THE 2ND (H.S.) GARRISON BATTALION

A battalion was also raised under the above title, presumably as a draft-finding unit for the 1st Garrison Battalion when serving overseas.

APPENDICES

I—VI

THE GREEN HOWARDS

APPENDIX I

THE GREEN HOWARDS ASSOCIATION

The Association was founded by Colonel A. de S. Hadow in 1909, under the patronage of The Rt. Hon. The Marquis of Zetland, K.T., The Earl of Londesborough, and The Earl of Carlisle, for the purpose of maintaining connection between the officers, W.O.'s, N.C.O.'s and men, past and present, of the Regiment, to foster Esprit de Corps, and to assist those of its members who were in want. In 1909 the membership was about five hundred and eight, which number increased gradually until the Great War, when to all intents the activities of the Association ceased until 1919.

Since that date more members have been enrolled, and at the present time there are about one thousand four hundred names on the list of members, and the Association is now in the process of reorganization on a much larger scale.

The Headquarters of the Association are now at The Barracks, Richmond, Yorkshire, where any further information regarding it can be obtained from the Secretary.

THE COMFORTS FUND

This Fund was started in October, 1914, and was run by Mrs. Cecil King, assisted at first by Mrs. Maurice Tomlin and later by a Committee of ladies of The Yorkshire Regiment from that date on until the end of the War (with the exception of a few months when it was run by Mrs. Alexander).

The object was to supply comforts to the 2nd Battalion Yorkshire Regiment at the Front. The money, clothing, etc., was contributed almost entirely by relations and friends of the Officers past and present and friends in Yorkshire interested in the Regiment.

Many thousands of shirts, socks, vests and other garments and regular weekly supplies of cigarettes, note paper, chocolate, etc., were sent out, and in addition, at the request of the Officer Commanding, periscopes, watches, wire-cutters, barbers' scissors and a vast number of other articles were supplied.

The 2nd Battalion kept the Committee informed of their wants, and thanks to the generosity of a large number of people connected with or interested in the Regiment, who either supported the " Comforts Fund " or gave in kind, the Battalion was kept well supplied.

The value of these contributions to the Battalion was inestimable, especially during the winter months of 1914–15, when the demand for socks, shirts and other such stores was, for a variety of reasons, largely in excess of the supply, and the work of the Committee was thoroughly appreciated by all ranks.

APPENDIX II

THE BATTLE HONOURS

The following are extracts from the Army Orders issued in regard to the award and allocation of Battle Honours.

" A.O. 338/1922   *September* 1922.

H.M. the King has been graciously pleased to approve of the award of Battle Honours to Regiments and Corps under the following conditions:

(*a*) Regiments and Corps will have awarded to them, and recorded in the Army List in addition to those already shown, the Honours due to them for taking part in the battles enumerated in columns headed (1) ' Operations ' and (2) ' Battles ' (' Name ' and ' Tactical Incidents Included ') of the tabulated list of engagements given in the Report of the Battles Nomenclature Committee.

(*b*) Following the Honours previously earned, and at the head of the List of Honours granted for the Great War to be recorded in the Army List, will be placed ' THE GREAT WAR,' and the number of the battalions of the Regiment taking part.

(*c*) Within the meaning of Regiments and Corps will be included Cavalry and Yeomanry Regiments. An Infantry Regiment or Corps will include the Regular, Militia (or Special Reserve), Territorial and Service Battalions of the Regiment concerned. There will be only one Honours List for a Regiment or Corps.

(*d*) Regiments of Cavalry and Yeomanry, Battalions of Infantry, Regular, Militia (Special Reserve), and Territorial, will have emblazoned on their Standards, Guidons and Colours not more than 24 Honours, of which not more than 10 will be ' Great War ' Honours, to embrace the whole history of the Regiment concerned from the date on which it was raised to the end of the Great War, such Honours to be selected by Regimental Committees from the List of Honours to be shown in the Army List. The Honours emblazoned on the Colours will be the same for all units comprising the Regiment concerned, and will be shown in thicker type.

(*e*) The guiding principle in the selection and allotment of Battle Honours will be that Headquarters and at least 50 per cent. of the effective strength of a unit in a theatre of war (exclusive of drafts, which, although in a theatre of war, had not actually joined the unit) must have been present at the engagement for which the Honour is claimed.

(*f*) Regimental Committees under the chairmanship of their regimental colonels, or of representatives to be nominated by the regimental colonels, will be set up to select the particular Honours for Regimental Colours."

" A.O. 470/1922   *December* 1922.

To obviate the necessity of removing Honours at present emblazoned on the
    Colours of Regiments and Corps, His Majesty the King has been graciously
    pleased to approve that the following shall be substituted for sub-para-
    graphs (*d*) and (*f*) of A.O. 338 of 1922.

(*d*) Regiments of Cavalry and Yeomanry will have emblazoned on their Standards
    and Guidons, Battle Honours earned by them in the Great War up to a
    maximum of 10, in addition to those already carried.

(*f*) Battalions of Infantry, Regular, Militia (Special Reserve) and Territorial,
    will have emblazoned on their King's Colour, Battle Honours up to a maxi-
    mum of 10, to commemorate their services in the Great War, such Honours
    to be selected by Regimental Committees from the list of ' Great War '
    Honours to be shown in the Army List. The Honours emblazoned on the
    King's and Regimental Colours will be the same for all units comprising the
    Regiment concerned, and will be shown in the Army List in thicker type."

The first announcement that Battle Honours had been awarded to the Green
Howards for the Great War was made in Army Order 49/1924 (February 1924), List
No. 1 ; and for the Campaign in Afghanistan, 1919, known as The Third Afghan
War, in Army Order 97/1924 (March 1924).

The tabulated detail of the Battle Honours allotted was issued by the War Office
on 13th March, 1924, the ten awards selected to be borne on the Colours and Appointments being printed in CAPITAL letters.

Army Order 55/1925 (February 1925) notifies the cancellation of Army Order
49/1924, substituting a revised and complete list, in accordance with that compiled
from the War Diaries and Rolls furnished by the Regimental Battle Honours
Committee, which is as follows :—

THE GREAT WAR

BATTLES.	BATTALIONS PRESENT.
" YPRES, 1914 "	2nd.
" „ 1915 "	2nd, 4th, 5th.
" „ 1917 "	2nd, 4th, 5th, 6th, 8th, 9th, 10th.
" Langemarck, 1914 "	2nd.
" „ 1917 "	6th.
" Gheluvelt "	2nd.
" Neuve Chapelle "	2nd.
" St. Julien "	4th, 5th.
" Frezenberg "	4th.
" Bellewaarde "	4th, 5th.
" Aubers "	2nd.
" Festubert, 1915 "	2nd.
" Loos "	2nd, 8th, 9th, 10th.

BATTLES.	BATTALIONS PRESENT.
" SOMME, 1916 "	2nd, 4th, 5th, 6th, 7th, 8th, 9th, 10th, 12th.
" „ 1918 "	4th, 5th, 12th.
" Albert, 1916	7th, 8th, 9th, 10th.
" Bazentin "	10th.
" Pozières "	8th.
" Flers-Courcelette "	4th, 5th.
" Morval "	9th.
" Thiepval "	6th.
" Le Transloy ".	2nd, 4th, 5th, 8th, 9th.
" Ancre Heights "	6th.
" Ancre, 1916 "	12th.
" ARRAS, 1917 "	2nd, 4th, 5th, 7th, 10th.
" „ 1918 "	2nd.
" Scarpe, 1917 "	2nd, 4th, 5th, 7th, 10th.
" „ 1918 "	2nd.
" MESSINES, 1917 "	6th, 8th, 9th.
" „ 1918 "	13th.
" Pilckem "	2nd.
" Menin Road "	8th, 9th.
" Polygon Wood "	8th, 9th.
" Broodseinde "	10th.
" Poelcappelle "	6th.
" Passchendaele "	4th, 5th, 7th, 9th, 10th.
" Cambrai, 1917 "	12th, 13th.
" „ 1918 "	9th.
" St. Quentin ".	2nd, 4th, 5th, 13th.
" Bapaume, 1918 "	12th.
" Rosières "	4th, 5th.
" Lys "	4th, 5th, 12th.
" Estaires "	4th, 5th, 12th, 13th.
" Hazebrouck ".	4th, 5th, 13th.
" Kemmel "	2nd.
" Scherpenberg "	2nd.
" Aisne, 1918 ".	4th, 5th.
" Drocourt-Quéant ".	2nd.
" Hindenburg Line ".	9th.

BATTLES.						BATTALIONS PRESENT.
" Canal du Nord "	.	.	.	.	.	2nd.
" Beaurevoir "	.	.	.	.	.	9th.
" Selle "	.	.	.	.	.	2nd.
" VALENCIENNES "	.	.	.	.	.	2nd.
" SAMBRE "	.	.	.	.	.	2nd, 9th.
" FRANCE AND FLANDERS, 1914–18 "	.	.	.	2nd, 4th, 5th, 6th, 7th, 8th, 9th, 10th, 12th, 13th, 16th.
" Piave "	.	.	.	.	.	8th, 9th.
" VITTORIO VENETO "	.	.	.	.	8th.
" Italy, 1917–18 "	.	.	.	.	.	8th, 9th.
" SUVLA "	.	.	.	.	.	6th.
" Landing at Suvla "	.	.	.	.	6th.
" Scimitar Hill "	.	.	.	.	.	6th.
" Gallipoli, 1915 "	.	.	.	.	.	6th.
" Egypt, 1916 "	.	.	.	.	.	6th.
" Archangel, 1918 "	.	.	.	.	.	6th, 13th.

It will be observed that in several instances the Honour represents a battle of the same name fought in different years, but only counts as one Honour—e.g. " YPRES, 1914, 1915, 1917."

In the Table the three battles are shown below one another so as to indicate the individual Battalions which participated in each.

THE THIRD AFGHAN WAR

BATTALION PRESENT.

" AFGHANISTAN, 1919 " . . . .   1st.

APPENDIX III

THE VICTORIA CROSS

No. 8191 CORPORAL WILLIAM ANDERSON,
2nd Battalion.

For conspicuous bravery and devotion to duty at Neuve Chapelle on the 12th March, 1915, when he led three men with bombs against a large party of the enemy who had entered our trenches, and by his prompt and determined action saved what might have otherwise become a serious situation. Corporal Anderson first threw his own bombs, then those in possession of his three men (who had been wounded) amongst the Germans : after which he opened rapid fire upon them with great effect, notwithstanding that he was at the time quite alone. (*London Gazette*, 22nd May, 1915.)

SECOND-LIEUTENANT DONALD SIMPSON BELL,
9th Battalion.

For most conspicuous bravery at Horseshoe Trench, on the 5th July, 1916. During an attack, a very heavy enfilade fire was opened on the attacking company by a hostile machine gun. Second-Lieutenant Bell immediately, and on his own initiative, crept up a communication trench and then, followed by Corporal Colwill and Private Batey, rushed across the open under very heavy fire and attacked the machine gun, shooting the firer with his revolver and destroying gun and personnel with bombs. (*London Gazette*, 9th September, 1916.)

MAJOR STEWART WALTER LOUDOUN SHAND,
10th Battalion.

For most conspicuous bravery near Fricourt, on the 16th July, 1916. When his company attempted to climb over the parapet to attack the enemy's trenches they were met by very fierce machine-gun fire, which temporarily stopped their progress. Major Shand immediately leapt on the parapet, helped the men over it and encouraged them in every way until he fell mortally wounded. Even then he insisted on being propped up in the trench and went on encouraging the Non-Commissioned Officers and Men until he died. (*London Gazette*, 9th September, 1916.)

No. 12067 PRIVATE WILLIAM SHORT,
8th Battalion.

For most conspicuous bravery at Munster Alley, on the 6th August, 1916. He was foremost in the attack, bombing the enemy with great gallantry, when he was severely wounded in the foot. He was urged to go back, but refused and continued to throw bombs. Later his leg was shattered by a shell and he was unable to stand, so that he lay in the trench adjusting detonators and straightening the pins of bombs for his comrades. He died before he could be carried out of the trench. For the last eleven months he had always volunteered for dangerous enterprises and had always set a magnificent example of bravery and devotion to duty. (*London Gazette*, 9th September, 1916.)

CAPTAIN ARCHIE CECIL THOMAS WHITE, M.C.,
6th Battalion.

For most conspicuous bravery at Stuff Redoubt on the 27th September and the 1st October, 1916. He was in command of the troops that held the southern and western faces of a redoubt. For four days and nights, by his indomitable spirit, great personal courage and skilful dispositions, he held his position under fire of all kinds and against several counter-attacks. Though short of supplies and ammunition, his determination never wavered. When the enemy attacked in greatly superior numbers and had almost ejected our troops from the redoubt, he personally led a counter-attack, which finally cleared the enemy out of the southern and western faces. He risked his life continually and was the life and soul of the defence. (*London Gazette*, 26th October, 1916.)

CAPTAIN DAVID PHILIP HIRSCH,
4th Battalion.

For most conspicuous bravery and devotion to duty in attack near Wancourt on the 23rd April, 1917. Having arrived at the first objective, Captain Hirsch, although twice wounded, returned over fire-swept slopes to satisfy himself that the defensive flank was being established. Machine-gun fire was so intense that it was necessary for him to be continuously up and down the line encouraging his men to dig and hold the position. He continued to encourage his men by standing on the parapet and steadying them in the face of machine-gun fire and counter-attack until he was killed. His conduct throughout was a magnificent example of the greatest devotion to duty. (*London Gazette*, 14th June, 1917.)

No. 242697 PRIVATE TOM DRESSER,
7th Battalion.

For most conspicuous bravery and devotion to duty near Roeux, on the 12th May, 1917. Private Dresser, in spite of being twice wounded on the way, and suffering great pain, succeeded in conveying an important message from Battalion Headquarters to the front line of trenches, which he eventually reached in an exhausted condition. His fearlessness and determination to deliver this message at any cost proved of the greatest value to his Battalion at a critical period. (*London Gazette*, 27th June, 1917.)

No. 42537 CORPORAL WILLIAM CLAMP,
6th Battalion.

For most conspicuous bravery near Poelcapelle on the 9th October, 1917, when an advance was being checked by intense machine-gun fire from concrete blockhouses and by snipers in ruined buildings, Corporal Clamp dashed forward with two men and attempted to rush the largest blockhouse. His first attempt failed, owing to the two men with him being knocked out, but he at once collected some bombs and, calling upon two men to follow him, again dashed forward. He was first to reach the blockhouse and hurled in the bombs, killing many of the occupants. He then entered and brought out a machine gun and about twenty prisoners, whom he brought back under heavy fire from neighbouring snipers. This Non-Commissioned Officer then again went forward, encouraging and cheering the men and succeeded in rushing several sniper posts. He continued to show the greatest heroism until he was killed by a sniper. His magnificent courage and self-sacrifice were of the greatest value and relieved what was undoubtedly a very critical situation. (*London Gazette*, 18th December, 1917.)

LIEUTENANT-COLONEL OLIVER CYRIL SPENCER WATSON, D.S.O.

For most conspicuous bravery and devotion to duty at Rossignol Wood on the 28th March, 1918. His command was at a dangerous point, where continuous attacks were made by the enemy in order to pierce the line. A counter-attack had been made against the enemy position which at first achieved its object, but as they were holding out in two improvised strong points, Lieutenant-Colonel Watson saw that immediate action was necessary, and he led his remaining small reserve to the attack, organizing bombing parties and leading attacks under intense rifle- and machine-gun fire. Outnumbered, he finally ordered his men to retire, remaining himself in a communication trench to cover the retirement, though he faced almost certain death by so doing. The assault he led was at a critical moment, and without doubt saved the line. Both in the assault and covering his men's retirement he held his life as nothing, and his splendid bravery inspired all troops in the vicinity to rise to the occasion and save a breach being made in a hardly tried and attenuated line. Lieutenant-Colonel Watson was killed while covering the withdrawal. (*London Gazette*, 8th May, 1918.)

SECOND-LIEUTENANT ERNEST FREDERICK BEAL,
13th Battalion.

For most conspicuous bravery and determined leading at St. Leger, on the 21st and 22nd March, 1918, when in command of a company detailed to occupy a certain section of a trench. When the company was established it was found that a considerable gap of about four hundred yards existed between the left flank of the company and the neighbouring unit, and that this gap was strongly held by the enemy.

It was of vital importance that this gap should be cleared, but no troops were then available. Organizing a small party of less than a dozen men, he led them against the enemy. On reaching an enemy machine gun, Second-Lieutenant Beal immediately sprang forward and with his revolver killed the team, and captured the gun. Continuing along the trench, he encountered and dealt with another machine gun in the same manner; and in all captured four enemy guns, and inflicted severe casualties. Later in the evening, when a wounded man had been left in the open under heavy enemy fire, he, regardless of danger, walked up close to an enemy machine gun and brought in the wounded man on his back. Second-Lieutenant Beal was killed by a shell on the following morning. (*London Gazette*, 4th June, 1918.)

No. 9545 PRIVATE HENRY TANDY, D.C.M., M.M.,
5th Battalion.

For most conspicuous bravery and initiative during the capture of a village and the crossings at Marcoing and the subsequent counter-attack on the 28th September, 1918. His platoon was held up by machine-gun fire : he at once crawled forward, located the machine gun with a Lewis-gun team and knocked it out. On arrival at the crossings, he restored the plank bridge under a hail of bullets, thus enabling the first crossing to be made at this vital spot. Later in the evening, during an attack, he, with eight comrades, was surrounded by an overwhelming number of Germans, and though the position was apparently hopeless, he led a bayonet charge through them, fighting so fiercely that thirty-seven of the enemy were driven into the hands of the remainder of his company. Although twice wounded, he refused to leave until the fight was won. (*London Gazette*, 14th December, 1918.)

No. 13820 SERGEANT WILLIAM McNALLY, M.M.,
8th Battalion.

For most conspicuous bravery and skilful leading during the operations on the 27th October, 1918, across the Piave, when his company was most seriously hindered in its advance by heavy machine-gun fire from the vicinity of some buildings on a flank. Utterly regardless of personal safety, he rushed the machine-gun post single-handed, killing the team and capturing the gun. Later at Vazzola, on the 29th October, 1918, when his company, having crossed the Monticano River, came under heavy rifle fire and machine-gun fire, Sergeant McNally immediately directed the fire of his platoon against the danger point, whilst he himself crept to the rear of the enemy's position. Realizing that a frontal attack would mean heavy losses, he, unaided, rushed the position, killing or putting to flight the garrison and capturing a machine gun. On the same day, when holding a newly captured ditch, he was strongly counter-attacked from both flanks. By his coolness and skill in controlling the fire of his party, he frustrated the attack, inflicting heavy casualties on the enemy. Throughout the whole of the operations, his innumerable acts of gallantry set a high example to his men, and his leading was beyond all praise. (*London Gazette*, 14th December, 1918.)

APPENDIX IV
THE MEDALS FOR THE GREAT WAR
"The 1914 Star"

In November, 1917, Army Order No. 350 was published announcing that His Majesty the King had been graciously pleased to signify His pleasure to give a decoration—a Star in bronze—in recognition of the services of such of the military forces of the Crown as had served in France and Belgium under Field-Marshal Sir John French, during the earlier phase of the War, from 5th August, 1914, to midnight of the 22nd–23rd November, 1914. No clasp was originally issued with this Star, the riband of which was to be red, white and blue, shaded and watered.

In October, 1919, Army Order No. 361 was published announcing that His Majesty had been graciously pleased to approve the issue of a clasp to those who had actually served under the fire of the enemy in France and Belgium between the 5th August, 1914, and midnight 22nd–23rd November, 1914.

In undress and service uniform, when ribands only are worn, the grant of the clasp is denoted by the wearing of a small silver rose in the centre of the riband.

"The 1914–15 Star"

Rather more than a year later—in December, 1918—Army Order No. 20 of 1919 was published, stating that His Majesty was further pleased to recognize the services rendered by others of His military forces who served in theatres of war between the 5th August, 1914, and the 31st December, 1915, both dates inclusive. This decoration, except for the date, was in all respects identical (but no clasp) with the " 1914 Star," but those eligible for the first named were not to receive the second.

"The War Medal"

Then in July, 1919, it was announced in Army Order No. 266 that " His Majesty had been graciously pleased to signify His pleasure that a medal be granted to record the bringing of the War to a successful conclusion, and the arduous services rendered by His Majesty's forces," the medal being in silver and the riband being " centre orange, watered, with stripes of white and black on each side and with borders of Royal blue."

"The Victory Medal"

In the following month it was given out in Army Order No. 301, that the services of His Majesty's forces were to be further recognized by the grant of a second medal, to be designated " the Victory Medal," which was to be identical in design with that issued by the other Allied and Associated Powers. The medal was to be of bronze and without any clasps, the riband to be " red in the centre with green and violet on each side, shaded to form the colours of two rainbows."

"The Territorial Force War Medal"

Army Order No. 143, April, 1920, announced that His Majesty had been graciously pleased to approve of a special medal being granted to those members of the Territorial Force who volunteered for service overseas on or before the 30th September, 1914, and who rendered such service during the years 1914–19, providing they were serving with the Territorial Force on 4th August, 1914, or had completed a period of not less than four years' service with the Territorial Force before the outbreak of war and rejoined not later than 30th September, 1914.

The medal is in bronze, the riband being yellow with two dark green stripes. Those who qualified for the " 1914 Star," or " 1914–15 Star," were ineligible.

408

APPENDIX V

THE KING'S COLOUR—SPECIAL ISSUE

In accordance with Army Council Instruction No. 444, dated 21st July, 1919, Silk Union Flags were authorized to be issued to Service Battalions, Garrison Battalions, and Territorial Force Battalions which had served abroad during the Great War, the details of which are as follows :

> His Majesty the King has been graciously pleased to approve of the presentation of a silk Union Flag to each Service, Graduated and Garrison Battalion of the Regular Army, and to each Second and Third Line Territorial Force Battalion, which has served abroad during the war.

> His Majesty has been further pleased to command that these Flags, which will represent the King's Colour, are to be consecrated and to be granted all the salutes and compliments authorized to be paid to Colours.

> In the case of Battalions which have been disbanded or otherwise ceased to exist, the final disposal of the Flags rests with the Commanding Officer and Officers of the Battalion at the time of disbandment, subject to the proviso that they are to be deposited in some sacred or public building in the locality where the unit was raised.   It is to be distinctly understood that the Flags remain the property of the State, and are not to pass into the possession of, or be handed over for custody to, any private individual.

> The Flags as issued are plain Union Flags, and no additions (except titles and numerals) can be sanctioned.

The design for a King's Colour is as follows :
> " The King's Colour of every Battalion is to be the Great Union, the Imperial Colour of the United Kingdom of Great Britain and Ireland, in which the Cross of St. George is conjoined with the Crosses of St. Andrew and St. Patrick on a blue field, as modified by Her late Majesty Queen Victoria in 1900.   The Colour is to bear in the centre the Territorial designation on a crimson circle, with the Royal or other title within, the whole surmounted by the Imperial Crown.   The number of each Battalion is to be placed in the dexter canton.
> "When Regiments have not a combination of Territorial and Royal or other special designations, the number of the Battalion will be placed within the circle bearing the name of the Regiment, instead of in the dexter canton."

APPENDIX VI

THE REGIMENTAL WAR MEMORIAL

After the War a Memorial Fund was raised, subscriptions to which amounted to about £11,000. Practically all Battalions contributed, the largest sum being received from all ranks of the 1st Battalion, which realized over £3,000 alone.

The Fund was primarily allotted to assist ex-members of the Regiment to start in business or to relieve distress, but about one-fifth of the total was put aside for the erection of a permanent memorial.

The Regimental War Memorial takes the form of a Celtic Cross built of stone, and is situated at the top of Frenchgate, Richmond, Yorkshire.

It bears the following inscription :—

" To commemorate the gallant dead of The Yorkshire Regiment (The Green Howards) who fought and died for their Country in The Great War, and whose names are recorded in a book placed in the Richmond Parish Church."

The ceremony of unveiling the War Memorial took place on the 13th July, 1921, in the presence of a large and distinguished gathering.

A short service was first held in the Parish Church, when General Sir Edward S. Bulfin, K.C.B., C.V.O., handed over to the Rector, Canon Nevill Edgerton Leigh, the Memorial Book containing the names of 464 Officers and 7,036 Warrant and Non-Commissioned Officers and Men of the Regiment who gave their lives for King and Country.

The congregation then moved to the top of Frenchgate, where the unveiling of the War Memorial took place.

The Marquis of Zetland made an opening address in which he thanked the Committee and Colonel N. E. Swan for the great pains they had taken in assisting him in the work of producing this great Memorial. He also made a touching reference to the great sacrifices made by the gallant men whose memory this Memorial perpetuated, and called upon Sir Hugh Bell to unveil the Memorial.

Sir Hugh Bell, the Lord-Lieutenant of the North Riding, in unveiling the Memorial, spoke of the fine record of the Regiment in the Great War. He spoke of the Memorial as one for the North Riding of Yorkshire, for their own Regiment, The Green Howards, and how splendid it was that twenty-four Battalions should have been raised from such a sparsely-populated district.

The Rev. Canon N. E. Leigh then dedicated the Memorial, and the Mayor of Richmond (Councillor Hodgson) spoke on behalf of the Corporation.

The ceremony ended with the sounding of the " Last Post " by four buglers and the salutes of the troops and discharged soldiers present.

Many wreaths were then placed on the Memorial, including one graciously sent from H.M. Queen Alexandra.

THE GREEN HOWARDS WAR MEMORIAL, RICHMOND.

Unveiled 13th July, 1921.

INDEX

A

Adolfo, R.S.M., awarded R.H. Society Diploma, 231
Afghan Army, organization of, 16, 17
Afghan War, Third, 16–32
Agricultural Company formed, 385
Aisne, Second Battle of the, 143–146, 167, 168
Alexander, Lieut.-Col. W. L., commands 2nd Bn., 53; killed, 59
Allenby, Maj.-Gen., 3
Anderson, Corp. W., wins V.C., 55–58
Antwerp, situation at, Sept. 1914, 34, 35
Archangel, 208
Armistice, The, with Germany, 118, 325; with Austria, 286
Armstrong, Col. T. G. L. R., 327
Arras, Battle of, 89–92, 134–137, 241–243
Asbrey, Capt. and Qr.-Mr., 230, 231
Asiago Plateau, The, 273
Aspinall, Lieut.-Col. R. L., 3rd Bn., 386; 11th Bn., 393
Austrian Offensive in Italy, The, 273

B

Babington, Maj.-Gen. J. M., 251, 256, 263, 269, 279, 286–289, 311
Backhouse, Maj. M. R. C., assumes command of 8th Bn., 265; Lieut.-Col., 282–284
Baker, Maj. B. G., assumes command of 13th Bn., 363; Lieut.-Col., 366; wounded, 367
Balfour, Rt. Hon. A., 272
Barnes, Maj. A. C., commands 150th Composite Bn., 146
Barrett, Maj. L. A., assumes command of 1/4th Bn., 128; killed, 131
Battalions :
1st Bn., 9–31
  Afghan War, Third, 13–16, 31
  Barian, 9

1st Bn. (*contd.*)
  Dakka, operations near, 21–23, 25, 26, 30
  India, stationed in, 9–31
  Kohat, 11–13
  Landi Kotal, 21
  Peshawar, 15, 31
  Rawal Pindi, 11, 13
  Sherabad Cantonment, 27
  Sialkot, quartered at, 9
  Thal, 12
  Twin Peaks, action at, 29, 30
  Waziristan, trouble in, 11, 12
2nd Bn., 32–120
  Armistice with Germany, 118
  Arras, Battle of, 89–92
  Bernafay Wood, 77, 78
  Bethune, 70
  Bruges, stay at, 33, 35
  Cadre, returns home, 120; composition of, 120
  Canal du Nord, Battle of, 113, 114
  Casualties at Arras, 95; in last action, 118; at Loos, 69; at Second Somme Battle, 107, 108; at Ypres, First, 50; at Ypres, Second, 60
  Channel Islands, stationed in, 32
  Demobilization, 119, 120
  Dumbarton Lakes, at, 94
  Epinoy, attack on, 115
  Festubert, Battle of, 59, 60
  First shots in the War, 37
  Fleurbaix, 52, 53
  Fluquières, 102, 104
  Gheluvelt, 46; fighting at, 49, 50
  Givenchy, 61, 62
  Gueudecourt, 80
  Guillemont, 79
  Hamblain-les-Prés, 113
  Haspres, 117
  Hedge Street Tunnel, disaster in, 98, 99
  Hénin-sur-Cojeul, action at, 84–89
  Hulluch, attack upon, 67, 112

411

THE GREEN HOWARDS

1914—1919

The Cypher of H.R.H. Alexandra, Princess of Wales, in gold (thereon " Alexandra ") interlaced with the Dannebrog (Denmark) enscribed with the date 1875, and the whole surmounted by the Coronet of the Princess.

Printed in Great Britain by Butler & Tanner Ltd., Frome and London

Printed in the United Kingdom
by Lightning Source UK Ltd.
127376UK00001B/145-216/A